George J. (

GENERATIONS

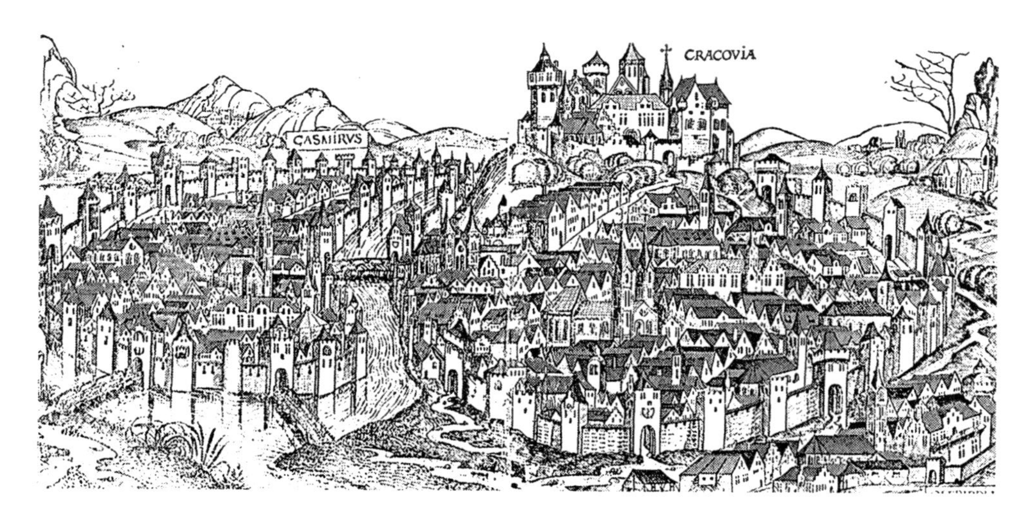

A millennium of Jewish history in Poland from the earliest times to the Holocaust told by a survivor from an old Krakow family

Congress for Jewish Culture
New York, 2008

George J. ALEXANDER

GENERATIONS

A millennium of Jewish history in Poland from the earliest times to the Holocaust told by a survivor from an old Krakow family

Design and layout by Boris Budiyanskiy

Publication of this book was made possible in part by funds from the Atran Foundation and the Department of Cultural Affairs, City of New York.

ISBN: 0-9724565-6-2

PRINTED IN THE USA

ACKNOWLEDGEMENT

I thank my wife and partner of fifty years, Rita Birnbaum Alexander, for her help in gathering data in Poland and for her patience with me when I got deeply involved in writing this work. Also, I want to express my appreciation to my son, Mark, for his understanding and helpful suggestions and my step-mother, Rózka Alexander, for sharing her recollections of pre-war Poland with me and for her unwavering encouragement. I wish to thank my many relatives and friends for providing me with important data about family relationships. My special gratitude goes to the Polish Archives in Kraków, Poland, and to the Manhattan office of the LDS Family History department for kindly allowing me to use their extensive archives of microfilmed data. I am indebted to Julian Schamroth and his associates for maintaining the extremely useful Jewish Genealogical Society's website with its remarkable record of reliability and accuracy. Finally, I wish to express my thanks to Shane Baker, Director of the Congress for Jewish Culture, for encouragement and help and to Boris Budiyanskiy. Art Director of The Yiddish Forward, for his invaluable work in having this book assembled, designed and ready for publication.

I dedicate this work to the memory of my mother,
Salomea (Scheindel) Rubin Aleksandrowicz (1900-1942),
and my little sister, **Anna Aleksandrowicz (1931-1942)**,
both of whom perished in the Holocaust
and
to my daughter, **Michele Anne Alexander (1960-1967)**,
a victim of childhood leukemia, which may have been due, in part,
to my wartime deprivations and damage to health.

TABLE OF CONTENTS

Part I. POLISH-JEWISH RELATIONS IN A HISTORICAL CONTEXT

Chapter 1. Introduction to a millennium of history

They lived side by side for a thousand years. Two very different peoples, Poles and Jews, intermingled, did not become comfortable with each other, did not become friendly, but they became acutely aware of each other. Over the centuries, from the early Middle Ages to the Holocaust, Poles have become accustomed to having Jews always among them, and Jews have adjusted to living dispersed throughout the country, surrounded by their not-always-welcoming Polish neighbors. At one level, the Poles looked at Jews as crafty, sly and untrustworthy and yet, somehow, on another level, they did admire and trust them. Throughout history, when a Polish aristocrat needed a loan, he turned to a Jewish money-lender and counted on getting a good deal. In a parallel yet very different situation, when an illiterate peasant in a rural hamlet needed to buy food and had no money, he turned to a Jewish shopkeeper in a small Jewish town, a *shtetl,* and received needed items on credit. Often, the peasant could not read but he trusted the Jew to properly record the debt and keep honest accounting of it. Proximity brought about a form of *modus vivendi*, which allowed the two groups to coexist. The coexistence was never easy, never far from violent eruptions, but for a thousand years these two peoples shared the land and its resources and developed it together. Given that today's polarized world is riven by a number of national, ethnic and/or religious conflicts, it is critical to study and try to understand how relations between disparate groups develop and how such groups manage to coexist for centuries.

Jews and Poles co-existed for a millennium. At one period of history, between 1500 and 1800 A.D. more that two thirds of all the world's Jews lived in Polish territories which then included Ukraine, Lithuania and Belarus and extended from Breslau (Wrocław) in Silesia to Kiev in Ukraine, from Riga on the Baltic to Odessa on the Black Sea. Kraków, Poland's royal capital, served as the epicenter of Polish Jewry. Near the middle of the twentieth century, in 1939, Poland's Jewish population (largely wiped out by the Nazis

between 1939 and 1945) consisted of more than three million souls and constituted over 10% of all people then living in the Polish Republic. Living among Poles but largely apart, Polish Jews created for themselves a remarkably vibrant, culturally exciting and stimulating society, nurturing large numbers of individuals who then contributed to human cultural, ethical, social and economic progress in a number of places, not least of them the United States.

It is hard to be fair and impartial in assessing Polish anti-Semitism and, conversely, Polish efforts to help Jews during the Holocaust, given the overwhelming fact of the demise of three million Polish Jews efficiently killed by the Germans on Polish territories, as some Poles watched with approval while others recoiled in helpless horror. We know that many Poles behaved abominably, yet a great many others sincerely attempted to help their Jewish neighbors. Helpful were many aristocrats in their country mansions and peasants in the villages and helpful were many urban residents, both members of professional elites and workers, members of labor unions. I found that during the Second World War in Warsaw an astounding proportion of urban Poles risked their own and their children's lives to protect beleaguered Jews from the Germans. In Warsaw, according to my estimate, as many as one family in six was active in sheltering hidden Jews (see supporting data in the next chapter). While we justly honor the many Danes, Hollanders and other Western Europeans who behaved courageously and helped their Jewish compatriots, we are not as aware of the efforts in Poland. The well-organized and ruthless German war machine did not make it easy to help Jews in occupied Europe, but it was particularly ruthless and cruel in Poland. The Germans shot entire Polish families caught sheltering Jews, including men, women and children, and bragged about it, proudly announcing such executions in wall posters and in the daily press. As an indication of how difficult it was to provide effective rescue anywhere under the efficient German occupation intent on ferreting and executing hidden Jews, note that even the iconic figure of the Dutch efforts to protect Jews, Anne Frank, did not survive. I do not know how many citizens of Amsterdam were actively involved in protecting Jews, but it could not have been as many as in Warsaw. Yet we all know how civilized and helpful were the Dutch during the War, but not many people appreciate the strenuous efforts made by a number of patriotic Poles at a much greater risk to themselves. The difference is that saving a few thousand Jews in Holland made a difference. Saving a few thousand out of three million in Poland was pathetic. It is sad that an admirable high-risk effort expended by a number of courageous Poles was able to save only a minute proportion of all Polish Jews.

In this book I try to illuminate selected aspects of the thousand years of Polish-Jewish co-existence intertwined with the history of an old Jewish family seen through the eyes of one of the last members of that family who grew up in Poland and survived the Holocaust. The story is centered in Kraków, an important historic center of Polish culture and once a world-renowned center of Jewish learning, the city of Nicholas Copernicus, the city of the prominent Jewish sage Remuh and, more recently, the city of the late Pope John Paul II. I am a Polish Jew and a Holocaust survivor, a first generation American citizen, a retired scientist and a part-time historian and genealogist. I am also a descendant of an old Jewish family that lost most of its members in the Holocaust, including my mother and sister. Having survived the Holocaust without help from outsiders, I am influenced by neither hatred nor gratitude toward Poles. Being always interested in history, I feel uniquely placed to try to evaluate the behavior of the Polish population during the Holocaust in the context of one-thousand-year long history of Polish-Jewish co-existence. I am obviously aware that the subject is complex, controversial and highly emotional. I do not expect to cover all aspects of Polish-Jewish interactions, but I do hope to illustrate some of them. Having lived as a child in the mediaeval Polish royal city of Kraków, a descendant of the old *Aleksandrowicz* family, I decided to try to explain my own take on the nuances of Polish-Jewish relations during the decades preceding the Second World War and the Holocaust and to place the latter in the context of the entire thousand years that Jews resided in Poland. To make the many strands of Polish-Jewish history easier to encompass I decided to concentrate mainly on what I know best, the story of Krakovian Jewry, using my family which lived in Kraków for many generations, as the prototype and example of the Jewish population. During the Second World War (1939-1945) most of my numerous relatives were killed, the survivors dispersed all over the world. In this my family was typical of my entire people. Also typical of one strand of this history is the fact that I survived the Holocaust in the ghetto and in concentration camps and that, after liberation, I came to the United States.

Having retired from the faculty of Columbia University's College of Physicians and Surgeons and the research staff of New York State Psychiatric Institute a few years ago, I decided to set down my recollections of the struggle to survive the war in Poland. Obviously, I knew that since the end of World War II many Holocaust memoirs, some very eloquent and emotional, had been written and not much that is new could be added. I was not interested, therefore, in producing yet another emotional war-time narrative. I felt an obligation, however, given my background and what I consider my unique immersion in the history of Poland and its Jews, to present a broad context of Polish-Jewish relations, covering not only the recent events which occurred during my and my parents' lives, but covering the entire millennium that Jews lived in Polish lands, from the early beginnings in tenth century to the present. I hoped to illustrate the historical forces that led Poland to become home to the largest concentration of Jews in the world, and that, subsequently, caused it to become a hotbed of virulent anti-Semitism. I believed that, in that broader context, my personal impressions may be of interest to a number of readers, having the additional dimension of describing not just the Holocaust, but the entire fabric of Jewish existence in Kraków, Poland's cultural capital, over the centuries. In this way, I hoped to present the interaction between Poles and Jews up to and during the Holocaust, from the vantage of a professional scientist, a naturalized American citizen who grew up in Poland and personally experienced life in Poland between two World Wars. I wanted my narrative to reflect my intense awareness of the historical background of unfolding events. In this way I hoped to make a valid addendum, not only to the already large Holocaust literature, but to the general European, Polish and Jewish history.

I was always interested in historical developments of forces that influenced the relationship between Poles and Jews. I grew up as a child in Poland in a politically and socially involved household. Both my parents were activists. In 1938 elections both of them, my father and my mother, ran for seats on the Kraków City Council on a Jewish socialist ticket. As a youngster, I was always acutely aware of historical developments in Central and Eastern Europe, of conflicts between economic strata within both Jewish and Polish populations, as well as of interactions between ethnic and national groups in Poland. I was also aware of the historic roots of these interactions.

During the years of World War II, I was deprived of formal education and when I arrived in the United States in 1946, I was eager to make up for the years of education that I had missed. Not being very conversant with English I chose a career in science. In accelerated studies I received a college degree (in 1949) and a doctorate in organic chemistry and microbiology in 1953. I became a research scientist and I was lucky to participate in and witness several exciting scientific discoveries. I was a doctoral student of Prof. Selman Waksman at Rutgers University (1949-1953), when he received the Nobel Prize in Medicine for discovery of the antibiotic streptomycin. I joined the laboratories of the Worcester Foundation for Experimental Biology in Massachusetts (1953-1958), during the exhilarating days when that Foundation fostered the development of the steroid contraceptive pill. While there, as associate of Dr. Erwin Schwenk, I helped to elucidate the mechanism of biosynthesis of cholesterol, competing and exchanging data with Prof. Konrad Bloch of Harvard, for which he then received the Nobel Prize in Chemistry. Four years later I joined the faculty of Columbia University in New York and the staff of the New York State Psychiatric Institute. My research in brain chemistry included, besides the biosynthesis of cholesterol, the workings of neurotransmitters, hallucinogens, opiates and other neuro-active substances. Among my research findings at Columbia was the discovery of the metabolic damage caused by the hallucinogen lysergic acid diethylamide (LSD). My findings, published in the journal *Science,* showing that LSD can be dangerous to the fetus, were instrumental in ending the LSD craze of the nineteen sixties. I was always interested in and conducted research in the chemistry of memory. Over the years I tested various new chemicals that enhance memory in experimental animal models and I had a whole colony of very smart rats. Unfortunately, my drugs, while enhancing memory in laboratory animals, showed significant toxic side effects and thus were not therapeutically useful. I have not given up hope of finding a safe memory enhancer and, while I formally retired in 1994, I still conduct part-time research in neuroscience. However, since retirement I have found time to start working on historical and genealogical research for this book.

In this account I attempted to combine my personal experiences with the historical background of my family and of Kraków Jews from the early beginnings ten centuries ago. Kraków, the city in which I grew up, has been central to both Polish and Jewish history and served as the cultural and political capital during the times of the great flowering of Polish power and Jewish cultural development from the Fifteenth Century. While trying to present an over-all sweep of early, medieval, Renaissance and modern history of Polish Jews, I chose to concentrate, in parts, on specific members of my family, the *Aleksandrowicz* family of Kraków and their putative ancestors and relatives. I have hypothesized about my almost legendary early forbears, incorporating oral family stories, using known historical details for a backdrop and I have researched documented family records in the archives. To that material I added my recollections of life in Poland prior to World War II and my experiences during the Holocaust. My narrative is set against the panorama of history of Jews in the city of Kraków, Poland, and of the interrelationship between Poles and Jews there, as reflected in my personal experiences, in the family documents that I collected and in sources that I consulted. I tried to correlate my family's history with contemporaneous historic events in Kraków, in all of Poland, in Europe and elsewhere, as they influenced the well-being of my family at the time or subsequently. I drew extensively on my own knowledge of history, which I acquired when growing up in Kraków and subsequently. As a child I revelled in old legends and stories of historic and pre-historic times. Now I took the opportunity to present some of these legends as they relate to my story. I expanded my remembered knowledge by using a number of primary and secondary sources, most of them written in Polish, which was my first language and in which I am still fluent. These historical and literary sources are listed in the Bibliography at the end of this work.

There were no published sources detailing the specific history of my family over the centuries. The foremost modern historian of Polish Jewry, Professor Mayer Bałaban, promised to research the origin of my family in 1938, but the 1939-1945 war intervened and he died before he was able to undertake this task. Many of the documents that might have been available in 1938 were destroyed during the Nazi occupation. I did not have the experience or the access that Prof. Bałaban might have had, thus my own research into my family history is fragmentary and only partly grounded in incontrovertible data. I supplemented my research with oral history notes from interviews with older family members and friends and I did archival genealogical study in Kraków. My wife and I examined original documents in the Kraków branch of the Polish National Archives. Earlier, I had written, in Polish, to the Main Office of the Archives in Warsaw, requesting permission to study in the Kraków branch, stating that I intend to write a book about the history of Kraków, using the history of my family as the starting point. I have received a formal response giving me the right of access to documents that I might need. In my search I found many relevant documents, written in an elaborate calligraphic script, in archaic Polish. I took the time to transcribe these hard-to-read texts and translated them into English. Copies of several are included in this work. Having lived as a child in Kraków from 1925 to 1943 and having survived the Holocaust in Europe, I knew that my ancestors lived in Kraków for a long time. I knew that there were three related branches of my Aleksandrowicz family living in Kraków prior to the World War II. There were also additional, more distant, relatives in Kraków as well. The three branches were grouped and colloquially known by the type of activity that they engaged in or by their place of residence. My branch was known as the Aleksandrowicz family with the wholesale leather business, politically active in the socialist Jewish Labor Bund. The second branch of my family was running a stationery-and-art-supplies enterprise and was very active in the Zionist movement and developments in the British Mandate of Palestine. The third branch, dealing in real estate, lived in Podgórze, an outlying region of Kraków located across the Vistula River from the city center. The most prominent member of that part of my family was a respected physician and medical researcher.

My extended family interacted with the larger Polish society and its institutions in many ways. Over the years, family members were economically and politically active. They wrote commentaries on the Talmud and dealt with ethical issues such as the propriety of charging interest on loans, an issue of critical importance to the accumulation of capital and the development of economy. They helped to develop commerce and industry, wrote historical treatises, helped edit books and journals, led political parties, did scientific and medical research at the Kraków university and elsewhere, run for elective offices, produced and promoted fine arts and literature, helped formulate and defend Polish constitution, took leading parts in anti-Nazi underground activities, served in Polish armies, participated in the 1944 Warsaw insurrection, joined partisans in the forests and otherwise contributed to Polish history, economy and culture in a variety of ways.

In conducting research in Kraków, I wanted to find out when Jews arrived there, how they lived and how they related to the broader Polish society. I wanted to determine how long have my putative ancestors resided in Kraków, what did they do, how did they affect the city and country, when did they begin to use the surname Aleksandrowicz, when did the surname first appear in official records and how was it derived. Also, I wanted to establish my exact relationship with the various branches of the extended Aleksandrowicz clan and with other Krakovian families, and, incidentally, to emphasize the ties between Kraków Jews like myself and the city, I wanted to revisit the places where I lived before and during the war. I was surprised to find out that it was a Jew who first reported the existence of Kraków and Poland in 965 A.D. I was able to establish a documented family tree of my Aleksandrowicz forebears in Kraków for hundreds of years back in time and I found when the name first appeared in official documents. I managed to collect a number of clues that eventually led me to formulate a hypothesis about the origin of the surname, a hypothesis that took me back in time to the fifteenth century and beyond. I found data about the assorted activities of early Jewish settlers in Kraków. In addition, during several trips to Poland, I paid visits to places in Kraków and vicinity, which I remembered from my childhood, as well as to places where I lived and struggled under German occupation during World War II.

Before he died in 1968 my father sat down with me and we made copious notes of family background and history, as well as of political, economic and religious events during his lifetime. Also, he and I took notes of our conversations with older relatives, including my father's aunt, Amalia Kaufer, nee Birnbaum, who came to America in 1938. I found these notes invaluable. Knowing the lifestyles, names and activities of the last three or four generations of my family, saved me a lot of time and made my search much easier. Knowledge of old and recent family stories and legends about family connections provided me with important clues. I believe that recording oral history from older family members should always be the first step in any genealogical research. There are certain obvious constraints in publishing a book that mentions a number of personal and family matters. There are some ethical considerations, pertaining to all biographical and genealogical publications. Thus, in keeping with these constraints, I have avoided providing ages (birth dates) for living individuals. In a few instances I have avoided using surnames of people who were included because of the way in which their lives impinged on mine, but whose permission has not been solicited.

Prior to going to Kraków to do research in the archives, I first recorded my personal recollections. Then I began to search for my roots in the Kraków branch of the Polish National Archives of Old Documents. In theory, the National Archives contain only documents which are at least one hundred years old; newer documents are supposed to be kept in regional and municipal storage centers, but I found that some more recent documents were also present in the archives. I began my search with the latest records. A lot of information in them was familiar to me and I worked my way back in time as far as I could go. I used the records to augment and, if necessary, correct the information that I remembered or that my father provided me with. Then I proceeded systematically back, checking records from 1900's, 1890's, 1880's and beyond, including lists of inhabitants, birth, marriage and death records, conscription lists, legal records and census books going back to 1790's, as well as court, tax, business and professional lists. I took copious notes and my wife did the same. We also checked some newer documents, which are not in the Archives but in the Kraków *Magistrat* (City Hall) located in the Wielopolski Palace and we examined the one cemetery list available in the office of the Jewish Community Council. The latter had only one such book of burials extant, partly singed, which survived the Nazi occupation hidden in a chimney. Most of the other Jewish communal books have been lost during the Nazi era, although some may yet be rediscovered in German archives. I have visited both the Remuh and the Miodowa Street Jewish cemeteries in Kraków and tried to read many of the tombstone inscriptions that remained after Nazi depredations, looking for ancestral graves. After my return to New York I re-examined a number of sources which I consulted prior to my trip to Poland and looked at them in the light of my Kraków findings, trying to fit my family's history into the over-all history of Poland and its Jews. When I needed specific historic dates, I found them in a book called "*The Timetables of History*" by Bernard Grun (1982). The one reference that I chiefly relied upon for background and for opinions about people and events was the monumental two-volume history of Kraków Jewry by the previously-mentioned Prof. Mayer Bałaban (1936). While these secondary sources have proved extremely useful in refreshing my memory and providing me with general background information, most of this work is not based on any specific source, but on my own general knowledge and opinion, my background and my lifetime of reading. The selection and interpretation of historical data is always my own, based on my own opinions as to their importance to the historical developments and relevance to my own and my family's background.

After coming home, I sorted my notes and began to write draft descriptions of my findings. Some preliminary accounts of my research in Kraków have been published. Three articles appeared in Yiddish translations in the New York monthly journal *Undser Tsait (Our Time)* published by the Undzer Tsait Ferlag (25 East 21-st Street, New York, NY 10010). I am indebted to Mr. Shane Baker, Director of the Congress for Jewish Culture, for the translations. Two of my stories appeared in *The Survivors' Chronicle* and one article appeared in the genealogical journal *Avotaynu*. Some of my early essays, which now need to be modified in view of recent research, are available on the Internet at www.jewishgen.org/Stetlinks/Poland/Krakow/essays.

In my search for Jewish history and family roots in Kraków, I found that my putative forebears lived in Kraków at least as early as 500 years ago. They were active at the time of a flowering of Polish Renaissance illuminated by the writings of Nicholas Copernicus, a graduate of Kraków University, and the commentaries on the Talmud by two of my relatives, the Krakovian Jewish sages, Reb Moshe Isserles (REMUH) and Reb Jozue Falk ben Alexander ha-Kohen (SMA). When the Second World War broke out in 1939 I had 21 *immediate* relatives living in Kraków, parents, grandparents, a sister, uncles, aunts, first cousins. Of these only three survived the War: my father and my father's oldest brother, Ignacy, and I. My father and uncle Ignacy escaped to the U.S. in 1941 prior to Pearl Harbor, I survived in German concentration camps. One of my uncles died of typhus, when he was deported by the Russians deep into the Soviet Union. The remaining 17 members of my immediate Krakovian family were killed in Poland by the German occupiers during World War II. Thus, my family can serve as rebuttal to those who claim that the Holocaust never happened.

Fig. # 001: (1a) The Aleksandrowicz house in Kraków, facing the royal castle

Fig. # 001: (1b) Rita and George Alexander in front of the Aleksandrowicz house in 1997

Chapter 2. Polish-Jewish relations, an overview. 965-1945 A.D.

My family, the *Aleksandrowicz* family of Kraków, lived in Poland for uncounted generations. It can serve as an example of old Krakovian Jewish families over the years. I grew up in Kraków prior to the Second World War. Polish was my first language and I speak it fluently. I am very familiar with Polish history and culture, yet I never considered myself a Pole. I was a Polish Jew. Poles never allowed the Jews to forget that they are not Poles but form a separate entity on Polish lands, a fact which usually suited the Jewish religious establishment as well. I loved the country and remember it with pleasure but my loyalty, such as it was, was not so much to Poland as to the lovely romantic city of Kraków, where I spent many happy years as a child before the arrival of German armies in 1939. Having grown up in Kraków, in the ancestral Aleksandrowicz residence on Bernardyńska Street, directly facing the ramparts of the royal castle on Wawel Hill, I could not help but be interested in history. As a child I played in the ramparts of the castle and read avidly of Polish princes and kings who resided there. Even now I believe that I know more about Polish history and culture than most Poles. I have read most of the important works of classic Polish literature. Yet, for all that, I never felt that I was a Pole, I was a Polish Jew. Interested in history, I read just as avidly about the long history of the Jewish people and, more to the point, about the long, often tragic, history of Jews in Poland and in Kraków.

As I see it, Poles and Polish Jews lived together, yet separately. I agree with the founder and former leader of the Solidarity movement and former President of Poland, Lech Wałęsa, who wrote in a 1988 letter to Marek Edelman, a surviving leader of the Warsaw Ghetto Uprising, that *"...For centuries, this land witnessed a coexistence for both better and worse of two communities – Polish and Jewish..."*, adding: *"This land, the Polish land, knows the truth about a struggle against slavery on behalf of freedom, against degradation on behalf of dignity, a struggle on behalf of hope fought without any chance of victory. The struggle of our Jewish brothers, the heroes of the Warsaw Ghetto, was such a struggle... In this land, the land of so many uprisings, the uprising of the Jewish fighters was the most Polish of all the Polish uprisings"* (translated by Mark Ehrlich, 1996). A copy of Wałęsa's letter, probably written with the help of his advisor, the Polish journalist of Jewish origin, Adam Michnik, is preserved in the Bund Archives section of the collection of YIVO, *Yiddisher Vissenshaftlikher Institut*, 15 West 16-th Street, New York, NY. The Poles and Polish Jews often shared similar fates, cooperating and intermingling, enriching each others' cultures, yet remaining separate and more often than not engaged in a cruel, though one-sided, conflict. Historically, Poland offered shelter to persecuted Jews in the Middle Ages and native Polish monarchs and high nobility showed an admirably enlightened attitude toward Jews, offering them protection of life and possessions. This policy led to Poland becoming home to the largest concentration of Jews in the world from the Fourteenth to the Nineteenth Century. The rulers and large aristocratic landowners obviously did not help Jews from some humane or altruistic motives, they must have derived significant financial benefits from having Jews around. Those benefits were sufficiently important to counter the influence of the powerful Church hierarchy, from the Pope in Rome to the local parish priests in villages, who saw the Jews as a subversive element. The Church expended considerable energy trying to ensure that the Polish "street" distrusted, and eventually hated, this "foreign" element residing among them. Unfortunately, even the enlightened and welcoming attitude of the ruling class did not survive into the present. The rise of Polish national and ethnic consciousness during the last one hundred and fifty years led to the rise of a widespread form of anti-Semitism in Poland and in formerly Polish territories taken over by Tsarist Russia, including Ukraine and Belarus. The vocal anti-Semitism at the time was not limited, however, to Poland and the former Jewish Pale of Settlement of the Russian Empire; it also flourished in neighboring Slovakia, Romania, Hungary, Lithuania and Latvia, as well as in Austria, Germany, France and other countries in Europe. It also thrived in Latin America as well as in the United States.

For the purposes of this discussion I have divided the history of the relationship between Jews and Poles into three vastly different phases: (1) Polish Kingdom and Crowned Polish-Lithuanian Commonwealth up to 1796, (2) partitioned Poland subject to foreign rule (1796-1918) and (3) newly reconstituted Republic of Poland between the First and Second World War (1918-1939). In the first phase, Polish rulers and aristocrats welcomed and protected Jews, often not very effectively and always against the wishes of powerful interests. These interests included the Roman-Catholic hierarchy, the burger merchants, who had to compete with Jews in the cities and the general populace, often incited against Jews by itinerant rabble-rousers like the (later sainted) Italian monk, John of Capistrano. Capistrano came to Bohemia, Silesia and Kraków in the 16-th century and saw fostering hatred of Jews as his mission in life, delivering hate-filled sermons to large crowds, thus inciting pogroms. In the second phase, treatment of Jews was controlled by the autocratic Russian Tsars, German Kaisers and Austrian Habsburgs. A heavy majority of Polish Jews lived in the Russian zone. The Tsarist Government used the Jews as scapegoats and it officially fostered anti-Semitism. In the third phase the Polish Government, faced with strong anti-Jewish feelings inherited from Tsarist times, was unable to come to terms with the large Jewish minority and ended up competing with nativist political parties in the anti-Semitic sweepstakes. I am not qualified to discuss the situation in Poland after the Holocaust because I left Poland during the Second World War, but the number of Jews left in Poland after 1945 is miniscule. Treatment of Jews under the Communist rule in Poland has been described by Arthur Wolak (2004).

In the Middle Ages and later, the social status of Jews in Poland and, I assume, in the rest of Catholic Europe, was rather unusual. Of course, Jews were outcasts, hated and persecuted. Yet, somehow, they were also admired for the steadfastness with which they clung to their ancient religion and their separateness. To begin with, the European society was rigidly stratified. In Poland there were four estates (castes): the nobles, the burgers, the clergy and the peasants. The peasants were *glaebe adscripti*, i.e. attached to the soil. They were serfs and part of a village. As such, they belonged to the village owner, could be sold and bought together with the land, and did not have the right to move away. They were subject to the infamous *"ius primae noctis"*, the right of the lord of the manor to be the first to bed all new peasant brides, which was supposed to improve the quality of the next generation. Burgers lived in cities and were usually of foreign (mostly Germanic) origin. The clergy was powerful, its higher ranks exclusively of aristocratic origin, while the lower ranks offered brighter peasants the only way of escaping serfdom. The nobles were divided between rich aristocrats with major land holdings (*latifundia*) and poorer rural petty country squires (*szlachta zaściankowa*), who usually owed loyalty to a specific aristocrat but who greatly cherished their patents of nobility and their right to participate in the country‘s parliament (*Sejm*). Jews existed outside of the caste system. They were protected by the ruler and by the aristocrats. Harming a Jew was treated as a significant crime. Since Church law prohibited Christians from collecting interest on lent money, considering it usury, it was left to the Jews to act as money-lenders, and there were laws, not often enforced, to protect Jewish lenders from non-repayment or bodily harm.

Jews were obviously considered special. The Church establishment was eager to convert them, by persuasion or by force. Thus, it is of interest that for a long time Polish Jews who converted to Christianity were almost automatically ennobled, receiving a coat of arms, landed estates and all the privileges of nobility. Of course, this served as an inducement, but it is also an indication of the peculiar respect in which the Jews were held, even while being treated cruelly as Jews. I understand that similar legal provisions also existed in Catholic Spain where, for a time, *converso* families rose to some of the highest ranks in Spanish society. There is in Spain a possibility that King Ferdinand of Aragon, husband of Isabella La Catholica and patron of Columbus, had some Jewish blood from his mother‘s Henriquez family, rumored to have been descendants of Jewish converts to Catholicism. Of course, usually only very rich and completely assimilated Jews, whether in Poland or in Spain, considered conversion. However, in addition, in Poland, a large group of rich as well as poor followers of the false messiah, Jacob Frank (described later), converted and joined the ranks of nobility. Apparently, they were able to overcome all obstacles and to fully blend with and loose themselves within the Polish society in very few generations. There is even in Poland a persistent, if unconfirmed, notion that the Polish bard, the pre-eminent national poet and patriot, Adam Mickiewicz, was of Frankist and, therefore, Jewish, origin. In his major opus, the book-length historic poem, *Pan Tadeusz*, Mickiewicz sympathetically describes a Jewish musician who plays so beautifully that his music continues to echo even after he stops playing.

The official Church doctrine did consider Jews unique. On the one hand the Church respected them because of their original special relationship with God, on the other

hand it hounded them and persecuted them because it feared the influence they might have over the faithful. On a more profound level, I believe, that many in the Church feared that the Jewish covenant with the Almighty might still be valid. Church theologians may have harbored dangerous thoughts that Jesus of Nazareth was another in the long line of false messiahs in Jewish history. He may not have been a charlatan like some pretenders, but may have honestly believe that he had a mission to save the world. It must have been painfully obvious even to the most devoted students of church and world history that Jesus left the world no better after his ministry than it was before it. Because of this manifest failure, the Church was forced to create the doctrine of a second coming, which had the effect of aligning Christianity with Judaism in that that both creeds are still awaiting the coming of an effective messiah, the Jews for the first time and the Christians for a second time. Both believe that the coming messiah will be a descendant of the ancient Jewish royal house of king David and that this time the coming will be for real. The idea of a coming redeemer can be comforting to those who believe that they will end up on the inside and scary to those who have reason to believe that they will find themselves outside of the charmed circle. In a way the Jewish idea is simpler because it does not require acceptance of a prior historic appearance of the messiah, or of the complex concept of a trinity and of the notion that the all mighty god has a need for a divine son. Thus, the Church had reason to worry that Jews might explain the tenets of their faith which, being easier to comprehend, might appeal to a wide audience. Hence, the eagerness over the years to get rid of the Jews and the need to demonize them. This, however, is not the place for an extended essay on the concept of a coming messiah or on the origins of catholic anti-Semitism, so this overly simplified summary will have to do.

Historically, Jews in Kraków, including my ancestors, served as biblical scholars and rabbis, as physicians, but mostly as money lenders, merchants and craftsmen. In the first case they exchanged ideas with more studious among the Roman Catholic theologians and learned priests. In the latter two occupations they competed with non-Jewish burgers and were engaged continuously in fighting off merchants' and guilds' attempts to restrict their ability to conduct trade or business in the city proper. The area of the original Jewish Ghetto in Kraków, was located near the *Rynek Główny* (Central Market Square), along today's St. Anne's Street, then known as the Judengasse. Eventually, in 1495, three years after the expulsion of Jews from Spain, Jews were expelled from the area in the center of the city of Kraków, which was given to the University. The Jews moved to the nearby Kazimierz that had a Jewish settlement since 1335, the time of King Casimir the Great. While forced to reside in the Ghetto in Kazimierz, the Jewish merchants continued to trade in the city proper and in the Central Market Square, which was within a brisk walking distance from Kazimierz. Among the important Jewish merchants in the first half of the 17-th century was one Aleksander Józefowicz. Other recorded merchants included Marek Aleksandrowicz (son of Alexander) and his sons and son-in-law. Given the combinations of names, and the rarity of these names among Jews, I believed that these merchants have been among my ancestors. The period of their documented commercial and political activities, XVI-th and XVII-th centuries, corresponded to the period of known religious, economic and political activities of one Alexander-ha-Kohen, son of Józef (i.e. Aleksander Józefowicz) and of his children and grandchildren. Alexander-ha-Kohen married Kendel (Hindl), an aunt of the great scholar, Reb Moshe ben Israel, known as Remuh (Bałaban I, 139). The activities

of Alexander and his family included service in the Kraków *Kahal*, Jewish Community Council, and participation in the Jewish autonomous legislature in Poland, the Council of Four Lands (*Vaad Arba Aratzot*).

Arguments and fights between Kraków Jews and burgers continued, with mixed outcomes: sometimes the Jews had to function in spite of restrictions, sometimes the restrictions were ignored. I need not dwell on the unfair treatment of the Jews by the courts, religious authorities and local officials, on pogroms, arrests, beatings and tortures, which followed after untrue and malicious accusations against the Jews which were common, for much has been written on this subject. Pogroms by incited mobs were fairly frequent. In a particularly heinous case, in 1663, a Kraków Jew, Matathias Kalahora, was martyred in a monstrously cruel way and burned at the stake. He was convicted of being the author of a blasphemous tract, which he could not have written, because it was handwritten in Old German, in an alphabet that he did not know. The Kalahoras were distant relatives of ours.

In the second phase, Poland lost its independence and the fate of the Polish Jews rested with outsiders. Until 1918 Poland was ruled by occupying powers and treatment of Jews was determined by the occupying powers. The Hohenzollerns of Prussia and Germany and the Habsburgs of Austria eventually learned how to live with their Jewish subjects and Jews in Berlin thrived. Many, like the Wertheimers, established department stores and others, like Heinrich Heine, wrote outstanding German poetry. A wealthy German-Jewish community arose in Breslau (now Wrocław in Poland), where the prominent Jewish historian Heinrich Graetz wrote his monumental six-volume Jewish history, a first modern re-telling of that history (Graetz, 1956). Other Jewish communities arose in cathedral cities of Speyer and Worms, in Koenigsberg in East Prussia (now Russian Kaliningrad), Fuerth in Bavaria, and in countless other places. In Koenigsberg my great-uncle Edward Birnbaum served as cantor, composer and historian of Jewish medieval lithurgical music. Fuerth near Nuernberg was the birthplace of Henry Kissinger, Richard Nixon's Secretary of State, and of my wife's father, Sigmund Birnbaum. Austrian Jews had, after 1867, gradually acquired all the civil rights, elected representatives to the Vienna Parliament, and joined local Diets and Chambers of Commerce and Industry, established important banks and joined Imperial councils. Jews in Vienna built railroads. Large Jewish communities thrived in Berlin, Hamburg, Frankfurt, Dresden, Leipzig, Koenigsberg, Breslau, Stuttgart, Offenbach, and in Vienna, Prague, Bratislava (German: Pressburg), Budapest, Kraków, Lwów (German: Lemberg), Czernovtzy (German: Tschernowitz), Brody and in a number of large and small places.

Only the Russian Tsars, who inherited a large Jewish populations when they swallowed the Eastern Reaches of the Polish-Lithuanian Commonwealth, including the Baltics, White Russia (Belarus) and Ukraine, never learned how to accommodate themselves to their Jewish subjects. To the contrary, they often resorted to the use of Jews as cover of their own shortcomings, using Cossack units of the *Black Sotnias* to foster pogroms. Their many Jews remained poor, living in hamlets, villages and small townlets (*shtetls*), without access to secular education. The shtetl Jews were led by a Jewish relious establishment, which was largely devoted to preserving the *status quo* and opposed to any opening of windows to the larger European civilization. Inspite of this opposition, subversive "Western" political and social ideas began to percolate to the Jewish villages, A large credit for this belongs to a Jewish national political and social organization, the

Jewish Labor Bund, founded in 1897-8 by a group of emancipated Jewish intelectuals in Vilna, then in Tsarist Russia, now Vilnius, the capital of Lithuania.

The role of the Jewish Labor Bund in modern Jewish history and its historic importance is largely underestimated. Most of it is due to the Holocaust and the consequent disappearance of the main centers of Eastern European Jewry and part of it is due to the dominance of the Israeli and pro-Israel historiography among the remaining Jewish centers in America and in Israel. With the passing of time, surviving members of the generation who knew and appreciated the contributions of the Bund are dying out and soon will disappear completely. It is imperative to record the seminal impact of the Bund on the world Jewry while there is still time. Within the limits of these next few paragraphs I present my view of the role of the Bund in Ashkenazic and world Jewish history. I will not deal with the details of Bund history, which had been amply described by others who know it better, but I will outline my view of the critical role played by the Bund in Jewish history in the last one hundred years.

The *Allgemainer Yiddisher Arbeter Bund of Poyln, Lite un Rusland* (the General Jewish Workers' Federation of Poland, Lithuania and Russia), generally known simply as *The Bund,* was founded by a secular group of Jewish socialists in 1898 in Vilna, then part of the Tsarist Empire. It prospered as an illegal but active political party in the Russian Empire, extending its activities to the educational and social sphere. It adopted and advocated Yiddish as the language of the Jewish masses. It grew and gained membership and popularity in the Tsarist areas of the Jewish Pale of Settlement, formerly territories of the Polish-Lithuanian Commonwealth annexed by Russia: Belarus, Ukraine, Lithuania, Latvia, Eastern Poland, parts of Moldavia, Bukovina, etc. Eventually, the Bund became the major political and social organization in its areas. A part of Bund's importance in Jewish history lies in the fact that these areas just happened to encompass a majority of the then existing world Jewry. Significant numbers of world Jews lived within the sphere of Bundist influence. It is sufficient to name just a few of the larger cities in these areas to appreciate the scope of Bundist activities. From Vilna, the Bund expanded to Warsaw, Białystok, Łódz, Riga, Smolensk, Vitebsk, Minsk, Kiev, Odessa, Zhitomir, Kishinev and a large number of smaller towns and communities. After 1918, because of Soviet persecution, the center of Bund activities moved to the newly freed Poland. Its headquarters was established in Warsaw where it printed its influential Yiddish daily, the *Folkstsaitung* (People's Newspaper) and a number of newsmagazines and literary publications. In Poland, the hitherto separate Galitzian Jewish Social Democratic Party voted to join the Bund, adding the cities of Kraków, Lwów, Tarnów, Rzeszów, Przemysl, Tarnopol, Kolomea, Stanisławów, Drohobycz as well as Czernovtsy (Tschernowitz) and other smaller towns to the roster.

At the time of Bund's founding the Jewish masses dwelt mainly in small townlets (*shtetls*) and rural areas. The shtetl Jews were mostly poor, their job and/or career prospects low to non-existent. Life was difficult, verging on desperate. Discrimination against Jews, official Tsarist anti-Jewish propaganda and not-so-rare pogroms, were a part of daily existence. Migration to cities offered some relief but the cities, too, offered only limited opportunities. Emigration, mainly to America, while popular, did not reach the proportion where it could serve as a major escape valve. A key factor, not stressed today, as we tend to emphasize the rabbinical/Hassidic Jewish history, was the isolation from and ignorance of the outside world by the Jewish masses. Local orthodox rabbis and local Hassidic *tzadiks* did nothing to diminish Jewish isolation and ignorance, actively discouraging assimilation, discouraging secular education and opposing western ideas then beginning to appear in the remote areas of rural Eastern Europe. Maintenance of the *status quo* always was, and still is, important to most existing religious hierarchies, whether Jewish, Christian, Muslim or otherwise, whose privileged positions often depend on keeping people in ignorance. This was certainly true of the Jewish religious authorities, both orthodox and Hassidic. The tsars did not establish secular government schools for their Jewish citizens and Jewish religious schools, the *cheders*, taught only prayers and rote recitation of religious texts. It became the historic role of the Bund, to challenge the religious establishment, to foster secular education and to spread contact with western ideas, including socialism and human rights of equality, freedom from anti-Semitism, religious liberty and the right to a job and a decent standard of living. The ideas were heady and it is not surprising that they attracted a following. A lot of hard work and a lot of complex struggles were necessary. The Russian government and later the authoritarian semi-fascist Polish government did not look favorably on the Bundist activities. Money was always a problem. Schools had to be established. Local rabbis and tzadiks in the shtetls had to be fought. Yiddish textbooks, grammars and dictionaries had to be written, Yiddish literature fostered. Success was far from certain, but dedicated work by inspired volunteers was having an effect.

There were other problems. Anti-Semites had to be fought. Relations with other leftist movements had to be rethought. In 1920, in the flush of excitement and high hopes after the Soviet Revolution, the Bund joined the Communist International (the *Comintern*), but after an intense internal discussion left it for the new anti-communist Labor and Socialist Internationale in 1923. The Soviet government then banned the Bund and communists everywhere strenuously opposed it. Stalin murdered Bundists who fell into his clutches including two outstanding Bund leaders, Henryk Ehrlich and Victor Alter. Equality of treatment in the new Poland was imbedded in the constitution, but was difficult to achieve in practice. In addition, the growing idea of Zionism, i.e. future emigration of Jews from Poland to Palestine, while attractive, diverted energy and resources from the critical and necessary fight for equality *in situ*, in Eastern Europe. This is where the majority of Jewish population resided and where it had to get educated and absorb modern western ideas and ideals. It was necessary to abandon the passivity encouraged either by religious dependence on a Higher Power or the Zionist consideration of Poland as only a temporary way station prior to the departure for Zion. It was the Bund position that mass migration of millions of Jews to Palestine was not feasible. Palestine did not have room for the entire Jewish people, comprising then approximately 16 million, and it was at the time a poor and arid land. In addition, Palestine was not empty but inhabited by Arabs, hostile to the Jewish immigration. The Bund was correct on both counts. Unfortunately, the Holocaust solved the first problem and the second one still haunts the Israeli existence.

As I see it, the main contribution of the Bund to history was waking up the sleeping giant of the large Jewish population of Eastern Europe, enabling it to emerge from the cocoon of generations of isolation, and engineering the striking entry of this population into the mainstream of European thought. It is astounding how much the world cultural, economic and artistic development of the last century owes to the energy of the Eastern European Jewry, which was awakened and incorporated into the human mainstream thanks to the activities of the General Jewish Workers Federation (Jewish

Labor Bund) of Poland, Lithuania and Russia. The historic importance of the Jewish democratic socialist movement of the Bund in Eastern Europe lay in steering the mass of Jewish population away from a religiously-induced passivity, fostering secular education and invigorating this population, leading it to become a part of modern Western thought. This awakening by the Bund was not limited to its members and other leftists but percolated through all the cities, towns and shtetls of Eastern Europe affecting the entire Jewish population. It affected Bundists as well as their opponents. The significance of this awakening can be measured by the subsequent contributions made in the world by members of this ethnic Eastern European Jewish group in Poland, in Russia, in Germany and elsewhere in Europe as well as in America and Israel. Attesting to this is the large number of Nobel Prize winners and statesmen, diplomats, writers, scientists, economists, artists and popular entertainers with origins within this population.

Thanks to the efforts of the Bundists and other like-minded people, in spite of the hostility of the Government, and perhaps because of it, the Jews in the Tsarist Pale of Settlement (Polish, Russian, Ukrainian and White Russian Territories) developed a vibrant cultural life of their own. European-class Yiddish and Hebrew newspapers appeared, novels and books of poetry were written, plays were performed before large audiences. Several political and religious parties sprung up in Warsaw, Łódź, Białystok, Vilna, Riga, Odessa, Kiev, Mińsk, and many smaller places. In addition to the new secular flowering, religious learning was also energized, and flourished in places like Vilna, "the Jerusalem of Lithuania", where the prominent sage the Gaon of Vilna, once excommunicated the new, and to him dangerously subversive, joyful and mystic movement of Hassidism, which originated and thrived in depressed Ukrainian-Jewish communities of Meziborzh, Leżajsk, Ostróg, Polonnoe, Lubavitch, Liady and others. All these territories once belonged to the Polish- Lithuanian Crowned Commonwealth, which disappeared from the map of Europe in 1796.

In 1790 the last Polish King ordered a census of Polish Jews; I examined the original of the part of this census that covered Kraków in the Kraków branch of the Polish National Archives. In 1794 Tadeusz Kościuszko, a Polish-Lithuanian nobleman, already a hero of the American Revolution, came to Kraków, visited the Jewish Ghetto, and took an oath on the Kraków Central Market Square to lead an armed fight for freedom and equality in Poland. In his speech he included an offer of emancipation for Poland's Jews. He created a Jewish battalion in his army, led by Colonel Berek Joselewicz. According to a persistent family story, told from one generation to the next, our documented ancestor, Joseph Aleksandrowicz (ca.1783-1827), served in Kościuszko's army. In 1796 Poland ceased to exist as an independent country. Kraków fell to the Austrians, who then ordered that a census of their new Jewish subjects be conducted. Unfortunately only half of that Austrian census survived to our times. In 1809 Kraków briefly joined a Napoleonic satellite, the Duchy of Warsaw (1809-1815), then existed for over thirty years as a semi-independent city-state, the Kraków Republic (1815-1846), and eventually, became a part of the Austrian Kingdom of Galitzia and Lodomeria. My great-great-great-grandfather, the Joseph Aleksandrowicz who may have been a fighter in Kościuszko's army and who was the first individual to actually carry the family surname as a surname, married Freindel Dobrysz, daughter of Jacob Gumpel, in 1802. The couple had at least eight children between 1805 and 1821. Joseph's parents must have done well financially, because, as a

very young man of 23, he was recorded as the owner of a sizeable apartment building in the Kazimierz Ghetto, building No. 203. Under Habsburg rule the fate of the Jews varied, depending on the attitude of the rulers. Empress Maria Teresa was hostile to Jews, her son Joseph was more liberal. As part of his reforms, Joseph insisted that all his subjects must have surnames, and his clerks were responsible for the many German-sounding names of Galitzian Jews. The rule of Franz Joseph (1848-1916) was generally beneficial. Kraków Jewish community grew in numbers and wealth under his rule. My great-grandfather, the second Józef Aleksandrowicz (1845-1940), grandson of the first Joseph, spoke glowingly to me of the old Franz Joseph in the 1930's in Kraków and I saw him read a Viennese newspaper until Hitler came to Vienna in 1938.

It was only in the third phase of Polish-Jewish history, when Poland regained its independence in 1918, that a government ran by Poles again controlled the treatment of Jews on Polish lands. At the time, Poland harbored within its new borders a large Jewish minority of more than 3 million, approximately 10% of the total population, a larger percentage of Jews than in any other place in the world. The presence of such a number of Jews, living among a devoutly religious Catholic majority, which was influenced by a strongly anti-Semitic Church hierarchy with poorly educated but virulently anti-Jewish parish priests, was bound to lead to problems. The enforced co-existence was always difficult and contentious. As nationalistic sentiments grew, Jew-baiting became a sure-fire method for ambitious politicians to garner votes. Similar phenomena occurred in other European countries, including Austria, where Vienna elected a mayor, Karl Lueger, from a party that had anti-Semitism as its only platform, and France, where a Jewish army officer, Captain Alfred Dreyfuss, was unfairly convicted of treason inspite of being innocent, primarily because he was Jewish.

Some honest Polish patriots believed that it was their patriotic duty to rid Poland of Jews and to accomplish it not by violence but through an economic boycott, hoping that impoverishing the Jews would encourage them to leave the country. Among those who called for such a boycott, were two prominent individuals, a politician and a cleric, the first a leader of the anti-Semitic National Democratic Party Roman Dmowski, the second a Roman-Catholic priest Maksymilian Kolbe. Dmowski, along with the pianist and politician Ignace Jan Paderewski, represented Polish interests at the Treaty of Versailles in 1918 and continued to play an important role in Polish politics. Kolbe spent a lifetime as publisher and editor of an anti-Jewish religious daily that he founded, which advocated a boycott of Jewish stores. Arrested by the Germans with many other Poles, Kolbe volunteered to serve as a hostage in place of a man with many children, hoping that his clerical garb will protect him. It did not and the Germans shot him. He was canonized by Pope John Paul II and is known now as Saint Maksymilian Kolbe.

In Warsaw's St. John's Cathedral I saw a memorial plaque to Roman Dmowski (1864-1959), quoting from his writings: "Catholicism is not an addition to Polonism – it is imbedded in its essence. Attempts to separate Catholicism from Polonism would destroy the very essence of the nation". This is a very strong statement. It implies that only Catholics can be true Poles. This quote goes a long way in explaining why this seemingly well-intentioned and seemingly intelligent Polish patriot engaged in such a virulent anti-Semitism. This quote also explains how this widespread belief, equating "Polonism" with Catholicism, automatically made it difficult for Polish Jews to become Polish patriots and to

simply become Poles, albeit Poles of Jewish origin. It insisted on keping Jews separate and continously confirmed their separate Jewish identity. It considered Jews not as a legitimate component of Polish state but as a problem preventing Poland from developing as a truly Polish society, a problem that has to be dealt with and solved somehow. Even today, in the United States, all ethnic Polish festivities and celebrations are wrapped up around the Catholic Church parishes and thus prevent formerly Polish Jews, like myself, who may harbor sentimental feelings for Poland, from participating. Dmowski's party was not always well-intentioned and often used less exalted methods to court votes by demagoguery, swaying the populace against the Jews by claiming that Jews owned all the wealth and lived well, while keeping Poles poor. I have a sample of an anti-Semitic flyer published in Kraków in the nineteen thirties, which says just that (see a copy at the end of this chapter). Reality was not so simple: there were some Jews who were well off, but most of the three million Jews were quite poor and eked a meager existence as peddlers, craftsmen or small shopkeepers. In small townlets, Jews who served as shopkeepers often owned the rickety wooden houses in which their shops were located, but these were not worth much.

Prior to 1939, Father Kolbe, the one who was later shot by the Nazis as a hostage, ran a large catholic publishing enterprise which included a journal *Dziennik Niepokalanej* (Daily of the Immaculate), that had as its primary purpose advocacy of a boycott of Jewish enterprises. He devoted all his considerable talents exclusively to this anti-Semitic activity. It is indeed a pity, that in a country as poor as was Poland between the two World Wars, so many honest patriots expended so much energy trying to impoverish 10% of the population, instead of welcoming the fact that Jewish citizens were taxpayers, and that many of them were innovative entrepreneurs whose domestic and international activities were enriching the country. And it is a pity that, as one of his first acts as Pope, the late John Paul II saw fit to canonize Maksymilian Kolbe.

Nationalism became a pernicious force. Relations between Poles and Jews were obviously strained. In 1939 Poland had more than 30 million people, 10% of them Jewish. However, Poland was then largely agrarian, with the population living on the land. The country was composed of a large number of small villages and hamlets, inhabited by poorly educated peasantry. The countryside was served by village churches as well as by taverns or inns, the latter often in Jewish hands. Scattered among the villages and hamlets were occasional mansions of local squires or palaces of important aristocrats. Also scattered among the hamlets were small towns most of them with a market square at the center. On market days, shtetl market squares were filled with area peasants, who brought chickens, eggs, milk, butter, some vegetables and grain to sell or barter for things that they needed, such as a Sunday suit and a pair of shoes for church, some metal tools or some fabric and notions. The population of these townlets was often more than half Jewish. A typical shtetl, such as *Jedwabne* in the Łomża district, which has lately been in the news because of revelations of a major pogrom there in 1941, had approximately 3,000 people, at least 1,600 of them Jews.

There is no question that Poles disliked and distrusted the Jews, and the Jews, in turn, did not like and did not trust their Polish neighbors. Yet, as I stated before, over the years they got used to each other. Over untold years a large number of Jews lived dispersed in the Polish countryside. The proximity of Poles and Jews brought about a form of conditional co-existence, a form of a working relationship. Poles have become used to

Jews and Jews have gotten used to living among Poles. It was not a friendly relationship, particularly in the countryside.

It may be difficult for an outsider to understand how these conflicting feelings on both sides produced a spectrum of cooperative behaviors that developed in the small *shtetls* and hamlets of the countryside, but it is a fact that mutually beneficial relationships usually prevailed, although without eliminating the underlying feelings of envy, rancor and suspicion. On occasion, violence did explode. The unstable situation lent itself, moreover, to manipulation by outside agitators, be it politicians or Church leaders, who fanned the underlying distrust of those who were "alien" and whose very strangeness was threatening to the deeply conservative peasantry. Pogroms occurred at times of stress, such as at the end of the First Word War (in Lwów, Kielce and other places), as well as during the inter-war period (1918-1939), most prominently in the townlet of Przytyk and the small town of Działoszyce. Major massacres occurred when the Nazis expelled the Russians in 1941 and proceeded to encourage Polish peasants to kill Jews, as in Jedwabne and several other *shtetls* in northeastern areas of Poland, near Białystok.

The cobbler or tailor workshops and the small food and notions stores in the shtetl market places were mostly Jewish, and Jews owned most of the houses in which their stores were located. The peasants may have thought that the Jews were rich, but given the poverty of the countryside, the Jews barely managed a living. They often had to sell on credit or through barter. A pair of scissors or some thread, ribbons, needles and buttons might have been exchanged for a scrawny chicken or two dozen eggs. Yet, the Jews had to pay for their supplies. The townlets also supported a small number of Polish professionals, a schoolteacher or two, a local politician/mayor, rarely a physician, and, of course, a church official and a parish priest. The Jews in the shtetl prayed in a synagogue, they were led by a rabbi assisted by a cantor and a *shahmes* who guarded, cleaned and maintained the synagogue building, a ritual slaughterer (*shoykhet*) and a *felczer*, a sort of barefoot doctor dealing with minor ailments, applying folk remedies like leeches or cupping, pulling teeth and often supervising the local Jewish ritual bath (*mikveh*). Poland also had cities inhabited by Polish and Jewish intelligentsia, craftsmen and industrial workers. These were growing in size and importance. By 1939 Jews constituted one-third of the population of Warsaw (400,000 out of 1.2 million). I believe that the textile manufacturing center of Łódź and the northeastern cities of Białystok and Vilna, the "Jerusalem of Lithuania", had a higher percentage of Jews. In Kraków there were 65,000 Jews in a population of 260,000.

Relationships in large towns and cities, where industrialization and migration of poor Jews from the *shtetls* in search of jobs created a Jewish proletariat, were more complicated. Polish workers fought for better living conditions, joining socialist (and communist) political parties, like the Polish Socialist Party (PPS), while Jewish workers joined the Jewish Bund. My parents were both very active in the Bund and I will describe their activities in the chapters dealing with my parents and my own childhood in Poland. Increasing access to lay education, fostered by the Bund among others, led to the formation of assimilated Jewish intelligentsia. Assimilated middle class Jews and Jewish professionals often formed social, economic and political bonds with their Polish counterparts and often forged common positions, confronting Government suppression of dissent and ignoring or opposing the official government support of political anti-Semitism. There were also a few inter-ethnic marriages between Poles and Jews, particularly among left-wing socialists and communists.

The Jews living in cities and towns were concentrated in commerce, industry, crafts and free professions beyond their percentage in the population-at-large and this was resented. Anti-Semitic excesses were often abetted by unscrupulous politicians and fostered by the powerful Catholic hierarchy. Pogroms and destructions of Jewish enterprises in the cities were not common, but occurred with some regularity. My father and my mother, as well as my uncle Ignacy, as enlightened social-democrats fought against discrimination, for security and for equal rights for minorities in Poland. In the 1930's the "Jewish Issue" was politically incendiary and aroused passionate feelings among the populace.

Of course, not all Polish patriots acted like Dmowski and Kolbe, although these two represented a majority of the Polish opinion of the time. Like the enlightened Polish rulers from the Middle Ages, Józef Piłsudski, the authoritarian leader of Poland until his death in 1935, did appreciate the major role Jews played in Polish commerce and industry and tried to moderate some of the more virulent anti-Semitic excesses and pogroms. Piłsudski was no friend to democracy; he believed in strongman rule (his own!). In 1918 he was the leader of Polish Legions which helped Poland achieve its independence and he became, subsequently, a towering figure in Poland after World War I, having the title of Chief of State as well as the military rank of Marshall of the Armed Forces. In 1925 he eliminated opposition figures and reestablished an elected Parliament (Sejm), but made sure that the elections were not exactly fair. The first democratically elected President of the Republic, a moderate statesman, Gabriel Narutowicz, was assassinated by a right-wing fanatic, who believed that Narutowicz was too friendly to the Jews. His successors did not repeat that mistake. Government fell into the hands of Piłsudski's henchmen, mostly mediocre former military men without much political vision, whose only claim to fame was their service in Piłsudski's Legion. They competed for popular support with not one but two anti-Semitic rightist parties, Dmowski's National Democracy (known from its initials as the "Endeks"), and the Church-supported Christian Democracy ("Chadeks"). Also in contention was a Peasant Party and the democratic socialist party, the previously mentioned PPS, which saw anti-Semitism as a tool that nativists used to divert workers' attention from their difficult economic existence. In 1936, when the Jewish Labor Bund started a campaign to fight the Nazi-inspired anti-Semitic propaganda, it received help from the PPS. On May 26, 1936, in the face of the Nazi-promoted anti-Jewish propaganda spread over all of Europe, the Central Executive Committee of the PPS sent letters, signed by the Chairman Thomas Arciszewski and the General Secretary Ksawery Pruszyński, to party locals all over Poland, stating: "*In connection with the large campaign being waged by our fraternal party, the Bund, against anti-Semitism, as one of the most pernicious factors acting besides fascism and for fascism and to the detriment of the working class and Socialism in Poland, we entreat you to extend to the Bund your assistance in the broadest meaning of that term...*" (a copy of this letter is available in the Bund Archives section of the YIVO collections).

I am personally aware that a measure of this cooperation between the Jewish Bund and the Polish Social-Democrats continued during the Nazi occupation in 1941 and 1942. My mother, Luśka Aleksandrowicz, was the leader of the Bundist Underground in the Kraków Ghetto in charge of relations with the Poles. Her contact on the Polish side was the secretary of the Kraków PPS, Józef Cyrankiewicz, a prominent political figure. Thanks to his influence with the Polish Government-in-Exile in London, my mother received, through an underground pipeline, funds from London which enabled her to expand some

of her Underground activities, including the setting-up of a children's nursery school for poor Jewish children in the Ghetto. I served as a courier between the Polish socialist underground, known then by its conspiratorial name WRN (for freedom, equality and independence) and the Bundist Underground, carrying conspiratorial messages, as well as illegal newsletters and pamphlets from the town center to the Jewish Ghetto. Incidentally, after the War Cyrankiewicz switched his loyalties from the Polish Government-in-Exile in London to the Stalin-imposed pro-Communist Polish regime and eventually became the Prime Minister of pro-Communist Poland.

Jews contributed, of course, to the development of Polish State and Polish culture from the very beginning of Polish statehood to its current existence. From the note about Poland by Ibrahim ibn Yakub in 965 to the modern Polish poetry by Julian Tuwim, Jews have enriched the country and its culture. Their primary contribution was to foster countryside commerce in a large numbers of little shtetls. In addition, many Jews defended Polish independence with arms, most famous among them Colonel Berek Joselewicz, the leader of a Jewish battalion in the army of Tadeusz Kościuszko and Napoleon. In a way, my 17-year-old cousin, Anna Aleksandrowicz, who fought, was wounded and died in the 1944 Polish Home Army Warsaw Insurrection against the German occupiers, also fought for Poland's freedom (a photo enclosed at the end of the chapter dealing with my early childhood shows this girl as a child in Kraków). Others Jews served as diplomats, like Meir Ashkenazi, who mediated between the Golden Horde of Crimean Tartars and King Zygmunt August. They served as parliamentarians, like Dov Ber Meisels who represented Polish Galitzia in the revolutionary Austrian parliament in Kromeriz (Krems) in 1848, and Ozjasz Thon, a Kraków Zionist member first of the Imperial Austrian legislature in Vienna and then of the Polish *Sejm* in Warsaw. They defended law and order as constitutional lawyers, like Ludwik Honigwill, who was a member of a defense team in the infamous political trial of the *Centrolew* activists, and my uncle, Ignacy Aleksandrowicz, a renowned defender of political prisoners. Many practiced as royal physicians, like Salomon Kalahora, Samuel bar Meshulam and my putative ancestor Samuel ben Baruch Aleksandrowicz in Kraków in 1648 and like my cousin once removed Julian Aleksandrowicz, dean of a Medical Faculty of the Jagiellonian University of Kraków in the 1970's. Many acted as royal bankers, like Levko Jordanis, financier of King Casimir the Great or Samson Wertheimer, Court Jew and "Oberfaktor" of King August II Mocny of Poland and Saxony. Development of Polish industry owed a lot to Jewish industrialists like the de Guinsbourgs, the Poznanskis and the Wawelbergs, who built railroads and textile factories, like Bertold Weinsberg, owner of the important Kraków-Bonarka brick factory, father of my schoolmate and friend Richard Weinsberg and like my uncle by marriage Isidor Wien, a co-owner of a petroleum refinery in Krosno in Galitzia. Many Polish Jews worked as engineers, among them the military construction expert, Mendel Izakowicz, who built pontoon bridges for the army of King Stefan Bathory, assuring Polish victories in the Russo-Polish war of the late XV-th century (had Napoleon followed Izakowicz example, he would not have had the trouble in crossing Berezina River in his retreat from Moscow). Among Polish-Jewish scientists was my relative Julian Aleksandrowicz, physician, specialist in hematology and expert on ecology at the Jagiellonian University of Kraków and Casimir Funk, a discoverer of Vitamin A. It was Funk, a candidate for a Nobel Prize, a long-time friend of my uncle Ignacy Aleksandrowicz, who discovered the first compound necessary to sustain life and he coined for it the term "vitamine", which now applies to all vitamins. In the flowering of Polish literature before 1939, the best known and beloved poets writing in Polish were Jews, Marian Hemar and the above mentioned Julian Tuwim. Tuwim was the author of a collection of poems called *Jarmark Rymów* (A Market of Rhymes) and of the delightful children's poem called *Lokomotywa*, which I knew by heart as a youngster. New editions of *Locomotywa* are still being printed in Poland and enjoyed by children to this day. Among the best prose writers was Józef Wittlin, a friend of my parents, author of the prize-winning novel *Salt of the Earth*. The editor of the foremost literary journal in Poland in 1939, the *Wiadomości Literackie*, was a Jew, Antoni Słonimski; the editor of the largest daily in Poland today, *the Gazeta Wyborcza,* is Adam Michnik. Numbers of others could be quoted. In addition, a large number of Polish Jews left Poland and they and their descendants contributed significantly to the development of commerce, industry, politics, banking, labor unions as well as comedy, literature, art, music and science in America, Israel, England, Germany, Russia and other countries.

I was born in 1925. My family lived in a desirable location, on Bernardyńska Street, directly opposite the Royal Castle on Wawel Hill. The Hill is also the site of the Kraków Cathedral, the See of the Roman-Catholic Archbishop Cardinal of Kraków. In the 1930's, when I was growing up, the See was occupied by John Paul II's predecessor as Archbishop of Kraków, Prince Adam Stefan Cardinal Sapieha, whom I met in Rome in 1945. As I grew up, I could see the castle towers from the window of my room, a view that made me interested in history. Also, as a child, I often played in the castle ramparts. Anti-Semitism was a fact we lived with, a quiet, ever-present menace, a source of mistrust, a pernicious trend, which had to be fought by all political and economic means available. I felt it even as a child in secondary school, where Polish language and grammar were among the subjects at which I excelled but for which, as a Jew, I was never given the top grade, which was reserved for one of my non-Jewish Christian classmates. Still, as I remember it, in spite of all the political and ethnic (and economic) problems in Poland, life in Kraków in the 1930's had its rewards for Jews and non-Jews alike. Kraków, a city of more than a quarter of a million inhabitants, was a center of culture with many outstanding cultural and educational institutions. Two of my uncles received law degrees from the Kraków Jagiellonian University. The town had many museums, theaters and parks and in them and in the Main Market Square there were many outdoor cafes. On weekends, my father took me to one of these, where he sipped coffee reading foreign newspapers mounted on bamboo frames, and I had ice cream. I attended many concerts, theater performances, operas, lectures, etc. I studied in the best public schools in Kraków.

The Jews fully participated in the town's lively cultural, social and political life. As I mentioned before, both my father and my mother ran (in 1938) for seats on the City Council on the list of the social-democratic Jewish Labor Bund, as did my uncle, Ignacy Aleksandrowicz. My uncle, Leibek Schmerler, my mother's brother, ran on the list of the left-wing Labor-Zionist organization, Poalei-Zion, and my cousin twice-removed, Zygmunt Aleksandrowicz, run as a "General Zionist". After being elected, Zygmunt became a member of the Praesidium of the Council. My father addressed large popular meetings of 20,000-30,000 people in the Kraków Central Market Square. Among my parents' friends were many outstanding writers, artists and politicians of the day, in Kraków as well as in Warsaw, among them Henryk Erlich and Victor Alter (leaders of the Bund, who were later killed by Stalin), the writer Józef Wittlin, Adam and Lydia Ciołkosz, Zygmunt Zaremba and Józef Cyrankiewicz (all leading members of the Polish Socialist Party), Leon Feiner (a prominent lawyer, a Bundist member of the Kraków City Council, who during the War became a co-leader of the entire Jewish Underground in Poland), Michał Schuldenfrei (a Kraków lawyer, later Chief Administrator of the Office of the Prime Minister of Poland), Stanisław Skrzeszewski (professor of education, after the War Polish Minister of Foreign Affairs and Ambassador to France), Marek Samuel (a local leader of the illegal Communist Party), Bolesław Drobner (lawyer, leader of the leftist political grouping of "Poles of Jewish Origin", after the War, Deputy Prime Minister of pro-Communist Poland), Ignacy Daszyński (a grand old man, former socialist member of Austrian, then Polish Parliaments), the thespians Ida Kaminska, Zygmunt Turkov, Diana and Jonas Turkov, Rachel Holzer and the remarkable Krakovian folksong-writer Mordechai (Mordche) Gebirtig.

My childhood in Kraków was a protected one. My parents provided love and security, assisted by a large number of close and distant relatives and friends. As can be seen from the photo at the end of the previous chapter, the windows of my room faced the Sandomierska Tower of the Royal Castle. I will provide later the details of my life in Kraków. What I did, what I ate, how I was dressed, what I did for entertainment, will be found in the chapter describing my own childhood. Here, suffice it to say that after being the first Montessori child in Kraków, I attended an excellent, experimental public primary school, *Swiętego Wojciecha* (St. Adalbert's) School, and went for two years to a distant but highly-rated public secondary school, the King John III Sobieski Gimnazjum. All this peaceful existence ended when the German troops entered in September 1939. From the beginning of the occupation schools were closed, Jews were persecuted, harassed, beaten, forced to wear armbands with a blue star, some were shot in the streets. Eventually, the remainder was herded into a Ghetto in the outlying district of Podgórze, prior to being sent to extermination camps.

My father was drafted into the Polish Army, fought against the Germans and retreated eastward before the German onslaught. When the Russians entered Poland from the East, the Polish army disintegrated. My father found that he could not return to Kraków, where the German Secret Police, the *Gestapo*, was looking for him because of his political activities, but he was not safe in the Russian zone either, because the Russian *NKVD* wanted him due to his public opposition to Stalinism. Eventually, he went to Vilna in the then briefly independent Lithuania. With the help of the Japanese consul, Chiune Sugihara, the Jewish Labor Committee in New York and the Committee to Save Endangered European Intellectuals, established under the patronage of Eleanor Roosevelt and Philip Green of the American Federation of Labor, he traveled through Siberia and Japan to the U.S. After a brief unsuccessful attempt to find a safer place, my mother, my sister and I remained in Kraków. From the Kraków Ghetto, most people, including all the elderly and all the children, were deported to the extermination center in Bełżec. The rest were taken to the concentration camp in Kraków-Płaszów. My mother, with her elderly mother, whom she would not abandon, my 11-year old sister Anna, three of my aunts and all my young cousins, were sent to Bełżec and never heard from again. I ended in the Płaszów camp, as did one of my uncles, Olek Aleksandrowicz. As the Russian armies were approaching Kraków in 1944, survivors of the camp were sent to camps in Hitler's "Alpine Redoubt" in Austria. My uncle died in February 1945 of beatings, exhaustion and starvation. I survived and was liberated by General Patton's army in May 1945.

During and after the war, Jews were not treated kindly in Poland, not only by Germans but also by Poles. The Poles, sandwiched geographically, with no natural boundaries, between two major enemies, with good historical reasons hate both the Germans and the Russians. There is, however, a difference: they hate the Germans but admire them, are jealous of them and look up to them – the Germans were always richer and better organized than the Poles and culture traveled to Poland from Southern and Western Europe through Germany. They hate the Russians and have a deep contempt for them and consider them uncivilized and uncouth, because for a long time the Russians were vassals of the Mongols and the Tsars never created an obligatory public education system. The majority of Russians were poorer and less educated than average Poles. Of course, the Poles were upset at having their country dominated by the "uncouth" Russians and concentrated their hate on "their" Jewish Communists. The popular anti-Semitic propaganda in Poland was not logical or internally consistent. The Jews were regarded as pro-Soviet and pro-Communist and yet, somehow, at the same time, as money-hungry capitalist exploiters. While there were in Poland some very wealthy Jewish owners of factories, the overwhelming majority of Polish Jews, living in small townlets, was desperately poor and the Jewish proletariat in the cities was exploited by Polish and Jewish capitalists, just as much as was the Polish proletariat. Many poor Jews were seduced by the myth of Communist workers paradise, with its pretence of having eliminated workers' exploitation and its pretence of having eliminated all vestiges of anti-Semitism. Given the dire choice available in 1939 between being occupied by the minions of Hitler or those of Stalin, Jews obviously preferred the latter.

In general, for obvious reasons Polish Jews preferred to be under Stalin rather than under Hitler, even though they had no illusions about the hardships of life in the Soviet Union. There were many stories about the famine in the Ukraine during the forced collectivization of agriculture. The infamous Moscow trials and executions of prominent Bolshevik leaders, such as Bukharin on trumped up charges that they were Nazi spies were not ignored in Poland. There were even jokes about Soviet peoples' dislike and contempt for Stalin. I remember one. Lenin was married to a well-known Communist leader in her own right, Nadezhda Krupskaya. Stalin was also married to a woman named Nadezhda. *Nadezhda* in Russian means "hope" (in Polish *nadzieja*). Nadezhda Krupskaya outlived Lenin by many years. When Stalin's wife died a statement was circulated that "when Lenin died at least Hope remained, while now Stalin is alive, but Hope died". Nevertheless, early in war many Jewish men moved from German areas to Russian ones.

In September 1939 Poland was divided between the Germans and the Russians. The Poles hated both with vehemence. Any appearance of collaboration with either of the hated occupiers was deeply resented. Poland is justly proud of never having produced a pro-German Quisling. No Polish auxiliaries fought along with the Germans and Austrians, as did Latvians, Ukrainians, Russians, as well as Spaniards, Frenchmen or Belgians. Poles did not give up the fight when Germans and Russians occupied their country. Polish pilots participated in the Battle of Britain. Polish soldiers participated in the battle for Monte Cassino in Italy and in the parachute drop at Arnhem in the Netherlands. In both places I have visited military cemeteries with large numbers of Polish and some Polish-Jewish tombstones. In Eastern Poland in 1939 Polish Jews, fearful of the Nazis, welcomed the arrival of the Soviet forces. When the Hitler-Stalin friendship soured, in 1941, the Germans conquered Soviet-occupied parts of Poland. Many local Poles, not having previously experienced German brutality or their contempt for the Poles, welcomed the Germans as liberators from the Soviet-Russian yoke and vented their anger by attacking Jews, unconsciously following an all-too-familiar historic pattern. The Nazis used the local anti-Soviet sentiments to fan the flames of pre-existing anti-Semitism among Polish peasants. In the shtetl of *Jedwabne* and in similar townlets they were remarkably successful. The local political and intellectual leadership was absent, having been arrested and deported by the Soviets. Nazi incitement. greed and expectation of takeover of the imagined Jewish wealth, mixed with ingrained traditional Jew-hatred, formed a combustible mixture. In July 1941, after the Russians were expelled from their share of Poland by the German Wehrmacht, anti-Jewish pogroms took place in many parts of post-Soviet Eastern Poland. Those in the Łomża district of the Białystok voivodship were particularly brutal. In Jedwabne up to 1,600 Jews were brutally beaten, tortured, and eventually herded by their Polish neighbors into a barn and burned alive (Gross, 2001). Among the participants in the Jedwabne pogrom were many of the neighboring peasants, who previously bought from, sold to and bartered with the Jews. The local priest, himself of peasant origin and a Jew-hater, refused to intervene. The killing of the Jews occurred in an almost festive atmosphere. What makes the Jedwabne story even more horrible for me, is the knowledge how participants in the pogrom hated the one family among them that did not participate but protected some Jews. The guilt-inspired hatred reached a point that the one decent family was threatened, and forced to flee and settled abroad. The few Jews returning from Soviet Siberia after the War were met with hostility and threats, their properties having been appropriated in the meantime. Pogroms and lynchings occurred. In Poland Jews were killed because they were Jews even after the Holocaust.

My stepmother heard a story, which may or may not be true, but which surely is indicative of the atmosphere in small Polish towns in the immediate aftermath of the War. It is said to have occurred in a small shtetl in the Warsaw district, which has not been identified. A young local Jew came back from an exile deep in Soviet Siberia and arrived in the shtetl inquiring about the fate of members of his family, all of whom have lived in this place for many years until killed by the Germans. The young man went to the house of the local *wójt* (mayor), whose family had before the War maintained friendly relations with his own. He was greeted pleasantly, but given the sad news that none of his relatives survived the Holocaust, their goods have been appropriated by the townspeople and a local Polish family lived in their house. The news of the young Jew's arrival had spread through the town and apparently was threatening to many people, because soon a mob had gathered in front of the mayor's house. The crowd was hostile and soon turned ugly. Its self-appointed spokesmen demanded that the young man be handed over to them, presumably for a beating or even a lynching. The mayor came out front and urged the mob to disperse, but was unsuccessful. When he refused to turn the Jew over he was told that his house would be burned with all those within it. The young Jew felt that he cannot endanger the lives of the mayor's wife and children and he stepped outside and confronted the mob. There was a moment of silence and then a shot rang out and the Jew, the only survivor of his family, fell dead. As I said, the story may be apocryphal, but it has the ring of truth.

We know now that the 1941 Jedwabne murders, long blamed on the occupying Germans, were actually perpetrated by the local Poles, albeit at the Germans' instigation. A local trial soon after the War showed this to be the case, but this unpalatable truth was buried and forgotten. The recently published book by the historian Jan T. Gross documented the Polish responsibility for the killing beyond any doubt and this has caused an uproar in Poland. Concern for Poland's reputation abroad was palpable. The President of Poland, its Foreign Minister and its Ambassador in Washington expressed their horror and issued apologies. Even the head of the Roman-Catholic Church in Poland, Józef Cardinal Glemp, not a great friend of Jews, published a sort of a hedged, conditional, apology.

There is no doubt that the Germans, with good reason, chose Poland for the killing field during the Holocaust. That is where most of the Jews were. There is no doubt that many Poles betrayed their Jewish compatriots to the Germans, mainly for financial rewards. Dregs of society, which exist in every country, blackmailed Jews who tried to hide as Christians, with false papers. Betrayals occurred with frightening frequency, often preventing decent people who wanted to save and protect Jewish friends from being able to help. Even Jews who escaped from the Ghettos and concentration camps into the deep woods were not safe there. Many Polish nationalist partisan detachments actually shot Jews who tried to join them to fight the Germans. All this is undoubtedly true and accounts for the current anti-Polish sentiments among Jews. There is no doubt that many Poles looked on but refused to help the beleaguered Jews. *But not all Poles*. My relative, Julian Aleksandrowicz, a physician, joined the partisans in the forests and was welcomed by them. It is unfair to ignore the significant number of Poles who risked their lives to help the beleaguered Jews. Many have been honored at the Yad Vashem in Jerusalem for their "righteousness". It must be recognized, moreover, that the need in Poland under the German occupation was overwhelming. Given a very efficient and very determined German administration, bent on killing the more-than-three-million Polish Jews and actively terrorizing the Poles who might have wanted to help their Jewish neighbors, there was no countervailing power in Poland that could have saved more than a small percentage of potential victims.

The commonly held impression that all Poles were (and are) hateful anti-Semites who did little to help their Jewish compatriots during the German occupation is obviously unfair. Large number of Poles did try to help. The Germans were particularly cruel in Poland. Poles did not placidly accept the German rule and did not simply wait to be liberated, without resistance. The Germans looked down on Jews as not deserving to be allowed to exist, but they also looked on Poles as lesser beings only fit to serve as manual laborers. From the beginning the German administration tried to decapitate the Polish nation by killing its intelligentsia. University and Gimnasium professors were arrested and many perished. Poland lost six million of its citizens, three million Polish Jews and an equal number of Catholic Poles. The difference is that three million Poles constituted approximately 10% of 30 million Poles while three million Jews constituted almost the entire Jewish population. While many Poles behaved abominably, we know that a sizeable number risked their lives to protect the Jews. The rescuers, while unable to save more than a small fraction of Poland's Jewry, constituted a rather significant proportion of Poland's manor houses, and also a significant percentage of average non-Jewish urban inhabitants, particularly in Warsaw. The size of the needed rescue effort has been described in detail in a book written in 1982 by Teresa Preker. The Jewish historian Emanuel Ringelblum (1900-1944), who was killed in the Warsaw Ghetto, stated in his notes which were hidden and then recovered after the War, that the "...more socially conscious large landowners hid... representatives of the Jewish society...". "Approximately 20% of all manors (and country estates) provided shelter to Jews as 'conspiratorial activists', not knowing that they are Jews, but half knowingly accepted and hid Jews" (Preker, 1982, 45).

Apart from those Jews who were hidden in country manors, I estimate that approximately 20,000 Jews survived by being hidden by Poles in Warsaw appartments. Quite mercilessly, the Germans executed not only all discovered Jews, but also all members of any Polish family found to have helped these Jews. The Germans deliberately posted announcements of these executions of entire families of Polish rescuers to scare any further volunteers. A copy of one such German announcement can be found in the Preker book, as illustration No. 41, near page 113. Yet, in spite of all these German efforts, 20,000 Jews survived hidden among Poles in Warsaw. They were helped by the Bundist underground and by individual Poles at first and, eventually, by a formal Polish underground rescue organization set up and funded by the Polish Government-in Exile in London specifically to help Jews, called *Żegota.* Created rather late in the War, this Polish Council to Help Jews (*Rada Pomocy Żydom*), was involved in distribution of financial support, search for safe housing, preparation of false documents, care of children separated from their parents and provision of medical care. It cooperated with the underground court system in a fight against blackmailers. The organization was staffed by patriotic Polish volunteers, some of them known anti-Semites, like the writer Zofia Kossak-Szczucka, who overwhelmed by the German cruelty towards the Jews felt that, their anti-Semitism notwithstanding, as humanitarians they had to help. The organization was engaged in finding hiding places for Jews. Hidden individuals could not work to support themselves in the inflationary economy, so the Council offered them financial assistance. It was a fact of life that hiding places were often rendered unusable due to denunciations by renegades serving as German agents. The hidden Jews had to be moved to new places often, sometimes every day. It is estimated that each protected Jew or small group of Jews had to change residence at least five times over the years of German occupation. I estimate that, over the last years of occupation, the 20,000 Jews must have been hidden in at least 40,000 apartments. The official Polish rescue organization felt obliged to tell the hosts of the risk and give them a choice of refusing. Warsaw, at the time a heavily bombed city which shrank from pre-War population of 1.2 million to 600,000 inhabitants, had a stock of approximately 240,000 housing units (Preker, p. 188). Even allowing for significant deviations and exaggeration in all numbers, these figures indicate that among Warsaw's urban population, as many as one in six heads of households were willing to risk death for themselves and their families in order to shelter their endangered Jewish compatriots.

Among those Jews hidden in Warsaw, protected and supported by the *Rada Pomocy Żydom* for several years, was my young cousin, Anna Aleksandrowicz (1927-1944), daughter of my uncle Ignacy. Jewish Bund Underground spirited her from Kraków, where she was known and risked being recognized, to Warsaw. She was hidden in Warsaw, using false papers, with the help of Jewish Underground and the *Rada Pomocy Żydom*. When Warsaw erupted in an anti-German Uprising in 1944 (not the Ghetto Uprising, but the later Polish insurrection), Anna joined the fighters, was wounded and taken by her combat comrades to a primitive field hospital. That was the last we heard of her. She did not survive the War. I will have more to say about her later when describing my uncle Ignacy and his family.

After the War ended in 1945, the remnants of the Jewish population began drifting back, some from German concentration camps, more from Russian exile. In their absence,

their possessions had been taken over and their reappearance was not welcomed. The Polish Communists, with some Jews prominent among them, ran a pro-Communist government imposed upon Poland by Moscow. Jewish Communists did not endear themselves to the religious Catholic and xenophobic population. All this led to a number of anti-Semitic outbursts as indicated in the story above told by my stepmother. The outbursts included a major pogrom in Kielce in Central Poland on the 4-th of July 1945, with 42 people killed, and one in Kraków on August 11, 1945, with "only" (sic!) one or two victims. Most of the remaining Jews emigrated from the then Soviet satelite a little later, when Stalin initiated an anti-Jewish campaign, the so-called "Doctors Plot". Only a few elderly Jews who had no options and some that intermarried with non-Jews remained.

After being liberated in Austria in 1945 I did not return to Kraków, but waited for my U.S. immigration visa in Italy and eventually joined my father in the United States in 1946. Given the known anti-Jewish sentiments in the Polish countryside, it would have been risky for me to try to reclaim my family's personal belongings, which were left not in Kraków but in a small shtetl nearby. I would not have felt confident of my safety while on a visit to this small town. Even years later, in 1958, when I visited Kraków, I did not go to the shtetl of Skała, where our family's belongings were stored. I assumed that all our valuables were taken and all personal keepsakes, which might have indicated their Jewish origin, were destroyed. To this day I feel sorry that I thus lost the opportunity to recover any of my family photographs and heirlooms.

Anti-Semitism, even without Jews, is still a potent force in Poland. A few years ago a visit to the United States by Joseph Cardinal Glemp, the Roman-Catholic Primate of Poland, was aborted because of his anti-Semitic pronouncements, decrying the power of the "Jewish international press", i.e. of the New York Times. Recently, the late Polish Pope has expended considerable effort trying to exorcise some of the Church's historic anti-Semitism. This is the same pope, however, who, as his first few moves, canonized the Polish priest, Maximilian Kolbe, whose main claim to fame was his life-long overt active anti-Semitism. The Pope's efforts to decrease anti-Semitism within the Polish Church and population are appreciated and I believe that, within his frame of reference, he has gone as far as he could. Too bad that even without Jews residual anti-Semitism is still rampant in Poland. There was recently in Poland a smoldering dispute about positioning of crosses at the gates of the concentration and extermination camp at Oświęcim (Auschwitz), in which many Jews and Poles died. In a special Catholic Jubilee Year session, the Polish Episcopate met in Częstochowa (in August 2000) and issued a letter of apology for its past anti-Semitic excesses. As mentioned above, the publicity surrounding the 1941 Jedwabne murders led to additional apologies and disclaimers by church leaders.

There is one more aspect of Polish-Jewish relations which has not been dealt with by the Poles and which remains as a sore point for the time being, This aspect concerns restitution for Jewish real estate properties confiscated first by the Nazis and then nationalized by the Communists. The Polish Parliament has steadfastly refused to acknowledge this debt of honor, inspite of pressure from the European Union and even from the U.S. Congress. I can appreciate the problems facing the Poles. At first, the country could not afford payment in cash but did not want to have a large proportion of its buildings owned by absentee landlords. Also, the Poles were worried by the irredentist territorial and financial claims of Germans who were removed as part of post-war exchange

of populations in the nineteen forties. The victorious Soviets moved Polish boundaries westward, expelling a large number of Poles from eastern territories taken over by Ukraine and Belarus, including the historically important Polish cities of Lwów, Wilno and Grodno. In exchange Poland was given ancient Slav areas of Prussia and Silesia, with Breslau and Stettin (in Polish Wrocław and Szczecin). Polish parliamentarians have made an attempt to fashion a bill that would offer restitution to some Jews without offering one to Germans, by specifying that only Jews who are current Polish citizens are entitled to it, but the law was not acceptable and was vetoed by the President of Poland. To the best of my knowledge fresh attempts to rewrite the bill are being made.

It is worth mentioning that along with the residual animosity toward Jews, I also found now in Poland a definite revival of interest among educated young Poles in things Jewish and in Jewish culture. They suddenly woke up to the fact that for a thousand years Poles and Jews co-existed and developed separate cultures, including literature and music, which often inter-acted and fertilized each other. The Kraków Jagiellonian University has a very active, well-staffed Institute of Jewish Studies. There is a Jewish Historical Institute in Warsaw and one in Kraków. In Kraków there is now a well-attended Jewish Cultural Festival, held each June, and an additional series of cultural Jewish events in October. Traditional Jewish Klezmer music is being taught in Poland. An impressive Jewish branch of the Polish National Museum is located in the Old Synagogue in Kazimierz. Also located nearby are Jewish restaurants serving "authentic" Jewish cuisine. When we visited Kraków in 1997 we found in front of one of these restaurants young catholic Poles, dressed in pseudo-Jewish pseudo-Hassidic garb playing some Klezmer music for the benefit of tourists, mostly young Germans, arriving in a long line of tour buses. The irony of this situation seems to elude everybody. The tourists are Germans coming to Poland to expiate for the wartime behavior of their parents. They are not paying to see what real Kraków Jews looked like, assimilated Kraków Jews like myself and my family, but to see strange, exotic people from another time, dressed in black caftans and capotes and sporting sidelocks (*peyes*) and *yarmoulkes* on their heads. What the tourists expect is being provided for them. I found this whole charade pathetic. There not being enough Jews in present-day Poland to satisfy the tourists' curiosity, anti-Semitic Poles, who always looked down on Jews, are now obliged to impersonate them for tourist money.

I do not believe that there is much of a future for Jews in Kraków. The official Kraków Jewish Community has only 189 registered members, mostly elderly. There are also in Kraków a few people of Jewish descent who do not necessarily consider themselves Jewish. I believe that the critical mass for a cultural revival just is not there. Krakovian Jewish survivors who emigrated to the U.S., Australia or Israel have not rushed to return. When I mentioned this gloomy forecast to some friends, I was contradicted and told that Poland's strong economic revival will create career opportunities and that some Jews may choose to take advantage of openings there and settle in the country again. Perhaps that might be true with respect to Warsaw, which is vibrant and developing new commerce and industry and has a small new Jewish presence already, but not Kraków which, while charming and elegant and a tourist mecca, does not seem to provide a suffiently stimulating economic milieu. I believe that a millennial history of Jews in Kraków has come to an end.

Polska dla Polaków!

Polacy!

Spójrzcie wokół siebie! Zobaczycie nędzę i biedotę wśród szerokich warstw polskich chłopów i robotników a sytość i zadowolenie wśród żydów. Zobaczycie w każdą sobotę i każde święto żydowskie suto zastawiony stół w żydowskim domu, a w każdą niedzielę i święto katolickie w domu Polaka taką samą — jak codzien — biedę, a coraz częściej i nędzę!

Czy tak być powinno? Czy inaczej być nie może? I my możemy być syci i zadowoleni, ubrani i nie głodni! Od nas to tylko zależy! Bo jeżeli

nigdy nie kupisz u żyda a zawsze i wszystko u Polaka

wówczas

dasz zarobić polskiemu kupcowi i rzemieślnikowi

a ten

kupi towar w polskim warsztacie i fabryce

w których

pracują robotnicy Polacy, wśród których jest też wielu synów wsi

wtedy będzie dobrze Polakom

bo będą mieli chleb i pracę a z nią i władzę w Polsce.

Wtedy żydzi sami wyjadą z Polski

a my zostaniemy gospodarzami na własnej polskiej ziemi, wówczas będzie

Polska dla Polaków!

Dlatego też

nigdy nie kupuj u żyda a zawsze i wszystko u Polaka!

Stronnictwo Narodowe.

Wydawca: Marian Markowski, Kraków, Tarłowska 12 m. 8.
Nakładem Stronnictwa Narodowego Kraków. Rynek Gł. 6 I p. m. 17.
Drukarnia „Mieszczańska" Kraków, Dolnych Młynów 3,

Fig. 002: An anti-Semitic leaflet, advocating a boycott of Jewish stores, 1936

AN ANTI-SEMITIC LEAFLET ADVOCATING BOYCOTT OF JEWS, 1936-9

Translated into English:

Poland for Poles!

Poles!

Look around you! You will see poverty and misery among wide segments of Polish peasants and workers but riches and satisfaction among Jews. Every Saturday and Jewish holiday you will see a richly set table in a Jewish home, and every Sunday and catholic holiday you will see the same - as always - poverty, and more and more often - misery!

Should it be that way? Can it be different? We, too, can be full and satisfied, dressed and sated! It all up to us! Because if

you never buy from a Jew but always and everything from a Pole

then

you will let a Polish merchant and craftsman earn money

and he

will buy supplies in a Polish workshop and factory

which

employs Polish workers among which there are also many of the sons of villages

then all will be well with Poles

because they will have bread and work and with it power in Poland

Then the Jews will leave Poland on their own

and we will become managers of our own Polish land, and then will be

Poland for Poles!

For this reason

never buy from a Jew but always and everything from a Pole!

National Party

Publisher: Marian Markowski, Kraków, Tarłowska Street 12/1

Issued by the National Party in Kraków, Central Market Square 6/1st floor, apt.17

Printed by „Mieszczańska", Kraków, Dolnych Młynów St. 3.

Part II. POLAND AND THE JEWS: EARLY HISTORY

Chapter 3. Travels of Ibrahim ibn Yakub

The year was 965 A.D. The caravan leader was a bearded middle-aged solemn man named Ibrahim-ibn Yakub. Although hailing from prosperous Arab Spain he was not an Andalusian, Castillian or Aragonese and he was not an Arab. He was a Spanish Jew. In that year, the Jew Ibrahim ibn-Yakub, one of many Spanish Arab and Jewish traveling diplomat-explorer-merchants, traveled for weeks through the heavily forested area of central Europe, keeping notes on his travels. In the settlement, which is today known as Prague, the main city of Bohemia, Ibrahim heard of a country to the north and of an important town located beyond mountains and forests, a commercial center on a trade route from Europe to the East that sounded like *Kracko*. In this way, in that year the earliest known formally recorded instance in which the Jews and the history of Poland and the city of Kraków became intertwined. Ibrahim's was the first ever written mention of Poland and of Kraków anywhere. Thus, Poland and Kraków owe their first appearance in written history to a Jew. We know very little about this Jewish merchant and traveler. His notes from travel to Slav areas in 965-966 have been lost and are known to us only from a transcription by a fellow contemporary traveler and chronicler, the Arab Al Bekri.

We can assume that, like most other literate Jewish inhabitants of the rich, cultured and tolerant Arab Spain, Ibrahim was largely assimilated. He probably spoke Arabic at home, dressed like all his Iberian contemporaries, but he remained faithful to his Jewishness. He kept Jewish traditions, read and wrote Hebrew, although he used Arabic in everyday life; he prayed on Friday evenings, he did not work or trade on Saturdays, he wore a cap or a fez and prayed in a shawl and he did not eat pork or mix milk and meat in one meal. Keeping these religious rules was easy in Muslim Spain but difficult while traveling through wild terrain and we can assume that Ibrahim ibn Yakub made certain necessary compromises. He did not eat non-kosher meat but he ate such food as he could obtain locally, including fish and eggs and he was, occasionally, forced to travel on Saturdays.

He sincerely prayed for forgiveness, and assumed that his Jewish God would appreciate the necessity for occasional compromises and recognize that exceptions to His rules are sometimes inevitable. Ibrahim learned his prayers from and followed the traditions of his Sephardic father. I assume that Ibrahim's father, Yakub, was an important member of the Spanish Jewish colony and a moneylender and advisor to Cordoban Caliph Abdul Rahman III. Poor people did not have the wherewithal to equip and mount a caravan and provide it with its merchandise. Ibrahim's family wealth, along with that of the Nagid of Cordoban Jews of the time, Hasdai ibn Shaprut (915-970), financed expeditions of Jewish as well as Moslem merchant travelers in many directions. Among the travelers, the two most famous were the Jew Benjamin ibn Yona of Tudela and the Muslim Ahmad ibn Fadlan, who went through the Mediterranean and Asia Minor to Persia and the lands of the Khazars.

The caravan of horse-drawn carts and armed horsemen, accompanying the Caliph's Jewish merchant envoy passed an active palisaded trading outpost (which in Roman times was called *Vindobona*) on the Danube River in Ostmark (Eastern March, border region of the Holy Roman Empire of the German People, ruled by a Margrave) and continued to the land of peoples speaking in a complicated tongue, which Ibrahim did not know. Through translators, Ibrahim found that the Slavic tribes were called Bohemians and Moravians. They formed a large powerful Great Moravian state with an administrative center on a small river, *Vltava*. It encompassed a ruler castle and below the castle a settlement of craftsmen and ducal servants. The natives called this center Praha. The state was ruled by a duke of the House of Przemyslids, Boleslav the Elder. In Prague, located in a huge oak forest, a visit of a merchant caravan from the distant Moslem-contolled western Mediterranean must have been an event worth noticing and the Duke himself would have met the new arrivals and admire their outlandish merchandise. One of the duke's young daughters, a girl named Dubrava, would have wanted to see the elegant fabrics and other goods that they brought with them, and eagerly listened to their stories about life in a distant and different world beyond the forests. We know of Dubrava's existence, because she soon entered history as the spouse of the first historic ruler of Poland. Her name, in Polish *Dąbrówka* or Oak Girl is derived from the word *dub* in Czech an *dąb* in Polish, meaning oak (by the way, I believe that the city of Dubrovnik on the Adriatic is also so named because it was situated in a grove of oak trees). The traveler, Ibrahim, would have been eager to hear from the locals about lands beyond the expanse of impenetrable forests to the north. The traveler was told of cities north of Prague, well worth a visit, but located many leagues further, beyond a chain of mountains known as Carpathians and beyond a nest of high, snow-covered peaks of the Tatras. The forested foothills of these rocky mountains were inhabited by fierce and dangerous mountaineers, the Górals, who were known to attack and rob travelers. While Ibrahim must have been interested in the countries beyond the mountains, it appears that he did not to venture beyond Prague. It is likely, however, that he eagerly questioned the natives about this northern country and carefully wrote down what they told him, hoping to use the information at a future time.

The inhabitants of Prague must have told him that the city beyond the mountains was wealthy and its prince powerful, ruling over a rich agricultural plain and a rich forested area, good for hunting. We now believe, that the city, Kraków, had hundreds of inhabitants, clustered around the wooden fortified residence of the ruler on a small hill, called Wawel, above a river called Wisła (Vistula). The ruler's castle was defended by earthwork surmounted by a wooden palisade. His subjects lived in wooden huts clustered

below the hill. The country had a number of other settlements and some thousands of inhabitants, eking a living by hunting wild animals, among them bisons, bears and boars, as well as rabbits, squirrels, beavers, elks and deer, ravens and crows. They also grew a few grains, mostly scraggly rye and groats and vegetables, mostly turnips, carrots, radishes and some beans. The inhabitants kept bees and collected honey, which they used to sweeten their food and fermented it into an alcoholic drink called mead. Trade, in which the locals offered food, slaves, furs, wax, honey, simple clayware, lumber and, the most desirable item, amber from the Baltic coast, was conducted mostly through barter, in exchange for fancy cloth fabrics, notions, damascene metal armor and swords, jewelry, beads and glassware. Some of this merchandise was brought from the Mediterranean, and some from the Middle East and Asia. Merchants came to this city of Kraków from the North, from the East (from an important trade center of Kiev located on the river Dnieper and beyond); as well as from the West. Ibrahim must have been told that this city was a meeting point for diverse cultures. Ibrahim could not have been sure but, finding a few Jews in Prague, he could have assumed that, as in Prague and Kiev and Constantinople and Cordoba, some of the merchants trading or even residing in that Krak town might be Jewish. He was probably confident that, should he decide to visit it next time, he would find welcome and important counsel and possibly shelter among his co-religionists, and they would provide him with valuable data about trade routes to lands beyond. That was one of the advantages of being Jewish: you could count on finding fellow-Jews almost everywhere.

Ibrahim was probably also told of other organized entities east and north of Kraków. One pre-historic state, located along the Vistula River, was centered around a town called Wiślica. A large pagan religious center was located upriver a short distance form Kraków at a place called Tyniec. The most powerful regional country was located in the plains further north, around Lake Gopło, its ruler living in a defensive castle of Kruszwica in the lake. This ruler, Mieszko of the House of Piast, a prince of the People of the Fields, or Polanians, called *Polaks* in their native language, must have been wealthy and powerful for it was stated that he had 3,000 armed men at his disposal, a very powerful force in those days. There were other states, large and small, in Silesia, at Wrocław and Opole as well as on the shores of the Baltic Sea, at Wolin, Rugia, Szczecin, Gdańsk and other localities.

Ibrahim knew that the capital of the Byzantine Empire, a grand city on the Bosphorus called Byzantium and once called Constantinopolis, was often visited by wild people dressed in furs who came from far north. They were called Vikings or Varangians. They came down in boats on the river Dnieper after a portage from the Baltic Sea. These Norsemen have built a fortified trading post in Novgorod and in time took over the cosmopolitan city of Kiev on the Dnieper from the Khazars. Kiev had a sizeable Jewish colony that continued to maintain an intimate contact with the Khazar Kaganate, where Jewish converts ruled over lands located north of the *Pontus Euxinus*, known today as *Kara Deniz* or the Black Sea. Ibrahim might have wanted to establish mercantile contact with the Vikings, these men in furs, through Prague and Kraków, thus by-passing the Byzantines, who exacted heavy taxes from transiting merchants. Also, he might have had grand dreams of establishing a new important commercial route from the Western Mediterranean, through Prague and Kraków to Kiev, then over the steppes of the Jewish Khazars to Persia, the oasis of Khorezm (Korasan) with its capital in Khiva, the emirate of Bukhara, eventually wending its way to Mongolia and the legendary Kitay, now known as China. Once established, such

a more northerly route would have avoided some dangerous desert crossings and would have, in time, served as a rival to, or might even supplant the about-to-be-established Silk Road to China. It would have immeasurably enriched the Spanish Jewish merchants who explored it, as well as increased the importance and wealth of all the places located along it. Unfortunately, Ibrahim never returned to the Slav countries and his large dreams remained unfulfilled. The northern route, while used extensively and helping the growing centers of Vienna, Prague, Olomouc in Moravia, Kraków, Lwów (today Lviv in Ukraine) and Kiev, never became as important as the more southern Silk Road from Byzantium.

When Ibrahim returned to Spain, he brought with him the first written notice of the existence of Kraków and of Poland. It is characteristic of the times that very few people, other than Jews, could read and write in Europe, and those few who could, were all Catholic monks, with little interest in what was happening in pagan areas. A Central European country, which must have obviously been quite powerful and important at the time, was never mentioned in writing until it got baptized, except for the short notice in the diary of a Jewish traveler.

Things moved rapidly in Polish and Jewish history shortly after Ibrahim‘s visit. In 966 the pretty Czech princess Dubrava, who may have greeted Ibrahim in Prague, was betrothed to the Duke Mieszko I of the Polanians. She joined Mieszko in his new capital in Gniezno. Mieszko abandoned his main pagan deity, the Swiatowid, who looked at four directions of the world, and the lesser gods residing in the old oaks in the forests, and converted to Christianity in its Roman-Catholic version. This meant that he accepted the Bishop of Rome as the final arbiter of God‘s will, entitled to anoint individual rulers as kings and emperors. Obviously, Christianity was making inroads elsewhere as well. In 988 Duke Vladimir of Kiev accepted Christianity from Byzantium in its Greek-Orthodox version. Geza, duke of the Magyars, followed in Mieszko‘s footsteps and also considered accepting Catholicism. Geza married Adelaide, the Polish “White Princess”, who was Mieszko‘s sister or daughter. Geza and Adelaide‘s son, Istvan, Hungary first crowned Catholic king, was later canonized as St. Steven. Mieszko‘s daughter Sigrid, known in Poland as Swiętosława, married Eric Victorious, King of Sweden. With Eric she had a son, Olaf, who became King of Norway, converted Norway to Catholicism and was eventually canonized as St. Olaf. When Eric died suddenly, young Swiętosława, as queen of Sweden, had many suitors. Eventually, she married Sveyn Forkbeard, King of Denmark. With Sveyn she had a son, Kanut, who became known as Canute the Great (995-1035), King of Denmark. Canute invaded the British Isles, defeated King Ethelred and became King of England. This was the Canute who, according to legend, tried to stop the waves. He was the son of a Polish princess.

In the East, the once powerful Khazar Kaganate located in the grassy steppes north of the Black Sea, whose ruling elite accepted Judaism and followed its precepts, lost most of its strength in fending off continuous attacks by the Vikings from the North and the Muslims from the South. After many exhausting battles, it disappeared from history around the year 1015 A.D.

While Ibrahim’s mention of the existence of Kraków denotes the start of written history of Poland, Polish-Jewish interactions significantly predate his travels. We can deduce a lot about them from available data from other areas, like the Rhineland in the west and Kievan Rus in the east and supplement it with stories that have come down to us in the form of oral traditions and folk legends.

Chapter 4. Legendary beginnings and early development

I have no way of establishing with any degree of certainty when the first Jews or when my first distant ancestors arrived in Kraków or where they came from. They may have been there before the inmigration of Slavic peoples from Asia. It is almost certain that they were there before Poland accepted Christianity in 966 A.D. Jews were travelling through Poland and are likely to have settled in Poland more than a thousand years ago. The area that is now Poland was in its pre-historic period. Legends from these times abound and archeological discoveries confirm the existence of palisaded old settlements being now uncovered, which had been buried in shallow lakes. In the north of Poland a major important prehistoric community has been discovered, well preserved by the waters of a lake. This community is today known as Biskupin. Another prehistoric settlement was found near Kraków, in south-central Poland near a village known today as Igołomia. Until further research brings forth new facts about the origin of Polish Jews in general, and those in Kraków in particular, all that I can do now is to elaborate on such scant information as exists. This information is derived from persistent old legends, from earliest written sources as well as from archeology and numismatics. I added some educated inferences, using data from other regions of the area, to create a plausible, though largely undocumented, story. Roman, Arab and Byzantine travelers and merchants moved through the area for at least two thousand years, and it is safe to assume that many of them were Jewish. Jewish merchant-travelers in the Slavic lands were known as Radanites or Rhodanites. I am not sure of the origin of that term, although the latter form implies that it was derived from the Latin name of the river Rhone in France (Lat. Rodan), an area from which many of the Jewish merchants must have come. Among the items of commerce that these Radanites sought in the Slavic areas were animal skins and furs, tall trees fit for masts of ships, a drink made from honey called mead, amber from the Baltic shore and slaves. In exchange they offered damascene swords, elaborate arms, jewelry, incense, Mediterranean fruits and such mundane items as scissors, glass beads, thread, notions, buttons, etc.

There exists a theory, enthusiastically embraced by the Hungarian-Jewish writer Arthur Koestler (1976), that Eastern European Jews are derived, not from the twelve Biblical tribes, but from Turkic people of the eastern steppes. In the steppes, located to the north of the Black and Caspian Seas, there was a realm of Turkic tribesmen, the Khazars, who accepted Judaism in the 8-th century A.D. The Khazars were somewhat related to other Turkic tribes, including the Magyars who founded the Hungarian Kingdom, so it was easier for Koestler to wholeheartedly believe that Hungarian Jews must be of Khazar origin, but the theory has not found wide acceptance. I do not think it likely that most of the Polish Jews came from Khazaria, but I accept the possibility that a few of the early Jewish settlers in Poland came, not from Western Europe, but from the east. They may have come to Poland from Persia and Bukhara, traveling through the area north of the Black Sea, which was a part of the Khazar Empire from around 700 to 1016 A.D. Among the reasons why I do not believe in the Khazar theory of origin of Polish Jewry is the almost total absence of Khazar or Turkic words in Yiddish. I believe that only a thin upper crust of the Khazar society, the ruling dynasty and some aristocrats, became Jewish, while the great mass of the population probably remained pagan and eventually accepted Islam. Also against the Khazar hypothesis is the personal fact that my ancestors were Kohanim, presumably direct descendants of the biblical Archpriest Aaron, brother of Moses. More recent studies of the genetic material of Polish Jews (Olson, 2002) also seem to indicate that the theory of Khazarian origin cannot be sustained, although the possibility that a minor percentage of Polish, Ukrainian, Lithuanian, Byelorussian, Roumanian or Hungarian Jewry may have been so derived cannot be dismissed.

What I know for certain from generations-old cherished family traditions, as stated above, is that I am a *Kohen* (plural: *Kohanim*), presumably a descendant of Aaron, brother of the biblical prophet Moses. Also, I know that according to Jewish tradition, this honor can only be transmitted through the male line. While the very existence of Moses and Aaron is known to us only from the legends imbedded in the biblical narrative, the tradition is very strong and the many Kohanim are duly proud of their origin. The Mosaic religion allows Kohanim a number of synagogue privileges but also imposes definite restrictions, such as prohibition of handling cadavers. Recently there have been attempts to compare the DNA of the Y chromosome of a number of male Kohanim, Levites and other Jews, with the results indicating that there seems to be some intriguing historical truth to the old stories (Olson, 2002).

Slavic tribes lived in Central-Eastern Europe between the Elbe and Dnieper Rivers for a long time, presumably after arrival from Asia. While the land was probably sparsely populated, I believe that it is likely that they found the land in possession of prior occupants, like the people of Biskupin and Igołomia, whom they replaced. Legends circulating in Poland today seem to tell a story of a gradual and largely peaceful take-over. There are no legends of heroic battles or conquests. The most common story, obviously trying somewhat simplistically to explain the origin of several of the names of Slav peoples, tells of three brothers travelling with their families through a wild and unoccupied area looking for a place to settle. The names of the brothers were conveniently said to be Lech, Czech and Rus. They came to a wide grassy plain by a lake surrounded by oak trees in the area that is today North-Central Poland and stopped for the night. In the morning they spotted a white eagle soaring above their camp and found it's nest on one of the tall oaks. Lech then said, "...if the eagles favor this spot, then here is where I will settle". The lake is said to be the Gopło, where indeed the historic Polish State had its origin. The area abounds in oak forests and fertile fields. The Polish word for a field is *pole* and the people of the fields, presumably descendants of Lech, came eventually to be knowns as Polanians (*Polaks*) and their country as *Polska.* The name ‚Lech' sounds archaic today, although it is still in occasional use and it has ancient sentimental connotations. Having that name may have been helpful in increasing the popularity of the founder of the free anti-communist workers trade union *Solidarność* and later president of Poland Lech Wałęsa. Poetically, the Poles sometimes refer to themselves as Lechites and the country was known in some languages, notably in old Turkish, as Lechistan, i.e. the country of the Lechs. The legend continued, with Czech settling to the south of Poland and Rus settling to the east. The white eagle is represented on the Polish flag and coat-of-arms. We know that other Slav tribes migrated from the Baltic area further south between the 5-th and 7-th centuries A.D. and that some have settled on the coast of the Adriatic where they came into contact with the Mediterranean culture and with Christianity.

There is another story about the origin of the name of Poland, this time a Jewish one. It may be a vaguely remembered reflection of an actual event. As the story goes, a tragedy befell Jews residing in the borderlands between France and Germany. Pogroms followed the outbreak of a plague and, as often in history, the Jews were blamed for it. A group of elders, having heard of a country to the east, that was rich in fertile lands and forests and inhabited by people speaking a strange tongue but said to be welcoming strangers, decided to travel there to explore the possibility of settling there. Seven wise men, distinguished rabbis, leaders of their communities spent many weeks on the road and arrived at the shores of Lake Gopło and requested an audience with the ruler. The duke was indeed welcoming, admiring their strange attire and listened to the description of their faith, so different from his. The duke believed that friendly spirits inhabited tall trees and he prayed to a four-faced deity called S*wiatowid.* As it happens, the country was in a prolonged period of drought and the grains were withering in the field yet somehow Swiatowid refused or was unable to help. The duke asked the visitors if their god could do something and they responded that they would pray for blessings for this land. They all woke up next morning to a heavy downpour. The delighted and impressed duke offered the visitors the right to settle in his domain and assigned them a piece of land, green with trees. The first day that they camped there they heard a deep heavenly voice from on high, speaking in their holly tongue and they interpreted it as "Poh-lin", i.e. here you rest. Thus, they called the country Polin or Poyln. *Poyln* is the Yiddish word for Poland. I found it interesting that the story may represent an echo of a historical event, an early visit by French Jewish leaders to Kraków (Rosenstein 2004, 38), to explore possibilities of settling there. Near the end of the XI-th Century, at a time of severe massacres by the Crusaders in the Rhineland, Rabbi Moses Aaron ben Mar Isaiah of Orleans led an exploration caravan of French and Rhineland Jewish elders to Poland. While some members of his entourage may have remained in Poland, he himself did not settle there, because records show his descendants lived in Orleans in the XIV-th century.

There must have been at least two areas where related Polish tribes created primitive state organizations, a large one around the Lake Gopło and another one at the

confluence of rivers Vistula and Rudawa. These two eventually coalesced to form the Polish Kingdom, but even today they are referred to as Greater Poland (*Wielkopolska*) and Lesser Poland (*Małopolska*). Legendary rulers of Greater Poland lived in Kruszwica on the lake and also had a castle in Poznań and a pagan religious center in Gniezno. Rulers of Lesser Poland built a castle on a hill in the bend of the Vistula (*Wisła*) River. The hill was (and is) called Wawel, the city below the hill Kraków. The city of Kraków must have been a significant center of statecraft and of economic activity, even prior to the end of the first millennium of Christian era. It was probably founded between the 5-th and 7-th Century. The origin of the name Kraków is unknown, and it is conveniently ascribed to its legendary founder, Prince Krak or Krakus, which does not really solve anything but only modifies the question to: where did the prince get his name? I am not aware of any etymological roots of the word, except possibly for the calls of ravens, which abound in Kraków and are said in Polish to sound like "*krah, krah*". The Polish word for a raven is *kruk*. The prince lived in a wooden castle on the Wawel Hill, pronounced "vah-vel". The name of the hill is also of unknown origin. There is a cave underneath the Wawel Hill. No castle on a hill in the bend of a river, with a cave below, can exist without a dragon. And no respectable dragon can exist without a steady diet of virgins. The Wawel dragon was certainly respectable. Prince Krak is said to have killed it with a ruse: he filled a goatskin with sulfur and left it for the dragon to eat. The beast became so thirsty that it drank itself to death with the river water.

Prince Krakus had a young daughter, called Wanda, a beautiful maiden, who ruled over Kraków after him. Wanda was obviously desirable both because of her beauty and because, as a dowry, she would have brought her Krakovian domain. A German magrave, named Rydiger or Ruediger, asked Wanda to marry him, and when she refused, invaded to force the issue. Wanda led an army and repulsed the unwanted suitor, who, however, would not give up and continued to insist on marriage. To spare her country a continuing ruinous war, Wanda is said to have committed suicide by jumping from the Wawel into the river below. Her patriotic sacrifice is remembered to this day. Once a year there is a festival in Kraków called *Wianki* (Wreaths) celebrated on the shore of the river with fireworks. Decorated floats sail on the river accompanied by a multiplicity of wreaths floating in the water with lit candles in them. This festival probably recalls an old pagan religious festival that survived to this day. As a child I enjoyed watching the fireworks and the floats from a balcony of our apartment overlooking the castle and the river.

It was an old Slavic custom to commemorate heroes with earthen mounds. In the vicinity of Kraków there are mounds dedicated to Krakus and to Wanda. Wanda is also remembered in songs, about the patriotic maiden buried in the Polish land because she "did not want a German". Incidentally, Kraków also boasts more recent mounds, one dedicated to Tadeusz Kościuszko, national hero of Polish (and American) struggles for independence, and to Joseph Piłsudski, leader of Polish legions in World War I and later authoritarian ruler of Poland until his death in 1935.

As the first millennium of Christian era was nearing its end, the world was undergoing rapid changes. Apocalyptic visions petrified Christian Europe, but the millennium fever did not affect pagan areas which then included Scandinavia and the British Isles, lands that form today's Germany and the Slav lands between the Elbe, Oder and Dnieper rivers, as well as most of Asia, incuding Kitay (China) and Hind (India). Also unaffected by the millennial fever were Moslems, whose domains included the Middle

East, North Africa and Spain, because they counted years from Hedjira, the trip of the Prophet Mohammed from Mecca to Medina, and Jews who followed their own ancient calendar. The Jewish population included then, not only the Diaspora Jews in the Moorish possessions and in Mediterranean Europe but also those living in the above-mentioned pagan lands and in the area of the Eastern European Khazar Empire, which followed the Mosaic Faith.

The first native Polish royal dynasty, the Piasts, who ruled from before 966 to 1370 A.D., originated in pre-historic times, i.e. before the existence of any written notices documenting the existence of Poland as a political entity. It is of interest that prior to the emergence of Poland as a country there were Jews there, either living permanently or at least traveling through and engaging in commerce. My preferred age-old legend from Poland's pre-historic past is the one that states that a Jew might have become Poland's ruler before the founder of the first dynasty, Kołodziej Piast, assumed the role. The story goes that a meeting of Polanian elders met on an island in Gopło Lake at Kruszwica in a conclave to elect a ruler to lead them. They argued and argued but could not agree on any one person and were finally reduced to let fate and chance decide. They decided that the first man crossing the bridge leading to their meeting place next morning shall be proclaimed ruler. As it happened, the first man to cross the bridge next day was an elderly Jewish merchant and the Polanians were constrained to ask him to become their ruler. However, the wise Jew argued against it and suggested instead that the oldest of the assembled Polanians be picked to rule. That man was Kołodziej Piast.

Both names of the newly selected ruler are of interest. They both carry connotations. A *kołodziej* in old Polish is a wainwright, a man who makes wagon wheels and puts rims on them. *Koło* in Polish is a wheel. In today's Poland that occupation is rapidly becoming obsolete, but undoubtedly it was a very important one at the time. The word *piast,* or more likely "piastun" in old Polish, denoted a tutor or care-giver and protector. In the context here, it implied a teacher and protector of an under-age heir to the throne, who may also have served as regent after a ruler's death until his pupil reached maturity. Roughly around this time, in France, one such tutor, Charles Martell, who had the title of *Maiordomo*, swept aside his young charge and ascended the throne himself. Perhaps this was also the case in Poland. According to legends, the dynasty that is said to have ruled Poland before the Kruszwica conclave, was that of Popielids, descendants of a ruler called Popiel. The Popielides are said to have ruled from a castle in Kruszwica. The last of them was killed before the Piasts assumed the mantle of leadership. It appears from the names of Kołodziej's successors, the legendary pre-historic rulers of the Piast dynasty, that they tilled the soil, as did most of their subjects. The Polish word for soil is *ziemia.* The dukes are said to have been called Ziemowit and Ziemomysł. The first historic ruler, presumably son of Ziemomysł, was Mieszko I (Mieczysław I). The word Mieczysław implies a man famous as a swordsman (*miecz* is a sword in Polish, *sława* is fame).

During the first millennium A.D. a migration of people took place throughout Central and Eastern Europe, including the areas that later became Polish, situated between the Oder and Vistula rivers. Slavic tribes settled the area all the way to and beyond the Elbe River. The proto-typical German cities of Hamburg and Bremen began as Slav settlements. Berlin is located on what was without a doubt Slav territory. Around the year 1,000 A.D. the area between the Oder and Elbe rivers and west of the Elbe was inhabited by related

Slav people: Sorbs, Lusatians, Lubushans, Veneds (Wends), and others. Beyond the Elbe (Pol.: Łaba, Czech: Laba) lived the PoLabians, i.e. people beyond the Laba. On the shores of the Baltic lived Rugians, Volinians and Prusans. All these people were eventually exterminated by the advancing Teutonic Margraves of Brandenburg and Mecklemburg and later by the German orders of religious/military monks, created by the Popes and given license to convert, expel or, better yet, kill the pagan tribes.

When Mieszko I died in 992 A.D., his son Bolesław the Great, called *Chrobry* (Boleslaus the Courageous) became the duke of the Polanians. Bolesław's realm included Kraków and the Vistulan territories. Apparently, Mieszko united the Polish-speaking Polanian and Vistulan territories before he died. Bolesław's united realm was rich and powerful, sufficiently so to demand recognition from the Pope and the Emperor as a sovereign entity: Bolesław was crowned King of Poland in 1025, and his son, Mieszko II was crowned after him. There exists in Poland a story dealing with Bolesław's crown. For the coronation, he needed a crown anointed by the Pope. However, on the way from Rome through Hungary, his emissaries carrying the crown were waylaid by soldiers of the Hungarian ruler Stephen, King of the Magyars, who grabbed the sanctified crown for himself. In the scuffle, as the story goes, the cross surmounting the crown was bent sideways and to this day the cross on the royal Hungarian crown, carefully preserved in Budapest, has remained bent sideways. Bolesław eventually received another blessed crown for his own formal coronation. Bolesław supported missionary activities by priests of his new religion. When one of his missionaries to the pagans, Wojciech (Adalbert) was martyred, Bolesław used the opportunity to press Rome to recognize the martyr as Poland's first Roman Catholic saint and to create the first independent Polish bishopric in his capital of Gniezno. There he built a cathedral with a grand golden tomb for the new saint. These actions solidified the importance of his country as a European power.

In 1058 his great-grandson, Bolesław II Smiały (the Bold), the first ruler who moved his capital to Kraków, faced an insurrection of powerful nobles, who found the centralization of power in royal hands a threat to their own positions. Among Bolesław's opponents was the haughty bishop of Kraków, Stanisław of the aristocratic family of Kostka. The imperious ruler brooked no opposition and, after defeating the rebels, had the bishop executed. The Church, which became very powerful in the meantime, responded with excommunication, relieved the nobles of allegiance to the ruler and thus forced him to flee. The murdered bishop was canonized and, for good measure, made the Patron Saint of Poland. It is of interest that a similar course of events played itself out in the West around this time, with the Emperor and the Pope competing for power. The Pope relieved the Emperor's vassals of allegiance forcing the Emperor to eat crow and humble himself before the pope at the castle of Canossa. That story did not end there. Unlike the Polish king, the Emperor regained power and had the Pope removed.

Chapter 5. From the Crusades to the Statute of Kalisz (1000 – 1264 A.D.).

When the last Exilarch, the autonomous Jewish prince in Babylon David ben Zacchai (921-945 A.D.) died, he was not replaced. For several centuries the center of Jewish learning and power, following the over-all Jewish population, wealth and importance, was gradually moving from Persia and the Middle East to Arab Spain and the lands bordering the river Rhine. The hereditary Exilarchy ended. Thereafter, the Jewish communities in Persia were led by Gaonim, learned religious men who also assumed civil and political functions. Saadia Gaon developed a famous Jewish academy in Suza. Other famous schools existed in Pumpeditha and Ecbatana. However, the importance of the Jewish community in Persia was declining. Jewish masses were moving to south-western Europe. The large and influential Jewish community in liberal, welcoming, Muslim-governed Spain produced political leaders as well as poets and writers. Salomon ibn Gabirol (1021-1070) and Yehuda ben Samuel ha-Levi (1086-11142) wrote poetry. The latter wrote a poetic story entitled "Khozari", following the correspondence of the Khazar King Joseph with Hasdai ibn Shaprut, the Nagid (leader) of Cordoban Jewry. In 1040 in Troyes in French Champagne a young Jew was born, who would grow up to become the pre-eminent sage and scholar, a rabbi of the large and important Jewish congregations in Mainz (Latin: Moguntia) and Worms (Lat.: Vormatia) in the Rheinland. He would be known to Jewish history as Rashi. The old synagogue in Worms is still known as the Rashi Synagogue. Also in Worms, there is a tower in a section of the medieval defensive walls that is known as the Jewish or Rashi Tower. Rashi was very proud of his ancestry. Among other studies, he did investigate his genealogy and claimed to have established, perhaps not very reliably, that he was descended from King David. Rashi died around 1105; he had no sons but he had at least three daughters who must have been quite prolific, because a great many of today‘s Jewish rabbinical elite claim descent from Rashi. Rashi‘s grandson, Reb Yaakov ben Meir, known as Rabbenu Tam (1100-1171), is celebrated even today in song and story. The modern Jewish poet, Itzik Manger, wrote

a poem and a song about a golden peacock, carrying messages to Rabbenu Tam from the Queen of Turkey. The most famous representative of Spanish Jewry, the philosopher, Moses ben Maimon (Maimonides, Rambam, 1135-1204) wrote a *Guide for the Perplexed*, but also became an expert in contemporary science, astronomy and medicine. Finally, around 1285, a Spanish Jew, Moses de Leon, wrote down one of the most important collections of mystical treatises ever, the founding book of the Jewish Kabalah, the *Zohar*, and attributed the origin of the contents to a biblical scholar, Simon ben Yokhai. I assume that De Leon must have become aware of sufism, a strain of Moslem ecstatic mysticism being elaborated at just about the same time by Jalal-el-Din Rumi, called the Mevlana (1207-1273), the founder of the sect of whirling dervishes in Asia Minor whose impressive green tomb I have visited in the town of Konya (Iconium), in central Turkey. I believe that sufism affected Islam in much the same way as the Kabalah affected Judaism.

In the year 1000 the story of Beowulf was written in the vernacular in England, while the Viking mariner, Leif Ericsson, landed in an unknown landmass across the Atlantic. In 1008 Mahmoud of Ghazni, a desert warrior from Afganistan, an early precursor of Babur, the Mughal conqueror and later emperor, conquered most of Northern India. In 1040 Duncan of Scotland was murdered by Macbeth, in 1045 the Spanish hero, El Cid, was born. In 1063, Alp Arslan became Chief of Seljuk Turks and in 1071 defeated the army of the Byzantine Empire at Manzikert, a battle that started the long slow decay of the Byzantines. Westminster Abbey was consecrated in London. In 1066 England was invaded, first by Harald Hardrada the Dane, and then by the Normans. The conqueror of England, the Duke of Caen and Bayeux, William of Normandy, was crowned King of England. In 1067, in Normandy, one of the great works of Western art, a tapestry depicting William's conquest, was created for Queen Mathilda at Bayeux. It is still on display in Bayeux. In 1077 the previously described quarrel for primacy in the Christian world broke out between Pope and the ruler of the Holy Roman Empire. The Emperor, Henry IV, humbled himself before the Pope, kneeling outside the Pope's castle at Canossa. To the east of Asia Minor, in the land of the Persians, in 1090, Sheikh-al-Jebel, the "Old Man of the Mountain" established a secret Muslim order of drugged and brain-washed assassins ("Hashishim"), who were promised guaranteed entry to paradise, if they died in the defense of their faith, killing infidels. The notion of paradise for those sacrificing themselves for Islam, described as a green garden with water fountains and available virgins, persists to this day. In the last years of the eleventh century, at the Pope's urgings, the entire Christian Europe mobilized to expel the Moslem Saracens from the Holy Land. The First Crusade, under the leadership of a relative of the Merovingian kings of France, a Provencal nobleman, Godfrey de Bouillon, began in 1096. According to far-fetched but very old stories the early kings of France, tried to claim descent from a child of Mary, possibly Mary of Magdala, said to have been pregnant when she escaped from the Holyland and came to southern France. Questions of legititimacy of Mary's child and its paternity were left to conjecture. It is said that Godfrey might have met and consulted Rashi prior to embarking on the crusade. Believing himself to be a descendant of Jesus and Mary he may have thought that he had some Jewish blood. For all that, he is known to have encouraged anti-Jewish pogroms. Jerusalem fell to Godfrey and the Crusaders in 1099. On Godfrey's orders all Muslim and Jewish inhabitants of the city were massacred and their wealth plundered.

The next century was a hard one for Jews in Catholic Europe. The Pope was exhorting kings, nobility and commoners to rally and go on crusades to keep the Holy Land

and Jerusalem from the hands of the Saracens. But the Moslems were far and difficult to get at, so in the meantime the crusading mobs turned against local heretics and local non-Christians, primarily Jews, and killed large numbers of them. The Jews were looking for new places to settle. The Rabbi of Orleans travelled to Poland. Many of the persecuted Jews in French-German borderlands along the Rhine and Rhone rivers moved eastwards to the relative safety of Silesia, Bohemia, Moravia and Poland. In the latter, they were said to have been welcomed and protected by local rulers. Jews, as the People of the Book, always taught their male children to read the Bible and its commentaries. During the Dark Ages in Europe, at a time when no lay people and only a few priests could read and write, the ability of Jews to read and to keep records plus their contacts all over the known world, made them invaluable as promoters of trade. The Polish princes were eager to have the Jews and protected them. Jews were completely dependent on the rulers for security and in return owed the princes loyalty and paid stiff taxes, thus enriching the rulers and the country. At the time of dire persecutions in the West, the arrangement in Poland was beneficial to both parties.

It is known that during the 11-th century, the wife of the Duke Władysław Herman, brother of Bolesław the Bold, dealt with travelling Jewish merchants, and bought slaves from them. The next Polish Duke, Bolesław Krzywousty (Boleslaus the Wrymouth, 1102-1138), a nephew of Bolesław the Bold, formally moved the country's capital to Kraków. In his will he divided the country among his sons, but made sure that the ruler of the capital city of Kraków remained as the premier among equals of all Polish princes. Fights among the princes and their progeny were fierce. Possession of Kraków was deemed important and Kraków changed hands frequently. Bolesław's oldest son, Władysław, ruled in Kraków from 1138 until he was defeated and expelled by his brothers in 1146, earning himself the nickname Władysław *Wygnaniec* (the Exile). He escaped to Germany and in 1147 joined the Emperor Konrad III of Hohenstaufen and King Louis VII of France on the Second Crusade. Kraków fell to his brother, Bolesław Kędzieżawy (the Curly, 1146-1173). In 1154 another son of Bolesław Krzywousty, a brother of Bolesław Kędzieżawy, Henry, Duke of Sandomierz, also joined the Crusaders and traveled to Jerusalem. In 1173 Duke Bolesław of Kraków died and was replaced by his brother, Mieszko III Stary (the Old) who ruled for four years, before being forced out by the powerful Kraków bishop Gedko and the local nobles. The victorious nobles called on Kazimierz Sprawiedliwy (Casimir the Just, 1177-1194), Mieszko's brother and the youngest of Bolesław Krzywousty's sons, to assume the throne. Kazimierz owed his accession to the throne to the clergy and nobility and he rewarded them in Łęczyca in 1180 with all manner of privileges and rights at the expense of peasants who became attached to the soil. We now suspect that Casimir the Just was a mediocre ruler, but he received his honorable nickname from the monks whom he favored and who were then the only writers and chroniclers.

In 1190 the influential and learned abbot of the Cistercian Abbey of Clairvaux, the later sainted Bernard, urged the entire Christian world to help the endangered Christian Kingdoms in the Holy Land. Among those who responded to his call and joined the Third Crusade were the Emperor Fredric Barbarossa and the son of Władysław Wygnaniec, Bolesław Wysoki (the Tall), duke of Wrocław (Breslau) in Silesia. Bolesław's sister, Ryksa, married the King of Castille, Alfonso VII. The ruler of Kraków, Kazimierz Sprawiedliwy, died in 1194 and was succeeded for five years by his son, Leszek Biały (the White, 1194-1199). In 1199 Mieszko III Stary returned to Kraków, punished his enemies and ruled until his death in 1202. Thus, Krzywousty's son, Mieszko III Stary, ruled over Kraków from 1173 to 1177, then lost the throne to Kazimierz Sprawiedliwy, then to Leszek Biały and then regained possession until 1202.

I mentioned all these details because it is known that Mieszko III and several other contemporary Polish rulers had Jewish minters. These Jewish minters struck coins with Hebrew lettering, flattering Duke Mieszko with inscriptions gloryfying him as King of Poland, "Mshka Poland's King", a dignity that he did not reach, for he was Duke of Lesser Poland and Kraków, not a King of the entire country. Other parts of Poland were ruled by others: Dukes Bolesław Kędzieżawy; Leszek I Biały, Konrad of Mazovia, Henryk Brodaty (the Bearded), Henryk Pobożny (the Pious), Bolesław Wstydliwy (the Bashful), etc. The coins could have been minted during any of the periods when Mieszko III was in possession of the senioral province.

The coins have been found, but little is known about their makers, although some of them put their own names on their coins (Dubnow, 2000, 15). Judging by the name of one, Abraham ben Isaac ha-Nagid, I assume that the minters may have come from Muslim Spain where the leader of a Jewish community, whether in Cordoba or Granada, was routinely referred to as a Nagid. Since Abraham did not call himself "Ibrahim ibn Issa" but "Abraham ben Isaac", I infer that he had abandoned Arabic Spain, perhaps to learn coin processing metallurgy in Venice, which was then rapidly becoming the primary Mediterranean center of commerce and industry. I also assume that when he came to Kraków, he brought some of his own silver, bronze and copper sheets. In Kraków, basking in the ruler's favor, he and fellow minters created the first local currency in Poland. They served as *servi camerae*, servants of the court, strongly protected by the ruler. Here is an example of the degree of this protection, indicative of the special respect that Jews received in Poland in the XII-th Century. Around 1173, during the rule of Mieszko III, a Jew had been attacked and beaten by students. Upon complaint to the ducal court, the crime was adjudged very severely, the assailants punished as for the most heinous of crimes, namely sacrilege, and heavily fined (Dubnow, 2000, 15). It is likely that, besides leasing the ducal mint, Abraham ha-Nagid and the other Jews lent money, charging interest, thus creating the first Jewish banks in Poland. Judging from the names on the coins, probably more than one Jewish family came to Poland. The coins were minted over time, thus it is likely that the minters settled to stay, establishing a Jewish colony in Kraków. In a few years they must have petitioned the rulers to allow them to build a house of prayer and a ritual bath. They must have bought land to serve as a cemetery. We know in which area of Kraków they settled, because the Jewish community was located there for years to come with documentary evidence available. The area was north of the Ducal Palace and central market, centered on today's street of Saint Anne where a Jewish Ghetto existed until 1494.

The Jewish minters, merchants and bankers were obviously important to the rulers. It did not matter who occupied the ducal castle and how much these occupants fought among themselves and how cruelly they punished adherents of their opponents. While they used castration, cutting of the tongue or gouging out of eyes as the milder forms of punishment of their enemies, the Jews, even those who served their opponents previously, remained unharmed. Ruler after ruler availed themselves of their services and, in turn, protected them against the clergy, burgers and peasants whom the clergy often incited against them. Coins with Hebrew lettering were issued by Mieszko's rivals, Dukes Casimir the Just, Bolesław the Tall, and Władysław Laskonogi (Ladislaus the Spindleshanks), who ruled Kraków between 1202 and 1228. While the Polish princes were preoccupied with internecine struggles, the

German Margrave Albrecht the Bear (1100-1170) and Duke Henry the Lion (1129-1195), conquered and largely exterminated pagan Western Slav tribes of Połabians, Sorbs and Lusatians. On these conquered borderlands of Germany the margraves established the German March of Brandenburg and duchies of Mecklemburg and others, which in future years played a significant role in the German *Drang nach Osten* (i.e. Push to the East),

In the push to the East the early margraves and dukes were later supplemented by German religious-military orders, among them the Teutonic Order of Knights of the Cross known in German as *Kreuzritter* and in Polish as *Krzyżacy* and the Knights of the Sword known in Polish as *Kawalerowie Mieczowi.* These orders, like the Knights Hospitaliers, were originally supposed to defend the Christian Kingdoms in the Middle East and tend the sick and wounded. When the Holyland fell to the Moslems around 1300 A.D., these monastic military orders were expelled and were searching for new missions and places to call their own. The Knights Hospitaliers moved first to Cyprus and then to Malta, the Knights of the Sword went to Livonia and Courland (today's Latvia and Estonia), while the Knights of the Cross came to what was then Northern Poland. They were invited there by the Polish prince Konrad of Mazovia. Their mission ostensibly was to baptize and civilize the pagan people called Prusans living on the shores of the Baltic. They went at it with great cruelty and thoroughness. The end result was that they enslaved and eventually exterminated these people and took their place, even adopting their name. This process was originally encouraged by the Church as part of the Crusades. At the urging of the abbot Bernard of Clairvaux, the mission of the Crusaders was expanded from fighting the Saracens for possession of the Holyland to fighting any and all non-Catholics, including pagan tribes along the Baltic, heretics in South of France (Albigensians, Cathars and others), Muslims in Iberia, and even the Eastern Orthodox Christians in Constantinople and elsewhere. It also prominently featured attacks on the hapless Jews scattered all over Christian Europe – attacks which led to massacres of Jewish communities on the Rhine along the French-German borderlands and to mass migrations of Jews to the East to Bohemia and to Poland and its eastern borderlands of Ukraine and White Russia. My own family legends repeated orally over generations mention an ancestor who was killed in Koblenz on the Rhine around 1140, during the Second Crusade and a Jewish sage, Alexander Suslin ha-Kohen, killed around 1238 as the aftermath of the Black Plague which was blamed on the Jews.

As part of their efforts at converting the neighboring pagan tribes the Knights of the Sword eventually turned to the east, against the Muscovites in the land near the river Neva, and were stopped in a classic winter battle on ice by a semi-indepenent vassal of the Mongols, the Russian Duke Alexander later called Nevski. The Knights of the Cross, who settled on Polish lands at the mouth of the Vistula, built a number of impressive fortressses, including one in Malbork (Marienburg), which in its time was said to be the most powerful in Europe. They grabbed territory at the expense of Poland and Lithuania and became a significant military force. It took many years for the combined forces of the Kingdom of Poland and the Grand Duchy of Lithuania to reduce their power in battles, first by the Poles at Płowce in 1331 and then by both nations together at Grunwald in 1410. The Knights of the Cross, not only killed off the Baltic Prusans, they appropriated their name. Eventually, in 1525 the Knights abandoned their Roman Catholic religious vows of chastity and celibacy, accepted Lutheranism and kept the land as a lay fief of the king of Poland. In due course they created a German country on the shores of the Baltic. There are

still some remnants of the Slavic Sorb and Lusatian populations in Eastern Germany. They managed to resist Germanization and retained traces of their Slavic heritage. Most of the other Slavs who lived between the Elbe and Oder perished long ago.

As I indicated, the Polish dukes fought each other but they all depended on the services of Jewish merchants, minters and money managers. The minters' origin is not certain. I have several reasons for assuming that while originally they may have come from Spain, they learned their trade in Venice, because there the arts of fine metallurgy, like that of silvering mirrors and glass-blowing, were most developed. It is unlikely that the first minter could have learned his trade in Kraków, thus he must have acquired the know-how before arrival. At the time Venice has become a maritime power. In 1202 it provided an armada of Venetian ships to carry the participants in the Fourth Crusade toward the Saracen East. The Venetians took advantage of the presence of the Crusaders and diverted the ships from the Holy Land to their commercial rival, Constantinople, the capital of the Eastern Greek Byzantine Empire. The Western Catholic Crusaders did not consider the Greek Orthodox Christians as true believers and landing there in 1204 they sacked and burned Constantinople. For a time the great city became a capital of a Latin Kingdom, then returned to Byzantine control, but it never regained its one-time power and splendor. It finally succumbed to the Ottoman Turks in 1453 and was renamed Istanbul. Recently, the head of the Roman-Catholic Church, Pope John Paul II, apologized to the Greek Orthodox for the 1204 sack of Constantinople by Roman Catholic crusaders.

Around 1200 Venice created a major ship manufacturing facility in its Arsenal. The heavy metallurgical industry was well developed, as was the fine metal craft, including minting of gold and silver coins. Another reason for assuming that the Krakovian minters came from Venice is the fact that the Venetian coin of the day, the *grosso*, gave its name to the Polish coinage and even today the small Polish coin is called *grosz*. In Venice the Jews (Ital.: *Giudei*) gave the name to the big island off the harbor, the Giudecca. However, by 1200 the Jews were confined to the area of the old foundry (*Ghetto Antico*) of the lagoon city and I assume that that is where they were trained in metallurgy. After the fall of Constantinople, the *Serenissima* Republic of Venice had a near-monopoly on commerce with the Muslim Near East and served as the main conduit of merchandise from Christian Europe to the Crimea, Persia and the Hind. Within a few years, in 1271, the brothers Polo and their young nephew Marco, took their Venetian trade to Kitay, to the court of Kublai Khan, a grandson of Djingis Khan. The Venetian fleet ruled the Adriatic and the Mediterranean. Its ships traveled to Palestine ruled, in turn, by Christian Crusader princes and by Muslim Saracens. With its wealth, Venice was in a position to develop crafts and industry. Venetian glass, Venetian precious metals and Venetian mirrors, production of which called for skills in both industries, were justly famous. Over the years Venice jealously guarded its secret formulae for making glass, for silvering mirrors and for purifying silver and gold, as well as producing assorted alloys of baser metals, copper, zinc and tin, i.e. brass and bronze. Revealing trade secrets was an offense punishable by death and Venice did not hesitate to send hired asassins abroad after expatriates who might end Venetian monopoly on production of certain high technology goods. I believe that among the most skilled Venetian craftsmen, with the most advanced science and technology, particularly in metal work, were Venetian Jews.

Abraham ben Isaac had an advantage that Ibrahim ibn Yakub more than a century before him did not have. Well travelled roads were created after the baptism of Poland in 966

A.D. Having been baptized Poland acquired some literate monks. It became a known entity with a lively trade with the West. Trails and roads leading from the Mediterranean to the key Polish city of Kraków had been improved and many travelers routinely used them. Still, not unlike Ibrahim ibn Yakub, his namesake, Abraham ben Isaac ha-Nagid followed a route which led through the Eastern German March, the Ostmark or Oesterreich, today's Austria, crossed the Danube, and continued further north. After several days he reached the area inhabited by Slavs. There, he may have met some Jewish traders who gave him precise information about the Vistula River and the city called Kraków. They also may have suggested that he approach the ruler and use his knowledge to start a metal workshop, which most likely would not have any competitors and would be beyond the reach of Venice. The trip would have been an exhausting one but the destination would have turned out to be a nice town, located on a river, with a Ducal castle on a Karst hill named Wawel with houses of burgers below. While the skilled metal worker was probably not the first Jew to reach Kraków, he may have been the first to come there to settle. As settlers, he and the other minters would have acquired or built wooden houses located below the castle, near a wooden Bernardine Cloister, and they would open a workshop. Soon, they would have become well known in town as skilled craftsmen in metal and as honest money-lenders. They would have been in contact with emissaries of the Duke, the old man, Mieszko III *Stary*. Duke Mieszko III the Elder was not happy with the use of coins of foreign origin, ducats, gold tallars, old Roman cesterses and others in Poland. He wanted to have his own coinage made locally with his name on it. He needed honest skilled minters to accomplish this and he found them in the Jewish immigrants.

Assured of the duke's favor, the Jews created the first Polish bracteates. Because their preferred written alphabet was Hebrew and they did not feel comfortable with Latin letters, the coins that they designed had Hebrew letters. Hebrew lettering was perfectly acceptable at the time in newly Catholic Poland, where many monks learned to read the Bible in the original Hebrew and Aramaic. The minters became rich and settled. They moved to more spacious quarters near the central market, creating a Jewish Street. They were ready to start families. At that time a large wave of new Jewish families began arriving in Kraków, escaping from the Crusaders and their pogroms in France and the Rheinland, among them possibly descendants of the famous seers of Worms, the previously mentioned Rashi, and his grandson, Rabbenu Tam. I assume that some of these families had young daughters and marriages have been arranged. After discussions of appropriate dowries, a number of marriages took place in Kraków, possibly with the duke in attendance. I believe that this is how a Jewish community began. After a while, the Jewish community was well established, protected by the rulers. Eventually, with the Dukes' permission, the community built a synagogue. The permission must have contained a proviso that the building not be higher than the towers of any church in town. Indeed, an easily recognizable synagogue architectural style evolved in Poland to satisfy this requirement. For centuries synagogues built in Poland had low roofs and no spires.

Books of Moses ben Maimon (Maimonides), born in 1135 in Arab Spain, eventually reached Kraków and his teachings became influential. To the east of Poland the duke who ruled in Kiev on the Dnieper River, Prince Yuri Dolgoruki (Yuri of the Long Arms), traveled north and in 1147 founded Moscow. In 1150 the University of Paris was established. Jews were expelled from France, although the edict could not have been fully enforced, because repeated expulsion orders were promulgated subsequently. In 1190

King Bela of Hungary briefly conquered the Polish-Ruthenian fortresses of Halicz and Włodzimierz (in Ruthenian: Galich and Vladimir, in German Galitch and Lodomer) and he named his son, Andrew, King of Halicz, or, in Latin *Rex Galatiae*. The name was revived hundreds of years later by the Austrian Empress Maria Teresa, when she participated in the partitions of Poland and occupied Southern Poland and Ruthenia, including Galich and Vladimir as well as Lwów (Lviv, Lemberg) and neighboring areas, and crowned herself Queen of Galitzia and Lodomeria.

During most of the twelfth century the Moslem world enjoyed the fruits of the tolerance and cosmopolitan nature of the rulers and their people. Characteristically, when the Muslim warrior Saladin reconquered Jerusalem from the Crusaders he ordered his troops to refrain from harming the civilian population of the city. To this day Muslims proudly compare his civilized behavior with that of Godfrey de Boullion who ordered a massacre of all inhabitants when he conquered Jerusalem a century earlier. The scientific and cultural developments in the Moslem lands followed the centers of power and wealth, shifting from Arabia to Syria (Damascus) to Mesopotamia (Bagdad) and south-eastern Asia (Bukhara, Samarkand) and then to Northern Africa (Kairouan, Fez) and to Spain (Cordoba, Seville). The old emirate of Khiva in the Khorasan (Khorezm) valley, where in 810 A.D. Muhammed ibn Musa wrote a mathematical treatise called *al gebr*, which gave its name to a new mathematical science of algebra, lost its pre-eminence to Cordoba and Grenada in Spain. At the time the development of science and medicine in Christian Europe was interfered with by religious restrictions, while it thrived in Muslim areas including Spain. Catholic Europe sunk into Dark Ages. The Church was opposed to any innovations and zealously persecuted anybody suspected of heresy. In Europe mathematics, as well as record keeping, were hampered by the use of the old Roman numbering system, which did not lend itself to easy computations. For example, 966, the year of Poland‘s baptism was written CMLXVI. The year of Maimonides‘ birth, 1135 A.D., one hundred sixty nine years later, was written as MCXXXV. There was no easy way to add one hundred sixty nine (CLXIX) to (CMLXVI) to obtain (MCXXXV). The Jewish system of numbering assigning numerical values to letters of the Hebrew alphabet was no better. An important breakthrough in European mathematics occurred when, around 1200, a traveling mathematician from Pisa in Italy, Leonardo Pisano Fibonacci (1180-1250) introduced modified Arabic numerals including the Indian concept of zero to Europe.

In the meantime, the Jewish population of Poland must have grown considerably, but no written records survived to attest to that. The capital city of Kraków was a hub of commercial activity and Jews were undoubtedly in the midst of it. The oldest official written Polish document dealing with Jews and attesting to their importance in fostering commerce, *the Statut Kaliski*, was issued not in the national capital of Kraków, but in the old city of Kalisz. It was issued by its local ruler, Duke Bolesław Pobożny (the Pious) in 1264. It earned him a prominent mention in Polish-Jewish history. In 1190 the Pope Gregory VII called for a Crusade to protect the Christian kingdoms in the Hollyland. He instituted far-reaching church reforms aiming at preventing church dignitaries from forming dynasties and deeding wealth to descendants. Among these reforms perhaps the most important was the introduction of the novel requirement of priestly celibacy. The Pope sent Peter, Cardinal of Capua, to enforce these rules in Poland. In 1206 Temudjin son of Yeziguey became Dzhingis Khan, the Supreme Ruler of all Mongols in Asia. In an incredible burst of energy, in a few years Dzhingis Khan's Mongols conquered China. His son Hulagu and grandson, Batu Khan, continued the conquests. In 1241, having overrun Moscow and Kiev, Batu Khan invaded Poland and Hungary. In Poland the Tartar invasion must have been quite traumatic, because it left memorable imprints, persisting to this day. Legends recounting miracles, such as the saving of nuns by rocks, which enclosed and protected them from the Mongols, are still being told today. Folk festivals, like the *Lajkonik*, commemorating defeat of the Mongols, are celebrated in Kraków annually, with a rider dressed as a Tartar riding a caparisoned wooden horse. The honor of riding on the "Lajkonik" is said to be hereditary, passed from the hero of the defense against the Tartar invasion to his descendants to this day. The most interesting reminder of the Mongol invasion in Kraków to this day is the trumpet melody of the *Heynal.* Every hour on the hour, a trumpeter mounts the tower of the Marian Church in the Central Square of Kraków and plays a melody that is being interrupted in mid-tune. The interruption is said to commemorate an event that occurred in 1241, when a man in a tower saw the approaching enemy army and alerted a sleeping city with a trumpet air called the *Heynal.* He was hit in the throat by a Tartar arrow, which stopped the trumpet call. Today, a trumpeter repeats the interrupted tune four times in four directions of the world. It is claimed that this tradition has been followed regularly since 1241. The Tartar invasion was stopped by the Polish Duke Henry the Pious in a battle at Legnica.

In 1215 King John signed the Magna Carta at Runnymede; in Poland in 1232 the church organization, although not it's individual dignitaries, received the right to hold property in perpetuity. In 1242 Prince of Novgorod Alexander Nevski defeated the armed German Order of Knights of the Sword. In 1246-8 work began on the Sainte Chapelle in Paris, the Alhambra in Moorish Granada in Spain, the El Transito synagogue in Toledo and on the Rashi synagogue in Worms on the Rhine. In 1271 the 17-year old Marco Polo (1254-1324) joined his uncles in a trip to the capital of China ruled then by Kublai-Khan, a descendant of Djingis Khan. Upon his return he wrote a chronicle of his voyage. In 1273 Rudolf of Habsburg was crowned in Aachen (Fr.: Aix-la-Chapelle, Lat.: Aquisgran) as Emperor of the Holy Roman Empire, starting a dynasty that ruled Germany and then Austria until World War I, when Emperor Karol abdicated in 1918 in Vienna. In 1290 the

Fig. 003. Sketch of Cracovia from Schedel Chronicle

philosopher-mathematician William of Ockham (1290-1349) was born. He articulated his well-known principle of "Ockham's Razor", stating that, absent other factors, the simplest solution to a problem is also the most likely to be the correct one. Around 1285 the *Zohar*, the key Jewish mystical treatise appeared. Of importance to subsequent Jewish history, the *Zohar* was used many centuries later by Israel ben Eliezer of Medziborz, better known as Bal-Shem-Tov, and his disciples Beer of Meseritch, Jacob Josef of Polonna and Elimelech of Leżajsk (Lezhaysk), as the basis for the development of Hassidism.

The issuance of the "Statut Kaliski" (Statute of Kalisz) in 1264 by Bolesław the Pious (1221-1279), declaring that crimes against Jews are to be treated like crimes against the ruler and describing commercial rights of Jews, was followed by issuance of similar statutes by the dukes Henry Probus of Wrocław (1273-1290), Henry of Głogów (1274-1299), Henry of Legnica (1290-1295) and Bolko of Legnica (1295) The year 1264 marks the end of the early era of Jewish settlement in Poland, an era known to us mostly from legends and suppositions. After 1264, we have historical evidence, documents, census lists, conscription lists, tax assessments, trading permits, court decisions, mentions in chronicles, incised tombstones and other sources.

In the next century, King Casimir the Great extended the protections of the Statute to the entire country and actively encouraged Jews to settle in his realm. This marked the beginning of a significant migration of European Jews east. Over the next several centuries a large proportion of world Jewry settled in Polish cities, towns, villages and hamlets in territories which by 1500 A.D. included Greater Poland, Galitzia and Lithuania, but also lands which are now the Baltic States, Belarus, Ukraine and Moldova. Over the next four hundred years the center of gravity of the Jewish people had moved to central and eastern Europe and that is where the future important Jewish geopolitical and cultural developments took place.

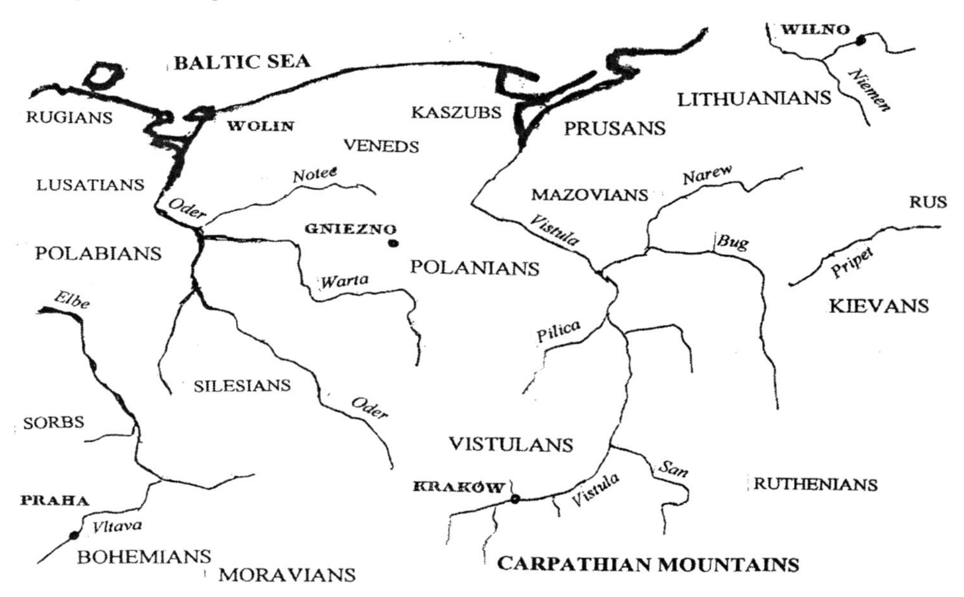

Fig. 004. A map of lands between Oder and Vistula rivers near 1,000 A.D.

Fig. 005. "Statut Kaliski", by the graphic artist Arthur Szyk

Part III. Flowering of Jewish Life in Kraków, 1300-1600 A.D.

Chapter 6. Levko Jordanis, *Argentier* to King Casimir the Great

The number of Jews in Polish territories was increasing significantly as the Jewish communities in Western Europe were being attacked first by would-be crusaders and then decimated by mass pogroms during the time of bubonic plague (1348-9 A.D.), which was, of course, blamed on Jews accused of poisoning wells and rivers. Hapless Jews were emigrating eastward to Bohemia, Silesia and on to central Poland and its eastern regions. In the 13-th century Poland was poor and backward, subdivided into small principalities, most of them ruled by related princelings of the Piast dynasty, descendants of the duke Bolesław Krzywousty. Most of these local rulers tried to occupy Kraków, the country's capital city, and all of them dreamed of unifying Poland and restoring the Polish kingship. Many of them welcomed Jews to their principalities and issued statutes protecting them. The first such statute on Polish lands was issued in Kalisz in 1264. After several attempts at unifying the country by these local rulers, one of them, Ladislaus the Short (Władysław I Łokietek) (1260-1333), a Piast duke of Kujawy, was successful. Łokietek managed to combine several provinces, fended off an invasion by Wacław II of Bohemia (*Good King Venceslaus*) and was ultimately crowned King of Poland in Kraków. It became the task of his son and successor, Casimir the Great (Kazimierz III Wielki, 1310-1370) to consolidate the newly united, sparsely populated poor country. Ascending the throne in 1333 Casimir needed time to increase the country's population and wealth by inviting settlers and increasing commercial activities. Newly arriving Jews seemed just what he needed and he was glad to welcome them. First, the young 23-years-old king compromised outstanding foreign feuds and then proceeded to establish security, law and order, reform administration, strengthen defenses and, most of all, increase the royal treasury and the country's over-all wealth by fostering commerce. He succeeded brilliantly. When he died, he left the country rich, powerful and respected. In his endeavors he was helped immeasurably by his Jewish subjects, primarily by the royal *argentier* or money manager and financial advisor, Levko son of Jordan.

Casimir invited Jews to settle in his kingdom, set up several formal Jewish communities and even established, in 1335, a purely Jewish settlement in a township that he founded near Kraków, named after him Kazimierz, which was incorporated into the city of Kraków in 1791. This Jewish community of Kazimierz by Kraków prospered and eventually became by 1550 A.D. the most important center of Jewish population and Jewish culture in Poland, and perhaps in all of Europe, if not the world. Casimir was the last member of the Polish Piast dynasty, which began with Kołodziej Piast, and ruled Poland for 400 years, until 1370. Under the Piast rule Poland reached great power status, declined into a series of small warring principalities, and, united once again, became strong and economically successful. During all this time Jews lived in Poland and shared the country's fate, contributing to the country's prosperity. As one of Poland's wisest rulers, the only one referred to as "Great", Casimir appreciated the role of Jews in fostering intra-state and international commerce, increasing his realm's wealth. He supported them, protected them and established special settlements for them. During his long reign, Casimir established many new towns, several of which were named after him. From their beginnings, with encouragement from the king, these towns boasted significant Jewish populations. In them, with royal help and encouragement impressive large brick synagogues were erected, several of which survived to this day and can be visited now. One of them is the easily accessible Old Synagogue (*Stara Bóżnica*) located in the Kazimierz part of Kraków. There being few Jews left in Kraków now, the Old Synagogue currently serves as a repository of Jewish artifacts as a Jewish branch of the Polish National Museum. Casimir was a builder best remembered for his encouragement of construction with brick rather than wood. His structures, town fortifications, castles guarding key strategic points, granaries, administrative buildings such as town halls, public structures, churches, monasteries and abbeys as well as synagogues, were built to last and many can still be visited today in Polish river towns, mostly along the Vistula. Among them are the old Town Hall (now the Ethnographic Museum), the just mentioned Old Synagogue in Kazimierz/Kraków, the Royal Granary, Town Hall and Synagogue in Sandomierz, a number of structures in Kazimierz Dolny on the Vistula, and many others.

Almost immediately after his accession to the throne in 1334, Casimir issued a series of privileges to Jews, modeled on those of the 1264 Statute of Kalisz, extending them first to Kraków and then to his entire kingdom. The Casimir statute, confirmed subsequently by most Polish kings, became the bedrock of Jewish legal and commercial rights in Poland. Among other points the statute forbade kidnapping of Jewish youngsters for forcible baptism, a provision that one could only wish were in force around 1850 when a Roman Pope did just that. Indeed, Casimir's statute decreed the death penalty for such kidnapping. The statute entitled Jews to lend money against merchandise, valuables or real estate, limited the percentage they could usually charge for loans, protected them from violence against persons and property and proscribed desecration of synagogues and Jewish cemeteries. Most importantly, the king removed Jews from the jurisdiction of city councils (which were run by their burger competitors and were bound to be unfriendly) and subjected them instead to the jurisdiction of royal governors for issues between Jews and gentiles and directly of the king for cardinal crimes. Issues between Jews remained the province of rabbis and the autonomous Jewish authorities.

Casimir expanded his kingdom through conquests but he is mostly remembered not for his military prowess but for his economic policies which enormously enriched the country and its citizens. Encouraging commerce and inviting Jews to settle in Polish cities led to a significant accumulation of wealth. His Jewish financier, Levko son of Jordan, was only the first in a long line of Jewish bankers serving rulers of Poland. Jewish advisors and financiers were present at the time in many European courts. Among the most important ones were Samuel Abulafia, an aide to Pedro the Cruel of Castile around 1350 and Don Isaac Abrabanel (1437-1509), finance minister to, of all people, Ferdinand and Isabella, the Catholic monarchs of Aragon and Castile. When Ferdinand and Isabella expelled the Jews from Spain they made an exception for Don Isaac and his family, who were given the right to remain there. Don Isaac proudly rejected the offer and went into exile. He died in Venice. The tradition of Jewish financiers and diplomats continued in Europe. Many served later Polish Kings and a number of other European rulers into the XIX-th century.

Levko was rich. He managed the royal mint. He conducted business activities on a very large scale, Alone and in partnership with other Krakovian Jews he loaned money to important aristocrats and important merchants like Nicholas Wierzynek, and also to princes and dukes of neighboring states, among them Ziemowit III of Czersk, the sovereign Duke of Mazovia, then an independent principality, now a part of Poland centering around Warsaw. In Kraków Levko owned many houses and building tracts, some in the Jewish area and some elsewhere. Assured of royal protection, Levko felt free to lend sizeable sums of money to the King of Hungary Karol Robert of Anjou, his wife (Casimir's sister), Elisabeth Piast, and their son (the future King of Hungary Louis the Great). The influence of Levko and his financial enterprises can hardly be exaggerated. It continued after Casimir died because Levko was owed monies by his successors, including the first ruler of the next dynasty, Grand Duke of Lithuania and then also King of Poland, Władysław Jagiełło. Indeed, the signal victory of Jagiełło's armies over the Teutonic Knights of the Cross at Grunwald in 1410, one of the greatest military achievements of combined Polish and Lithuanian forces, was made possible, in part, by Jewish money provided by Levko and his partners (Bałaban, I, 22).

Under Casimir's wise rule the cities of the realm, particulary Kraków, grew in wealth and importance. In 1365 Casimir asked many crowned heads of Europe to meet him in Kraków on the occasion of the marriage of his granddaughter Elizabeth. While in town all the royals were invited to a feast in the house of a rich burger merchant, the later ennobled Nicholas Wierzynek, located on Grodzka Street at the point where it enters the Main Market Square. Nicholas Wierzynek was a rarity, a Polish (not German or Jewish) burger in Kraków around 1360 A.D. He was not a nobleman, but he was rich. He set out to impress all of the foreign dignitaries with his wealth and savoir-faire as well as with his menu. Among the invited royals, besides Casimir the Great, were Emperor Charles IV of Habsburg, King of Bohemia John of Luxemburg, King of Hungary Louis of Anjou, King of Denmark Waldemar, King of Cyprus Peter de Lusignan, Duke of Austria Rudolf IV, Margrave of Brandenburg Albrecht, Duke Otto V Wittelsbach of Bavaria, Duke Ziemovit III of Mazovia, Duke Bolko II of Swidnica, Duke Władysław of Opole, Duke Kaźko of Szczecin and others. There are many records indicating that Wierzynek borrowed lots and lots of money from Levko, the King's financier, and thus it was Jewish money that helped to fund the feast. According to Prof. Bałaban (I, 19-20, 24), not only Nicholas but also his son, Thomas, and his brother, Jan (*Janusz*) Wierzynek, owed large sums to Levko and were not able to repay them. It was Levko's sons, who took all the Wierzyneks to court in 1398. All of these transactions have been carefully noted in preserved municipal accounts books. Obviously, this *Uczta u Wierzynka* (Feast at Wierzynek's) was quite an event and the memory of it is still being cherished in Kraków today and it is one of stories inevitably told to tourists. A restaurant bearing Wierzynek's name, located in the original restored Wierzynek building, still serves fine food. My wife and I can testify that the restaurant, where we had an epicurean meal in 1997, still deserves its reputation as a Kraków landmark. The tradition of fine feasts continues to this day at Wierzynek's. The Wierzynek restaurant with its crystal chandeliers and fine décor and service, is the most elegant and the most expensive in town.

We know that Casimir was a capable warrior and diplomat and a superb administrator. He enlarged his kingdom by conquering the area of the castles and land of Red Ruthenia (*Grody Czerwienskie*). He established up to forty fortresses at the peripheries of his kingdom. He helped his nephew become ruler of Kiev on the Dnieper. He fostered development of large profitable industries among them the salt mines in Wieliczka and Bochnia by Kraków. These elaborate historic mines provided the royal treasury with a large proportion of its income not only during the reign of Casimir but the reigns of all Polish rulers thereafter. Casimir needed a reliable and efficient administrator for the salt mines and he trusted Levko, so in 1368 he asked him to reorganize and then run these enterprises (Bałaban, I, 18). With Levko's help, the king also expanded iron and copper mines and smelters in the foothills of the *Góry Swiętokrzyskie* (Mountains of the Holy Cross), now referred to as the *Zagłębie Staropolskie* (Old Poland Basin), which he defended with fortresses, including one at Chęciny near Opoczno. By the way, the tallest mountain of this Holy Cross chain was and is called *Łysa Góra* (Bald Mountain) and legends have it that it was a nightly meeting place of witches and spirits and it was not an accident that after baptism of Poland the mountains were declared "Holy" and a large iron cross was erected on the bald top of the Bald Mountain.

For obvious reasons the King was very eager for a male heir and tried hard with several wives and concubines without success and the dynasty died out with him. It is, therefore, ironic that, according to persistent stories, he may have fathered several sons with a most unlikely partner, a Jewish girl names Esterka.

Prominent among the many semi-historical stories about Polish Jews is a persistent legend going back many centuries that the king Casimir the Great had a young beautiful Jewish mistress. Supposedly, he met her while hunting in the woods. The king was a large, corpulent man. He loved to hunt, mostly for wild boars, and seems to have spent a considerable time on a horse, hunting in the many large forests of oaks, beeches, maples, birches, poplars, pines and firs, which abounded in his Kingdom. He also traveled all around his domain, inspecting and enlarging many castles. I assume that at times he stayed in castles other than his primary one in Kraków. During one of his hunting trips Casimir must have traveled north along the Vistula, from the impenetrable Niepołomice Forest with its large bison population past the ruins of pre-historic Igołomia and past the *shtetl* of Proszowice with its known Jewish population. Abandoning the Vistula he must have turned north to the newly established community of Kazimierza on the Nidzica River and to the Kazimierzan fortress, now a ruin near the town of Działoszyce. The king continued

to Szydłów, with its still extant XIV-th Century brick synagogue and royal castle. All this hard riding and hunt must have made him tired and thirsty and it is not surprising that the king finally stopped for a drink and a rest in the local pub and inn in the nearby town of Opoczno and it is logical to assume that, like a great many inns in Poland, this particular country tavern was operated by a Jew. Most inns were indeed run by Jews then and later. In the inn the king was likely to have been served a draft of the locally made beer or honey wine named mead by the publican's daughter, said to be very bright as well as unusually beautiful and charming. Her name was Esterka. The legend has it that the king was smitten and first built for her a house in a village called Bohotnica near Kazimierz Dolny on the Vistula and eventually brought Esterka to Kraków and built for her a palace in Łobzów, then a suburb of Kraków, now incorporated as a section of the city. There is no question that a royal palace had existed in Łobzów from the time of king Casimir and sketches of its ruins dating to 1806 and 1820 are available in the Kraków Historical Museum, but by now all traces of it have disappeared. The legend continues, stating that Esterka bore the king several children, including two boys, which is interesting because the king had no legitimate male children and the dynasty ended with his death. Esterka's existence remains an interesting legend. All attempts to properly document it were unsuccessful. There exists a number of literary works written about her by Jews and non-Jews alike (Shmeruk, 1988). There is a possibility that the whole story was invented by the king's enemies, as a means of slandering him, but there seems to be some historical truth to it and it obviously caught the imagination of many. Of course, there was always the Biblical story of Queen Esther. It is of interest, therefore, that Casimir's mistress' name was said to be Esterka, and that Casimir's detractors referred to him as the Polish Ahasuerus. Queen Esther had a protector and advisor, her uncle Mordechay. Casimir's Esterka had such an advisor in the king's premier aide, the financier Levko.

Casimir the Great died when he fell ill after a hunting accident in 1370. The direct male line of the Piast dynasty died with him. Prior to his death he made a complex deal arranging for his succession. The throne passed to his nephew Louis, King of Hungary, son of Carol Robert of the French family of Anjou and his wife, Elizabeth Piast, who was Casimir's sister. As Ludwik Andegaweński, Louis ascended the Polish throne in 1370. In 1373 he sent his daughter, Hedwig, in Polish *Jadwiga*, to become ruler of the country. Jadwiga married the Lithuanian Grand Duke, Yogaillo, grandson of the duke Gediminas and a nephew of the first wife of Casimir the Great, the Lithuanian princess, Aldona. At the time, Lithuania was a major pagan power, with its hegemony extending over lands that are today known as Latvia, Lithuania, Belarus and Ukraine. Yogaillo converted to Catholicism and was crowned, in a most unusual process, as co-King of Poland along with Jadwiga, as Władysław II Jagiełło. A dynastic union combined Poland and Lithuania into a joint realm. The combination became rich and powerful. Unlike Kazimierz, Jagiełło, as a new convert to Christianity, was not friendly to Jews and failed to appreciate their economic contributions to Poland-Lithuania, although he continued to use the services of Levko Jordanis and his sons.

Casimir the Great laid the foundations of Polish wealth and power which manifested itself in the next two centuries under the new rulers, the Jagiellonian dynasty. The country first mentioned by Ibrahim ibn Yakub around 965 A.D., rapidly became a prime mover in European history and a home to a large number of Jews, escaping from intolerable conditions in the Christian Western and Southern Europe during the Crusades and later. Both the country and its Jewish population reached an apogee of their power and wealth between 1500 and 1600 A.D. Around 1550 A.D. Kraków served, in a certain sense, as the main focus of the worldwide Jewish diaspora. It became a critical center of Jewish population, Jewish commercial and trade activity, Jewish political and diplomatic efforts as well as the center of Jewish religious learning and theology. It was the site of the main Hebrew and Yiddish publications. After the fading in importance of Jewish colonies in Persia, Syria, Mesopotamia and North Africa, and after expulsions from France, Germany, Austria, Spain and Portugal the center of gravity of World Jewish life, along with population, moved to Poland, with Kraków then as the main city in Poland. I believe that the importance of Kraków in Jewish history, during the European Renaissance and beyond, has not been sufficiently appreciated.

Chapter 7. Rachel Fischl, advisor to two queens in XVI-th Century Kraków

Wife of a royal financier and confidante of two Polish queens, Rachel Fischl, must have been very personable, very bright, very clever and very well-educated, to achieve the most unusual and influential position that she held at the royal court during the reigns of four Polish kings and two of their consorts. Powerful women relied on her advice and appreciated her friendship. I am not aware of any other Jewish woman around the year 1500 A.D., who had a career parallel to but largely separate from that of her husband.I am aware of two other wealthy Jewish Renaissance woman, Donna Grazia in Portugal, Venice and Istanbul and Pacienza (fictionalized as Grazia dei Rossi) at the court of Isabella d'Este in Mantua, but Rachel was unique in the scope of her influence. I find her a tantalizing subject and wish I could find out more about her. I am surprised how little is known about her today. Apart from some comments in Mayer Bałaban's history of Kraków Jews (I, 71) very little has been written about her. Yet, she deserves a careful study.

The basic facts about her husband's family are relatively well known. Moses Fischl, was well connected, wealthy and influential. It is Rachel's own background and education, her personality and many of her activities that are elusive, One is left wishing that she put down her experiences on paper, the way Gluckel of Hammeln (1646-1725) did one hundred years later. Her husband and partner, Moses Fischl, served for many years as a key royal banker and factor at the royal court in Kraków while at the same time he served as leader of the Jewish community. She was affectionately known by her Polonized diminutive nickname as *Raszka*. Rachel became a confidante and a sort of lady-in-waiting (member of the court entourage) to the Polish queen Elizabeth II of Bohemia, a descendant of both Habsburg and Luxemburg dynasties who married the king of Poland Casimir IV Jagiellon. Queen Elizabeth became the mother of Polish kings Jan Olbracht, Alexander and Zygmunt I, who ruled from 1492 to 1548. Moses Fischl advised the royal family about financial and economic matters, provided or arranged royal loans, directed investments and manage royal wealth. His wife provided advice not only in matters of costumes, palace décor and purchases of jewelry and art but also in matters of domestic policy and back door intrigues at the court. She was surprisingly active in royal foreign policy, mainly offering suggestions for advancing the dynastic interests of the royal family through advantageous marriages of royal children. We know that Rachel followed the same policies at home that she advocated in the palace and she carefully arranged the marriages of her own children. After Moses died she became the *de facto* leader of Kraków Jews. Thanks to queen Elizabeth's acumen and partly thanks to the advice that she received from her Jewish confidante, after the death of king Casimir IV three of the queen's sons became kings in succession. Rachel's influence during their reigns must have been exerted primarily by influencing the Dowager Queen, their mother. When the last of the three kings, Zygmunt I, married Bona Sforza of the family ruling in Milan, Rachel also became an advisor to the new queen, accompanied her in travels to Italy and Belgium to purchase jewelry and Renaissance art for the palace and, in turn, helped her secure the future of her children. Eventually, in her old age, Rachel introduced Chwałka (nicknamed Falka), the young wife of her son Efraim Francis to the young queen Bona and helped Falka become a lady-in-waiting to the new queen. I believe that Rachel's position was most exalted and most unusual for a Jewish woman, even during the enlightened times of the European Renaissance. Inasmuch as it is unlikely that either Elizabeth the Queen Mother, or Bona, an Italian girl, knew any Polish, it is obvious that Rachel Fischl must have been quite accomplished in colloquial German and Italian and probably also fluent in post-mediaeval Italianized Latin.

As described above, with the end of the Piast dynasty at the death of Casimir the Great, the Polish throne was inherited by Casimir's nephew, Louis of Hungary. Louis preferred to stay in Esztergom in Hungary and sent his young daughter *Jadwiga* to Kraków, where she was crowned as Queen. For reasons of state and against her wishes she was made to marry the pagan ruler of the Grand Duchy of Lithuania, instead of marrying her favorite, young Maxymilian of Habsburg. The Duke *Yogaillo* accepted Christianity and all of Lithuania converted to the Roman Catholic faith. He was baptized as Władysław II Jagiełło and was crowned king of Poland with Jadwiga, thus the two of them uniting in their persons the thrones of both Poland and Lithuania. After Jadwiga died, King Jagiełło had other wives and with them became the founder of the Jagiellonian dynasty of Polish kings and Lithuanian Grand Dukes. Two of his sons ascended the double throne after him. The first one, Wadysław III "Warnenczyk" (ruled in Poland 1434-1444) became also ruler of Bohemia and Hungary. He died young battling Turks at Varna (hence his cognomen) in today's Bulgaria on the shores of the Black Sea. His domain was divided after his death. His brother Casimir IV (Kazimierz Jagiellonczyk (1427-1492, ruled 1447-1492) became king of Poland, while his son Louis Jagiellon succeeding him as king of Bohemia and Hungary. In 1454 Casimir IV married 16-year-old Elizabeth II of Bohemia (1438-1505), daughter of Albrecht II Habsburg and Elizabeth of Luxemburg. These dynastic connections insured that the young woman had an independent power base and that her opinions mattered. Just the same, the future queen of Poland had a difficult childhood. Her father died when she was one year old, her mother when she was four. As a child heiress to both the Habsburg and the Luxemburg names, she was protected and given a modern humanistic education but little personal love or affection. She grew up aware of royal intrigues and incessant manipulations, but it is reasonable to assume that she also grew up suspicious of all courtiers and aristocratic ladies-in-waiting who may have conspired to take advantage of her. It is not surprising, therefore, that after she came to Poland the one companion that she could trust was a bright well-educated Jewish girl, not much older than herself, who obviously could not have any dynastic aspirations. That girl was young Rachel Fischl, wife of Moses Fischl, the king's financier. The queen trusted her and enjoyed her company.

Rachel was married to Moses Fischl, son of the first Efraim Fischl and that fact facilitated her entry into the court circle. The Efraim Fischl family arrived in Poland around 1450, from Germany. One by one the German cities were expelling their long-established Jewish communities: Cologne in 1426, Speyr in 1435, Mainz in 1438, Augsburg in 1439. In 1500 Jews were expelled from all of Bavaria ruled then, as during the Feast at Wierzynek in 1364, by the Wittelsbach dynasty which continued to rule Bavaria until the end of the First World War in 1918. While the situation of Jews in Poland was uneven and often difficult and while many Poles looked down upon Jews, nevertheless the situation in Poland was incomparably better than in the West. In Poland, while the Church and the burgers were doing their best to make Jewish life difficult if not impossible, the reigning monarchs and their governors tried to restrain the anti-Jewish campaigns and to protect Jews from pogroms. These efforts at protecting Jewish lives and Jewish commerce were not very effective but they did take place. The migration of western European Jews to Poland proceeded apace and the Jewish population of Poland grew and grew. We know that the Fischls came to Poland from Bavaria prior to the expulsion of all Bavarian Jews in 1500 A.D. We do not know where Moses Fischl met Rachel, but it is likely that Rachel, was also of German-Jewish origin.

Moses and Rachel had many children. One of their sons, Efraim Francis (called *Franczek* to distinguish him from his grandfather), followed in his father's and grandfather's footsteps and conducted business on a very large scale. Rachel arranged to marry her daughters to two learned men, Jacob Pollack and Asher Leml, both of whom, thanks to her influence, became chief rabbis of Kraków in succession. Interestingly, another of her and Moses's sons, Steven, chose to abandon Judaism and converted to Catholicism, apparently at first not creating any major intra-family conflicts. Thanks to what I assume was Rachel's arrangement or at least acquiescence, Queen Mother Elizabeth became his baptismal sponsor. Such conversions among the sons of very wealthy Jews were not unheard of at the time. Some might even have been planned as a family business tactic. I take it as an indication of the enlightened spirit of the times that elite Jewish families were so culturally assimilated in speech, apparel, appearances and behavior that their members were easily able, after having been baptized, to meld into the Christian society. In 1507 Steven, as a new Christian, augmented his inherited wealth by receiving royal privileges, including a right to collect certain specific taxes from Jews. He became a nobleman and shared a coat of arms called Korab with the important family of the Polish Crown Chancellor Jan Łaski, whose sister he married. Indicative of the respect with which Jews were looked upon even while hated as Jews, Steven, as a Fischl, was regarded as an equal by the most noble families of the realm inspite of his Jewish origin. He bought some landed property from one of the wealthiest Polish aristocrats of the time, Anne, Countess Lubomirska, and, after his first wife's death married the heiress Appolonia of Zgierz. He moved among the highest levels of Poland's nobility. However, to his mother's mortification, he befriended the most notorious of anti-Semites, the German-Jewish convert and apostate, Johann Pfefferkorn,

and helped him write scurrilous anti-Semitic pamphlets against the Talmud. It was because of Pfefferkorn's efforts that the Pope condemned the Talmud as blasphemous and had it publicly burned in Rome.

In 1453 an itinerant preacher, the monk John of Capistrano came to Silesia. He was a spell-binding speaker and rabble rouser, and the rousing that he did was mostly directed at Jews living among the Christian majority in Central Europe. In Silesia he fostered pogroms, massacres, accusations of blasphemy, arrests and lynchings of falsely accused Jewish leaders and expulsions of whole Jewish populations from cities and towns. In Kraków an important church dignitary and politician, Zbigniew Cardinal Olesnicki, extremely hostile to Jews, decided that Capistrano was what he needed to persuade the king to sign off on all manner of anti-Jewish decrees. Olesnicki urged Capistrano to come to Kraków, which he did in 1453. A series of massacres ensued and the king was forced to abolish some old Jewish privileges. In 1469 the University was given Jewish buildings within the Judengasse and the Jews were made to abandon their key synagogue which then became and may still be today a part of the University buildings.

With her international connections, Rachel was able to serve as a diplomat using Jewish channels, cleverly advising the king and queen in matters of importance to the realm without being too obvious about it. For example, in 1475 both Fischls, Moses and Rachel, using their Bavarian connections were instrumental in advocating and arranging the marriage of princess Jadwiga (Hedwig), daughter of Casimir IV and Elizabeth of Bohemia to the heir of the Wittelsbach kingdom of Bavaria. The marriage of the Polish princess to George the Rich took place, amid much splendor, in Landshut in Bavaria. To this day the anniversary of this wedding is celebrated in Landshut with massive public dance performances in Renaissance costumes. When we visited Kraków in 1997 we witnessed one such staged costumed performance by a large visiting troupe of Bavarian actors and amateur youngsters who came to Kraków to perform it in the courtyard of the royal palace. Elizabeth the queen, as well as Rachel were well read and aware of the new humanist trends developing in Italy and elsewhere, ripe for Reformation. The royal offspring were taught by an influential modern liberal thinker named Kallimach. Around 1488 a humanist discussion group at court gathered around Kallimach which he called *Societas Vistulana*. The group was willing to question and challenge existing dogmas and to pursue truth wherever it might lead. I assume that participation by the queen served to protect the group from attacks by the Church and conservatives at the court. It is likely that the queen's Jewish companion also participated in the group's meetings. In fact, it is known that Kallimach and his group expressed a strong curiosity about then current Jewish religious and philosophical views and were interested in the original biblical texts in Hebrew and Aramaic. Although there is no written record attesting to this, it is likely that the group queried Rachel and valued her stimulating contributions to its discussions.

In the meantime Rachel had problems at home. In 1496 she bore the last of her children, a girl named Sarah. Trying to insure Sarah's future in turbulent times, Rachel engineered her wedding at the ripe age of six to a rich Hungarian Jew, David of Buda. This turned out to have been a costly mistake. At the age of 12, in 1508 Sarah renounced and rejected the marriage and was granted a divorce (a *ghet*) by her brother-in-law Jacob Pollack, then Rabbi of Kraków, a recognized prominent Talmudic scholar. Rumors began to circulate that Sarah renounced the marriage because she had a lover although married.

This led to scurrilous songs by wandering troubadours. The divorce was then challenged by other Talmudic experts. Pollack and the entire Fischl family were excommunicated by Juda Mintz, chief rabbi of Padua in Italy, a seat of a great university favored by many Poles and Polish Jews and also then a recognized center of Jewish learning, and by rabbis Pinkas of Prague and Jacob Margulies of Nurnberg. Mintz was the father of MaHaRaM Padua and the founder of the Katzenellenbogen religious dynasty. Pollack was forced to temporarily leave Kraków and gave up the position of chief rabbi but returned after Rachel secured for him a royal protective "iron letter". After his return he founded the first Talmudic academy in Kraków. Pollack (1460-1530 or 1541) was a learned, brilliant but controversial character, who tangled with many rabbinical authorities. He was an influential inventive Jewish scholar, who created a system of exegesis known as *pilpul,* which came to be used extensively thereafter. His obvious talent and deep learning, including his pioneering method of interpreting the Talmud attracted students from all over Europe. Rachel, undaunted by troubadour ridicule and by excommunications from abroad, successfully insisted that her other son-in-law Asher Leml be named new chief rabbi of Kraków.

In 1522 a new scandal roiled the Jewish community, again involving Jacob Pollack, then the *Rosh Yeshiva* (head of the Talmudic academy) that he founded. Malicious rumors accused one of queen Bona's Italian-Jewish physicians, Samuel bar Meshulam, of consorting with a married woman (Bałaban I, 116-8). The rumors were formally denied, but that only fueled the rumor mill and, as stated by Bałaban, the affair again gave rise to derisive songs by wandering minstrels. In 1522 the libeled physician sued for retraction in Jewish religious courts, claiming that the primary spreader of the malicious gossip was no other than the learned Jacob ben Josef Pollack, head of *yeshiva* and husband of Ester, daughter of the richest Jewish couple in town, the late royal factor Moses Fischl and his widow Rachel, then still an advisor to the queen-mother. The case against Pollack became ugly. Among witnesses against him was his own brother-in-law, then chief rabbi of Kraków, Asher Leml, husband of another of Fischls' daughters, Hindl. Pollack denied that he spread the rumors. The *beth-din* (Jewish religious court) asked him to appear before it to swear that he did not spread calumnies against bar Meshulam. Pollack considered this an insult and chose not to appear, but left town. He died in Palestine; his death is given variously as 1530, 1532 or even 1541.

King Casimir IV and his queen Elizabeth of Bohemia had several sons. One became a church dignitary and a cardinal, another led an ascetic life and after he died was declared a saint and patron of Lithuania, but three other sons became rulers of Poland in succession after their father's death: John Albert (Jan Olbracht, ruled 1492-1501), Alexander (1501-1506) and Sigismund I the Old (Zygmunt I Stary, 1506-1548). The first two died without heirs. The last of queen Elizabeth's sons to become king, Zygmunt I was crowned in 1806, one year after his mother's death. None of the three sons had any children, and the last one was not getting any younger, having ascended the throne at the age of 39, after two of his brothers. Obviously, his then ailing long-time wife Barbara Zapolya was not going to have any children. When the sickly queen Barbara died a search began to find him a suitable new mate. Even before her demise, the queen-mother Elisabeth actively investigated potential new wife candidates with the obvious help of her Jewish lady-in-waiting. Eventually, the king's advisors settled on Bona Sforza, a young, healthy and well educated heiress to the Sforza, Visconti, Chiaromonte and de Lusignan dynasties,

heiress to the Duchies of Bari and Bassano in Italy. Bona's father. Gian Galeazzo II Sforza, died when she was an infant, leaving his widow without much support from his successor Lodovico "Il Moro" (1451-1508), Gian Galeazzo's brother, Bona's uncle. Lodovico was a typical cunning Renaissance ruler, intriguing to get ahead, switching alliances as required for success and marrying his own children off to the ruling houses of Europe. His daughter married the Emperor Maxymilian I of Habsburg and his son Giovanni Sforza married Lucretia Borgia, daughter of the Borgia Pope Alexander VI (that latter marriage was quickly annulled). Bona's fate was not of his concern. However, Bona was a child of an exceptional lineage. She was a cousin of Francis I of France. One of her cousins married the emperor Maxymilian I of Austria. Her mother, the remarkably beautiful Isabella of Aragon (1470-1524) was a descendant of the de Lusignans and carried the hereditary titles of Queen of Jerusalem and of Cyprus. She was a strong woman with her own rights to the dukedoms of Bari and Bassano in the south of Italy. There was no future for her in Milan so she took her daughter away from the nest of intrigues at the Sforza court and went to the quiet heaven of Bari. There she provided the girl with an exceptional humanistic education. She saw to it that Bona's interests were protected and maneuvered to find a suitable marriage for her. In this endeavor she recruited powerful allies, including the Habsburg emperor. A suitable marriage was eventually arranged and in 1518 the 24-year old Bona married the 51-year old childless king of Poland and Grand Duke of Lithuania. With a splendid entourage, Bona travelled to Kraków where she was greeted with pomp by the king and an assembly of Polish nobles.

In the meantime in Milan, Lodovico had a young mistress, a fifteen year old girl of a prominent family by the name of Cecilia Gallerani. For a time. Lodovico also had a court artist, one Leonardo born in the small Italian community of Vinci (1452-1519), who painted a wall image of the Last Supper on a refectory of a Milanese church. There is a fascinating connection between Lodovico Sforza, Leonardo da Vinci, Cecilia Gallerani and Kraków. In 1490 Leonardo painted a portrait of the young mistress, oil on wood, holding a nearly hairless pet ermine in her lap. There is evidence that Lodovico ordered the painting, called *Lady with Ermine* to give it to Cecilia, perhaps as a souvenir, because he was about to give her up in order to marry Beatrice d'Este of the ruling family of Ferrara (Zoellner, 2004). What is fascinating is that today Leonardo's painting of Cecilia is in Kraków in the Czartoryski Museum established by this pre-eminent Polish aristocratic house. It has been in the possession of the Czartoryski aristocrats for many generations, a tribute to that family's wealth and good taste. I would love to know when and by what route did this particular painting end up in a Krakovian museum. I believe that there are too many coincidences for that painting to have found its way there purely by serendipity. Fate eventually caught up with Lodovico; he was defeated by the French, who conquered Milan in 1500, and imprisoned him in France until his death in 1508. The artist Leonardo eventually moved to France where he died.

By the way, I have always wondered about another of Leonardo's subjects, the sitter for the painting now known as Mona Lisa (La Gioconda) in the Louvre in Paris, known for her enigmatic smile. How come that Leonardo who was then a court painter at the Sforza court in Milan and painted primarily princely ladies connected one way or another to the Sforza family painted the wife of a merchant Il Giocondo? And how come that Leonardo never delivered the painting of La Gioconda to Il Giocondo but kept it and eventually took it with him to France? Was Il Giocondo so rich that he could commission a painting from a painter as famous as Leonardo was then, and if so then why did he not acquire the painting when it was finished? I am not aware of any record of Il Giocondo's sudden death or bancruptcy or of any notes by Leonardo that he was not paid but used the merchant's beautiful wife as a model or that he refused to deliver the finished portrait to the rich patron who ordered it. The sitter's currently accepted identity was not established during Leonardo's life but much later. Several art historians have suggested that, judging from the painting itself, the sitter may have been pregnant when posing. Recently it has been suggested by one maverick art historian that "Mona Lisa" was not the wife of a mere Milanese merchant but the Duchess of Milan herself, Isabella of Aragon, wife of Gian Galleazo II, which might have been then pregnant with the future Polish queen Bona. This would explain why Il Giocondo did not receive that portrait to which he would have had no rights. History of Isabella of Aragon also might explain why Leonardo could not sell it but kept it with him when he left Milan. We know that the husband of the painting's newly proposed subject, the Milanese duchess, if that is who it was, count Gian Galleazo II died, the duchess herself had no available funds to redeem it and left Milan for Bari. Her brother-in-law Lodovico would not have been interested in purchasing a portrait of his late brother's wife. Without claiming any expertise in this area, I am partial to that explanation why Leonardo brought the painting to France and it ended up in the Louvre. If true, it would mean that the woman with the most famous smile in the art world was the pregnant mother of a Polish queen who, in turn, became a friend and patroness of two outstanding Jewish women in Kraków.

With Bona Sforza as queen and the wealth of the combined Polish-Lithuanian Commonwealth available to her, the Kraków court became a center of modernity and learning. The queen seems to have had an exquisite taste and used many Jewish advisors and jewelers, who also displayed sound financial judgement and artistic taste. On her many shopping trips to Italy to buy jewelry and art works, she was accompanied by her Jewish financial advisors and by Chwała (*Fałka*) Fischl, Rachel's daughter-in-law, one of Bona's own court ladies and special advisors. Bona did not hesitate to use lots of money to get what she wanted. She brought with her to Poland an array of Italian architects and also several Jewish physicians and bankers. Her architects converted the old gothic buildings of the Krakovian royal castle into a spectacular Renaissance palace with a large arcaded courtyard that is to this day among the largest, most opulent and best decorated in Europe. With financing provided by Jewish bankers, my ancestors and relatives among them, she commissioned and brought to Kraków a large collection of Belgian Arras tapestries, among the most beautiful in Europe, comparable to the *Unicorn* series in the Louvre. Indeed, when the Metropolitan Museum of New York held recently (in 2002) an exhibition of the best of European Renaissance tapestries, chief among the displayed works were large tapestries from Kraków. The poster published by the Museum for its tapestry exhibition featured one of the Krakovian tapestries, indicative of their remarkable appeal.

Thanks to queen Bona, not only walls, but also ceilings of royal chambers were elaborately decorated. One chamber had its ceiling decorated with sculptured heads of known personalities and legendary characters. Looking up at the ceiling, it is easy to see that one of the heads has a gag over its mouth. An explanation told in Kraków to this day has it that when Bona's son, King Zygmunt II August (1548-1571), held court in this

room and was about to condemn an innocent man, the head spoke up and urged him "to judge justly" (in Latin, *Rex Auguste, iudica iuste*). To prevent any further interference by the head with the King's justice, a tape was sculpted over its mouth. Many of the original heads were destroyed over time and, during renovation of the palace at the beginning of the Twentieth Century, substitutes were carved by one of Poland's foremost sculptors, Xawery Dunikowski, and his students. Among Dunikowski's student assistants who helped to sculpt the replacement heads at that time was my aunt by marriage, Sala Klipper Aleksandrowicz, a talented sculptress, wife of my uncle Ignacy, described later.

Zymunt I Stary (1467-1548) ruled for 42 years, from 1506 to his death. This was the time when Poland and its Lithuanian partner were militarily and economically secure, among the richest and largest countries in Europe. Their dominions extended from Courland on the northern Baltic coast to the Black Sea, from the river Oder to the Dnieper. Commerce thrived. As proof of Poland's power and importance a public ceremony of the "Prussian Homage" took place in Kraków. Northern Poland was occupied by the powerful religious/military Teutonic Order of Knights of the Cross, originally invited to Poland by Polish duke of Mazovia. The order, originally created to fight Saracens in Palestine and invited to convert pagan tribes on the Baltic shore, was bound by Roman-Catholic vows of poverty, celibacy (chastity) and service. The knights exterminated the pagans, ignored their vows, occupied the land and grew into a military power threatening Poland and Lithuania. It took several campaigns and many battles to defeat the Order and limit its ambitions. In 1525 the last Grand Master of the Order, Albert of Brandenburg, an ancestor of the Kaisers of Germany, decided to abandon Catholicism, disband the Order and convert to Lutheranism. Originally, the Order was settled on lands legally owned by Poland, Now, the last Grand Master asked to receive the Prusan lands conquered by the Order from their legal owner and feudal overlord, the Polish King, as a hereditary lay ruler. Thus, he would become a lay Duke of "Prussia" as a vassal of the King of Poland, Zygmunt I the Old. To receive this land as a fief in his new capacity, he was obliged to promise eternal allegiance to the Polish crown and pay public homage to his liege at the Main Market Square of Kraków, the Polish capital. He swore fealty for himself and all his successors in the presence of massed dignitaries, foreign rulers and representatives of the Pope. The event, of great historic pride to Poles, is depicted in a huge patriotic painting by Jan Matejko, which hangs in the museum located on the second floor of the Sukiennice (Cloth Halls) in the center of the Main Market Square (*Rynek Główny*), of Kraków. This unique public Prussian Homage (in Polish, *Hold Pruski*) represents the peak of Polish power and importance.

Around 1520 Kraków became a center of cultural and economic developments, among the most important in Europe. The country's wealth, mostly due to grain exports, was a magnet for Spanish, Italian and German philosophers, physicians, artists, scientists, architects, astronomers and astrologers, and, among them, many Jews. Craftsmen, scholars and artists came to Kraków in droves. The Jagiellonian University of Kraków had few, if any, peers in Europe. Among its students at the time was the brilliant Toruń-born astronomer, Nicholas Copernicus (1473-1543), who also received a doctorate in theology from the Italian University of Ferrara in 1503. The atronomer and mathematician Wojciech of Brudzew, a professor at the Kraków Jagiellonian University, taught many students, among them Copernicus. Later, in 1543, Copernicus published his revolutionary *De revolutionibus orbium celestium libri 6* in the year of his death, thus escaping the clutches

of the papal Holy Office of the Inquisition, which did not exactly approve of it. Copernicus' later supporter, Galileo Galilei (1564-1642) was not so lucky. He was forced to formally recant the theory that the earth may not be the center of the Universe. His *Dialogue on Two Chief World Systems*, published in 1632, even though pretending to be neutral between the Ptolemaic Earth-centered and Copernican Sun-centered world systems, was placed on the Index and proscribed in all Catholic countries. The late Krakovian Pope, John Paul II, only recently brought the Roman Church to acknowledge that the Church was wrong in denying the reality of world cosmography and that, as Galileo insisted, the Earth rotates around the Sun and not *vice versa,*

The flowering of wealth and culture in Kraków in the XVI-th century was also reflected in the Jewish street. Just as Italian architects converted the royal palace into a Renaissance architectural masterpiece, other Italian architects directed the rebuilding of the Old Synagogue in Kazimierz into an impressive edifice, which can still be visited today. Jewish cultural as well as economic activity on European scale took place in Kraków. An astounding numbers of important Jewish personalities of the period were either born or lived in Kraków, or came to Kraków to study and stay for a time. The Jewish population of Polish cities, towns and villages grew in numbers and contributed significantly to the country's developing wealth. The earlier Jewish area near the Main Market Square in the center of Kraków (not Kazimierz) had several houses of worship, a public bath and a cemetery. A tower, part of Kraków's defensive walls was known as the Jewish Tower, and the Jews were responsible for manning their section of the walls. The Jewish area, the Jewish Street, was very well located, off the main market next to the University, and it was very desirable. It was coveted by the University eager to expand its main campus. Eventually, during the rule of Jan Olbracht in 1495, an era rendered memorable in world history by the voyages of Columbus and in Jewish history by the expulsion of Jews from Spain by the Catholic Monarchs, Ferdinand and Isabella, the Jews were forced to abandon the area in the center of Kraków and move to the nearby town of Kazimierz, where a number of them lived since the time of Casimir the Great. We may assume that Rachel Fischl, as the most influential personality in the Jewish Street and as friend and companion of the queen-mother, protested this expulsion but could not avert it. The net effect of her protests was that she alone of all the Jews was allowed to remain in the city along with her entire family. In fact, when Rachel's daughter Hester married Jacob Pollack in 1501, Rachel gave the couple one of the elegant houses that she owned on the old Jewish street next to the palace in which lived her baptized Catholic son Steven, the new Polish nobleman. After 1495 the Jewish Town in Kazimierz hosted a large concentration of Jews. In a way, Kraków-Kazimierz became the capital city of the Jewish diaspora, becoming richer, more vibrant and thus more important than such other contemporary centers of Jewish thought as Safad, Damascus, Cordoba, Padua, Amsterdam, Istanbul or Regensburg. It became the foremost center of Jewish culture and commerce, perhaps the largest in the world.

Within two years of her marriage, in 1520, queen Bona had a male child, Poland's long awaited male heir to the throne, named Zygmunt II August. She saw to it that he was assured the throne after his father by having him crowned as the king's successor at the age of 9. She also maneuvered, with Rachel's daughter-in-law Chwałka's help, to marry off her other children, all girls, while they were very young. Thus, Anne Jagiellon was married to Stefan Bathory, Duke of Transylvania, and Catherine to John III Vasa, King of Sweden.

Both marriages turned out to have been prescient. After Zygmunt II August died without an heir and his successor Henri de Valois left the Polish throne, Anne's husband Stefan Bathory became king of Poland and after him members of the House of Vasa ascended the Polish throne. In 1526 the Jagiellon king of Bohemia and Hungary Louis the Jagiellon, Zygmunt's cousin, died fighting a Turkish army at Mohacs. With his death the wide dominion of the Jagiellon dynasty ended. As per previous dynastic arrangements, Bohemia and Hungary were taken over by the Habsburgs.

As an example of how rapidly the status of the Jews could change, among all the apparently favorable quiet conditions, a sudden disaster striked in 1485. When the king Casimir IV Jagiellończyk was away in his alernative capital, the Lithuanian Vilna, Krakovian Jewish elders, a Dr. Alexander among them, were imprisoned and presented by Kraków Catholic authorities with a document to sign which severely restricted Jewish rights to trade in the city proper. Pressured, under duress, abandoned by the local royal governor and not having any choice, they agreed to sign away Jewish commercial rights in the city. This extorted agreement came to haunt Krakovian Jewish merchants over the centuries; it was often invoked by Kraków burgers against their Jewish competitors. The prohibitions were so restrictive that the Jews could not abide by them and had to find ways to circumvent them, legally or otherwise. They used bribery, the influence of Rachel Fischl and her queen over the king and the influence of the bribed Kraków voivode, Peter Kmita. They fought the hostility of the local archbishop and learned how to temporarily mitigate some of the worst provisions of the agreement, but it remained a bane of their descendants until 1867, when it was formally rescinded.

During the reign of Zygmunt I an additional problem arose. Poland had its own, milder, version of the problem that ostensibly led to the expulsion of Jews from Spain. A few Polish aristocrats, among them an elderly heiresss, became interested in the tenets of Judaism. The Church was appalled, considered it all a fault of proselytizing by Jews and moved to punish them for supposedly encouraging "Judaization". One elderly Catholic woman who gravitated towards Judaism was convicted of apostasy and publicly burned at a stake. The entire Krakovian Jewish community council was imprisoned on order of the local ecclesiastic authorities and tortured in jail from 1539 to 1542. Even during the presumably enlightened Renaissance, the Senior of the community, Dr. Moses Fischl, son of Efraim Francis Fischl and grandson of Moses and Rachel, died after release from jail, as a consequence of the treatment in prison and the tortures that he suffered. He was not the first nor the last senior Jewish official to be tortured by the Church authorities. However, unlike Spain and its New World colonies, Poland did not establish local Inquisition Offices and, with few exceptions, did not engage in any prolonged hunt for apostates, Jewish converts to Christianity, who might have continued secretly to follow the customs of Judaism, or Catholics who quietly followed some Mosaic religious precepts. In Poland the elderly convert was the only one to die in flames for apostasy. Many, many more died in Spain and elsewhere in Europe. I find it fascinating that today, some 500 years later, apostasy can still be punishable by death in Moslem countries ruled by the strict *sharia* religious law of the Koran.

Kraków's role as a center of Jewish learning, religious and semi-religious literature, publishing and printing, is well documented. In distant Safad in Palestine Joseph Caro (1488-1575) wrote the key set of religious regulations, a treatise called *Shulkhan*

Arukh, which soon arrived in Kraków and inspired many commentators, of whom later. In 1534 Anschel of Kraków wrote the first book in Yiddish, mainly addressed to women who spoke Yiddish and knew little Hebrew. In 1622 Jacob ben Isaac of nearby Janów (1550-1628) wrote the *Tsene U-rene*, a compilation of Biblical stories written in Yiddish. The first book printed in Hebrew in Kraków appeared in 1534 in the establishment of Jewish printers, the brothers Halicz. The brothers converted to Catholicism but continued to print Hebrew prayer books. The local Jewish community tried to boycott these books but the brothers sought the help of the king and in 1537 received a royal order forcing Kraków Jews to continue buying the Halicz *siddurs.*

King Zygmunt I Stary, i.e. the Elder as well as many high aristocrats, had Jewish financiers and Jewish physicians, including some who came from Germany and some from Italy. Jews, being able write and keep accounts, held leases on toll and tax collections, were tenants and sub-tenants of royal mint and royal salt mines. In fact, it appeared to many courtiers that the king and the nobles favored Jews over Christians. In 1521 the king's secretary and chronicler, Justus Decius, complained that "there is hardly any toll or tax for which they [*the Jews*] would not be responsible". Zygmunt I and his son and successor, Zygmunt II August, had several Jewish physicians, among them Isaac of Spain and Salomon Ashkenazi of Udine. The latter left Poland in 1565, six years before the king died, and joined the court of the powerful Ottoman Grand Vizier Ahmed Sokolli in Istanbul. Zygmunt the Elder and Zygmunt August also had a number of Jewish *argentiers*, among them the above-mentioned Moses Fishl and Lazar of Brandenburg. Three prominent Krakovian Jewish family surnames appeared in written records around 1500 for the first time: the Isserles, the Jekeles and the Kalahoras. I believe that my ancestors can claim relationship with all three and I will deal with the nature of this relationship below. I also believe that the origin of the surname Aleksandrowicz dates to this time, as I will try to demonstrate.

At the time, the court of Zygmunt I and Bona became embroiled in a private scandal when the King's only son, also Zygmunt, who later ascended the throne as Zygmunt II August, fell in love with one of Bona's ladies-in-waiting, the reputedly very beautiful and vivacious Lithuanian Princess Barbara Radziwiłł. Barbara was an aristocrat, but the queen did not consider her good enough to marry the heir to the throne because she would not bring any new territories as dowry and thus would not advance the royal dynastic interests. Her family, the Radziwiłłs, was descended from the Lithuanian ducal house, and carried a hereditary right to a princely title. Her father, Jerzy Radziwiłł served as the Grand Marshal of Lithuanian armies. The Radziwiłł family grew in power and wealth. It owned huge estates in eastern Poland and western Ukraine. It aspired to sovereignty, which it, however, never achieved. To this day, the Radziwiłłs own large tracts of land and a number of castles and palaces; they are rich and powerful. One of the present-day Radziwiłłs, Prince Stanisław (Stash), married Jackie Kennedy's sister, Lee Bouvier. However, in 1500 the old King and Queen felt that a marriage of their heir to a subject Polish-Lithuanian princess was not good enough. Zygmunt August married Barbara secretly and their semi-public love affair provided choice gossip for the European courts. Barbara died almost immediately after Zygmunt II August accession to the throne and rumors had it that Bona, by then a widowed Dowager Queen may have had a hand in her poisoning. Later Zygmunt August married twice consecutively to two Austrian Hapsburg prinesses, but he died without an

heir. The Jagiellonian dynasty died with him. As a Lithuanian Princess, Barbara became a patriotic icon. There is now in the Lithuanian capital of Vilnius a street named after Barbara Radziwillaite, presumably as Grand Duchess of Lithuania. The relation between Bona and her son the king became strained, Bona was by then mistrusted by many Poles and she eventually left Poland and went to her Italian possessions where she died shortly.

Under the last of the Jagiellons, Zygmunt II August, Polish Jews received a great deal of formal autonomy. A powerful country-wide Jewish Council, the *Vaad Arba Aratzot,* was established around 1549. It lasted until 1764. As King, Zygmunt August dealt with several important foreign Jewish diplomats. He must have appreciated their skills, their abilities to secure compromise outcomes in international disputes, as well as their loyalty to their sovereigns and their fairness in all their dealings. Among these diplomats were Don Joseph ha-Nasi, Duke of Naxos, adviser to the Sultan Selim III of Turkey and Meir Ashkenazy, at one time a formal representative of the Khan of the Crimean Tartars, Devlet Givrey Bey. The King's contact with these Jewish dignitaries must have colored his attitude towards his Jewish advisers and his Jewish subjects. Meir Ashkenazy was influential and active in many European diplomatic maneuvers, among them a negotiated treaty between the Most Serene Republic of Venice and the Turkish Sultan. During the interregnum after the death of Zygmunt August, he was instrumental in securing an offer of the Polish crown for the French prince, Henri de Valois, younger son of Catherine de Medici, later French King Henry III. Henri became king of Poland and served from 1573 to 1575 as Henryk I Walezy. However, when his brother, the king of France died, Henri decided he would rather rule France than Poland, and left Kraków for Paris, abandoning his Polish possessions. The Poles then met in a diet, and chose a Transylvanian duke, Steven Bathory as King (1575-1586). Steven was the husband of Anna Jagiellonka, daughter of Zygmunt I and Bona Sforza. It was a lucky choice. Bathory turned out to be a competent ruler and, like his predecessors, he respected the important role of Jewish craftsmen, traders and merchants in Polish commerce and he confirmed Jewish commercial privileges. He extended Polish souzerainty after a winning campaign against Russia. When he successfully invaded Muscovy he employed a Jewish engineer to build semi-permanent pontoon bridges over rivers, a small item that, to his regret, Napoleon neglected to do some 230 years later. Bathory promoted education as a great equalizer. In one case he offered to ennoble a peasant boy should he learn Latin (*disce puer Latine, ego te faciam Mości Panie*). The engineer who build his pontoons, Mendel Izakowicz, had many grand designs. Among other projects, he also unsuccessfully proposed to build a bridge over the Danube in Vienna.

Mieszko I - 992
+Dubrawa
.. Bolesław I Chrobry (the Brave) 967 - 1025
.. +Emnilda
.... Mieszko II 990 - 1034
.... +Ryksza 993 - 1063
.... Kazimierz I Odnowiciel 1016 - 1058
.... Bolesław II the Bold 1042 - 1082
.... Władysław Herman 1042 - 1102
.... Bolesław III Krzywousty (Hare-lipped) 1086 - 1138
.... +Salomea of Berg
.... Władysław II Wygnaniec (the Exile) 1105 - 1159
.... Bolesław IV Kędzierzawy (the Curly) 1122 - 1173
.... Henryk Pobożny (the Pious) 1123 -
.... Mieszko III Stary (the Old) 1125 - 1202
.... Kazimierz II Sprawiedliwy (the Just) 1138 - 1194
.... Various Princelings
.... Władysław Łokietek (the Short) 1260 - 1333
.... Kazimierz III Wielki (the Great) 1310 - 1370
.... Elizabeth Piast
.... +Charles Robert of Anjou, King of Hungary
.... Louis of Anjou (the Great) 1326 - 1382
.... +Elizabeth of Bosnia
.... Jadwiga (Hedwig) 1374 - 1399
.... +Władysław II Jagiełło of Lithuania 1352 - 1434
.... Władysław III Warneńczyk 1424 - 1444
.... Kazimierz Jagiellończyk 1427 - 1492
.... +Elizabeth of Habsburg
.... Jan Olbracht (John Albert) 1459 - 1501
.... Alexander 1461 - 1506
.... Zygmunt I Stary (the Old) 1467 - 1548
.... +Bona Sforza
.... Zygmunt II August (last of the Jagiellons) 1520 - 1572

The male line of the Piast dynasty of Mieszko I died out in 1370 with Kazimierz the Great. The Jagiellon dynasty began with Wladyslaw Jagiello and Hedwig, great-niece of Kazimierz the Great and died out with Zygmunt August in 1572.

Fig. 006. Listing of Polish royal dynasties

Chapter 8. Alexander ha-Kohen (ca. 1525-1574) and his contemporaries

Among the individuals living in mid-sixteenth century Kraków-Kazimierz, Alexander ha-Kohen was of particular interest to me because of his name. While we know a great deal about the Kraków Jewry of the time, our specific knowledge of Alexander ha-Kohen is scant. He married Kendel, daughter of the rich banker Lazar of Brandenburg. She was a sister of Izrael Lazar's known as *Isserl* and aunt of the great Krakovian sage known as *Remuh*. Alexander was important in the Jewish community. He was an acknowledged leader. He was not a physician, although he was referred to as Doctor Alexander (Bałaban, I, 190, 543). Apparently, being called "doctor" (Latin for *very learned*), was an honorific, an indication of respect for the wisdom and learning of an individual, not an indication of a university degree, whether medical or otherwise. Alexander was not a rabbinical scholar, inasmuch as he left no known works of biblical exegesis. Yet, to marry into as prominent a family with access to the royal court as that of Isserl, Alexander must have been *yikhes*, i.e. of an elite origin. Essentially, this implies that he was rich.

I believe that he must have been a scion of a wealthy and important family to be allowed to marry Kendel, who became an aunt of the budding genius and future sage, Remuh. Among the likely ways in which his father and grandfather could have made money, was through lending it to gentiles at high interest rates and through leasing tax-collecting functions from the royal house and important aristocrats. Since both his father and grandfather became ill and died suddenly in the plague of 1552, it is likely that young Alexander inherited a fortune and must have been quite a catch as a potential bridegroom. We know that his sons and his famous grandson, Dr. Samuel ben Baruch Aleksandrowicz ha-Kohen, were very wealthy. Alexander's success and wealth and membership in the leadership of the Jewish community are attested to by his having served as a Senior of the Jewish Community Council in 1553 and 1554 (Bałaban, I, 543) and, of course, by the prominence attained by his children and grandchildren. From Bałaban, we know that he had at least two sons, one of them (Jozue Falk ben Alexander-ha-Kohen, known as SMA) a recognized first-rank religious scholar, writer and Talmudic interpreter and statesman, another (Baruch ben Alexander ha-Kohen) a businessman. From published commercial Kraków records for the year 1593 (Małecki and Szlufik, 1995), it appears that he also had a third son, Marcus (called in Polish *Marek Aleksander,* in Yiddish probably Mordekhay). This Marcus seems to have been perhaps the most astute businessman in the family; he traded on a very large scale with Bohemia and Moravia as well as with Ukraine. From tombstones in the Remuh cemetery we know that Alexander also had a daughter, Sarah (Sarele or Serl) who died in 1630. Rich and successful, a progenitor of a large and important family, Alexander ha-Kohen died in 1574.

I have always been aware of the existence of a family story stating that we (the Aleksndrowicz family) were related to the scholar and sage Remuh. We were not descended from Remuh, but related to him in some way. Indeed, this relationship to the most famous of Kraków's Jews has always been a matter of pride. Also, I have always been aware that we are Kohanim. I believe that my evidence strongly indicates that Alexander ha-Kohen was the ancestor, whom we have obliquely referred to for generations, although I have not been able to document it unequivocally with an unbroken chain. His being the forefather of the Aleksandrowicz family would vindicate the old story. Conversely, the fact that the story has survived in my family for generations, adds weight to the assumption that Alexander, husband of Remuh's aunt, Kendel, was indeed the original Alexander, at the beginning of the history of our family's surname. As husband of Kendel, Alexander ha-Kohen was related to the Isserles. As uncle-by-marriage of Remuh, who was married sequentially into the Shalom Shachna and then the Mordechai Gershon families, Alexander was also distantly related to the Jekeles and the Kalahoras, the Spiras, the Lurias, the Rapaports and the Horowitzes.

I have mentioned before that, as a general rule, there were no formal surnames in the Krakovian Jewish community of the day, however, prominent families tried to keep the memory of an important ancestor alive by a continued use of his name in a form that we would today consider a surname. In addition, patronymics were used routinely both in Hebrew as in Alexander ben Yehoshuah ha-Kohen, and in formal Polish registries and in commercial transactions with outsiders. In the Polish form common at the time, the father's name was either used following the individual name or used with the ending "wicz" as in Aleksander Józefowicz, a name I encountered in a 1636 registry of commerce edited by Małecki and Szlufik (1995, 152). Jewish individuals were often recorded in the Jewish annals using the first form and in the Polish ones using the other two. Thus, the sons of Alexander ha-Kohen, Baruch ben Alexander ha-Kohen, Marcus ben Alexander ha-Kohen and Jozue Falk ben Alexander ha-Kohen, would have been recorded in Polish annals as Baruch Aleksander or Baruch Aleksandrowicz, Marek Aleksander or Aleksandrowicz and Józef Aleksander or Aleksandrowicz. It is not far-fetched to assume that when our first definitive ancestor, Józef son of David, was obliged in 1805 to choose a family surname, he chose to be known as Józef Alexander and, eventually, as Józef Aleksandrowicz, the name being tied to a family tradition.

Besides a mention of Baruch in Mayer Bałaban's history as being a cousin of Remuh and the father of a famous son, I found no other mention of Baruch ben Alexander.

We know that he saw to it that his son, Samuel ben Baruch ha-Kohen, received a first-class education. We know that Baruch was sufficiently wealthy and aware of the world beyond the confines of the Jewish ghetto, to send his son to study medicine in Italy, but we have no data about any of his other activities. By contrast, activities of his brothers, Jozue Aleksandrowicz, nicknamed Falk, and Marek Aleksandrowicz, have been amply recorded. Falk made a name for himself as a scholar and an educator, a recognized interpreter of the Bible and the *Shulhan Aruch.* He was pragmatic, adept in adjusting religious commandments to practical everyday needs. He studied under Salomon (Shlomo) Luria of Lublin and under Remuh and was active in the *Vaad Arba Aratzot* (the Council of the Four Lands, the Jewish over-all governing body in Poland). As a recognized halakhic authority he was among the leaders, in 1587, who issued a decree against purchasing of rabbinic positions (Encyclopedia Judaica, VI, 1158) and he dealt with an issue which was critical to the development of Jewish commerce in the future. While, the Roman-Catholic Church looked askance at collecting interest on lent money, considering it usury, Jews always felt free to lend money to non-Jews, often at usurious rates. However, Jews were long constrained by their ethic from charging interest to their co-religionists, which interfered with intra-Jewish conduct of business and made consolidation of funds and partnerships difficult. It was my putative relative, Jozue Falk ben Alexander ha-Kohen (a.k.a. Józef Falk Aleksandrowicz), who wrote a treatise on business ethics, *Heter Iska* (Bałaban, I, 234), which stated that the lender in effect becomes a business partner of the borrower, becoming vitally interested in the borrower‘s business success and ability to repay the loan, and thus entitled not only to a return of the loaned sum, but also to a just share (up to 10%) of the profits from the financed enterprise which he can collect instead of interest. This convoluted interpretation, which allowed Jews to lend money to other Jews, and thus to pool finances, was approved by a council of religious authorities, convened during the meeting of the *Vaad Arba Aratzot* in 1607. Jozue Falk wrote several other treatises, including an important interpretation of the *Shulkhan Arukh*, called *Sefer Meirath Aynayim* (1615). As author of the latter, he became known by its initials as SMA. While his family was important in Kraków and his father served as a senior of the Kraków Kahał at about the time he was born, he is said to have been born not in Kraków but in Lublin. At some point Jozue Falk moved to Lwów (Lemberg, later chief city of Austrian Galitzia, now Lviv in Ukraine), where he became Rosh Yeshiva. There, he married the daughter of a rich merchant, Israel son of Eidele. It was probably his son, named Alexander after his grandfather, who was known as Alexander ben Jozue or Aleksander Józefowicz, that was listed as a merchant in 1636.

I have not been able to find out how Jozue acquired the nickname Falk. In Yiddish *falk* is a hawk, in Latin a falcon, a bird of prey. May be he was compared to a falcon because of his sharp intellect and cunning. The nickname Falk was quite popular at the time and its use by several contemporaries led to a considerable confusion. I would like to postulate another possible explanation. In Yiddish it is spelled not with an "f" but with two "yids" vocalized in Yiddish as "v", thus rendering the name as "valk" or even "vilk". The latter, in Polish denotes the animal, wolf. The wolf, in turn, in German is Wolf and in Hebrew Zev. It is therefore possible that Jozua ben Alexander had a second name Zev or Wolf. This interpretation of the name Falk as Wolf is a distinct possibility, fortified by the fact that another individual known as Falk was also known as Zev (see the next paragraph for details). The name Falk or its Polonized form, Falek, remained in continued use among

Kraków Jews. I am related to one Falek family. My aunt Pola, my mother's older sister, married Maurice (Maniek) Falek, a furrier in Kraków, after the First World War. Pola and Maniek moved to Paris, but the remainder of Maniek's family continued to live in Kraków and I knew his sister, Reba Falek, who died in the Holocaust. The Falk name continued in use among descendants of the line of Jozue ben Alexander ha-Kohen. Jozue had several sons, among them Feivel (Feibush) and Alexander, polonized to Alexander Józefowicz. Jozue's grandson, Samuel ben Feibush Falk wrote *Leket Shemu'el* and *Derush Shemu'el*. Samuel ben Feibush's son, Chaim Abraham became a rabbi of Vienna. When Jews were formally expelled from Vienna in 1670, he settled in Hebron in Palestine, where he wrote a commentary on *Shir ha-Shirim* (Song of Songs) and on the Psalms, called *Erez ha-Hayim*. The other sons of Alexander ha-Kohen, SMA's brothers, Mordche (Markus) ha-Kohen and Baruch ha-Kohen and their descendants continued to live in Kraków/ Kazimierz.

Initially, I confused Alexander ha-Kohen's famous son, Jozue (Yehoshuah) Falk ben Alexander, with his equally famous younger contemporary and a student of his, Yehoshuah Heshel ben Jozue (Zev) Katz. This Yehoshuah Heshel became Rosh Yeshiva in Kraków and author of *Meginei Shlomo,* and the responsa called *Pnei Yehoshuah*. He died in 1648, as indicated on his tomb in Remuh cemetery. I was not the only one who was so confused. My confusion was compounded by an article written about "Falk, Joshua ben Alexander ha-Kohen" by Solomon Schechter and M. Seligsohn for the Jewish Encyclopedia published in English after 1900 and now fortunately available on the Internet under www.Jewishencyclopedia.com, which credited Joshua Falk ben Alexander ha-Kohen with the authorship of *Pene Yehoshu'a*, which were in fact written by his student, author of *Meginei Shlomo*. I believe that the confusion was due to the fact that this Yehoshuah Heshel ben Jozue's descendants chose to use the nickname Falk, perhaps to honor his teacher and mentor. Thus, his grandson, a rabbi in Lwów and then, sequentially, in Berlin, Metz and Frankfurt, was called Jacob Joshua ben Tzvi (Hirsh) Falk (1680-1756). This latter rabbi Falk published a learned work, which he entitled, *Pnei Yehoshuah II,* thus honoring his grandfather. He himself was, in turn, known as *Pnei Yehoshuah II*. In 1718, he succeeded Tsvi Hirsch Ashkenazi (*Chacham Tsvi*), father of Jacob Emden as rabbi of Lwów. It is of interest that in Metz, *Pnei Yehoshuah II* was succeeded as rabbi by Yonathan Eybenschutz (1690-1764), a scion of another famous Kraków Jewish family, descendants of the cabalist, Nathan Nate Spira, and his daughter Dobrysz, who died in Kraków in 1642.

Like Remuh, Nathan Nate ben Salomon Spira, (1585-1633), author of *Megale Amukot*, claimed descent from Rashi, and thus from King David, through his ancestor Matathiahu of Treves, Rabbi of Paris, 1325-1385. He was a recognized Krakovian scholar and a supporter of the Kaballah. I assume, based on the name Spira, that his distant ancestors came from the cathedral city of Speyer in the Rheinland, called Spira in Latin. He married Roza, daughter of Moses Jacobowicz Jekeles. Nathan and Roza had a daughter called Dobrysz, the same name as that of my ancestress Dobrysz, daughter of Jacob Gumpel and wife of Joseph Aleksandrowicz. Dobrysz, daughter of Nathan Spira, married Yeshaya Ashkenasi (Joseph the German) from Hildesheim. Either their daughter or granddaughter married Isaac Zelig Spira. Their son, also Nathan (Nosson) Nate Spira, also known as Chalfon, became rabbi of the Moravian community of Ivancice, known in German and Yiddish as Eybenschutz. He died in 1707. His sons, Aaron, Yonathan and Yehuda Leib, adopted the name Eybenschutz as their surname. The most famous of the three, Yonathan

Eybenschutz born in 1690 was a known scholar, Talmudist and expert on the Kaballah. In 1725 he signed an excommunication document against the followers of Sabbatai Tsvi, the false messiah of Smyrna, in concert with other rabbis. Later, he became a supporter of the mystical strain of Judaism. He was said to have written a book called *Kameyot* (Amulets). In defense of his mystical beliefs, he engaged in a prolonged, acrimonious theological feud with Jacob ben Tsvi Ashkenazi (1697-1776), son of Chacham Tzvi (Hirsch) Ashkenazi (1660-1718), the rabbi in Lwów who later became the leader of the Ashkenazi community of Amsterdam. Jacob ben Tsvi (Yakov ben Zvi, called Yavez) was a strong opponent of the mystic and Sabbatean trends in Judaism. For a while he served as Rabbi of Emden in Germany and hence also became known as Jacob Emden. He wrote an outstanding commentary on the Mishnah, an autobiography *Megillat Sefer* and also edited a new prayer book, *Siddur beit Yaakov*. The dispute about mysticism and effectiveness of amulets and incantations between Emden, who opposed them, and Eybenschutz, who advocated them, became personal, with mutual excommunications. They were both rivals for the rabbinical seat in Hamburg/Altona. Several different biblical experts tried to adjudicate the dispute, including the renowned R. Yechezkiel Landau (1713-1793), author of *Noda B'Yehuda*, the chief rabbi of Prague. Among those who in 1756 also excommunicated Yonathan Eybenschutz was the above-mentioned Jacob Jehoshuah ben Tsvi Hirsch Falk (1680-1756), author of *Pnei Yehoshuah II*. At one point the dispute between Eybenschutz and Emden reached the Vaad Arba Aratzot, the Council of Four Lands, which supported the Eybenschutz position thanks to superior numbers, if not logic. A granddaughter of Yonathan's brother, Aaron Eybenschutz, Sarah Eybenschutz-Geldwerth (1792-1854) married Nathan Silberfeld in Kraków in 1811. In 1813, Yonathan's granddaughter, Reisl Eybenschutz, married Hirsh Zelig Birnbaum, a brother of my direct ancestor Berek Birnbaum, great-grandfather of my grandmother Hanna Hinda Aleksandrowicz, nee Birnbaum. Hirsh Zelig and Reisl's son, Nathan Birnbaum, married Frieda Eibenschutz-Ehrenpreis (see the chapter on the Birnbaum family history below).

Of the famous Krakovian Jewish families around 1500 it is likely that the Kalahoras came from Spain and we know that the Isserles came from Regensburg. I have not been able to ascertain where the family of Alexander ha-Kohen, the husband of Kendel, sister of Isserl, came from. Perhaps this family lived in Kraków for a long time prior to 1500. The family's connection to Kraków is not in question, as Alexander ha-Kohen served as a member of the Kraków Jewish community council, along with the sons of reb Ayzik reb Jekeles. According to Bałaban (I, p. 462), Alexander's grandfather was Elimelech ha-Kohen who died in Kraków during the plague epidemic of 1552. It is likely that he had many children, but we know that he had at least two, a daughter Miriam who died in 1574 and a son Jozue, Alexander's father, who perished in the same plague of 1552 along with his father. The name Jozue was on occasion rendered in Polish as Józef, in German as Joseph, in Yiddish as Josl, and in Hebrew as Yehoshuah, Yeshuah or Yeshayah. Jozue ben Elimelech ha-Kohen was the father of Alexander ben Jozue ha-Kohen. The epidemic of 1552-3 was obviously deadly. It decimated the Jewish population of Kraków. There was no drainage in town and offal and garbage of all kinds were thrown into the streets, there to putrefy and poison the air. Rats infested the old wooden buildings. We know that among those who succumbed to it were Dr. Samuel bar Meshulam, the above-mentioned much maligned physician to the King and Queen Bona Sforza. Also, among the plague's victims was the mother of Isserl and Kendel, grandmother of Remuh, Gitl; the wife of Isserl and mother of Remuh, Malka; the first wife of Remuh, Golda, daughter of Shalom Shachna; and the daughter of Remuh, Dreizl. Also, among the victims of the plague was Moses Charif, the Rosh Yeshiva who married the daughter of another Rosh Yeshiva, Józef ben Mordechai Gershon Katz and Jozef's wife Sprinza Eberl's. This Józef (Jozue) ben Mordechai Gershon Katz, who died in 1591, is not to be confused with Alexander's father, Jozue ben Elimelech Katz, who died in 1552, or with that Jozue's grandson, Jozue Falk ben Alexander-ha-Kohen, who died in 1614.

A young man, Israel ben Josef, nicknamed *Isserl*, whose grandfather, Moses Auerbach, arrived in Kraków from Regensburg (Ratisbon) in Germany a few years earlier, married in Kraków (Dina) Małka, the daughter of the great Jewish financier Eleazar (Lazar) of Brandenburg. He was known henceforth in Kraków as Israel Lazar‘s. Jews were formally ordered expelled from Regensburg in 1519 and that must have spurred Moses Auerbach, the leader of this Bavarian Jewish community to move to Kraków. Obviously, his family and Lazar‘s family came to Kraków with considerable financial resources and appropriate connections to reach the highest levels of both Polish and Jewish communities. The families were both wealthy and remarkably progressive, familiar with both Western Renaissance and traditional Jewish biblical and Talmudic lore. To serve the King, bankers had to be able to communicate with their patron, i.e. they must have known some Latin, some Italian and some Polish, besides Hebrew, German and/or Yiddish. With Moses Auerbach came his entire family to Kraków, his wife Gitl, his son-in-law Josef and several grandchildren, among them Isserl and his sister Kendel. Lazar, referred to by Mayer Bałaban as Lazar of Brandenburg and by Neil Rosenstein as Eleazar Schrentsel (Rosenstein, 2004, 277ff) was married to Dreisel, daughter of Yechiel Luria (who died in 1470), rabbi of Brest Litovsk (*Brisk*) and of Ostróg (*Ostrev*) in Volhynia. According to Rosentein, Yechiel Luria's family, descended from Salomon (Samson) Luria who lived in Orleans in France around 1300–1350 and had to move temporarily to Erfurt when Jews were ordered expelled from France. Yechiel‘s father was Aaron ben Natanael Lurie. His mother was Miriam Spira, a daughter of Salomon Spira (1375–1452) and greatgranddaughter of Matathiahu Treves (of Troyes in France), rabbi of Paris. Among Salomon Spira's descendants was the above-mentioned Nathan Nate Spira, *rosh yeshiva* in Kraków, author of *Megale Amukot* (1585-1633).

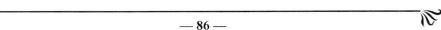

The most famous progeny of both Lazar of Brandenburg and Moses Auerbach was their great-grandson, Isserl's son Moses (1525-1572), born in Kraków in the year that Albert von Hohenzollern swore eternal loyalty to the Polish crown. Moses Isserles studied with Shalom Shachna of Lublin and became famous as a Talmudic scholar at an early age. His fame grew and he became widely known and respected even as a very young man, drawing students and acolytes from all over Europe and beyond. He became revered as a teacher and interpreter of Jewish Law under the name of Reb Moshe ben Yisroel (*Remuh*). Remuh set out to codify all Jewish religious laws in one work, but Joseph Caro of Safad in Palestine did that first. Caro‘s book was called *Shulhan Arukh*. Scooped by Caro, Remuh was reduced to a publication of his work as commentaries to the *Shulhan Aruch* in *Mappah*, which became important by adapting the rules to the Ashkenasi geopolitical conditions. Together, the Caro/Remuh regulations became generally accepted and followed by the Eastern European Jewry, which then constituted a large majority of all Jews. Remuh fame and recognition of his knowledge were such that at the extremely young age of 25 he became the Rabbi of Kraków and, simultaneosly head of the yeshiva that was founded by Jacob Pollack. As a descendant of Isserl's, Remuh and his entire family became henceforth known in Kraków as the family Isserles. Isserl funded a prayer house, the only one active to this day, known as the Remuh Synagogue.

The historian Mayer Bałaban (I, 139) presented the Isserles family tree and in it mentioned that Isserl had a sister, Kendel (Hinda?), who married Alexander ha-Kohen. Both Isserl and his sister Kendel died in 1568. This Kendel, Isserl's sister and Remuh's aunt, is not to be confused with her niece, also Kendel, sister of Remuh, who died in 1572. Another of Remuh's sisters and a niece of Kendel and, by marriage, of Alexander ha-Kohen, Miriam Bella, who lived until 1617, married Pincus Horowitz, who died in Kraków in 1618. Their daughter, Hinda Isserless (also Kendel? Horowitz, the name Hinda seems to have been popular then), married Meir Wahl a descendant of R. Meyer ben Yitzhak Katz of Ellenbogen, rabbi in Padua, called MaHaRam Padua, who died in 1565. It was his father, Judah Mintz that tangled with Jacob Pollack a generation earlier. Meyer's son, Samuel Juda Katz, rabbi in Venice, took on the name Katzenellenbogen. In turn, his son Saul, father of Meir and father-in-law of Miriam Bella Isserless, took on the name Wahl. Saul Wahl was an important businessman in Kraków, active in Polish civic affairs and influential in the elections of the King by the Polish diet of nobles. It is said that for one night during the *interregnum* of 1572-3 he acted as a royal substitute. The surname Wahl which he chose (in Yiddish and German Wahl means election) may very well have referred to his famous activities during the royal election in which he played a critical role. In 1580 he was the concessionaire of all the royal Wieliczka salt mines near Kraków (Bałaban, I: 160, 212).

It seems, not surprisingly, that all the important Jewish families of the time were interrelated. Saul Wahl's grandaughter, Dina (died 1617), married Abraham Jozua Heshel (died 1663), rabbi in Kraków. Heshel had three well-connected children, sons, Isachar Beer (died 1691) and Saul (died 1704) and a daughter who married Nathan Spira. Isachar Beer's grandson Berush ben Gabriel Eskeles, rabbi in Mainz, married Dina (Hana?) Rifka, daughter of Samson Wertheimer (1658-1724), a court Jew, *Oberfaktor* of the Emperor Charles VI and of King August II of Poland and Saxony. In 1712 the Kraków community formally offered the wealthy and learned Samson Wertheimer the position of Chief Rabbi of Kraków, an honor which he declined. Samson Wertheimer was a nephew of another important "Court Jew", Jud Suess, Samuel Oppenheimer, financier of Princes Eugene of Savoy and Ludwig of Baden. The son of rabbi Heshel, Saul (died in 1704), was also a rabbi in Kraków. His granddaughter married Isaak ha-Levi, rabbi in Kraków, from 1776 to 1799. For many of the above, we know the dates of their deaths but not their births, from their tombstones in the Remuh and other cemeteries. I will have more to say about the Horowitz and Katzenellenbogen families when discussing their descendants, the Birnbaums of Kraków, the family of my paternal grandmother, Hancia Birnbaum Aleksandrowicz.

Incidentally, Remuh was interested in his family's origin and, after some study, claimed descent from Reb Shelomo ben Isaac, known as Rashi (1040-1105), the sage of Troyes, Worms and the Rheinland. Like Remuh, a great many of today's Orthodox and Hassidic dynasties claim descent from Rashi. This is important to them, because Rashi stated that he was descended from the biblical King David. According to Jewish tradition, the coming Messiah will be a descendant of King David. The presumed First Century Jewish preacher and healer, Jesus of Nazareth called Christ, was said to have been a descendant of

King David and Christian biblical literature mentions a fanciful *Tree of Jesse*, presumably documenting that descent. The tree is clearly shown in the Nurnberg Chronicle of Schedel, one of the first books printed after the Guttenberg Bible. The false messiah of Smyrna, Sabbatai Tzvi (1626-1676), also claimed descent from King David. In our times, so did the late Chabad Lubavitcher Grand Rebbe, Menachem Mendel Schneerson, many of whose followers believe him to be the Messiah. Unlike the honor of being a Kohen, which can be transmitted only through the male line, the honor of descent from the Royal House of Judah apparently has no such limitations, inasmuch as Rashi had no male heirs and all royal descent had to be either through his daughters or perhaps through his male siblings and other relatives.

Remuh married Golda, a daughter of his teacher, Reb Shalom Shachna of Lublin (known as *RShaCh*), a famous disciple of Jacob Pollack. When Golda died at 20, in the epidemic of 1552, Remuh married a second wife, daughter of Mordechai Gershon ha-Kohen (Katz) (Bałaban, I, 492). She was a sister of Józef ben Mordechai Gershon Katz (1510-1591). This Józef Katz, Remuh's brother-in-law, for 50 years head of the Kraków yeshiva and author of *She'erit Yosef*, married Sprintza (Speranza), sister of reb Jacob ben Moshe known by his diminutive "reb Jekele" (pronounced *yekeleh*). In this way Josef Katz became a brother-in-law of both Remuh and reb Jekele, the founder of the Jekeles clan of Kraków.

This brings me to another family, which played a significant role in Jewish history in Kraków, the Jekeles, descendants of Jacob ben Moyshe known as reb Jekele. He was the son of Moyshe Eberls in Kraków, and was know as *Jakubek Bogaty* (Rich Jake). His uncle, Jacob Eberls, married Gitl, daughter of Jekutiel Landau ha-Levi, progenitor of the Krakovian family Landau. Reb Jekele had two sons, Isaac (Ayzik) and Moses. Both played important roles in Kraków history, both served on the Kraków Jewish governing body. Isaac ben Jacob (Jakubowicz), known as reb Ayzik reb Jekeles (nicknamed Rich Ayzik), married Breindl Rapaport, daughter of Israel Yechiel and granddaughter of Gerson Rapaport. According to Bałaban, this was the beginning of ties between the Jekeles and the Rapaports. From 1633 for eleven years Reb Ayzik reb Jekeles tried to build a synagogue in Kazimierz, and dedicated large sums of money to the task. It took a lot of effort and more money to overcome the objections of local Catholic clergymen who violently opposed consecrating the new large and elegant building. Finally, in 1644, permission was obtained from the King and the new synagogue was open. Today, the Ayzik Synagogue still stands, as impressive as ever, restored from the neglect of its recent past. There being very few Jews left in Kraków now, it serves mostly as a museum and a concert hall, with its great accoustics. Isaac/Ayzik died in 1653. Reb Ayzik reb Jekeles' son, grandson of reb Jekele, Moses ben Ayzik (Izakowicz) Jekeles, married another Sprintza, daughter of the rabbi of Lwów, Abraham Schrentzl Rapaport, author of *Eytan ha-Ezrahi*. When Sprintza died, he married her cousin, Chaya, daughter of Nachman Rapaport (Bałaban, II, 128-9). When Chaya died (obviously women died often in childbirth or in plagues and their husbands, left with small children, needed to remarry quickly), Moses married Sarah, daughter of Zachariah Mendel. Moses died in 1691. Moses' grandson, also called Moses, as an old man and widower, married the young Ita (Yuta) Kalahora, daughter of Dr. Aaron Kalahora and granddaughter of the martyr, Matatiahu Kalahora (see below).

Moses ben Jacob (Jakubowicz) (reb Moyshe reb Jekeles), the other son of reb Jekele, also served as a member of the Jewish leadership for many years. His daughter,

Roza, married the cabalist Nathan Nate Spira, the Rosh Yeshiva in Kraków who claimed descent from Rashi. Roza died in 1642 and is buried in the Remuh cemetery, along with her grown up daughter, Dobrysz, wife of Yeshayah of Hildesheim who died the same year. It was Nathan Spira who sent his son, Isaac, to Smyrna (today Izmir in Turkey) to learn more about the possibility that a messiah, Sabbatai Tzvi, has appeared there. Isaac Spira met Sabbatai and was very impressed by him. Sabbatai was obviously quite charismatic and possessed of personal magnetism, which accounted, in part, for his success as a leader and a purported messiah.

An ancestor of Yuta Kalahora Jekeles, Dr. Salomon Kalahora, was among the Jewish physicians at the court of King Zygmunt August. Apparently, the Kalahora family came to Kraków from Italy and its members spoke Italian. The name indicates, however, that the family originated in Spain prior to 1492. The Kalahoras prospered in Kraków and became a family of physicians and pharmacists. A terrible tragedy befell them in 1663, when the family patriarch, Matatiahu Kalahora, was accused of being the author of a blasphemous anti-Catholic tract. Although the tract was written in old German, an alphabet Kalahora did not know, he was convicted of having authored it, a serious charge of blasphemy. The crime called for draconian penalties. The local verdict being so patently unjust, it was appealed to the highest tribunal in the realm which sat in the central Polish town of Piotrków Trybunalski but the appeal was rejected and the poor accused was martyred in the most cruel way, torn to pieces, tortured and burnt alive. His ashes were dispersed by being shot from a canon. A small sample of the ashes was saved by his co-religionists, brought to Kraków and buried in the cemetery. For many years Kraków Jews prayed regularly for the peace of his soul. The martyr‘s two grandsons, Aron and Mendel Kalahora, practiced medicine in Kraków. It was Dr Aron‘s daughter, Yuta (died 1776) who married Moyshe Jekeles, a relative of my putative ancestor Alexander-ha-Kohen, through his wife Kendel of the Isserles. Yuta‘s marriage was not a happy one, and did not last long. Dr Aron's brother, Mendel Kalahora, had a daughter named Hanna Temerl, born in 1775. According to Bałaban, Hanna Temerl Kalahora, the last in the Kalahora line, married a man who in 1805 adopted the surname Loebenheim. The name Temerl was also that of one of my ancestor Józef Aleksandrowicz's daughters, born 33 years after the birth of the last of the Kalahoras. The Aleksandrowicz and the Kalahoras were distantly related through the Jekeles and through Remuh, but there may also have been a closer relationship and both girls may have been named after a common ancestress. The Loebenheims continued to live in Kraków. Around 1900 the last of the Loebenheims, Marya Loebenheim, married Paweł (Saul) Aleksandrowicz, born in 1877 in Kraków. Pawel's family came from the oil town of Gorlice in the southwest of Kraków. I believe that we are related to the Gorlice branch of the Aleksandrowicz family through another daughter of my ancestor Joseph, whose offspring, after only a religious marriage not recognized by the state, were recorded in Gorlice under her surname and not that of her husband and thus continued to carry the surname Aleksandrowicz. According to the 1920 census, Paweł Aleksandrowicz and his wife Marya nee Loebenheim, lived in Kraków on Starowiślna Street. I understand that Paweł and Marya's children moved to England and, like me, abbreviated their family name to Alexander. Thus, the descendants of the illustrious Kalahora family of Kraków became Aleksandrowicz and today carry the surname Alexander, just as I do.

Jewish commerce in Kraków was quite extensive and well documented. In a register of collected custom duties dating to 1593 and 1636, there are listings of many Jewish merchants and of a lively trade which they conducted, not only with nearby areas, but also with Central and Northern Poland and Lithuania, Silesia, Bohemia, Slovakia and Ukraine, as well as with the Netherlands, England, Saxony, Italy and Turkey. The out-of-town Jewish commerce was thriving, with the number of entries listing Jewish merchants during one year reaching 521 in 1593 and almost 700 in year 1636. Among the goods that Jews brought from Bohemia was cloth of many kinds, including velvet, and finished items such as stockings, gloves and notions suitable for sale in street stalls. In exchange they took furs and leather to the Czech and German lands. Among prominent merchants of the time, besides my putative ancestors mentioned earlier, were reb Ayzik reb Jekeles, Marek Gimpel and Jurek Gimpel, merchants listed in the customs book for 1636 and Salomon Gimplo who came to Kraków from Silesia in 1680. Any of these may have been related to my ancestress Dobrysz Gumple Aleksandrowicz.

There are many records of Jewish traders in Kraków, dealing in goods from Holland, Spain, Bavaria, Saxony, Venice as well as from Turkey. Merchandise from Nurnberg in Bavaria (*towary norymberskie,* i.e. Nurnberg wares, mainly notions and sewing supplies: scissors, pins and needles, thread, buttons, ribbons, etc) was among the staples in Jewish stalls. In general, Poland, and specifically the city of Kraków, maintained close commercial (and political) ties with Dresden and Leipzig in Saxony (two Saxon rulers of the Wettin dynasty served as kings of Poland). Leipzig conducted then as now a large annual trade fair, in which many Krakovian Jewish merchants participated. The family of two of my great-grandmothers must have come to Kraków from Dresden because the family became known in Kraków as the Drezners. There are also reliable records of Jews dealing with merchandise produced in the countryside surrounding Kraków, including salt from Wieliczka, where Jews were often holding unique concessions.

Records of transactions and of bridge tolls and customs duties (*"rogatkowe"*) paid in Kraków by Jewish importers and exporters near the end of XVI-th Century, transcribed by Małecki and Szlufik (1995), indicate that the family of Alexander ha-Kohen conducted commerce on a very large scale. It was Marek Alexander and his sons Hirsch (# 451) and Salomon (# 497) and son-in-law Abram (# 39, 91, 108, 183, 296), who were particularly active. Their trades stood out as being on a scale larger than those of most of the other recorded merchants. While most custom transactions involved merchandise carried by one or two horse-drawn wagons, transactions of Marek Alexander (# 43, 57, 128, 168, 331, 350, 368, 387, 410) and his relatives were invariably much larger. In one instance (# 57, Małecki and Szlufik, 1995, 63) 12 horses were used, in another (# 296, p.81) the caravan consisted of wagons drawn by 24 horses. The numbers of items transported were surprisingly large. For example in the latter trade, # 296, in July 1593, "*Abram of the Markuses, Jew of Kraków, declared 1,900 gray squirrels, 1,000 brown squirrels, 8 otters, 10 martens*" and in the same transaction added an additional 8,000 (!) squirrel skins and 19 foxes. The value of the merchandise was very high. The custom duties were calculated as being 1% of the value of transported merchandise. In one instance, on March 16, 1593, "*Abram, son-in-law of Marek declared for Moravia 124 oxen, 3,900 gray squirrels, 9 otters*", merchandise for which he paid customs of złp 3/24/00 (i.e. 3 Polish *złotys*, 24 *groszys*, zero *denarii*). This custom payment implies that the merchandise was valued at approximately 380 złp.

(# 91, p. 66). The Polish word *złoty,* the name of the Polish currency to this day, means "golden"; the then circulating coin was made of gold. One złp consisted of 30 *groszy* or 540 *denarii.* To provide an indication of the purchasing power of the sums involved, Małecki and Szlufik stated that one Polish *złoty* (złp) (a unit also known as gulden or *florin*) was then sufficient to support 25 men for a year. I assume that these numbers were based on the average modest cost of living. Thus, the indications are that the cargo carried by Abram son-in-law of Marek Alexander on that one day four hundred and fourteen years ago could have sustained as many as 9,500 people for a year.

Baruch ben Alexander ha-Kohen (Baruch Aleksandrowicz) sent his son, Samuel ben Baruch, born sometimes around 1590, to study medicine at the Univerity of Padua in Italy. Padua, an old city from Roman times, known in Latin as *Patavium,* was then a part of the territory of the Republic of Venice and faced fewer religious fundamentalist restrictions than comparable papal territories. It had a large prominent Jewish colony. The University, second oldest in Italy, founded in 1238, served as a center of innovation and development in science and technology. Young Samuel must have been fluent in Latin and possibly also in Italian, and probably conversant with mathematics and Western philosophy. In Italy, Samuel was known as "*Iudeus Cracoviensis*", a Krakovian Jew in Latin. According to Bałaban, he became friendly with David Morpurgo, a contemporary, the son of the rabbi of Padua, also a student of medicine, who later came to Kraków. I assume that the two curious young medical students, Samuel and David, took courses and attended lectures in Padua from the then most prominent university faculty member, a professor of mathematics already famous as a scientist and inventor, Galileo Galilei (1564-1642). Galileo came to Padua in 1592 and taught there for 18 years. Most of those attending his lectures were students of medicine. Thus, I consider it likely that one of my ancestors studied with Galileo and perhaps may have been among the people who talked to Galileo about the then novel idea of the central role of the Sun in the solar system propounded a few years earlier by another student from Kraków, Nicholas Copernicus. Copernicus also had studied in Padua and Ferrara in addition to his being the most famous graduate of the Jagiellonian University of Kraków. I also assume that the two young Jewish students took advantage of their stay in Italy and visited the most important center of the Renaissance art and science, Florence of the Medicis.

Samuel ben Baruch Aleksandrowicz finished his studies in Padua and, having become formally certified as a physician, returned to Kraków. At the time, being a physician essentially meant that he was a diagnostitian and an internist, often using astrological star charts as a help in diagnosis. Surgery was the province of surgeon-barbers (*cyruliks* in Polish) and *felczers,* sort of barefoot doctors who applied folk medicines like leeches and prescribed herbs. Birthing was the province of midwives. In Kraków Dr. Samuel became known, in deference to his studies in Italy, as Dr. Samuel *Patavinus* (Samuel the Padovan). He soon became important as a physician, a banker (money-lender) and a philanthropist. His standing in the community can be inferred from the fact that he was chosen and served as an Elder (Senior), i.e. a member of the Krakovian Kahał (Jewish Community Council), longer than almost anyone else. He served for at least twenty-four years, from 1623 to his death in 1648 (Bałaban, I, 544 ff). In 1638 he was entrusted with and became responsible for a formal charitable aid program for indigent Jews. In the Kahał budget there was a provision of the large sum of złp 50 annually, funds given to Dr. Samuel for distribution

among the poorest inhabitants of Jewish Kazimierz (Bałaban, I, 461). He married Sława, daughter of Asher Selig. Dr. Samuel and Sława Asherówna had several children, who took over their father's lending business after he died. One son, Mojżesz, died young, in 1617. The sons who inherited Dr. Samuel's business, died much later, Baruch ben Samuel in 1672 and Naphtali Hirsh in 1686. Dr Samuel's daughter, Rebecca, married a man named Aron. She had a son Mordechai. Rebecca Samuelówna died in 1632, perhaps in childbirth. According to Bałaban (I, 70), Naphtali Hirsh had two sons, Arie Leib (died 1684) and Jacob Moses (died 1685).

Bałaban refers to Dr. Samuel mainly when discussing medical service in Jewish Kraków, thus stressing Dr. Samuel's most important attribute, the medical degree from Padua. Bałaban does not deal with the issues which were of interest to me, namely, his family history, ancestors and descendants, the way the good doctor was referred to in Kraków and whether he was using a patronymic or a surname. In the 1930s Bałaban was asked by my great-uncle Filip Aleksandrowicz to research the history of the Aleksandrowicz family of Kraków but Professor Bałaban died before he could perform the research. As I have stressed, the Polish patronymics mostly involved the addition of the ending "wicz" to one's father's name. Writing in Polish, Prof. Bałaban routinely converted patronymics through the use of the "wicz" ending into pseudo family surnames, anticipating in many cases their actual usage, which only occurred after 1805. Thus, Bałaban did not hesitate to refer to Jacob Gumple as Jacob Gumplowicz, even though in all contemporary documents during his lifetime this individual was only referred to as Jacob Gomple or Gumpel. The use of the full name *Gumplowicz* did not appear until after 1805 when it was used by Jacob's son, Lebl. Many similar examples in the Bałaban books can be cited. Following this Bałaban usage, I believe that Dr. Samuel would have been known in Poland as Dr. Samuel, son of the rich merchant Baruch Aleksandrowicz. He died in 1648. His last direct known descendant, as listed by Bałaban, died in 1686. There were no listing of descendants of Marcus Alexander, besides the daughter who married Abram, probably because they only used patronymics and not the surname.

The time period from 1500 to 1700 saw a great many upheavals in Europe. The discovery of America by Columbus and the expulsion of Jews from Spain and Portugal in 1492 and 1498 changed the power and wealth relationship among the countries of Europe. Spain became temporarily ascendant, benefitting from gold plundered in the Americas, but eventually it lost the cultural vitality, which was among the benefits of cross-fertilization between Christian, Jewish and Muslim cultures. Spanish ascendance did not survive the disastrous expeditions of the Grand Armada against England in 1588 and 1597 under the command of the Duke of Medina Sidonia. The sixteenth century also saw the development of a great schism within Western Christianity. In 1517 a brilliant, though strongly anti-Semitic, German monk, Martin Luther (1483-1546), propounded a series of 95 accusatory theses protesting the sales of papal indulgences. Openly challenging the Pope, he nailed these theses publicly, on the door of the Palast Church in Wittenberg. This started a discussion which eventually evolved into a series of religious wars. While residing for his own safety in an isolated castle, Luther translated the Bible into vernacular German, making it accessible to people who did not know Latin, Aramaic or Hebrew. The Catholic Church did not advocate laymen reading the Bible. It preferred that they rely on the churchmen for interpretation of biblical narratives. Luther, having made the Bible easily accessible

to everybody, decreased the importance of official Catholic theology and opened the way for common people to make their own interpretations of the "inerrant" words of God, although those words came to them in the often inaccurate translations. As a result of the schism, Germany was torn by religious wars and Sweden turned Lutheran. In France the Huguenots and the Catholics fought for supremacy, with the eventual re-conversion of the Huguenot leader Henry of Navarre to Catholicism to become King, with the statement that "Paris is well worth a Mass".

The encroaching Turkish Ottoman Empire was embroiled in a continuous tug of war with Christian Europe. In 1526 the Jagiellonian King of Hungary, Louis II, was killed in a battle with the Turks at Mohacs. Most of Hungary became Turkish. In 1551 and in 1565 the Turks besieged the Knights Templars on the island of Malta, a key to the hegemony over the Mediterranean. The defenders, led by the Grand Master Jean de la Valette managed to hold on until relief arrived. The victory of the Christian fleet under Don Juan of Austria at Lepanto in 1571 ended the Turkish threat to the Mediterranean. A long conflict between the Turkish Porte and the Serenissima Republic of Venice ended in 1573, thanks to the efforts of the Jewish diplomat, Meir ben Salomon Ashkenazi, the Turkish Ambassador to Venice. I mentioned earlier that the same diplomat also represented the interests of the Crimean Tartars at the Court of the Polish King Zygmunt August and helped Henry of Valois to become King of Poland after the death of the last of the Jagiellons. In Europe arts and literature flourished. Leonardo da Vinci (1452-1519) painted the *Last Supper* on a wall of a church refectory (dining area) in Milan, Michelangelo Buonarotti sculpted the *Pieta* in 1498. Miguel de Cervantes Saavedra wrote *Don Quijote de la Mancha.* In 1569 the first atlases, collections of maps, were published by Mercator and by Ortelius. The *Duomo* (Milan Cathedral) was consecrated by Cardinal Carlo Borromeo in 1587. William Shakespeare wrote *Henry V* in 1556, *Hamlet* in 1600. In 1531 the appearance of Halley's Comet caused a great deal of commotion throughout Europe. In 1547 Nostradamus prophecied the end of the world. In Poland and Ukraine, comparable prophecies were being propounded by a man called Wernyhora. To indicate Poland's importance and power, in 1600, France had 16 million inhabitants, Poland 11 million, Spain 8 million and England with Ireland 5.5 million.

In the world outside of Western Europe, in 1519 Hernan Cortez entered Tenochtitlan and was welcomed by the Aztec Emperor Montezuma. In 1524 Giovanni da Verazzano sailed into New York harbor. In 1536 Jacques Cartier started exploration of the Saint Lawrence River country and Pedro de Mendoza founded Buenos Aires. Akbar the Great (1556-1605) became the Moghul Emperor of India, while Totoyomi Hideyoshi (1536-1598) united Japan and built Osaka Castle in 1583. In 1598 Hideyoshi was succeeded by Ieyasu Tokugawa, who restored the Shogunate. And in Eastern Europe and adjoining Asia a new power was growing. The Russian Cossacks continued their eastern expansion, through Siberia, reaching the Sea of Okhotsk. Saint Basil's Cathedral was built between 1534 to 1561 in Moscow, which replaced Kiev as the key center of Eastern Slavs. Despite temporary setbacks, such as the defeat of the Muscovite armies by the Polish King Stefan Bathory in 1582, and the "Time of Troubles" after the death of Boris Godunov in 1605, Russia became more and more powerful. With the elevation of Michael Romanov to the throne of the Tsars in 1613, Russia was eventually destined to play a large role in subsequent history of the world and of the Eastern European Jewry.

In Spain the Inquisition began a hunt for apostates, Jews who officially converted to Catholicism but secretly continued to observe Jewish religious customs. The Grand Inquisitor Tomas de Torquemada, appointed in 1482, even before the expulsion of Jews from Spain in 1492, earned himself a special place in the annals of human cruelty with his unremitting efforts at torturing and burning luckless individuals. In 1499 75 converts (Marranos) were burned at the stake in Avila in central Spain, with many more to follow. Persecuted and expelled Jews felt that their world was falling apart and they easily fell pray to false messiahs who promised succor and bliss. An adventurer named David Reubeni at first claimed to be an envoy from a Jewish kingdom somewhere in North-east Africa or South-west Asia. At one point he began to claim that he himself was a Messiah who would recruit a Jewish army. An associate, Salomon Molcho, followed in his footsteps. Both died in prison or at the stake. In 1553 Pope Julius III decided that the Talmud contains anti-Christian writings and Jewish religious books were burned at *auto-da-fe's* in Rome and elsewhere. Jews were expelled from Kraków proper to Kazimierz in 1495, but Jewish life continued inspite of difficult conditions. In general, Jews lived in crowded ghettos with minimal hygienic amenities. When in 1552 and 1563 bubonic plague swept through Europe, many Jewish lives were lost, some to the disease and some to pogroms engendered by the accusations that the Jews were responsible for the plague by poisoning wells.

I stated above that in XVI-th Century, the Polish Jews had a considerable degree of autonomy. In a way they constituted a state within a state. They were not a part of the feudal caste system. They were not bound by the Church decrees against usury and money-lending. They were hated and persecuted, yet admired and feared at the same time. Their taxes were negotiated with the King and/or Legislature of Nobles (*Sejm*) by a Jewish Parliament, the *Vaad Arba Aratzot*, the Council of Four Lands, established in 1549, which met for more than two hundred years. This Jewish Parliament was unique in Jewish history from the time of the Biblical Sanhedrin to the modern Israeli Knesset. At times, meetings of the Vaad served as occasions for a gathering of biblical experts to deal with religious matters, such as the above-mentioned lending money on interest to fellow-Jews and adjudication of disputes between Jewish mystics and their opponents.

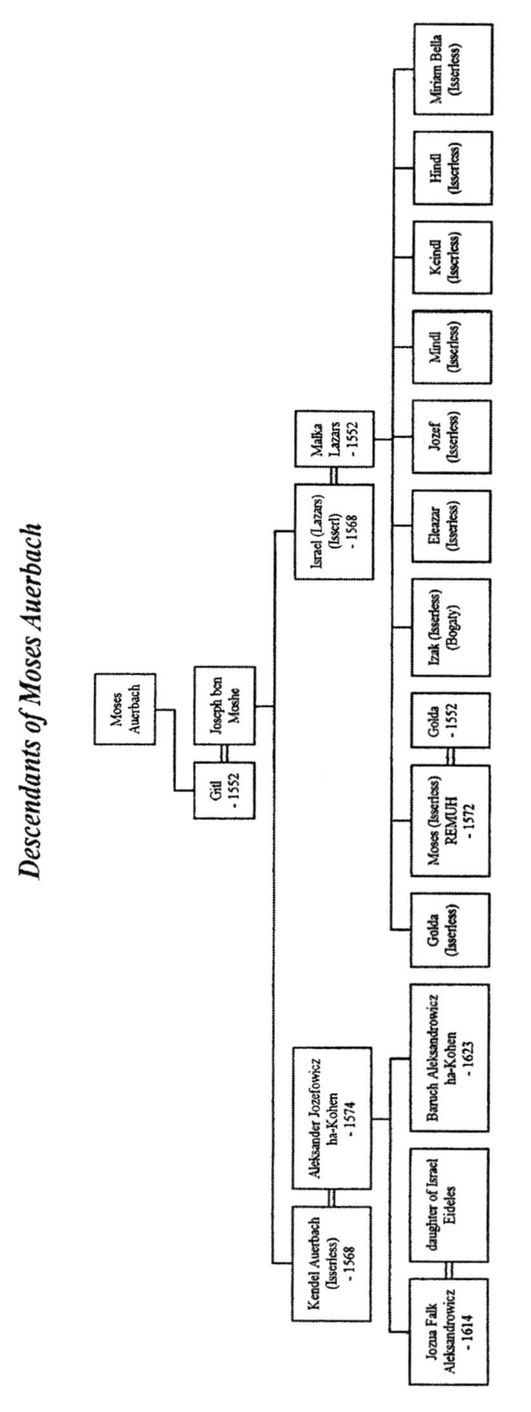

Fig. 007. Family tree of Auerbachs and Isserles

Family tree of Alexander ha-Kohen and Kendel sister of Isserl

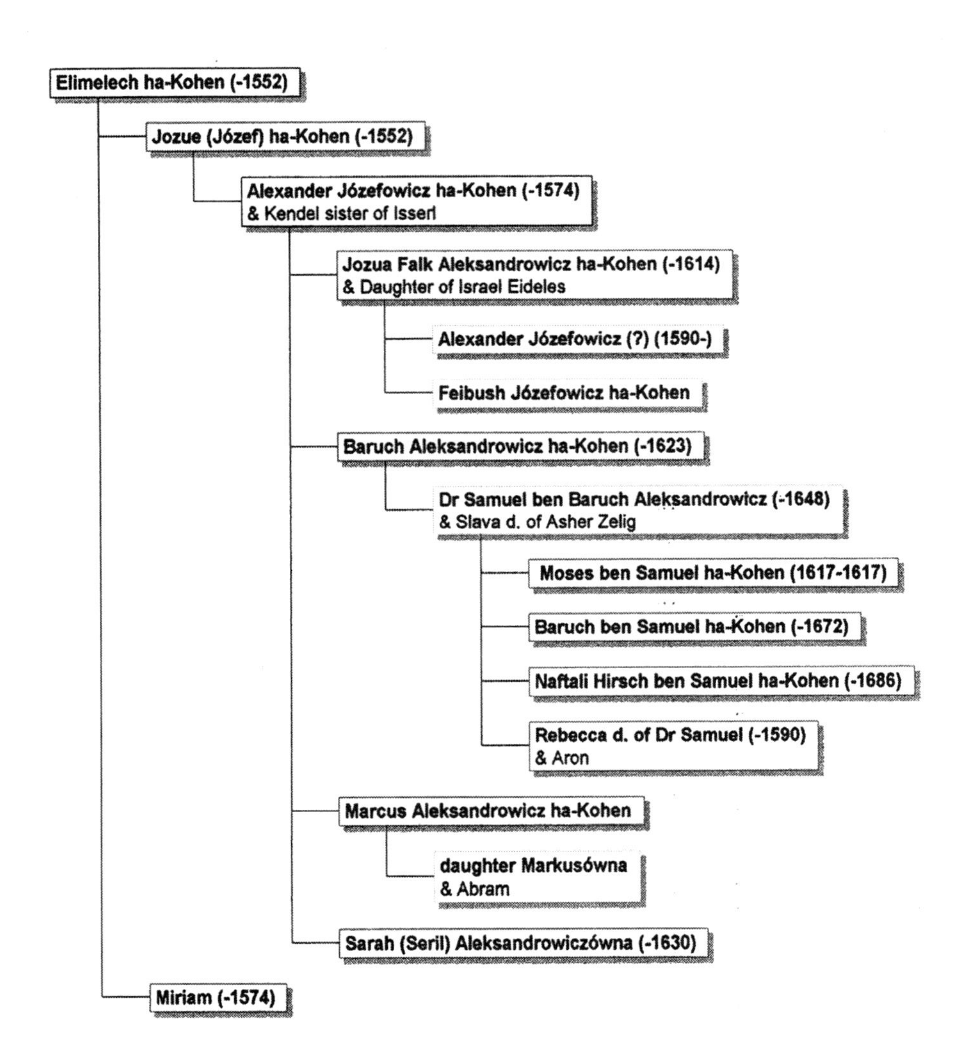

Fig. 008. Family tree of Elimelech ha-Kohen, grandfather of Alexander ha-Kohen;

Chapter 9. Decline of the Polish-Lithuanian Crowned Commonwealth (1648-1796)

In 1648 deeply religious Eastern Orthodox peasants and Cossacks in then Polish Ukraine rebelled against their mostly Catholic Polish aristocratic overlords, under the leadership of Bogdan Chmielnicki. Chmielnicki, a minor noble wronged by a Polish aristocrat and eager for revenge, turned out to be an inspiring leader and a capable military tactician. He is now revered as the founder of Ukrainian national consciousness. Chmielnicki's rebels, not being able to reach the hated magnates who were safe in their palaces in Warsaw or Kraków, wreaked their vengeance on local Jews, "arendars" (holders of rights to collect taxes owed to the nobility), rural merchants, moneylenders, tavern keepers and others. Large numbers of Jewish men, women and children in the eastern reaches of the Polish territories were massacred, many escaped west, some came to Kraków. The Cossack depredations have been described in a book, *Yavein metsulah,* by Nathan Hanover, a refugee from Eastern Poland who lived in Kraków for a while. A Swedish invasion and occupation of Poland that followed the Cossack attacks contributed to the general impoverishment of the country, which included Kraków's Jewish population. Both the Cossacks and the Swedes were inimical to the Jews. The Swedes had previously been converted to Protestantism of the Lutheran variety, which meant that they did not subscribe to the Roman-Catholic near-deification of Mary, mother of Jesus and in Poland they tended to desecrate Marian monasteries. The Swedish invaders were expelled after a successful defense of the fortified monastery of Our Lady of Częstochowa, an event that converted the monastery into a national shrine. The bejewelled portrait of the Black Madonna of Częstochowa became a national icon. The Swedish war ended with re-confirmation of Poland as a strongly Catholic country with Virgin Mary as the "Queen of the Polish Crown".

The misery brought about by the twin disasters of the Cossack Uprising and the Swedish invasion, produced a deep yearning for a deliverer among the Jews. Conditions deteriorated rapidly. Belief that the end of the world must be near and thus that the coming of

a messiah's was approaching prepared the ground for the claim by Sabbatai Tzvi (1626-1676) of Smyrna (now Izmir in Turkey). Sabbatai (Shabse) declared himself a messiah and created a stir among the downtrodden and fearful Jews all over Europe, North Africa and the Middle East. Because the times were bad all-over, with pestilence and wars and pogroms, and seemed ripe for the appearance of a messiah, Sabbatai, who must have been a very convincing and uncommonly charismatic orator, was taken seriously, both by Jews and by the various temporal powers including the Sultan of Turkey. The *Rosh Yeshiva* in Kraków, Nathan Spira, sent his son to Smyrna to find out if Sabbatai is indeed the anointed one. The number of supporters of Sabbatai grew and they became more fervent. Eventually, the Sultan became concerned, had Sabbatai brought to him and offered him a choice of imprisonment and death or conversion to Islam. Sabbatai chose the latter, which considerably cooled the enthusiasm for him among the Jews, although it failed to stop his movement completely. In Turkish prison, Sabbatai held court and received visitors in nearly royal splendor. Eventually, the Sultan had enough of it and Sabbatai was executed. Some of his supporters, however, refused to abandon hope and continued to believe that he would rise and lead the Jews into the millennium. Rabbis tried to exorcise the specter of mystical Sabbateanism with mixed success. Other purported messiahs, and supposed miracle workers arose to fan the flames of mysticism and cabbalistic incantations meant to speed up the millennium. One of these miracle makers, "Masters of the Good Name", a charismatic speaker, Israel Baal Shem Tov from Meziborz in Eastern Poland, started a movement that we now know as Hassidism.

Joseph Caro's dissertation called *Shulhan Arukh,* which codified Jewish religious laws and traditions, was modified by a book, *Mappah,* produced in Kraków by Remuh in 1571. These two works defined traditional orthodox Jewish religious practice for the diaspora. However, there always was another strand of Jewish tradition, involving mystical powers and assorted superstitions, propagated by charismatic preachers claiming to be able to perform miracles. Hundreds years earlier, in 1280, Moses de Leon in Spain (1250-1305) wrote the *Zohar*, the founding treatise of the *Kabbalah* (Hebrew: tradition), a combination of Greek philosophy and Jewish mysticism dating to biblical sages, advocating secret incantations to speed up the coming of the messiah. The profound messianic expectations were responsible for the appearance of several false messiahs. Eventually, the *Zohar* became the inspiration for the creation of a new Hassidism, persisting to this day. A number of wandering Jewish *bal-shems,* self-proclaimed miracle-makers, were popular among Jewish masses (Bałaban, II, 490). Charismatic personalities, among them David Reubeyni and Salomon Molkho, mentioned earlier, made claims of being the long- and eagerly-awaited messiahs, but both were condemned and executed by the Roman Pope. It took a very charismatic figure like Sabbatai Tsvi from Smyrna (1626-1676) to really stir the Jewish masses. The mystical Sabbatean movement continued to thrive even after Sabbatai Tsvi converted to Islam and even after he died in a Turkish prison. The Jewish Parliament in Poland, the *Vaad Arba Aaratzot*, excommunicated Sabbatean mysticism and belief in *Tsaddikim* (miracle men) in 1722. In eastern Poland and western Ukraine two very different men tapped into the surviving mystical messianic beliefs and both had significant impact on Polish Jewish history, Jacob Leibowicz Frank and Israel ben Eliezer Baal Shem Tov (*Besht*). Of the two, the impact of the latter being far more lasting.

Jacob Frank (1726-1791) declared himself a messiah and gathered a number of followers. Like some previous false messiahs in the long Jewish history, he preached that

the Jewish commandments and religious restrictions and obligations have been fulfilled with his coming and need no longer be observed. It is said that Frank and his followers engaged in sexual orgies, group debauchery and such. He was persecuted by the Jewish establishment and turned to the Christian authorities for help and protection, accusing Talmudic scholars of heresy. In 1757, at his instigation, the local Bishop of Kamieniec Podolski ordered a religious-philosophical disputation and as a result had the Talmud proscribed and many copies were burnt at an *auto-da-Fe*. In the end, Frank and his followers converted to Catholicism. As I stated earlier, it is interesting, that in Poland at the time the Jews were held in contempt and yet in some way also held in high esteem. Of course, they were knowledgeable, deeply religious, well-connected, able to read and write (in Hebrew) and, in a few cases, very wealthy. Polish laws reflected both an eagerness to convert them and a respect for their refusal to convert and the steadfastness in their beliefs. Any Jew that converted could, almost automatically, receive the highly-valued patent of nobility, a piece of land and usually a nomination to an honorary state office. It appears that, upon conversion, the Frankists became Polish nobles and joined the ranks of minor aristocracy. There is a likelihood that some of the most exalted individuals in subsequent Polish history and literature were descendants of the Jewish followers of Jacob Frank, among them Poland's foremost national poet, Adam Mickiewicz (1798-1855), a mystic if there ever was one.

The other man, (Izrael) Baal Shem Tov (ca.1700-1760) was born in Medzyborz in the district of Podolia. He never wrote any religious tracts himself but was charismatic and had a knack of expressing himself simply yet joyfully. He attracted brilliant students and successors, Magid Dov Beer of Mezeritch (1698-1772), Jacob Josef ha-Kohen of Polonnoe (1724-1784), who published the first Hassidic work, *Toledot*, Elimelech of Lezhaysk (1717-1786) and the founder of the Chabad Lubavitcher movement, Shneur Zalman of Liady (1745-1813). Together they created a deeply religious, mystical, joyful, religious-ecstatic movement lasting to this day. The movement was popular and spread widely but it was considered heretical and dangerous by the contemporary orthodox Jewish religious establishment. The Gaon of Vilna (1720-1797), the foremost Jewish religious authority of the day, excommunicated Hassidism in 1772. In 1785, noticing the appearance of a Hassidic *shtibl* ("little room") in Kraków, the Krakovian Chief Rabbi, Izak ben Mordechai ha-Levi had an excommunication of Hassidism read in all Kraków synagogues. Among the leaders of Kraków Hassidim was the very rich and influential Ber Luxenburg, owner of important parcels of land and housing in Jewish Kazimierz and elsewhere, related by marriage to both Dr Aron Kalahora and to the Jekeles family. The feud between the traditional orthodoxy and the Hassidim was fierce but excommunications did not stem the growth of the latter. Hassidic sects proliferated, led by miracle-maker Tsadikkim from *shtetls*, inluding Góra Kalwaria (Yiddish: *Gher*), Opatów (*Apt*), Tykocin (*Tiktin*), Nowy Sącz (*Santz*), Bobbova, Sadogóra (*Satma*r), Kotzk, Liady and Lubowicze. The successor of Schneur Zalman of Liady's moved to Lubowicze, hence the sect's current name. All Lubavitcher Grand-rebbes, including the last, Menachem Mendel (1902-1997), were either natural or adopted descendants of Schneur Zalman and all used the surname of Schneerson. All the Hassidic Grand-rebbes were believed to be able to communicate more-or-less directly with the Almighty and to serve as intermediaries for their believers. Each was supported by his followers in grand style. Some of the Tsaddikim maintained elaborate courts, with princely mansions, uniformed armed guards, students, acolytes and hundreds of supporters. In exchange they performed some important functions, sometimes interpreting biblical injunctions in surprisingly liberal way, thus making difficult life easier and providing hope that the good Lord will indeed provide for the truly faithful. In my childhood in Kraków I was aware of the existence of scores of small Hassidic prayer rooms (*shtibls*) in the Jewish areas of town, each filled at prayer time with followers of and believers in a given holy miracle maker and guru.

For centuries, registers of inhabitants of Poland were kept by Roman-Catholic parish priests, as part of their obligation to make sure that all parishioners attend mass and undergo required sacraments. These priests were also expected by the State to keep records of people of other religions, Protestants, Jews and Moslems. The Jews were mostly registered by the local rabbis, under supervision of the priests who were supposed to check the accuracy of these census lists. The Polish royal governors also occasionally attempted to list all Polish Jews. Several state census listings of Polish Jews dating to early and middle of the seventeen hundreds have been made, but these were incomplete, unreliable and are now available only in fragments. In 1790, under the last Polish King, Stanisław August Poniatowski, a complete census of Jews was undertaken, listing by name not only those living in royal towns like Kraków and Kazimierz, but also those living in privately owned small towns and villages whose owners were ordered to certify the listing of "their" Jews. I have examined an original copy of this census, more than 200 year old, covering the area of Kraków and its neighboring towns and villages, which is preserved in the Kraków Archives on Sienna Street. I found that my reliably documented ancestors were listed in Kraków at least since 1725. There is a later census, made by the Austrians when they came to Kraków in 1796. In this census, too, there are indications of my forebears living in Kraków at least from 1725, and probably much earlier. It is likely that Alexander ben Yehoshuah ha-Kohen and his grandson, Dr Samuel ben Baruch (Patavinus) are among my direct ancestors but there is a gap of more than sixty years between the death of the last known descendants of Dr Alexander and the birth of the first fully documented ancestor of mine, Joseph, son or grandson of David, who later in life became known as Aleksandrowicz. Until additional data are found, I am limited to suppositions. I find the juxtaposition of names suggestive. I know that there was a prominent line of Alexanders in Kraków's early Jewish history. I assume that, just as I have always been fully aware of my ancestors for the past one hundred years, so Joseph Aleksandrowicz must have been aware of his ancestors in 1805 when he chose to register a family surname.

More often than not, the Jewish Community Council of Kraków (the Kahał) was run dictatorially and corruptly by cabals of greedy rich men, who took advantage of opportunities to get rich by squeezing the poor. They bribed non-Jewish supervisory officials such as the royal governor, secured special privileges for themselves and enriched themselves at the expense of the community. This was particularly true during the unsettled times just prior to the disappearance of Poland as an independent entity, when royal authority was weakened. There were in Kraków two groups vying for control of the Kahał. When successful, each dealt brutally with the other. They did not play by the rules; cruelty and brutality, lack of compassion, and torture were common. Often, however, being a member of the Kahał also led to danger. It meant being exposed to abuse by conquering armies, Russian, Prussian, Swedish and Austrian, as well as by armed Polish factions, such as the Bar Confederates (1768-1772) (Prof. Bałaban wrote a chapter about the Bar Confederacy).

The latter extorted huge sums of money from the Jews and felt free to enforce the extortion by arrest and torture of Kahał seniors.

The executive power in the declining Polish "Crowned Republic" in the 17-th and 18-the centuries formally resided with the kings, each of whom was directly elected by all of the country's gentry. The king appointed royal governors (voivods, in Polish "*wojewoda*"). It was these royal governors who were in charge of local Jewish affairs. In addition, in large private land holdings, powerful aristocratic families, such as those of the Princes Radziwiłł, Sapieha, Zamoyski, Wiśniowiecki, Potocki, Czartoryski, Poniatowski, Ossoliński, Sanguszko and others, exercised almost sovereign powers. Individual petty nobles (*szlachta zaściankowa*) cherished their right to sit in the country's parliament and exercise their right to veto not only the proposal under discussion but the entire ouput of the parliamentary session. Foreign powers, mainly Russia, took advantage of this quirk in the Polish constitution, bribed individuals and prevented the country from appropriating funds to maintain an army or modernize commerce and industry. The country eventually went under because of this *liberum veto*. There was, however, a mechanism for by-passing the regular parliament, by forming a so-called "Confederacy" of nobles, in reality a rump parliament, where the right of veto did not apply and a simple majority of those present made decisions. In 1768, in desperation, a group of Polish patriots formed just such a confederacy in Bar on the Ukrainian border and mobilized an army. In Polish history, the Bar Confederacy is remembered as a last-minute glorious but futile patriotic attempt to save Poland. Unfortunately, as part of their Polish patriotism, the Confederates held strong anti-Jewish sentiments and were convinced that Polish Jews were harmful to the country. Russia, which saw the Bar Confederacy as a hostile endeavor, sent in armies to crush it. The Russians, like the Confederates, saw the Jews as enemies. In Ukraine in 1768 the rabble "*haidamaks*" massacred scores of Jews including the entire Jewish population, men, women and children, of the town of Uman, an event known to history as "*Rzeź Umańska*", i.e. Uman massacre. Kraków was alternately in the hands of the Confederate and Russian armed forces. Both sides arrested, beat and tortured Jews, particularly the senior members of the Kahał.

Acccording to Bałaban, in 1768 and for many years previously, the Kahał was run by members and friends of the Jekeles family. Among the "seniors" were Gutman Rakowski (Rakower), son of Berl and grandson of Izak of Raków, Feibush Giess, Izrael son of Aron Manasses (Pitzele?), Dr. Mendel Kalahora and old Moses Jekeles. Gutman Rakowski served as the chief senior. In 1771 the Confederates arrested and tortured him so cruelly that he died of wounds suffered in beatings. In 1772 the Bar Confederacy was defeated by the Russians with help from those Poles who wanted to defend the use of the *liberum veto* and who formed a competing confederacy at Targowica. Eventually, Kraków was occupied by Russian armies. On February 2, 1772 a group of opponents and rivals of the Jekeles faction took over the Kahał, with connivance of bribed Russian officers, and placed Hershel Stobnicki, Feibush son of Abraham and Moyżesz Braciejówka as seniors. Once in power, Stobnicki arrested his opponents, kept them in prison and extorted money from them. In 1773 a major fire swept through Kazimierz not only destroying a number of wooden houses but also causing the loss of a lot of stored Kahał documents, including critical originals of precious royal privileges.

Moyżesz (Yiddish: Moyshe) Braciejówka, son of Pincus (Bałaban, II, 390), the patriarch of a rich and powerful family in Kraków, was born in 1722. He and his wife Ester

had several sons, Jankel born 1745, Ghetzel (Gecel) born 1752, Berek born 1762 and Judka born 1766. The Austrians occupied Kraków in 1796. It appears from a certificate of death dated 1816, that in 1805 when Kraków Jews were obliged to select family surnames, Getzel Braciejówka, owner of building No.1 in Kazimierz, chose to adopt the name Moyzinger or Mosinger. It is not known why he had abandoned the old nickname, perhaps because its Polish sound was inappropriate for a Jewish family living under Austrian domination. It is also not known why he picked the surname Moysinger. It may be that he knew that the family originated in some town or village of Mossin, Meissen or similar, several of which exist in Silesia, Bohemia and Poland, or simply because his father was called Moyshe. There is evidence that a descendant of Ghetzel's, Hirsch Mosinger born around 1817, married Hana Aleksandrowiczówna, i.e. Miss Hana Aleksandrowicz. Hana, born in 1813, was a daughter of Joseph Aleksandrowicz and his wife Dobrysz, a sister of my great-great-grandfather Menashe and an aunt of my great-grandfather Józef. A copy of Hana's birth record is enclosed below, along with copies of birth and death certificates of her little daughter Marya. I have received these from one of their descendants, now living in Australia, along with copies of records of some of Hirsch and Hana Mosinger's other children, among them Manele, born 1845, David Jacob born 1850 and short-lived baby Rifka Moysinger (1852-1853).

The First Partition of Poland took place in 1772. Kazimierz by Kraków and its Jewish Ghetto, but not the center of the city of Kraków, were occupied by the armies of Maria Theresa, Empress of Austria. The separation of Kazimierz from Kraków meant that Jews lived in a foreign (Austrian) territory, but had their stores in Kraków, which remained, for the time-being, a part of Poland. The situation was untenable, and eventually, in 1775 Kazimierz reverted back to Poland until the Third Partition in 1796. The impoverished Jewish population of Kraków had more problems. In the partition, Polish Kraków and Kazimierz lost their natural market and supply area to the south, which became Austrian. This meant that the entire commerce had to be reoriented to the north, towards Warsaw. The entire merchant class, Jewish as well as non-Jewish, was in deep trouble. The Christian merchants, in their difficulties, decided that most of their problems would be eliminated and their economic situation improved if they could only get rid of their Jewish competitors in Kraków. They filed a suit to enforce a two-hundred-years-old regulation that barred Jewish store-owners and craftsmen from the city proper. The suit, in the Assessors Court in Warsaw, took a while coming to a head, but in 1776 the Court ruled against the Jews. In Jewish Ghetto in Kazimierz there was desperation. The entire livelihood of the Jewish Town was at risk. In this extremity the Jews took a desperate step: they negotiated with the town government of the Christian non-Jewish part of Kazimierz to allow Jews to rent stores on the main non-Jewish thoroughfare, Krakowska Street. Krakowska Street led directly from Kazimierz, past the royal palace, to Kraków main market square, a walk of 20-30 minutes. When the Kraków city government began enforcing the court ruling, confiscating Jewish stores, the Jews moved all their stores and craft shops to Krakowska Street in Kazimierz (Bałaban, II, 395). With them, almost the entire Krakovian economic activity moved to Kazimierz. Customers followed the Jews. Houses on Krakowska Street, which heretofore merited little rent, now started bringing money. The house-owners in Kazimierz profited, while house owners in the city of Kraków now had empty stores and workshops and collected no rent. The trade moved out of Kraków. If Kraków Christian merchants thought that getting rid of Jews would bring them prosperity, they were sorely disappointed.

Not all the Jews moved out of the center of Kraków, only the sellers of merchandise and specified craftsmen. Others, mostly bankers and moneylenders, among them some of my Gumple and Alexander ancestors, remained. Eventually, the others drifted back. In 1791 Kazimierz was incorporated into the Kraków municipality and the Jewish merchants had to fight for their rights all over again. The pattern repeated itself, the Jews again lost their rights for a while and gradually drifted back to the center of the city. The difficulty of Jewish existence were compounded by internal disputes. At the time, the Polish Jewry, including that of Kraków, was riven by emotional disputes concerning deeply held religious convictions. The traditional orthodox rabbis were excommunicating the Chasidim who nevertheles were gaining adherents, mostly among the poor.

As if the argument between the orthodox and Hassidim were not enough, Western assimilationist tendencies began to appear in Kraków. Austrian authorities began to reward those Jews who were groomed and dressed in Western manner, eschewing the long hair and beards and side-locks (*peyes*), black capotes, *yarmoulkes* and fur-hats (*shtramels*). In Germany Moses Mendelssohn (1729-1786) translated the Jewish Bible and wrote commentaries on it in German, thus making it generally available and understandable. This started a modern reformist Jewish movement, the *Haskalah*. Supporters of the Haskalah in Kraków started gaining strength after 1800. One of the strongest future supporters of the modernization of Kraków Jewry, was Abraham Gumplowicz, born in 1801, son of Lebl Gumplowicz, grandson of Jacob Gumpel and cousin of Menashe Aleksandrowicz, my great-great-grandfather.

The old, stable political and economic system of balance of power in Continental Europe around 1750 was about to be shaken by three major upheavals, the disappearance of Poland and revolutions in North America and France. Poland was getting weaker because of the selfishness and greed of its ruling class of petty nobility. Polish kings were elected by special convocations of the entire nobility. At these convocations the nobles were divided into a pro-Russian party, a pro-Austrian party and a group that hoped to preserve Polish independence by aligning itself with France. The last ruler who commanded strong Polish forces was King John III Sobieski (1624-1696, ruled 1674-1696), an ally of France, married to a French princess Marie whom he called by the diminutive Marysienka. He helped to save Vienna besieged by the Turks in 1683. This was arguably the last of Poland's great successful battles. The next king was August II the Strong of the Wettin dynasty of Saxony, so-called not because he was a strong ruler but because he was physically strong. It was said that he broke iron horseshoes with his bare hands for fun and the sheer satisfaction of it. After his death the pro-French party pushed through the election of a Polish magnate, Stanisław Leszczyński, father-in-law of the King of France, Louis XIV, whose election was immediately contested by the Russians, who favored the son of August II. The "War of Polish Succession" (1733-1735), pitted two Polish factions against each other, one aligned with France and the other with Saxony, Russia, Austria and Sweden. Even Spain and the Kingdom of Sardinia became involved. A balance of power in Central Europe was at issue. All of Europe was watching with interest. Great Britain sent George Woodward, Esq., as an "Envoy Extraordinary to the Kingdom and Republic of Poland" to collect intelligence and influence events. In January 1735 Woodward submitted a bill for 100 pounds for his expenses, a large sum of money for the time (see photostat at the end of this chapter). France was far and Russia was near. The pro-French faction lost, Leszczyński abdicated

and was compensated with the Duchy of Lorraine as a fief of the King of France, with capital at Nancy. August III *Sas* (of Saxony) became king of Poland. As king, August III confirmed the ancient Jewish privileges, originally issued by Casimir the Great and previously confirmed by John III Sobieski in 1676. The period of rule by the two Saxon kings was characterized in Poland as an era of selfishness and gluttony of the nobility: "*Za króla Sasa, jedz, pij i popuszczaj pasa*" (During the reign of the Saxon king, eat, drink and let out the belt). The next and last Polish king, a Polish nobleman, Stanisław August Poniatowski, was a handsome, dapper man, always impeccably dressed, who was said to have been a secret lover of the Russian *tsaritsa*, Catherine the Great He was favored for the Polish throne by the increasingly powerful pro-Russian party. Of interest to Jews, he was an educated liberal man, aware of being responsible for the well-being of a large number of Jews. When he visited Kraków, he made a point of also visiting the Jewish Kazimierz. As king, he faced impossible conditions, was ineffective and was forced to abdicate after the third partition of Poland in 1795-6.

Unlike Poland, the other major Continental European powers surrounding her, Russia, Austria and Prussia, had governments entirely controlled by "divinely anointed", hereditary autocratic rulers. Their standing armies were strong and their governments powerful. Poland's weakness was inviting interference in its internal affairs and, eventually, led to partitions of its territory among the three neighbors. The demise of the country was gradual, from 1772 to 1795. For Polish Jews each successive loss of territory had dire economic consequences. Thus, the first partition led to Russian occupation of large area of eastern Poland with its large concentration of Jews who from then on had to contend with animosity of the Tsarist regime. Poznan (Posen), the Polish Baltic coast and the mouth of the river Vistula fell to the Prussians cutting the rest of Poland from a sea outlet. A lot of Krakovian exporters used the Baltic ports to send their merchandise abroad on barges floating on the Vistula. Thus, lumber from the Carpathian Mountains, with its straight tall trees suitable for ship masts, sold to Holland and England, were traditionally shipped by water to Gdańsk (Danzig) on the Baltic. After 1772 the river ceased to be the cheapest and most direct transportation route. Kraków lost its natural hinterland to Austria, including the salt mines of Wieliczka, towns of Skawina, Brzesko (*Brisk*), Nowy Sącz (*Sanz*), Nowy Targ, Rabka, etc. The entire local trade had to be reoriented first towards Warsaw and central Poland, then towards Moravia, Bohemia and Austria. Krakovian Jews lived in Kazimierz but routinely traded in Kraków markets.

While the strong Central European powers enjoyed apparent stability thanks to their military prowess and centralized governments, beneath the surface there was ferment. Intellectuals began broaching the revolutionary ideas of government by consent of the governed, of equality of all people, of freedom of expression, etc. The existing system was unable to deliver the good life to its peoples and it was showing signs of sclerosis and atrophy. A small minority of aristocrats, courtiers, high clergy and other members of the ruling elite were primary beneficiaries of the system, while most people lived in dismal poverty. Inhabitants of townlets and villages were living in hovels with floors of beaten earth. The towns lacked the most rudimentary hygiene. Streets were not paved and in bad weather were mired in mud, with sewage freely flowing in the middle. Diseases were endemic. Most of the population lived not in the cities but in the countryside and all European economies were largely rural. Peasants in the countryside were not only

desperately poor, but as serfs they were treated like chattels, unable to improve their lot. As long as people were kept in ignorance and the established churches supported the *status quo*, the kings, emperors and tsars continued to rule and their subjects continued to suffer in quiet resignation. Then an impetus for change came from a totally unexpected source, from a rebellion of a batch of distant British colonists in North America.

The American colonies were ruled in a way that was not substantially different from their European counterparts, but the colonists had several advantages. Their sovereign was distant and largely ignorant of local conditions. He had no rapid way of enforcing his wishes. As happens occasionally in history, serendipitously, the colonies had a number of literate outstanding minds among the ruling British-American elite, aware of the latest writing of John Locke and Jean-Jacques Rousseau. Like the European models, the colonial economies depended on the availability of cheap labor. The Southern plantation system used African slaves. The New England small factory and craft system needed a continuous infusion of cheap immigrant and indentured servant labor. What rendered the system unstable in 1772, however, was not the condition of the poor masses but the resentment of regulations (and taxes!) imposed on the ruling groups by representatives of the absentee king. The slogan of "No taxation without representation" was catchy and the idea that all men are created equal, stirred educated liberal men not just in the Americas but all over Europe as well. A strong faction in England supported the colonists' quest for freedom and separation from England. Volunteers came to fight "*For our freedom and yours*" from France and Germany. Poland was represented by Casimir Pułaski and Tadeusz Kościuszko. French help, the impact of the cost to the British treasury of trying to reclaim America with hired Hessian mercenaries, the opposition in Britain itself and the valor and sheer endurance of the army under George Washington, ensured a victorious outcome for the United States. A new constitution was written and Washington was inaugurated as the first President of the United States in New York in 1789. The first ten amendments to the Constitution, the Bill of Rights, were ratified in 1791. Jews had the same rights as everyone else. The new nation was already home to a sizeable number of Jews, with synagogues in Newport, Charleston and Savannah.

At the time, the Jews of Kraków were only vaguely aware of America. My ancestor, Józef Aleksandrowicz, was only six years old in 1789. Little could his parents guess that their son's descendants would one day live in the New World beyond the ocean. They must have been much more concerned about their daily problems, aggravated by the situation in Warsaw and Vienna and St. Petersburg. In 1781, after the death of the Habsburg Empress Maria Teresa, who was hostile to Jews, her son Joseph II ascended the Austrian throne and issued a Patent of Religious Tolerance, decreasing somewhat the anti-Jewish ordinances. It is of interest that Pope Pius VI found this edict which allowed assimilated Jews to live outside special Jewish areas so troubling, that he journeyed to Vienna to persuade Joseph II to rescind it. He was unsuccessful. The old Jewish section of Prague, Jozefov, to this day bears the name honoring Joseph II. At the time, Kraków, unlike Prague, was not Austrian, but became so a few years later, in 1796. The Jews, including the Aleksandrowicz family, were about to be profoundly affected by events about to occur in France.

The stirring message of the American experiment was not lost on liberals in Europe. Many of the European volunteers who helped the Americans, like the Marquis de Lafayette, did not remain in the United States but returned to their countries of origin. The next explosion occurred in France. It is difficult to exaggerate its impact on Western

Civilization. In the same year that Washington was inaugurated, France changed world history and along with it, the history of European Jewry. France was ruled by King Louis XVI, a descendant of the Constable of Bourbon, who was married to an Austrian Princess, Marie Antoinette, daughter of the Empress Maria Teresa. Seething unrest and vocal opposition of many, forced the King to call a meeting of the Estates General, an ancient form of parliament that met only rarely. Even as the Estates met, however, it became clear that the popular discontent and impatience with royal ineptness would not be appeased by half-measures. A Parisian mass demonstration ended with the sack of the cruel royal fortress prison, the Bastille, which was burned. The so-called Third Estate assembled in Versailles declared itself an *Assemblee Nationale* entitled to represent, and perhaps rule, the country. A stirring Declaration of Rights of Man and Citizen was written. French Jews were granted all civil liberties. A slogan, that reverberated throughout Europe, "*Liberte, Egalite, Fraternite*" was adopted. A French poet, Rouget de Lisle, wrote a revolutionary hymn, called "*La Marseillaise*", which soon became known all over Europe and served to rally men to the new cause of freedom and equality for all. The *Marseillaise,* which became the national anthem of France, has remained a truly stirring song of individual liberty and opposition to oppression. Even during the Second World War, in Nazi concentration camps, prisoners, myself included, hummed the *Marseillaise* as a song of protest and defiance. In a development that shocked royalist Europe, the Bourbon King and his Austrian wife were executed in 1793 in a reign of terror. In 1800 Napoleon Bonaparte, as First Consul and Commander of French armies, conquered Milan and Rome, in 1801 he dissolved the Holy Roman Empire. In 1804 he crowned himself Emperor of the French. As leader of revolutionary armies, he became the bearer of the new revolutionary ideas of equality and freedom. His ideas and his armies were invincible for a time. Vienna, Berlin, Madrid, Lisbon, Amsterdam, Naples, Venice, fell to the French. Napoleon's armies included a sizeable Polish contingent under the command of Prince Józef Poniatowski, a nephew of the last king. Prince Józef became a Marshal of France.

Napoleon established a legal commission, which created a modern code of laws, now named after him, *Code Napoleon.* He assembled a congress of learned Jews and referred to it as a *Sanhedrin,* after the old biblical assembly of sages. He encouraged and funded French science and arts. In Rome, he abolished the Inquisition, after the pope, Pius VII, fled. He abolished the venerable *Serenissima* Republic of Venice which had outlived its usefulness. When he successively invaded the Iberian Peninsula, the Portuguese royal house of Braganza escaped to Portuguese South America and there established a Portuguese Brazilian Empire. In 1803, the French army fought a black slave insurrection in Haiti under Toussaint l'Ouverture, then abandoned the island allowing it to become the first independent black republic. Napoleon sold a large swath of conquered Spanish land in North America, including the city of New Orleans, Louisiana, to the new nation of United States. After defeating the Prussians at Jena, Napoleon established an independent Polish Duchy of Warsaw. Five years later, in 1809, after defeating the Austrians at Wagram, Polish troops led by Prince Józef entered Kraków, which was added to the Warsaw Duchy. Included in the Polish army was a Jewish battalion, originally created by Tadeusz Kosciuszko, commanded by a Jewish officer, Colonel Berek Joselewicz. There exists a family legend that one of our ancestors served in the Joselewicz battalion. Colonel Joselewicz died in 1809 in a battle against the Russian army at Kotzk.

Napoleon's successes could not last. France was getting exhausted both financially and in its human resources. All her enemies united against her. The last and most important of these was the Tsar of All Russias, Alexander I. Napoleon assembled a *Grande Armee* and marched on Moscow, which he conquered, but from which he had to retreat because it burnt and offered no protection from the Russian winter with its snows and winds. Defeat at the crossing of the frozen Berezina River and later of the river Elbe at the Saxon city of Leipzig, ended the Napoleonic era. The Emperor was exiled first to the island of Elba, then to the island of St. Helena. His enemies met at a Congress in Vienna and divided the spoils. Louis XVII became king of France. The Pope returned to Rome and promptly reinstated the Holy Inquisition. Tsar Alexander I became king of a rump Polish Kingdom, wholly under Russian domination. Prussia got Pomerania and the Duchy of Posen, Austria took all of southern Poland, except for Kraków, which became a small, semi-independent city-state, the Kraków Republic, under the protection of the surrounding autocracies. The victors tried to discredit the ideals of the French Revolution and reverse all its innovations. They succeeded, but only briefly. The power of ideas cannot be defeated by force. The world was changed by the American and French Revolutions and it was never to be the same.

While the French were spreading their novel social notions, scientists and inventors were busy, as were writers, poets and musicians. In 1783, the year of the birth of my ancestor, Józef Aleksandrowicz, the brothers Montgolfier ascended in a balloon, using coal-heated air. The Viennese court enjoyed the music of Haydn and the youthful Mozart. In 1786 Mozart's *Marriage of Figaro* was presented in Vienna. In 1789, a French chemist, Antoine Lavoisier, discoverer of oxygen, cathegorized all the primary elements and created a logical table of 31 elements. We have since added many more elements to the table but we are essentially using the same table with Lavoisier's categories today. In 1801 in Spain, Francisco Goya painted the Duchess of Alba as *Maya Vestita* and *Maya Desnuda*. In 1803, Robert Fulton built his first steamboat. During the first two decades of the 1800's Friedrich Schiller wrote *Wilhelm Tell*, Johan Wolfgang Goethe wrote *Faust* and Washington Irving wrote *Rip van Winkle*. In 1808 Ludwig van Beethoven wrote the Fifth Symphony *(Eroica)*, in honor of Napoleon. In 1811 Amadeo Avogadro (1776-1856) postulated the molecular composition of gases. The economist Thomas Robert Malthus (1766-1834) publicized his worry that the rise in food production will not keep up with population increase. Since the time of Malthus we have made large increases in agricultural output, but I have no doubt that this only postponed the inevitable and that, in the long-run, Malthus will be proven to have been right. Unless we override the political opposition to family planning by the Catholic Church, the Christian evangelicals and the Muslim (and Jewish) fundamentalists and develop rational programs limiting population growth, I am convinced that not only the availability of food, but availability of livable land, energy, clean air and clean water will also fail to keep up with the increase in population, if not in the developed countries, then certainly in the less-developed areas of the globe.

The brothers Grimm published their *Fairy Tales*, Jane Austen wrote *Pride and Prejudice,* Lord Byron wrote *Childe Harold's Pilgrimage*. Samuel Taylor Coleridge published his poem *In Xanadu did Kublai Khan...* in 1816. In 1820 Sir Walter Scott wrote *Ivanhoe,* Alexander Pushkin wrote *Ruslan and Ludmilla* and Keats the *Ode to a Nightingale*. Heinrich Heine published a collection of poems and Thomas de Quincy wrote the *Confessions of an English Opium Eater*. Alessandro Manzoni's *I Promessi Sposi*, a tale of love during the

time of plague was published in 1825, James Fenimore Cooper wrote *Last of the Mohicans* in 1826, Alexandre Dumas pere wrote *The Three Musketeers* and Victor Hugo wrote about Quasimodo in *Notre Dame de Paris*. Charles Darwin (1809-1882) sailed for the Galapagos Islands on the H.M.S. Beagle, while Michael Faraday (1791-1867) established the possibility of electromagnetic induction of current. After the voyage, Darwin published his theory of natural selection, which by now has been amply documented in the fossil record, yet remains controversial because, like the Copernican sun-centered world design, it ran into fundamentalist religious opposition. Thanks to Faraday's discovery we now have electricity to light our streets and power our home appliances. Washington Irving wrote the *Tales of the Alhambra*, Alexander Pushkin wrote *Eugene Onegin,* Alfred Lord Tennyson wrote the *Lady of Shalott*. In the distant empire of Japan, my favorite Ukiyo-e artist, Ando Hiroshige, created *The Fifty-Three Stages of the Tokkaido.* When we visited Japan, we made a special point of hiking a portion of the Tokkaido. While we walked there, rain came down on us in sheets, and the Tokkaido looked just as depicted in Hiroshige woodcut drawings.

The effect of the political and military changes on Polish Jews and on my family in Kraków was quite profound. The immediate changes in their existence were brief and transient, but the changes in their outlook were long lasting. They allowed themselves to hope that overt anti-Semitism would decline and their future and that of their children would improve significantly and that made all the difference. Tadeusz Kościuszko, as Polish Supreme Commander and Chief of State, visited the Kraków Jewish area and was greeted with jubilation. In his oath to fight for Polish independence, which he took on the Kraków Central Market Square, he called for complete emancipation of Jews and for freeing of serfs. For brief periods Kraków Jews enjoyed all the rights and privileges then enjoyed by Jews of America, Britain or France. These were withdrawn after Napoleon's defeat. After the death of the Jewish colonel, Berek Joselewicz, the Jewish battalion was disbanded. I have no doubt that my ancestors were proud of the battalion's existence and sympathized with Kościuszko and then with Napoleon. Of immediate concerns to my forebear Józef Aleksandrowicz and his family was their personal sefety, as different armies marched through Kraków, each being cruel to and exacting tributes from the Jewish community. Housing for soldiers and provision of food were mandatory. Large amounts of cash were contributed to avoid massacres. Protecting the house owned by the family was a constant problem, as was the family's livelihood in the continuously changing environment. It appears that to avoid obvious dangers, my ancestors chose not to accept membership on the Jewish Community Council, although their status may have entitled them to one. They knew from long experience, that Council members were always exposed to harsh treatment by all invading forces. Council members were frequently arrested, often beaten and tortured in attempts to extort money from the Jewish community. In spite of all the military and political upheavals and dangers, daily life continued. Józef's trading activities were being continuously re-aligned to keep up with the changing international boundaries. Prior to 1772 most of the buying and selling was directed to the south of Kraków towards the foothills of the Carpathian Mountains, Slovakia and Moravia. Later it was re-directed to the north towards Kielce, Radom and Warsaw. After 1815, when Kraków became a separate small semi-independent entity, commerce tended to atrophy and the city as a whole, of course also including its Jews, was impoverished. Even its proud ancient University fell on hard times. In 1802, Joseph later known as Aleksandrowicz and Dobrysz

of the Gumplowicz were married in Kraków. Their history and the history of their progeny will be described in the following chapters. In 1800 the population of London was 864,000, of Paris 547,000, of Vienna 231,000. Impoverished Kraków had only 26,000 inhabitants, among them around 4,300 Jews.

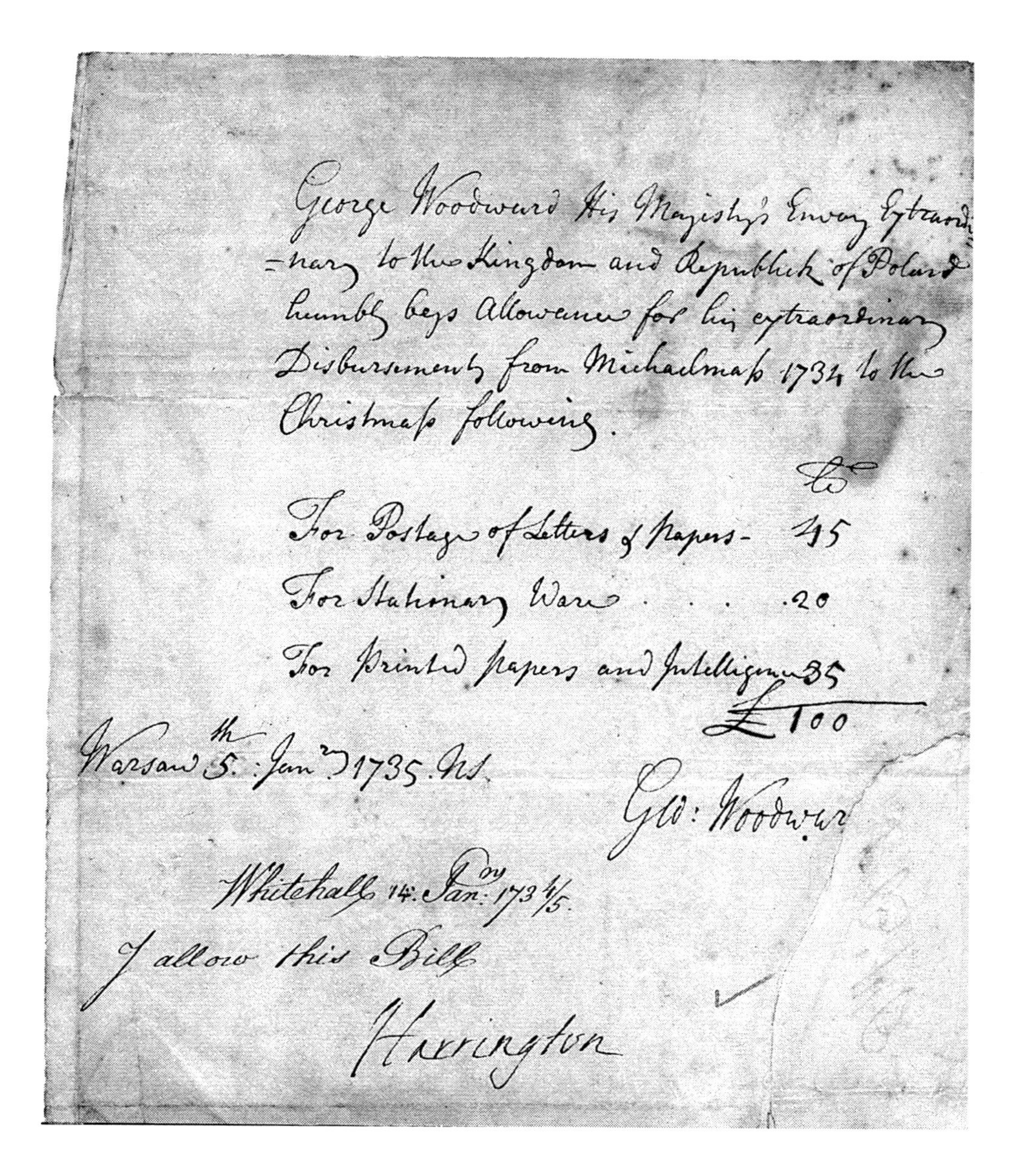

George Woodward His Majesty's Envoy Extraordi-
-nary to the Kingdom and Republick of Poland
humbly begs Allowance for his extraordinary
Disbursements from Michaelmass 1734 to the
Christmass following.

	£
For Postage of Letters & Papers -	45
For Stationary Ware . . .	20
For Printed papers and Intelligence	35
	£100

Warsaw 5th: Jan.ry 1735. N.S.

Geo: Woodward

Whitehall 14: Jan.ry 173 4/5.

I allow this Bill

Harrington

Fig. 009. Bill of the British Envoy to the Kingdom and Republic of Poland.

BILL OF THE BRITISH ENVOY TO POLAND 1735

In the War of Polish Succession (1733-1735) several European countries were fighting to insure that the selection of the next Polish King would not influence the balance of power in Europe to their disadvantage. Vital interests of Russia and Austria were at stake, as well as the interest of France, a key player. The contestants for the Polish crown were: Stanisław Leszczyński, a Polish magnate, and August Wettin, king of Saxony. Leszczynski had the support of the King of France, whose daughter he had married. August of the Saxon Wettin dynasty, was the son of the previous King of Poland and King of Saxony, August II the Strong. Leszczyński was elected as King of Poland in a contested election. The outcome of the War was of vital interest also to other powers, including Great Britain, whose security depended on not allowing any one European continental power to become dominant.

In 1733-5 Britain kept an Envoy in Warsaw observing the ongoing diplomatic machinations and trying to influence the course of events by spending money on collection of intelligence and dispatch of letters to participants. In January 1735 this envoy, George Woodward, submitted the following bill to the Secretary of the British Foreign Office, William Stanhope, Earl of Harrington. The text of the bill follows:

"George Woodward His Majesty's Envoy Extraordinary to the Kingdom and Republic of Poland humbly begs allowance for his extraordinary Disbursements from Michaelmass 1734 to the Christmass following.

For Postage of Letters and Papers	45
For Stationary Ware	20
For Printed Papers and Intelligence	35

	£ 100

Warsaw the 5 Jan'ry 1735 Ins.

Geo. Woodward

Whitehall, 14 Jan'ry 1734/5
I allow this Bill

Harrington "

Part IV. SEARCH FOR FAMILY ROOTS IN POLAND

Chapter 10. Wedding of Joseph Aleksandrowicz and Dobrysz Gumplowicz

Two attractive young people, offspring of old Krakovian families, were about to be married, joining the family of Jacob Gomple (eventually known as Gumplowicz) with that of David Alexander, eventually known as Aleksandrowicz. The Jewish community of Kazimierz, an area that was recently incorporated into the city of Kraków itself, was in a festive mood on the 15-th day of September 1802, inspite of the generally difficult times. All the members of the community were invited to attend the religious nuptials and to participate in the shared cakes and wine in the Synagogue. Afterwards, relatives, members of the community council (the *Kahal*), and other community luminaries were invited to a reception at the home of the bride's parents, building No. 205, one of the newest houses in Kazimierz.

Standing under the *hupeh* (wedding canopy) were Joseph (also called Josl) Alexander and Dobrusch (also using two names, Freindl Dobrysz), daughter of Jacob called Gomple (sometimes spelled as Gumpel or Gimple). He was listed as being 19, she as 18 years old. Below his name in the civil register which they filled out that day appeared the name of David, his father, below her name the name of Jankel, a diminutive of Jacob, which we know was her father's first name. Exact spelling of names was obviously not considered important: in later documents Dobrusch's name was also spelled as Dobrysz, Dobrysch, Doba, Dobosch or Dobress. Her mother was Sarah daughter of Abele. Joseph's mother was not mentioned in any of the known documents – she must have died some time before. It is likely that David, Joseph's father, was ailing because he died within a short time after the wedding. In 1806 Joseph, at 23, was recorded as the owner of the family residence, one of the large new buildings in Jewish Kazimierz, building No. 203. It is unlikely that he would have been so listed, unless his father who originally had the house built had died and left it to him. It appears that Joseph also died in his middle age. He died before reaching 44, because in 1827, at the marriage of his daughter Temerle, he was recorded as deceased and

his wife Dobrysz listed as a widow. It can be inferred from the listings of births, weddings and deaths that in 1802 Kraków Jews did not use surnames but they must have been aware that, as Kraków and Galitzia had been incorporated into the Austrian Empire six years earlier, the Emperors' edict that all his subjects must adopt surnames would apply to them. They probably discussed the coming adoption of surnames among themselves. The Austrian authorities made the surnames mandatory in Kraków in 1805.

It is easy for us to guess who were the likely wedding guests of Joseph of the Alexanders and Freindl Dobrysz, daughter of Jacob Gumpl. The *shadkhen* (marriage broker, usually female) who arranged the joining of the Gumples and the Alexanders must have been pleased and congratulated herself. Because a large crowd of relatives and friends were expected, the wedding ceremony most likely took place in the Isaac Synagogue which, being the newest and largest in Kazimierz at the time, was best equipped to handle the large party. The old chief Rabbi of Kraków, Ayzik ha-Levi, who had excommunicated Hassidism in 1785 and again in 1794, died three years earlier, in 1799. A successor, Moses Salomon Zalman, had been selected but did not yet assume his position. For the time being, the official functions of the rabbinate were being performed by the old rabbi's son, Hirsch (Zev) David ben Ayzik ha-Levi, and it was he who must have officiated at the ceremony. Records indicate that Hirsch David ha-Levi, who eventually served as the official Rabbi of the Kraków Kahał from 1816 until he died in 1832, was a brother-in-law of the bride's mother. Hirsch David's wife, Feigl, was a sister of Sarah, the wife of Jacob Gumple and thus a maternal aunt of the bride, Freindl Dobrysz.

Even though at the time of the wedding the groom's father David was not well, he enjoyed the happy occasion and his hopes were high. He was accompanied by his brothers and cousins. Kalman Alexander and his wife Lea were present, Lea still weak from her latest confinement, but proud of her new-born son, Moshe. Isaac Alexander came with his wife Tauba. Wolff Alexander, a widower, brought his young daughter, 7-year-old Rivka. The bride's father, Jankl Gumple, was accompanied by his large family, among them sister Feigl and brother-in-law Lazar ben Moshe and another sister, Liebe, and her husband Mordechay ben Monash. The 34-year-old Genendel (*Gentzl*, Little Goose in Yiddish) came with her husband Leib ben Judah, and Jankl's brother Liebman came with his wife, Zelda Wolfówna. The brides mother Sarah, in a new wig and dressed in a elaborate velvet gown, was accompanied by her father Abele and her stepmother, his young new wife Ester. Also present were Sarah's sisters and their husbands, Feigl accompanying her husband, Hirsch David ha-Levi, who conducted the wedding, and Rebecca (Rivka) with husband Samuel (Simon) later known as Goldstoff, owner of two large buildings in Kazimierz, No. 53 and 67. The Goldstoffs lived in building No. 53, as did rabbi Hirsch David. Also present at the reception were Jacob and Sarah's children, the bride's siblings, her older sister Hana, 24, with her new husband Abe, later known as either Zimzer (Cymcer) or Fischlowicz, her brother Lebl, 22, and her little sister Feigl Gumpel, 10.

I assume that among the invited guests were the brothers Braciejówka, sons of old Moses, Jankl, Getsel, Berek and Judka, with their wives. The Braciejówka family's feud with the Gumples has been consigned to history and the relationship of the two families was reasonably cordial. Indeed, one of old Moses's great-grandsons, Hirsch, would eventually marry Hana, a future daughter of Dobrysz Gumplowicz and Józef Aleksandrowicz, the young couple getting married, and thus a future granddaughter of Jacob Gumpel. It appears that Getzel ben Moyshe Braciejówka, who lived in an old building in Kazimierz, No. 1, was concerned that the old, Polish-sounding family name has become inappropriopate since Kraków had became a part of Austria and toyed with the idea of selecting a new surname. It seems that he later chose to adopt "Moysinger" as that surname.

Other prominent guests would have included Jacob called Bader, the community *felczer*, who was paid by the community to take care of the town ritual bath, the *mikveh (*in Yiddish and German *Bad)*, and for applying leeches and cupping to patients in the Jewish Contagious Diseases Hospital. With him came his wife Leah, and their sons, Joseph, engaged to Golda Enselówna (eventually to be known as Golda of the Birnbaums Bader), and Moses, engaged to Małka Abrahamówna. His brother Józef Abraham Bader came with his wife Reizl, another sister of the bride, a daughter of Jankl Gumpl and Sarah Abele's. Also present were brothers Saul and Moses Rakowski, who owned the double house, number 109/110, located just outside the ghetto walls. Their father and grandfather once feuded with both Herschel Stopnicki and Moses Braciejówka, over the leadership of the Jewish Community Council. Eliachim Getzel Rakowski brought his wife, Hinda, daughter of Szymon Peysach, and his 10-year-old son Leibl. Eliachim (Chaim) also considered modifying his surname to a more Germanic-sounding Rakower. Simon called Pitzele (perhaps because of his small stature) brought his sons, 17 year-old Israel and 11 year-old Ruben (the latter eventually married the bride's little sister, Feigl Gumpel) and daughter Feigl Pitzele, who later married the *melamed*, Asher Drezner. That couple, Asher Drezner and Feigl Pitzele, later had several daughters, two of them became my greatgrandmothers. Among other invited guests were Izak later known as Weiskerz, Hersch Hertzig and wife Rivka, Icyk Fischl and wife Chava, Szachna Orgler, son of Abraham and Chana, with his wife Rachel Chaimowna, Zelig Wolf Katzner and his wife Małka. Several brothers who would soon chose the surname Birnbaum came together, Ensel came along with his brother Joel and wife Beyla, Berek and his wife Mirl. Salomon soon known as Baum came with Eliasz Isaac, a neighbor who lived in building 202 and with Hirsch Uberall, son of Moses and Dobressa. Dr. Aron Kalahora and his cousin Abraham known as Kolhari were accompanied by another physician, Dr. Filip Bondy who just acquired the house No. 87. Ayzik soon called Dattelbaum brought his wife Ester daughter of Zelig. Joel Weindling and Szachna Markusfeld came with the already-famous 36-year-old biblical scholar Jonathan Eybenschutz and his wife Małka. Among the bride's friends were the young daughter of Jonathan and Małka, Rachel Eybenschutz, not quite 18 yet, and Reisl, daughter of Izak, later known as Schnitzer, who was engaged to the bride's brother, Lebl, later known as Gumplowicz. The Horowitz family was represented by Israel son of Jacob and his wife Gitl Lea and the sons of old Pincus, Leibel, Getzel, Aron and his wife Scheindl, and Isaac and his wife Nechama. Also present were friends of the bride, 20-year-old Schachna Horowitz and Gershon Samuelowicz later known as Baum. Gershon had the distinction of being able to speak and write in fluent grammatical Polish. Samuel later known as Schamroth came with his wife, Sarah, and the three Tilles brothers, David, Lebl and Jacob.

I cannot be sure, if the largest landowner and the richest Jew in Kazimierz, Berl Luxenberg, had been invited to the wedding. Berl was the largest property owner and probably the richest man in town. He owned large pieces of property both in the Jewish area and outside of it. He was certainly important enough to be invited. However, he was controversial, because he was receptive to the newly arrived mystical aspect of Judaism, known as Hassidism, which originated in poor Ukrainian shtetls and has been strongly condemned by orthodox rabbinical establishment only a few years earlier. Indeed the rabbi's late father excommunicated Hassidism eighteen years earlier and again twelve years after that. The Hassidim, newly arrived in Kraków from surrounding small villages, did not join existing synagogues but formed small prayer rooms, *shtibls*, loyal to Hassidic miracle maker rebbes from Gher (Góra Kalwaria), Sanz (Nowy Sącz), Tiktin (Tykocin), Apt (Opatów), Lubavitch (Lubowicze), Sadogóra (Satmar) and other Hassidic centers. By projecting joyous extatic religious feelings and promising direct intercessions with the Almighty these sects were rapidly gaining adherents, appealing mostly to the poor and new arrivals in town from outlying shtetls. The one exception to the latter, was the extra-rich but excentric Berl Luxenberg. Thus, it is likely that he had been ostracized and not invited to the religious ceremony in the synagogue, but whether he was or was not invited to the reception at the house is a matter for conjecture. It probably depended on how deep was the antagonism between the young rabbi and his relatives and the Krakovian supporters of Hassidism at the time.

Chapter 11. Jewish life around 1800: Research in the Kraków Archives

In 1997 my wife and I sat in the spacious attractive, bright ground-floor reading room of the small palace that houses the local branch of the Polish National Archives on Sienna Street in Kraków, excitedly perusing some old original handwritten documents. Unlike research into the general Jewish history in Poland over the centuries which largely involved checking a number of published secondary sources, research for family roots called for personal visits to the Archives in Kraków and elsewhere. We found the personnel of the Kraków Archives uniformly polite and most helpful. In particular, without the courteous and efficient assistance of the Kraków archivist Ms Aneta Szpilka (see photo at the end of this part), we would not have been able to do as well as we did. We were told which documents were available in the Archives and were shown all that we requested. We examined the record of the census of of Jews of 1790-2, the oldest listing of individuals house by house, albeit only with patronymics, because surnames were not yet in use. Kraków was a part of the Habsburg Empire from 1796 to 1809 and again from 1846 to 1918 and was under strong Austrian influence from 1815 to 1846. While Jewish rabbinical and communal records of these periods, which had been kept in the Kraków Kahał (Community Council), have been largely destroyed by the Nazis during the Second World War, civil Jewish records, which were kept by the Imperial Austrian officials designated to keep Jewish data, remained largely intact and most are now kept in the Kraków branch of the Polish National Archives. These records are mostly in Polish. The loss of the Jewish communal and religious records means that hardly any data about purely religious rites, whether births, marriages or burials, that were not simultaneously recorded by the civil authorities, are extant.

My knowledge of Polish, which was my first language and in which I am still fluent, was of tremendous help in my search in Kraków. Use of a translator, while necessary for anyone who does not know Polish, is not completely satisfactory, because besides knowledge of the language, knowledge of spellings and permutations of Jewish names and awareness of Kraków Jewish history and customs is helpful in understanding the available records. Most current Polish translators, even those who are fluent in Polish and English, do not have a thorough grounding in Krakovian Jewish lore.

For example, traditionally, Kraków Jews did not name their children after living relatives but named them after recently departed ones. Thus, first names tend to repeat themselves in Kraków Jewish genealogy every two or three generations. This is often helpful in determining relationships, especially when the names are unusual but part of a family tradition. However, this tradition was modified with time, to permit use of names other than those of departed ancestors, as long as the new name began with the same or vaguely similar letter. In the more recent times as parents wanted to give their children more modern-sounding names, they often availed themselves of this option. It was often enough for the first letter to correspond to a Hebrew or Yiddish name of the departed relative. It was also customary for even non-religious Kraków Jews to have, in addition to their everyday first names, religious "Hebrew" names. These Hebrew names were more likely to correspond to that of the deceased. Thus, my father, Max Alexander, born in Kraków in 1902, who used in everyday life in Poland the name of Maksymilian (abbreviated to Maks) Aleksandrowicz, was also given the Hebrew name of Menashe ben Yaakov ha-Kohen (Menashe son of Jacob, descendant of the Biblical High Priest Aaron, brother of the prophet Moses). The name Menashe was that of his great-grandfather Menashe, son of Joseph, born in Kraków around 1817. The fact that my father carried that name told me that his great-grandfather Menashe, whose date of death I could not find, must have died before 1902. I was named Jerzy (in English, George) Aleksandrowicz, with a diminutive Jurek (pronounced Yooh-reck), and also given a Hebrew name of Yitzhak ben Menashe ha-Kohen (Isaac son of Menashe), after my mother's father, Isaac Rosenberg, who must have died prior to my birth, in 1925.

In the search for my family history I had the advantage that most genealogists do not have: I was able to span a considerable amount of time in only a few generations. I was 82 years old in June 2007, which means that I was born in 1925. I spent my childhood in Poland and as a child I knew my great-grandfather, Józef (1845-1940) who died in his 96-th year. His father, Menashe (1817-<1901) named him, his first-born, after his father, the family patriarch, Joseph Aleksandrowicz (1783-1827), who had been the first man to officially carry the Aleksandrowicz surname. The surname was not common but it was distinctive. Thus, there were only a few individuals with that surname in each generation and the documentation was fairly straight-forward. I began with a great deal of knowledge about the last two hundred years of my family's past. Having grown up in Poland, I also knew a great deal about the history of Polish Jewry and about the kind of milieu in which the Polish Jews existed.

Prior to 1805 only a handful of Kraków Jews used surnames. A few descendants of famous men, who wanted to remind everyone of their ancestry, continued to append the famous ancestor's name or nickname to their regularly-used patronymics, indications of their occupations or places of family origin. Among the latter were the Isserles descendants of Remuh, the Jekeles descendants of reb Isaac reb Jekeles, the Kalahora family of physicians and a few more. It is likely that a few others, less obvious, also retained a famous ancestor's name or nickname. In the latter category I would place my relatives, the family of Gumple later known as Gumplowicz and the family of Alexander later known as Aleksandrowicz, the latter my surname when I lived in Poland.

Thus, the main difficulty in investigating family origins prior to 1805 lies in the absence of surnames. Without knowing the forefathers' sequential first names one is reduced to interpretations of vague clues and to informed guesses. Certainty is rare. First names can take many forms, vary from Yiddish/Hebrew to Polish or German. Confusion abounds. While occasionally both men and women were given dual first names, in most cases the second name in official documents was the name or nickname of the individual's father or, when the father was deceased, a grandfather or other important relative. I have reason to believe that that was the case when the second name was Gumpel or Alexander.

I shall start with the Alexanders (or Aleksanders, replacing the "x" with "ks", the Polish way). The name Alexander was not very common among Kraków Jews in the eighteenth century. Documentary indications of the existence of Jews with the possible family name of Alexander come from assorted documents mostly from the end of the 18-th and the beginning of the 19-th centuries, which I found in the official records in the National Archives. Thus, a Wolff Alexander served as a witness to a wedding on January 15, 1799. To serve as a witness he must have been an adult, and he must have had an official permit to reside in the Jewish Town in Kazimierz by Kraków. An Isaac Alexander witnessed a wedding in March 1799. In 1801, on the 20-th of June a baby was stillborn to this Isaac Alexander and his wife Tauba. As described above, in 1802 19-year-old (i.e. born in 1783) Joseph, later known as Alexander and eventually as Aleksandrowicz, was married. In the listing, his father was listed as David. In 1806 this Joseph Alexander was listed as the owner of the house No. 203 in Kazimierz. In 1817 a child, Bazia, was born to Izrael Lieberls and his wife Rivka of the Alexanders, age 23, i.e. born in 1795. In 1821 Moses Alexander, son of Kalman, married Ester Frager. This Moses Alexander served in 1831 as a member of a municipal civil guard (Bałaban, II, 736). In 1828 a son, Siskind Alexander, born to Moses and Ester daughter of Wolf, died as an infant. In 1828 Liebe, daughter of Salomon Alexander died.

Collecting all those strands together and trying to make some sense of them required a lot of informed guesswork. Using the Principle of Ockham's Razor, which states that all else being equal, the simplest explanation is also the most likely to be correct, I believe that the simplest explanation is that David, Wolff, Kalman, Isaac and Salomon were siblings, or possibly, cousins. Given the modest number of Jews in Kraków (4,300 in 1804), it would have been too much of a coincidence to believe that they were not related. The next generation of Alexanders included my ancestor, Joseph (or Józef in Polish), born in 1783, father of Menashe and grandfather of Józef II, my great-grandfather whom I knew as a child in Kraków. Other members of that generation were Rivka Alexander born in 1795, Israel born on 20 January 1799, Samuel born on 13 June 1799 and Moses born around 1800. Interestingly, documents for the year 1852 show that this Moses Alexander, 50, son of Kalman and Leah, died on 16 October 1852, and Ester, his wife, daughter of Wolf and Chaya Frager, died four days later. It is likely that they both died victims of then rampant cholera epidemic. The descendants of Joseph (1783-1827), my line of the Aleksandrowicz family of Kraków, will be described later.

In 1796 when the Austrian Army entered Kraków, a census of Jews was ordered. Unfortunately, only the first half of that census has been preserved. Based on my experience genealogists should be wary of accepting as reliable the data in this census and in birth, marriage and death registers. The information contained therein is often only approximate and at times conflicting There are several reasons why the numbers should be treated as only approximate and other recorded data, such as the occupations of servants, butlers and maids, may even have been deliberately inaccurate. The authorities tried to limit the number of their Jewish subjects by limiting the number of marriages, thus limiting the establishment of new households and decreasing the natural population growth. Among the deliberate obstacles created by the civil authorities I will mention only two. Prior to marriage a potential couple had to establish possession of means of support, such as family wealth or the groom's profitable job, occupation or profession. Possession of these means of support had to be certified in writing by the *wójt (*local catholic district chief). Another limitation was the minimum age at which a marriage was permitted. At one point the authorities decreed that girls may not marry until they reach the mature age of twenty although it was obvious at the time that Jewish and not only Jewish girls were often married at 15 or 16 and bore many children before reaching 20. Thus, often civil registration of marriages were considerably delayed. As the ghetto was crowded and hygiene minimal, infant and child mortality was high and a number of offspring did not survive to adulthood. Particularly vulnerable were children of these very young brides. Nevertheless, it appears that seven children per household was obviously considered a low number and 15 or 16 was not unusual. Social mores of the time were such that a religious (though not a civil) marriage was absolutely obligatory. Unfortunate children born out of wedlock and their progeny for up to ten generations (sic!) would have been forever ostrasized as bastards and treated with great cruelty. Group morality, however, was satisfied by a religious marriage performed by a rabbi and registration of the wedding with civil authorities was a largely superfluous luxury, except for the moneyed classes which needed legal state protection for their activities. Given all the obstacles to civil registration, it is not surprising that most poor people did not bother with it, or postponed it, often for years. Poor couples often opted for only a religious ceremony and did not register their marriage, or reported it, if ever, many years later. They also felt very free to be vague about the ages of the bride and groom. As most Krakovian rabbinical records have been lost and only civil Austrian or Polish record are preserved, this created a nightmare for present-day genealogists. Birthdays of several children are often found to predate the officially registered date of their parents' marriage. These children were considerate legitimate by the Jewish society, but illegitimate by the State. If recorded by the civil clerks these children were recorded under their mother's surname. When the parents eventually chose to register their marriage, the children may have been re-registered or not. Thus, surnames as well as all dates and ages of bride and groom and their parents must be treated with caution.

Absent Jewish religious records, without a civil listing, the family history is often incomplete and difficult to ascertain. Children born to couples with a non-recorded religious nuptials were registered under their mother's maiden name. This can be extremely confusing. My mother's case can serve as an example. Her birth certificate from the year 1900, which I remember seeing as a child, stated that Salomea Scheindel Rubin was born as an illegitimate daughter of Keila Hinda Rubin. Then it added: "As father presented himself one Izak Rosenberg". As it happens, Keila Hinda and Izak Rosenberg were properly married by a rabbi, but at the time the State did not considered that official and my mother carried the surname of her mother, not her father. Sometime later either Keila Hinda and Izak Rosenberg must have either recorded their marriage or the state decided to recognize religious marriages, because their youngest daughter, born in 1908 was recorded as Sarah Rosenberg. There was an additional complication: neither Keila Hinda's nor Izak's parents had recorded their marriages with the civil authorities, so their recorded surnames were not those of their fathers but of their mothers. As the state came to recognize that these older people were indeed married, as often happened, additional family names appeared. This kind of confusion occurred generation after generation and it can enormously complicate genealogical search of a Jewish family tree.

There is another item in the census that requires explanation, namely the large number of servants, butlers, maids, etc., even in households that were not wealthy. As stated above, the Kraków ghetto was overcrowded and both the civil authorities and the Kahał tried to limit the number of newcomers from surrounding shtetls and hamlets and from other areas of Galitzia by limiting the number of permits for new households. Yet, the shtetls were poor, and life there was boring, opportunities were limited and the Kraków ghetto, for all its problems, acted as a magnet for young people from near and far. I believe that one of the ways in which these people could come to and stay in the Kraków Kazimierz ghetto was by being registered as servants or distant family members. This may explain the statistically surprising large percentage of people recorded as servants (up to 20 %) among the Jewish population. Some of these may indeed have been servants. There is, however, no doubt that, as in most societies, the wealthy were few and the majority of Jewish population was poor. In fact, the Community Council always had a large budget position of monies to be distributed to the poor and these monies were never sufficient to ameliorate the conditions of the poor. While we know of events in the lives of the financial or rabbinical elites, the records are largely silent when it comes to the very poorest part of the population. We do not know how they made ends meet, how they fed their children or paid rent. We know that there were sizeable numbers of beggars (Yiddish : *shnorrers*) in the ghetto and a number of people without steady employment who lived from day to day by looking daily for small opportunities to earn a few pennies.

In the surviving portion of the Austrian 1796 census there are no listings of Alexanders, but several listings of Gumpels. Given the custom in Kraków of not using names of living relatives but only of deceased ones, the founding father of the Gumplowicz family, Gumpel or Gimple, must have died on or before 1829, because in that year Ruben, son of Simon Pitzele, and his wife "Feigl of the Gumpels" named a child Gumpel. Listed in the 1796 census was Feigl's father, Jacob Gumpel (1759-1829), married to Sarah born Abele. Jacob was also the father of Dobrysz (born in 1784) who married Joseph Aleksandrowicz. Both Jacob Gumple and Simon Pitzele were my direct ancestor. Jacob Gumpel had many siblings, among them Feigl (born in 1762), not to be confused with the above-mentioned Feigl of the Gumpels who married Ruben Pitzele. Of other sisters, Liebe, was born in 1765 and Genendel (Gendzl) in 1768. A brother, Liebman, was born in 1771. Also in the 1796 census a few children were listed. Jacob and Sarahh Gumple had Lebel, born in 1780 and Liebman and Zelda Gumple had two sons, Samuel and Wolf, the latter born in 1787. They all had other children later but very few youngsters born immediately before 1796 were counted in the 1796 census. Simon Pitzele, Ruben's father, had a son Israel and a daughter also named Feigl (obviously a very popular name, meaning "a little bird" in Yiddish) born in 1783, who later married Asher Drezner. As stated, Asher Drezner and Feigl nee Pitzele were grandparents of two of my great-grandmothers, Rachel Drezner Aleksandrowicz and Małka Drezner Birnbaum. This places Feigl's father Simon Pitzele among my direct ancestors, not once but twice.

In addition to the Gumpels (later known as Gumplowicz) listed in the 1796 census, Prof. Mayer Bałaban (II, p.591) mentions Joachim Gumplowicz, a rich merchant who offered to buy monopoly rights to the alcohol trade in Kraków in 1811. Possibly, he was the same individual as the one later known as Chaim Gumplowicz-Edelstein, a member of the leadership of the Jewish Community Government (the Kehillah, in Polish Kahał) in 1803. The traditional Yiddish name *Chaim* was often transcribed into Polish or German as *Joachim*. Obviously, the Gumple clan was very rich and very influential. Bałaban (II, p. 422) describes how Jacob Gumplowicz, in partnership with a certain Pesach, supplied noble metals to the Kraków mint since 1765, and lent money on usurious rates. Among those to whom they lent 30,000 złp (Polish gold currency units, złotys), an astronomically large sum, were two sons of Hershel Stopnicki, the senior of the Kahał. When the Kraków economy took a dive in 1790, the Stopnicki brothers could not pay back the loan and the Gumple partnership went bankrupt. Their bankruptcy created such a major economic problem for Poland that the then King of Poland, Stanisław August Poniatowski, had to appoint a special commission to investigate and adjudicate the affair. In the meantime, the powerful leader of the Kahał, Stopnicki, had the partners taken to the Kahał jail, and confiscated their store with all its merchandise, leaving the doors broken. The commission ordered a restoration of all the removed or stolen goods. The upshot of this affair was that the Gumplowicz clan now joined the opposition to Stopnicki, more about which later. Somehow, the bankruptcy did not cause Jacob Gumple to loose wealth or reputation, because in 1793 he received (purchased) the exclusive right to collect tax on vodka sold in bottles. The Jacob Gumple listed in the 1796 census was born around 1759, he would have been too young to be a supplier of the mint in 1765. It thus appears that there were two individuals named Jacob Gumple in Kraków, perhaps cousins or an uncle and a nephew, named after the same ancestor. However, only one is listed in the 1796 census, the father of Dobrysz, wife of Joseph Aleksandrowicz, and the age of this man and his progeny are fully documented in Kraków archives for subsequent years. Thus, I assume that the older Jacob died prior to 1796. Again, collecting all these items together, I assume that the family patriarch, Gumpel, was a rich man and his sons and grandsons, Jacob, Liebman, and probably also Chaim (Joachim) were all also very, very wealthy. Not surprisingly, his daughters and granddaughters, Feigl, Liebe and Genendel, were married to prominent and rich members of the community.

Jacob Gumpel's wife, Sarah, was listed in the 1796 census as the daughter of Abele, a diminutive form of Abe (Abraham). Sarah was listed as being 30, i.e. she was born in or about 1766. Also in that census, Sarah's father Abele was listed as the son of Jacob who, I assume, must have died prior to 1788, because in that year Abele and Ester Nachumowna named a son Jacob Hirsch (Tzvi). From later records and assorted mentions in Prof. Bałaban's book, I assume that Sarah had siblings who married into important Kraków families. I can list two of her sisters, Feigl and Lea. Feigl married Hirsch David ha-Levi and Lea married Samuel later known as Goldstoff. Hirsch David (1760-1832) was the son of the official rabbi of Kraków, Ayzik ben Mordhe ha-Levi who excommunicated Hassidism twice. In the Austrian census of 1796 Hirsch David and Feigl were listed as

family # 285. They had a son Jacob, born in 1781 and two daughters, Dina born in 1789 and Ester born in 1793. In the listing of 1798 births, on November 28, 1798, Hirsch David and Feigl were listed as parents of a girl, whom they named Nachama Golda, probably named in honor Feigl's grandfather Nachum, father of Feigl's mother Ester, as shown in the 1796 census (family # 550). Abele's other daughter, Lea, was married to Samuel, son of Simon, born in 1763. In the list of births for 1798, on December 20 Lea and Samuel were recorded as having had a girl whom they named Rivka, they lived in building 53, the same building as her sister Feigl and Hirsch David. In the 1796 census Samuel is shown as being 33, i.e, born in 1763 and Lea as 26, i.e. born in 1770, a mere six year discrepancy. According to Bałaban (II, 589), Samuel, who after 1806 became Samuel Goldstoff, was elected in 1810 to serve as a Senior of the community council, the Kahał, an honor indicating recipient's wealth and important position in the community.

There is a controversy concerning Abele, father of Sarah Abele's Gumple. To begin with I was told by some of his descendants who researched the family tree that his wife was Hanna, yet the 1796 census show his wife as Ester daughter of Nachum. However, there appears in the census listing a significant disparity in the ages of husband and wife. Abele is said to be 71, Ester 40. Could Ester be his second wife? If so, was she the mother or stepmother of Feigl, Lea and Sarah? Abele may have later adopted the surname Pufeles, a view that was tentatively accepted by the *<www.Jewishgen.org>* web site. Originally, I thought that the surname was Abeles, a name with a long and distinguished Krakovian Jewish history, but I could not find any supporting data. I have not been able to independently either confirm or deny the possibility that Pufeles was indeed Abele's adopted or assigned surname. The Gumplowicz descendants of my ancestor, Jacob Gumple (Gumplowicz) and his wife Sarah daughter of Abele will be described separately.

To summarize, I found that the first historically certain ancestor of mine, who came to use the definitive family surname *Aleksandrowicz,* was born around the year 1783. His wife, born a year later, was Dobrysz, daughter of Jacob Gumple. At the time of their births family surnames were not in general use among Kraków Jews. For identification the Jews mostly used patronymics. Dobrysz was referred to as *Dobrysz Jacobowna*, i.e. daughter of Jacob or *Dobress z Jacobów*, i. e. Dobress of the Jacobs. Only much later (in 1831) was she listed in a document as *Dobress z Gomplowiczów*, i.e. of the Gomplowiczes. Around 1800, only a limited number of families, were using a surname. Examples of the latter include names such as Rotschild, Louria, Katzenellenbogen, and in Kraków, Isserles, Kalahora and Jekeles. At the time of his marriage in 1802 Józef lived in Building 203 in the area of Kazimierz which three years earlier became a part of the City of Kraków. For a long time, since its founding in 1335, Kazimierz was a separate town, with its own administration, an elaborate Town Hall (used today as a Museum of Ethnography) and all the appurtenances of a lively community. All Jews had to live within the walls of the Jewish section of Kazimierz. Buildings in Kazimierz were not listed then by street locations but by consecutive numbers, based on the date of their construction. I believe that sometimes between 1780 and 1790 a new large house was built for David Alexander. When David died, after 1802 but before 1806, the building was inherited by his oldest son, Joseph. In a listing of houses dated from approximately 1806, Joseph Alexander is shown as owner of the building, No. 203, where his sons and daughters were born. Joseph died during or prior to the year 1827, but as shown in subsequent census lists, his widow lived in the house

No. 203 for many years after his death and families of his sons, Menashe and Israel Eliasz, lived in that building in 1827, 1831 and 1844. According to the Polish census of 1790, No. 203 was a substantial building occupied by at least eight extended families, with grown married children and their children (see Chapter 13 below).

In 1800 the Kraków Jewish community purchased land for a new cemetery, the old one located behind the Remuh synagogue being full. In 1801 Napoleon forced the dissolution of the Holy Roman Empire, and its Emperor, Francis II of Habsburg, abdicated that title and assumed the reduced position of Emperor Francis I of Austria.

In 1802 when Joseph married Dobrysz Freindel or in 1805 at the birth of their daughter Scheindl, neither Joseph nor Dobrysz used surnames. Surnames only began to appear among Kraków Jews after 1805 and gradually all Jews acquired them, as ordered by the Austrian authorities. In an 1807 listing Joseph was shown as "Joseph Alexa...". In the detailed 1811 and 1813 birth records of daughters, Gele and Hana, he was listed as "Alexander", in 1818 and 1821 he was listed by the registering clerk as "Josef Alexandrowicz" but signed himself as "Joseph Alexanderr". Joseph's wife Dobrysz Aleksandrowicz was born in 1784 in the listing of her wedding, but her brthdate varied in the records of births of her children. In an 1831 document, the marriage record of their daughter Rivka Polner, nee Aleksandrowicz, to Faivel Orgler, Dobrysz was listed as Dobress z Gomplowiczów (Dobress of the Gomplowiczes), widow, living in Building 203. In 1844 she was again listed as a widow living in building 203, engaged in dealing in "assorted merchandise".

As mother in the birth listing of her daughter, Scheindel, in April 14, 1805, Dobrysz was listed as Freidl. As mother of Temerle, on September 21, 1807 she appeared as Freindel. In 1809 she had another daughter, Rivka, but the birth certificate is missing. We know of Rivka's existence from the record of her second marriage of 1831. On February 6, 1811 and on February 3, 1813, in detailed records of the births of her daughters Gele and Hana, the mother was listed as Dobrysz, daughter of the Jacobs, but interestingly, in both documents recorded two years apart, her age was recorded as being 26, thus born in either 1785 or 1787 (see copies at the end of the chapter). In or around 1817 a son named Menashe was born to Joseph and Dobrysz, but his birth record has not been recovered. In a detailed record of the birth of her son, Samuel Aron, on July 23, 1818 she was shown as "Dobrosz of the Jacobs", age 34, i.e. born in 1784. In 1821, in the record of birth of her youngest son, Izrael Elias, born on August 11, 1821 she was listed as "Dobresz Jacobowna" (Miss Jacob), age 30, i.e. born in 1791. So much for accuracy of peoples' ages in the data as stated to, and recorded by, the Austrian civil state clerks. For a while, I was not certain if Freindl Aleksandrowicz and Dobrysz Aleksandrowicz were one and the same person. It was not beyond the realm of possibility that Freindl died and her husband married again. This possibility was put to rest after perusal of a document dated 1827, in which she was listed as "double-named" Freindel Dobrysz.

With the passage of time, usage of surnames increased, although the surnames were not necessarily shown in all the records. At the wedding of Temerle Aleksandrowicz with Mojżesz Hercig in 1827, it was stated that the bride's father, Josel Aleksandrowicz, was "already dead" but the mother "with two names", Freindel Dobrysz, was alive and living in Building 203 in Kazimierz. In the next family document that I found, the marriage record of Rivka, nee Aleksandrowicz, widow of Michael Pollner, dated March 1, 1831, the bride's mother was listed as Dobress of the Gomplowicz, widow, living in Building

203 and dealing in assorted merchandise. This was my first firm indication that Dobrysz, daughter of Jacob and wife of Joseph Aleksandrowicz, was the daughter of the merchant and businessman, Jacob Gumplowicz of Kraków.

In the basic history of Kraków Jewry by Professor Meyer Bałaban, Jacob Gumplowicz was described as a rich man. The family was obviously prominent and remained as such even after a bankruptcy of one of its members. To marry a Gumplowicz in 1802, a young man must have been either a scion of a wealthy family or a famous scholar. Like his putative ancestor, Alexander ha-Kohen before him, Joseph Aleksandrowicz did not make a name for himself as a scholar, hence, his parents must have been well off. In most existing records, Joseph was listed as a merchant, but in the list of Kazimierz real estate of ca. 1806 he was listed as owner of building No. 203. This finding was confirmed in the wedding announcement of his son Menashe to Lea Katzner, dated March 3, 1844, where the late father was also listed as the deceased owner of a building in Kazimierz. The Jewish area of Kazimierz was very crowded. Each house had many tenants. To own a building implied wealth. We know from the 1790 census that the building that Joseph owned, the one in which he lived, was a substantial apartment building with many residents. Also, we know that several family members lived there for many years. I believe that today the building is listed as 22 Józefa Street, a four-story structure, even today in good repair. When we visited Kraków in 1997, we were told by its inhabitants that it is the oldest building in Kazimierz still in use.

I mentioned two useful listings of Kraków Jews dating to 1790 and 1796, useful because they show building numbers, family relationships and some of the householders' businesses, occupations and/or professions, allowing for some identifications of future surnames of the listed individuals. The first census was performed in Kraków-Kazimierz "by the Chief Rabbi and Clergy of the Synagogue". Listing of Jews in nearby private small towns and villages was the responsibility of the noble owners, who certified the accuracy of the count of "their" Jews. As shown in the photographs at the end of this part, that census is available at the Kraków branch of the Polish National Archives. It is a large collection of individual sheets for the villages and a bound booklet of several pages for the city of Kraków, all wrapped up in a loose fabric cover. The 1796 census, *"Verzeichnis der saemtlich in der Judenstadt Kasimir, den Vorstaedten und naher Dorfen befindlichen Juden"* (Index of Jews residing in the Jewish town of Kazimierz, its suburbs and nearby villages), was taken when the Austrians entered Kraków, after the last (third) partition of Poland. It is written in Old German handwriting, often illegible. Between the two listings there are large areas of agreement and also large discrepancies. I mention some of these discrepancies in the next chapter describing the Aleksandrowicz houses in Kazimierz by Kraków around 1805-6. A photostat of a page from the 1796 "Austrian" census is appended to a later chapter dealing with the lateral family, the descendants of Jacob Gumplowicz.

Sometimes prior to 1798, the civil authorities created a special position: a lay, civil official, paid by the government, whose exclusive duty it was to keep records of Jewish births, marriages and deaths. This "Civil Record Clerk appointed for the Old Covenant Community of Kazimierz by Kraków" was not a Jew but usually an educated Pole (or Austrian), who spoke Polish and German but not Yiddish or Hebrew. This clerk maintained an open office near the Jewish area and he meticulously recorded Jewish births, wedding announcements, marriages and deaths as they were reported to him. He wrote these in bound books, sometimes in archaic Polish, always in an elaborate calligraphic script, often extremely difficult to read. The bound volumes of these records are preserved at the Kraków branch of the National Archives, except for the volume covering the years 1809-1810, which is missing. Birth records from the years 1798-1808 consist of one-line listings, but after 1811 each birth is recorded in great detail, covering at least half a page, with much useful information, such as parents ages and addresses, the father's occupation and the name of the mother's father or both parents.

Fig. 010. Photos of the National Archives building in Kraków, census of 1790 and of the author with Archivist Aneta Szpilka;

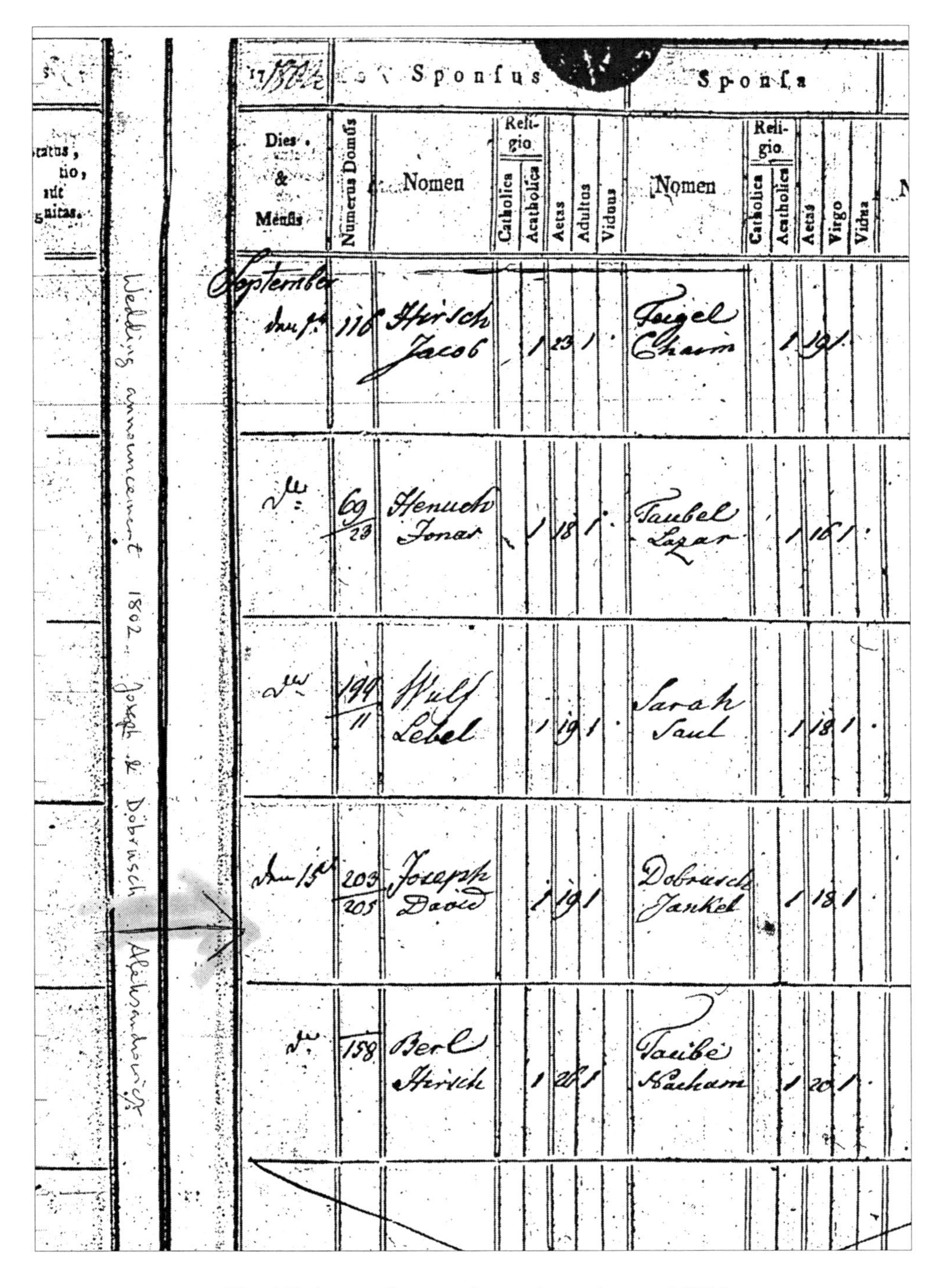

Wedding announcement 1802. Joseph & Dobrusch Aleksandrovich

1802 Dies & Mensis	Numerus Domus	Sponsus Nomen	Religio Catholica	Religio Acatholica	Aetas	Adultus	Viduus	Sponsa Nomen	Religio Catholica	Religio Acatholica	Aetas	Virgo	Vidua
September die 7th	116	Hirsch Jacob		1	23	1		Feigel Chaim		1	19	1	
do	69/23	Henuch Jonas		1	18	1		Taubel Lazar		1	16	1	
do	199/11	Wulf Lebel		1	19	1		Sarah Saul		1	18	1	
die 15th	203/205	Joseph David		1	19	1		Dobrusch Jankel		1	18	1	
do	158	Berl Hirsch		1	20	1		Taube Nacham		1	20	1	

Fig. 011 A page from registry of marriages of 1802 (marriage of Joseph and Dobrusch is item 4 on the page).

MARRIAGE CERTIFICATE OF JOSEPH AND DOBRUSCH – 1802

In the list of marriages in the Old Covenant Community of Kazimierz by Kraków for the year 1802, there is a listing, dated September 15, of a marriage between Joseph, son of David, age 19, living in house No. 203 and Dobrusch, daughter of Jankel, age 18, living in house No.205, neither of them catholic:

1802

		Groom	Religion Cath. Non	Age	Adult	Spouse	Religion Cath. Non	Age	Maiden
Day Month	House Nr.	Name				Name			
Sept. 15	203/ 205	Joseph David	x	19	x	Dobrusch Jankel	x	18	x

Descendants of Joseph and Dobrysh

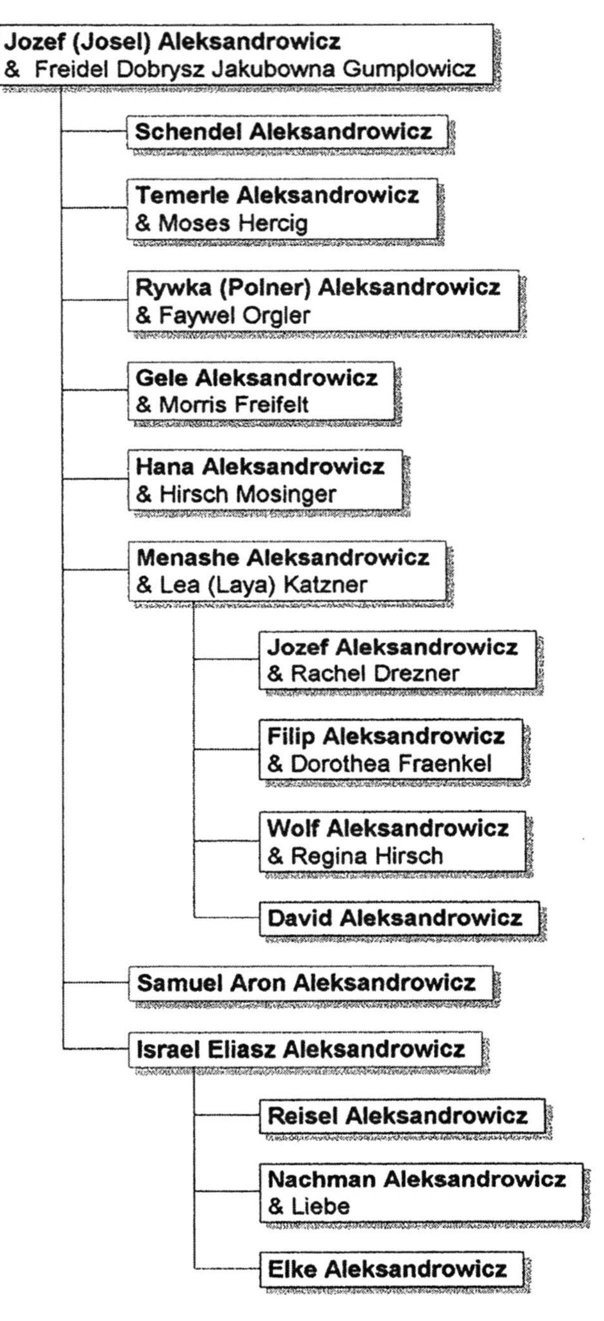

Fig. 012. Descendants of Joseph and Dobrysz Aleksandrowicz

Chapter 12. Origin of the name Aleksandrowicz and other Jewish names in Kraków

My present name is George Alexander. As you know by now, I am a survivor of the Holocaust and a naturalized citizen of the US. Before the World War II (1939-1945) I lived in Kraków, Poland and was known there as Jerzy Aleksandrowicz. My family lived in Kraków for hundreds of years. My wife and I have visited Kraków several times so that my New York-born wife could see where I grew up. In October 1997 we went to Kraków to research the history of Kraków Jewry with particular attention to the history and genealogy of my family and the origins of the family names in the archives. Here are the results of our search in the Kraków Archives.

Surnames began to appear among Kraków Jews after 1805. Until the fall of Poland in 1796 Kraków Jews did not use last names; to identify themselves they mostly used patronymics, nicknames, places of origin or professions. In English usage, patronymics took the form of adding an "s" after an apostrophe at the end of the father's name, thus the son of William was known as William's, son of Steven as Steven's. These designations, with the apostrophe omitted, often came to be used as family surnames, thus Williams and Stevens. In Yiddish, which was then the *lingua franca* among Kraków Jews, as in German, apostrophe was not used. Thus, the famous Kraków sage, Remuh, as the son of Israel nicknamed *Isserl* became known as Moses Isserls or Isserles. Because he was so famous, his descendants continued to use the name Isserles as the family designation. The children or descendants of a man named Gimbel were known as Gimbels. In Polish, the term comparable to the added "s", is the word "*z*" meaning "of". Thus, Dobrysz, daughter of Jacob Gumpel, was listed in the birth certificates of her children as "Dobrysz **z** Jacobów", i. e. Dobrysz of the Jacobs. In other documents she was also listed as Dobrysz "Jacobowna", i. e. Miss Jacobs. In conformity with the then common Polish usage the father's name could also be used with the ending "-wicz". Thus, as I eventually discovered, Dobrysz was also referred to as Dobrysz Gumplowicz.

The use of this patronymic ending "wicz" was in very common usage and can be inferred even if actual records do not show it. In his history of Kraków Jews Prof. Mayer Bałaban freely converted fathers' names to surnames that ended with "wicz". For example, he referred to Jacob Gumple, who in his own life was recorded only as Gumpel (for example, in the 1796 Austrian census, building # 106, family # 551), as Jakób Gumplowicz (Bałaban II, 422). In another example, from history, Berek, son of Josel, the leader of a Jewish battalion in Kościuszko's and Napoleon's army, became known as Berek Joselewicz. My ancestor Saul Birnbaum, son of Berek, was described in one document as Saul Berkowicz. The Polish word for butcher is "*rzeźnik*". In the 1790 census of Kraków Jews the butcher's son living in building 203 was listed as Jebel Rzeźnikowicz. The son of a Jewish physician was recorded as Doktorowicz. In line with the above, it is reasonable for me to assume that Baruch, son of Alexander, was known as Baruch Aleksandrowicz. Prior to 1805 these were not family names, but patronymics. After 1805 many of these terms eventually ended up by being adopted as surnames. In the light of the above, I came to believe that the simplest explanation for the origin of the name Aleksandrowicz, first used in 1807, was that of having an important ancestor named Alexander, and searched for such an ancestor.

Exact spelling was not considered critical at the time. Transcription from Hebrew, which uses no vowels, to the Latin alphabet was always haphazard. In 1805 when Kraków Jews began to adopt surnames, the civil clerks knew German, little Polish, but no Yiddish or Hebrew. Thus names were often spelled interchangeably in their Polish or German variants and often changed arbitrarily. The first name of the first man to use the surname Aleksandrowicz (pronounced by accentuating the "o") was spelled Joseph by Germans and Józef (pronounced "Yoo'-zef") by Poles. In Polish, the accent is always on the second syllable from the end, i.e. the penultimate sylable (thus Kra'ków, but Warsza'wa) except in some words of foreign derivation). Jacob was called in Polish Jacob, pronounced "Yah'-koop". In Polish grammar the genitive case of Józef (i.e. Joseph's) is Józefa, of Dobrysz is Dobryszy. All of these usages appear in assorted documents. The name Aleksandrowicz (or Alexandrowicz), changes in the genitive singular to *Aleksandrowicza* or in plural, to *Aleksandrowiczów*. In one document Dobrysz of the Gumplowiczes was referred to as *Dobressa z Gumplowiczów*. In Polish, the name of a married woman ends in "owa" and of an unmarried woman in "ówna", thus Dobrysz after her marriage was *Pani* Aleksandrowiczowa and her maiden daughter in her 1827 wedding record was *Panna* Temerl Aleksandrowiczówna. In the index at the end of the yearly record of weddings Temerl was entered as Temerl, daughter of Józef Alexander. Hana, daughter of Dobrysz and sister of Temerl, was listed as (Miss) Aleksandrowiczówna. From all the above, it becomes obvious how useful the knowledge of Polish grammar and usage can be in interpreting old records.

The use of an ancestral profession, which eventually became a family surname is mirrored in many Jewish family names today. In German / Yiddish the family whose ancestor was a tailor may now bear the name Schneider, the descendants of a carpenter (tablemaker) may be called Tischler, descendants of a teacher Lehrer, descendants of a jeweler working with gold Goldman or Goldschmidt. In the Russian part of Poland the same families may bear the names of Kravetz or Stolar or Uchitel or, from the Polish word for gold *złoto,* Zlotnik, today often spelled Slotnick. The place of origin of a family was denoted in German or Yiddish by the ending "er", in Polish or Russian by the ending "ski" or "cki". Thus, when a Jew from Dresden in Saxony came to Kraków, he became known

as Dresdner or Drezner (my great-grandmother's maiden name), if he came from Pinsk he would be referred to as Pinskier, if he came from Frankfurt as Frankfurter. If a Kraków Jew left for Vienna or Berlin he would be referred to as Krakauer; if he went to Warsaw or St. Petersburg, he might be known as Krakowski. A Jew from the border post of Brody between Galitzia and Ukraine would be referred to as Broder or as Brodsky, and a Jew from Białystok as Bialystocker or Białostocki. It is important to remember, however, that prior to 1806 these were not family names but patronymics, indications of professions, places of origin or nicknames. In Russian Poland both endings "-wicz" and "-ski" were used not only for patronymics but also for places of origin. Thus, a Jew from the town of Aleksandrów, of which there were several in Poland, could be know as Aleksandrowski or more often as Aleksandrowicz. Thus the name Aleksandrowicz, first encountered for my family in official records in Kraków as a family surname after 1800, denoted having an ancestor named Alexander or of having an ancestor who came from a town named Aleksandrów or from a village near Kraków called Aleksandrowice. Not just Jews but others who had such an ancestor or who came from such localities would have been known as Aleksandrowicz. Noblemen who owned the manors or castles located in such places would also be known as Aleksandrowicz. However, the most likely origin of the surname was to have had an ancestor named Alexander.

There are comparatively few historical references to rabbis, talmudic scholars, merchants and other prominent Kraków Jews named Alexander, or Aleksander, which made my search for either an immediate or more distant family founder named Alexander easier. There is a family legend, preserved over the years, of an ancestor who was killed in Koblenz on the Rhine by the Crusaders during the 2-nd Crusade around 1140. The most respected Catholic scholar of the time, Bernard of Clairvaux, suggested that Crusaders need not be limited to fighting the Muslims in the Holyland, but might as well turn on other infidels, both pagans living at the outer reaches of Christian Europe and Jews who lived interspersed among Christians in Europe. What followed was a series of massacres of the Jewish populations in the Rhineland and elswhere. I found of specific interest the fact that pogroms of 1348 occurred in Koblenz and in Kraków. In the XIV-century there was a prominent Jewish scholar named Alexander (Suslin) ha-Kohen, author of a treatise titled *Sefer ha-Agudah*, hence remembered as Agudah. He was said to have died in a pogrom during an outbreak of the plague in 1348 A.D. The plague, of course, was blamed on the Jews. Details are scant about these distant times.

Of more immediate interest was the fact that there lived in Kraków, in XVI century, Alexander-ha-Kohen, son of Jozue or Józef, a rich, respected and learned man, married to a prominent woman, Kendel, sister of Isserl. He became the father and grandfather of famous merchants, scholars, physicians, administrators and writers. This Alexander son of Józef was described earlier. Also, in 1642, Dobrysz, daughter of Natan Spira, also a possible ancestor of ours, died in Kraków and her tomb is preserved in the old Remuh cemetery. Prof. Mayer Bałaban mentions in his history of Kraków Jewry that a Solomon Gomplo, a possible ancestor of the Gumplowicz side of my family, came in 1680 from Silesia to Kraków.

In 1787 the Austrian Emperor Joseph II issued an order that all his subjects must have family names. Kraków was not Austrian at the time but became Austrian in 1796. Eventually, in 1805, the Emperor's edict was being enforced and Kraków Jews began

adopting surnames. Most of these were assigned by Austrian officials and have a deliberate Germanic flavor: Altman, Baumgarten, Bader, Goldberg, Rosenwald, Schwartzstein, etc. The names, when not referring to patronymic, origin or profession, refer to gardens, mountains, forests, fields, flowers, trees, etc. Sometimes they show inventiveness and imagination. In the birth records that I have consulted in Kraków surnames began to appear in 1805. The first Jews with surnames that I found were Berl Luxenberg (perhaps named after place of origin of his family?), Hillel Rosenzweig and Abraham Anisfeld. The first use of the name Birnbaum (my grandmother's maiden name) occurred in 1806.

As mentioned before, the first use of the name Aleksandrowicz (actually Alexa...) occurred in 1807. Of course, I was very interested in finding out why the family patriarch, Joseph Aleksandrowicz, selected or was given such a non-Germanic aristocratic-sounding surname. He was born around 1783. At birth he did not have a family surname but it appeared, from his wedding record in 1802 and later records that he was probably the son of David of the family of Alexander. The name David appeared in the register of marriage of Joseph and Dobrysz in 1802. According to Kraków records from around 1806, the building No. 203 in District 10 in the area of Kazimierz was owned by Joseph Alexander. Thus, it is quite certain that this Joseph or Józef was the one who eventually became known as Aleksandrowicz.

Joseph's eventual surname, Aleksandrowicz, appeared in the records in an informative piecemeal fashion. In the Civil Register for Year 1805, when his daughter Scheindel was born he was listed only as Josef and his wife as Freidel. In 1807 when the second daughter, Temerle, was born, his name was recorded in an abbreviated form as Joseph Alexa... or Alexe... By 1811 and 1813, in the books of yearly birth records kept in the Kraków Archives, the half-page long birth certificates of his daughters, Gele and Hana, respectively, gave the father's name as Josef Alexander. At the end of these certificates, Joseph signed himself, in Latin alphabet with two "r's": "Joseph Alexanderr"(!). There is no question that in 1813 this was considered Josef's full name, because in the index to the volume of records the event is listed as "*Hana, córka Josefa Alexandra*", i.e. "Hana, daughter of Josef Alexander", using the grammatically correct Polish genitive form of the words Josef and Alexander, dropping the "e" before the "r". The development of the name continued. In the 1818 book of birth certificates, the page for July 30 showed a listing of the birth of Samuel Aron. The child's father was listed as Josef Aleksandrowicz, but the signature at the bottom continued to be Joseph Alexanderr. Similarly, the 1821 certificate of the birth of Israel Elias showed the name of the father as Josef Aleksandrowicz and the signature as "Joseph Alxanderr", again with two "r's" but missing the first "e". Obviously, this ancestor of ours spelled his name in this fashion. He could write Hebrew, but was not fluent in the Latin alphabet in common usage outside of the Jewish community. Most birth certificates were witnessed by two Jewish adults and most wedding certificate by four. With few exceptions, these witnesses could not write at all or wrote only in Hebrew. This shows that Joseph Aleksandrowicz was, for his place and time, more in touch with the outside world than most of his contemporaries. Temerle Alexa..., born in 1807 was later known as Aleksandrowicz. This is confirmed by the record of her marriage, in 1827, to Moses Hercig, which listed her as Temerle Alexandrowiczówna (Miss Temerle Aleksandrowicz), daughter of the late Josel Alexandrowicz and of "doubly-named" Freindel Dobrysz, his widow, living in the Jewish Town in Kazimierz by Kraków in District 10, building Nr. 203.

Thus, by 1818, the year of the birth of Samuel Aaron, the official family name was fixed as "Alexandrowicz". The documents show (copies of several were included in the previous chapter) when the name first appeared in official records and how it gradually assumed the final form. It is likely that Joseph knew his family history of the previous one hundred years, and knew that he had important ancestors, possibly even a grandfather, who used Alexander and/or Aleksandrowicz, as a quasi-surname. It is likely that he was proud of his descent and wanted to insure that it would be remembered.

I believe that Joseph adopted the surname after 1805 to commemorate his Aleksandrowicz ancestors, specific ancestors that he knew of. However, these specific ancestors are no longer a part of current family memory. None of the surviving members of the Aleksandrowicz clan know anything about them, and neither, apparently, did the previous generation. Thus, to seek a reason for the adoption of Aleksandrowicz as a family surname, I faced the difficult task of finding an Alexander who was a historical figure of some importance, active in the Kraków Jewish past, fitting several specific requirements. I had described the quest and the findings in the chapter dealing with the early Alexanders in the XVI-th century. In the meantime, however, I had to deal with alternate theories of the origin of the surname.

There exists a persistent romantic family legend that an ancestor of ours was befriended by a Polish aristocrat named Aleksandrowicz, that the ancestor may even have saved that nobleman's life in a battle and then was given permission to use that name as his own. If so, the battle must have occurred around 1800, when Joseph Aleksandrowicz was old enough to fight (he was born around 1783), yet before his wedding in 1802 or the subsequent arrival of his children. The Jewish battalion in Kościuszko's and Napoleon's army was active from 1794 to 1809 or to 1813, dates which encompass the period of Józef's possible military service. Moreover, the story that Józef saved an aristocrat's life may well be true without postulating that he was a soldier engaged in heroic battles. In the unsettled times around 1800 many Polish patriots fighting for a free country often had to hide from invading Russian or Austrian armies. It is not unlikely that one of them would have sought shelter among Jews and that in one such encounter a young Jew helped him hide. The Jew could then have been allowed to adopt this aristocratic Polish name. Against this legend, is the fact that this early ancestor of ours did not immediately use the full name Aleksandrowicz but both he and the registering Austrian clerks considered the word "Alexander" as the proper form of his last name. And it was the Polish usage of the "wicz" ending that led, eventually, to the adoption of the full term *Aleksandrowicz* as the family surname. Joseph's use of the name Alexander justifies the contention that the family name Aleksandrowicz simply means "of the family of Alexander" and that it is legitimate, in countries where the long Polish version of the name is difficult to spell and pronounce, to shorten the name and use the form "Alexander", as I have done.

While I believe that the name evolved naturally, I have been told not by one but by several members of the family that it was originally the surname of a high Polish aristocrats, who allowed one of our ancestors to adopt it as his own. I never heard that story from my father or grandfather, but I have heard it from a granddaughter of my great-uncle Wolf Aleksandrowicz and also from a grandson of another great-uncle, Filip Aleksandrowicz. I decided, therefore, to explore it further. In my search I found that indeed there was a Polish aristocratic house with the name Aleksandrowicz arising around 1700,

which rightfully claimed, the right to the title of count or baron. This family and their relatives described below seem to have frequently interacted with their Jewish neighbors and one collateral descendant played a role in the Vatican passivity during the Holocaust of the Second World War.

Jukasz Antoni, count Aleksandrowicz, was born in 1684 in the domaine of Chrzastów near Kielce, in Central Poland. His noble coat-of-arms was also known as the *Aleksandrowicz,* however I could not find the design of that coat-of-arms anywhere. Count Jukasz lived to a ripe old age and died in his 80-th year. His younger brother, Martin, also count Aleksandrowicz, was born around 1690. We know more about this count Martin. He maried Helena Bachminska, born in 1700, who had a coat of arms called *Jastrzębiec.* Martin became a *starosta* (a district leader) of Bronowiec in Eastern Poland. He died in 1770. Martin and Helena had several sons. Jan Aloyzy, count Aleksandrowicz (1728-1881) became a bishop of the Lublin-Chełmno diocese and thus, as far as I can tell, did not have any children. Neither apparently did his brothers Stanisław, Antoni Felicjan and Franciszek Witold. Another brother. Józef, rose to be a major–general of Polish armies and probably participated in the desperate and unsuccessful attempts to save Poland from the Tsarist armies in 1792 as well as in the Kościuszko Insurrection of 1794 which ended in the second and third (final) partition of the country. The youngest son of Martin and Helena, Tomasz Valerian, Count Aleksandrowicz, coat-of-arms *Aleksandrowicz,* born around 1740 (?) continued the line of counts Aleksandrowicz and rose to prominence in Poland at the time of the last Polish king, Stanisław August Poniatowski (Polski Słownik Biograficzny, I, p.70). Tomasz Valerian became a governor (voivod) of the Podlasie region and a senator and a participant in the Great Parliament also known as the Four-Year Parliament (*Sejm Czteroletni*, 1788-1792). This historic *Sejm* attempted to reform Polish government and field a strong army. On May 3, 1791 it passed a new strikingly liberal democratic constitution for Poland, the first in Europe and only the second in the world after that of the United States. Unfortunately, this constitution could not be put into effect. The king who advocated and supported it was eventually forced to renounce it and abdicate the throne. Subsequently, Poland, having wasted this last opportunity to save itself, lost its independence by 1795.

Count Tomasz Valerian married Marianna Countess Halka-Ledóchowska, coat of arms *Shaława*, who was born around 1765 in Ledóchów in the eastern Polish province of Volhynia, now on the border between Ukraine and Byelarus. Marianna's parents were Józef Antoni Count Ledóchowski and Maria nee Zakrzewska. Marianna had a brother, Stanisław Count Halka-Ledóchowski, born in 1764, who married Apolonia, countess Aleksandrowicz, count Tomasz Valerian's daughter, thus adding Aleksandrowicz genes to the Ledóchowski line. Marianna also had an older brother, Antoni Halka-Ledóchowski (1755-1835), owner of large estates in Byelarus and Ukraine and a member of the Polish parliament who married Julia Princess Ostrowska (1766-1803), a descendant of very high aristocracy. An ancestor of hers, Prince Alexander Ostrogski (the name, derived from the family estate and castle of Ostróg on the border between Volhynia and Podolia, could be spelled in many ways), had a daughter, Anna Aloysia Ostrowska, born in 1600. This Princess Ostrowska, at the age of 20, married the 60-year-old Jan Karol Chodkiewicz (1560-1621), the *Wielki Hetman Koronny* (Grand Crown Marshal of the Armies) of the Polish Commonwealth, one of the most illustrious Polish military commanders, famous victor over Swedes at Kirchholm in Courland (1602) and over Turks at Chocim (Khotzim) in Ruthenia (1621). As it happens,

the manor of Ostróg in Volhynia / Podolia lies in an area of heavy concentration of Jewish *shtetls*, such as the towns and villages of Meziborz, Polonna, Bratslaw, Zhitomir and others, an area where Hassidism originated and thrived. Count Ostrowski and his progeny were the lieges and therefore also landlords, employers and protectors of a large proportion of the Jewish population in Polish-Ukrainian borderlands.

Princess Julia Ostrowska and Count Antoni Halka-Ledóchowski had many sons and daughters, among them Joseph (1786-1859), Ignaz (1789-1870), Apollonia (1790-?) and Franciszek, born 1802. Ignacy (Ignaz) Halka Ledóchowski served in Napoleon' army and served as a brigadier-general during the Polish November 1830 Insurrection against the Tsar. A nephew, Mieczysław Halka Ledóchowski (1822-1902), made a career as a priest in the Roman Catholic Church, joining the Vatican Curia. In 1861 he was the Papal Nuncio in Brussels and in 1874 was named Archbishop in Gniezno and Poznań (Gnesen and Posen) in the then Prussian part of Poland and made a Cardinal and Primate of Poland. As a Polish patriot, he opposed Germanization of the Poznań province and was arrested and expelled from his See by the Prussian Government, although retaining his title of Cardinal. Eventually he settled in Rome, becoming the Prefect of the Sacred Congregation (*Propaganda Fidei*) at the Vatican. When Poland was partitioned, one branch of the counts Ledóchowski family stayed in Russian Poland, while another branch moved to the Austrian parts of Poland and to Bohemia and Transylvania that became a part of the Austrian Empire. Ironically, in view of their uncle's arrest for being such a strong Polish patriot and opponent of Germanization, the Austrian branch, moving in aristocratic Viennese court circles, took on a definite Germanic tinge. For example, one of their descendants, born in 1904, living in Klausenburg in Transylvania (now Cluj in Romania), styled himself Graf Anton Maria Franz von Ledochowski. Members of this branch also served the Church. Graf Włodzimierz (Vlodimir) von Ledochowski (1866-1942) became the 26-th Superior (General) of *Societa Gesu*, the Jesuit Order in Rome and a key advisor to Popes Pius XI and XII. In that capacity he apparently played an unsavory role, preventing the Vatican from publicly condemning the Nazi racism leading to the Holocaust. It appears that Pope Pius XI proposed to issue an anti-Nazi encyclical, strongly condemning racism and anti-Semitism. He asked his advisors to write an appropriate text and to present it to him for signature prior to its publication. The document was written and given to Ledochowski for presentation to the Pope. However, Pius XI was then terminally ill and it became obvious that a new pope would take over soon. It is said that it was Father Włodzimierz Ledochowski, the head of the Jesuits, deliberatly caused a delay in presenting the written document to Pius XI during the illness, thus prevented its issuance (Passlecq and Suchecki, 1997; Kertzer, 2001). The dying pope's successor, Pius XII (Cardinal Pacelli), was less concerned about the fate of Jews than about the danger of "godless" Communism, and he was intent on maintaining Vatican relations with Hitler's Germany which he hoped would attack the Soviet Union. After his accession to the Papacy, he refused to consider the encyclical. The document is now stored in the Vatican Archives and referred to as the "Secret Encyclical", an indication of the Vatican's hesitation during World War II to openly confront the Nazis, particularly about their treatment of Jews. It is impossible to tell whether issuance of that document would have made much difference and how it would have affected the Nazis but I do believe that it would have influenced some Polish Catholics, lay and priests, and may have saved more Jewish lives in Poland, Hungary, Slovakia and other places where the Church was strong.

Włodzimierz, who prevented the publication of the encyclical, was a nephew of Mieczysław Ledochowski, the Cardinal Archbishop of Poznań and Gniezno I find it interesting that two of Włodzimierz's sisters became prominent nuns and being well-off, both funded convents and both founded new religious orders and both were beatified by the church in a step towards sainthood. Blessed Maria Teresa Ledóchowska (1863-1922), "Mother of Black Africa", a founder of Klaverian Sisters was formally beatified by Pope Paul VI in 1975. Saint Julia Ursula Ledóchowska (1865-1939), founder of the Order of Ursuline Sisters of the Sacred Heart of Dying Jesus, was beatified by Pope John Paul II in 1983 and canonized in 2005. Thus, one close relative of the Counts Aleksandrowicz became a Catholic saint and another is on the way to become one.

Tomasz Walerian and Marianna Aleksandrowicz had several children, among them a son, Stanisław Witold Count Aleksandrowicz, who was also born near Kielce, in 1781. This Stanisław Witold had a son, named Stanisław Aloyzy Tomasz. Stanisław Witold married Countess Apollonia Ledóchowska, probably a niece of Marianna who married his father Tomasz Valerian Aleksandrowicz. In 1800 Stanisław Witold, count Aleksandrowicz, formally received from the Hapsburg Emperor Francis II the Imperial Austrian title of baron, which was, in turn oficially recognized by the Polish Kingdom under the Tsar in 1819. In 1803 Count Stanisław Witold was appointed an Austrian chamberlain. During the existence of the Warsovian Duchy, in 1811-1812, he was a member of the *Sejm* (Parliament). In 1825, when the Russian Tsar carried the title of King of Poland, Count Stanisław was a member of the Polish Senate. His son, Stanisław Aloyzy, became a member of the State Council (i.e. a member of the Tsar's Cabinet). His daughter, Maria Teresa Aleksandrowicz (1812-1845), married Tomasz Alexander Adam Count Potocki (1809-1861), a a scion of one of the highest aristocratic families of Europe. The Potockis had at least five offspring who thus continued to carry the Aleksandrowicz genes. At the time of the Kościuszko's Uprising, Tomasz Walerian Count Aleksandrowicz was 34 years old, Stanisław Witold was only 13. In Napoleonic times in Poland (1806-1812), Stanisław Witold would have been 25-30. Either one of them could have been the Polish patriot with divided loyalties, who was helped by a young Jew in these unsettled times.

Given the fact that in earlier times Jews who converted received noble titles and coats of arms, it is not beyond the realm of possibility, that counts Aleksandrowicz had a distant Jewish ancestor and that their name, just like ours, reflects descent from the same Aleksander Józefowicz, the rich Krakovian merchant who lived in the 16-th century. We know that rich Jewish Renaissance families in Kraków, like the Fischls, were partly assimilated, it is likely that their sons knew Polish and Italian, French and Latin and that they dressed like their Polish or Italian counterparts. We know that a grandson of Alexander Józefowicz, Samuel son of Baruch, studied medicine in Italy and thus must have known Italian and Latin, and he must have been tempted to abandon the faith of his forefathers for the greener pastures of baptism and membership in Polish aristocracy, He must have been aware of the example of Steven Fischl and of the favors of the Dowager Queen Elisabeth and the privileges bestowed upon him by the King and the Crown Chancellor. He may also have had an Aleksandrowicz relative who converted. We know that Dr. Samuel resisted the temptation after his return from Italy and rejoined the Jewish community of Kraków in which he rose to prominence as a physician. It is possible, however, that one of the descendants of Alexander-ha-Kohen had converted and became a founding member of a Catholic branch of the Aleksandrowicz family, but no records of such conversion have surfaced. It is obvious, however, that it would have been to the the Counts' Aleksandrowicz advantage to keep their Jewish origin, if any, very quiet. Having maintained a careful family history they would have been aware of it and, when in need, may have felt free to ask a young Jew for help, particularly if they had met him earlier in the Napoleonic army. I assume that aristocratic families kept a careful log of their family ancestry. Members of the lines of Counts Aleksandrowicz, Ledóchowski and Potocki are likely to have records that might show if they had a hidden Jewish ancestor or ancestress in their past. I am tempted to speculate that the Ledóchowskis' knowledge of having had some Jewish ancestors in the past, may explain their interest in proving their loyalty to the Church through devoted service and their apparent hostility to Jewish interests.

The name Alexander is, of course, of Greek-Macedonian origin. It was introduced to Jewish history when Alexander of Macedon (356-323 BC) conquered Jerusalem. In his brief life Alexander made a lasting impression on history. A large number of cities were founded by and named after him, starting with Alexandria in Egypt, which for a while was the effective capital of the known Western world. Other cities named after Alexander, whose name in Arabic was Iskander, include Iskanderun, Sandjak (Alexandretta), even Kandahar in Afganistan, the city in the news recently. Alexander is one of a few non-Biblical names that are acceptable to religious Jews. One of the Hasmonean kings was called Alexander, one of Herod's sons was named Alexander. The Polish-Lithuanian crowned Commonwealth had a king, Alexander of the Jagiellonian dynasty (ruled 1501-1506), who expelled Jews from Lithuania and was obliged to cancel the expulsion order a few years later because Lithuania needed the commerce that the Jews conducted. And, of course, the Romanov Tsar of Russia at the time Joseph was picking a surname was named Alexander (ruled 1801-1825). The tsar was at first a partner and then an implacable enemy and nemesis of Napoleon. Tsarist troops marched through Kraków several times.

The name of Joseph Aleksandrowicz's wife, Dobrysz, was new to me, as was the name Temerle. However, I have since found that both names were not uncommon in the early XIX-th Century among Kraków Jews, and that both were sort of a family tradition. Temerle Aleksandrowicz's nephew, Nachman, named one of his daughters Temerl. Dobrysz's grandson, Wolf, named one of his daughters, Dora or Dobrysza. In the old Jewish cemetery in Kraków, near the Remuh synagogue there are two tombstones to Dobrysz, or Dobrosz, who died in 1642, daughter of Nathan Spira (1585-1633). The Polish word "dobroć", roughly pronounced "dobrotch", means "goodness", so the name Dobrosz may be a translation of the common Jewish name of Guta or Gitl. Dobrysz Aleksandrowicz nee Gumplowicz may have been a descendant of Dobrysz, daughter of Nathan Spira. Both Remuh and Nathan Spira claimed that they established their descent from Rashi. Rashi, in turn, claimed descent from the Royal House of Judah. Thus, allowing for a little poetic license, Joseph Aleksandrowicz may have been a descendant not only of Aaron ha-Kohen but also of King David, and so was his wife.

My first name is George. Prior to World War II I lived in Poland where I was known as *Jerzy* (pronounced Yeh-zhee) Aleksandrowicz. As a child I was called by a diminutive *Jurek* (pronounced Yoo-reck). Following a standard Kraków Jewish custom, I was also given a Hebrew name *Yitzhak ben Menashe ha-Kohen.* The first name was that of my mother's late father, Yitzhak (Isaac) Rosenberg (1866-<1925). In America I translated

my first name *Jerzy* to George. This is a *verbatim* translation. *Swięty Jerzy* was the saint depicted in religious paintings as the one who fought a dragon. My names were fairly typical examples showing how Kraków Jewish children were named prior to 1939.

The name of a daughter born in 1807 to Joseph and Dobrysz, Temerl, was also fairly common around 1800. I have come to believe that it is a diminutive form of the biblical name Tamar. In Yiddish the addition of an ending "l" or "ele" to a word converts it to a diminutive form. Thus, the Yiddish word *shtoht* means town (in German *Stadt*). Adding an "l" and, in the process, changing the vowel, which occurs often in Yiddish, converts it to a diminutive, "a little town", namely a *shtetl (*Germanic/English plural *shtetls*, proper Hebraic plural*: shtetlekh).* The name Temerl seems to have been a tradition in our family. Nachman Aleksandrowicz's daughter, Temerle, was later known as Tenna.

Hebrew writing uses only consonants, no vowels. Thus, a Polish or Austrian clerk doing transliteration of Hebrew names into the Latin alphabet, had problems, As I mentioned earlier, the nickname of Dobrysz's father, Gimple, has been, in different documents, written as Gumpl or Gimpel. Dobrysz was once inscribed as Dobress z Gomplowiczów, i.e. of the family Gomple. The name or nickname Gimpel or Gimbel must have been fairly common, because it often appears in unexpected places, as in the now defunct department store in New York named Gimbels. It was probably used as a nickname and it eventually became a family surname. A son of Jacob and Sarah Gumple, a brother of Dobrysz Aleksandrowicz, Lebel, born in 1780 was the first to use Gumplowicz as a family surname. He was the father of Abraham Gumplowicz, born in 1803, and the grandfather of Prof. Ludwik Gumplowicz (1838-1909), the founder of the modern science of sociology.

For reasons that are not always clear, a number of individuals went through life using first names other than those registered in their original birth certificates. Perhaps the children did not like the names given them by their parents. More likely, they wanted a more westernized name or perhaps they had some valid legal reasons concerned with official permits, taxation, conscription to military service, etc. Some of theses name changes obviously followed a fixed pattern. For example, the name Shaya was always changed to Jozue. Thus, Dobrysz's Aleksandrowicz's sister Feigl married Ruben son of Simon Pitzele. Her sister-in-law, Simon's daughter also named Feigl, married my ancestor, Asher Drezner, born in 1777. It was Asher and Feigl's son, registered at birth in 1813 as Shaya, father of my grandmothers, Rachel Drezner Aleksandrowicz and Małka Drezner Birnbaum, who went through life known as *Jozue* Drezner. Similarly, another Shaya, grandson of Menashe Aleksandrowicz, son of Józef, went through life known as *Jozue.* Thus, the Hebrew name Shaya, an abbreviated form of Yeshaya, Yehoshuah, or Yeshua, was usually Polonized to Józef or Jozue.

Names were frequently translated in an arbitrary way, at other times in a way that was so literal as to be grotesque. For example, the common Jewish name Hirsch, of German and Yiddish origin, translates into English as "stag". The Hebrew equivalent is *Tzvi*, spelled in Poland as *Cwi*. A stag in Polish is *jeleń*, and many Jewish merchants in Kraków, in the XVII-th century, were inscribed in written Polish documents as *Jeleń*, a most unusual name. I doubt if it was ever used that way by the Jews themselves, today it sounds peculiar even in Polish. It is of interest that there was in Poland a Jewish family, descendants of a rich man called Hirsch, which converted in 1764 and, becoming officially ennobled, adopted the surname of *Jeleński*. Literal translations of names from other languages into Polish were not unusual. The common Latin name Felix, which means *Lucky* in English, was

often translated into Polish as *Szczęsny*. *Szczęście* means *luck* in Polish, in Yiddish the word would be *glick,* in German *Glueck.* The latter was also used as a name. For example, there was a German Jewish woman, Gluckel of Hamelin (1646-1724), who wrote a remarkable memoir in Yiddish. These translated names, *Jeleń* and *Szczęsny*, as well as *Glueckel*, have an archaic feel to them and are not used today.

Between 1772 and 1796 Poland was being invaded by the armies of Russia, Austria and Prussia. In 1794, the Polish patriot and hero of the American Revolution, Tadeusz Kościuszko, led an uprising against Tsarist armies from Kraków. Initially successful, the Kościuszko armies were eventually defeated by superior forces and by 1796 Poland was erased from the map of Europe. Kraków was occupied by the armies of Austria.

In my search for roots in Kraków, I have been able to establish that our family name has ancient roots, possibly going back in Kraków to around 1500. In its present form, the surname appeared in official documents in Kraków more than 200 years ago, at first as "Alexa...", then as "Alexander" and, eventually, as "Aleksandrowicz". I have been able to find a prominent ancestor named Alexander, whose name was probably used to develop the family surname. I have been able to correlate events in the history of Poland and Kraków and the Kraków Jews with events in the history of our family, which was large and prominent in that town from the sixteenth to the twentieth century. Also, I have established the exact relationship between the various existing branches of the family.

Joseph Aleksandrowicz became the progenitor of a large family. His son Menashe Aleksandrowicz had four sons: Józef, David, Filip and Wolf. Their children and grandchildren continued to live in Kraków until 1939. The Aleksandrowicz family tree contains several hundred names. While many family members perished during World War II, the survivors now live in New York, Hawaii and California, in Israel and in Poland, Argentina and in many other places.

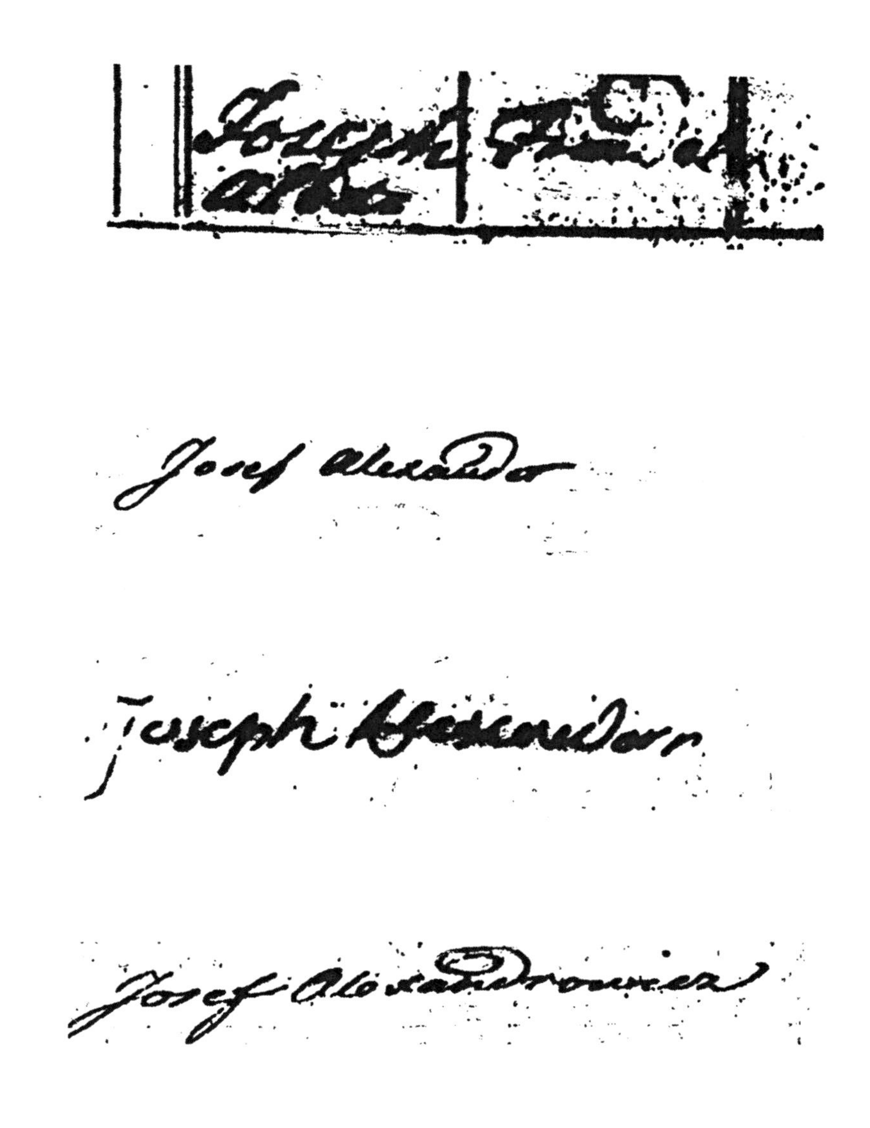

Fig. 013. Gradual appearance of the surname Aleksandrowicz in official records

Chapter 13. Two hundred years of Aleksandrowicz residences in Kraków

In 1802, when Józef soon known as Alexander and later as Aleksandrowicz, and Dobrysz, daughter of Jankl Gompel, eventually known as Gumplowicz, were married, the brief record of their marriage stated that they lived in the Jewish Town in Kazimierz, a part of Kraków, in buildings 203 and 205, respectively.

According to the census of 1804, quoted by Jan Małecki in the third volume of his and Bieniarzówna's monumental opus on Kraków history (Bieniarzówna and Małecki, III, 1979), the Jewish Town had only 207 buildings. The entire town of Kraków, including Kazimierz, had 1,772 buildings. Thus, the Jewish Ghetto contained 11.7% of the total housing stock. It is of interest that the population of Kraków in 1804 was 25,750, of which 4,300 were Jewish. The Jews constituted 16.7% of the total population but occupied only 11.7% of the housing. Not surprisingly, this indicated that the Jews, hemmed in, as they were in a Ghetto, were more crowded than everybody else. While in Kraków as a whole, there were 16.7 people per house, in the Jewish section the ratio was 20.8, a significant difference.

In the family document from the Kraków Archives, the 1831 record of the second marriage of Rivka Aleksandrowicz, a young widow, the bride's deceased father, Józef Aleksandrowicz, is said to have been an owner of building 203 in Kazimierz. In all the documents, for sixty or seventy years after 1802 the address of all the Aleksandrowicz families was invariably given as building 203. It was logical for me to assume that this was the building that Józef's family owned. Not only did he live there on the day he married, but he also lived there in 1821 when his son Israel Eliasz was born and then until his death sometimes around 1827, when he was listed as deceased. His widow, Dobrysz, lived in this building until her death sometimes after 1847 and the families of both their surviving sons, Menashe and Izrael Eliasz, lived there in 1850 and beyond. Only the census of 1881 showed a different Aleksandrowicz address.

A list of owners of houses in Kazimierz, said to date to 1805-6 has been found. In it,

building No. 203 is shown as being owned by Josef Alexander. This was surprising, because Józef was only 22 in 1805 and when I read about wedding in 1802, I had assumed that the building was owned by his father. Indeed, I hoped to be able to establish for sure what were his parents' and perhaps his grandparents' first names by perusing the list of Kraków householders. I checked the building inhabitantsin the last (1790) Polish census but found no people named Alexander or Aleksandrowicz living there. I assumed that the family purchased the building sometimes between 1790 and 1802. Having seen that 1805-6 list of building owners, I now assume that Josef's father must have died young and Józef inherited the building.

The building Nr. 203 is a large three-story structure. It stands, solidly built and in good repair. It is inhabited by many families. I believe that its present address is 22 Józefa Street. When I visited there in October 1997 I was told that it is the oldest occupied apartment building in Kazimierz. The structure is now approachable from one side, the neighboring building having been demolished. From that open side one can see that each floor has an open wooden outside corridor and the building is rather attractive although undoubtedly very old. The size of building 203 can be seen from its listing in the Polish census undertaken in 1790-1792, entitled: *"Spis ludności w Mieście żydowskim Kazimierzu, przy Krakowie, w Woiewództwie i Powiecie Krakowskim leżącym, przez Rabina Synagogi y Duchownych czyniony"* (Population census in the Jewish Town Kazimierz by Kraków, located in the District and Province of Kraków, performed by the Rabbi and Clergy of the Synagogue) (Table I):

TABLE I
Listing of inhabitants of Building 203 in Kazimierz by Kraków

(as copied from the 1790-2 census located in the Kraków branch of the Polish National Archives, in original Polish) [see Table II for an English translation]

No.domu	Nazwiska	Męszczyzny	Lata	Białogłowy	Lata
203	Maier Dranes	1	53		
	żona Keila			1	50
	Hierszel Pieczętarz	1	30		
	żona Sorla			1	20
	Fewel Kalmans	1	24		
	żona Hinda			1	24
	Mojzesz zięć Szmerla	1	30		
	żona Rochla			1	40
	Chaym Ayzykowicz	1	40		
	żona Fayga			1	36
	Abram Herszkowicz	1	45		
	żona Rochla			1	40
	Córka Tauba			1	22
	Jebel Rzeźnikowicz	1	40		
	żona Itla			1	36
	Syn Hierszel			1	20
	Mojźesz Krawiec	1	71		
	żona Rochla			1	30

Obviously, this particular listing, unlike some others in the same census (see below) omits children. It is likely that it also omits some adult inhabitants who did not want to be registered, for example, individuals who came from neighboring small towns and villages, but did not have the valuable and coveted permit to reside in Kraków. Such individuals lived as unregistered boarders, sheltered by registered friends, relatives or business associates; many got themselves apparently listed as cooks or servants, accounting for the unusually large number of "servants" recorded in the so-called "Austrian" census of 1796.

From the Polish census, we can infer that in 1790-2 at least eight families, a total of 18 adults lived in building 203. Several things can be deduced from this list. If Józef who became Józef Aleksandrowicz had lived in Building 203 in 1790-2, he would not have been listed, because he was too young to be mentioned in the census. However, if, as it appears from his 1802 wedding notice, his father's name was David, than this branch of the family did not live in this building and probably did not own it then. That is how I conclude that the family acquired this house after 1792 but before 1802, although other members of the family may have lived there. Specifically, we know from later documents, that Kalman Alexander lived in Kraków and one of his sons, Moses, eventually known as Moses Alexander was born around 1800. I have not been able to determine whether the Kalman mentioned in Tables I and II as the father of Feivel was also the father of Moses. As can be seen from Tables I and II, residents of the house did not have surnames in 1790-1792. Individuals were identified by their professions: such as "seal maker" or "tailor", their father's profession: "son of the butcher", their father's name: "Kalman's", "son of Hershel", "son of Isaac", or even by relationship to a better known person, such as: "son-in-law of Shmerl". I also found it interesting that the 71-year-old tailor had a 30-year-old wife, and that women were listed as white-haired. This may sound peculiar, but it is the exact translation of the Polish term used in the census.

TABLE II.
Inhabitants of building 203 in Kazimierz/Kraków in 1790-2. (English translation).

Building No.	Name	Male	Years	White-haired	Years
203					
	Mayer Dranes	1	53		
	Wife Keila			1	50
	Hershel the seal-maker	1	30		
	Wife Sorl			1	20
	Feivel of the Kalmans	1	24		
	Wife Hinde			1	24
	Moses son-in-law of Schmerl	1	30		
	Wife Rachel			1	40
	Chaim son of Isaac	1	40		
	Wife Feige			1	36
	Abram son of Hershel	1	45		
	Wife Rachel			1	40

Daughter Taube			1	22
Jebel son of the butcher	1	40		
Wife Itl			1	36
Son Hershel	1	20		
Moses the tailor	1	71		
Wife Rachel			1	30

Comparison of the data in the Polish census of 1790 and the Austrian census of 1796 show considerable concordance between the two but also some obvious discrepancies. As an example I have compared a family living in building # 9 in the Austrian census with their listing in the earlier Polish one (see Table III, below). I picked this family because of a possibility, however remote and difficult to prove conclusively, that it may represent some of my ancestors.

Table III

Comparison of data in the Polish and Austrian census lists of 1790 and 1796

Polish census		Austrian census (house # 9, families 46, 47)		
Name/Relationship or patronymic	Age	Name/Patronymic	Family status	Age
David Józefowicz	54	David / Joseph	Widowed father of Herschel	70
wife Toba	48	Taube	cook?	56
daughter Feigle	12			
Jacob Davidowicz	36	Jacob / David	head of family # 47	37
wife Judysz	30	Judith	wife, nee Jekel	36
daughter Hindle	3	Kendel	daughter	10
Herszla Davidowicz	30	Herschel / David	head of family # 46	32
wife Rivka	28	Rifka	wife, nee Jekel	31
		Feigl daughter	18	
		Joseph son	10	
		Kendel daughter	17	

I have also compared the data in the two census listings for another family, this one in building, # 46 (Table IV). In the Polish census of 1790 there is only one family listed residing in this building, in the Austrian census, six years later, there are 5 additional households listed. The family whose listings I have compared is shown in the Austrian census as No. 237.

Throughout most of the nineteenth century Dobrysz, Józef's widow, and both her sons, Menashe and Izrael Eliasz, and their families lived in building 203. The first indication that the family moved, perhaps after the death of the matriarch Dobrysz, the first record of a different address occurred in the birth certificate of Malka Reisel Aleksandrowicz, born on January 23, 1874, granddaughter of Menashe, daughter of his son, Józef Aleksandrowicz and Józef's wife Rachel nee Drezner. Józef and Rachel lived in 1874 in a desirable building, No. 169, on today's Kupa Street, next to the Isaac Synagogue.

The census of 1881, Volume 100-174, of District VIII of Kraków shows that building No. 168 housed the Isaac Synagogue (Bóżnica Izaka) and no inhabitants. The building listed next, No. 169, on Kupa Street, had only three apartments. In apartment No.1 lived Menashe Aleksandrowicz. Menashe was born around 1817, so in 1881 he was 64 years old. According to the census, he lived alone, a widower, his wife, Lea nee Katzner, having died earlier.

TABLE IV.

Additional comparison of Polish and Austrian census listings (1790-6)

Polish census of 1790				Austrian census of 1796			
Name	Gender Male	Gender Female	Age	Name	Patronymic	Age	Status
Leyzer Szmulowicz	x		30	Lazar	Samuel	40	Head of family
żona Smalka		x	27	Malke	Isaiah	40	Wife
syn Rafal Nocha	x		13	–			
syn Józef	x		9	Joseph		18	Son
córka Leia		x	4	Lea		8	Daughter
syn Szmul	x		1	Samuel		6	Son
				Schoendel		1	Daughter
				Sarah		50	Cook

On a separate page of the 1881 census, Józef, Menashe's son, was listed as living in apartment No. 2. This Józef, born in 1845, was named after his grandfather, Menashe's father. With him in apartment No.2 lived his wife Rachel, daughter of Szaia (Jozua) Drezner, born in 1847, and their children, Jacob, born 6 June 1866, David, born 24 June 1867, Hana, born 1869, Malka, born 1873, Sziya (later known as Jozua), born 1877 and Rivka, born 1879. Attached to the page was a separate sheet of paper, issued and glued in on May 1, 1881, containing the birth certificate of "Jacob Aleksandrowicz, son of Józef and Rachel", certifying that he was born in Kraków on June 6, 1866. The document was signed by one "Wenner, deputy clerk maintaining Israelite metrical records in Kraków". This Jacob Aleksandrowicz was a grandson of Menashe and my grandfather.

In apartment No. 3 of building 169 lived the family of Izrael Eliasz Aleksandrowicz, brother of Menashe, son of the first Józef Aleksandrowicz. Izrael Eliasz was born in 1821. He was listed as a commercial agent. With him lived his wife Ester and children Reisel, born 1860, Nachman, born 24 November 1864 and Elke, born 1867. Attached to this page, on a separate sheet was a document issued 30 December 1880, stating that "Aleksandrowicz Nachman, son of Izrael Eliasz and Ester", was born in Kraków on November 24, 1864. This document was also signed by the deputy clerk Wenner. While I was in Kraków in 1997 I visited the Miodowa Street cemetery and there I saw an elaborate new tombstone, erected after the War, commemorating Nachman Aleksandrowicz.

Thus, Menashe lived in an apartment in the same building as his oldest son Józef. His other sons, Filip and Wolf, lived elsewhere. Records show that they gradually moved further and further away from the crowded Jewish area in Kazimierz. Filip's family moved to the outlying area of Podgórze and Wolf's son Sinai moved to St. Gertrud's Street near the Royal Castle. Wolf's widow, Regina, nee Hirsch, established a store in the northern area of Kraków, near the Kleparz market. Records show that Jacob Aleksandrowicz, grandson of Menashe, son of Józef, moved to the area of Stradom, which is located between the old Jewish Town in Kazimierz and the city center of Kraków (*Sródmieście*). Stradom area approaches the royal palace and castle hill of Wawel. In 1874 Jacob lived on Dietla Street, a street that was created by filling the old bed of the Vistula River, the river that used to separate Kraków from Kazimierz (the river bed moved further south and now separates Kraków, including Kazimierz, from the district of Podgórze). In 1890 Jacob and family lived on Koletek Street, only one block away from the castle hill. Sometimes around 1906 Jacob Aleksandrowicz purchased from a family named Metzger two cream-colored apartment houses directly opposite the Royal Castle on Wawel Hill and overlooking the Vistula River, on Bernardyńska Street, corner of Smocza Street. This is the premier location in Kraków. Bernardyńska Street borders the southern access to the castle. It is named after the imposing old Bernardine Cloister located at its corner with Stradom Street. Smocza Street is named after a dragon (Polish: *smok*), which, according to legend, lived in a cave under the Wawel Hill. After my grandfather Jacob's death in 1935, the two houses, with elaborately carved walls, many balconies and original artistic stained-glass windows in the staircases, were inherited by his sons and daughters, i.e. by my father and his siblings. Three of my uncles and an aunt died in the Holocaust, one died in Soviet Central Asia. One uncle and my father, Maksymilian Aleksandrowicz, known later as Max Alexander, survived the War and died in New York. All their spouses and children (except myself) perished. I therefore consider myself a rightful inheritor of the houses, even though they were taken over after the 1939-1945 war by the Polish Communist authorities as "abandoned property" and I have not been able to recover them yet.

The houses have been kept in good repair, and their location is absolutely fabulous. As can be seen from photographs, the houses are as close as possible to the Royal Complex, its ramparts, Renaissance palace and Baroque cathedral (See of the Cardinal/Archbishop of Kraków). In the 1930's, Prince Adam Stephan Cardinal Sapieha was the archbishop. His successor was the late Karol Cardinal Woytyła, who became Pope John Paul II. The two houses together have 26 apartments. In 1939 my father, mother, my sister and I lived on the second floor of the corner house, Bernardyńska 11. Our apartment had a balcony facing the Castle and the Vistula River. From my bedroom window I could see the round castle keep, the so-called Sandomierska Tower. My uncle Józek and his family lived next to us. On the ground floor lived my aunt Sonka, with her husband Stefek Neuger and son and my grandmother on my mother's side. On the top floor, in an apartment with a spectacular view of the castle and the Vistula River lived my aunt Lola. In the next building, Bernardyńska 10, my uncle Olek lived with his family, and my step-grandmother, Toni. The German occupation changed everything. We were expelled, When we came over after the War, the houses were fully occupied but I do not know the present inhabitants or administrators. Our old apartment is occupied by a real estate company, which posted a big and unsightly advertising sign on the balcony. When we came to Kraków in 1997 we could not move into our own house and we had to rent an apartment on Rajska Street, a cross-street from Karmelicka, north of the Central Market Square, but within easy walking distance from the town center.

Other branches of the family had comparable histories. Menashe Aleksandrowicz had three surviving sons. My father was a grandson of the eldest son, Józef. The next son, Filip and his wife, Dorothea, nee Fraenkel, moved to the area of Podgórze, on the other side of the Vistula. There, they became major owners of real estate, including a flagship house, still in family hands, the building overlooking the river, at Przy Moście 1 (By the Bridge). The street was named after a wooden bridge then spanning the Vistula, but the wooden bridge was destroyed by the flood of 1813. A new bridge, subsequently reinforced and still currently in use, was not built on the same site but further down the river. The Filip and Dorothea Aleksandrowicz house, however, stands on its old site facing the spot where the old bridge once stood. The house is in good condition and is fully occupied. The widow and children of the third son of Menashe Aleksandrowicz, Wolf, moved away from the Jewish area of Kazimierz. Wolf's son, Zygmunt (Sinai), lived on St. Gertud's Street, which begins at the royal enclave on the Wawel Hill and leads towards the main railroad station of Kraków (Dworzec Główny) at Lubicz Street. Wolf's other son, David and his wife Róża nee Groner, moved to the northern part of Kraków and lived with their family in the stylish house they owned at 4 Biskupia Street in the Krowodrza/Kleparz area of Kraków. The house at 4 Biskupia Street designed by the architect Tomasz Pryliński in 1872 in the so-called "Krakovian palace style", has since been modified several times. As a school child, attending the primary school on Biskupia Street, along with David's son, Richard (Dov) Aleksandrowicz, I spent a lot of time in that house. Parenthetically, the school, which was located in an old-fashioned wooden structure, is no longer in existence.

Chapter 14. "*Starozakonny*", a polite Polish word for "Jew" in old documents

The late Roman Catholic pope John Paul II, while praying at the Wailing Wall during his historic trip to Jerusalem on March 26, 2000, committed himself to "a genuine brotherhood with the People of the Covenant". It so happens that reference to Jews as the People of the Covenant came naturally to the Polish Pope, because the term, "people of the Old Covenant" was for a long time the standard polite form of speaking about Jews. Anybody who has examined old Jewish documents from Poland dating from around 1820 to 1860 and from the Free Kraków Republic from 1815 to 1846 must have encountered the word *starozakonny* and wondered what it implies. Several genealogists have asked me to explain it to them. The word, a popular old polite term for a Jew, is not found in modern Polish dictionaries, because it is no longer in use. I will try to put it within its historic context.

As used in Kraków, the word *starozakonny* (male, singular) and its other forms, *starozakonni* (male, plural), *starozakonna* (female, singular) and *starozakonne* (female, plural) is derived from two Polish (and general Slavic) roots. *Stary* (m, sing.) or *stara* (f., sing.) means old, as in the name of the Old Synagogue in Kraków, "*Stara Bóżnica*", or the Alt-neu Synagogue in Prague, called in Czech "*Staro-nova Synagoga*"). The other root is the word "*zakon*", which in this context means "covenant" or "testament" or "order" as used in the phrases "The Old Testament", "religious order" or "knightly order" (ex. *Stary Testament*, the Benedictine Order" or "Order of the Knights of Malta" (in Polish "*Zakon Benedyktynów*" or "*Zakon Kawalerów Maltańskich*"). Thus, the word *starozakonny* refers to a person of the old order, Old Covenant or the Old Testament, i.e. to a Jew.

While it is quite proper today in translating old Polish documents into modern English to translate *starozakonny* as "Jew", this does not convey the archaic, pedantic and overly proper sense of this word. In my translations I have preferred to use the rather clumsy but evocative terms such as "Old Covenanter" or "Old Testamenter" or, in plural, "people of the Old Testament". I have not established when the word first appeared in the Polish language. In Kraków it came into official use when the Kraków Senate established a *Komitet Starozakonnych* (Committee of the People of the Old Testament) around 1818.

In documents from pre-Partition Poland, from sixteenth and seventeenth centuries, the word used for a Jew was *"Żyd",* the same word as used today. For example, in 1636 the merchant Alexander Józefowicz was called *"Żyd przy Krakowie*", i.e. "a Jew from near Kraków", as quoted in a book dealing with Jewish commerce in Kraków, published in 1995 by the Kraków Academy of Arts and Sciences (Bieniarzówna and Małecki, 1979). In documents dating to the eighteenth century a Jew is mentioned either as "*Żyd*" or as "a person of the Mosaic Faith". The last census of Jews made in independent Poland in 1790, a part of which is kept in the Kraków branch of the Polish National Archives, refers only to the population "*żydowskiego Miasta*" (of the Jewish Town). The next census, in 1796, run by Austrian occupiers, did not use any Polish terms, it used only German: "*Verzeichnis der saemtlich in der Judenstadt Kasimir, der Vorstaedten und nahen Doerfer befindlichen Juden"* (Listing of Jews found in the Jewish Town Kazimierz, the suburbs and nearby villages).

In the first two decades of the nineteenth century, records of Jewish births, marriages and deaths in Kraków were kept by a government clerk specifically appointed to keep records "for persons of Mosaic Faith", but individuals were not additionally described as Jews. For example, the birth record of Samuel Aron Aleksandrowicz, dated August 30, 1818, stated "*...przed Nami, Stanisławem Dudzicz, Urzędnikiem Stanu Cywilnego... dla osób Wyznania Moyżeszowego ustanowionym... stawił się osobiście Józef Aleksandrowicz, kupiec..."* (...before Us, Stanisław Dudzicz, Civil State Clerk... designated for persons of Mosaic Faith ...appeared personally Józef Aleksandrowicz, merchant..."). As yet, the word *starozakonny* was not used.

However, in the very next document in my possession, the birth record of Israel Eliasz Aleksandrowicz, dated only three years later, on August 17, 1821, the word *starozakonny* made its appearance. Thus, the document stated: *"...przed Nami, Staniławem Dudzicz, Urzędnikiem Stanu Cywilnego...dla* Starozakonnych *ustanowionym...stawił się osobiście Józef Aleksandrowicz, kupiec* (...before Us, Stanisław Dudzicz, Civil State Clerk...appointed for *persons of the Old Testament...* personally appeared Józef Aleksandrowicz, merchant...)". As stated, during this period the government of the newly-established Free City of Kraków abolished the traditional Jewish Community Council, the *Kahal,* and created a Committee of the People of the Old Testament, to deal with Jewish issues. From that time on, individuals were routinely described as "*starozakonni*". Thus, the announcement of the second wedding of Rivka Polner, nee Aleksandrowicz, and Faywel Orgler, dated 11 March 1831, contained the following: *"...przed Nami Woyciechem Kucięskim, Urzędnikiem Stanu Cywilnego w Mieście wolnem Krakowie dla Starozkonnych ustanowionym... stawił się osobiście starozakonny Faywel Orgler,...z księgi urodzenia Starozakonnych ...dowodzi...syn Starozakonnych Szachny Orgler,...i Racheli Chaimowney, ...stawiła się także Starozakonna Rivka z Aleksandrowiczów Polnerowa... wdowa po niegdy Starozakonnym... Michale Polner... córka Starozakonnych Josela Aleksandrowicz już zmarłego... i żyjącey Dobressy z Gomplowiczów Jego Małżonki nateraz wdowy.*" (before Us, Woyciech Kucięski, Civil State Clerk appointed in the free City of Kraków for *people of the Old Testament...* appeared personally *Old Testamenter* Faywel Orgler...as proved by the book of births of the *People of the Old Testament*...son of the *Old Testamenters* Szachna Orgler and Rachel daughter of Chaim...also appeared the *Old Testamenter* Rivka of the Aleksandrowiczes Polner... widow of the late *Old Testamenter* Michael Polner...daughter of *Old Testamenters* Josel Aleksandrowicz already deceased and living Dobress of the Gomplowiczes His Spouse and now widow...").

Similarly, on May 5, 1845, the birth of Józef Aleksandrowicz was recorded by Franciszek Gawroński, the clerk appointed "*dla Starozakonnych*" (for the *People of the Old Testament*). Before him personally appeared *starozakonny* Manasses Aleksandrowicz, the act was witnessed by *Starozakonni* Herschel Grifl and Saul Prigiel. Every Jew was always identified as *starozakonny.* Polite though the term may have been, there is no escaping the fact that it was invariably used to make sure that in all official documents there was never any question that a Jew was a Jew.

Over the years the Government clerks in Kraków changed: Stanisław Habdank Dudzicz was succeded by Franciszek Gawroński, then by Woyciech Kucięski and Filip Etgins, but usage of the term *starozakonny* continued. The term was still used in the birth certificate of Wolff Aleksandrowicz in 1852, six years after the Free City of Kraków ceased to exist and became a part of the Austrian Empire. Later, as the Jewish population grew, the office of the specially appointed clerk was superceded in Kraków by an Israelite Regional Registry Office (in Polish, *Izraelicki Okręgowy Urząd Metrykalny*). All documents that I have, dated 1866 and later, were issued by that office, which, being "Israelite", did not have the need to use any special terms to denote Jews and did not refer anymore to Jews as *starozakonni.* The word gradually disappeared from everyday language, although it survived as a testimonial to the persistence of old anachronistic terms, even to my time.

I have a small personal recollection of the overly polite use of this term. In 1931, when I was 6 years old I began grammar school located quite far from our home. My parents wanted to allow me some freedom to grow up and assume responsibilities, so after a very few days they trusted me to find my own way to school. Most of my classmates, however, were accompanied on their way to school by parents, nannies or governesses. When I arrived at school one day there was a typewritten notice on the class door, which I ignored, my reading skills at the time being rather limited. In class, instead of the regular teacher, there came a priest, a Jesuit. He began the class by asking all to stand up and say a prayer. I already knew that during a Roman-Catholic prayer, which in Polish schools of the time was said daily, Christian pupils held their hands together and recited the "*Ojcze Nasz, któryś jest w niebie...*", i.e. Our Father who art in heaven... loudly, but Jewish students were expected to stand quietly with hand at their sides. So when the priest ordered a prayer I stood without praying. He came up to me and asked me quietly, whispering into my ear, "Are you a *starozakonny*?", a word that was not in use and which I did not know when I was six. Therefore, I assured him that I am not. He gave up and continued with his catechism lesson, but obviously must have realized that I did not know the catholic routine, so after a few minutes more he again came to me and this time asked me if I am "*a żydek*", i.e. a little Jew. This, of course, I knew. So I told him that I am indeed a Jew. Not wanting to be accused of attempting to proselytize a child, he very politely told me that it would be better if I not remain in his class but wait outside for it to be over. It was only when I went outside that I found all my Jewish classmates there (a quarter of the class was Jewish) and discovered that the notice on the door stated that a Catholic religious class will take place

and recommended that Jews wait it out in the hallway or in the school playground. This was my only personal experience of ever being called a *starozakonny.*

The above anecdote illustrates my statement that the word *starozakonny* was no longer in use in Poland when I was a child, except in situations, which may have called for the use of extremely tactful, somewhat artificial, politeness. It was perfectly proper when I grew up in Poland to use the word *"żyd*", pronounced zhid, (pural *żydzi*") to describe a Jew. There were no pejorative connotations of that word in modern Polish, apart from a general anti-Jewish sentiment. In fact, there was no other proper word to use. It is of interest, that unlike in Polish (or Serbo-Croatian), that word does have negative connotations in Russian, where the word "Zhid" is considered insulting, and where the polite term for a Jew is *Yevrey* (a Hebrew). In Poland prior to 1939 we have occasionally used both *yevrey* and *starozakonny,* treating both as somewhat ironic, archaic terms. For example, "*uczony yevrey*" (an educated Hebrew) was a pedant and a know-it-all, and there was an old satirical song about an army in retreat: "*Dziesięc tysięcy kawalerii, czternaście pułków artylerii, pułk Mameluków z Afryki skwarnej i Starozakonny oddział sanitarny*" ("Ten thousand cavalry, fourteen battalions of artillery, a battalion of Mamelukes from scorched Africa and an Old Testament medical unit").

The usage of the term *starozakonny* is today of purely historical (and genealogical) importance, primarily for people interested, for whatever reasons, in old Jewish institutions and old Jewish documents from Poland and the Kraków Republic, dating to the mid-nineteenth century.

Chapter 15. Surprise in the Archives: A new ancestor, Jacob Gumple (Gumplowicz)

It is always a thrill when you find something unexpected in old documents, a surprising connection to another family or, in this instance, both a connection to a prominent Krakovian Jewish family and to a historical personality who turned out to be among my direct ancestors. The family was Gumplowicz and the personality was the founding father of that family, Jacob called Gumple (ca. 1759-1830), progenitor of the family later known as Gumplowicz. I met several people with the Gumplowicz surname as a child in Kraków. At the time, in the nineteen thirties, I did not know, however that I, too, am counted among Jacob Gumple's descendants. It took me a lot of effort to find out that the wife of my ancestor Joseph Aleksandrowicz was a daughter of Jacob Gumple.

The first historically fully documented definitive recorded document of my family, the Alexander – Aleksandrowicz family, that I found in my research in Kraków was a listing of a wedding on September 15, 1802 of Joseph, son of David, and Dobrysz, daughter of Jankel. While early in my research I found that Joseph's eventual surname was Aleksandrowicz, the maiden surname of his wife remained a mystery and took a lot of search time before I was able to track it down. In most listings only her patronymic was given. Thus, in various documents she was shown as Dobrysz Jakubowna or Dobress z Jacobów, i.e. as Miss Jacobs or as a daughter of the Jacobs. That established that her father's first name was Jacob. But the surname of her father's family remained a mystery, until I found a much later document, dated March 11, 1831. In that document, a wedding announcement of Rivka, daughter of Joseph and Dobrysz Aleksandrowicz, the bride's mother was listed not as Dobress z Jacobów but as Dobress z Gomplowiczów, i.e. Dobress of the Gomplowicz. This was my first indication that Jacob, Dobrysz's father, was Jacob Gomple, later referred to as Jacob Gumplowicz, who was among the most important members of Kraków Jewry in the years 1765-1830. I have described my search for Dobrysz's surname and my surprise at finding that it was Gumplowicz in an article entitled "How I found a new ancestor in

Kraków, Poland", published in the genealogical journal *Avotaynu* in 1998.

My descent from Dobrysz Aleksandrowicz, nee Gumplowicz, is quite straightforward. Her son, Menashe (1817-<1902) had a son, Józef (1845-1941), my great-grandfather, who in turn had a son Jacob (1866-1935), my grandfather. Jacob's son, Maksymilian (1902-1968) was my father. I knew my great-grandfather Józef Aleksandrowicz as an old man in Kraków. He died in his 96-th year, when I was almost 16. Dobrysz was his grandmother.

The origin of the Gumplowicz family is lost to history. The form "Gumplowicz" is obviously a Polish variant of the word Gumpel, using the Slavic ending for a patronymic. Apparently the surname was derived from the first name of a man called Gumpel, Gumpl, Gompel or Gimpel. That name was not uncommon. Even now, in America, there are many Gimpels, Gumbels and Gimbelses around. I have found the word "Gimpel" in Cassell's German-English Dictionary (MacMillan, 1978). It refers to it as a colloquial term meaning "dunce, ninny, noodle, simpleton". I have not found it in any modern Polish or Yiddish dictionary, but the root words of "gimp" and "gump" are listed in the Webster Unabridged Dictionary (Random House, NY). A *gimp* is a limp, a person who limps, a lame person. A *gump* is a foolish or stupid person. The Dictionary adds that the latter term, of unknown origin, was used colloquially between 1815 and 1825. This confirms my belief that historically it was used in Yiddish as in German as a nickname for either an easy-going man, perhaps easily fooled, or else, for a man with a physical deformity. In either case, it must have been quite common. Since there are no vowels in Hebrew, the name, as pronounced, could have been and was spelled in either way. In Yiddish the addition of an "l" at the end converts either word to an diminutive *gumpl* or *gimpl*.

The earliest recorded mention of any Gumpels in Kraków occurs in the 16-th century, according to a book on Jewish trade of the 16-th and 17-th centuries published by the Polish Academy of Arts and Sciences (Małecki, 1995). In that book, among Jewish merchants entered as having paid commercial taxes and duties, were two with a patronymic or a nickname Gimpel. Marek Gimpel (No. 391, p.136) was a dealer in spices who imported 3 lapis (?) of anise for general sale in Kraków. Jurek Gimpel (No. 587, p.151) dealt with leather and paid duties on calf and rabbit skins. I mentioned these Gimbel merchants in an earlier chapter. In his monumental history of Kraków Jewry, Prof. Majer Bałaban, mentions (II, p. 165) that in 1680 a Salomon Gimplo arrived in Kraków from Silesia. Other than similarity of name, I found no direct proof that any of these individuals were in any way related to my ancestor Jacob Gompel.

The Polish census of 1790 listed Jankel (a diminutive form of Jacob), son of Gumpl and son-in-law of Abele (item # 1260), living in the house No. 106. Jankel was said to be 33 years old. His wife, Sissl (Sarah), daughter of Abele, was 28. Among her siblings were two sisters, Leah Abele's, who married Samuel (Shmul) later knowns as Goldstoff, a Kahał Senior, and Feigl Abele's, who married David Hirsch ha-Levi, a rabbi, who later took on the surname of Lewin. All three sisters might have been daughters of Abele who later adapted the surname of Puffeles, when Austrian officials insisted that Jews must adopt surnames. I have not been able to confirm this. Should it turn out that my ancestor Abele, father of Sarah Gumplowicz and grandfather of Dobrysh Gumple Aleksandrowicz was indeed named Abel (Abraham?) Puffeles, then the family surname Puffeles will *ipso facto* become a part of my family tree.

In the 1790 census Jankel and Sarah were listed as having two girls, Hana, 13 (i.e. born in 1777), and Pesl, 11 (b. 1779), and a son Lewek (Levko, Lebl), 8 years old, i.e. born around 1782. The dates listed in the census cannot be correct, as they imply that Sarah conceived her first child before she was 15, which is not likely. Women had children at 15 and 16. not unusual at the time, but not much earlier. In the Austrian census of Kraków Jews from 1795-6 there were several Gumpels listed, all living in different houses in the Kazimierz district. That census mentioned that Jacob Guempel, 36, and his wife, Sarah, born (*geboren*) Abele, 30, had children: Lebelle, 15, and Dobosch, 9, i.e. born around 1786 (this is the girl that later married Joseph Alexander). Again, it showed Sarah as being too young. She had Lebel at 15 and we know that she had children before Lebel. This census, omitted her older girls, Hana and Pesl, possibly because they were married in the meantime and established their own separate households. It listed Lebl as having been born around 1780 and adds Dobrysz, who was not mentioned in the Polish census of a few years earlier (see photostat of a page of the Austrian census at the end of this chapter). The discrepancies between the two census listings, taken approximately six years apart clearly demonstrate the cavalier approach to birth dates and ages of those listed and confirm that extreme caution is indicated when accepting census data.

The Austrian census also showed Liebman Gumpel, born 1761, Feigl, daughter of Gumpel, born in 1762, Liebe, daughter of Gumpel, born in 1765, and Genendel Guempel, born in 1768. I mentioned that there is a time discrepancy between the Polish and Austrian census lists, indicating that data for each list were collected over several years. Prof. Bałaban described Jacob Gumplowicz as a rich man, a supplier of the Kraków mint in 1765, whose company went bankrupt in 1791 and who received (purchased), in 1793, the coveted monopolistic right to collect taxes on alcohol sold in bottles. He was obviously a prominent citizen even after his bankruptcy. However, in the two census lists Jacob was shown as having been born around 1757-60, too young to be a supplier of the mint in 1765. Either the dates are totally wrong or there were two Jacobs and the younger man may have been a relative, perhaps a nephew and a namesake of the ther Jacob, also called Gumpel, who died before the time of the censuses. Indeed, it is possible that the younger Jacob was called by the diminutive Jankel to distinguish him from his older relative of the same name.

Prior to 1805 most Kraków Jews did not use surnames, they used patronymics, nicknames, professions or places of origin. My ancestor Jacob Gumplowicz was recorded in different official documents throughout his life as Jacob or Jankel Gimple, Guemple, Gumpel or Gomple. In 1791 he lived in building No. 205. The birth records for year 1801 that I found in Kraków showed that on November 11 Jacob Gomple and his wife Sarah, living in building No. 205, had a child named Abele. The child was probably named after Sarah's father, Abele, who died. In 1801 their son Lebel was around 21, their daughter Dobrysz around 17 and they had a younger daughter Feigl, age 9. The next birth record showed that in 1803 Jacob Gimpl and Sarah had a son whom they registered as Juda Leib. The name as used was Gimpl. Only after 1805, when the Austrians insisted on surnames, did the full name Gumplowicz appear as a surname in the official records. The first use of that surname that I found occurred in April 15, 1806, when the above-mentioned son of Jacob and Sarah, Lebel (Levko, Lebelle) Gumplowicz, then recorded as being 26, and his wife Roesl (Reizl), also living in building No. 205, had a daughter named Hanna. Eventually, I found out that Reizl who married Lebl Gumplowicz was the daughter of Izaak later known as Minzer.

Jacob and Sarah Gumplowicz had many children, but I could find documented records of only some. Two older girls Hana and Pesl were listed in the Polish census of 1790. Hana married Salomon Fiszlowicz (Fischlovitz, maybe even Tischlowitz?}. The daughter Dobrysz, born in 1784, married Józef Aleksandrowicz in 1802; the other daughter Feigl, born in 1792, married Ruben Pitzele in 1808. A son, Manasses, born in 1796, married Cyperl, daughter of Izak Schnitzer in 1812, the year in which Napoleon's *Grande Armee* marched through Poland to assail Russia and then retreated after a defeat by the Russian winter, an important series of events that impacted Poles and Polish Jews severely. The son Abele, the one who was born in 1801, married sixteen-year old Hanna Dattelbaum on March 21, 1820. Hanna Dattelbaum was born on 29-th of January 1804, daughter of Izak Dattelbaum and his wife Ester daughter of Zelig. The name Dattelbaum may possibly be a variant spelling of the eventual surname Teitelbaum. As far as I can tell, Juda Leib born to Jacob and Sarah on April 3, 1803, was their last child. Jacob and Sarah's daughters, Dobrysz and Feigl had many children. Dobrysz Gumplowicz with Józef Aleksandrowicz had Schoendel, born 1805, Temerl born 1807, Rivka born 1809, Gele born 1811, Hana born 1813, Menasse born 1817, Samuel Aron (1818-1824) and Izrael Eliash born 1821. Feigl Gumplowicz and Ruben Pitzele, son of Simon Picele of Kraków, living in building 134 in Kazimierz, had a large number of children, many of whom did not survive to adulthood. Records collected by a descendant of theirs, Ben Weinstock, show births of Monish (1807), Aba (1809), Józef (1811), David (1813), Israel (1814), Hirsch (1817), Juda Saul (1819), Chaya Sora (1820), Józef Manasses (1821), Abraham Feibus (1822), Kalman (1824), Elias (1825), Gitl Ester (1826), Naftali Hirsch (1827), Gompel (named after greatgrandfather, 1829), Jacob (1830), Salomon (1831), Dina Rivka (1832) and Izak (1833). A copy of a birth record of one child of Feigl Gumplowicz and Ruben Pitzele is shown at the end of this chapter, as is a copy of the record of Feigl Gumplowicz Pitzele's death at 52 in 1844. I have seen business documents of the Picele family and find it of historical interest that Picele women were just as active in business as their male counterparts. Obviously, in the Jewish milieu in Kraków, women were as free to own property and deal in assorted transactions as men and the Austrian authorities had no problem with that. I enclose below a copy of a business certificate, showing that Jewish women owned property and businesses in their own names.

According to later Kraków data, Abraham Shaya Gomplowicz was born in Kraków around 1800 to Leibl Gomplowicz, Jacob and Sarah's son, and his wife Roesl (Reizl) Izakowna Minzer. Abraham Shaya was a nephew of both Dobrysz Aleksandrowicz and Feigl Pitzele, as well as of Manasses Gumplowicz, husband of Cyperl Schnitzer, and Abele Gumplowicz, husband of Hanna Dattelbaum. Leibl and Reisl Gumplowicz had several other children, some of whom died as infants. Daughter Hanna, whose birth certificate was the first document to use the full family surname Gumplowicz, was born in 1806. She married Moses Frommer in 1825. Other children of Leibl and Reizl include a son, Izaak, born in 1813, and then a daughter Sarah born in 1817 and a boy Judka born in 1820, both of whom died young.

Abraham Shaya Gumplowicz, son of Leibl, married 17-year-old Dobresh Hanna Neuman, daughter of Hirsch and Lieba Lea Eliaszówna on the 14-th of February 1819. With Dobresh Hanna he had several children, some of whom died as infants, such as Rachel Lea who died soon after birth in 1831. In 1827 Abraham and Dobresh Hanna

had a daughter, Cerel (pronounced *Tsirl*, a variant of Sarah) Breindl, who later called herself Szarlotta (Charlotte). This Szarlotta married Feivel (Ferdynand) Kestel in 1851. Dobresh Hanna Neuman Gumplowicz died in 1830. According to the banns posted on the 15-th of July 1832, and recorded by the Civil State Clerk Woyciech Kucieński in the marriage records of the year 1832 on page 105, under the number 55, the 33-year-old Abraham [Shaya] Gomplowicz, "son of Lebel Gomplowicz and Reizl daughter of Izak, a widower whose first wife Dobres Hanna Neuman died", became engaged to marry "Hanna Inlainder, 23 years old, daughter of Moyżesz Inlander, a bank clerk, and Gosel his wife living in Brody" on the Galician-Ukrainian border (see enclosed photostat). Hanna Inlainder's parents came to Kraków for the marriage ceremony. It is of interest that in the record of these banns Abraham was listed as being 33, i. e. as having been born in 1799, ten years older than his second wife. Hanna Inlainder was born in 1809. She later called herself Henrietta. With the two wives, Abraham [Shaya] Gumplowicz had many children, including Edward, Felix, Ludwik, Ignacy and Maksymilian Teofil, besides the above-mentioned daughter, Szarlotta.

I mentioned before that Abraham [Shaya] Gumplowicz, liberal in his religious beliefs and aware of and interested in word cultural developments, founded a privately-owned for-profit lending library of modern European novels and non-fiction books. As a child, in Kraków in the 1930's I used to borrow books from the two Gumplowicz private libraries. In 1840 Abraham Gumplowicz helped to found the modern Reform Jewish synagogue in Kraków, the Tempel. The Tempel had a then shocking mixed-gender choir and an organ. I remember visiting it as a child in the 1930's and I visited it again in 1997. The Tempel has been impressively renovated by the Ronald Lauder Foundation to serve as a synagogue and a concert hall. Abraham Gumplowicz was a leader of those Krakovian Jews who believed that knowledge of and involvement in the surrounding Western-European culture will benefit Jewry and help it develop economically and culturally. He believed that this acculturation can occur without the Jews abandoning their faith (as shown below, his own son did not quite follow his father's path).

Abraham's son, Ludwik Gumplowicz, whose birth was recorded in the 1838 book of Jewish births in Kraków, page 34, # 100, was born on the 8-th of March 1838 (see photostat). He was the son of Abraham's second wife, Henrietta of the Inlainders, 28. In this document Abraham is listed as being 35, i.e. born in 1803, a discrepancy of mere four years from the data in his wedding banns, showing again that exact dates were not considered crucial at the time. Ludwik Gumplowicz grew up in Kraków. He became a world-renown scholar and an innovator. He became an early expert on population trends and group dynamics and is generally credited with being the founder of a new discipline, sociology. He became a Polish patriot, while remaining always interested in Jewish affairs. He is the author of an important source book on Polish laws relating to Jews. During the Polish patriotic uprising of 1861, which took place in the Russian part of Poland, but which caused patriotic ferment in Kraków as well, Ludwik run afoul of the Austrian authorities by becoming involved in helping the insurrectionists and had to leave Kraków. He hoped to secure a university appointment in Kraków, but his being Jewish prevented that. Whether out of conviction or to advance his career, he abandoned Judaism at one point and converted, a step widely considered as obligatory prior to receiving an Austrian university appointment at the time. Perhaps thanks to this step, he eventually did receive a university

appointment. The Encyclopaedia Judaica (Keter Publ., Jerusalem 1972, VII, 975-977), mentions that Ludwik Gumplowicz received a full Professorship in Political Science at the Graz University in Austria in 1893. The article in the Encyclopedia states that he "was one of the first to achieve full emancipation for sociology from the non-social sciences by insisting that social phenomena and evolution are distinctive and can be understood only by reference to social causes". He is considered as "the father of sociology".

Even after baptism and conversion to catholicism, which mocked his father's conviction that Jews can remain Jewish, while being assimilated, Ludwik Gumplowicz showed continued interest in Jewish affairs. His sociological writings became widely known and he was quite influential worldwide. He corresponded with the founder of modern Zionism, Theodor Herzl, and in a letter to the latter written in 1899 he expressed his opinion, as a sociologist, that Jews are not a nationality and reiterated his opposition to Jews acquiring a territorial base, whether in Palestine or elsewhere. Of course, his letter did not convince Herzl, who continued to advocate a Jewish state. Gumplowicz had talented students, among them Franz Oppenheimer, who expanded on his sociological theories. His books have been translated into English and published in the United States. One of them was reprinted recently (Encyclopaedia Judaica VII). His professional success did not translate into a happy personal life. He was depressed, partly because of poor state of his and his wife's health. Ludwik's wife, Frances, was blind, sick and bed-ridden for years. Ludwik took care of her. When he discovered that he had cancer, life became too difficult for them and both he and Frances took poison. My second cousin trice-removed, Ludwik Gumplowicz, along with his wife, died in Graz in Austria in 1909.

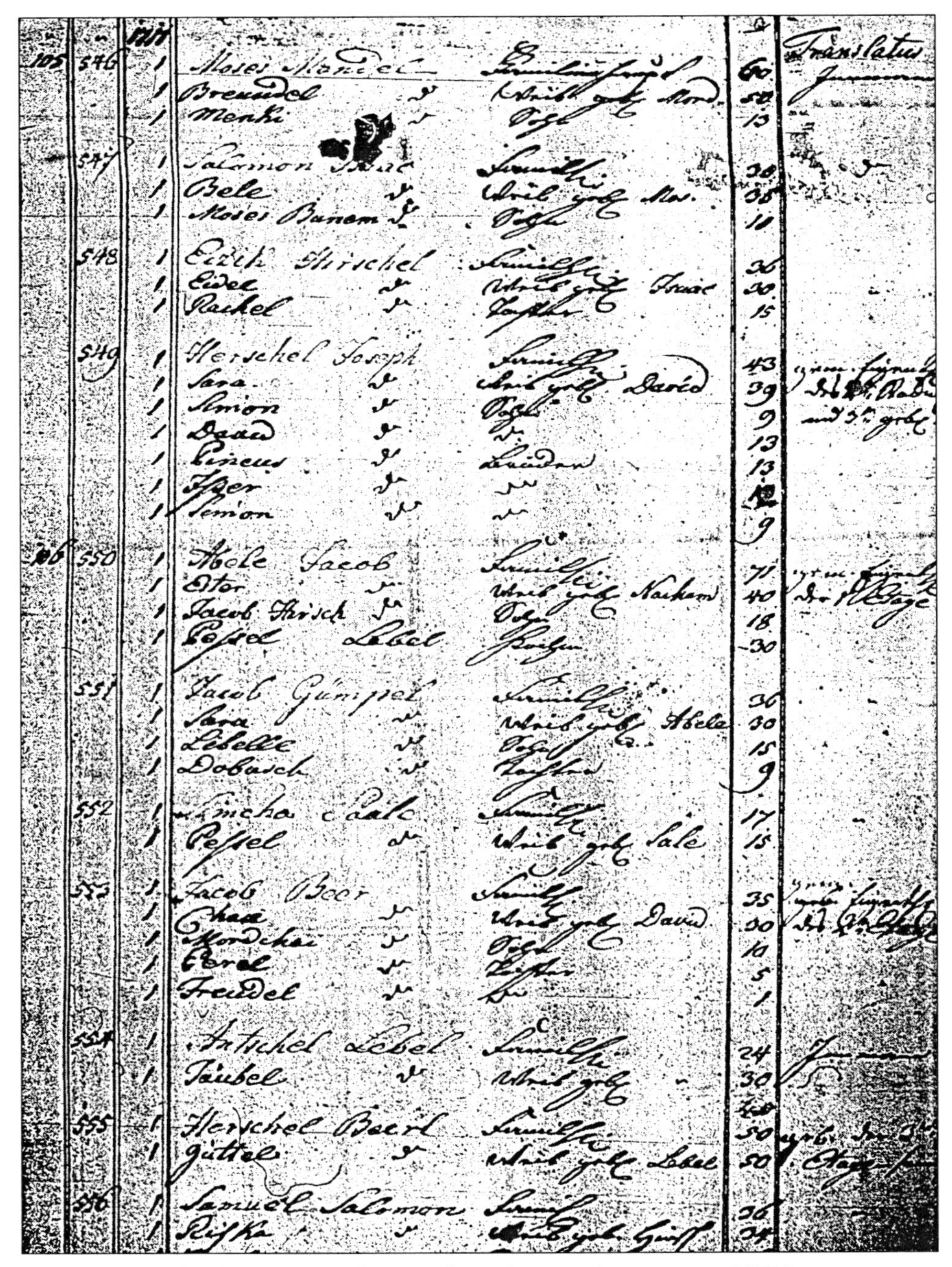

	No.	Name	Age
105	546	Moses Mandel	60
		Breundel	50
		Menki	13
	547	Salomon [illegible]	38
		Bele	35
		Moses Banem	11
	548	Eizik Hirschel	36
		Eidel	30
		Rachel	15
	549	Herschel Joseph	43
		Sara	39
		Simon	9
		David	13
		Pincus	13
		Isser	[illegible]
		Simon	9
106	550	Abele Jacob	71
		Ester	40
		Jacob Hirsch	18
		Pessel Lebel	30
	551	Jacob Gümpel	36
		Sara	30
		Lebelle	15
		Dobosch	9
	552	Simcha Saale	17
		Pessel	15
	553	Jacob Beer	35
		Chaie	30
		Mordchai	10
		Perel	5
		Freudel	1
	554	Antschel Lebel	24
		Taubel	30
	555	Herschel Beerl	50
		Güttel	50
	556	Samuel Salomon	36
		Riffka	34

Fig. 014. A copy of a page from the Austrian census of 1796, showing Jacob Guempel and family listed as # 551 (Dobrysz, who later married Joseph Alexander, shown as Dobosch, age 9);

Fig. 015. Formal certificate of wealth of Leah Picele; 1822]

I am indebted to Messrs. Ben Weinstock and Julian Schamroth for the 1818-1822 business documents of a company of widow Leah (Laja) Picele and her partners, which clearly show that women could conduct business in their own name.

LEAH PICELE: CERTIFICATE OF BUSINESS WEALTH – KRAKÓW 1822

M. Dobiński, R.P.S. Pieczęć zapłaty/ groszy dziesięć

Swidectwo

Mocą którego My niżey podpisani Zaświadczamy i zeznaiemy sumiennie i Sprawiedliwie jako Starozakonna Laja Picele Kupcowa w Mieście Żydowskim przy Krakowie pod L. 56 w Gminie X-ey mieszkaiąca, posiada w Handlu swem własnego czystego Fundusza w Zaspokojonych Towarach Zło. Pięć Tysięcy Złp 5000. Podług nam w dniu dzisieyszym okazanego stanu maiątku swego – Po ninieyszym zaświadczaiąc dla większey wiary i xxx Własnoręcznie podpisuiemy

W Krakowie dnia 22 Kwietnia 1822 r.-

Herszel l. Binenfeld

Kalman Reinhold

Rabin Obwodu Kazimierskiego zaświadcza jako podpisy świadczących osób ninieysze świadectwo, s xxx własnemi wyżądzone rękami potwierdza tak jak wyżey

H David Lewy

Rabin

Podpisy powyższe za własno ręczne zaświadcza

Michał Mohr, Z.W.G.X.

M. Dobiński, R.P.S. Tax stamp: ten groszys

Certificate

(Polish word is misspelled)

With this certificate we the undersigned declare and testify honestly and justly that the Jewess Laja Picele merchant living in the Jewish Town by Kraków in bldg 56 in the X-th Community possesses in her business of own clear funds in all-paid merchandise Pol. Zło. Five Thousand Złp 5000 According to the state of her wealth as shown to us today – after the above, certifying for greater faith and xxx we sign with our Own hands

In Kraków, 22 April 1822

Herschel L. Binenfeld

Kalman Reinhold

The rabbi of the Kazimierz District testifies that the signatures of the persons witnessing this certificate are xxx by their own hands confirmed as above

H David lewy

Rabbi

Certifying that the signatures were by own hands

Michael Mohr, Z.W.G.X.

Note that the Polish word for a certificate, *"swiadectwo"*, is misspelled in the above Pitzele document

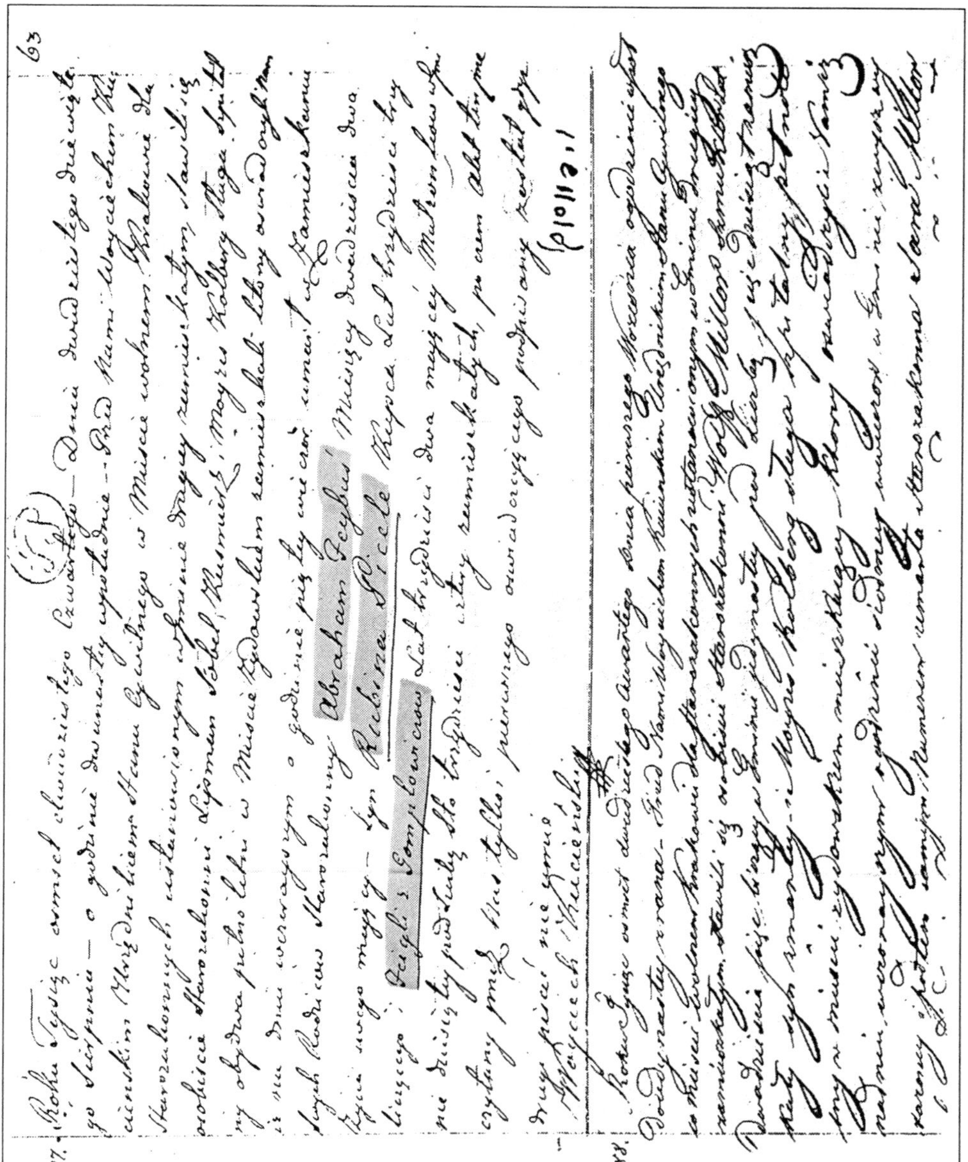

Fig. 016. Death certificate of Abraham Feybus Pitzele, age 2, 1824

Death certificate of ABRAHAM FEYBUS Pitzele, 2, 1824

Roku Tysiąc ośmset dwudziestego Czwartego – Dnia dwudziestego dziewiątego sierpnia – o godzinie dwunastey wpołudnie – przed Nami Woyciechem Kucieńskim Urzędnikiem Stanu Cywilnego w Mieście wolnem Krakowie dla Starozakonnych ustanowionym w Gminie drugiey zamieszkałym, stawili się osobiście Starozakonni Lipman Sobel, Kuśnierz i Moyżesz Kolberg Sługa Szpitalny obydwa pełnoletni w Mieście Żydowskim zamieszkali którzy oświadzyli Nam iż w dniu wczorayszym o godzinie piątey wieczór umarł w Zamieszkaniu Swych Rodziców Starozakonny Abraham Feybuś Miesięcy dwadzieścia dwa życia maiący – Syn Rubina Picele Kupca Lat trzydzieści trzy liczącego i Feigli z Gomplowiczów Lat trzydzieści dwa maiącey Małżonków w Gminie dziesiątey pod Liczbą Sto trzydzieści cztery zamieszkałych, po czem Akt te przeczytany przez Nas tylko i pierwszego oświadczającego podpisany został gdyż drugi pisać nie umie.

Woyciech Kucieński Lipman Sobl (Hebrajskie litery)

In English:

In the year One thousand eight hundred twenty Four – on the twenty ninth of August – at twelve noon – before Us, Woyciech Kucieński, Civil State Clerk in the free City of Kraków, appointed for the people of the Old Testament, living in the Second Community, personally appeared Old Testamenters Lipman Sobel Furrier and Moyżesz Kolberg Hospital Orderly both adults living in the Jewish Town who announced to Us that yesterday at five o'clock in the evening died in their parents domicile Old Testamenter Abraham Feibus having twenty two months of his life – son of Rubin Picele Merchant thirty three years old and Feigl of the Gomplowicz thirty two years old, spouses living at the building number one hundred thirty four, after which this Act was read by Us and signed by Us and only by the first announcer because the second can not write.

Woyciech Kucieński Lipman Sobl (in Hebrew letters)

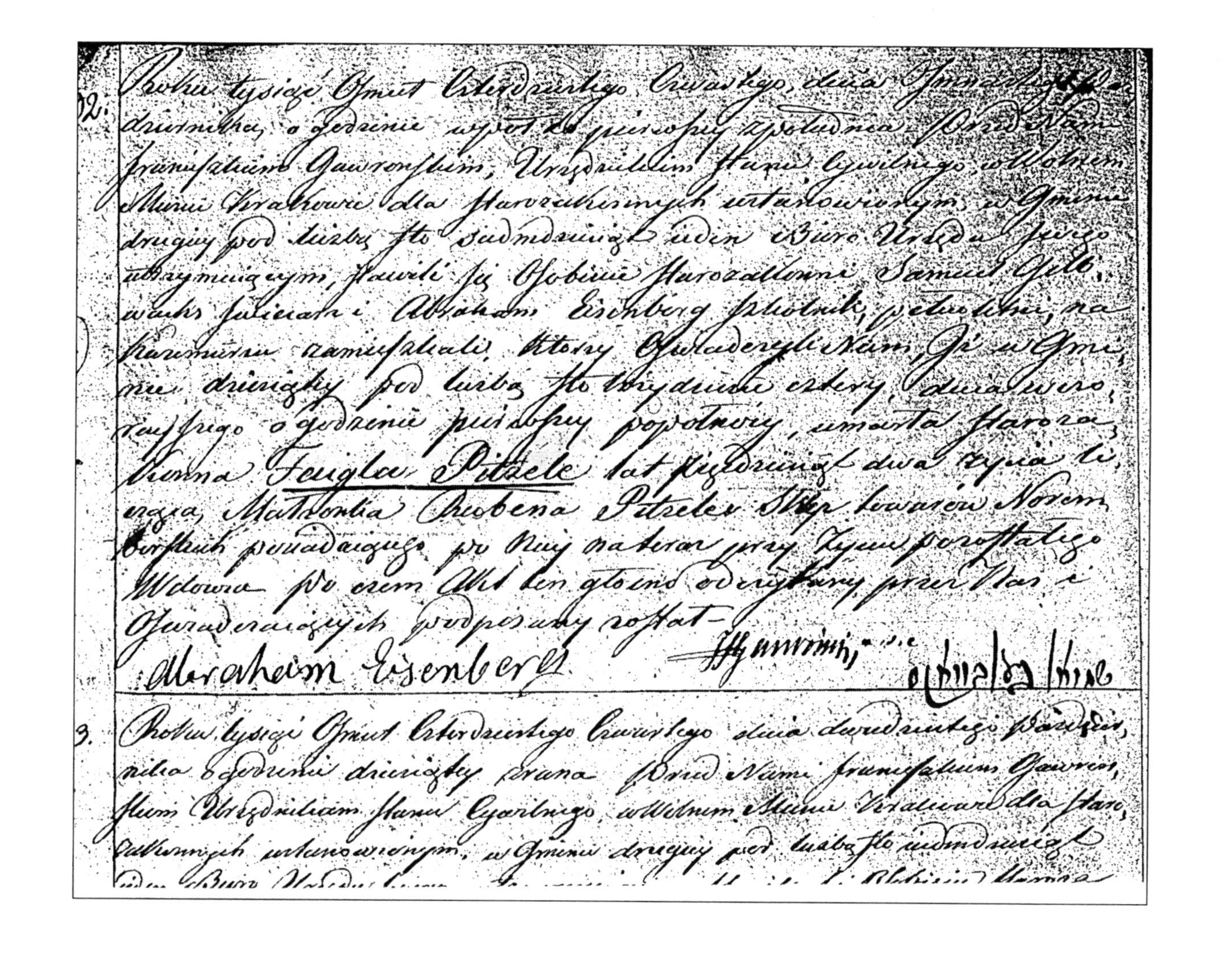

92. Roku tysiąc Ośmset Czterdziestego Czwartego, dnia Ośmnastego Października, o godzinie wpół do pierwszej z południa. Przed Nami
Franciszkiem Gawrońskim, Urzędnikiem Stanu Cywilnego, Wolnem
Miasta Krakowie dla Starozakonnych ustanowionym, w Gminie
drugiej pod liczbą sto siedmdziesiąt jeden w Biuro Urzędu swego
utrzymującym, stawili się Osobiście Starozakonni Samuel Gello-
wanka Jubilarz i Abraham Eisenberg Szkolnik, pełnoletni, na
Kazimierzu zamieszkali, którzy Oświadczyli Nam, Iż w Gminie drugiej pod liczbą sto trzydzieści cztery, dnia wczo-
rajszego o godzinie pierwszej popołudniu, umarła Starozakonna Feigla Pitzele lat sześćdziesiąt dwa licząca licząca, Małżonka Rubena Pitzeler Kupca towarów Norym-
bergskich posiadającego po Niej na teraz przy życiu pozostałego
Wdowca. Po czem Akt ten głośno odczytany przez Nas i
Oświadczających podpisany został.

Abraham Eisenberg — Gawroński — [illegible]

3. Roku tysiąc Ośmset Czterdziestego Czwartego dnia dwudziestego Października o godzinie dziewiątej z rana. Przed Nami Franciszkiem Gawrońskim Urzędnikiem Stanu Cywilnego, Wolnem Miasta Krakowie dla Starozakonnych ustanowionym, w Gminie drugiej pod liczbą sto siedmdziesiąt
jeden w Biuro Urzędu [illegible]

Fig. 017. Death record of Feigl Pitzele, nee Gumplowicz 1844

DEATH CERTIFICATE OF FEIGL PITZELE, NEE GUMPLOWICZ, 1844

Roku tysiąc Ośmset Czterdziestego czwartego, dnia Ośmnastego Października, o godzinie wpół do pierwszey zpołudnia – Przed Nami Franciszkiem Gawrońskim, Urzędnikiem Stanu Cywilnego w Wolnem Mieście Krakowie dla Starozakonnych ustanowionym, w Gminie drugiey pod liczbą sto siedemdziesiąt ieden Biuro Urzędu Swego utrzymuiącym, stawili się Osobiście Starozakonni Samuel Gelbwachs świecarz i Abraham Eisenberg Szkolnik, pełnoletni, na Kazimierzu zamieszkali, którzy Oświadczyli Nam, Iż w Gminie dziesiątey pod liczbą sto trzydzieści cztery, dnia wczorayszego o godzinie pierwszey popółnocy, umarła Starozakonna Faigla Pitzele lat pięćdziesiąt dwa życia licząca, Małżonka Rubena Pitzele Sklep towarów Noremberskich posiadaiącego po niey nateraz przy życiu pozostaiącego Wdowca po czem Akt ten głośno odczytany przez Nas i Oświadczaiących podpisany został

FGawroński, u.s.c
Abraham Eisenberg. Szmuel Gelbvaks (po Hebrajsku)

In English:

In the year one thousand eight hundred and forty four, on the eighteenth day of October, at half past noon – before Us, the Civil State Clerk in the Free City of Kraków, appointed for people of the Old Testament, maintaining an Office in the Second Community under the number one hundred and seventy one, personally appeared Old Testamenters Samuel Gelbwachs, candle maker and Abraham Eisenberg, school employee, adults, living in Kazimierz, who declared to Us that in Community Number Ten under the number one hundred thirty four, yesterday at one o'clock after midnight, died Old Testamenter Feigl Pitzele, fifty two years of age, wife of Ruben Pitzele, owner of a store of Nuremberger wares and now living widower – After which this Act was read aloud and signed by Us and the Declarers

FGawroński, c.s.c.
Abraham Eisenberg (in Hebrew) Shmul Gelbvaks

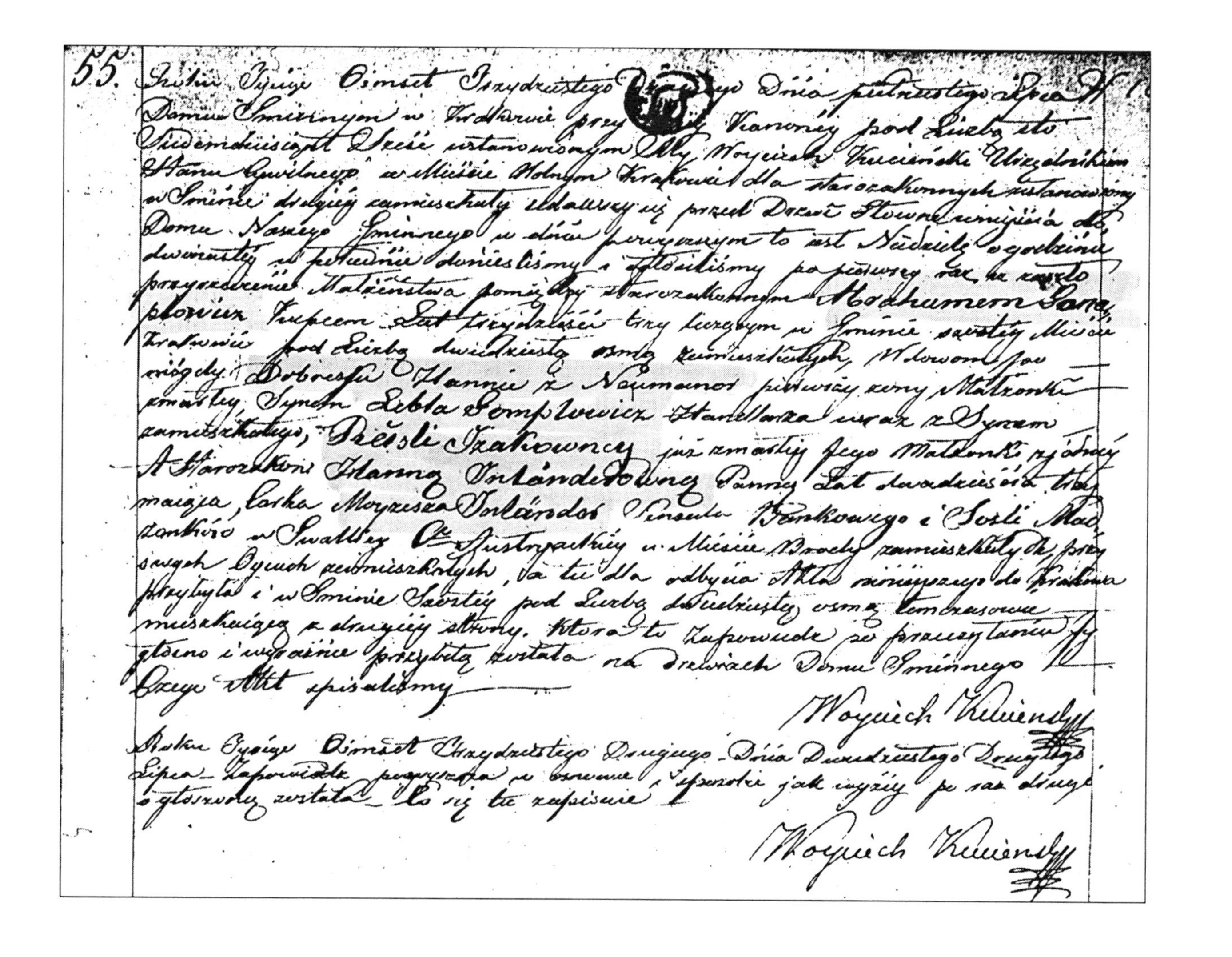

55. Roku Tysiąc Ośmset Trzydziestego [illegible] Dnia piętnastego Lipca W
Domu Gminnym w Krakowie przy [illegible] Kanoniczey pod Liczbą sto
Siedemdziesiąt Trzecie ustanowionym My Woyciech Kuciński Urzędnikiem
Stanu Cywilnego w Mieście Wolnym Krakowie dla starozakonnych ustanowiony
w Gminie drugiey zamieszkały oświadczamy iż przed Drzwi Głowne wniyścia do
Domu Naszego Gminnego w dniu pierwszym to iest Niedzielę o godzinie
dwunastey w południe donieśliśmy i ogłosiliśmy po pierwszy raz o zamierzonym
przyrzeczeniu Małżeństwa pomiędzy Starozakonnym Abrahamem Gumplowicz Kupcem Lat trzydzieści trzy liczącym w Gminie szóstey Miasta
Krakowie pod Liczbą dwudziestą ósmą zamieszkałym, Wdowcem po
niegdy Dobrysi Hannie z Neumanów pierwszey żony Małżonki
zmarłey, Synem Lebla Gumplowicz Handlarza wraz z Synem
zamieszkałego, Dziesli Izakowney już zmarłey jego Małżonki z jedney
A Starozakonną Hanną Inländerówną Panną Lat dwadzieścia trzy
mającą, Córką Moyżesza Inländer [illegible] Bankowego i Sosli Małżonków w Swalbey [illegible] Austryackiey w Mieście Brody zamieszkałych, przy
swoich Oycach zamieszkałych, [illegible] dla odbycia Aktu niniejszego do Krakowa
przybyłą i w Gminie Szóstey pod Liczbą dwudziestą ósmą teraźniejszo
mieszkającą z drugiey strony. Która to Zapowiedź po przeczytaniu
głośno i wyraźnie przybitą została na drzwiach Domu Gminnego
Czego Akt spisaliśmy

Woyciech Kuciński

Roku Tysiąc Ośmset Trzydziestego Drugiego Dnia Dwudziestego Drugiego
Lipca Zapowiedź powyższa w ówczas i sposobie jak wyżey po raz drugi
ogłoszoną została. Co się tu zapisuje

Woyciech Kuciński

Fig. 018. Wedding of Abraham Gumplowicz and Hanna of the Inlainders

WEDDING BANS OF ABRAHAM GUMPLOWICZ AND HANNA INLANDER

In original Polish, document # 55, page 105, 1832 register of births of Jews in Kazimierz:

Roku Tysiąc Ośmset Trzydziestego Drugiego Dnia piętnastego Lipca w Domu Gminnym w Krakowie przy Ulicy Kanoniczey pod Liczbą sto Siedemdziesiąt Sześć ustanowionym, My Woyciech Kucieński ustanowiony Urzędnikiem Stanu Cywilnego dla Starozakonnych, w Gminie drugiey zamieszkały, udawszy się przed drzwi główne wejścia do Domu Naszego Gminnego w dniu powyższym to iest w Niedzielę o godzinie dwunastey w południe donieśliśmy i ogłosilimy po raz pierwszy iż zaszło przyrzeczenie Małżeństwa pomiędzy Starozakonnym Abrahamem Gomplowicz kupcem Lat trzydzieści trzy liczącym w Gminie szóstey w Mieście Krakowie pod Liczbą dwadzieścia ośm zamieszkałych, Wdowcem po niegdy Dobresie Hannie z Neumanów pierwszey żony, Małżonki zmarłey, synem Lebla Gomplowicz Handlarza wraz z Synem zamieszkałego, i Reizli Izakowney już zmarłey Jego Małżonki z jedney strony --- A Starozakonną Hanną Inlanderówną Panną Lat dwadzieścia trzy maiącą, Córką Moyżesza Inlander Genanta Bankowego i Gosli Małżonków w Galicyi Austryackiey w Mieście Brody zamieszkałych, przy swych Ojcach zamieszkałą, a tu dla odbycia Akta ninieyszego do Krakówa przybyłą i w Gminie Szóstey pod Liczbą dwudziestu ósmu tymczasowo mieszkaiącą z drugiey strony, która to zapowiedź po przeczytaniu Jej głośno i wyraźnie przybitą została na Drzwiach Domu Gminnego – Czego Akt spisaliśmy -

Woyciech Kucieński

Roku Tysiąc Ośmset Trzydziestego Drugiego – Dnia Dwudziestego Drugiego Lipca – Zapowiedó powyższa w osnowie i sposobie jak wyżey po raz drugi ogłoszona została – Co się tu zapisuie -

Woyciech Kucieński

Translated into English:

In the Year One Thousand Eight Hundred Thirty Two, on the fifteenth day of July in the Community House established in Kraków on Kanonicza Street under the Number one hundred Seventy Six, We Woyciech Kucieński, Clerk appointed for the People of the Old Testament, living in Community Number Two, having come to the front of the Main Entry Door of our Community Building on the above-mentioned day, that is Sunday at twelve noon have announced and declared for the first time that there occurred a promise of Marriage between the Old Testamenter Abraham Gomplowicz, merchant, thirty three Years old living in Community Number six of the City of Kraków in building number twenty eight, Widower of the late Dobres Hanna Neuman, first wife, his deceased Spouse, Son of Lebl Gomplowicz, commercial agent, living with the Son, and Reizl daughter of Izak, deceased his Spouse on the first part – And Old Testamenter Hanna Inlander, Maiden, twenty three Years old, Daughter of Moyżesz Inlander, Banking Agent and Sosla, Sspouses living in Austrian Galicya in the Town of Brody, living with her Parents, and has arrived in Kraków in order to conclude this marriage Act temporarily living in building twenty eight in Community Six on the other part, this Announcement after having been read loud and clear

was attached to the door of the Community House – which Act we herein entered –

Woyciech Kucieński

In the Year One Thousand Eight Hundred Thirty Two on the Twenty Second day of July this Announcement, in the manner as above was announced for the second time – as we now enter.

Woyciech Kucieński

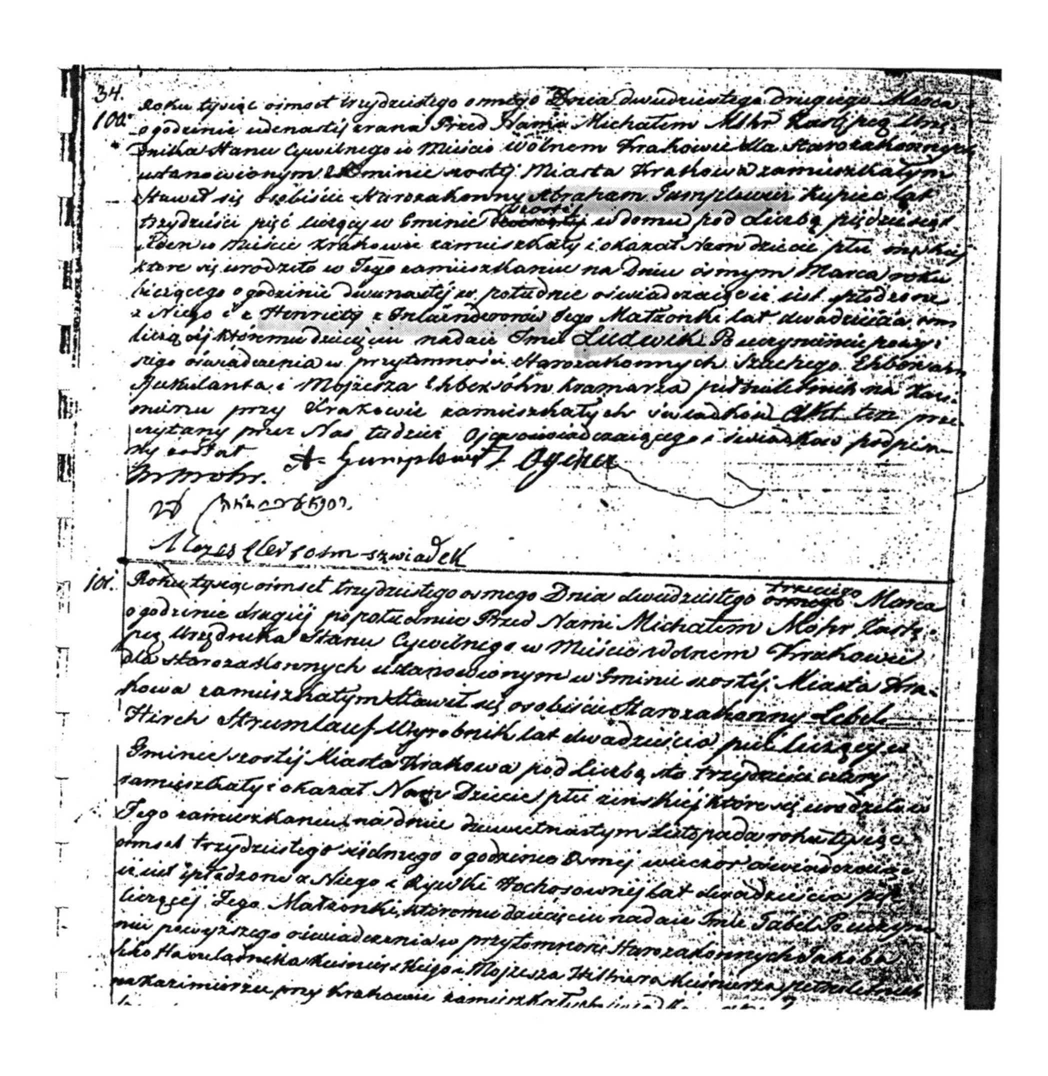

Fig. 019. Birth record of Ludwik Gumplowicz, 1838

BIRTH OF PROFESSOR LUDWIK GUMPLOWICZ – 1838

Document # 100, page 34, Birth Records of Kraków Jews, year 1838:

Roku tysiąc ośmset trzydiestego ósmego Dnia dwudziestego drugiego Marca o godzinie iedenastej zrana Przed Nami Michałem Mohr, zastępcą Urzędnika Stanu Cywilnego w Mieście Wolnem Krakowie dla Starozakonnych ustanowionym w Gminie szóstej Miasta Krakowa zamieszkałym stawił się osobiście Starozakonny Abraham Gumplowicz kupiec, lat trzydieści pięć liczący w Gminie Szóstej w domu pod Liczbą pięćdziesiąt ieden w Mieście Krakowie zamieszkały i okazał Nam dziecię płci męskiej które się urodziło w Jego zamieszkaniu na Dniu ósmym Marca roku bieżącego o godzinie dwunastej w południe oświadcząc iż jest spłodzone z Niego i z Henriety z Inlainderów Jego Małżonki lat dwadzieścia ośm liczącej któremu dzieciąciu nadaie Imię Ludwik. Po uczynieniu powyższego oświadczenia w przytomności Starozakonnych Szachego Ehbersohn spekulanta i Mojżesza Ehbersohn kramarza pełnoletnich na Kazimierzu przy Krakowie zamieszkałych świadków Akt ten przeczytany, przez Nas tudzież Ojca oświadczaiącego i świadków podpisany został.

A. Gumplowicz Oyciec
[Hebrajski podpis]
M. Mohr Mozes Ehbersohn szwiadek

In English:

Year one thousand eight hundred thirty eight on the 22-nd day of March at eleven in the morning before Us, Michał Mohr, Deputy Civil State Clerk appointed for person of the Old Testament in the Free City of Kraków living in the Sixth community of the City of Kraków personally appeared the Old Testamenter Abraham Gumplowicz merchant, thirty five years old, living in the sixth Community in building fifty one and showed us a baby of male gender which was born in his domicile on the eighth day of March of the current year at twelve noon declaring that it was born to him and to Henrieta of the Inlainders his spouse twenty eight years old to whom he gives the name Ludwik. Having made the above declaration in the presence of Old Testamenters Szacha Ehbersohn speculant and Mojżesz Ehbersohn stall keeper adults living in Kazimierz by Kraków as witnesses, and having this act read, it was signed by Us, as well as by the declaring father and witnesses.

A. Gumplowicz, father
[a Hebrew signature]
M. Mohr Mozes Ehbersohn, witness

Chapter 16. Children born to Józef and Dobrysz Aleksandrowicz (1802 – 1827).

As far as I could determine, Joseph and Freindel Dobrysz Aleksandrowicz had five daughters, born in 1805, 1807, 1809, 1811 and 1813. Around 1817 they had a son, Menashe, in 1818 another, Samuel Aron, and in 1821 a third son, Izrael Eliasz. Joseph died aged 44, around 1827. His son, Samuel Aron, died as a six-year old child, in 1824. In 1844 Joseph's first-born son, Menashe Aleksandrowicz, married Lea Katzner and in 1845 he and Lea had a son, my great-grandfather Józef Aleksandrowicz (1845–1940), whom I knew as a child. In 1847 Menashe and Lea had another son, David, who died as a baby, in 1849 a son, Feibus, who later adopted the name Filip, and in 1852 a fourth son, Wolf. In 1854 a Jacob Aleksandrowicz was born in Kraków but the records are not clear if he, too, was a child of Menashe and Lea.

In 1846, a brief revolt of Polish aristocrats and urban patriots in Kraków was suppressed by the Austrians, who then incorporated the Kraków Republic into the Habsburg Kingdom of Galitzia and Lodomeria. Two years later, in 1848, a general discontent all over Europe erupted in almost simultaneous popular uprisings, which broke out in Paris, and spread to Rome, Berlin, Vienna, Budapest as well as Kraków. Vienna was subdued after bombardment by the imperial Habsburg army under General Count Windischgraetz, Kraków gave up after bombardment by the imperial army under General Castiglione. When a second uprising took place in Vienna, the Emperor resigned and 18-year-old Franz Joseph of Habsburg became Emperor of Austria. Franz Joseph ruled for many years (until 1916). He eventually learned how to compromise with his restive subjects, pacified most of his political opponents, instituted liberal reforms, satisfied Hungarian patriots with a far-reaching autonomy and became a constitutional ruler. In the end, he was well liked by his subjects.

I have not been able to find out when Dobrysz Aleksandrowicz, nee Gumplowicz, died. She is listed in the census of 1847 as living with her son, Manasse Aleksandrowicz, in Apartment 2 in Building 203, in District 11 of Kraków. In that census, she has given her year of birth as 1790, making her 57 years old, although if she were born in 1784, as shown in a predominance of existing records, she was really 63. After that, the trail grows cold. I found no further documents listing Dobrysz Aleksandrowicz. Inasmuch as most of Kraków Jewish tombstones as well as funeral and cemetery records were destroyed by the Nazis, it is unlikely that any Jewish records of Freindel Dobrysz Aleksandrowicz, daughter of Jacob Gumplowicz, and great-grandmother of the Aleksandrowicz clan of Kraków, Poland, will be found. Her name does not appear in any civil death records that I have been able to examine, but I understand that there exists somewhere a mention of the death of a Dobrisch Aleksandrowicz dated 1871, at which time Dobrysz, wife of Joseph, would have been 87 years old.

It appears that Joseph and Dobrysz had a nephew, son of Joseph‘s brother Kalman, Moyżesz (Moses), born around 1790, but he appeared only in later Kraków records, including a listing of members of the Jewish municipal guard in 1831, and no record of his birth was found. In 1821 Moses Alexander married Ester Wolfówna Frager. He died in 1852. It appears that a daughter of Joseph and Feigle (Dobrysz), Scheindel, was born in 1805; as recorded in birth records for that year. As mentioned above, the next child, Temerle Aleksandrowicz, was listed in the 1807 record of births as a daughter of Joseph "Alexa..." and Freindel. There is no doubt that "Alexa..." stood for Alexander and later Aleksandrowicz, because Temerle was later recorded in the volume listing marriages for 1827, as Tamerl Aleksandrowiczówna (i.e. Miss Tamerl Aleksandrowicz). We know that Rivka Aleksandrowicz was born in 1809, Gele, daughter of Joseph Alexander and "Doba of the Jacobs", was born in 1811 and daughter Hana was born in 1813.

A son, Menashe, was born around 1817, I have more to say about him in the next chapter. The next child of Joseph and Dobrysz, a boy named Samuel Aron, was born on July 23, 1818. He was the first one to be listed in official records as a son of ‚Józef Aleksandrowicz‘, not of ‚Joseph Alexander‘. I wonder if Joseph named this child Samuel because he was aware of having had an ancestor, Dr. Samuel Aron ben Baruch Aleksandrowicz, in the 17-th century. Little Samuel Aron died in 1824. Finally, in 1821 Joseph and Dobresz had another surviving son, whom they named Izrael Eliasz.

Thus, Joseph Aleksandrowicz, born in 1783, was a progenitor of a large Kraków family, his daughters married well, his sons had many children. His grandson Menashe started three current branches of the Aleksandrowicz clan. While a number of their descendants died in the Holocaust, the others, with one exception, left Kraków and live today dispersed all over the world, primarily in the USA and Israel. When Joseph was born, Poland was still an independent country, a crowned republic of nobles, subject to repeated invasions by neighboring autocracies. The First Partition of Poland created a demand for major changes in the country's governance. A reformist parliament sat for an unprecedented four years, 1788-1792. On the 3-rd of May 1791 it produced a remarkable liberal constitution, promising freedom to serfs and emancipation to Jews. In 1793 Louis XVI and Marie Antoinette, the latter one of many daughters of the Austrian Empress Maria Teresa, were executed. In 1794 a Polish hero of the American Revolution, Tadeusz Kościuszko, led a national Polish insurrection against Russian invaders, beginning with an Oath on the Main Market Square in Kraków. Kościuszko recruited a Jewish battalion commanded by Berek Joselewicz. I mentioned before an old family story that our ancestor Joseph Aleksandrowicz was a soldier in Joselewicz's battalion.

In 1802 Józef married Freindel Dobrysz in Kraków. In 1807, a few months before the birth of their second daughter Temerle, Napoleon Bonaparte met Tsar Alexander at Tilsit, then created the Duchy of Warsaw consisting of lands which Prussia took from Poland in the partitions. In 1809, after defeating the Austrians at Wagram, Napoleon added the Kraków region to the Varsovian Duchy. Józef and Dobrysz's daughters, Rebecca (Rivka and Gele were born in the Varsovian Duchy. A disastrous 1812-1813 Moscow Campaign ended the Napoleonic era. Berek Joselewicz died in battle in 1809. The Commander-in-Chief of Polish Army who also became a Marshal of France, Count Józef Poniatowski, died at the battle of Leipzig in Saxony in 1813, the year Hana Aleksandrowicz was born. In 1815 at the Congress of Vienna, the victorious Russians took most of Poland with the Tsar as ruler of the so-called Congress Kingdom. Because the Austrians would not let the Tsar take Kraków, the latter became a city-state, the "Free, Independent, and Strictly Neutral Kraków Republic". It remained a free city until 1846, when it was again taken over by Austria. Menashe Aleksandrowicz in 1817, Samuel Aron in 1818 and Israel Eliasz Aleksandrowicz in 1821 were born in the new Kraków Republic. Józef died before 1827, the year his daughter Temerle married Moses Hercig (Hertzog). Menashe was then 10 years old. In 1845 Menashe named his first born, my great-grandfather, Józef, after his father. I knew this latter Józef, my great-grandfather born in 1845, personally in Kraków in 1935. He was then 90 and I was 10.

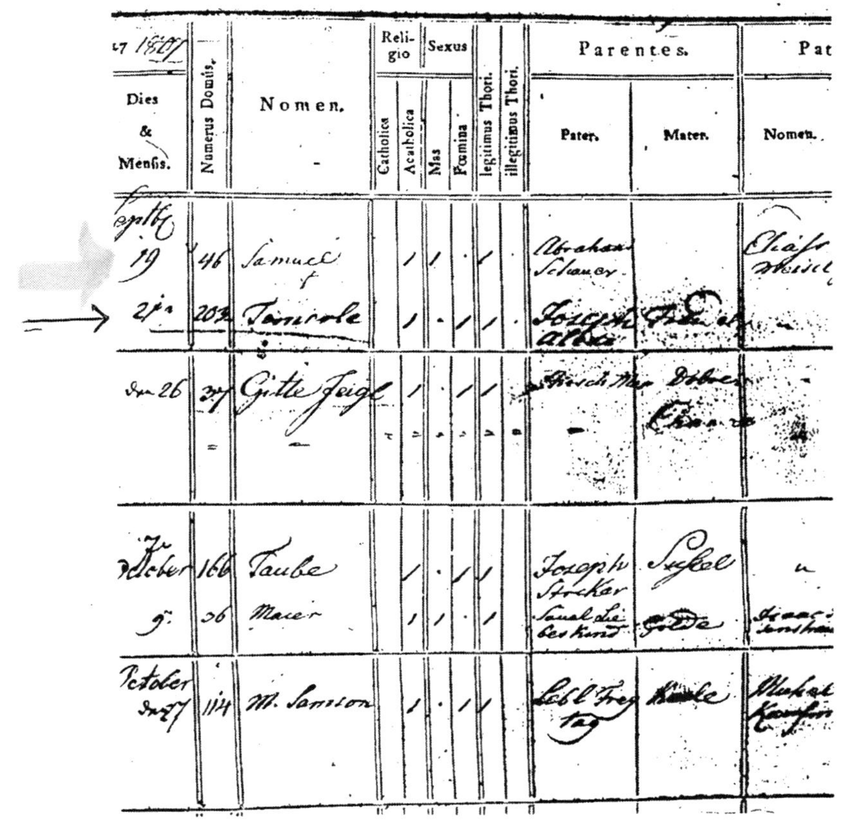

1807 Dies & Mensis	Numerus Domus	Nomen	Religio: Catholica	Religio: Acatholica	Sexus: Mas	Sexus: Foemina	legitimus Thori	illegitimus Thori	Parentes: Pater	Parentes: Mater	Pat… Nomen
Septbr 19	46	Samuel		/	/		/		Abraham Schauer		[illegible]
21	203	Temerle		/		/	/		Joseph Alexander	[illegible]	[illegible]
Dec 26	37	Gitte Feigl		/		/	/		[illegible]	Dobrysz [illegible]	[illegible]
October 7	166	Taube		/		/	/		Joseph Stricker	Sichel	
9	36	Maier		/	/		/		Samuel Liebeskind	Golde	[illegible]
October 27	114	M. Samson		/		/	/		Leibl Freytag	[illegible]	[illegible]

Fig. 020. Birth certificate of Temerle Aleksandrowicz, 1807

BIRTH OF TEMERLE ALEKSANDROWICZ – SEPTEMBER 24, 1807

In the book recording births of Jewish children in Kraków / Kazimierz, available in the Polish National Archives branch in Kraków, under the Year 1807, folio 149, there is a notice of birth of Temerle, non-catholic female, legitimate daughter of "Joseph Alexa..." and Freindel (?), his spouse:

1807

Day/mo.	House number	Name	Religion Cath.	Religion Non	Sex M	Sex F	Legit?	Parents Father	Parents Mother	Witnesses Name
Sept 24	**203**	**Temerle**		x		x	yes	**Joseph Alexa...**	**Freindel**	

The appearance of the abbreviated name "Alexa..." is the first time that the official records in Kraków show the family surname as a surname. That "Alexa..." was meant to indicate Alexander or Alexandrowicz, used interchangeably, is confirmed by the fact that at her wedding in 1827, the same young woman was referred to as Tamerl Alexander in the index and as Tamerl Alexandrowicz in the full-page marriage record. Obviously, the term Alexandrowicz, later Polonized to Aleksandrowicz, was used at first only as a patronymic and indication of origin, implying "of the family of Alexander", and only gradually became accepted as a surname.

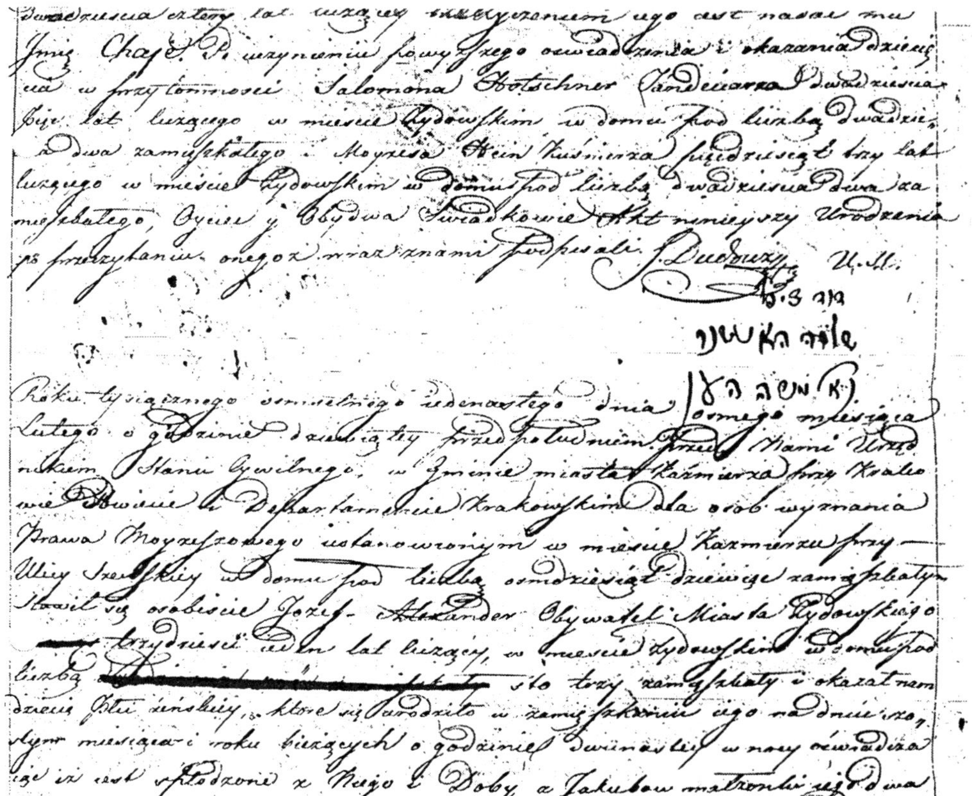

dwadzieścia cztery lat liczący, a życzeniem jego jest nadać mu
Imię Chaje. Po uczynieniu powyższego oświadczenia i okazania dziecięcia w przytomności Salomona Hotschner Kandelarza dwadzieścia
pięć lat liczącego w mieście Żydowskim w domu pod liczbą dwadzieścia dwa zamieszkałego i Moyżesza Hein kuśnierza pięćdziesiąt trzy lat
liczącego w mieście Żydowskim w domu pod liczbą dwadzieścia dwa zamieszkałego, Ojciec y Obydwa Świadkowie Akt niniejszy Urodzenia
po przeczytaniu onegoż wraz z nami podpisali. J. Duczuży U.M.

שלמה האטשנר

משה הײן

Roku tysiącznego ośmsetnego jedenastego dnia ósmego miesiąca
Lutego o godzinie dziewiątej przedpołudniem. Przed Nami Urzędnikiem Stanu Cywilnego, w Gminie miasta Kazimierza przy Krakowie Powiecie i Departamencie Krakowskim dla osób wyznania
Prawa Moyżeszowego ustanowionym w mieście Kazimierzu przy
Ulicy Szerokiej w domu pod liczbą osiemdziesiąt dziewięć zamieszkałym
Stawił się osobiście Józef Alexander Obywatel Miasta Żydowskiego
trzydzieści jeden lat liczący, w mieście Żydowskim w domu pod
liczbą sto trzy zamieszkały i okazał nam
dziecię płci żeńskiej, które się narodziło w zamieszkaniu jego na dniu szóstym miesiąca i roku bieżących o godzinie dwunastej w nocy oświadczając
iże iż jest spłodzone z Niego i Doby a Jakubów małżonki jego dwadzieścia sześć lat liczącej, i że życzeniem jego jest nadać mu
Imię Gele. Po uczynieniu powyższego oświadczenia i okazania dziecięcia w przytomności Świadków Moyżesza Teufel faktora trzydzieści jeden
lat liczącego w mieście Żydowskim pod liczbą dziesięć zamieszkałego i
Leibel Salafgut faktora czterdzieści lat liczącego w mieście Kazimierzu pod liczbą sto dziewięć zamieszkałego, Ojciec i Obydwa świadkowie
Akt niniejszy Urodzenia po przeczytaniu onegoż z nami podpisali.

Joseph Alexander

J. Duczuży

page 18 a 120

Fig. 021. Birth record of Gele Alexander, Kraków-Kazimierz, 1811

1811 – BIRTH RECORD OF GELE ALEXANDER – KRAKÓW / KAZIMIERZ

(Akty Urodzenia Osób Wyznania Moyżeszowego w Miescie Kazimierzu, 1811, str. 18).

Roku tysiącznego omsetnego iedenastego dnia ósmego miesiąca Lutego o godzinie dziesiątey przed południem przed Nami Urzędnikiem Stanu Cywilnego w Gminie miasta Kazimierza przy Krakowie w powiecie i Departamencie Krakowskim dla osób wyznania Prawa Moyżeszowego ustanowionym, w mieście Kazimierzu przy Ulicy Szewskiej w domu pod liczbą ośmdziesiąt dziewięć zamieszkałym, stawił się osobiście Józef Alexander, Obywatel Miasta Żydowskiego trzydzieści ieden lat liczący, w mieście Żydowskim w domu pod liczbą xxxxxxxx sto trzy zamieszkały i okazał Nam dziecię płci żenskiey, które się urodziło w zamieszkaniu iego na dniu szóstym miesiąca i roku bieżących o godzinie dwunastey w nocy, oświadczaiąc iż iest spłodzone z Niego i Doby z Jacobów małżonki iego dwadzieścia sześć lat liczącey, xxxx i że życzeniem iego iest nadać mu Imie **Gele.** Po uczynieniu powyższego oświadczenia i okazania dziecięcia w przytomności Swiadków Moyżesza Teufel faktora trzydzieści ieden lat liczącego w mieście Żydowskim pod liczbą diesięc zamieszkałego i Leibel Szlafgut faktora czterdzieści lat liczącego w mieście Kazimierzu pod liczbą sto dziewięć zamieszkałego, Oyciec i Obydwa świadkowie Akt ninieiszy urodzenia po przeczytaniu onegoż z nami podpisali

S. Dudzicz UST Joseph Alexander
(dwa hebrajskie podpisy)

(Index of births of persons of Mosaic Faith in the Town Kazimierz; Year 1811, p.18)

In the year one thousand eight hundred and eleven, on eighth day of the month of February at ten o‘clock in the morning appeared before Us, Civil State Clerk in the Community of the town of Kazimierz by Krakow, in the Krakow district and department, appointed for persons of Mosaic Faith living on Szewska Street in house number 89, personally appeared Jozef Alexander, citizen of the Jewish Town, thirty one years old, living in the Jewish Town house number xxxxxx one hundred and three and showed Us a baby of female sex, who was born in his domicile on the sixth day of the current month and year at 12 o‘clock at night, declaring that it was born to him and Doba of the Jacobs, his spouse, twenty six years old, xxx and that it is his wish to give it the name **Gela.** Having made the above announcement and presenting the baby in the presence of witnesses Moyzesz Teufel, factor, thirty one years old, living in Jewish Town in house number ten and Leibel Szlafgut, factor, forty years old, living in the Jewish Town in building number one hundred and nine, Father and both witnesses signed this Birth Document after reading it with us.

S. Dudzicz CSC Joseph Alexander
(two Hebrew signatures)

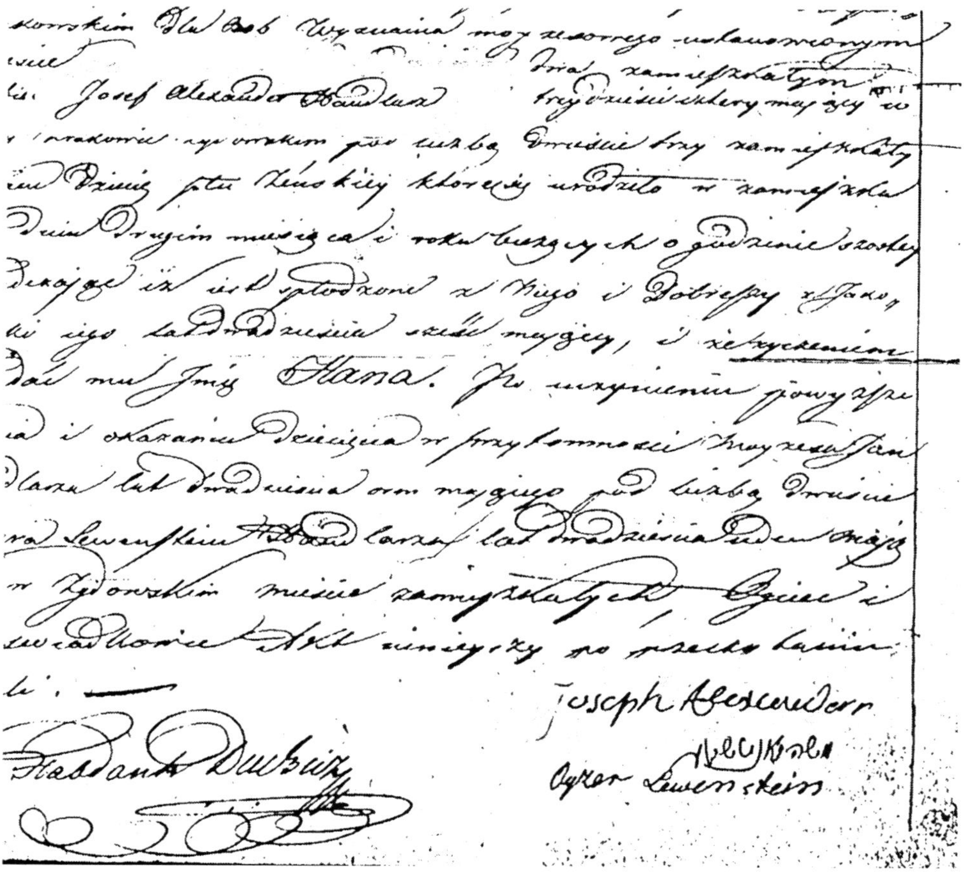

...owskim dla Bob... Wyznania Mojżeszowego ustanowionym
...wie ... Brial zamieszkałym
...li. Josef Alexander Handlarz trzydzieści lat mający w
...Krakowie Żydowskim pod liczbą dwieście trzy zamieszkały
...nam dziecię płci żeńskiej które się urodziło w zamieszkaniu
...dnia drugim miesiąca i roku bieżących o godzinie szóstej
...deklarując iż jest spłodzone z niego i Dobrejszy z Jakow...
...ki jego lat dwadzieścia sześć mającej, i że życzeniem
...dał mu imię Hana. Po uczynieniu powyższe
...a i okazaniu dziecięcia w przytomności Mojżesza Jan...
...dlarza lat dwadzieścia osim mającego pod liczbą dwieście
...ra Lewensteina Handlarza lat dwadzieścia jeden mając
...w Żydowskim mieście zamieszkałych, Ojciec i
...świadkowie akt niniejszy po przeczytaniu ...
...li.

Joseph Alexander

Oyzer Lewenstein

Fig. 022. Birth record of Hana Alexander, 1813

1813- BIRTH RECORD OF HANA ALEXANDER – KRAKÓW / KAZIMIERZ

(Akty Urodzenia Osób Wyznania Moyżeszowego w Mieście Kazimierzu, 1813, str. 3/1)

Roku tysiącznego ośmsetnego trzynastego dnia trzeciego Lutego o godzinie dwunastey w południe przed Nami Stanisławem Habdank Dudziszem Urzędnikiem Stanu Cywilnego w Kazimierzu przy Krakówie w powiecie i Departamencie Krakowskim dla osób wyznania moyżeszowego ustanowionym, i w tymże mieście pod liczbą sto dwadzieścia dwa zamieszkałym, stawił się osobiście **Josef Alexander**, Handlarz, lat trzydzieści cztery maiący, w Kazimierzu żydowskim pod liczbą dwieście trzy zamieszkały i okazał Nam Dziecię Płci żenskiey, które się urodziło w zamieszkaniu iego na dniu drugim miesiąca i roku bieżących o godzinie szóstey rano, oświadczaił iż iest spłodzone z Niego i **Dobryszy z Jacobów** małżonki iego lat dwadzieścia szść maiącey, i że życzeniem iego iest nadać mu Imie **Hana.** Po uczynieniu powyższego oświadczenia i okazaniu dziecięcia w przytomności świadków Moyżesza Kanczotek Handlarza lat dwadzieścia ośm maiącego pod liczbą dwieście cztery i Ozera Lewenstein Handlarza lat dwadzieścia ieden maiącego tamże w żydowskim mieście zamieszkałych, Ojciec i Obydwa świadkowie Akt ninieiszy po przeczytaniu go podpisali.-

Joseph Alexanderr
Stanisław Habdank Dudzicz

(hebrajski podpis)
Oyzer Lewenstein

In the year one thousand eight hundred and thirteen, on third day of February at twelve noon before Us, Stanisław Habdank Dudzicz, Clerk of the Civil Record in Kazimierz by Kraków, in the district and department of Kraków appointed for persons of Mosaic Faith living in same town under number twenty two, appeared personally **Josef Alexander**, Merchant being thirty four years old, living in Kazimierz by Kraków under two hundred and three and showed Us a baby of female gender, which was born in his domicile on the second day of the current month and year at six in the morning, declaring that it was born to him and his wife **Dobrysz of the Jacobs**, twenty six years old, and that it is his wish to give it the name **Hana.** Having stated that and having presented the baby in the presence of witnesses Moses Janczotek, merchant, twenty eight years old, under number two hundred and four, and Ozer Lewenstein, merchant twenty one years old, also living in the Jewish Town, Father and both witnesses after having read it signed this Document.

Joseph Alexanderr
Stanisław Habdank Dudzicz

(one hebrajski podpis)
Oyzer Lewenstein

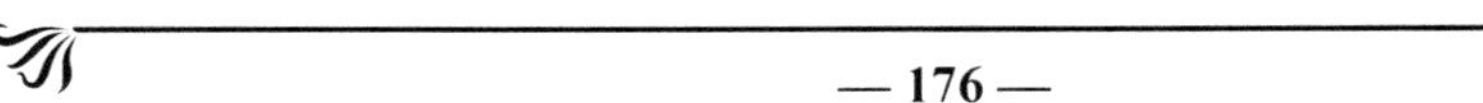

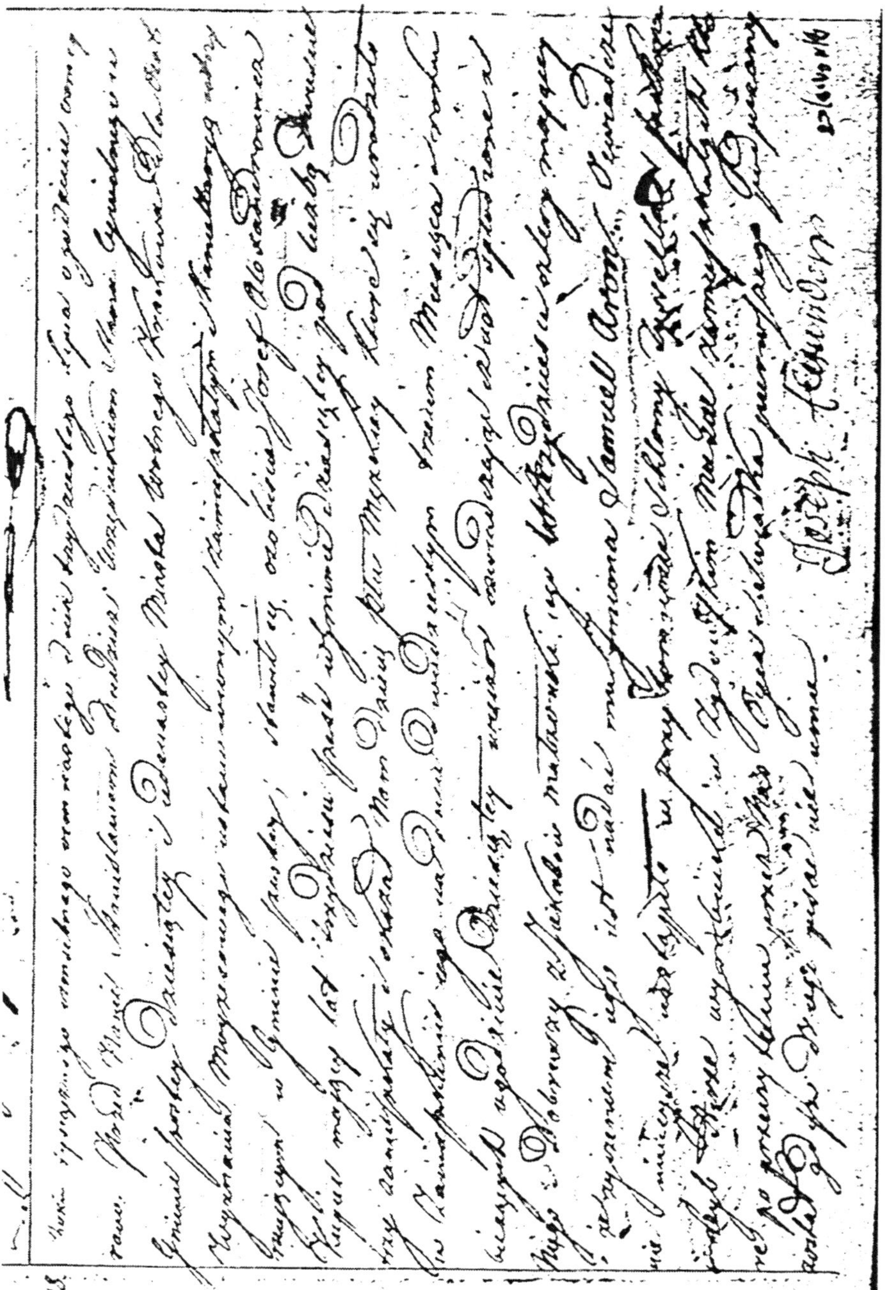

Fig. 023. Birth record of Samuel Aron Aleksandrowicz, 1818

BIRTH OF SAMUEL ARON ALEKSANDROWICZ 1818

Extract from Civil State Records, Year 1818,
Free City of Kraków, page 101, Nr. 207:
In the original Polish:

"Roku tysiąc ośmset osiemnastego trzydziestego lipca o godzinie ósmej rano przed Nami Stanisławem Dudzicz Urzędnikiem Stanu Cywilnego w Gminie Szóstej, dziesiątej i jedenastej Miasta Wolnego Krakowa dla osób Wyznania Mojżeszowego ustanowionym zamieszkałym i Kancelaryę utrzymującym w Gminie szóstej – stawił się osobiście Józef Alexandrowicz, kupiec mający lat trzydzieści sześć w Gminie dziesiątej pod liczbą dwieście trzy zamieszkały – i okazał Nam dziecię płci męskiej które się urodziło w zamieszkaniu iego na dniu dwudziestym trzecim miesiąca i roku bieżących o godzinie dziesiątej wieczór oświadczając iż iest spłodzone z niego i Dobryszy z Jacobów Małżonki iego, lat trzydzieści cztery maiącej, i że życzeniem iego jest nadać mu imiona Samuel Aron – Oświadczenie niniejsze nastąpiło w przytomności Schlomy Tiselobis faktora i Leyb Hirze wyrobnika w żydowskim Mieście zamieszkałych – którzy po przeczytaniu przez Nas ojca i świadka pierwszego podpisany został gdyż drugi pisać nie umie.-

Joseph Alexanderr
Schlomo Tislovis
Stanisław Dudzicz

in English:

Year eighteen hundred eighteen on the thirtieth day of July at eight o'clock in the morning before Us, Stanislaw Dudzisz, Civil Registry Clerk in the sixth, tenth and eleventh district of the Free city of Kraków, appointed for persons of the Mosaic Faith and living and maintaining an Office in District six – personally appeared Jozef Alexandrowicz, merchant, thirty six years old and living in District Ten, building two hundred and tree – and showed Us a baby of male gender which was born in his domicile on the twenty third day of the current month and year at ten o'clock in the evening, declaring that it was born to him and Dobrysz of the Jacobs, his spouse, thirty four years old and that it is his wish to give it names Samuel Aron. This declaration occurred in the presence of Schlomo Tiselobis, merchandise broker, and Leyb Hirze, laborer, living in the Jewish Town – and having been read by Us, has been signed by the father and one witness because the other does not know how to write.

Joseph Alexanderr
Schlomo Tislovis
Stanisław Dudzicz

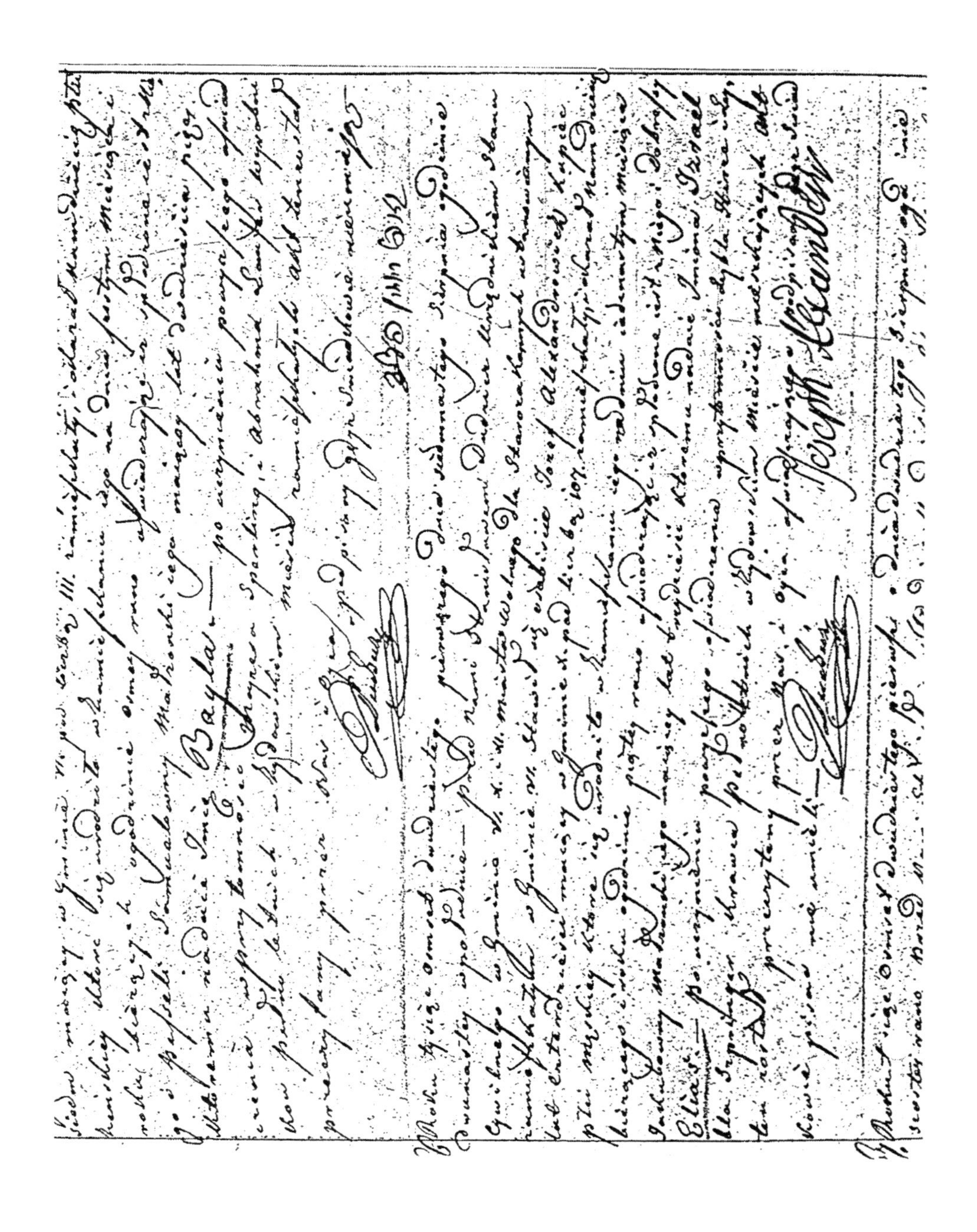

Fig. 024. Birth record of Izrael Elias Alexandrowicz, 1821

1821 – BIRTH CERTIFICATE OF IZRAEL ELIASZ ALEXANDROWICZ

From "Akta Stanu Cywilnego Gminy Starozakonnych na Kazimierzu przy Krakowie, Rok 1821":

Roku tysiąc ośmset dwudziestego pierwszego dnia siedemnastego sierpnia o godzinie dwunastey w południe – przed Nami Stanisławem Dudzicz Urzędnikiem Stanu Cywilnego w Gminie VI, X i XI miasta Wolnego dla Starozakonnych ustanowionym zamieszkałym w Gminie VI stawił się osobiście Józef Alexandrowicz kupiec lat czterdzieści maiący w Gminie X pod liczbą 107 zamieszkały, i okazał Nam dziecię płci męskiey które się urodziło w zamieszkaniu iego na dniu iedenastym miesiąca bieżącego i roku o godzinie piątey rano oświadczając iż spłodzone iest z niego i Dobryszy Jacobowny małżonki iego maiącey lat trzydzieści któremu nadaie Imiona **Izrael Elias**. – Po uczynieniu powyższego oświadczenia w przytomności Leybla Hirze i Leybla Szpringer krawca pełnoletnich w żydowskim Mieście mieszkających Akt ten został przeczytany przez Nas i Oyca oświadzającego podpisany gdyż świadkowie pisać nie umieli -

S.Dudzicz Joseph Alxanderr

In English;

Year one thousand eight hundred twenty first seventeenth day of August at twelve o'clock noon – before Us Stanisław Dudzicz Civil Recording Clerk in Community VI, X and XI of the Free city appointed for people of the Old Covenant living in Community VI, appeared personally Jozef Alexandrowicz, merchant forty years old and showed Us a baby of male gender which was born in his domicile on the eleventh day of current month and year at five o'clock in the morning stating that it was conceived by him and Dorysz Jacobowna his spouse thirty years old whom he gives the names of **Izrael Elias**. – After making this declaration in the presence of Leybl Hirze and Leybl Szpringer tailor adults living in the Jewish Town this Act was read and signed by Us and by the declaring Father because the witnesses could not write -

S. Dudzicz Joseph Alxanderr

Part V. GENERATIONS: THE *ALEKSANDROWICZ* FAMILY OF KRAKOW

Chapter 17. Nineteenth Century : Menashe Aleksandrowicz and his siblings

Menashe Aleksandrowicz was born into a family of girls. At birth he had five sisters. The oldest, Scheindl, was fourteen. Next came Temerl, almost ten, Rivka, eight, Gele six and the youngest, Hana, only four. He was apparently the first boy. When Menashe was one year old, his mother had another child, a second boy named Samuel Aron. When he was four, on August 11, 1821, his mother bore another boy, named Izrael Eliasz. Samuel Aron died when Menashe was seven, in 1824. His father, Joseph, must have died soon after, before Menashe was 10, because the next document in my collection, a record of marriage of his sister, Temerl Aleksandrowicz, in 1827 shows the father as deceased. We know about Menashe's oldest sister, Scheindel, from a vague listing in the Kazimierz birth records for April 14, 1805. She may have died young, because so far, I have not found any further records of her. There may have been an earlier child or children, because the parents were married in 1802, but there are no indications of it in the existing data, as well as of any later children, born after 1821 and before 1827 when Józef died.

My father's namesake, his great-grandfather Menashe Aleksandrowicz, was apparently born in Kraków around 1817. The history of the city of Kraków and its Jewish inhabitants and the history of my family have been intimately intertwined from way back and fully documented since the year 1802, the year of the wedding of Joseph Aleksandrowicz and Freindel Dobrysz Gumplowicz, described in a previous chapter. Józef and Dobrysz were representative of a stratum of Jewish population and can serve as an example of the lives of many of Kraków Jews. Menashe's father was thirty-four at the time, his mother was thirtythree. They lived in the Jewish area of Kazimierz in an appartment in their own house, building # 203. It appears that both his father's and his mother's families were well off, even though the times were difficult, city economy in tatters and diseases rampant. His grandfather on his mother's side, Jacob Gumplowicz, was an important businessman, mentioned in historical sources by name. His paternal grandfather, David, was also well off, but he apparently died young, because in 1806, Joseph, at 23, was listed as the owner of the family building.

I have not been able to find any record of Menashe's birth. However, his existence is well established. There are many official documents, census lists, conscription lists and records of births and marriages of his children in which he is listed, but a certificate of his birth is missing. In 1817 Kraków was in turmoil. The Polish-Napoleonic Warsaw Duchy ceased to exist and Kraków with its immediate vicinity was converted into a small city-state, the last, somewhat free, sliver of Polish territory, dubbed "The Free, Independent and Strictly Neutral Kraków Republic", created at the Congress of Vienna in 1815 by Napoleon's enemies after his defeat. The three autocracies, Austria, Russia and Prussia, after many significant defeats were finally victorious over Napoleon and his Polish supporters. They could not decide who should get Kraków, so they set it up as a weak and poor, purportedly independent city. The free city was governed by a Senate, serving at the pleasure of envoys of the three protecting courts, the Habsburgs of Austria, Romanovs of Russia and Hohenzollerns of Prussia. The city, as well as its Jews, were impoverished because of the preceding political and ideological turmoil and the continuous need to quarter and feed contending armies marching through and occupying the area: French (Napoleon's *Grande Armee*), Polish, and then Russian, Austrian and Prussian. Life in the free city of Kraków was very complicated. Commerce with surrounding areas was restricted. The presiding officer of the governing city Senate, Stanisław Wodzicki, was openly anti-Semitic and hostile to Jews, thus limiting their ability to enrich the city through their commercial activities. At the insistence of the Church and the neighboring autocracies Jews had absolutely no voting rights and all had to live in the narrow confines of the ghetto in Kazimierz. Any privileges that they may have received during the brief Napoleonic interlude were withdrawn. Taxes were heavy and many were imposed exclusively on Jews. In 1818 the Senate abolished the autonomous Jewish Kahał and replaced it with a more restricted *Komitet Starozakonnych* (Committee of the People of the Old Testament), thus introducing to Kraków this overly polite term for Jews, mentioned above. Not trusting the Jews to govern themselves, the Senate required that the Committee have a non-Jewish chairman. In addition, the Committee consisted of the Chief Rabbi of the City and two other members, rich Jewish owners of real estate. Eventually, two more members were added as alternates, who also participated in Committee deliberations. For several years starting in 1823 my relative, Gershon Baum, served as Secretary of the Committee. Gershon's sister, Gitl Baumówna Birnbaum, wife of Saul Birnbaum, was my diect ancestor, grandmother of my grandmother, Hancia Birnbaum Aleksandrowicz.

The next sibling, Temerle Aleksandrowicz, was listed in the 1807 record of births as a daughter of Joseph "Alexa..." and Freindel. She was born Sept. 21, 1807. There is no doubt that "Alexa.." stood for Alexander and later Aleksandrowicz, because Temerle was later recorded on December 18, 1827 as marrying Mojżesz Hercig (Moses Hertzog?), son of Hersh and Rivka Hercig, living in building No. 8 in Kazimierz. In the wedding announcement page she was listed as Tamerl Aleksandrowiczówna (i.e. Miss Tamerl Aleksandrowicz), living in building 203, daughter of the late Josel Aleksandrowicz and Dobresz z Jakubów). In the index to the 1827 volume of marriages, page 49, she was listed as Temerel Alexander, indicating that either or Alexander or Aleksandrowicz was then acceptable as a surname. In the wedding announcement she was recorded as having

been a maiden, living until then with her widowed mother, Freindel Dobrysz, in Building 203 of the Eleventh District of Kraków. It is obvious from that document and others about the surname of the groom, that at the time there were no firm rules about spelling. Jewish names were arbitrarily transliterated from Hebrew. In later documents, the groom's name was written as Hercog, and later as, the more modern sounding, Hertzog. According to later records, Temerl Hertzog, nee Aleksandrowicz, died in 1877.

We know that the next of Menashe's sisters, Rivka (Rebecca) Aleksandrowicz was born in 1809, but the book listing the entire Kraków Jewish records for most of 1809 and 1810 is missing from the Kraków archives. We know of her existence thanks to a record of her second marriage. As mentioned earlier, Rivka had a complicated existence: sometimes prior to 1830 she married Michael Polner, who died soon after. In 1831 she was recorded as a young widow living with her widowed mother in Building 203. On March 11, 1831, at the young age of 22, she re-married to one Fayvel Orgler, son of Schachna Orgler and Rachel, daughter of Chaim, living in building 128 in Kazimierz. Schachna Orgler owned a tavern in Kraków, serving liquor. The groom was 25 and was listed as a bookbinder. Rivka was listed as the "daughter of the late Josel Aleksandrowicz and Dobress of the Gomplowicz, his spouse and now widow, living in building 203". In 1832 Feivel and Rivka had a son, David Orgler (listing # 150), in 1836 another son, Jacob and in 1838 Gimpel (!). They may have had other children but the records I could find list only those few. In 1844 there was a listing of a "Rebeka Orgler" who died (# 109). Rivka would not have given her own name to a newborn, hence, I assume that it was Rivka Orgler, nee Aleksandrowicz, who died in 1844 at the age of 35, perhaps in childbirth.

Gele, daughter of Joseph Alexander and "Doba of the Jacobs", was born on February 6, 1811. As recorded in Kraków the number of the building in which she was born has been written in, then crossed out, then written in again as # 103. Given the fact that in all other documents, before and after, the building was # 203, I assume that this was a mistake by the clerk, and that the family continued to live in building 203. Gele married Herschel Freifelt (Griffel?) in 1837. The Freifelt name appears many times in the records; Hirsch (Herschel) Freifelt served frequently as a witness in births, weddings, etc. as shown in documents recording assorted events from this period.

On February 2, 1813 Joseph Alexander and "Dobresz of the Jacobs" had a daughter, Hana, also born in building 203. No record of her marriage has been found, but this Hana had been married to a man named Hirsz (Tsvi) Moyzinger in 1845, when the birth of their son Manele has been recorded. She had several more children in Kraków, including a girl named Marya, who died as a child. Marya's birth record confirms that her mother Hana, was born Miss Aleksandrowicz (see Marya's birth and death records below). It appears that two of Hana's children, grandsons of Joseph and Dobrysz Aleksandrowicz, eventually emigrated to America. I understand that one of them lived in St. Louis, the other in Vicksburg on the Mississippi. The origin of the name Moyzinger or Mossinger is uncertain, but as mentioned earlier a possibility has been broached, based on housing records and a death record of Getzel Mossinger in 1816, that Hirsz was a grandson of Moses Braciejówka, important merchant mentioned earlier as a Kahał senior.

It appears from an 1844 record of his wedding as well as later records of his children that Menashe, son of Joseph and Dobrysz, was born around 1817. Thus, at the age of 25, on June 13, 1844, "Manasses, son of the late Józef, owner of a building in

Kazimierz, and Dobresz, his wife and currently widow, spouses Aleksandrowicz, living in building 203", married "Lea Katznerówna, [*i.e. Miss Katzner*], age 28, daughter of Wolff and Małka, spouses Katzner, merchants living in the 10-th district [*Kazimierz*], building 18". In this document, Lea is shown as being three years older than her husband. Menashe and Lea had at least four sons, Józef, David, Filip and Wolf (Zeev). His eldest, Józef, was my great-grandfather. This Józef was born on April 6, 1845. In the record of Józef's birth, Menashe was listed as being 28 years old, but interestingly so was his wife, Lea nee Katzner, also listed as being 28. In their wedding announcement she was 3 years older than her husband, but she managed to shed those three years in the intervening 10 months. In the listing of the birth of Józef, Manasses Aleksandrowicz was described as "a writer of the lottery office" (*pisarz kantoru loteryi*), living in building 203. This second Józef, born in 1845, named after his grandfather, died of natural causes in 1940. As a child in Kraków I knew him as an old man.

The next child of Joseph and Dobrysz, a boy named Samuel Aron, was born on July 23, 1818. He was the first one to be inscribed in official records as a son of ‚Józef Alexandrowicz', not of ‚Joseph Alexander'. I wonder if Joseph named this child Samuel because he was aware of having had an ancestor, Dr. Samuel ben Baruch Aleksandrowicz, in the 17-th century. Little Samuel Aron died in 1824, at the age of 6.

Finally, on August 11, 1821 Joseph Aleksandrowicz and Dobresz Jacobowna had another son, whom they named Izrael Elias. Izrael Elias married Ester Lack, daughter of Leib (Lebl), as shown in the 1848 certificate of the birth of their son, also named Józef after the grandfather. That baby Józef died young. Izrael Elias had at least five other children, probably more. One of his sons was Nachman, living in building 203. Nachman Aleksandrowicz married Liba Herzog. Near the entrance to the Cemetery on Miodowa Street stands today a large impressive tombstone of Nachman Aleksandrowicz.

I have previously indicated a complex web of relationships between Kraków Jewish families around the year 1800, as seen in the listing of wedding guests in 1802. At any given time, at least three generations of any family are likely to have existed at the same time. The couple married in 1802 seems to have had at least six surviving children. It is likely that they had more children, but child mortality was obviously very high and I found hard evidence for survival of only six. The next generation, assuming that they all married and continued to live in Kraków and had a similar number of surviving children, would number thirty six, not counting their grandparents. In one more generation the number would reach two hundred and sixteen. With spouses, the number would be double. Thus, the total for three generations of the Aleksandrowicz family would have been at least 600, and they would have been related to a large number of other families. Between the Aleksandrowicz and Gumplowicz families I have listed at least 12 surnames of relatives by marriage. If these twelve families behaved similarly, the number of third generation relatives living in the Jewish Town in Kazimierz by Kraków, not counting spouses, would have been at least 3,048. According to Małecki (Bieniarzówna and Małecki, 1979), in 1804 Kraków had 4,300 Jews, in 1815 4,862. My relatives obviously constituted a significant portion of that total. Increasing with time, not quite in a geometric progression, the number of Kraków Jews rose by 1835 to 10,952, representing 30.4% of the total population of 36,027. In 1850 the Jewish population of Kraków, 13,425, constituted 33.8% of the total number of inhabitants. In 1939, after three or four more generations, the number of Jews

in Kraków was approximately 60,000, in a total population of 240,000. A large number of these must have been descendants of my relatives.

The Jewish Town was very crowded. Life was not easy. Almost everything that a family needed had to be brought in from the outside. The area was walled in, passage through the gates was restricted so that fees could be collected when bringing merchandise or foodstuffs into the Ghetto. Rich men in the Ghetto paid annual fees for monopoly rights to bring in alcohol, cattle, poultry, flour, as well as leather, cloth, notions (Nurnberger wares), etc. They also paid for monopoly right to collect city taxes, including *podymne* (per chimney), *świeczkowe* (for the right to light candles), *czopowe* (general tax to the city) and others. The chimney tax was unfair, the Jews were taxed at a higher rate that Christians for comparable houses. The right to slaughter cattle for kosher meat and to sell such kosher meat was vested exclusively in Ber Luxenburg, owner of many houses in the Ghetto. Luxenburg collected that tax ruthlessly for many years until 1823 and paid a fee to the *Komitet Starozakonnych* for the right. That fee helped support the committee's activities. In 1818 the right to collect the city "*czopowe*" tax was vested in Hirsch Neuman and Józef Bader who paid the huge annual sum of 30,000 Polish złotys for it. Józef Bader was the father of Henna who married Shaya Drezner. Shaya Drezner and Henna nee Bader were the parents of two of my great-grandmothers, Rachel Drezner Aleksandrowicz and Małka Drezner Birnbaum.

In November 1830, when Menashe was about thirteen, a Polish insurrection broke out in Warsaw, the capital of a rump Polish Kingdom of which the Russian Tsar was King. The army of that kingdom rebelled against its Russian overlords and the local *namiestnik* (governor, vice-roy), the tsar's brother, the Grand Duke Konstantin Romanov. Among the leaders of this so-called "November Insurrection" was General Ignacy Ledóchowski, a relative of the Counts Aleksandrowicz. The insurrection had no chance of success against the powerful Russian forces, but it temporarily liberated Warsaw and caused unrest in other parts of Poland, including Kraków. Support for the Polish patriots was also voiced in Western Europe. In Kraków lots of help was sent to Warsaw. Insurrection leaders asked that the city remain neutral and thus able to serve as a conduit of supplies. To protect the city, a Civil Guard was created, including a number of Jews. According to Bałaban, among its Jewish members were Menashe's cousins Moses Alexander and Ruben Pitzele. Also in 1830 a revolution broke out in Paris ousting the Bourbon King and replacing him with a cousin, Louis Philippe of the Bourbon-Orleans branch of the family.

In 1830-1831 a severe cholera epidemic broke out in Kraków. The crowded and unhygienic Jewish Ghetto suffered terribly. According to Bałaban (II, 617) of 1,464 deaths in Kraków, 591 were in the Jewish Town. One can surmise that Michael Polner, the first husband of Menashe's sister Rivka Aleksandrowicz, who died so very young, succumbed to this cholera epidemic, raging through Kraków and its Jewish Town. In 1832 the Chief Rabbi of Kraków died and a fight broke out among the contenders for the position. The ultra-orthodox residents supported Saul Rafał Landau (Reb Shioel), while the more moderate elements offered the nomination to Dov Ber Meisels (1798-1870), who played a large role in subsequent history as a Polish patriot and a member of the Austrian revolutionary parliament in Krems (Kromeriz) in 1848. Meisels became "acting" rabbi and retained the Chief Rabbi's position until his resignation in 1856. To this day there is a street in Kazimierz named after Rabbi Meisels. In 1835 a great celestial spectacle was visible at night over

Kraków, when Halley's comet appeared in the night sky. In 1843 Abraham Gumplowicz, a cousin of Menashe Aleksandrowicz and a vocal supporter of reform Judaism, founded a civic association, which built the Kraków reform synagogue, called the Tempel. This Tempel has great acoustic resonance and has recently been renovated. During our visit to Kraków in 1997, we heard a concert there.

On Sunday March 3, 1844 at noon, in front of the main entrance to the Government Office of the Second District of Kraków, Franciszek Gawroński, the Civil State Clerk "appointed to keep records of people of Mosaic Faith", publicly announced for the first time the bans, i.e. "a promise to join in marriage [by] an Old Covenanter (*Starozakonny*) Manasses Aleksandrowicz, bachelor, youth of twenty five, son of the late Józef, owner of a building in Kazimierz, already deceased, and of Dobresz, his wife, now living, widow, spouses Aleksandrowicz, residing with his mother in Building 203 *on one side* and Lea Katzner, unmarried, maiden, twenty eight years old, daughter of Wolff and Malka, spouses Katzner, merchants, residing with her parents in Building 18 *on the other side*". The obligatory second public announcement took place the next Sunday, March 10, 1844. There being no objections, the wedding took place on June 13, 1844 (see end of chapter).

Menashe and Lea had four sons, maybe five or even more. The oldest, Józef, was born on April 6, 1845. David, born in 1847, died as an infant. Feibush (Filip) was born on February 26, 1849 and Wolf was born in 1852. These three sons married and became the founding fathers of three branches of the Aleksandrowicz family that I knew as a child in Kraków. The birth record of the first, my great-grandfather Jozef, shows that his father was employed as a writer or broker in a "Lottery Bureau". Józef and his wife, Rachel nee Drezner, will be described below, as will Józef's brothers, Filip and Wolf and their families. Also described later will be Józef's son, my grandfather, Jacob, followed by descriptions of Jacob's children.

In 1846 another Polish insurrection broke out, this time in the supposedly free city/state of Kraków and the surrounding Galitzian countryside, confined largely to the sophisticated urban population and the country squires and aristocrats, newly aware of their nascent Polish nationalism. A revolutionary government was established. On 23 February 1846 it issued an "Appeal to Brothers Israelites" asking them to join the insurrection and offering them full citizenship and all human rights. There is no indication that Menashe Aleksandrowicz, then a newly-wed with a ten-month old baby, responded in any way to this appeal. The insurrection did not last. Austria's wily Chancellor, Prince Klemens Metternich, stirred Polish peasants against Polish aristocrats with the result that all over the area peasants rebelled against nobility and burned manor houses. The armies of all three surrounding autocracies entered Kraków and, to avoid any further Polish patriotic activities in Kraków, abolished the autonomous Kraków Republic. Kraków was joined to the Austrian Kingdom of Galitzia and Lodomeria. Two years later, Vienna erupted twice in demonstrations, which eventually led to the formation of the Austro-Hungarian Dual Monarchy, to Toleranz-Patent of 1867 and to unification of Italy under King Victor Emmanuel of Savoy.

In 1851 in distant America *The New York Times* began publication. Menashe Aleksandrowicz could not have predicted that his descendants will one day read it every day. In 1864 the *Neue Freie Presse* began publishing in Vienna. Menashe's son, Józef, continued to read it until Hitler came to Vienna in 1938. In the census of 1881, Menashe

was listed as a widower. He lived to see his first grandson, Jacob Aleksandrowicz, who was born in 1866 to his oldest son Józef, and many other grandchildren. Menashe's death certificate is missing, but after the turn of the century Menashe's grandson Jacob gave his fourth son, born in 1902, the Hebrew name Menashe, which he would not have done had Menashe been still alive. Thus, Menashe ben Josel ha-Kohen must have died before 1902. His namesake and great-grandson, Menashe ben Yakov ha-Kohen, was my father.

Fig. 025. Wedding of Temerle Aleksandrowiczówna and Moses Hercig – 1827

WEDDING OF TEMERLE ALEKSANDROWICZ AND MOSES HERCIG – 1827

Roku tysiąc ośmset dwudziestego siódmego dnia ośmnastego miesiąca grudnia o godzinie dziesiątey przed południem w domu gminnym w Krakowie przy ulicy Grodzkiey pod liczbą dwadzieścia dziewięć stoiącym, przed Nami Szymonem Józefem Białeckim, zastepcą Urzędnika Stanu Cywilnego w mieście wolnem Krakówie dla Starozakonnych ustanowionem, tudzież Woytem Gminy pirwszey Miasta Wolnego Krakowa, stawił się osobiście Starozakonny Moyżesz Hercig, młodzian lat dziewiętnaście maiący skończone co Metryką urodzenia z Ksiąg Urzędu Stanu Cywilnego w Sądzie pokoyu Wolnego Miasta Krakowa okręgu drugiego za byłego Cesarsko-Austryjackiego rządu przy Kahałe i Synagodze Kazimierskiey utrzymywaney wypisaney dowodzi **Allegat 1** Syn Starozakonnego Herszka i Rywki Hercigów małżonków żyjących w Krakówie na Kazimierzu w Gminie Iedenastey pod liczbą ośm zamieszkałych w ich Assystencyi i upoważnieniu xxxxx strona iedna. Stawiła się także Starozakonna Tamerle Aleksandrowiczówna stanu wolnego panna lat dwadzieścia maiąca, to metryką urodzin z Ksiąg Urzędu Stanu Cywilnego w Sądzie Pokoyu Wolnego miasta Krakowa okręgu drugiego za byłego Cesarsko Austryjackiego Rządu, przy Kahałe I Synagodze Kazimierskiey utrzymywaney wypisaney dowodzi **Allegat # 2.** Córka starozakonnego Josela Aleksandrowicza oyca już zmarłego to odpisem metrykalnym z Ksiąg Urzędnika Stanu Cywilnego w mieście Wolnem Krakówie wypisanym dowodzi **Allegat 3** i Freindli Dobrysz matki żyiącey tu w Krakowie na Kazimierzu w Gminie iedenastey pod liczbą dwieście trzy zamieszkałey w iey Assystencyi i upoważnieniu xxxxx strona druga. Strony stawiaiące okazawszy Nam Konsens na zawarcie Związku pomiędzy sobą Małżeństwa, przez Wóyta Gminy iedenastey Wolnego Miasta Krakowa na dniu dziesiątego Listopada tysiąc ośmset dwudziestego siódmego roku wydanym **Allegat 4** Żądaiąc abyśmy przystąpili do obchodu ułożonego pomiędzy niemi małżeństwa którego zapowiedzi wyszły w Krakówie przed głównemi drzwiami domu naszego Gminnego na to przeznaczonego pierwsza dnia ośmnastego a druga dnia dwudziestego piątego Listopada. Gdy żadne tamowanie przeciw żeczonemu małżeństwu nie zaszło, a asystuiący rodzice Aktem ninieyszym na obchód iego zezwalaią, Zaczem My przeyąwszy wzwyż wymienione Akta z których ocenia iż wszystkie formalności iakie Prawo wymaga zachowane zostały przychylaiąc się do mienionego Małżeństwa po przeczytaniu stronom i świadkom wzwyż wymienionych dowodów iako też działu szóstego Kodeksa Cywilnego w tytule o małżeństwie zapytaliśmy przyszłego małżonka i przyszłey małżonki czyli chcą się z sobą połączyć węzłem małżeńskim na co każde z nich oddzielnie odpowiedziało Iż taka iest ich wola Ogłaszamy w Imieniu Prawa iż Starozakonny Moyżesz Hercig i Tamerle Aleksandrowiczówna połączeni są z sobą węzłem małżeńskim z czego wszystkiego spisaliśmy Akt w obecności pełnoletnich świadków potrzebne przymioty z prawa maiących iako też Starozakonnego Markusa Etwanika przekupnia Jakóba Misor handlarza Abrahama Gatonnach handlarza Berla Botenberga Szmuklerza, którzy po przeczytaniu wszystkiego Akt ninieyszy przed nami i stronami podpisali

Szymon Joz. Białecki. Zastępca
Urzędnika Stanu Cywilnego (Pięć hebrajskich podpisów

TEMERLE'S WEDDING, 1827,

English translation

Year one thousand eight hundred twenty seven, eighteenth day of December at ten o'clock in the fore-noon in the Community House in Kraków located on Grodzka Street number twenty nine, before us, Simon Joseph Bialecki, deputy civil state clerk appointed for persons of mosaic faith in the Free City of Kraków, and also the Mayor of the Community number one of the Free City of Kraków, appeared the Old Covenanter Moses Hertzig, a young man who finished nineteen years as documented by the certificate from the Book of Births of the Civil State Office of the Peace Court of the Second District of the Free City of Kraków kept by the former Imperial Austrian Government in the Kahał *(Jewish Community governing body*) and synagogue of Kazimierz in Community number eleven **Claim 1** Son of the Old Covenanters Hersh and Rivka Hertzig, spouses, living in Kraków in Kazimierz in Community Eleven house number eight, appearing with their help and authority First Party. Also appeared Old Covenanter Tamerle Aleksandrowicz, single, maiden, twenty years old as established by the certificate of birth from the books of the Civil State Office in the Peace Court of the Free City of Kraków Second District of the former Imperial Austrian Government kept by the Kahał and Synagogue **Claim 2.** Daughter of Old Covenanter Josel Aleksandrowicz, father, already departed proved by a copy of certificate from the records of the Civil State Clerk in the Free City of Kraków **Claim 3** and Freindel Dobrysz mother living here in Kraków in Kazimierz in Commmunity eleven house number two hundred and three, appearing with her help and authority Second Party. The Parties having shown Us a Marriage Consent form issued on the tenth day of November one thousand eight hundred twenty seven by the Mayor of Community eleven of the Free City of Kraków **Claim 4** Request that we proceed to the ceremony of marriage agreed upon between them, inasmuch as announcements of this marriage have appeared in Kraków in front of the Main Gate of the Community House designated for this purpose, the first on the eighteenth and the second on the twenty fifth day of November. Since there were no objections to the said marriage and parents are assisting and with this document assent to the ceremony Therefore, we, having read all the above-mentioned papers, and having decided that all formalities required by Law have been satisfied, favorably inclined to grant the said marriage, after having read to the parties and to the witnesses the above mentioned proofs as well as the Chapter six of the Civil Codex dealing with marriage, we asked the future husband and the future wife if they wish to be united in a matrimonial bond, to which each separately answered that that is their wish We declare in the name of the Law that Old Covenanters Moses Hertzig and Tamerle Aleksandrowicz are united in marriage, which we have recorded in this Act in the presence of adult witnesses having all the legally necessary attributes, to wit. Old Covenanters Markus Etwanik, salesman, Jacob Misor merchant, Abraham Gatonnach merchant, Berl Botenberg jeweler, who after having read everything signed this certificate in front of Us and the parties.

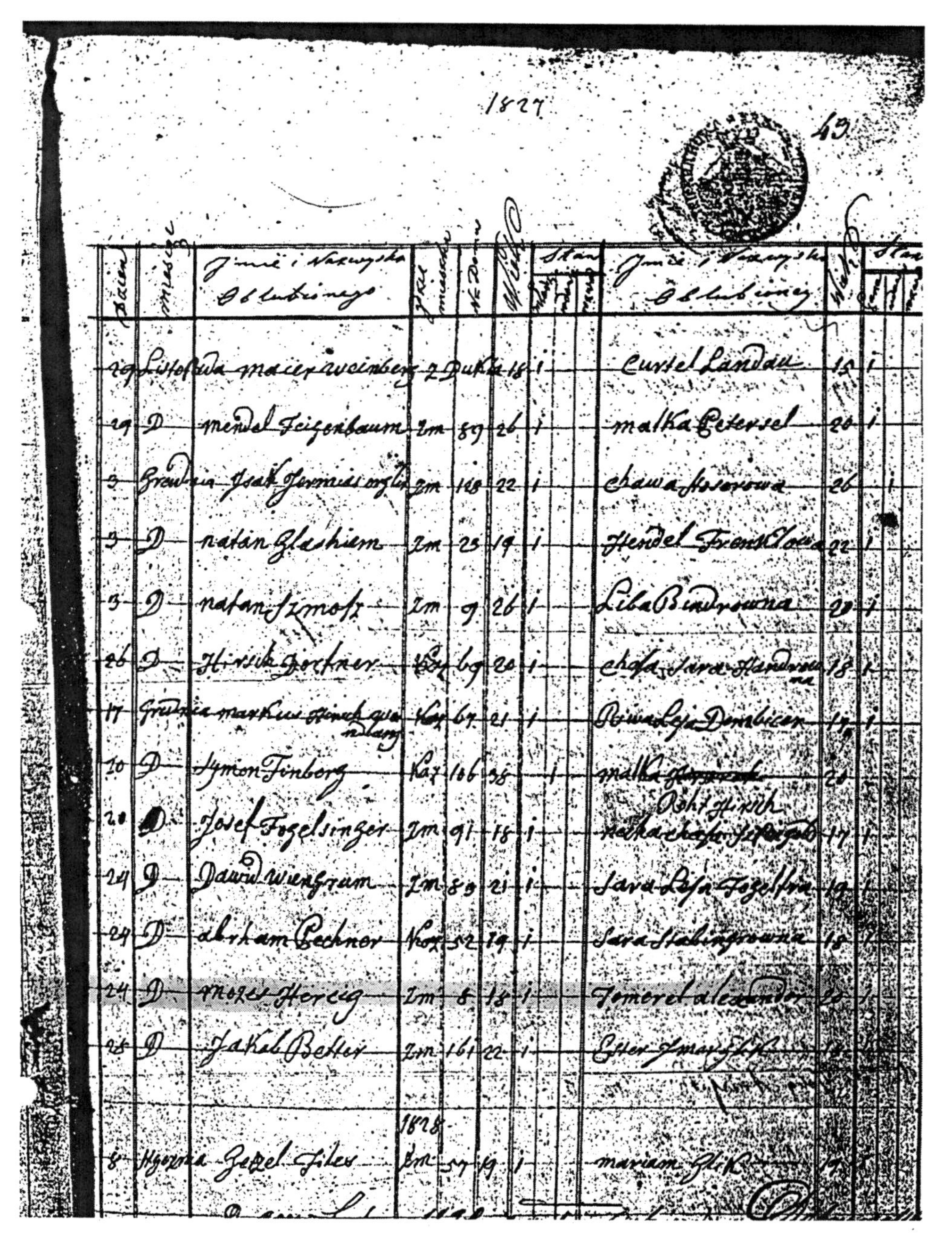

1827

43

Dzień	Miesiąc	Imię i Nazwisko Oblubieńca	Z	№ Domu	Wiek	Stan			Imię i Nazwisko Oblubienicy	Wiek	Stan
19	Listopada	maciej weinberg	Z	[illegible]	18	1			Curtel Landau	15	1
29	D	mendel Feigenbaum	Zm	89	26	1			malka Petersel	20	1
3	Grudnia	Isak [illegible]	Zm	168	22	1			chawa [illegible]	26	1
3	D	natan Glashiem	Zm	25	19	1			Hendel Frenkl[illegible]	22	1
3	D	natan Szmosz	Zm	9	26	1			Liba Bindrowna	20	1
26	D	Hirsch Gortner	Kaz	69	20	1			chafa Sara Handrowna	18	1
17	Grudnia	markus [illegible]	Kaz	67	21	1			[illegible] Leja Dembican	19	1
10	D	Szymon Tinberg	Kaz	166	38		1		malka [illegible]	[illegible]	
20	D	Josef Fogelsinger	Zm	91	18	1			[illegible]	17	1
24	D	Dawid Weingram	Zm	89	21	1			Sara [illegible]	19	[illegible]
24	D	abrham Pechner	Kaz	52	19	1			Sara Stalingrowna	18	[illegible]
24	D	Mozes Hercig	Zm	8	18	1			Temerel alexander	20	1
28	D	Jakob Better	Zm	161	22	1			Ester [illegible]	[illegible]	
			1828								
8	Stycznia	Getzel Filer	Zm	57	19	1			mariam Glik	19	

Fig. 026. Index page from the 1827 volume of Jewish Kraków marriages showing that on December 24-th Moses Hercig and Temerel Alexander were married;

24.
N° 24

Roku Tysiąc osmset trzydziestego pierwszego — Dnia Siedemnastego Marca o godzinie trzeciej po południu — Działo się w Domu Gminnym w Krakowie przy Ulicy Kanonniczej pod Liczbą Sto siedmdziesiąt szesć stojącym — Przed Nami Woyciechem Kucieńskim Urzędnikiem Stanu Cywilnego w Miescie wolnem Krakowie dla Starozakonnych ustanowionym w Gminie drugiey zamieszkałym stawił się osobiscie Starozakonny Fajwel Orgler, z professyi Introligator młodzian, lat dwadzieścia pięć liczący, co wypisem z Księgi Metryk Urodzenia Starozakonnych, za tytęgo Cesarsko-Austryackiego Rządu przy Kahale i Synagodze Kazimierskiey utrzymywaney wydanym, dowodzi Allegat N° 1° Syn Starozakonnych Szachny Orgler Szynkarza Trunków i Racheli Chaimowney Małżonków w Gminie dziesiątey Miasta Krakowa pod Liczbą Sto dwadzieścia osm zamieszkałych, przy swych Rodzicach mieszkający — Strona jedna — Stawiła się także Starozakonna Rywka z Alesandrowiczów Polnerowa lat dwadzieścia dwa licząca co Aktem Znania w Sądzie Pokoju Miasta wolnego Krakowa Okręgu drugiego, w dniu osmnastym Stycznia Roku bieżącego zdziałanym udowadnia Allegat N° 2° Wdowa po niegdy Starozakonnym Michale Polner jak Wywod słowny w Sądzie Pokoju wyżey powiedzianym w celu udowodnienia Zeyscia jego z Swiadków na dniu dwudziestym Stycznia Roku bieżącego wyprowadzony okazuje Allegat N° 3° córka Starozakonnych Jozela Alesandrowicz już zmarłego, jak wyciąg Akta Zeyscia Jego z Księgi Cywilnych Akt Krakowskich wydany swiadczy Allegat N° 4° i żyjącey Dobrechy z Gomplowiczów Jego Małżonki, a teraz Wdowy, rożnym handlem trudniącey się, w Gminie dziesiątey pod Liczbą Dwieście trzy zamieszkałey, przy Swojey Matce zostająca, strona druga — Strony stawające okazawszy Nam Konsens, na Zawarcie Związku pomiędzy sobą Małżeństwa przez Woyta Gminy Dziesiątey Miasta Krakowa w dniu trzecim Lutego Roku bieżącego wydany Allegat N° 5° Żądają abyśmy przystąpili do Obchodu ułożonego pomiędzy niemi Małżeństwa, którego Zapowiedzi wywieszony przed Głownemi Drzwiami Domu Naszego Gminnego to jest Pierwsza — Dnia Trzynastego, a druga dnia dwudziestego Lutego Roku bieżącego Gdy żadne tamowanie przeciw rzeczonemu Małżeństwu nie zaszło, a Oyciec i Assystujący Rodzice zaslubić się mającego, tudzież Matka zaslubić się mającey, po odebraniu w Obecności naszey od Swych Dzieci Akta uszanowania na Obchod tego Małżeństwa zezwalają. Zaczem My przeyrzawszy wszystkie wyżey wymienione akta z których okazuje się, iż wszelkie formalności jakich Prawo wymaga zachowane zostały, przychylając się do namienionego żądania, po przeczytaniu Stronom i Swiadkom wszystkich wyżey wyrażonych Dowodów, jako też Działu Szostego Kodexu Cywilnego w Tytule o Małżeństwie — Zapytaliśmy się przyszłego Małżonka i przyszłey Małżonki chcą się z sobą połączyć Związkiem Małżeńskim, na co gdy każde z nich oddzielnie odpowiedziało, iż taka jest Ich wola — Oswiadczamy w Imieniu Prawa iż Starozakonni Fajwel Orgler i Rywka z Alesandrowiczów Polnerowa połączeni są z sobą Związkiem Małżeństwa — Czego Akt spisaliśmy w obecności pełnoletnych Swiadków potrzebnie przyniosły z Prawa mających jako to Starozakonnych: Samuela Storn przekupnia Starzyzny — Markusa Hochwald handlarza — Mendla Finkor Bakałarza, i Samuela Joskowicza Kusniera — na Kazimierzu przy Krakowie zamieszkałych Którzy po przeczytaniu wszystkiego Aktu niniejszy wraz z Nami i Stronami podpisali oprócz Matki zaslubioney, gdyż ta oswiadczyła że pisać nie umie. —

Woyciech Kucieński Urzędnik Stanu Cywil.

Faiwle Orgel

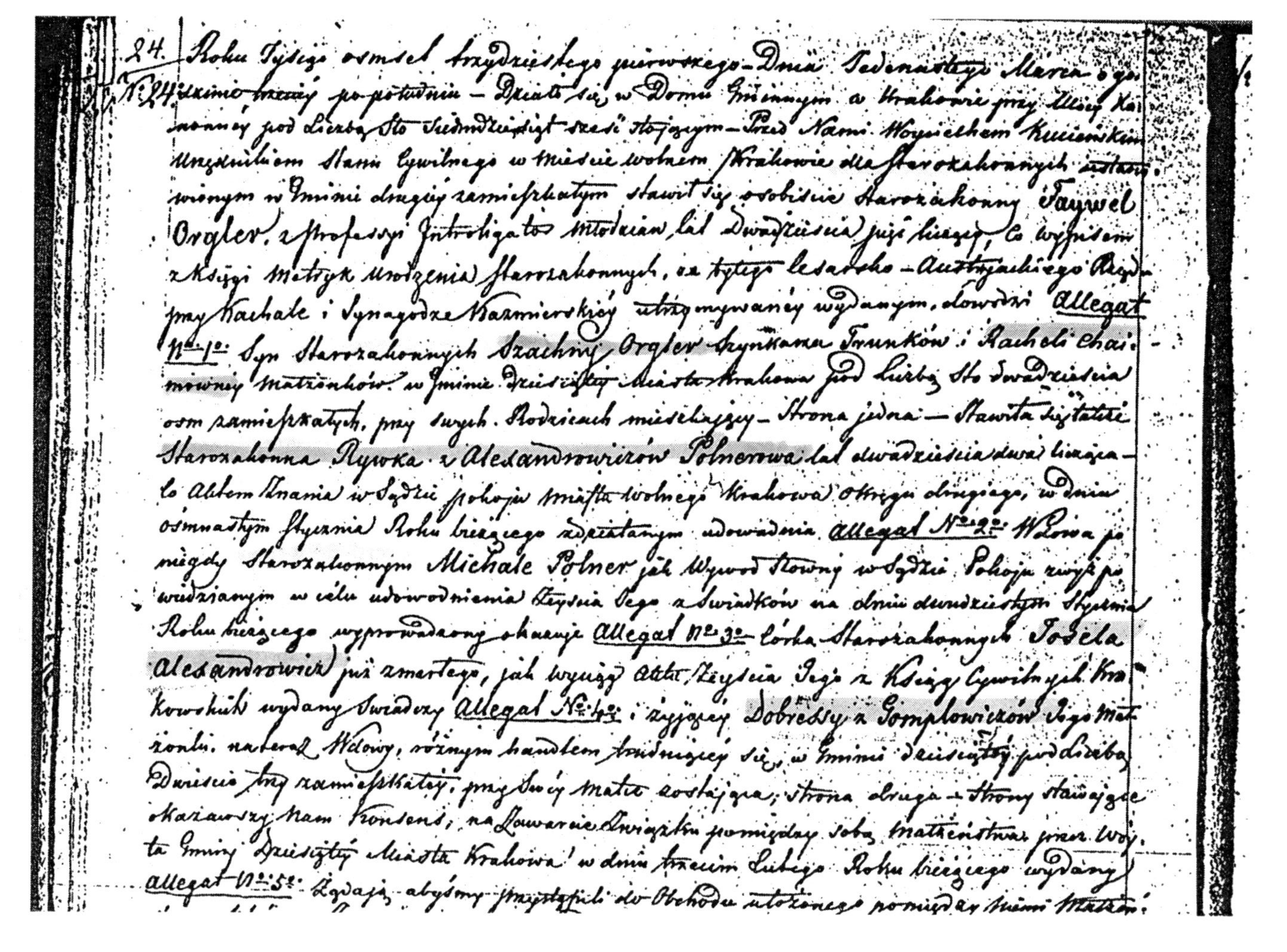

24. Roku Tysiąc ośmset trzydziestego pierwszego — Dnia Jedenastego Marca o go-
N° 24 dzinie trzeciej po południu — Działo się w Domu Gminnym w Krakowie przy Ulicy Kanonniczej pod Liczbą Sto Siedmdziesiąt sześć stojącym — Przed Nami Woyciechem Kucieńskim
Urzędnikiem Stanu Cywilnego w Mieście wolnem Krakowie dla Starozakonnych ustanowionym w Gminie drugiej zamieszkałym stawił się osobiście Starozakonny Fayvel
Orgler, z profesyi Introligator Młodzian, lat dwadzieścia pięć liczący, co wypisem
z Księgi Metryk Urodzenia Starozakonnych, za tytułem Cesarsko-Austryackiego Rządu przy Kahale i Synagodze Kazimierskiej utrzymywanej wydanym, dowodzi Allegat
N° 1° Syn Starozakonnych Szachny Orgler szynkarza Trunków i Racheli Chai-
mówny małżonków w Gminie dziesiątej Miasta Krakowa pod Liczbą Sto dwadzieścia
osm zamieszkałych, przy swych Rodzicach mieszkający — Strona jedna — Stawiła się także
Starozakonna Rywka z Alesandrowiczów Polnerowa lat dwadzieścia dwa licząca,
co Aktem Znania w Sądzie pokoju Miasta wolnego Krakowa Okręgu drugiego, w dniu
osmnastym Stycznia Roku bieżącego zdziałanym udowadnia Allegat N° 2° Wdowa po
niegdy Starozakonnym Michale Polner jak Wywód słowny w Sądzie Pokoju wyżej powiedzianym w celu udowodnienia Zeyścia Jego z świadków na dniu dwudziestym Stycznia
Roku bieżącego wyprowadzony okazuje Allegat N° 3° Córka Starozakonnych Josela
Alesandrowicz już zmarłego, jak wyciąg Aktu Zeyścia Jego z Księg Cywilnych Krakowskich wydany świadczy Allegat N° 4° i żyjącej Dobreszy z Gomplowiczów Jego Małżonki, naterąz Wdowy, różnym handlem trudniącej się, w Gminie dziesiątej pod Liczbą
Dwieście trzy zamieszkałej, przy Swej Matce zostająca; strona druga — Strony stawające
okazawszy Nam Konsens, na Zawarcie Związku pomiędzy sobą Małżeństwa przez Woyta Gminy Dziesiątej Miasta Krakowa w dniu trzecim Lutego Roku bieżącego wydany
Allegat N° 5° Żądają, abyśmy przystąpili do Obchodu ułożonego pomiędzy niemi Małżeń-

Figs. 027, 028 Record of wedding of Fayvel Orgler and Rivka Aleksandrowicz, widow of Michael Polner.

MARRIAGE RECORD OF RIVKA POLNER ALEXANDROWICZ – 1831

Roku tysiąc ośmset trzydziestego pierwszego dnia iedenastego Marca o godzinie trzeciey po południu działo się w domu gminnym w Krakowie przy ulicy Kanoniczey pod liczbą sto siedemdziesiąt sześć stoiącym – Przed Nami Woyciechem Kucieńskim Urzędnikiem Stanu Cywilnego w Mieście Wolnem Krakowie dla Starozakonnych ustanowionym w Gminie drugiey zamieszkałym stawił się osobiście Starozakonny Faywel Orgler, z profesyi Introligator Młodzian lat dwadzieścia pięć liczący, co wypisem z Księgi Metryk Urodzenia Starozakonnych, za byłego Cesarsko-Austryjackiego Rządu przy Kahałe i Synagodze Kazimierskiey utrzymywany wydanym dowodzi **Allegat No. 1** Syn Starozakonnych Szachny Orgler szynkarza trunków i Racheli Chaimowney Małżonków w Gminie dziesiątej Miasta Krakowa pod liczbą sto dwadzieścia ośm zamieszkałych, przy swych Rodzicach mieszkaiący – Strona jedna – Stawiła się także Starozakonna Rivka z Alexandrowiczów Polnerowa lat dwadzieścia dwa licząca – co Aktem Znania w Sądzie Pokoju Miasta Wolnego Krakowa Okręgu drugiego w dniu ośmnastym stycznia Roku bieżącego zdziałanym udowadnia **Allegat No. 2** Wdowa po niegdy Starozakonnym Michale Polner jak wywód słowny w Sądzie Pokoju zwyż powiedzianym w celu udowodnienia Zeyścia Jego z świadków na dniu dwudziestym stycznia Roku bieżacego wyprowadzony okazuje **Allegat No. 3** Córka Starozakonnych Josela Alexandrowicza już zmarłego, jak wyciąg Aktów Zeyścia Jego z Ksiąg Cywilnych Krakowskich wydany świadczy **Allegat No. 4** i żyjącey Dobressy z Gomplowiczów Jego Małżonki a teraz Wdowy, różnym handlem trudniącey się, w Gminie dziesiątey pod liczbą dwieście trzy zamieszkałey, przy Swey matce zostająca; strona druga – Strony stawiające okazawszy Nam Konsens na Zawarcie Związku pomiędzy sobą Małżenstwa przez Wóyta Gminy dziesiątey Miasta Krakowa w dniu trzecim Lutego Roku bieżącego wydany **Allegat No. 5** żądają abyśmy przystąpili do Obchodu ułożonego pomiędzy niemi Małżenstwa, którego Zapowiedzi wyszły przed Głównemi Drzwiami Domu naszego Gminnego to jest Pierwsza – dnia trzynastego a druga dnia dwudziestego Lutego Roku bieżacego. Gdy żadne tamowanie przeciw rzeczonemu Małżenstwu nie zaszło, a obecni i assystujący Rodzice zaślubu się mającego, tudzież Matka zaślubu się mającey, po odebraniu w obecności naszey od swych dzieci Akta Uszanowania na obchód tego Małżenstwa zezwalają. Zaczem My przeyżawszy wszystkie zwyż wymienione Akta z których okazuje się, iż wszelkie formalności jakich Prawo wymaga zachowane zostały, przychylając się do namienionego zadania po przeczytaniu Stronom I świadkom wszystkich zwyż wyrażonych dowodów, jako też Działu szóstego Kodeksu Cywilnego w Tytule o Małżenstwie – Zapytaliśmy się przyszłego Małżonka i przyszłey Małżonki czyli chcą się z sobą połączyć Związkiem Małżenskim, na co gdy każde z nich oddzielnie odpowiedziało , iż taka jest ich wola – Oświadczamy w Imieniu Prawa iż Starozakonny **Faywel Orgler i Rivka z Alexandrowiczów Polnerowa** połączeni są z sobą Węzłem Małżenstwa – Czego Akt spisaliśmy w obecności pełnoletnich świadków potrzebne przymioty z Prawa mających jako to Starozakonnych: Samuela Stern, przekupnia starzyzny – Markusa Hochwald handlarza – Mendla Tinker Bakalarza i Samuela Joskowicza Kuśnierza – na Kazimierzu przy Krakowie zamieszkałych którzy po przeczytaniu wszystkiego Akt ninieyszy w raz z Nami i Stronami podpisali – oprócz Matki zaślubionego, gdyż oświadczyła że pisać nie umie.-

Woyciech Kucieński Urzędnik Stanu Cywil
Faiwle Orget

MARRIAGE RECORD OF RIVKA POLNER, NEE ALEXANDROWICZ – 1831

English translation:

In the year one thousand eight hundred thirty one on the eleventh day of March at three in the afternoon – occurring in the Community House in Kraków located on Kanonicza Street number one hundred seventy six – before Us Woyciech Kucienski Civil State Clerk in the Free City of Kraków, named for Persons of the Old Covenant and living in the Second Community, appeared personally the Old Covenanter Faywel Orgler, bookbinder by profession, a young man of twenty five years, which he proved with an extract of the metrical book kept by the former Imperial Austrian Government in the Jewish Community Council and Synagogue. **Claim Nr 1.** Son of the Old Covenanters Szachna Orgler, tavern keeper selling drinks, and Rachel, daughter of Chaim, spouses, domiciled in the tenth Community of the City of Kraków house number one hundred twenty eight, living with his parents – first party. – Also appeared before Us Old Covenanter Rivka Polner, nee Alexandrowicz, twenty two years old, – which she established with a document from the Peace Court of the second district of the Free City of Kraków, issued on the eighteenth day of January of the current year. **Claim Nr. 2** . Widow of the late Old Covenanter Michael Polner, as shown by the verbal proof by witnesses in the above mentioned Peace Court establishing his demise. **Claim Nr. 3**. Daughter of the late Old Covenanter Josel Alexandrowicz, his demise corroborated by an extract of the Cracovian Civil Deaths Records. **Claim Nr. 4.** and of the living Dobress nee Gomplowicz his spouse and now widow, dealing with assorted merchandise in the tenth Community and domiciled in house number two hundred and three, living with her mother, second party – the parties have shown us consent form for marriage issued on the third day of February of the current year by the Mayor of the tenth Community of the City of Kraków **Claim Nr. 5**. Request that we proceed with the ceremony of the agreed upon marriage., prior announcements of which appeared before the Main Gate of our Community House, first on the thirteenth and second on the twentieth of February of the current year. Since no objections against the forthcoming marriage occurred, and the present and assisting parents of the to be married man and the mother of the to be married woman, having been shown respect from their children in our presence, have assented to this marriage, thus, we, having looked over all the above mentioned documents from which it appears that all formalities required by law were performed, leaning toward fulfilling the request, after having read to the parties and to the witnesses all of the above documents as well as the sixth chapter of the Civil Code dealing with marriages – we queried the future husband and the future wife whether they wish to be united in marriage, to which each separately responded that that is indeed their wish – we declare in the name of the law that the Old Covenaters **Faywel Orgler and Rivka Alexandrowicz Polner** are united in marriage – the Certificate of which we wrote in the presence of adult witnesses having the legally required attributes, thus the Old Covenanters: Samuel Stern, dealer in old clothing, Markus Hochwald , merchant, Mendel Tinker, bakalar. and Samuel Joskowicz furrier, living in Kazimierz by Kraków, who , after having read everything, signed this certificate along with Us and the Parties – except for the mother of the groom, who stated that she does not know how to write.-

Woyciech Kucienski Civil State Clerk
Faiwle Orget

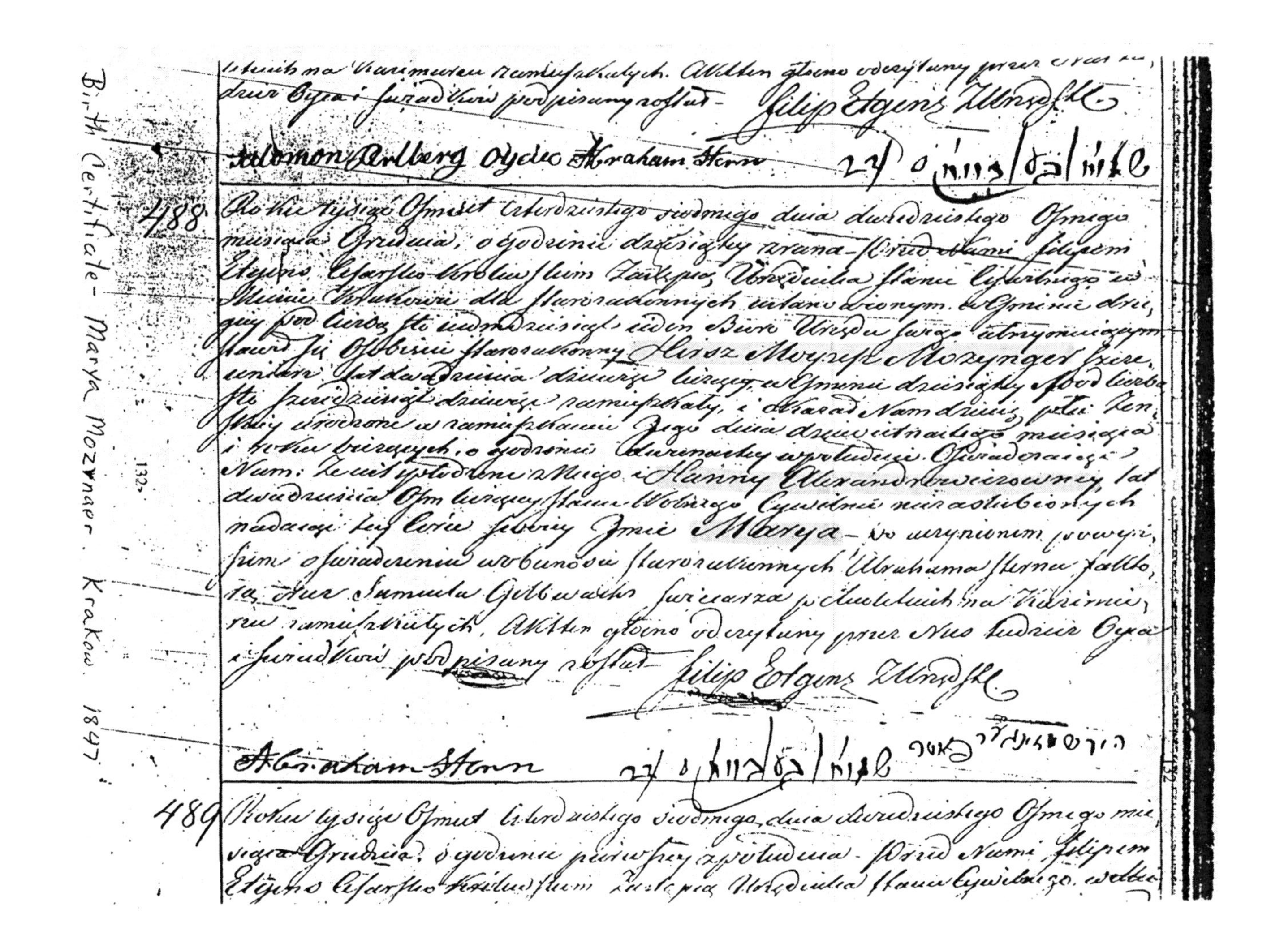

...na Kazimierzu zamieszkałych. Akt ten głośno odczytany przez [illegible] Ojca i Świadków podpisany został. — Filip Etgens [illegible]

Salomon Arlberg Ojciec Abraham Stern [illegible]

488. Roku Tysiąc Ośmset Czterdziestego siódmego dnia dwudziestego Ósmego miesiąca Grudnia, o godzinie dziesiątej zrana. Przed Nami Filipem Etgens, Cesarsko-Królewskim Zastępcą Urzędnika Stanu Cywilnego w Mieście Krakowie dla starozakonnych ustanowionym, w Gminie drugiej pod liczbą sto siedmdziesiąt jeden w Biurze Urzędu Jego [illegible] stawił się Obywatel starozakonny Hirsz Moyżesz Mozynger [illegible] lat dwadzieścia dziewięć liczący, w Gminie dziesiątej pod liczbą sto [illegible] zamieszkały, i okazał Nam dziecię płci żeńskiej, urodzone w zamieszkaniu Jego dnia dziewiętnastego miesiąca i roku bieżących, o godzinie [illegible] w południe. Oświadczając Nam: że jest spłodzone z Niego i Hanny Aleksandrowiczówny lat dwadzieścia ośm liczącej, stanu wolnego, cywilnie niezaślubionych, nadając temu dziecięciu Imię Marya — po uczynionym powyższym oświadczeniu w obecności starozakonnych Abrahama Sterna [illegible], tudzież Samuela Gelbwacha [illegible] na Kazimierzu zamieszkałych. Akt ten głośno odczytany przez Nas [illegible] Ojca i Świadków podpisany został. — Filip Etgens [illegible]

Abraham Stern [illegible]

489. Roku tysiąc Ośmset Czterdziestego siódmego dnia dwudziestego Ósmego miesiąca Grudnia, o godzinie pierwszej z południa. Przed Nami Filipem Etgens Cesarsko Królewskim Zastępcą Urzędnika Stanu Cywilnego [illegible]

Fig. 029. Birth record of Marya Mozynger, daughter of Hana Aleksandrowicz

1847- BIRTH RECORD OF MARYA MOZYNGER, DAUGHTER OF HIRSZ MOYZESZ MOZYNGER AND HANNA ALEXANDROWICZ

(Akty Urodzenia Osób Wyznania Moyżeszowego w Mieście Kazimierzu, 1847, # 488)

Roku tysiąc Ośmset Czterdziestego siódmego dnia dwudziestego ósmego miesiąca Grudnia, o godzinie dziesiątey zrana – przed Nami Filipem Etgins, Cesarsko-Królewskim Zastępcą Urzędnika Stanu Cywilnego w Mieście Krakowie dla starozakonnych ustanowionym, w Gminie drugiey pod liczbą sto siedmdziesiąt ieden Biuro Urzędu swego utrzymuiącym, stawił się Osobiście starozakonny **Hirsz Moyzesz Mozynger**, szczeciniarz, lat dwadzieścia dziewięć liczący, w Gminie dziesiątey pod liczbą sto sześćdziesiąt dziewięć zamieszkały, i okazał Nam dziecię płci żeńskiey, urodzone w zamieszkaniu Jego, dnia dziewiętnastego miesiąca i roku bieżących, o godzinie dwunastey w południe. Oświadczaiąc Nam: że iest spłodzone z Niego i **Hanny Alexandrowiczówney** lat dwadzieścia ośm liczącey, stanu Wolnego Cywilnie niezaślubionych, nadaiąc tey Córce swoiey Imię **Marya** – po uczynieniu powyższem oświadczeniu w obecności starozakonnych Abrahama Sterna, faktora oraz Samuela Gelwachs świecarza pełnoletnich na Kazimierzu zamieszkałych Akt ten głośno odczytany, przez Nas tudzierz Oyca i świadków podpisany został.

Filip Etgins Z Urzęd StC.
Abraham Stern
(Dwa hebrajskie podpisy)

In English:

In the year one thousand eight hundred and forty seven on the twenty eighth day of the month of December at ten o'clock in the morning – before Us, Filip Etgins, Imperial-Royal Deputy Clerk of the Civil Record in the City of Krakow, appointed for persons of the Old Testament, living in the second community, maintaining an office under number one hundred seventy one, appeared personally Old Testamenter **Hirsz Moyzesz Mozynger**, [broom maker?], being twenty nine years old, living in the tenth Community under the number one hundred sixty nine and showed Us a baby of female gender, born in His domicile on the nineteenth day of the current month and year, at twelve noon. Declaring to Us: that it was born to Him and **Hanna Alexandrowicz,** twenty eight years old, single, not married according to civil records, giving this Daughter of his the name **Marya** – having made this statement in the presence of Old Testamenters Abraham Stern, trader, as well as Samuel Golwachs, candle maker, adults living in Kazimierz, this Akt having been read aloud, was signed by Us as well as by the Father and the witnesses.

Filip Etgins, Dep. Clerk C.Rec.
Abraham Stern
[two Hebrew signatures]

Little Marya Mosinger, lived only for one year, died in January 1849

... [illegible] po nim przy życiu
pozostały Wdowy Matrumlców [illegible] w Gminie [illegible] według
[illegible] siedmdziesiąt jeden wraz z swą Matką zamieszkałą, z drugiej strony - Która to Zapowiedź głośno i wyraźnie odczytaną będąc, u drzwi
Domu w którym Biuro Urzędu Naszego utrzymujemy dla wiadomości
przybitą została. Czego Akt podpisaliśmy. [signature] m.p.

Dziś to jest w niedzielę, dnia dziesiątego miesiąca i roku bieżących, Zapowiedź
powyższa w tymże samym sposobie i u tychże Drzwi ogłoszoną zostawszy
po raz drugi, tu się umieszcza i zapisuje - [signature] m.p.

nb Odbył się ślub d. 20. Marca r.b.

18 Roku tysiąc Ośmset Czterdziestego Czwartego dnia trzeciego Marca
Działo się w Domu Gminy drugiej pod Liczbą sto siedmdziesiąt jeden
stojącym My Franciszek Gawroński Urzędnik Stanu Cywilnego w Wolnem Mieście Krakowie dla Osób Wyznania Mojżeszowego ustanowiony udawszy się przed drzwi główne Wejścia domu powyżej wzmian-
kowanego w którym Biuro Urzędu Naszego utrzymujemy, dziś to jest w
niedzielę o godzinie dwunastej w południe, donieśliśmy i ogłosili po raz
pierwszy: Iż zaszło przyrzeczenie Małżeństwa którym się stające postanowili, Starozakonny Manasses Alexandrowicz stanu Wolnego, lat dwadzieścia pięć liczący Syn nieżyjącego Józefa Właściciela Domu na Kazimierzu nie zmarłego i [illegible] Matronlii
po nim na teraz przy życiu pozostałej Wdowy Matrumlców Alexandrowiczów w Gminie drugiej pod Liczbą [illegible] trzy wraz z Matką mieszkający z jednej - i Lea Katznerówna stanu Wolnego, Panna lat
dwadzieścia Ośm liczącą, córka Wolffa i Matlei żyjących Małżonków
Katznerów handlem się trudniących w Gminie drugiej pod Liczbą
Ośmnaście przy swych Rodzicach mieszkającej z drugiej strony - Któ-
rato Zapowiedź głośno i wyraźnie odczytaną będąc, u drzwi głównego Wejścia do Domu gdzie Biuro Urzędu Naszego utrzymujemy
dla wiadomości przybitą została. A czego Akt podpisaliśmy.
[signature]

Dziś to jest w Niedzielę dnia dziesiątego miesiąca i roku bieżących, Zapowiedź powyższa w tymże samym Sposobie i u tychże Drzwi po raz drugi
ogłoszoną zostawszy, tu się umieszcza i zapisuje
[signature] m.p.
nb Ślub był d. 13. Marca r.b.

Fig. 030. Wedding announcement of Manasses Aleksandrowicz and Lea Katzner

BANS – 1844: MANASSES ALEKSANDROWICZ AND LEA KATZNER

Roku tysiąc Ośmset Czterdziestego Czwartego dnia trzeciego Marca Działo się w Domu Gminy drugiey pod liczbą sto dwadzieścia ieden stoiącym My Franciszek Gawroński Urzędnik Stanu Cywilnego w Wolnem Mieście Krakowie dla Osób Wyznania Moyżeszowego ustanowiony udawszy się przed drzwi główne Weyścia domu powyżey wymienonego w którym Biuro Urzędu Naszego utrzymuiemy, dziś to iest w niedzielę o godzinie dwunastey wpołudnie, donieśliśmy i ogłosili po raz pierwszy: Iż zaszło przyżeczenie Małżeństwa którym się złączyć postanowili, Starozakonny Manasses Aleksandrowicz Stanu Wolnego, Młodzian lat dwadzieścia pięć liczący Syn niegdy Jósefa Właściciela Domu na Kazimierzu iuż zmarłego i Dobreszy tegoż Małżonki po niem na teraz przy życiu pozostałey Wdowy Małżeństwa Aleksandrowiczów w Gminie dziesiątey pod Liczbą dwieście trzy wraz z Matką mieszkaiący z iedney – I Lea Katznerówna Stanu Wolnego, Panna lat dwadzieścia ośm licząca, córka Wolffa i Małki żyiących Małżeństwa Katznerów handlem się trudniących w Gminie dziesiątey pod Liczbą ośmnaście przy swych Rodzicach mieszkaiąca od drugiey Strony – która to Zapowiedź głośno i wyraźnie odczytana będąc u drzwi głównego Weyścia do Domu gdzie Biuro Urzędu Naszego utrzymuiemy dla wiadomości przybita została – A czego Akt powyższy spisaliśmy.

(-) FGawroński

Dziś, to iest w Niedzielę dnia dziesiątego miesiąca i roku bieżących, Zapowiedź powyższa w tymże sposobie i w teyże Osnowie po raz drugi ogłoszona zostawszy, tu się umieszcza i zapisuie. FGawroński u.s.c.

Slub był .2.13. Iuni r.b.

In English:

On March third of year one thousand eight hundred and forty four in the Community House located at number one hundred twenty one, We, Francis Gavronski, appointed as Civil State Clerk of the Free City of Kraków for Persons of Mosaic Faith, having come before the front door of the main entrance of the building in which We maintain our Office, today, i.e. Sunday at noon, We publicly announced and gave the first notice: that there is an intention of marriage uniting the Old Covenanter Manasses Aleksandrowicz unmarried, bachelor, young man twenty five years old, son of the late Josef owner of a building in Kazimierz deceased and Dobresz his wife currently living widow, spouses Aleksandrowicz, living with mother in building two hundred three in Community ten on one side – and Lea Katzner, unmarried, maiden, twenty eight years old, daughter of Wolff and Malka, living, spouses Katzner, merchants, living with parents in building eighteen in Community ten on the other side – this notice having been read loudly and clearly at the door of the main entrance to the building in which We maintain our Office was tacked to the door – after which we wrote this act

Today, i.e. Sunday the tenth of current month and year, this notice in the same manner and the same sense was published for the second time, hereby confirmed and recorded.

Wedding took place 13 June of current year.

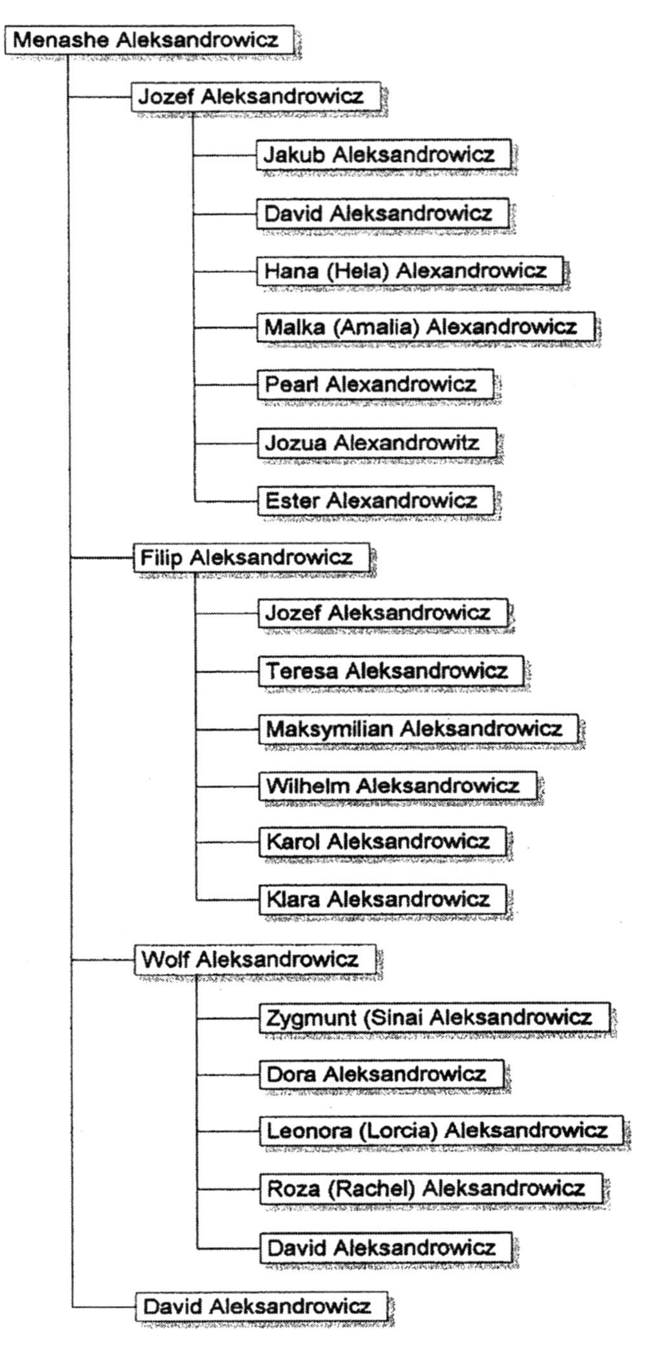

Fig. 031. Family tree: descendants of Menashe Aleksandrowicz

Chapter 18. Aleksandrowicz Family: Next Generation, Józef II, Filip and Wolf

(a) Józef Aleksandrowicz, my great-grandfather (1845-1941)

I was lucky to know my great-grandfather Józef. I remember him as a kind elderly white-haired gentlemen, always dressed in a white shirt with a soft collar and a black pair of pants and a long black jacket and a cap, wearing thick glasses and sporting an unruly white beard. I was born in 1925, Józef Aleksandrowicz died in 1941 when I was almost 16. My memories of him are quite vivid. As a genealogist trying to establish my family's background I find that my having a direct personal knowledge of an individual born in the middle of the XIX-th century helped me to span a period of a hundred and fifty years of history and four generations of my family with ease and confidence.

Józef Aleksandrowicz was born in 1845. He lived to be 96. In 1844 his father Menashe Aleksandrowicz, a broker at the Kraków state lottery, married Lea Katzner and started a family. Within less than a year of their formal wedding registration they had their first son. As noted in the civil records of the district of Kazimierz by Kraków for the year 1845, item # 143, page (folio) # 49, Menashe appeared before the civil clerk Francis Gawronski and stated that a male baby was born at one o'clock at night on April 4, 1845 in his domicile, house # 203 in Kazimierz, to him and his spouse Lea nee Katzner. Both Menashe and Lea were reported as being 28 years old at the time, which implied that they were both born in 1817. They named the child Józef (Josl ben Menashe ha-Kohen).

It appears that Józef was the first male child born in our family after Menashe's father Joseph Aleksandrowicz died in 1827 when Menashe himself was only around ten years old. Following an old Kraków Jewish tradition, when Menashe married, he and Lea named their firstborn Józef. It is of interest that the next male Aleksandrowicz child, a boy born to Menashe's younger brother Izrael Eliasz and his wife Ester Lack, who was born in building # 203 three years later, on June 8, 1848, was also named Józef. That Józef son of Israel Eliasz died as a baby.

The "Free and Independent and Strictly Neutral City of Kraków" (Kraków Republic) lost its autonomy in 1846, when Kraków had become the center of political ferment and the scene of an uprising by Polish patriots. Serving as the last reasonably free piece of Polish territory, Kraków became a center of conspiratorial activity aiming at reconstitution of a free and independent Poland. It is of interest that in 1846 this activity was largely confined to landed nobility and educated urban intelligentsia awash in national Polish awareness and grand aspirations, while the majority of the future nation, the peasants in the countryside displayed no national consciousness. The peasants, still subject to the will of the nobles and obligated to perform serfdom services for manor owners had, however, a burning desire to be free of serfdom. Thus there were at the time two parallel drives, that of Polish nobles and literate city dwellers for a Polish state and that of peasants for ownership of land and abolition of vestiges of serfdom. The nationalist patriotic activity in Poland was led by Ludwik Mierosławski, the local one in the Kraków Republic by Jan Tissowski. The uprising began in Kraków. Mierosławski was not available, having been interned by the Prussians, and a national Polish "government" was inaugurated by Tyssowski, who declared himself "Supreme Leader of a Provisional Revolutionary Government" and a self-appointed dictator. He published several revolutionary decrees, incuding one proclaiming an unconditional end to serfdom and equality for all (male) citizens. A Jewish delegation, led by Rabbi Dov Ber Meisels, met with Tyssowski and his secretary Edward Dembowski, and asked for a clarification of the new government's policy toward Jews. The Provisional Government emphasized the abolition of all unequal treatments and the next day (February 23, 1846) published a manifesto to "*Brothers Izraelites! Poles! The hour of unity of families of our society has struck. Under enemy rule you were considered as a separate nation. The Revolution accepts you to the bosom of society, assures you, as brothers of one soil, human rights and welcomes you as Sons of the Fatherland, worthy of liberation and grant of unconditional equality. Inasmuch as enjoyment of rights and obligations is appropriate, so the Revolutionary Government calls upon you to join the ranks of Defenders and declares that all manifests issued so far and to be issued in the future apply also to Poles Israelites*" (Bałaban, II, 101). A stirring public appeal in the Old Synagogue in Kazimierz led to enlistment of a number of Jews.

The Austrian general Kolin, who led an Austrian garrison in the supposedly free Kraków Republic, faced with an armed insurrection, at first withdrew from Kraków, then returned with reinforcements after a few days. The Austrian provincial governor issued an order abolishing serfdom in the name of the Emperor, with compensation for nobility. This order which had force behind it, unlike the one by Tyssowski, was widely publicized in the countryside. Polish aristocrats opposed abolition of serfdom without compensation, and many turned against Tyssowski. Peasants, incited by the Austrian authorities under Prince Metternich, believed the Austrians and turned angrily against the nobility, attacking country palaces. The three autocratic regimes could not tolerate Polish irredentism and authorized Austrian and Russian Governments to send in armies and eventually decreed annexation of the Free Kraków Republic to the Austrian Galitzia. The Austrians used the animosity between landowners and peasants in the Polish areas of the Austrian Empire and incited the peasants to rise. Manor houses burned in the Galitzian and Slovak countryside. Tyssowski was caught and the Polish uprising squelched. Once this was achieved, the Habsburg authorities decided that the peasant uprising had gone too far, and it, too, had to be stopped. Troops were sent against the peasants whose rebellion the Habsburgs originally encouraged. The brief but intense conflict between the Austrian and Hungarian army now defending the nobles and Polish and Slovak peasants in the countryside and mountaineers at the foothills of the Carpathian mountains and the High Tatra range ended with suppression of the peasants and execution of their leaders.

The conflict led to songs and legends about several folk heroes. Historical and legendary exploits were ascribed to Polish and Slovak peasant leaders who were said to have robbed the rich and distributed the bounty to the poor. These were immortalized in folksongs. Particularly famous were the exploits of the Polish peasant leader Jacob Szela and the even better-known Slovak Mountaineer folk hero, *Janosik*, whose Robin-Hood-like exploits had been described in a number of folksongs, books and movies. Janosik was eventually captured by the Hungarian army, tortured and publicly cruelly executed by impaling on the market square in the town of Rużomberok (Rosenberg) in Slovakia. To this day he is revered in the Polish and Slovak Tatra Mountains. I remember from my childhood a song about Janosik, *Jęczą góry jęczą, Janosika męczą (*Moaning are the mountains, moaning, Janosik is being tortured).

The exploits of the Polish and Slovak peasant heroes and their 1846 uprising against the aristocrats and large landowners were generally ignored by most Polish historians because they represented a non-patriotic, even anti-patriotic event in Polish history, but they were grist for the mill of Polish communists and their view of history. As a child I read about Jacob Szela and his role in the peasant class struggle against Polish and Hungarian landowners in a book by a young Communist poet and writer Bruno Jasienski. Jasienski was not admired by the then reactionary Polish government, but his books were nevertheless published and circulated in Poland. My parents obviously admired Jasienski and I remember reading, besides *The song about Jukub Szela*, a book entitled *Palę Paryż* (I burn Paris), a fictional account obviously inspired loosely by the history of the Paris Commune of 1870. It describes a revolt of Parisian workers, who then created a veritable egalitarian workers paradise in that city, while surrounded by a ring of outside bourgeois forces kept from entering the city by false claims of a deadly epidemic raging there and maitaining a quarantine around the city. I did not know then that Jasienski was a Polish Jew, an exile, living in Paris. I recently found out that he was expelled from France and moved to the Soviet Union where at first he was greeted as a hero. Eventually, however, he suffered the fate of most Polish and Jewish communists who expected to be greeted as comrades if not as heroes. The Soviet dictator Joseph Stalin did not thrust them, suspected them, as he did most of the old Bolsheviks, of disloyalty and lack of respect for his rule. He had them arrested and executed in the basement of the Moscow Lubianka prison. Jasienski died there soon after his arrest.

The events of 1846 left the elite Polish patriots in despair. Particularly galling was the fact that the aborted uprising not only failed to generate support among Polish peasant masses, but was suppressed mostly through peasant actions. A soul-searching was in order. A re-acquaintance of the urban and aristocratic educated classes with surrounding countryside peasant masses (which then constituted most of the Polish speaking population) was obviously urgent. In this unhappy period patriotic songs were created using very strong language to express the depression felt. Other songs attempted to comfort the divided nation by recalling its former glories. All three neighboring enemies occupying Polish territories came up for condemnation. In the Austrian zone, where Polish landed estates were set on fire by Polish peasants, a desperate patriotic "*Chorale*" was written, vividly expressing the feelings of its authors. The music was written by Józef Nikorowicz, the words by Kornel Ujejski, as follows:

Z dymem pożarów,	With smoke of fires,
Z kurzem krwi bratniej,	With ashes of fraternal blood,
Do Ciebie, Panie, płynie ten głos.	To You, Oh Lord, this voice is raised.
Skarga to straszna	The lament is horrible
Jęk to ostatni,	The moan terminal,
Od takich modłów bieleje włos!	From such prayers hair turns grey!

More or less at the same time, in the face of the policy of Germanization pursued by the Prussian Government in its section of Poland, the poet Maria Konopnicka wrote the "*Rota*":

Nie rzucim ziemi skąd nasz ród,	We will not abandon the land of our birth,
Nie damy pogrześć mowy,	We will not let our language be buried,
Polski my naród, Polski lud,	We are a Polish nation, Polish folk.
Królewski szczep Piastowy.	The regal tribe of the Piasts.
Nie będzie Niemiec pluł nam w twarz,	Germans will not spit in our face
Ni dzieci nam Germanił,	Nor Germanize our children
Potężny stanie hufiec nasz,	Powerful will be our force
Bóg bedzie nam hetmanił	With God marshalling our strength
Twierdzą nam będzie każdy próg,	Every doorstep will serve us a fortress,
Tak nam dopomóż Bóg,	So help us God.

Finally, in the Russian zone, the patriots sung the anti-Muscovite anthem, remembering the glorious victories of Tadeusz Kościuszko against Tsarist armies:

Patrz, Kościuszko na nas z nieba	Look at us, Kościuszko, from heaven
Jak w krwi wrogów będziem brodzić	As we'll wade in enemy blood,
Twego miecza nam potrzeba	We need your sword
By Ojczyznę oswobodzić.	To free the fatherland.
Kto powiedział że Moskale	Anybody who says that Muscovites
Są to bracia nas Lechitów	Are brothers to us Lechites,
Temu pierwszy w łeb wypalę	I'll be the first to shoot his head
Pod kościołem Karmelitów!	In front of the Carmelites church!

All these songs were used by liberal Krakovians, Poles and Jews, in patriotic demonstrations in Kraków as a form of protest and as indication of contempt for the autocratic occupying authorities. On festive occasions commemorating assorted Polish patriotic anniversaries, usually held with significant Jewish participation, singing these Polish protest songs served as a way to express the anti-Austrian feelings. Austrian authorities formally forbade their public singing, but did not forcefully enforced the ban.

In a census of 1847, done after Kraków was incorporated into the Austrian Galitzia, the city had a total population of 40,310 inhabitants, of whom 13,066 or 32.4% were Jewish. All the Jews had to live in the tight confines of the Jewish Town in Kazimierz, although they moved freely throughout the city and many of them had stores, food stalls and other commercial interests in the city of Kraków proper. Many of these were located in the Main Market Square (*Rynek Główny*) in the center of town and also on the St. Thomas Street nearby.

In 1848 the people all over Europe exploded in a rage against the old autocratic order. European historians refer to this series of events as the "*Spring of Peoples*". Popular revolts broke out in Paris, Vienna, Berlin, Rome, Venice, Milan, Budapest as well as in Kraków and many other places. News of uprisings in one place fed the flames in the next. In Paris, following hostile demonstrations, King Louis Philippe abdicated and a republic was declared. Prince Louis Napoleon, a nephew of Napoleon Bonaparte, was eventually elected President of republican France (He then declared himself Emperor as Napoleon III). In Berlin, the Polish patriot, Ludwik Mierosławski, who was arrested by the Prussians in 1846, was forcibly liberated from the Moabit Prison. In Rome, a popular uprising forced the ruling Pope Pius IX to flee, while Giuseppe Mazzini declared a republic. In 1848 the Austrian Emperor Ferdinand I, fired the hated reactionary Chancellor Prince Metternich and promised to issue a new constitution. In Budapest, Lajos Kossuth proclamed Hungarian independence. In Kraków, people gathered in the streets. Again, a Civil Guard was created to police the city, including a separate Jewish Guard division. The Austrian troops under the command of General Castiglione withdrew from center of Kraków to the Wawel Hill, then began bombarding the city, which surrendered, ending the rebellion. In Vienna, the imperial Austrian army under General Count Windischgraetz, also used cannon shots from surrounding hills, to suppress the rebellion. Tsarist troops helped to subdued Budapest. Kossuth escaped to Turkey. French Bourbon troops restored the Pope in Rome. A few months later, a second Vienna uprising led to the Emperor's abdication in favor of the youthful (18 years old) Franz Joseph, but the *Spring of Peoples* was effectively over. With the help of Tsarist armies, the old autocratic regimes were restored, but not for long. Like the French Revolution fifty years earlier, the *Spring of Peoples* left its mark on European people, including its Jews, for years to come.

In 1853, a rich friend of Menashe Aleksandrowicz, Mojżesz Feintuch, trader in so-called "colonial" merchandise (wine, tea, coffee, spices, etc.) converted to Catholicism. His conversion was greeted in Kazimierz with a mixture of contempt and envy. Feintuch was very rich and, after conversion, largely accepted into the Kraków Christian burger society. Unlike earlier in Polish history, he did not aspire to nobility but chose to become a wealthy burger. He owned a truly venerable Krakovian landmark building in the Central Market Square, the Grey Stone Building (Pol.: *Szara Kamienica*) in which his store was located. The building stands proudly to this day, still grey, supported by abutments. Abandoning

his Jewish surname, Feintuch adopted a surname from the building, and henceforth his family was known in Kraków as Szarski. The Szarski store with colonial merchandise continued in business and the Szarski family remained prominent in Krakovian society for generations.

In January 1863 a Polish Insurrection broke out in the Russian zone of Poland. This was a hopeless quixotic endeavor. Unlike the previous Polish Uprising against the Tsar in November 1830 when the Poles had an autonomous standing army able to hold territory and keep Warsaw free until defeated by larger Tsarist troops, this January Uprising was a guerilla effort, led by isolated aristocratic partisan groups in the forests. Cities remained in Russian hands and the Polish partisan units were eliminated one by one. Support rallies did take place in the Western E!urope, without much effect. As a result of this uprising, the Tsar abolished the Polish Kingdom entirely and began a forcible Russification of the country. Even the word "*Polska*" was eliminated; the Russians called the area officially The Land by the Vistula (*Privislenskiy Kray*). By contrast, in 1867 the Habsburgs in Vienna were forced to enact a Constitution and losen the autocratic laws. They allowed freedom of languages and cultures in the Habsburg territories. Hungary became co-equal with Austria under the Habsburg rule, and Franz Joseph became, besides being the Emperor of Austria, king of an autonomous Hungary. The Government was henceforth styled as *Kaiserlich-und-Koeniglich*, i.e. Imperial-and-Royal. In semi-autonomous Galitzia with provincial capital in Lwów, Polish language and culture were allowed to flourish. Jews, who dressed in Western manner and whose children attended public schools, had citizenship rights. In Kraków, the elected City Council consisted of 72 members, 12 of them Jews. In 1869 Kraków had 50,000 inhabitants, Jews constituted 23% of the population (Bieniarzówna and Małecki, III, 233).

All zones of partitioned Poland were poor and economically underdeveloped. Life in the Russian Zone was particularly grim. Illiteracy in the countryside was widespread. Economic conditions in the Austrian Zone was not much better. However, while the Austrian area (Galitzia) was also economically depressed, it enjoyed a great cultural revival and a great deal of political activity. School attendance was high, standards of literacy elevated, and the population, Polish peasants as well as poor Jews in the *shtetls*, had full access to schooling in Polish and access to a free and lively Polish press. Almost all the towns and cities of the Dual Monarchy had a significant Jewish population. There were obvious material advantages to living in a large and varied country, such as the Dual Monarchy of Austria-Hungary (Vienna, Budapest), which then included, besides Eastern and Western Galitzia (Lwów/*Lemberg*. Kraków, Tarnów, Przemysl, Rzeszów, Tarnopol, Brody, Stanisławów, Kołomyja), also Bohemia (Prague, Plzen, Karlsbad), Moravia (Brno, Ostrava, Olomouc), Slovakia (Bratislava/*Pressburg*, Kosice/*Kasha,*) and Ruthenia (Uzhorod/*Ungvar,* Mukacevo/*Munkacs*). Further south the dual monarchy included Slovenia (Lubljana/*Laibach*), Croatia (Zagreb/*Agram*), Dalmatia (Dubrovnik/*Ragusa*, Split/*Spalato*), Bosnia and Hercegovina (Sarajevo, Kotor, Budva), large parts of Northern Italy and Tirol (Trieste, Rijeka/*Fiume*, Bolzano, Trent). It also included parts of modern Romania, Moldavia and Ukraine: Bukovina (Czerniowce/*Tschernowitz*), Moldavia-Bessarabia (Jassy/*Iasi*, Kishinev/*Chisinau*), Banat (Timisoara/*Temesvar*), Voivodina (Novi Sad), Sanjak (Novi Pazar), Varad (Oradeia/*Grossvardein*), Transylvania (Cluj/*Klausenburg/ Kolozsvar*) and other areas. It was possible for Krakovians to export merchandise via the

Austro-Hungarian Adriatic harbors of Trieste and Fiume or to travel easily by train without passports and border controls to Vienna, Salzburg, Prague, Budapest, Zagreb, Sarajevo, as well as to the spas of Karlsbad and Marienbad, to resorts of Semmering, Innsbruck and Bad Ischl, or to the beaches of Dubrovnik, or Abbazia (today *Oppatija*). Travel and commerce within the even larger Russian Empire, say from Smolensk or Vitebsk to Kiev or Odessa, was difficult, unlike that in Austria-Hungary, and the economic advantages, while there, were not as pronounced.

Polish culture flourished in Kraków. Because the Austrian zone was the only part of Polish lands in which Polish language was not officially forbidden and could be used freely, Polish writers and artists from all Polish territories flocked to Kraków. A school of patriotic painters, most prominent among them Jan Matejko (1838-1893), produced large canvases of art on patriotic themes. One of Matejko's paintings, dealing with the Prusian homage of 1525 called *Hold Pruski* hangs today in the Museum on the second floor of the *Sukiennice* in the Main Market Square of Kraków (see the description of the event in the chapter about Rachel Fischl above and the description of the painting itself below in the chapter on Kraków *Rynek*). The next generation of artists, the so-called "*Młoda Polska*" (Young Poland) School of Art, included Henryk Siemiradzki (1843-1902), painter of the spectacular fire-curtain in the Kraków Municipal Theater. Among others, two artists, Teodor Axentowicz (1859-1938) and Jacek Malczewski (1854-1929), benefited from the largesse of my relative Regina, widow of Wolf Aleksandrowicz. In exchange, both painted portrtaits of Regina's daughter, "*Panna Róża*".

Attempts were made to unite Polish intelligentsia with Polish peasants and Polish Jews, instilling Polish patriotism in the latter two groups. Among other writers, a prominent Krakovian artist, Stanisław Wyspiański (1869-1907) showed a truly multi-faceted talent as a painter and writer. He designed a modern stained glass windows for the age-old Franciscan Church in Kraków, painted many canvases and wrote poems and plays. In a powerful appeal for unity among Poles and an appeal to the intelligentsia to show greater interest in and contact with the Polish peasantry, Wyspiański used the occasion of a wedding of a friend, the poet Lucjan Rydel, to a country girl in the village of Bronowice near Kraków, as the background for a stirring play designed to wake his compatriots from despair and apathy and push for a rebirth of united Polish patriotism. The play, The Wedding (Pol.: *Wesele),* is a parable, reminding people of their former glory and current depressed, almost somnolent state:

Miałeś, chamie, złoty róg, miałeś, chamie, czapkę z piór,
Czapkę wicher niesie, róg stuka po lesie, ostał ci się jeno sznur!

(You, jack, you had a golden horn, you had a feather hat,
Wind carries that hat, the horn knocks in the forest, all you got left is a string!)

Wyspiański is buried in the crypt of the Church of St. Stanisław *na Skałce*, reserved for only the most prominent and deserving Polish artists and patriots. Writers of the "Young Poland" group became interested in the peasant culture, concentrating on mountaineers in the developing mountain resort of Zakopane in the High Tatras. Jan Kasprowicz and Kazimierz Przerwa-Tetmajer wrote about the mountaineers and their folk art and legends.

The most famous Polish writer of the time, Stefan Żeromski, lived for a while in Zakopane in the mountains in 1913. As a child I enjoyed his many novels, but I particularly liked his short story about Wałgerz Udały of Tyniec by Kraków, written in archaic language about a medieval heroic knight.

Kraków also enjoyed a renaissance of popular folk literature. A number of satirical folklore plays were written by Stefan Turski (1875-1945), a Polish counterpart to Gilbert and Sullivan, though perhaps not of the same caliber. My mother used to sing some of Turski's songs from *Krowoderskie Zuchy* and *Lola z Ludwinowa,* two musicals about simple Krakovian folk from the working-class suburbs of Krowodża and Ludwinów. Lola from Ludwinów became a folk heroine, a sassy free-wheeling sexy young hoyden

Zdradzi ciebie I mnie i coś pól z Krakowa	*Will betray you and me and half of Kraków*
Właśnie ta dziewczyna, właśnie ta jedyna	*Just this girl, only this one*
Lola z Ludwinowa	*Lola from Ludwinów*

While the cultural life was in ferment, the political scene was even more complex. To begin with, the voting rights were tightly restricted, reserved by categories for the landowners and wealthy burgers, Polish, Austrian or Jewish. The political life in the newly semi-democratic Kraków was dominated at first by ultra-conservative aristocrats, grouped in a political faction called the *Stańczyks* (court jesters), after a published manifesto of that title in which they outlined their program, mainly featuring their loyalty to the Habsburg throne. Their main organ, a venerable Krakovian daily, was called *Czas* (Time). Opposition to the Stańczyks was led by more democratic forces grouped around a weekly called *Kraj* (the Country), founded by the liberal aristocrat, Adam Count Sapieha, and then edited from 1869 to 1874 by my second cousin twice removed, Ludwik Gumplowicz (1838-1909), a Jew, and a strong Polish patriot whom I described earlier in the chapter about the Gumplowicz family. His leading role in the Galitzian democratic movement is an indication that educated assimilated Jews were welcomed and could rise to top positions. Gumplowicz's Polish patriotism led him to problems with the Austrian police and eventually forced him to leave Kraków for a professorship at the University of Graz in Austria, where he became the founder of the field of Sociology. By the 1890's, Democratic Socialism began making inroads in Kraków. The leader of the Polish Social Democratic Party, Ignacy Daszyński (1866-1936), an almost exact contemporary of my grandfather, Jacob Aleksandrowicz (1866-1935), founded a social-democratic newspaper called *Naprzód* (Forward). In 1897, thanks to an outpouring of Polish *and Jewish* liberal votes, Daszyński was elected to represent Western Galitzia in the Austrian Federal Parliament in Vienna. In 1905, the Jewish Social Democrats, including two of my young uncles, both future lawyers, Ignacy and Wilhelm Aleksandrowicz, formed a separate Jewish Social-Democratic Party of Galitzia, which continued to work with and support Ignacy Daszyński.

When resurrected Poland became united and independent again in 1918, politicians and statesmen from the three former ocupation zones vied for national leadership. Roman Dmowski from the Prussian zone advocated ultra-conservative, anti-Semitic policies. Ignacy Daszyński from Galitzia was the chief liberal and democrat. Józef Piłsudski from Vilna and the Russian Poland, while nominally also a Social-democrat, became a military man and head of the Polish Legions, which he formed into the nucleus of a new Polish army.

After 1918, in free Poland, Piłsudski became Head of State, Dmowski led the majority Polish parliamentary party, the anti-Jewish nationalists, and Daszyński led the opposition Polish Socialist Party. Piłsudski engineered a coup d'etat, after which Daszyński withdrew from politics. He was not forgotten and served as a symbol and a rallying point for all those opposed to Piłsudski's semi-autocratc rule. Racing ahead to my own recollections, I remember that in 1935-6, when I was 10 and 11, both Piłsudski and Daszyński died and both had elaborate funerals in Kraków. I observed both. As I remember it now, Piłsudski's funeral featured numbers of armed soldiers, marching infantry, canons and horse-mounted troops. By contrast, Daszyński's funeral a year later had none of the military display, but it had thousands upon thousands of crying people slowly marching in a display of loyalty to his ideals as opposed to those of Piłsudski and his government.

In 1858, when the second Józef Aleksandrowicz was only 13, an event took place in Italy which produced reverberations among Jews and non-Jews in Kraków and in Vienna, as well as in Paris, London and even in America. Apparently, a Jewish boy, Edgar Mortara, born in Bologna in 1851, was a sickly child and his Christian maid, concerned that the child might die and go to hell, pronounced an incantation over him, using words somewhat similar to those pronounced by a priest at the rite of baptism. The child recovered and nothing further was said about this until a few years later. The maid told someone about the pseudo-baptism and the word got out that this Jewish boy had been properly or improperly baptized. Bologna at the time was a part of the Papal States and under the civil legal secular as well as ecclesiastical jusrisdiction of the Pope. The Church decided that such a baptized boy should not be left to his Jewish parents. Over the parents' vehement protests, the local office of the Holy Inquisition (reconstituted by the Pope after the defeat of Napoleon), forcibly removed the child and placed him in a Catholic orphanage in Rome. This took place, not in the Middle Ages, but in the middle of the nineteenth century, years after the French Revolution, in the age of presumed enlightenment. Protests erupted all over the world. The French Emperor Napoleon III and the young Austrian Emperor Franz Joseph sent urgent appeals to the Pope, Pius IX. From distant America President James Buchanan urged the Pope to relent and send the child back to his parents. All to no avail. Pius IX was adamant, reaffirmed his rigid medieval position and the soul of the abducted child was forcibly saved; he was raised as a Catholic and eventually joined the priesthood. The Jews in Kraków were deeply affected by this incident, mounted protests and joined Viennese Jews in petitioning the Austrian Emperor to intervene with the Pope, which he did. Kraków Jews were deeply grateful for his intervention. The incident tended to enhance their loyalty to the Austrian Imperial government and to the then 28-year-old Emperor Franz Joseph. Józef Aleksandrowicz remained a Habsburg supporter all his life.

As he grew up, Józef Aleksandrowicz, son of Menashe, became a dealer in foodstuffs and married Rachel (Reizl) Drezner, daughter of Shiya Jozua Drezner, a tavern keeper in Kraków, and his wife Henna Drezner nee Bader. Rachel was born August 12, 1847, thus was two years younger than her husband. Rachel's grandfather Asher Drezner served in Kraków as a teacher of Jewish children. His family were lease-holders of a mill in Sub-Carpathian Slovakia. Henna Bader's family traditionally operated the local Krakovian Jewish community ritual bath and served as attendants in the hospital for contagious diseases. I do not have the marriage certificate of Józef and Rachel but it must have taken place sometimes around 1865 because their first child, a boy named Jacob, was born June

6, 1866. Jacob was followed by another boy, David, born June 24, 1867. A girl, Hana, was born in 1869, another girl, Małka (Amalia), in 1873, a third girl Pearl in 1875, a boy Shiya (Jozue) in 1877 and the last child, a girl named Rivka (Rebecca) in 1879. Pearl may have died young because after her birth no further records exists. Eventually, all surviving members of the family married and had many children. The oldest, Jacob, became my grandfather. He married Hanna Hinda (Hancia) Birnbaum and had seven children described later. The second son, David, born on September 7. 1867 married Anna Gumplowicz and had one daughter, Hela. He lived on Józefa Street Nr. 9 in 1900 and was recorded in the 1900 census as a shoemaker dealing exclusively with the shoe soles (the Polish term for this was *cholewkarz)*. This was a profession separate from the shoe craftsman who cut upper parts of the shoe leather or the one who then assembled the whole shoe from its constituent parts. The youngest boy Shiya changed his name after he grew up and moved to Vienna, to its more Westernized form, Jozue. Jozue Aleksandrowicz married Zofia (Sophie) Wunderlich (Fortreflich?) and became the father of Herbert, Fritz, Frantz and Lilli. Franz died of natural causes in Vienna before Hitler took it over in 1938; Herbert Aleksandrowicz married his second cousin, Halina Weindling, daughter of Roman Weindling and Eleonora (Lorcia) Aleksandrowicz, daughter of Wolf ; Lilli Aleksandrowicz married Bernard Fried with whom she had two daughters: Michele, living in England and Catherine living in France. Józef's daughter Mania (Amalia) Aleksandrowicz married Henry Kleinhaendler. The Kleinhaendlers operated a dry-goods store and lived on Rabbi Meisels Street in Kazimierz. When Józef became old (in the nineteen thirties, when I visited him) and could not live alone, he lived near this daughter. He had a separate apartment in the Kleinhaendler house, over their store. The Kleinhaendlers had two daughters and three sons, Manny, Henry and Shaya. Their daughter Hela married Abraham Frisch and had a son, Wilhelm. Their daughter, Lola, married a man named Kalman Wasserberger.

According to the list of inhabitants of Kraków for the year 1881, entries Nos. 100-174, Józef Aleksandrowicz, then 36, lived in apartment II in building No. 169, on Kupa Street. The building was located next to No. 168, which had no inhabitants but housed the Izak Synagogue in the impressive large building founded by Izak Bogaty (the Rich), Reb Eizik reb Jekeles, one of our early relatives. In apartment I in building No. 169 lived Menashe, Józef's father, listed as a widower and in apartment III lived Józef's uncle Israel Eliasz with his wife and children. In the list of 1900, volume XV for District VIII (Kazimierz), Józef Aleksandrowicz was listed as an owner of a food stall, born April 6, 1845 in Kraków, living at Józefa Street 22. Apparently, he moved from Kupa to family-owned 22 Józefa Street in the interval. As listed, he lived with his wife Rachel, born 1847 and three youngest children, Amalia, 26, Jozua, 23, and Ester, 14 (?).

I remember my great-grandfather Józef well. I must have been around four or five, when my father first took me to visit his grandfather. In the 1930's my father and I visited him often, in his apartment above the Kleinhaendler store. I liked the old man but hated to visit there not because of him, but because his son-in-law, "uncle" Henry Kleinhaendler had a habit of pinching my cheeks and twisting them painfully. While he obviously must have considered this '*knipping*'a friendly gesture and I had inviting full rosy cheeks, I sure did not think of this as friendly. Great-grandfather Józef, 90 years old in 1935 was quite spry, lively and alert. I understand from my father that as a younger man he was tall and slim, but when I saw him, as a man in his nineties, he was stooped and rather rotund. As

I mentioned earlier, he sported a long white beard and wore a small black cap. He wore a soft white shirt with a starched removable collar. His suit consisted of a long shiny black jacket (a *capote*) and black trousers. He needed thick glasses. He subscribed to the daily Viennese *‚Neue Freie Presse‘* until 1938 and was very aware of European events. My father discussed the Polish political situation and latest developments in Nazi Germany with him in German or Yiddish. He had so many grandchildren and great-grandchildren, at least thirty seven by my count, that he could not be sure which was my father and who was I. At the beginning of every visit he would have to be told that my father was Maks, the fourth son of Jacob, his oldest.

Józef Aleksandrowicz was born just before Kraków was forcibly incorporated into the Austrian domain. He lived for nearly a hundred years of astounding changes in Europe and in Kraków. The autocratic Austrian Empire morphed in 1867 into an Imperial-Royal Dual Monarchy of Austrian Empire and Hungarian Kingdom, which fell apart at the end of the First World War in 1918. The old Emperor Franz Joseph began his rule during a general chaos of the Spring of Nations in 1848, when Austrian military had to use artillery to subdue popular rebellions in Vienna as well as in Kraków. He died in 1916 as a well-liked old man. He had seen his heirs to the Austrian throne die one by one. His son Rudolph died in a suicide pact with his love, Maria Vetsery, in the castle at Mayerling. His nephew Ferdinand was assassinated in 1814 in Sarajevo in Bosnia by a young Serb, an act that led to the First World War. His wife, the beautiful and loved Empress Elisabeth (Sissi) was also assassinated, by an anarchist. Eventually, Franz Joseph was succeeded by another of his nephews, Karl of Hapsburg, who abdicated within two years. Parts of the Hapsburg Empire, either opted for a republican form of independent existence, joined other liberated areas as new states or picked a regent to keep alive a fiction of a monarchical form of government. The Bohemian and Moravian areas joined the Slovak areas as Czechoslovakia, under the guidance of a democrat, half-Czech and half-American, Thomas Garrigue Masaryk. Polish Galitzia joined Polish areas liberated from Russian and German occupations as a united Poland which became immediately engaged in a fierce survival battle with the revolutionary Red Russia. Hungary underwent a revolution under a Jewish Communist Bela Kun and then reverted to a fascist regime presided over by Admiral Nicholas Horthy as Regent, pending restoration of a monarchy, which never happened. Italy took Trieste and South Tyrol. Croatia, Slovenia and Bosnia-Hercegovina joined Serbia and Montenegro as a Serb-Croat-Slovene Kingdom (*Srba, Hrvata i Slovenaca)*, eventually called Yugoslavia, with Alexander Karageorgevich of Serbia as King. Bukovina and Transylvania joined Romania. A truncated Austria, including Tirol, became a republic.

While Warsaw became the capital, Kraków regained its place as the primary center of Polish culture in a Polish Republic. The Treaty of Versailles created an independent Poland with guaranteed minority rights. These were not always respected. In the new Poland, Jews constituted as much as 10% of the population. From inception, the new Poland had trouble forming a reliably democratic government. Anti-Semitism was rampant and used by demagogues to garner votes and power. A democratically-elected President, Gabriel Narutowicz was assassinated by a Jew-hater who believed that the new President favored Jews too much. Eventually, the democratic Government was turned aside in a putch conducted by Józef Piłsudski, the former democratic socialist turned into a hero of the fight for independence as the founder of the Polish Legions in World War I. Piłsudski

became *the* Marshal of the Polish Army and the strongman of the new Polish regime. From the beginning of independent Poland in 1918 Jews (and women!) had all the formal legal rights: to vote, to form political parties (except for Communists, whose party was banned), to run for office, to attend public schools and universities, to trade and conduct business, to own real estate and factories, to travel, etc. etc. Restrictions, such as existed were not legal but social. Animosity against Jews was prevalent. Jewish enterprises faced boycotts. Jewish university students were ostracized, faced unofficial quotas (*numerus clausus*), and were forced to stand rather than assume assigned inferior seats. Violent murderous pogroms were not common, but occurred with frightening frequency. Kraków was also rife with anti-Jewish sentiments, but these seemed to have been more gentil than in other Polish areas. In 1939 Poland had 32 million people, among them more than three million Jews. Kraków had approximately 260,000 inhabitants, of whom about 60,000 were Jewish.

Józef Aleksandrowicz lived through all these times, saw his children succeed in business, acquire important parcels of real estate in Kraków, have many grandchildren. His health was good. He was a widower, having lost his wife earlier, and he lived alone. In the last years of his life he saw the disintegration of Jewish Kraków in World War II, after the entry of the German Army and Hitler's Waffen-SS troops. Recently, I received from the U.S. Holocaust Memorial Museum in Washington a copy of an ID card (*Kennkarte*), dated 30 April 1941, all blurred and hard to read but it must have belonged to my great-grandfather because it specifies that the card's possessor was born on 6 April 1845 in Kraków. The card has an official stamp stating that according to the best medical opinion the card's owner is unable to be moved and cannot travel (the word used was *Transportunfaehig)*. To the best of my knowledge, Józef Aleksandrowicz, son of Menashe, father of Jacob, grandfather of Maksymilian and great-grandfather of George Alexander, died in 1941 of natural causes in German-occupied Kraków, in his own apartment, in his 96-th year. I am aware of his seven children, three sons and four daughters. My grandfather, Jacob, was his oldest child. Jozef's descendants are shown in the family tree at the end of this chapter.

(b) Filip Aleksandrowicz, son of Menashe (1849-1909)

The second son of Menashe Aleksandrowicz and his wife, (Gitl) Lea nee Katzner was Filip, born on February 26, 1849 and given the name of Faibus. He was born with the assistance of a midwife in the family home, building # 203 in the Kazimierz area of Kraków. Eventually he abandoned the very Jewish name Faibush in favor of a more Westernized name Filip, characteristically retaining however the first letter of the name. In 1873 Filip married Pesel (Dorothea) Fraenkel, daughter of the Rabbi Jonas Fraenkel of Loeslau in Prussia, a descendant of the *Tzadik* (Hassidic miracle maker) of Raciborz. I understand that around 1800 this Tzadik wrote a Hassidic classic "*Ziv Harutzim*", dealing with special Talmudic rules pertaining to ritual killing of fowl. In a census of 1880, Filip was listed as a merchant, 31, living in house # 10. In 1905 he was living on Sebastyana Street, outside of but near the Jewish Quarter. Around 1908 his family moved to the outlying area of Podgórze, on the other side of the river Vistula.. Filip and Dorothea acquired several houses in Podgórze, beyond the Vistula, most notably the house at No. *1 Przy Moście* Street (Street by the Bridge), overlooking a wooden bridge over the river. The bridge, built in 1802, was washed away in the flood of 1813 and never replaced, but the street retained its name. A new stone bridge was built later a few blocks away. The old house still stands, as does the stone bridge. In a book of addresses in Kraków-Podgórze for 1909 Filip's occupation was given as owner and administrator of real estate. He died that year, at 60, so that in the subsequent list of inhabitants, in 1910, his wife, Dorothea, was listed as a widow, owner of real estate, living at Przy Moście 1.

In the history of Kraków, Filip and Dorothea are also known as the one-time owners of The First Galitzian Manufactory of Patented Matresses ‚Polonia', one of the few modest early industrial enterprises in Kraków and vicinity, employing a number of people. Filip and Dorothea had several children. The boys were Józef (b. 1878), Maksymilian/ Matyasz (b. 1880), Wilhelm (b. 1881), Isidor (b.1885), Jacob and Karl. The girls were Teresa and Klara. Teresa married Ueberall, Klara married Zeliger.

Filip and Dorothea's oldest son Józef Aleksandrowicz, also described in official records as owner of real estate in Podgórze, married Rose. They had one son, Julian (1908-1988), who became a physician specializing in hematology and a scientist concerned with effects of environmental pollution, lack of minerals in the soil and, in general, in the role of trace minerals in health and disease. In 1940 when the Germans required that all Jews living in Kraków register, Julian Aleksandrowicz filed a registry protocol, a copy of which I received from the US Holocaust Memorial Museum in Washington (see the end of this chapter). In the Ghetto Julian directed the official hospital. As the war continued and the Germans moved to eliminate the Ghetto Julian and his family escaped through the sewers. His wife, Maryla nee Tischlowicz, and child hid with non-Jewish friends and former patients, while Julian himself joined the Partisans in the woods and used his medical skills in the service of the partisan Underground Army in Poland. His conspiratorial war alias was *Dr. Twardy* (in English: Dr. Hard or Dr. Tough). After the War, he received Poland's highest honor, the medal of the *Order of Virtuti Militari*. He published a book of memoirs of his war experiences, *Pages from the diary of Doctor Tough* (Aleksandrowicz, 1967). He dedicated the book to *true* people, people who remained faithful to real humanity. In the book he bemoaned the general degradation of human behavior, complaining that in German-occupied Kraków human life had hardly any value as individual and mass executions and murders were all too common. He stated that it was a time when cruelty and meanness were extolled and more civilized behaviors had largely disappeared. Yet, he ended the book with a restatement of his belief in science and the future, saying that he believed that a vision of world without war as a mechanism for solving conflicts is not a naive hope. *"I am convinced that advances in science in all areas are continuous and will lead, in the end, to a world in which aggressiveness and genocide will be replaced by activities that foster positive development of man and humanity"*.

Eventually, in post-war Poland, Julian Aleksandrowicz founded and became Chairman of the Division of Hematology of the Medical Academy of the Jagiellonian University in Kraków. He published more than 300 scientific papers dealing with leukemia and other blood disorders as well as with the social impacts of diseases and with social ecology. In 1979 he published a book entitled *Sumienie Ekologiczne* (Ecological Conscience). In the nineteen fifties he was recognized as one of Poland's foremost scientists, physicians and researchers. Julian lived on Copernicus Street, near the Kraków Botanical Garden. He visited us several times in the United States and we visited him and his wife Maryla in Kraków. They had a summer home in the country, on Rożnów Lake and we visited them there also. Julian was a collector of old religious icons painted on wood, which he saved from small rural churches, that were being renovated or abandoned. His son, Jerzy Aleksandrowicz, a very young child during World War II, survived the War in hiding. Afterwards, he formally testified to the cruelty of the German occupation and described his life as a hidden child during the war in a testimony collected in Poland as part of war crimes trials. His testimony was published as part of a book "Children of the Holocaust speak", edited by Wiktoria Sliwowska (1993). Jerzy Aleksandrowicz is the last member of my extended family to have remained and now lives in Kraków. Dr. Julian Aleksandrowicz died and is buried at the Rakowicki cemetery in Kraków. In 1990 his friends and the Polish Ministry of Health and Social Welfare established a not-for-profit public Julian Aleksandrowicz Leukemia Foundation in Kraków, honoring Julian (in Polish: *Fundacja Imienia Juliana Aleksandrowicza*). A bronze plaque honoring him is on display at the medical school. Recently he was voted the second most prominent citizen in modern Kraków history (after the Pope John Paul II). There is now in the Krowodża district of Kraków a street named in his honor, Dr. Twardy Street (*ulica Doktora Twardego).*

Filip and Dorothea's second son, Maksymilian Matjasz, was listed in the 1932 address book of Kraków as an engineer-industrialist, living at Przy Moscie 1. He married Ernestyna Siódmak. They had a son Filip, named after his grandfather. Like their nephew Julian, Maksymilian Matjasz and Ernestyna also registered in German-occupied Kraków in 1940 and their registry forms are preserved in Warsaw, with copies at the Washington Holocaust Museum. Their son, Filip, survived the War deep in Russia, married Bertha (Blima) and had a son, Ignatz. Filip, Blima and Ignatz came to the US in the late fifties and moved to California.

Filip and Dorothea's next child, Wilhelm Aleksandrowicz, married Ellie Mannheim, emigrated to Germany, then when the Nazis took over, moved to the United States. He and Ellie lived in Queens. When my father arrived in the United States in 1941, Wilhelm met him at the train station in New York City. However, contact was not maintained afterwards. I have no information on Filip and Dorothea's other sons, Isidor, Jacob or Karl Aleksandrowicz.

The older daughter of Filip and Dorothea Teresa married Joachim Ueberall in Kraków. They had two children, a boy named Mieczysław and a daughter, Leontyna. Joachim must have died before 1926, because in the address book of 1926 he is not mentioned but, instead, the listing for the building at Przy Moście 1, shows his widow living with the family. She is shown as *"Uberall z Aleksandrowiczów Teresa*", i.e. Uberall of the Aleksandrowiczes Teresa. Teresa and Joachim's son, Mieczysław Uberall had one daughter, Magda Joanna, who came to the United States, became a physician, expert in marital relations and author of several books on medico-social subjects. She married Darryl Polenz and had three children: Theresa, Darryl Jr. and Elizabeth (Libby). All three children are married. Theresa married Blake Delany and has four children, a daughter, Hadley and a boy, Forbes, a girl Margo and a new baby, Seth. Elizabeth married Scott Rappaport.

Although Magda lived near us in Westchester we did not know her, until a few years ago when our common relative from Poland, Jerzy, great-grandson of Filip Aleksandrowicz, visited us and asked if we could drive him to see his cousin living nearby. That cousin was Magda Polenz, a granddaughter of Joachim Ueberall and Teresa Aleksandrowicz and also a great-granddaughter of Filip Aleksandrowicz. We found Magda and her family delightful and we have been in friendly contact ever since. Both Magda's daughters are pursuing professional careers, Teresa is a lawyer, Elizabeth an architect. Magda died after a long illness in November 2007.

The other daughter of Filip and Dorothea, Klara, married a man named Zeliger. The Zeligers had four girls: Wanda, Teresa, Elisabeth and Rose. Wanda's married name is Landau, Teresa's name is Huppert. The Landau family lives in Israel.

Filip's family tree, photographs of Filip and his wife obtained from his great-granddaughter and a registry page of Filip's grandson, Julian Aleksandrowicz, in the Kraków Ghetto, are appended below.

(c) Wolf Aleksandrowicz, youngest son of Menashe and Lea (1852-1888)

In the late nineteenth and early twentieth centuries Kraków attracted a number of talented young artists, painters and sculptors, of the so-called Young Poland school of arts. When an impecunious Polish artist needed a canvas and paints and had no funds to purchase them, he routinely turned for help to Wolf Aleksandrowicz, and after his death to his widow, Regina. Wolf and then Regina owned and run a store of paper goods and art supplies, which grew into a superstore and a factory of paper and art and craft supplies on the corner of Basztowa and Długa Streets in Kraków, eventually occupying the entire ground floor of the large Chambers of Commerce and Industry Building. In time Regina achieved a reputation as a patroness of a generation of young Polish artists.

Extant records in Kraków indicate that Menashe Aleksandrowicz and Lea Katzner had three surviving sons and no daughters living in town. It is likely that they had other children – most Jewish families at that time had many children – but these may have died at birth or early in childhood or emigrated to England or America. Their youngest surviving child was Wolf, now referred to in Israel as Zev. Wolf married Rivka (Regina) Hirsch (1853-1940), daughter of a tavern keeper from Tarnów. Wolf and Regina had five children. Wolf died at 36, just as his last child was being born. His widow, Regina, lived long and was a very successful businesswoman in Kraków, she enlarged the store and its line of art supplies. Wolf and Regina's first child, Sinai, was born in 1877. According to his birth record, his name was immediately changed to Zygmunt; it reverted to Sinai when he moved to Israel. Then in sequence were born Dora (Dobrysza) (1880-1942), Lorcia (Leonora) (1882-1964), Róża (Rachel) (1886-1973) and David (1888-1947). Only Róża, the subject of portraits by Polish artists – recipients of free

painting materials from her mother, remained single. All the others married. Wolf earned a living as a shopkeeper. His widow, Regina, converted his stationery store into the premier wholesale-and-retail paper-and-art-supplies establishment in Kraków, serving generations of school children and artists.

Austrian Galitzia was freer than either the German or the Russian areas of Poland. After 1867, the Austrians allowed the official use of Polish, which was banned in German and Russian zones. Between 1867 and 1914, Kraków served as a center of Polish culture, with almost every important Polish writer, painter and sculptor residing, studying or visiting Kraków. When impecunious painters of the so-called *Młoda Polska* (Young Poland) group, students of the famous School of Fine Arts in Kraków, could not afford art supplies, they often received them free from the *R. Aleksandrowicz fabryka i skład papieru i magazyn papieru i przyborów piśmiennych* (R. Aleksandrowicz factory and paper warehouse and store of paper and writing supplies). In recompense for the free supplies, many of the artists painted or sketched portraits of Regina's young daughter Róża, who was 14 in 1900 and 28 when World War I broke out in 1914. Several such portraits exist. A life-size, full figure, oil painting of Róża Aleksandrowicz by the later famous Polish painter, Jacek Malczewski (1854-1929), hangs at the second floor entry to the main dining room of the elegant Kraków restaurant Hawełka in the Main Town Square (Rynek Główny)(see photos after the chapter dealing with the Rynek of Kraków). Another painting of Róża, this one by Teodor Axentowicz (1859-1938) is in a private collection. I have also seen several watercolors, pastels and pen-and-pencil sketches of Róża in Kraków. As Regina aged, the running of the paper enterprise was taken over by her sons, Zygmunt and David, and the store's name was changed to "R. Aleksandrowicz sons", as listed in the 1930 Kraków telephone directory. In the 1930's "R. Aleksandrowicz sons" was credited with having donated the paper for printing of the two volumes of the authoritative history of Kraków Jewry by Prof. Mayer Bałaban, as shown on one of front pages of the book. Regina Hirsch Aleksandrowicz died in 1940, at the beginning of World War II as a refugee in Lwów.

Her son, Zygmunt Aleksandrowicz (1877-1946), married Helena (Hinda) Rakower (1884-1968) in Kraków. The Rakowers were a prominent Kraków family, with a long and distinguished history. The name implies that a distant ancestor of theirs came from the town of Raków. Earlier members of the family were referred to, in the Polish style, as Rakowski, later ones, in the German (or Yiddish) style, as Rakower. As described earlier, Gutman Rakowski, a martyred ancestor of the Rakowers, served as the Elder of the Kahał during the difficult time of the Bar Insurrection and was arrested and tortured to death. As a child I went to school and was a friend of one of the Rakowers, Józek. Recently, I was shown a history and genealogy of the Rakower family prepared by Roman Rakower of California.

Zygmunt (Sinai) Aleksandrowicz was an ardent Zionist and supporter of Zionist causes. In 1904, in Kraków, he published a small pro-Zionist Hebrew newsletter. In 1905 Zygmunt and Helena had a son whom they named Wilhelm (Wilek). As a wealthy man with a conscience and interest in social causes Zygmunt became a promonent philanthropist. He was instrumental in helping the Jewish Palestinian *Yishuv* to purchase land in Palestine, including many orange groves. He funded schools and youth centers for poor Jewish youngsters both in Poland and in Palestine. I recently came across a specific example of Zygmunt's generosity. Apparently, one day he came across the small square near Brzozowa

Street in Kraków where young religious youths argued about fine points of the Talmud and the Torah. Zygmunt stopped and listened for a while, was impressed with the acumen and knowledge of one of the young men and asked him where he would like to go to study. He was told that the youth dreams of going to the Chachmei Yeshiva in Lublin but that his family is too poor to send him there. Zygmunt then offered to sponsor him and pay for his education. When the young man applied to the school he was tested by then Rosh Yeshiva Rabbi Meir Shapiro who was astounded by his vast proficiency in all aspects of the Torah and knowledge of the Talmud by heart. Zygmunt then paid the school for his protegee's education. The young man, Chaim Kreisworth (1918-2001), grew up to become and Orthodox rabbi who founded and led the Merkaz ha-Torah Yeshiva in Jerusalem. In 1947 he became Rosh Yeshiva in Skokie, Illinois and in 1953 he was called to become the Chief Rabbi of the respected Orthodox Jewish community of Antwerp in Belgium.

In Kraków, Zygmunt was elected Vice-President of the Jewish Community Council (Kahał) and served as an elected member of the Presidium of the over-all Kraków City Council. Zygmunt and Helena were caught in Kraków at the outbreak of the war in 1939. Early during the war they moved through Lwów and the USSR to Palestine where they had properties. Also, their only son, Wilhelm lived there. Zygmunt died there in December 1946. In 1968 in New York, the World Committee of the TOZ charitable organization published a commemorative booklet honoring Sinai Aleksandrowicz. Another commemorative booklet was published in Tel-Aviv in 1987. A bronze tablet honoring him was unveiled in 1999 in Kraków, thanks to the efforts of his grandchildren.

Zygmunt's son Wilhelm (1905-1992), born in Kraków, was also an ardent Zionist. At 17, in 1922 he produced a hand-written little journal advocating migration to Palestine and stressing the dangers of assimilation in the Diaspora. He left Poland soon after and moved to Jerusalem. Eventually, he married Lea Chelouche (*Shlush*), whose Sephardic family lived in Palestine for generations and was important in early Jewish settlement of the land. The Chelouche family lived in Jaffa when it was a mostly Arab town, one of the largest and most important in Palestine. They used Arabic as their everyday language. One of the Chelouche became governor of the Jaffa region and was among the founders of the new exclusively Jewish town of Tel Aviv. Tel Aviv grew to become the largest city in what is now Israel. Now Jaffa is only a quaint old suburb of Tel Aviv. Lea Chelouche was a known beauty and her marriage to Wilhelm Aleksandrowicz, the heir to Zygmunt Aleksandrowicz fortune was treated as a major social event. Wilhelm, known in Israel as Zeev, was an accomplished photographer. He travelled widely and left a large number of stunning photographs, among them a series of striking photos of early Jewish settlements and evocative portraits of ragged Arab children. Among famous people that he photographed was the poet Chaim Nachman Bialik (1873-1934) and the political leader Vladimir Jabotinsky. Some of his photos, of Palestine, Japan and elsewhere are about to go on display in Poland and elsewhere. Zeev and Leah had four children, a son Joseph (Yossi) (1938-2007), another son Daniel and twins, Sinai and Rachel. Zeev Aleksandrowicz continued to be active in Jewish Yishuv in Palestine, and was helpful in the establishment of the State of Israel. He was friendly with most of Israel's founding fathers. He died at 87. I never met Zeev but I have met all his children. The meetings came about in an interesting fashion.

My wife and I were working in the National Archives in Kraków in 1997, when Jerzy, the son of Julian Aleksandrowicz, who lives in Kraków, announced that we would have an opportunity to meet another Aleksandrowicz relative, who was arriving from Israel. This turned out to be Dr Joseph Aleksandrowicz, known as Yossi, son of Zeev. This was a pleasant surprise and we enjoyed meeting Yossi and his second wife, a famous artist, Tithy. We found out that we have a lot in common and we exchanged information about our family tree and discovered, among other items, that Yossi's sister, Rachel, lives in the United States across the George Washington bridge in New Jersey. After our return to New York we met her and her husband, Chaim Shimshowitz, their beautiful daughter, Avital, and Avital's daughter, Shir. Eventually, in Rachel's house we also met Rachel's son, Dror and Rachel's brothers, Dani Aleksandrowicz and Sinai Aleksandrowicz.

Yossi, Zev Aleksandrowicz's son, first married Lisa Degens. They had a daughter, named Vanessa. His second wife whom we met in Krakow, Ernestine (Tithy) Hasson is a painter, who had many exhibitions of her artwork. Yossi's brother, Dani, whom we met recently, married Elen Jaffe. They have three daughters, Michal, and twins, Esther and Tami. Dani married again. His wife is Sylvia nee Weissman, born in Wrocław, Poland. Michal married Robert Rabinowitz. They have three children, Lilli. Jack and Ben. Zev's youngest son, one of twins, Sinai, named after Zeev's father who died in 1946, was sick as a child and spent some time in rehabilitative clinics in Switzerland. Eventually, fully recovered, he married and has three children, Or, Nili and Gadi. It is his twin sister, Rachel Shimshowitz, who lives in New Jersey. Or Aleksandrowicz married Miri, Nili married Zechiel Yaban.

Wolf and Regina's oldest daughter, Dora (Donia) married Gustav Scheller. In 1919 they had a child, Ursula, who married Alexander Anhalt. Donia, Gustav and the Anhalts perished in the Holocaust in 1942. Donia's sister, Eleonora (Lorcia), married Roman Weindling in Kraków. Like his wife, Roman Weindling was also born in Kraków in 1882. He was the son of Marcus (Mordhe) Weindling and grandson of Joel Weindling. Roman was an architect. He and Lorcia had three children, Halina (1913-1997), Władysław (Walter) and Jadwiga. Halina Weindling, daughter of Roman Weindling and Eleonora nee Aleksandrowicz, granddaughter of Wolf and great-granddaughter of Menashe Aleksandrowicz, married her relative Herbert Aleksandrowicz of Vienna, son of Jozue, grandson of Józef and great-grandson of the same Menashe Aleksandrowicz of Kraków. When Herbert died, Halina remarried. Her second husband was Kees Driessen whom she married in Rangoon in Burma, today Yangoon, capital of Myanmar. With Herbert she had Eva Alexander, with Kees Michael Driessen. Walter Weindling moved to England. He married Gail and has three children: James, Richard and John Weindling.

The next child of Wolf and Regina, Róża , never married. I met her in Kraków, but I have only a vague recollection of what she looked like. I believe that she was far from beautiful, but in her youth she was lively and vivacious and a fit subject for many portraits. Prior to the Germans' entry into Kraków, she moved east to Lwów and eventually ended in Palestine, where she died in 1973. I have enclosed a photo of a large oil portrait of Róża (which hangs in the restaurant Hawełka) at the end of the description of the Central Square of Kraków below. A photo of RóżaAleksandrowicz is on display in an exhibit of artifacts pertaining to Jews of Kraków currently (in late 2007) open in the Kraków Rynek Główny (Central Market Square).

The youngest child of Wolf and Regina, David (1888-1947), ran the paper and art goods enterprise in Kraków with his brother Zygmunt. David Aleksandrowicz married Róża

Groner (1898-1994). They lived in Kraków on Biskupia Street 4, in a house they owned. David and Róza had three children, Maryla, Ryszard and Witold. The children's early years were spent in Kraków. Richard attended the same grammar school as I and we saw each other daily. Once a week he and I and two of our classmates, Adam Scharf, grandson of Napoleon Telz, and Józek Rakower mentioned above, had lunch in Richard's home, which was located in the immediate vicinity of the school, right on Biskupia Street. When we both finished the grammar school (in 1937), our paths diverged. I went to a public secondary school, while Richard went to a private Hebrew Gimnasium in Kraków. He finished two years of that school when the war broke out and our peaceful Kraków existence ended abruptly. After escaping through the Soviet Union, the David Aleksandrowicz family moved to Palestine. Maryla (Miriam) became an engineer, married and has a son, David. David Miloh married Dalia Karoh. They have two children, Hadar Miloh and Doron Miloh. My classmate Richard (Dov) became a physician, married Malka Krol. They have three children, Orly, Ann and Dani Aleksandrowicz. Orly married Assaf Maron. They have Keren, Tal and Ayelet Maron. Anna married Yoad Brisker. They have Ariel Brisker. Witold (Zev) Aleksandrowicz, the youngest child of David (Dov), a talented chemist, married Mira and then Gabriela (Gabi). He has Daphna, Ronan and Gil Aleksandrowicz. Daphna married Dan, then Avi. She has Carmel and Naaman. All those listed here live in Israel. The descendants of Wolf (Zeev) Aleksandrowicz constitute the largest group of family members, many of them proudly carrying the Aleksandrowicz family name. It is likely that in the not-too-distant future they will be the only ones left to carry that name.

mili, lat dwadzieścia jeden liczący w Gminie dziewiątej pod liczbą trzechset
mieszkający, i okazał Nam dziecię płci żeńskiej, urodzone w zamieszkaniu
Jego dnia dwudziestego trzeciego Kwietnia bieżącego roku, o godzinie pierwszej wrano, Oświadczając: Iż spłodzone jest z niego i Brajndli Gitli
z Szmelcerów lat dwadzieścia dwa liczącej Jego Małżonki prawej, o
czem Nas Aktem ślubu Cywilnego przekonał - nadając mu [illegible] Imie
Estera. Po wyczytaniu powyższem oświadczeniu w obecności Szachna
Gerstenfelda profesyi Rzeźnicy i Eliasza Koral Wyrobnika Obywateli
tutejszych na Kazimierzu zamieszkałych, Akt ten głośno odczytany przez Nas
Ojca i świadków podpisany został — [signature] m.s.c.

[Hebrew signature] Samuel Feiwowicz Gottlieb [illegible] Józef Gerstenfeld

3 Roku tysiąc Ośmset Czterdziestego piątego dnia piątego Maia, o godzinie
pierwszej popołudniu - Przed Nami Franciszkiem Gawrońskim Urzędnikiem Stanu Cywilnego w Wolnem Mieście Krakowie dla Starozakonnych ustanowionym
w Gminie drugiej pod liczbą sto siedemdziesiąt jeden Biuro Urzędu swego utrzymującym. Stawił się Osobiście Starozakonny Manasses Alexandrowicz
pisarz w Kantorze Loteryi, lat dwadzieścia Ośm liczący w Gminie dziewiątej
pod liczbą dwieście trzy mieszkający, i okazał Nam dziecię płci męzkiej urodzone w zamieszkaniu Jego dnia piątego Kwietnia bieżącego roku, o godzinie pierwszej wrano, Oświadczając: Iż spłodzone jest z niego i Lei z Klatene-
rów lat dwadzieścia Ośm liczącej jego Małżonki prawej, o czem Nas Wyciągiem Aktu ślubu Cywilnego przekonał - nadając temu Synowi swemu
Imie Józef. Po wyczytaniu powyższem oświadczeniu w obecności Starozakonnych Herszla Grifla [illegible] i Saula Mygel [illegible] Obywateli tutejszych na Kazimierzu zamieszkałych, Akt ten głośno odczytany przez Nas
Ojca i świadków podpisany został - [signature] m.s.c.

[Hebrew signature] Menasses Alexandrowicz ojciec

4 Roku tysiąc Ośmset Czterdziestego piątego dnia piątego Maia, o godzinie po
pierwszej popołudniu - Przed Nami Franciszkiem Gawrońskim Urzędnikiem
Stanu Cywilnego w Wolnem Mieście Krakowie dla Starozakonnych ustanowionym, w Gminie drugiej pod liczbą sto siedemdziesiąt jeden Biuro Urzędu
swego utrzymującym. Stawiła się Osobiście Starozakonna Sara z Lea [illegible]-
wnówna, Stanu Wolnego Szwaczka, lat dwadzieścia pięć licząca w Gminie
dziewiątej pod liczbą sto dwadzieścia jeden mieszkająca, i okazała Nam dziecię płci męzkiej urodzone w Gminie piątej pod liczbą trzydzieści trzy to jest w
Szpitalu Żydowskim dnia piętnastego Maia tysiąc Ośmset trzydziestego Ósmego roku, o godzinie dziewiątej wrano, Oświadczając: Iż spłodzone jest z niej
[illegible] Abraham

Fig. 032. A copy of the birth certificate of Józef Aleksandrowicz, son of Menashe

1845 – BIRTH OF JóZEF ALEKSANDROWICZ, SON OF MENASHE

From Jewish Civil Records, Kraków-Kazimierz, Year 1845, Item 143, folio 49:

Roku tysiąc Ośmst Czterdziestego piątego dnia piątego Maia o godzinie pierwszey popołudniu przed Nami Franciszkiem Gawrońskim Urzędnikiem Stanu Cywilnego w Wolnem Mieście Krakowie dla Starozakonnych ustanowionym w Gminie drugiey pod liczbą sto siedmdzisiąt ieden Biuro Urzędu Swego utrzymuiącym stawił się Osobiście Starozakonny **Manasses Aleksandrowicz** pisarz w Kantorze Loteryi, lat dwadzieścia ośm liczący w Gminie dziesątey pod liczbą dwieście trzy mieszkaiący, i okazał Nam dziecko płci męskiey urodzone w zamieszkaniu Jego dnia Szóstego Kwietnia bieżącego roku o godzinie pierwszey w nocy, Oświadczaiąc iż spłodzone iest z niego i Lei z Katznerów lat dwadziescia ośm liczącey iego Małżonki prawney, o czem Nas Wyciągiem Aktu ślubu Cywilnego przekonał – nadaiąc temu Synowi swemu Imie **Józef** – po uczynionym powyższym oświadczniu w obecności Starozakonnych Herszla Grifla faktora i Saula Prygiel Kucharza pełnoletnich na Kazimierzu zamieszkałych, Akt ten głośno odczytany, przez Nas, Oyca i świadków podpisany został –

F. Gawroński, u.s.c.
Menases Aleksandrowicz, ocyec

In English:

Year one thousand eight hundred forty five, fifth day of May at one o‘clock in the afternoon before Us, Franciszek Gawroński, Civil Record Clerk appointed for persons of the Old Testament in the Free City of Kraków, maintaining an office in the Second Community under the number one hundred seventy one, appeared in person Old Testamenter Manasses Aleksandrowicz, writer in the lottery office, twenty eight years old, living in the Tenth Community under the number two hundred and three, and showed Us a child of male gender, born in his domicile on the sixth day of April of the current year at one o‘clock at night, declaring that it was born to him and to Lea nee Katzner, twenty eight years old, his legal wife, which he proved to us with a copy of an Act of Civil Marriage – giving this Son of his the name Józef – after making this declaration in the presence of the Old Testamenters Herszl Grifel, broker, and Saul Prygiel, cook, adults living in Kazimierz, this Act, having been read aloud, was signed by Us, the father and witnesses.

F. Gawroński, c.r.c.
Menases Aleksandrowicz, father

Descendants of Józef Aleksandrowicz (1846-1942)

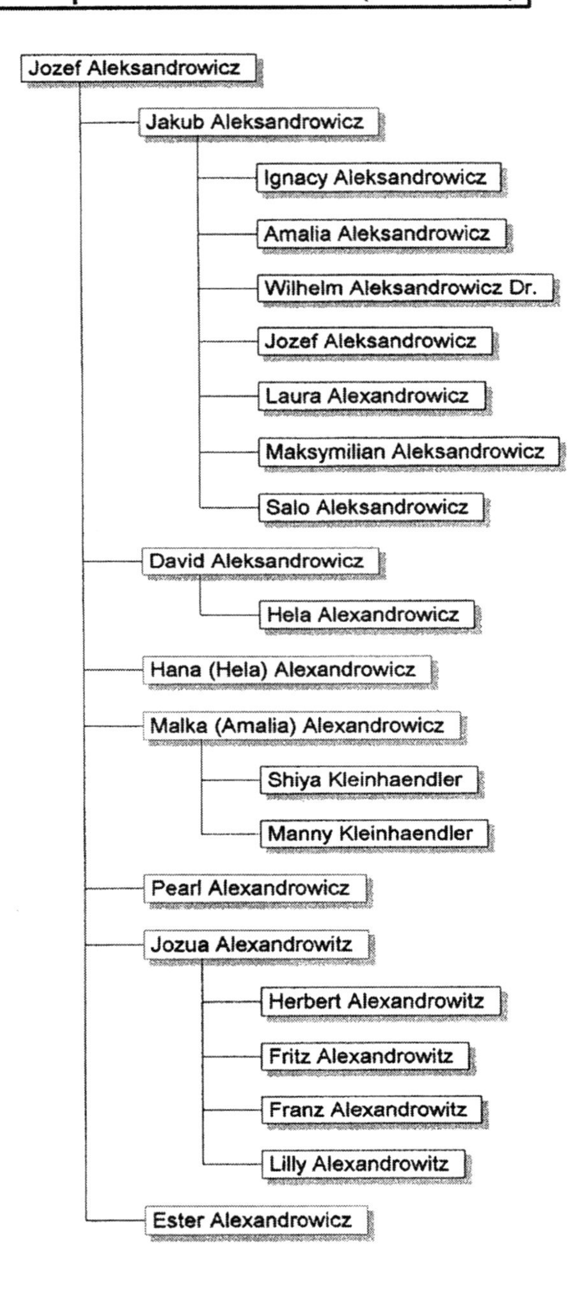

Fig. 033. Family tree of Józef and Rachel (Drezner) Aleksandrowicz

[illegible handwriting — conclusion of preceding record, signed:] Filip Etgens Urzędnik

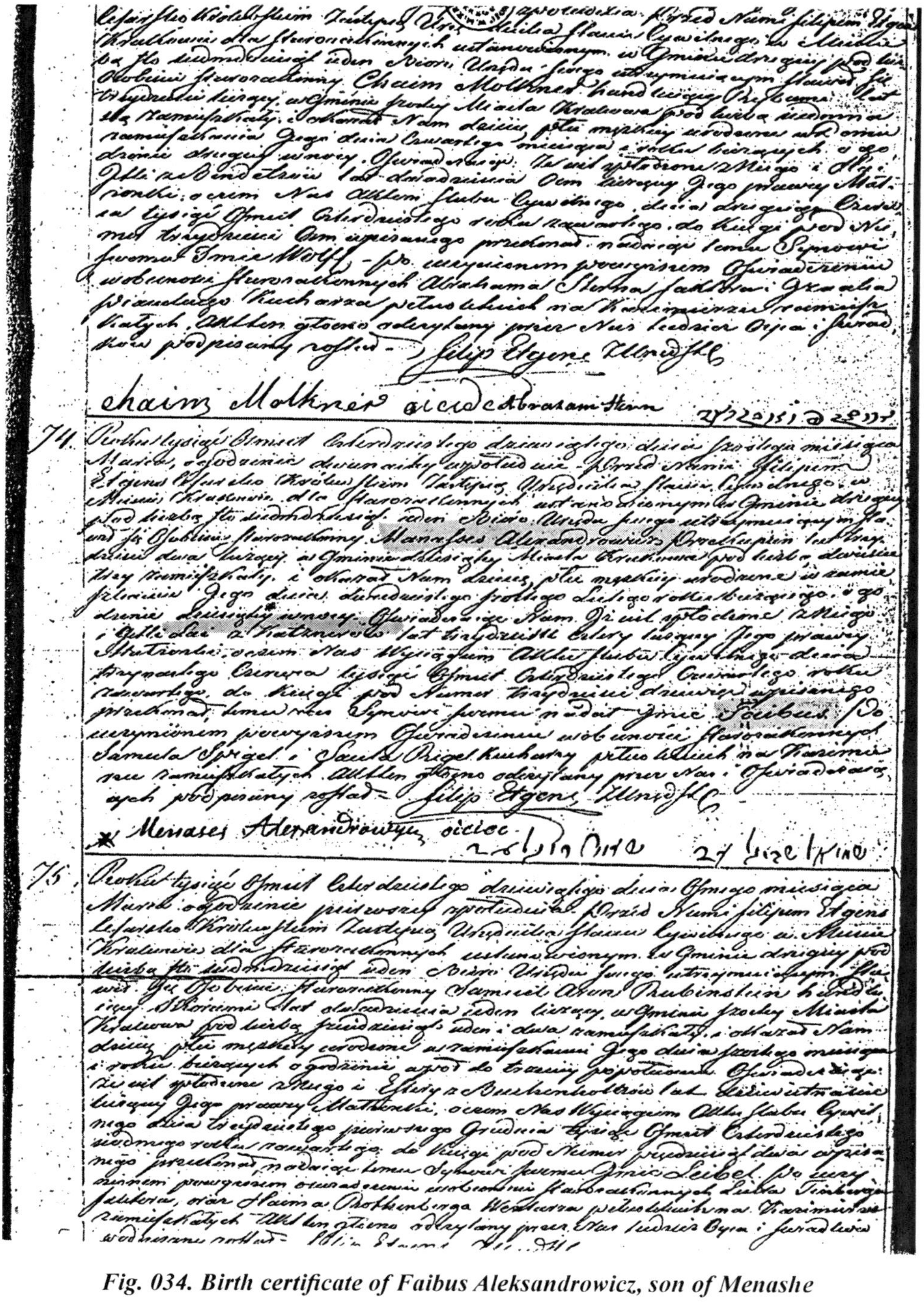

Chaim Molkner ojciec Abraham Stern [Hebrew notation, illegible]

74. Roku tysiąc ośmset czterdziestego dziewiątego dnia [illegible] miesiąca Marca, o godzinie dziewiątej wpołudnie. Przed Nami Filipem Etgens [illegible] Urzędnikiem Stanu Cywilnego w Mieście Krakowie dla Starozakonnych ustanowionym w Gminie drugiej pod liczbą sto siedmdziesiąt jeden [illegible] Urzędu Jego stawił się osobiście Starozakonny Manasses Aleksandrowicz Przekupień lat trzydzieści dwa liczący w Gminie dziesiątej Miasta Krakowa pod liczbą [illegible] zamieszkały, i okazał Nam dziecię płci męskiej urodzone w zamieszkaniu Jego dnia [illegible] Lutego roku bieżącego o godzinie dziesiątej wieczór. Oświadczając Nam iż jest spłodzone z Niego i Gitli Laj z Katznerów lat trzydzieści cztery liczącej Jego prawej Małżonki, o czem Nas wyciągiem Aktu Ślubu Cywilnego dnia trzynastego Czerwca tysiąc ośmset czterdziestego czwartego roku zawartego, do Księgi pod Numer trzydzieści dziewięć wpisanego przekonał, temuż zaś Synowi swemu nadał imię Faibus. Po uczynionem powyższem Oświadczeniu w obecności Starozakonnych Samuela Szpigel i [illegible] Rigel kucharzy pełnoletnich na Kazimierzu zamieszkałych. Akt ten głośno odczytany przez Nas i Oświadczających podpisany został. — Filip Etgens Urzędnik

Menases Aleksandrowicz ojciec [Hebrew notation, illegible]

75. Roku tysiąc ośmset czterdziestego dziewiątego dnia ósmego miesiąca Marca o godzinie pierwszej popołudniu. Przed Nami Filipem Etgens [illegible handwriting — remainder of record]

Fig. 034. Birth certificate of Faibus Aleksandrowicz, son of Menashe

1849 – BIRTH CERTIFICATE OF FEIBUSH (FILIP) ALEKSANDROWICZ

Roku tysiąc Ośmset Czterdiestego dziewiątego dnia szóstego miesiąca Marca, o godzinie dwunastey wpołudnie – przed Nami Filipem Etgins Cesarsko-Królewskim Zastępcą Urzędnika Stanu Cywilnego, w Mieście Krakowie dla Starozakonnych ustanowionym w Gminie drugiey pod liczbą sto siedemdziesiąt ieden Biuro Urzędu Swego utrzymuiącym stawił się Osobiście Starozakonny Manasses Aleksandrowicz Przekupień lat trzydzieści dwa liczący w Gminie dziesiątey Miasta Krakówa pod liczbą dwieście trzy zamieszkały i okazał Nam dziecię płci męskiey urodzone w zamieszkaniu iego dnia dwudziestego szóstego Lutego roku bieżącego, o godzinie dziesiątey w nocy, Oświadczaiąc Nam iż iest spłodzone z Niego i Gitli Lai z Katznerów lat trzydzieści cztery liczącey Jego prawney Małżonki, o czym Nas Wyciągiem Aktu ślubu Cywilnego dnia trzynastego Czerwca tysiąc Ośmset Czterdziestego Czwartego zawartego do Księgi pod numer trzydzieści dziewięć wpisanego przekonał, ...temu Synowi swemu nadał Imię Faibus. Po uczynionem powyższym Oświadczeniu w obecności Starozakonnych Szmula Sprigiel i Saula Prigel kucharzy pełnoletnich na Kazimierzu zamieszkałych Akt ten odczytany przez nas i oświadcziących podpisany został

Filip Etgins
Menasses Aleksandrowicz oiciec

In English:

In the year one thousand eight hundred forty nine on the twenty sixth of March, at twelve noon – before Us Filip Etgins, Imperial-Royal deputy Civil State Clerk appointed in the City of Kraków for persons of the Old Testament and maintaining his Office in the Second District under the number one hundred seventy one, personally appeared the Old Testamenter Manasses Aleksandrowicz, merchant, thirty two years old, living in the Tenth District under the number two hundred and three and showed Us a baby of the male gender born in his domicile on the twenty sixth of February of the current year at ten o'clock at night, declaring that it was born to him and to Gitl Lea of the Katzners, thirty four years old, his legal spouse, which he proved to us with an extract from the Civil Marriage Record of thirteenth of June one thousand Eight hundred Forty Four, entered into the Record under the number thirty nine...he gave do this son of his the Name Faibus. Having made the above announcements in the presence of Old Testamenters Szmul Sprigiel and Saul Rigiel, cooks, adults living in Kazimierz, this Act was read by us and by the witnesses was signed

Filip Etgins
Menasses Aleksandrowicz, father

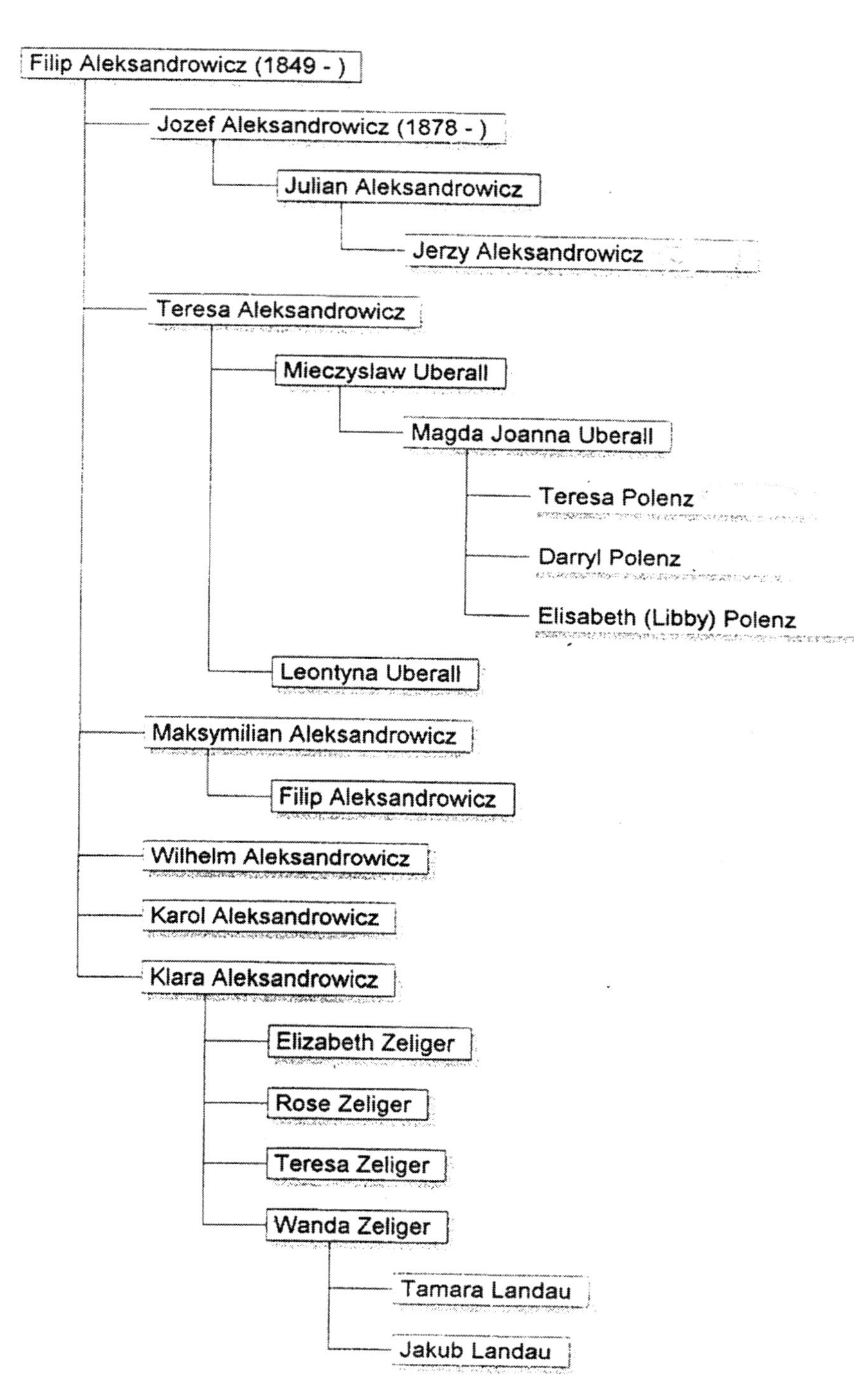

Fig. 035. Family tree of Filip Aleksandrowicz

Fig. 036. Portraits of Filip and Dorothea Aleksandrowicz;

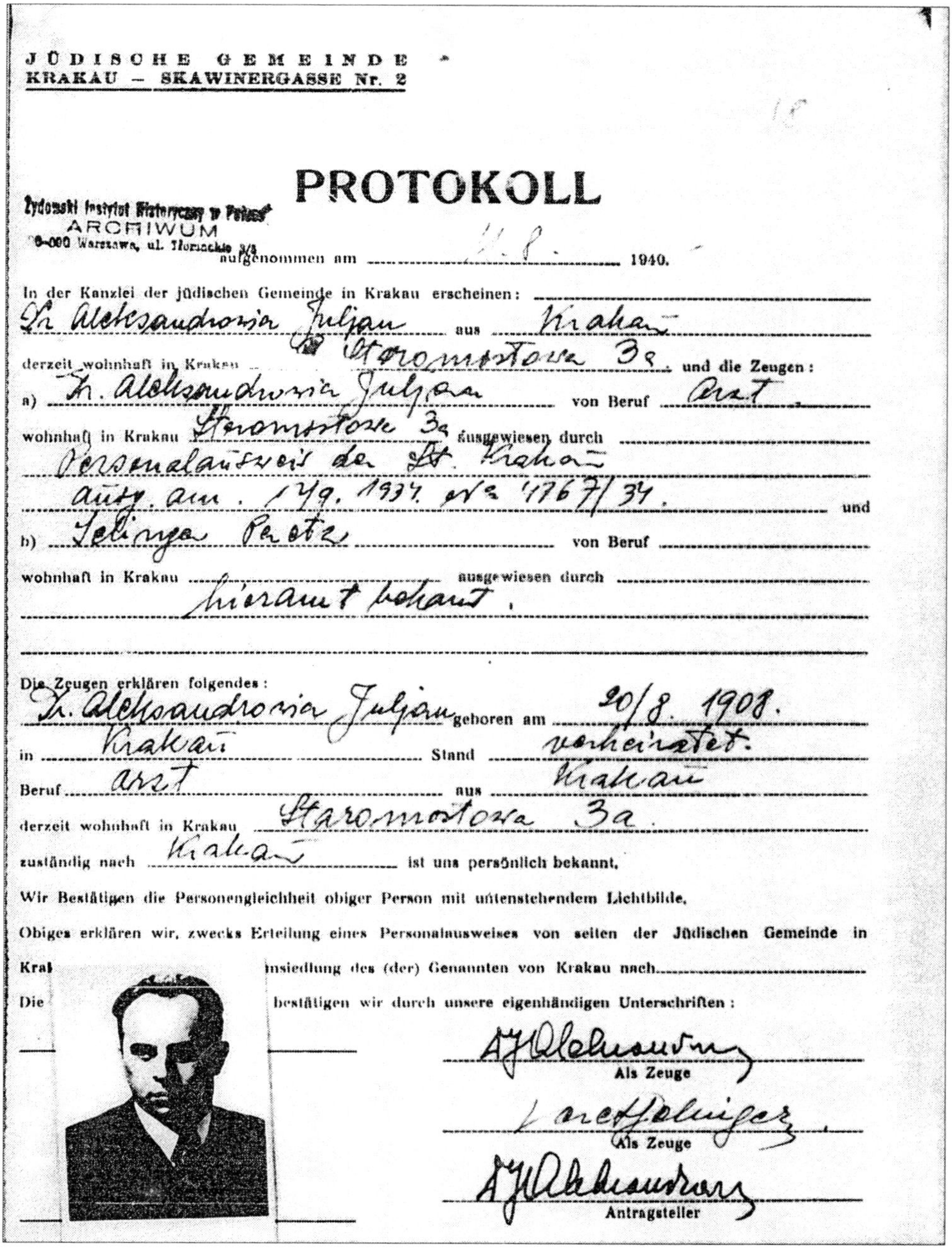

JÜDISCHE GEMEINDE
KRAKAU – SKAWINERGASSE Nr. 2

PROTOKOLL

Żydowski Instytut Historyczny w Polsce
ARCHIWUM
00-090 Warszawa, ul. Tłomackie 3/5

aufgenommen am 21.8. 1940.

In der Kanzlei der jüdischen Gemeinde in Krakau erscheinen: Dr. Aleksandrowicz Juljan aus Krakau

derzeit wohnhaft in Krakau Staromostowa 3a und die Zeugen:

a) Dr. Aleksandrowicz Juljan von Beruf Arzt

wohnhaft in Krakau Staromostowa 3a ausgewiesen durch Personalausweis der St. Krakau ausg. am 17/9. 1934 Nr 4767/34. und

b) Zelinger Peretz von Beruf

wohnhaft in Krakau ausgewiesen durch hieramt bekannt.

Die Zeugen erklären folgendes: Dr. Aleksandrowicz Juljan geboren am 20/8. 1908.

in Krakau Stand verheiratet.

Beruf Arzt aus Krakau

derzeit wohnhaft in Krakau Staromostowa 3a

zuständig nach Krakau ist uns persönlich bekannt.

Wir Bestätigen die Personengleichheit obiger Person mit untenstehendem Lichtbilde.

Obiges erklären wir, zwecks Erteilung eines Personalausweises von seiten der Jüdischen Gemeinde in Kra[…] […]nsiedlung des (der) Genannten von Krakau nach

Die […] bestätigen wir durch unsere eigenhändigen Unterschriften:

Dr. J. Aleksandrowicz
Als Zeuge

Peretz Zelinger
Als Zeuge

Dr. J. Aleksandrowicz
Antragsteller

Fig. 037. A sheet from the Kraków ghetto registry of 1940 showing registration of Filip's grandson, Dr. Julian Aleksandrowicz

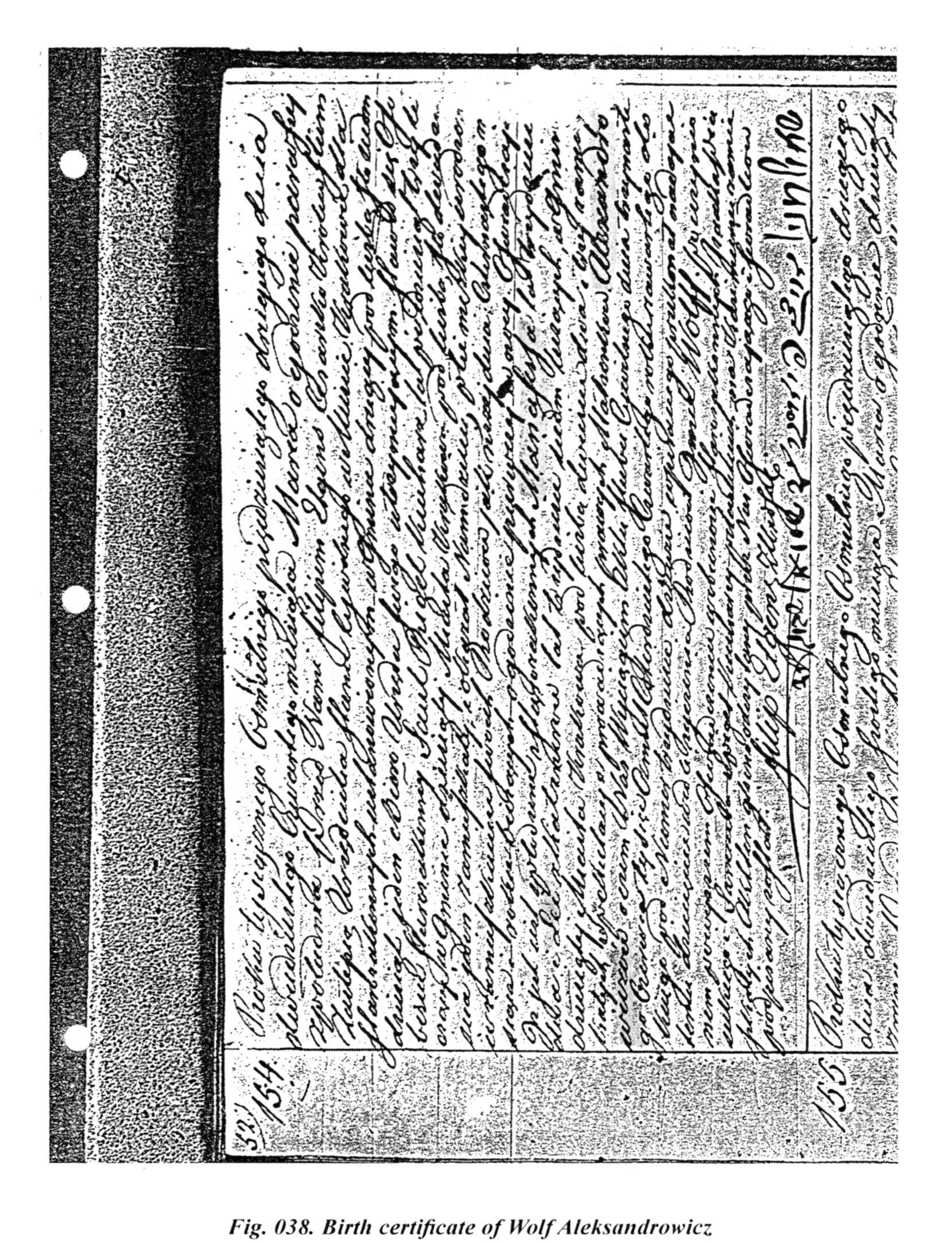

Fig. 038. Birth certificate of Wolf Aleksandrowicz

BIRTH CERTIFICATE OF WOLFF ALEKSANDROWICZ – KRAKÓW 1852

(from the Kraków Civil Records, Year 1852, page 52, item # 154):

Roku tysiącznego ośmsetnego pięćdziesiątego drugiego dnia dwudziestego Czwartego miesiąca Marca o godzinie pierwszey zpołudnia przed Nami Filipem Etgins Cesarsko- Królewskim Zastępcą Urzędnika Stanu Cywilnego w Mieście Krakowie dla Starozakonnych ustanowionym w Gminie drugiej pod liczbą sto siedmdziesiąt jeden Biuro Urzędu swego utrzymującym stawił się Osobiście Starozakonny Saul Prigel kucharz lat pięćdziesiąt trzy liczący w Gminie dziesiątej Miasta Krakowa pod liczbą sto dwadzieścia jeden zamieszkały, i okazał Nam dziecię, płci męskiej urodzone w zamieszkaniu swoich Rodziców jak niżej dnia Czternastego miesiąca i roku bieżących o godzinie pierwszej w nocy. Oświadczając: Iż jest spłodzone z starozakonnych **Manasessa** lat trzydzieści dwa i Lei z Katznerów lat trzydzieści siedm liczącey, w Gminie dziesiątej Miasta Krakowa pod liczbą dwieście dwa i trzy zamieszkałych, spekulację prowadzących prawnych Małżonków **Aleksandrowiczów** o czem Nas Wyciągiem Aktu ślubu Cywilnego dnia trzynastego Czerwca tysiąc Ośmset Czterdziestego Czwartego roku zawartego do księgi pod Numer trzydzieści dziewięć wpisanego przekonał nadając temu dziecięciu wedle życzenia Rodziców Imię **Wolff**. Po uczynionem powyższem Oświadczeniem w obecności Starozakonnych Izaka Piaseckiego i Samuela Prigel Kucharzy pełnoletnich na Kazimierzu zamieszkałych Akt ten głośno odczytany przez Nas Oświadczającego i świadków podpisany został.

Filip Etgins, ZCKUrz SC

In English:

In the year one thousand eight hundred fifty two, on the twenty fourth day of the month of March at one o'clock in the afternoon before Us, Filip Etgins, Deputy Civil State Clerk in the City of Kraków, appointed for the Old Testamenters and maintaining an office in the second Community under the number one hundred seventy one, personally appeared the Old Testamenter Saul Prigel, cook, fifty three years old, living in the tenth Community of the City of Kraków under the number one hundred twenty two, and showed us a baby, of male gender, born in the domicile of his parents, as below, on the fourteenth day of the current month and year at one o'clock at night, declaring that it was born to the Old Testamenters Manasses, thirty two years old, and Lea of the Katzners, thirty seven years old, living in the tenth Community of the City of Kraków under the numbers two hundred two and three, conducting trades, legal spouses **Aleksandrowicz**, which was proven to Us by an extract of the record of a civil wedding contracted on the thirteenth day of the month of June one thousand eight hundred forty four, entered into the book under the number thirty nine, and giving this baby, according to the parents' wishes, the name **Wolff**. After having read the above statement aloud, in the presence of Old Testamenters Isaak Piasecki and Samuel Prigel, cooks, adults living in Kazimierz, this Act was signed by Us, by the declarer and witnesses.

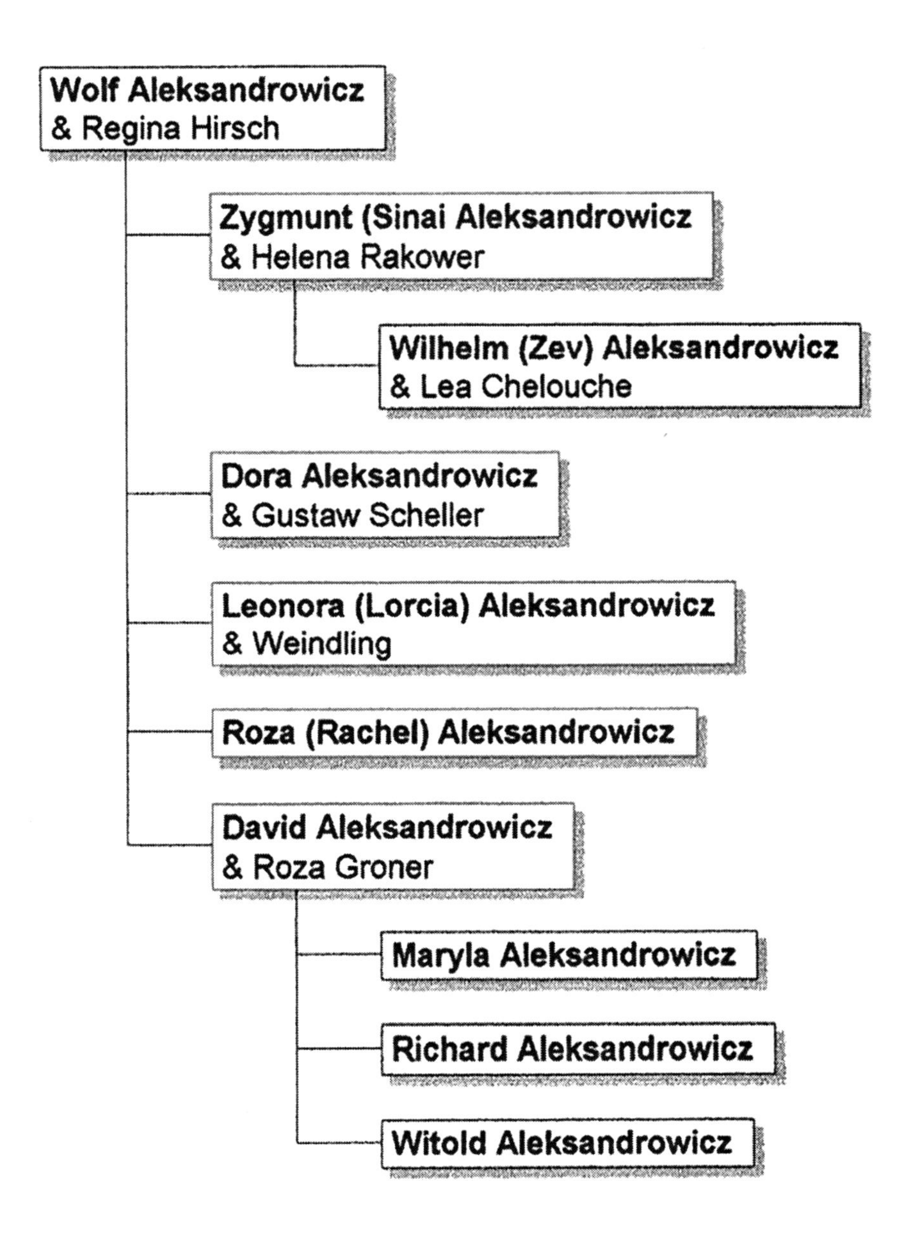

Fig. 039 Family tree of Wolf Aleksandrowicz

A page from the Kraków 1930 telephone directory with Aleksandrowicz listings.
At the bottom: an ad for the R. Aleksandrowicz paper goods enterprise

ROZMÓWNICE PUBLICZNE:

Rejonowy Urząd Telefoniczno-Telegraficzny, Wielopole 2.
Kraków 2, dworzec kolejowy, (westybul).
Kraków 4, Podwale 3.
Kraków 5, Rynek Kleparski 16.
Kraków 6, Augustiańska 20.
Kraków 7, pl. Bernardyński 1.
Kraków 8, Friedleina 1.

1 11 11 Pogotowie ratunkowe.
1 22 22 Straż pożarna.
1 21 11 Straż pożarna.
1 19 13 Sypanie kopca Marsz. Piłsudskiego, wszelkie informacje dla wycieczek, biuro komitetu, Lubicz 4.

A

1 27 62 **Abderman Zygmunt**, dr, adw., Nowowiejska 31 a.
1 30 17 **Abeles Albert**, prokurent firmy Kamsler, Św. Gertrudy 18. (p. Kamsler Herman).
1 43 61 **Abeles Alojzy**, dr, dyr. banku, Dietlowska 83.
1 63 63 **Abeles Berta**, pracownia sukien damskich, Koletek 7.
1 13 66 **Abeles i Poser**, fabr. guzików, Dietla 37.
1 76 30 **Abeles Juliusz**, dr, adw., Florjańska 15.
1 82 32 **Abeles M. i S-ka**, „Blachometal", Św. Gertrudy 15.
1 22 85 **Abend Henryk**, dr, adw., Sienna 7.
1 26 37 **Abend Józef**, dr, lekarz, Rynek Podgórski 11.
1 28 44 **Abend Salomon**, dr, adw., Wielopole 26 m. 1.
1 60 99 **Abend Wiktor**, dr, lekarz, Bol. Limanowskiego 19.
1 45 09 **Ablamowicz Włodzimierz**, dr, adw., Sławkowska 10.
1 29 44 **Ablamowicz Włodzimierz**, dr, adw., Łobzowska 57.
1 42 72 **Abraham D.**, wytw. art. modeli tłoczonych, Zacisze 16.
1 07 50 **Abrahamer Alfred**, mgr, Garncarska 9.
1 24 14 **Abrahamer Dawid**, właśc. piekarni elektromotor., al. 29 Listopada 37.
1 27 68 **Abrahamer E.**, dr, adw., Kanonicza 16.
1 78 39 **Abrahamer Emanuel**, cegielnia, Smolki 18.
1 06 32 **Abrahamer Izrael**, młyn i piekarnia, Łobzowska 5.
1 72 40 **Abrahamer Józef**, Sarego 24.
1 17 98 **Abrahamer M.**, Krasickiego 14.
1 87 81 **Abrahamer Natan**, m., Kalwaryjska 28.
1 65 39 **Abrahamer Szymon**, al. Słowackiego 4.
1 32 70 **Abrahamowicz Leon**, Św. Krzyża 3.
1 18 18 **Abramowicz A.**, dypl. inż. budow. i zaprzys. biegły sądowy, Wrzesińska 9.
1 09 05 **Absler Ed. i Uher Fr.**, naprawa maszyn biurowych, Św. Jana 11.
1 74 84 **Abusz Józef**, „Sanit", perfumerja, Wielopole 12.
1 03 49 **Ackermann Adam**, dr, lekarz, specjalista chorób kobiecych i akuszer, Garncarska 1.
1 79 83 **Adamczyk Gustaw**, konc. zakład instalacji wodociągu, Dunajewskiego 7.
1 54 39 **Adamczyk Mieczysław**, konc. przedsiębiorstwo elektrotechniczne, Krowoderska 23.
1 67 42 **Adamowicz Paweł**, dr, lekarz chorób wewnętrznych i zakład Roentgena, Potockiego 5.
1 24 81 **Adamski Andrzej**, pracownia stolarska, Pułaskiego 14.
1 34 37 **Adamski Józef**, urzędnik zarządu miasta Krakowa, Felicjanek 27.
1 42 30 **„Ad-dulcia"**, Wojciechowski Jan i Sp., Urzędnicza 42, II p.
1 27 65 **Ader Ernest**, dr, adw., m., Straszewskiego 25.
1 22 29 **Ader Erwin**, dr, przemysłowiec, Św. Tomasza 30.
1 75 51 **Ader Irena**, Biskupia 14.
1 15 31 **Ader Jakub**, dr, Grabowskiego 5.
1 87 48 **Adler Aleksander**, dr, adwokat, m. Ambrożego Grabowskiego 7.
1 04 08 **Adler Aleksander**, dr, **Sternbach Edward**, dr, **Sternbach Ludwik**, dr, adwokaci, Straszewskiego 26.
1 76 04 **Adler Dawid**, mgr farm., Kołłątaja 2.
1 40 26 **Adler Joanna**, położna, Krakowska 33 i Augustiańska 25.
1 58 14 **Adler Leopold**, prok. Banku Hip., Kołłątaja 4.
1 64 53 **Adler Markus**, wytwórnia kołder i waty, Grodzka 2.
1 20 99 **„Adler"**, maszyny do pisania, Św. Marka 25 (róg Szpitalnej).
1 15 88 **Administracja nieruchomości Zakładu Ubezpieczeń Społecznych**, Pomorska 1.
1 00 06 **Administracja przedsiębiorstw handlowych towarzystwa „Nasz dom"**, dział skupu butelek, Starowiślna 97.
1 27 02 **Administrator nowej fund. księży spowiedników przy kościele N. P. M.**
1 16 27 **Adolf Beniamin**, kupiec, Pijarska 5.
1 61 08 **„Adria"**, handel papieru, Meiselsa 9.
1 10 21 **A. E. G.**, powszechne towarzystwo elektryczne, Św. Tomasza 8.
1 72 80 **Aeroklub Krakowski**, lotnisko w Rakowicach.
1 06 11 **„Aeskulap"**, węgierska wytwórnia szczotek i pendzli, Sp. z o. o., Berka Joselewicza 21.
1 32 83 **Affenkraut Chaim**, wytwórnia bielizny, Stradom 15.
1 60 42 **Affenkraut I.**, fabryka kapeluszy damskich, Stradom 17.
1 71 12 **Affenkraut S.**, płaszcze, kostiumy, Florjańska 32.
1 01 60 **Affenkraut Salomon**, kupiec, Retoryka 26.
1 44 47 **Affenkraut Stefania**, handel galanteryjny, Krakowska 5.
1 17 39 **„Afka"**, fabryka parasoli, Abraham Frühauf, Miodowa 10.
1 13 63 **Aftergut Dora**, cukry i owoce, Długa 51.
1 14 19 **Agencja cukru**, Binzer S., Radziwiłłowska 15.
1 08 57 **„Agraria"**, S-ka z o. o., pl. Kossaka 2.
1 07 86 **„Agromechanika"**, Sp. z o. o., pierwsza polska fabryka części maszyn rolniczych, Św. Filipa 13.
1 28 62 **„Aida"**, skład fabr. tutek i bibułek, Skałeczna 7, (p. Hulles).
1 62 79 **Ajencja handlowa M. Hoffmanna**, Nast., Florjańska 49.
1 45 10 **Ajencja wschodnia**, oddział, kier. Wł. J. Dembowski, Czapskich 1.
1 81 44 **Akademicki Związek Sportowy**, sekcja wioślarska i kajakowa, Kościuszki 12.

Akademia Górnicza.
1 46 62 — gabinet rektora, al. Mickiewicza 30.
1 50 40 — centrala, al. Mickiewicza 30.
1 33 85 — centrala, Podgórze, Krzemionki 11.
1 81 47 — gospodarz gmachu, Podgórze Krzemionki 11.
1 44 90 — laboratorium maszynowe, Reymonta 7.
1 00 57 **Akademia Sztuk Pięknych**, pl. Matejki 13.
1 81 44 **Akademicki Związek Sportowy**, Kościuszki 12.
1 52 10 **Akcyjny Bank Hipoteczny**, filia w Krakowie, Rynek Gł. 21, Bracka 1, (p. Bank).
1 42 74 **„Akfal" — „Zdrowie"**, zakłady przem. L. Schneidera, Chocimska 17/19.
1 44 58 **„Akiba"**, biuro centralne i wydawnictwo, Wielopole 24.
1 26 38 **„Akropol"**, zakłady reprodukcyjne, Grzegórzecka 23.
... m., Św. Teresy 8.
... towarów ga... r., Wiślna 4.
... stal. wodoc., ... ewań, pra... a dla robót ... ochodowych, Zacisze 9.
1 32 88 **Aksman Ludwik**, skład maszyn biurowych, przyborów i warsztaty mech., Jagiellońska 7.
1 49 39 **Aksman R.**, zakład instalacyjny i blacharski, Sp. z o. o., Garbarska 15.
1 81 51 **Akumulatorów skład i naprawa**, autostart, Zwierzyniecka 29.
1 68 13 **„Akwa"**, konces. zakład instalacyjny wodociągowy i blacharstwa, Felicjanek 4.
1 70 72 **„Aladin"**, przedsiębiorstwo elektrotechn. handlowe, Bracka 10.
1 34 50 **„A la Ville de Paris"**, S. Horowitz, Florjańska 3.
1 24 07 **„Alba"**, zakład fryzjerski, Szczepańska 7.
1 70 20 **Albertynki siostry**, al. 29 Listopada 75.
1 32 13 **„Albertynów"**, schronisko dla ubogich mężczyzn i fabrykacja mebli giętych, Krakowska 43.
1 01 08 **Albiński Franciszek**, przeds. wiertniczo-studniarskie, Cystersów 3.
1 38 52 **Aleksandrowicz Dawid**, m., Biskupia 4.
1 41 16 **Aleksandrowicz Ignacy**, dr, adw., Wrzesińska 4.
1 78 08 **Aleksandrowicz Jakub**, dr, adw., Przy Moście 1.
1 43 04 **Aleksandrowicz Jakub**, skóry, Dietla 57.
1 01 79 **Aleksandrowicz Józef**, Przy Moście 1.
1 89 99 **Aleksandrowicz Julian**, dr med., specjalista chorób wewnętrznych (analizy krwi), Podgórze, Warneńczyka 14.
1 11 18 **Aleksandrowicz Maksymilian**, inż., Przy Moście 1, (p. cegielnia).
1 83 84 **Aleksandrowicz Maksymilian**, inż., Wola Duchacka 18.
1 64 79 **Aleksandrowicz Nachman**, kupiec, Krakowska 36.
1 23 60 **Aleksandrowicz Paweł**, właśc., mgr. Marcel Aleksandrowicz, przybory piśmienne, rysunkowe, Starowiślna 43.
1 19 42 **Aleksandrowicz Paweł**, Rynek Kleparski 4.
1 53 10 **Aleksandrowicz R.**, synowie, fabr. skład papieru, Długa 1.
1 03 11 — magazyn papieru i przyborów piśmiennych, Basztowa 11.
1 36 12 **Aleksandrowicz Regina**, m., Długa 4.
1 04 33 **Aleksandrowicz Wilhelm**, dr, adw., Basztowa 15.
1 10 86 **Aleksandrowicz Zygmunt**, św. Gertrudy 8.
1 86 26 **Alexandrowicz Karol Witold**, dr, Kujawska 8.
1 28 10 **Alexandrowiczowa Maria**, Łobzowska 29.
1 06 65 **Allerhand Maurycy**, handel korzenny i delikatesów, pl. Szczepański 2.
1 07 33 **Allerhand Maurycy**, kupiec, Br. Pierackiego 4.
1 27 15 **Allerhand Zygmunt**, inż., radca kolei, Basztowa 23.
1 61 04 **Allerhandowa Stefania**, handel dziczyzny i drobiu, Szczepańska 7.
1 69 56 **„Alliance"**, salon fryzjerski, Basztowa 18.
1 05 28 **Altendorf Szymon**, dr, adw., Św. Krzyża 3.

Fig. 040. Krakow telephone directory page with R. Aleksandrowicz store ad

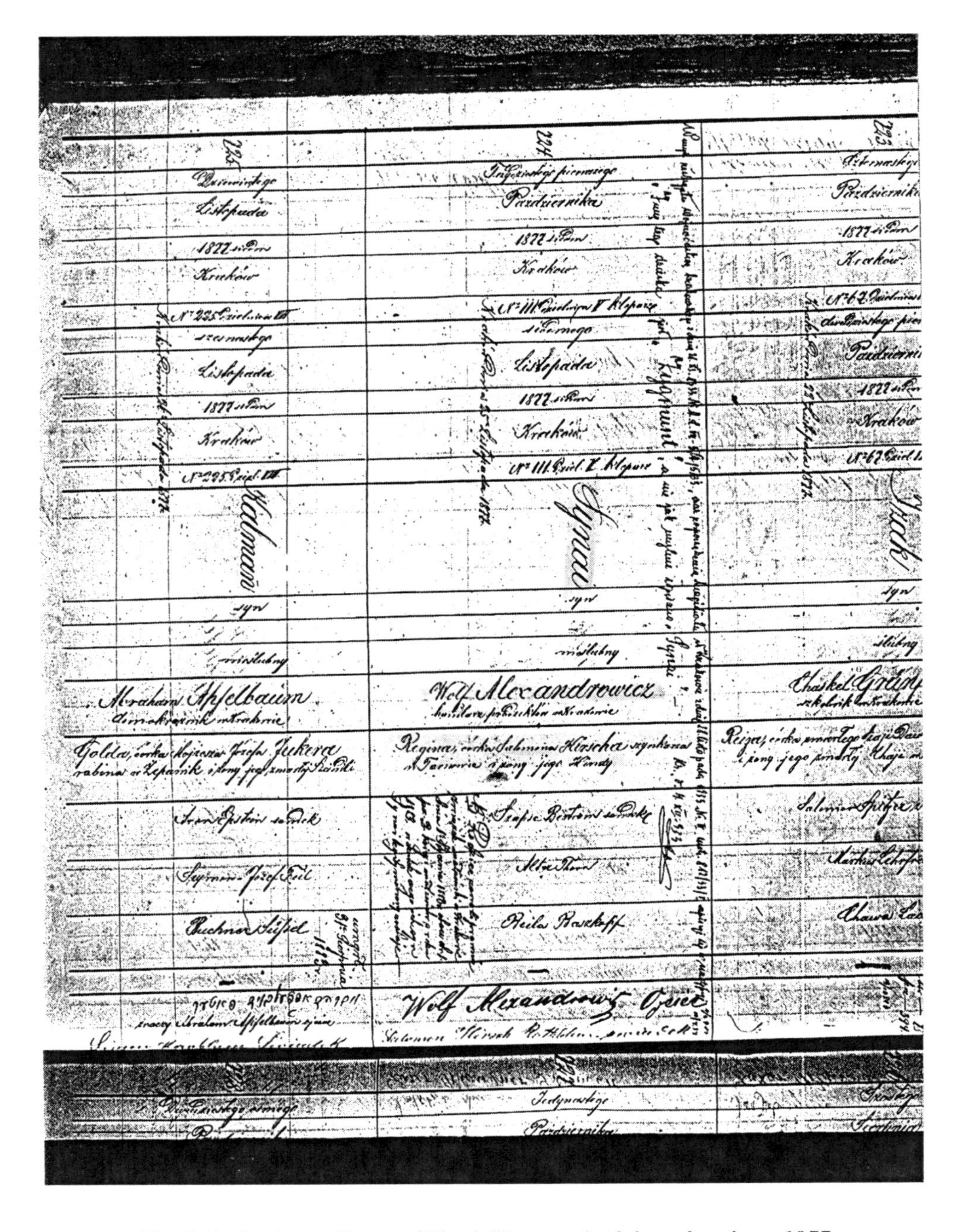

Fig. 041. Birth certificate of Sinai (Zygmunt) Aleksandrowicz – 1877

BIRTH REGISTER OF SINAI (ZYGMUNT) ALEKSANDROWICZ – 1877

From the Civil Registry of Births, Kraków 1877, Act # 724 :

Kraków No.111 Dzielnica V Kleparz Siódmego Listopada 1877 siedem
Synai Syn – nieślubny
Ojciec: Wolf Aleksandrowicz, handlarz produktów w Krakowie
Matka: Regina, córka Salomona Hirscha szynkarza w Tarnowie i żony jego Hindy

Shapse Bertram świadek, Alter Thorn, Reila Baszkopf
Wolf Aleksandrowicz Ojciec
Salomon Hirsch Rothblum świadek

Późniejsze komentarze na boku dokumentu:

Rodzice zawarli prawnie związek małżeński w Krakowie dnia 1-go Stycznia 1878 r obacz dr1pm.2. Księgi małżeństw z roku 1923, wskutek czego ich syn Synai legitymowany zostaje- -

W myśl reskryptu Województwa Krakowskiego z dnia 21.XI.1933 No.Ad.Vii-5/A-5/33, oraz rozporządzenia Magistratu w Krakowie z dnia 28 listopada 1933 No. Tr. Regstr. 812/33/V zapisuje się następujące "Imię tego dziecka jest **‚Zygmunt'**, a nie jak mylnie wpisano **‚Synai'** – Kr.d.4.XII.933

In English:

Kraków Nr 111 area V Kleparz Seventh Of November 1877 seven
Sinai Illegitimate son

Father: Wolf Aleksandrowicz Seller of merchandise in Kraków
Mother: Regina, daughter of Salomon Hirsch, bar owner In Tarnów and his wife Hinda
Szapse Bertram witness Alter Thorn Reila Rashkopf
Wolf Aleksandrowicz Father
Salomon Hirsch Rothblum witness

Later comments on the side:

Parents entered into a legal marriage in Kraków on January 1, 1863 , see dr.1.pm.2. book of marriages for year 1863, as a result of which their son Synai is to be considered legitimate.-

According to the registry of the Kraków district of 21.XI.1933 No.A.d.Vii-5/A/5/33, as well as a decree of the Kraków City Government of 28 November 1933, No. Tr inst. 812/33/V the following is entered: "The name of this child is ‚Zygmunt' and not ‚Sinai' as was wrongly recorded" – Kr.d.4.XII.933.

Fight for Health of Jewish People / 50 Years of TOZ (OZE)
(New York, 1968 pamphlet in Yiddish, honoring Zygmunt Aleksandrowicz)

אין קאַמף פאַרן געזונט פון אידישן פאָלק

(50 יאָר „אזע")

ניו־יאָרק, אויסגאַבע פון וועלט־פאַרבאַנד "אזע", 1968

זיגמונד אַלעקסאַנדראָוויטש
(1946 — 1877)

אין דער שטאָט קראָקע, אין מערבֿ־גאַליציע, אינעם פאַר־מלחמה׳דיקן פוילן, איז דער נאָמען פון זיגמונד אַלעקסאַנדראָוויטש געווען איבעראַל גוט באַקאַנט.

ער איז געווען באַוואוסט אַלס פײַנער, אידעלער מענטש מיט גוטע מידות, נאָבעלער באַנעמונג און מיט אַ געפיל פון האַרציקן מיטליד מיט יעדן נויטבאַ־דערפטיקן. ער האָט פאַרנומען פאַרשיידענע אָנגע־זעענע פּאָזיציעס אין אָרטיקן געזעלשאַפטלעכן לעבן, וואו ער האָט אויסגעפירט זײַנע פליכטן מיט גרויס ערנסט און פאַראַנטוואָרטלעכקייט. אַזוי איז ער געווען וויצע־פּאַרזיצער פון דער יידישער קהילה אין קראָקע, פּרעזידיום־מיטגליד פון אָרטיקן שטאָט־ראָט, וויצע־פּאַרזיצער פון „מזרחי", פון „צענטאָס" און מיטגליד פון פאַרשיידענע אַנדערע אָרגאַניזאַציעס און אינסטיטוציעס אין שטאָט.

Fig. 042. TOZ pamphlet, honoring Zygmunt Aleksandrowicz

Chapter 19. Two lateral branches: the families Drezner and Bader

Family relations can get quite complicated at times. My ancestry can serve as an example. Asher son of Abraham, known after 1806 as Asher Drezner, born in Kraków in 1777, married Feigl daughter of Simon later known as Simon Pitzele. Asher and Feigl had a son Shiya, also known as Jozua. Shiya Jozua Drezner's daughter Rachel married my great-grandfather, Józef Aleksandrowicz. Thus, both Abraham Drezner and Simon Picele are direct ancestors of mine. Jacob Aleksandrowicz, the oldest son of Józef and Rachel was my grandfather. In addition, another daughter of Shiya Jozua Drezner, Rachel's sister Małka, married Izak Mendel Birnbaum. Izak Mendel and Małka's daughter, Hanna Hinda, married her first cousin, Jacob Aleksandrowicz, Rachel's son. Thus, Simon Pitzele and Abraham Drezner are my ancestors twice, through Rachel Drezner Aleksandrowicz and her sister Małka Drezner Birnbaum, whose children, Jacob Aleksandrowicz and Hanna Hinda nee Birnbaum, are my paternal grandparents.

In Kraków documents, Asher Drezner was referred to as a teacher of Jewish children. A search of old family records by Asher's grandson, Edward Birnbaum (described later), found that the Drezner family leased and operated, i.e. were *arendars* of a large lumber mill somewhere in the heavily forested area south of the Carpathian Mountains, today Slovakia. They did not own the mill, they leased it. The mill in question was large, it was a regionally important major economic enterprise. It was probably owned by one of the wealthy aristocratic Hungarian families, like the Esterhazy or Zapolya, but was leased and operated by a Jew, in this case Asher Drezner's grandfather. Asher even mentioned to his son Shiya that he visited the mill as a child, but he was vague about its location and I have not been able to find out exactly where that mill was. Asher's father, Abraham, moved to Kraków, which was then the main urban center of this area of Western Austro-Hungarian Galicia and Slovakia and Asher was born and grew up in Kraków. I assume that the Drezners in Slovakia had many children and Asher's father was not the eldest,

was not scheduled to take over the lease and operation of the mill and found few other opportunities in the poor Slovak countryside and thus migrated to Kraków prior to 1776. Around 1804 Asher married Feigl Pitzele, born in 1783. My records are far from complete, but I found that Asher and Feigl had at least five children, two girls, Scheindl born May 2, 1806 and Reisl born August 20, 1809, and three boys, Simon born August 8, 1812, the above-mentioned Shiya Jozua, born September 12, 1813, and Shachna, born in 1818.

Feigl Pitzele Drezner had a brother, Ruben born in 1788. On the 6-th of February 1808 this Ruben Pitzele (or Picele, as it was spelled in Polish) married another Feigl, daughter of my ancestor, Jacob Gomple of Kraków. The marriage of Ruben and this Feigl was of interest to me because her father, who was called Jacob Gomple in 1792 when Feigl was born, was the progenitor of an important Kraków family later called Gumplowicz. His older daughter, Feigl's sister Dobrysz, married Joseph Alexander, who became known as Joseph Aleksandrowicz, the key ancestor of the Aleksandrowicz clan of Kraków, grandfather of the second Józef who married Rachel Drezner in 1865. Ruben and Feigl Pitzele had a number of children, listed above in the chapter devoted to the Gumple/Gumplowicz family. Jacob Gomple had other children, among them Lebel, born in 1780, grandfather of Professor Ludwik Gumplowicz (1838-1909), the founder of the modern science of sociology, born in Kraków. Ludwik's brother Ignacy Gumplowicz and his children ran a lending library in Kraków where as a child I used to borrow books.

Asher Drezner's son Shiya Jozua Drezner was eighteen when he married Henna Bader on June 17, 1832. He became a tavern keeper and a liquor merchant. Henna Bader was born on June 17, 1816. Thus, she was exactly sweet 16 on her birthday and wedding day. Her parents were Abraham Józef Bader and Reizl Gumplowicz of Kraków. Reizl, the bride's mother, was also a daughter of Jacob Gomple and a sister of Dobrysz Gumplowicz, wife of Joseph Aleksandrowicz and of Feigl Gumplowicz, wife of Ruben Picele and a sister-in-law of Feigl Picele, wife of Asher Drezner. The Bader family is described below. There is a gap in existing Drezner records for the next few years, but it can be filled from later information gleaned from the records of the next generation. According to that information and data available on the Internet (at www.Jewishgen.org) Shiya Jozua and Henna Drezner had a daughter in 1833 whom they named Małka. This Małka married Isaac Mendel Birnbaum in Kraków in 1853. Next Shiya Jozua and Henna had Lea, who died as a small child (1835-1837) and Asher, born in 1837. The name of the latter child indicates that Shiya's father Asher must have died prior to 1837. Next born was Hana who died four years later (1939-1843), Salomon who died at three (1842-1845) and Izak born in 1844. Next we have the interesting phenomenon of a child being born and named Feigl Reisl (1846, Act # 177), and dying as an infant with the names then being reused and given to the next two girls born in 1947 and in 1849. Rachel (Reisl) Drezner was born 12 August 1847 in Kraków, Feigl Golda Drezner born in 1849. Rachel Drezner married Józef Aleksandrowicz and became my great-grandmother. This other girl, Feigl Golda, in 1879 married Isaac Mendel Birnbaum, a widowed husband of her older sister Małka after Małka died in 1876. After Feigl Golda Shiya and Henna had one more daughter, Hana, born in 1851. Małka, while married to Isaac Mendel Birnbaum, had seven children and then she died, presumably during a cholera epidemic. Her husband, Isaac Mendel Birnbaum, then married her sister Golda and with her he had four more children. All these children, except one, married into important Kraków Jewish families and they had many children in turn. As indicated above, one of Isaac Mendel and Małka's daughters, Hanna Hinda (Hancia) Birnbaum, married her first cousin Jacob Aleksandrowicz, son of Małka's sister Rachel, thus also becoming my grandmother. In this fashion two of the Drezner girls, Rachel, wife of Joseph Aleksandrowicz and mother of my paternal grandfather Jacob Aleksandrowicz and Małka, wife of Isaac Mendel Birnbaum and mother of my paternal grandmother Hancia Birnbaum Aleksandrowicz, wife of Jacob, became my great-grandmothers. In addition, a third Drezner sister, Feigl Golda, married the widowed Isaac Mendel Birnbaum and had several children with him. Her children were also full cousins of my father. It is obvious that the family relationships became quite complex. My father had a large number of cousins and *double cousins* in Kraków. Without exaggeration, I can state that a great many of Kraków Jews were my relatives. The genealogy of the Birnbaum family will be described in a separate chapter.

To recapitulate, little Hanna Bader was sixteen in 1832 when she married Shiya Jozua Drezner in Kraków. Her parents were Abraham Józef Bader and Reizl nee Gumplowicz. His parents were Asher Drezner and Feigl daughter of Szymon Pitzele. Shiya Jozua and Henna's daughter, Rachel Drezner married Józef Aleksandrowicz. Józef and Rachel's son, Jacob Aleksandrowicz married his cousin Hancia Birnbaum, daughter of Rachel's sister Małka Drezner, also daughter of Shiya and Henna. Jacob and Hancia had seven children. Their sixth child, fifth boy, whom they named Maksymilian (Menashe ben Yaakov), was my father.

Jacob called Gomple and Sarah nee Abele were the parents of Reizl Gumplowicz. I am not sure who were the parents of Henna Bader's father. I assume that Abraham Bader was born in Kraków around 1790. There were several individuals, *patres familias*, living in Kraków at that time, who assumed the surname Bader when the Austrian clerks were assigning names to Kraków Jews in 1805-1806. I can guess at the rationale behind their selection of this surnames. An ancestor of the Drezners must have come from Dresden at one point in the past. An ancestor of the Baders must have operated the Kraków communal *mikveh* or *bad* in Yiddish. In investigating my family's genealogy at the Polish National Archives in Kraków in 1997 I found out that Shiya Jozua Drezner, son of Asher, married a young Bader girl, who thus became one of my great-great-great-grandmothers. The Baders were a large prominent Krakovian family. There were several important and wealthy Bader brothers and cousins in Kraków at the beginning of the nineteenth century. One of the Bader's couples emigrated in mid-nineteenth century (i.e, around 1850) to England. In England the Baders modified their surname by adding an "r", making it Barder. Perhaps they wanted to have their name pronounced "Baah-der", as it was pronounced in Kraków, rather than "Bay-der" as it would have been in England, and achieved that by adding a largely silent "r" in the middle of their name. One of the British Barders, descendants of the Kraków Baders, Brian, son of Harry Barder and Celia nee Hess, served recently as the United Kingdom's Ambassador to Poland. When Brian Barder was in Poland, he was apparently unaware of his family Polish-Jewish origin, which his wife discovered only after his tour of duty ended and he retired from the British Foreign Service. While researching my family origin, I found that Joseph Aleksandrowicz married a daughter of Jacob Gomple, Dobrysz, a sister of the Reisl who married Abraham Bader. Thus, it is likely that my ancestress Dobrysz was little Henna's maternal aunt, as was her sister Feigl who married Ruben Pitzele, and their father Jacob Gomple is an ancestor of the Bader (Barder), Aleksandrowicz, Pitzele, Birnbaum and Gumplowicz families. I find it fascinating how all these families were interrelated.

After occupying Kraków in 1796 the Austrian authorities ordered a census of all Kraków Jews, who then had to live in the Jewish Town in Kazimierz. There was a Jacob, son of Samuel, listed in the 1796 Austrian census, living in building # 11 in the Jewish Town. From later records that I found in Kraków, it appears that this Jacob son of Samuel Elias later assumed the surname Bader. Some of these records are now available on microfiche at the Family Research Centers of the Church of the Latter Day Saints (Mormon), including the LDS center in New York, and some are available on the Web at <jewishgen.org/shtetLinks/Poland/Kraków>. In the seminal history of Kraków Jewry, the prominent historian Mayer Bałaban mentioned that Jacob Bader was paid by the Kraków Kahał (Jewish Community autonomous governing body) to be a "*felczer*" and between 1809 and 1822 a bath attendant at what I assume was the communal religious "*mikva*". I know from personal experience, that in Poland a *felczer* was a cross between a barefoot doctor and a practical nurse, a healer who applied folk remedies like cupping and leeches and herbs to treat fevers and other ailments and often served as a barber as well. When after 1805 the Austrian officials insisted that all Jews must have surnames, it was only natural to give Jacob ben Samuel as an attendant at a bath the surname Bader.

There were several Baders and several Gumpels living in Kraków, listed in Jewish records maintained by the civil clerks after 1800. Henna Bader's father, Abraham, was probably the son of Jacob Bader, the Kraków *felczer*. Among other children of Jacob and Lea were Joseph born around 1785, Moses born around 1788, Samuel born in 1799, Herschel born in 1798 but registered in March 1799, and Chaya born in 1805. The Gumpels, later known as Gumplowicz, described earlier, included Henna's mother, Reizl, the daughter of Jacob Gumpel, her brother Lebel and her sister, Dobrysz, as well as other siblings, Feigl, Abele and Juda Gumplowicz.

Jacob Bader was born around 1756, his wife Lea around 1766. In the census of 1796 he was listed as being 40 years old, living in house # 85, family # 460. His wife, Lea, age 30, was listed as daughter of a man named Moses and alternately as Leah Lewkowicz. This latter discrepancy may be explained if we assume that Moses belonged to the tribe of Levi and thus was known as Moses Lewkowicz or Moses the Levite. Jacob's father, Samuel, must have died before 1796, Lea's father, Moses, before 1788, because Kraków Jews did not name their children after living relatives, and the 1796 census stated that Jacob and Lea had two sons, named Moses, 8, and Samuel, one year old. A list of house owners in Kraków, dating probably to 1806, available on the Web, showed Jacob Bader as owner of building # 11. In 1788 was born Moyżesz, son of Jacob and Lea. As Moses Bader, he was listed as a member in the Kraków civil guard in 1831 during a Polish November Uprising against Russia, which led to sympathy demonstrations and riots in Kraków. His future wife, Małka Abrahamówna was born in 1790. According to the often delayed civil records, Herschel, son of Jacob and Lea, was born on March 1799 in building 21. On March 25, 1805 in building 7 was born Małka, daughter of Jacob and Lea Bader. On July 7, 1805 Moses son of Jacob Bader, 16, living in building 7, married Małka, daughter of Abraham, 15 years old, who lived in building 102. On July 7, 1806 in building 7, Jacob and Lea had a daughter, whom they named Chaie. In 1809 in building 11 Moses Bader and Małka had a son, Abraham, who died next year. On 13 February 1814 in building 107, Józef Bader, 30, and his wife Golda nee Birnbaum (another example of the close relationships among Kraków Jews of a certain class!), 20, had a daughter whom they named Henna. On June 18, 1816, Abraham Bader and Reizl nee Gumplowicz had a daughter, whom they also named Henna (This is the Henna who eventually married Asher Drezner). Obviously, both girls, cousins, were named after a common ancestress. On 23 November 1817 in building 11, Herschel Bader, 19, son of Jacob and Lea, married Zelda Goldberg, 17, who lived in building 5 with her parents Aaron Abele and Kreindl Chaya nee Herszkowicz. It was Hershel and Zelda's descendants that migrated to England in 1853. In 1818 in building 103, lived Mozes Bader and his wife Rebeka Chaimowna, who probably was a cousin of the Moses Bader who married Małka Abrahamowna. Another Moses Bader married Rozla Fischer, daughter of Abele and Chaya Lewkowicz, likely a sister of Zelda, inspite of the confusing appearance of two differing surnames of Goldberg and Fischer. On April 18, 1818 Józef, son of Izrael Bader, and his wife Lea had a daughter, whom they also named Henna. This Henna later maried Moses Aaron Reinhold This is the third girl born in the Bader family to be named Henna. One must wonder whom they were all honoring. Who was the original Henna. Their grandmother? A beloved sister who died without having been recorded? This list shows how confusing can records be, particularly in cases of popular surnames, like Bader and popular first names like Henna.

Migrating from Austrian Kraków to England in mid eighteen fiftees was obviously a major undertaking but it cannot be compared to contemporaneous migrations from Polish-Russian territories to America. The latter were escapes from intolerable economic and social conditions, utter poverty, pogroms and threats of pogroms, official persecution, government-encouraged Kossack attacks and a dearth of educational opportunities. In Galitzia, by contrast, there was little official persecution and little threat to life. In Kraków school attendance became obligatory and literacy was high and knowledge of conditions in other European countries, including England, and America, was available. There was not much by way of economic opportunities in Galitzia, but nevertheless some Krakovian Jewish families were fairly well off. Contacts between emigrants and their families were continuing. In case of the Baders who left for England, the family obviously was sufficiently wealthy to allow travel back-and-forth between England and Kraków. We know that the English Baders, or Barders as they became known, returned to Kraków to visit their family, perhaps even more than once. Obviously, travel from England to Kraków was easier and less expensive than travel to and from New York. Hershel Bader and Zelda Goldberg had a son, Menachem Lazar around 1827. Known in Kraków as Lazar Bader and, after 1854 in Manchester as Louis Barder, he was trained as a furrier. According to a Barder chronicle prepared by Brian Barder's wife Jane, Louis married Hanna /Hala Hamburger. In Kraków in 1852 they had a son Israel and in England in 1855 another son, Levi. Levi Barder married Rebecca Waxman, daughter of Abe Warszawski. In 1883 Levi and Rebecca had Harry who married Rachel Hamburger and Celia who married Herbert Hess, a brother of Dame Myra Hess. Harry and Rachel were the parents of Brian Barder, the British diplomat and husband of Jane to whom I am indebted for a lot of this information about the illustrious British branch of an old Krakovian Jewish family.

As stated above, in Kraków the Baders were and remained a large and important family until the onset of World War II. Golda Augusta Birnbaum, a sister of my grandmother Hanna Hancia Aleksandrowicz nee Birnbaum, married Max Bader in Kraków, so that my father had Bader cousins: Alexander, Sigi, Rose and Charles Bader. Other branches moved from Kraków to Vienna. Some of these latter came to the United States before the Second World War. Some offspring of the British Barders also moved to the United States. There are now large numbers of descendants of Krakovian Baders in the United States as well as in England.

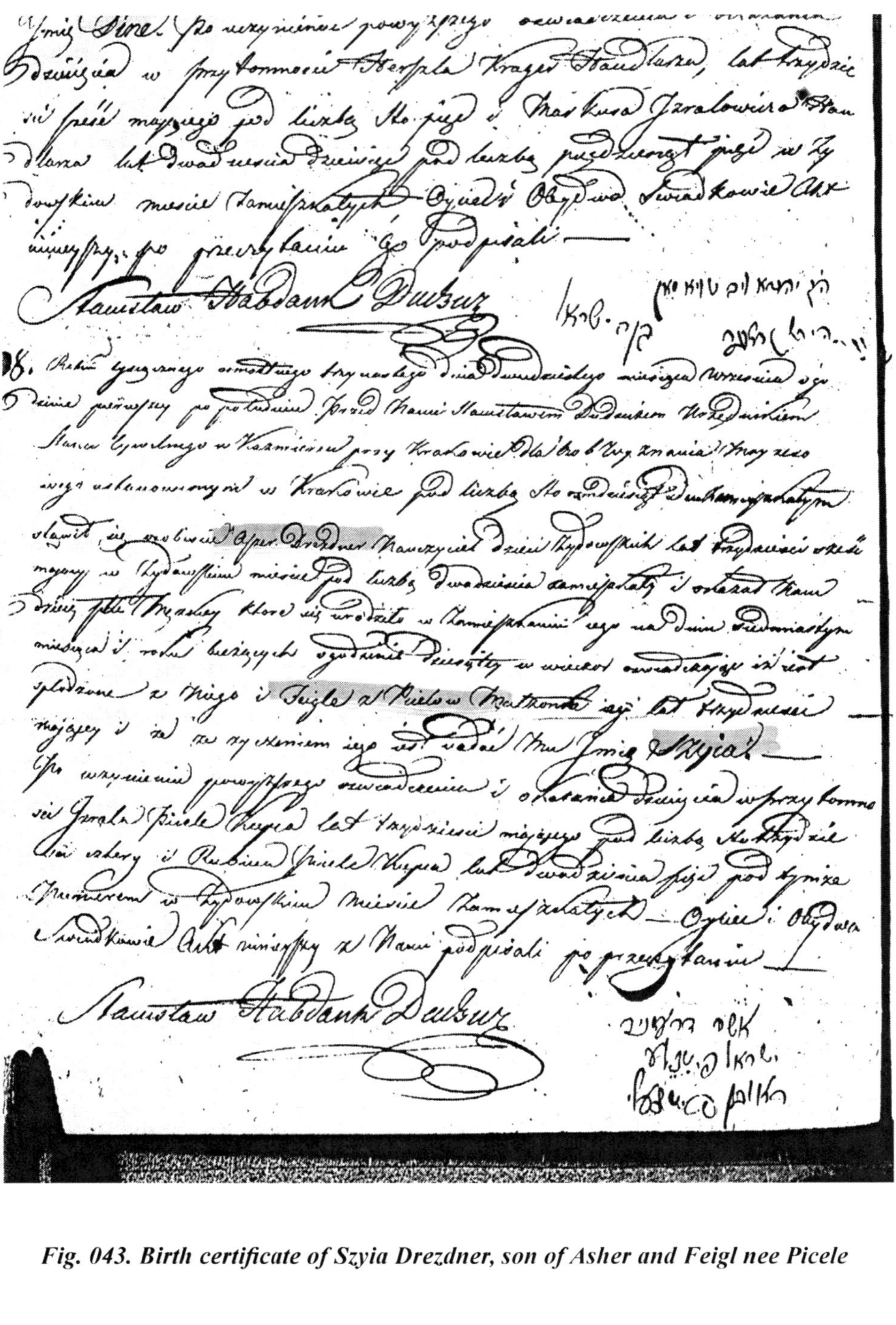

Imię Dwora. Po uczynieniu powyższego oświadczenia i okazania
Dziecięcia w przytomności Herszla Krager Handlarza, lat trzydzie
ści sześć mającego pod liczbą sto pięć i Markusa Izraelowicza Han
dlarza lat dwadzieścia dziewięć pod liczbą pięćdziesiąt pięć w Ży
dowskim mieście zamieszkałych. Ojciec i Obydwa Świadkowie Akt
niniejszy po przeczytaniu go podpisali —

Stanisław Habdank Dudzicz

18. Roku tysiąc ośmsetnego trzynastego dnia dwudziestego miesiąca września o go
dzinie pierwszej po południu. Przed Nami Stanisławem Dudzicem Urzędnikiem
Stanu Cywilnego w Kazimierzu przy Krakowie dla Osób Wyznania Mojżeszo
wego ustanowionym w Krakowie pod liczbą sto siedemdziesiąt dwa zamieszkałym
stawił się osobiście Asser Drezdner Nauczyciel dzieci Żydowskich lat trzydzieści ośm
mający w Żydowskim mieście pod liczbą dwadzieścia zamieszkały i okazał Nam
dziecię płci męskiej które się urodziło w zamieszkaniu jego na dniu siedmnastym
miesiąca i roku bieżących o godzinie dziesiątej w wieczór oświadczając iż jest
spłodzone z niego i Feigle z Picelów Małżonki jego lat trzydzieści
mającej i że za życzeniem jego jest nadane Mu Imię Szyia.
Po uczynieniu powyższego oświadczenia i okazania dziecięcia w przytomno
ści Izraela Picele Kupca lat trzydzieści mającego pod liczbą sto trzydzie
ści cztery i Rubina Picele Kupca lat dwadzieścia pięć pod tymże
Numerem w Żydowskim Mieście Zamieszkałych. Ojciec i Obydwa
Świadkowie Akt niniejszy z Nami podpisali po przeczytaniu.

Stanisław Habdank Dudzicz

אשר דרעזנר
ישראל פיצעלע
ראובן פיצעלע

Fig. 043. Birth certificate of Szyia Drezdner, son of Asher and Feigl nee Picele

1813 BIRTH CERTIFICATE OF SZYIA DREZNER

From the Birth Registry for Year 1813, folio # 8, for September 12:

Roku tysiącnego ośmsetnego trzynastego dnia dwudziestego miesiąca września o godzinie pierwszej po południu przed nami Stanisławem Dudziszem Urzędnikiem Stanu Cywilnego w Kazimierzu przy Krakowie dla Osób Wyznania Mojżeszowego ustanowionym w Krakowie pod liczbą sto sześćdziesiąt ieden zamieszkałym stawił się osobiście Aszer Drezner Nauczyciel dzieci żydowskich lat trzydzieści sześć maiący w żydowskim Mieście pod liczbą dwadzieścia zamieszkały i okazał nam dziecię płci męskiey które się urodziło w zamieszkaniu iego na dniu dwunastym miesiąca i roku bieżących o godzinie dziesiątey w wieczór oświadczaiąc iż iest spłodzone z niego i Feigle z Picelów Małżonki iego lat trzydzieści maiącey i że życzeniem iego iest nadać mu Imię Szyia – Po uczynieniu powyższego oświadczenia i okazaniu dziecięcia w przytomności Izrala Picele Kupca lat trzydzieści maiącego pod liczbą sto trzydzieści cztery i Rubina Picele Kupca lat dwadzieścia pięć pod tymże numerem w żydowskim mieście zamieszkałych – Ojciec i obydwa świadkowie akt ninieiszy z nami podpisali po przeczytaniu -

Stanisław Habdank Dudzisz

in English:

In the year one thousand eight hundred thirteen on the twentieth day of the month of September at one o'clock in the afternoon before us Stanisław Dudzisz, appointed as Civil Records Clerk in Kazimierz by Kraków for persons of the Mosaic Faith living in Kraków under the number one hundred and sixty one personally appeared Asher Drezner, teacher of Jewish children thirty six years old living in the Jewish Town under the number twenty and showed us a baby of male gender which was born in his domicile on the twelfth day of the current month and year declaring that it was born to him and to Feigle of the Picels his wife thirty years old and that it is his wish to name it Szyia – having made this declaration and having shown us the baby in the presence of Izral Picel merchant thirty years old living in the Jewish Town under the number one hundred and thirty four and Rubin Picel merchant twenty five years old living under the same number – After a reading, this Act was signed by Us with the Father and both witnesses -

Stanisław Habdank Dudzisz

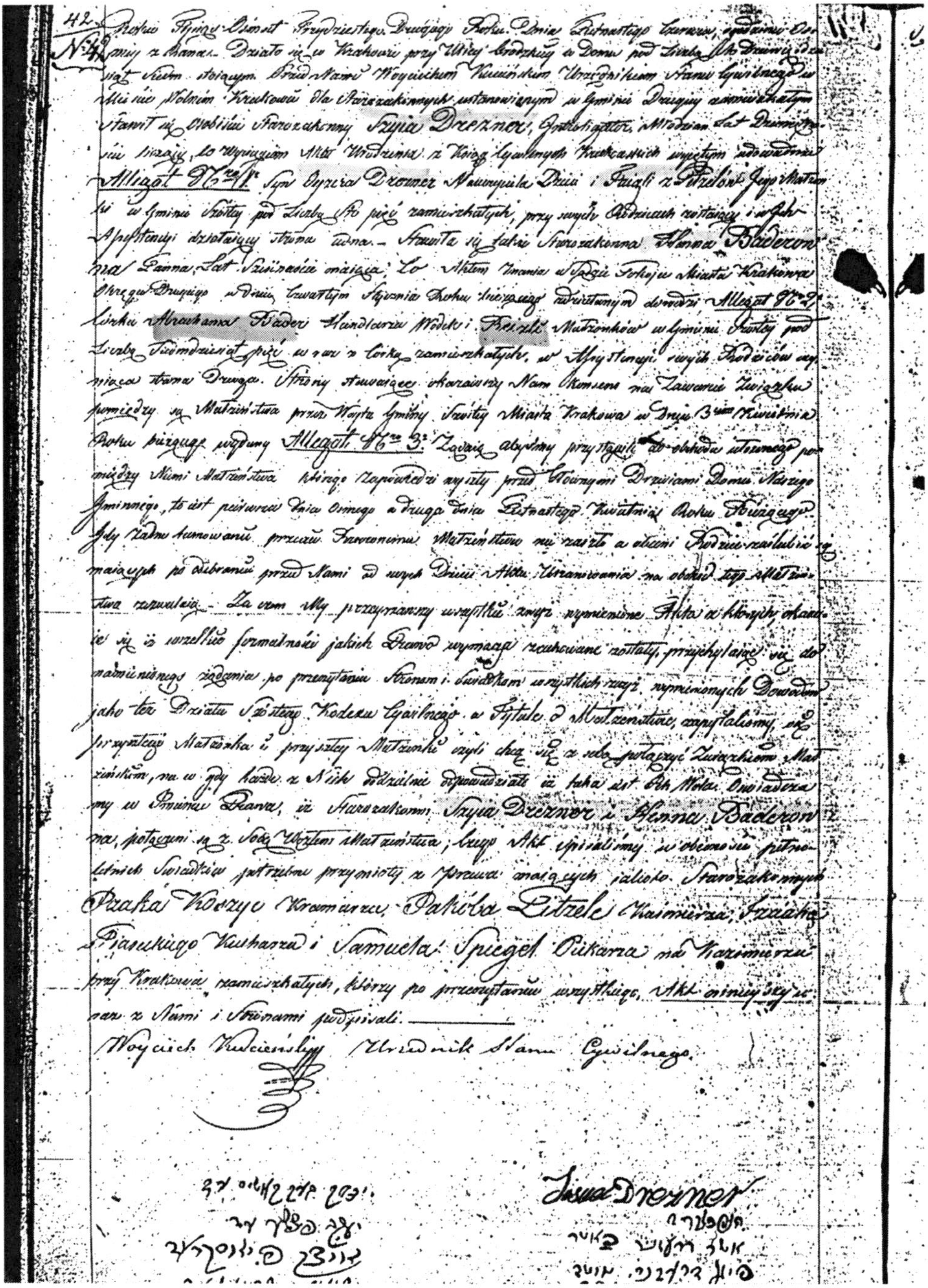

42

No 42

Roku Tysiąc Ośmset Trzydziestego Drugiego Roku. Dnia Piętnastego Czerwca, o godzinie Ośmey z Rana.- Działo się w Krakowie przy Ulicy Grodzkiey w Domu pod Liczbą Sto Dziewięćdziesiąt Siedm stoiącym. Przed Nami Woyciechem Kucieńskim Urzędnikiem Stanu Cywilnego w Mieście Wolnem Krakowie dla Starozakonnych ustanowionym w Gminie Drugiey zamieszkałym stawił się osobiście Starozakonny Szyia Drezner, Introligator, Młodzian Lat Dwadzieścia trzy maiący, co wypisem Aktu Urodzenia z Xiąg Cywilnych Krakowskich wyjętym udowadnia Allegat No 1. Syn Ozyasza Drezner Nauczyciela Dzieci i Fraidli z Pitzelów Jego Małżonki w Gminie Szóstey pod Liczbą Sto pięć zamieszkałych, przy swych Rodzicach zostający i w ich Assystencyi działaiący strona iedna.- Stawiła się także Starozakonna Hanna Baderówna Panna Lat Szesnaście maiąca, co Aktem Urodzenia z Xięgi Cyrkułu Miasta Krakowa Okręgu Drugiego w dniu Czwartym Stycznia Roku bieżącego wydanym dowodzi Allegat No 2. Córka Abrahama Bader Handlarza Wódek i Freidli Małżonków w Gminie Szóstey pod Liczbą Siedmdziesiąt pięć wraz z Córką zamieszkałych, w Assystencyi swych Rodziców czyniąca strona Druga. Strony stawaiące okazawszy Nam Konsens na Zawarcie Związku pomiędzy się Małżeństwa przez Woyta Gminy Szóstey Miasta Krakowa w Dniu 3cim Kwietnia Roku bieżącego wydany Allegat No 3. Żądaią abyśmy przystąpili do obchodu uroczystego pomiędzy Nimi Małżeństwa którego Zapowiedzi wywieszone przed Głównymi Drzwiami Domu Naszego Gminnego, to iest pierwsza Dnia Ósmego a druga dnia Piętnastego Kwietnia Roku bieżącego. Gdy żadne tamowanie przeciw zawarciu Małżeństwa nie zaszło a obecni Rodzice zaślubić się maiących po odebraniu przed Nami od nich Dnia Aktu Uszanowania na obchód tego Małżeństwa zezwalaią.- Za czem My przeyrzawszy wszystkie wyż wymienione Akta z których okazuie się iż wszelkie formalności jakich Prawo wymaga zachowane zostały, przychylaiąc się do nadmienionego żądania po przeczytaniu Stronom i Świadkom wszystkich wyż wymienionych Dowodów jako też Działu Szóstego Kodexu Cywilnego w Tytule o Małżeństwie, zapytaliśmy się przyszłego Małżonka i przyszłey Małżonki czyli chcą się z sobą połączyć Związkiem Małżeńskim, na co gdy każde z Nich oddzielnie odpowiedziało iż taka iest Ich Wola. Oświadczamy w Imieniu Prawa, iż Starozakonni Szyia Drezner i Hanna Baderówna, połączeni są z sobą Węzłem Małżeństwa; czego Akt spisaliśmy w obecności pełnoletnich Świadków potrzebne przymioty z Prawa maiących iako to Starozakonnych Izaaka Woszyc Kramarza, Jakóba Litzele Kaśmierza, Izaaka Piaseckiego Kucharza i Samuela Spiegel Piekarza na Kazimierzu przy Krakowie zamieszkałych, którzy po przeczytaniu wszystkiego, Akt niniejszy wraz z Nami i Stronami podpisali.

Woyciech Kucieński Urzędnik Stanu Cywilnego.

[illegible]

Jsua Drezner

[illegible]

Fig. 044. Wedding announcement of Szyia Jozua Drezner and Hanna Bader

WEDDING OF SZYIA JOZUA DREZNER AND HANNA BADER – 1832

Roku Tysiąc Ośmset Trzydziestego Drugiego Dnia Piętnastego Czerwca, o godzinie Ósmey z rana – Działo się w Krakówie przy ulicy Grodzkiey w Domu pod Liczbą Sto Dziewiędziąt Siedem stoiącym. Przed Nami Woyciechem Kucieńskim Urzędnikiem Stanu Cywilnego w Mieście Wolnem Krakowie dla Starozakonnych ustanowionym w Gminie drugiey zamieszkałym stawił się osobiście Starozakonny **Szyia Drezner,** Introligator, Młodzian Lat Dziewiętnaście liczący, to Wyciągiem Aktu Urodzenia z Ksiąg Cywilnych Krakowskich wyiątym udowadnia **Allegat Nro.1** Syn Oyzera Drezner Nauczyciela Dzieci i Faigli z Pitzelów Jego Małżonki w Gminie Szóstey pod Liczbą Sto pięć zamieszkałych, przy swych Rodzicach zostaiący i w Ich assystencyi działaiący strona iedna. – Stawiła się także Starozakonna **Hanna Baderówna** Panna, Lat Szesnaście maiąca; to Aktem Znania w Sądzie Pokoju Miasta Krakowa Okręgu Drugiego w Dniu Czwartym Stycznia Roku bieżącego zdziałanym dowodzi **Allegat Nro. 2.** Córka Abrahama Bader, Handlarza Wódki i Reizli Małżonków w Gminie Szóstey pod Liczbą Siedemdziesiąt pięć w raz z córką zamieszkałych w Assystencyi swych Rodziców czyniąca strona Druga. Strony stawaiące okazawszy nam Konsens na zawarcie Związku pomiędzy sobą Małżeństwa przez Wóyta Gminy Szóstey Miasta Krakowa w dniu 3-cim Kwietnia Roku bieżącego wydany **Allegat Nro. 3**. żądaią abyśmy przystąpili do obchodu ułożonego pomiędzy Niemi Małżeństwa którego Zapowiedzi wyszły przed głównymi Drzwiami Domu Naszego Gminnego, to iest pierwsza dnia Ósmego a druga dnia Piętnastego Kwietnia Roku Bieżącego. Gdy żadne tamowanie przeciw Rzeczonemu Małżeństwu nie zaszło a obecni Rodzice zaślubić się maiących po odebraniu przed nami od swych Dzieci Aktu Uszanowania na obchód tego małżeństwa zezwalaią – Za czem My przeyrzawszy wszystkie zwyż wymienione Akta z których okazuie się iż wszelkie formalności jakich Prawo wymaga zachowane zostały, przychylaiąc się do namienionego zadania po przeczytaniu Stronom i świadkom wszystkich zwyż wymienionych Dowodów jako też Działu Szóstego Kodexu Cywilnego w Tytule o Małżeństwie zapytaliśmy się przyszłego Małżonka i przyszley Małżonki czyli chcą się z sobą połączyć Związkiem Małżeńskim, na co gdy każde z Nich oddzielnie odpowiedziało Iż taka iest Ich Wola. Oświadczamy w Imieniu Prawa, iż Starozakonni **Szyia Drezner i Hanna Baderówna**, połączeni są z sobą Węzłem Małżeństwa, czego Akt spisaliśmy w obecności pełnoletnich świadków potrzebne przymioty z Prawa maiących jakoto Starozakonnych **Izaka Koszyc** Kramarza, **Jakóba Pitzele**, Kuśnierza, **Izaaka Piaseckiego** Kucharza i **Samuela Spiegel** Piekarza na Kazimierzu przy Krakowie zamieszkałych, którzy po pzeczytaniu wszystkiego, Akt ninieyszy w raz z Nami i stronami podpisali. –

Woyciech Kucieński Urzędnik Stanu Cywilnego
Josua Drezner
Cztery hebrajskie podpisy

in English:

DREZNER – BADER WEDDING

Year one thousand eight hundred thirty two, on the fifteenth day of June, at eight in the morning -- Occurred in Kraków in the house located on Grodzka street number one hundred ninety seven. Before us, Woyciech Kucieński Civil State Clerk in the Free City of Kraków appointed for persons of the Old Testament and living in Community Number Two appeared personally the Old Covenanter **Szyia Drezner**, bookbinder, a young man of nineteen years, which he proved to Us with an Extract of the Cracovian Civil Birth Records **Claim Nr.1**. Son of Oyzer Drezner, teacher of children and Feigl daughter of the Pitzeles, his wife, living in Community six in house number one hundred and five, staying with his parents and acting with their help – first party – Also appeared Old Covenanter **Hanna Bader**, maiden, sixteen years old, which she proved with a Statement issued by the Peace Court of the Second District of the Free City of Kraków on the fourth day of January of the current year **Claim Nr. 2** daughter of Abraham Bader, vodka seller and Reizl, his wife living with their daughter in Community six in house number seventy five, acting with the help of her parents – second party. The appearing parties, having shown Us a Consent form for said marriage issued on the 3-rd day of April of the current year by the Mayor of community six **Claim Nr. 3**. request that we proceed to the performance of the arranged between them marriage, of which announcements have been made before the Main Gate of this our Community House, the first on the eighth and the second on the fifteenth of April of the current year. Since no objections to this planned marriage occurred and the parents of the couple to be married, present here, having received in our presence an act of respect from their children, agree to this marriage – therefore, We, having examined above-mentioned documents proving that all formalities required by Law have been satisfied, favoring the request, after having read to the parties and to the witnesses all the above-mentioned proofs as well as Part Six of the Civil Code dealing with marriages, we asked the future husband and the future wife if they wish to be united with a marital bond, to which each of them separately answered that that is their wish. We declare in the name of the Law that Old Covenanters **Szyia Drezner and Hanna Bader** are united in marriage, which we certified in the presence of adult witnesses having all the attributes required by Law, namely Old Covenanters **Izak Koszyc** stall owner, **Jacob Pitzele**, furrier, **Izaak Piasecki**, cook and **Samuel Spiegel** baker, living in Kazimierz by Kraków, who, having read everything, signed this certificate along with us and the parties.-

Woyciech Kucieński, Civil State Clerk
Josua Drezner
Four Hebrew signatures Four Hebrew signatures

Descendants of Shaya Drezner and Henna Bader
(Rachel married Jozef Aleksandrowicz; Malka married Izak mendel Birnbaum)

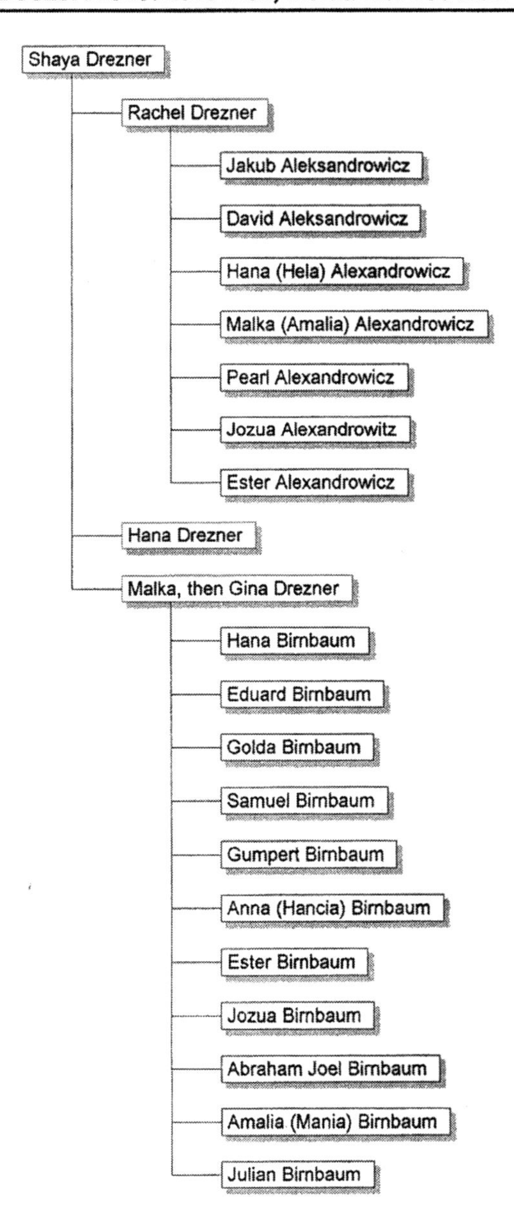

Fig. 045. Family tree of Szyia (Jozua) Drezner and Hanna Bader

Chapter 20. Jacob Aleksandrowicz, son of Józef (1866-1935).

In my grandparents' formal dining room stood an elaborate, elegant upright credenza made of highly polished dark wood, with beveled glass front. It was filled with small antiques, Japanese Satsuma ware, Dresden porcelain figurines and the like. Next to all these valuable collectors items sat a small set of a miniature table and chairs. The table and chairs were made of cork, covered in red velvet, their legs made of pins with beads as heads. The reason why this simple primitive set had a place of honor like this, was that it was handmade as a present to a grandfather by his 7-year-old grandson. I presented it to my grandfather on his 66-th birthday in 1932.

When I was born in 1925 my grandfather, Jacob Aleksandrowicz, lived in the house he owned on Bernardyńska Street No. 11, in the Second District of Kraków, between the Stradom area and the Wawel Hill, overlooking the river Vistula and facing the Royal Castle complex on the Wawel. He was an important and influential merchant in Kraków, the owner of a successful wholesale-and-retail leather export-import enterprise on Dietla Street at the edge of Kazimierz. Sometime after I was born he was getting married for the second time, to a widow named Toni Spitzer. I understand that all seven of his grown-up children, including my father, were strongly opposed to this marriage, but Jacob was a strong-willed man and very much a boss in his family and he did what he felt was appropriate for him. In perfect symmetry, he was also opposed to my father's marriage to my mother, who was not from a rich family, but my father, stubborn just like his father, proceeded with the marriage in spite of his father's displeasure. Before his death, Jacob acknowledged that he was wrong and my mother became his favorite daughter-in-law, but he never regretted his marriage to Toni.

The reasons why his children did not want their father to re-marry were obvious. It was also obvious that they loved and admired their late mother, who died two years before my birth, more than they admired their father. To them, she was irreplaceable. To hear them talk about her, she was not only a remarkable mother, a saint, an angel of a person,

she was also an acute businesswoman, better than her husband, and it was she who was responsible for the success of the family wholesale leather business. Her name was Hanna Hinda (known as *Hancia*) (1866-1924), nee Birnbaum, and she was Jacob's cousin as well as his wife. She was the daughter of Isaac Mendel Birnbaum of Kraków (ca.1830-<1891) and Małka Birnbaum, nee Drezner. Jacob was a son of Józef Aleksandrowicz and Rachel Aleksandrowicz, nee Drezner. To rephrase it, Shiya Jozua Drezner's daughter Rachel married Józef Aleksandrowicz and her sister, Malka, married Isaac Mendel Birnbaum. Thus Jacob and Hanna Hinda were first cousins, children of two sisters. Such marriages between first cousins are, apparently, sanctioned by Jewish religious rules. I found it of interest, when I arrived in the United States, to find that Franklin Delano Roosevelt and his wife Eleanor were also first cousins.

Shiya Jozua's daughter Rachel Drezner Aleksandrowicz had six children. Her sister Malka Drezner Birnbaum had seven. There was a further complication: when Malka died suddenly, her widowed husband Isaac Mendel Birnbaum married her sister, another of Shiya Jozua Drezner's daughters, Feigl Golda (Gina), who was also a sister of Rachel Drezner Aleksandrowicz. With her, Isaac Mendel had four more children. All these offspring married and produced many children. The number of first cousins that my father had, many doubly-related, simultaneously through his father as well as through his mother, was obviously very large. Inasmuch as most of them lived in Kraków and were of similar ages, they all knew each other, played together as children and helped each other. Then they, in turn, married and had children who were of my generation. It is not much of an exaggeration for me to assume that most of Kraków Jews must have been, in some way, my relatives.

Around 1906 Jacob and Hanna bought from a family named Metzger two elegant apartment houses on Bernardyńska Street, which were built approximately ten years earlier. These were the houses that I knew as the family residences. Jacob and later several of his grown-up married children resided in these houses. I understand that my grandparents loved each other and had a happy marriage. Jacob always conveyed the impression of being strong and authoritarian, but it appears from the stories of his children that Hancia was actually the stronger of the two and, in any disagreement, it was her will that usually prevailed. Her children all admired her and loved her and thought highly of her. Jacob was more distant and did not interfere with their upbringing. From photographs that survived to this day (see at the end of this chapter and the chapter dealing with my father) we can see that he looked very stiff, formal and dignified, and was always properly dressed. He always looked like our image of a proper wealthy Austrian burger. And like a proper Austrian burger, he was very involved in his mature children's futures and helped to arrange all their marriages, except that of my father.

Jacob's father Józef was not wealthy, he was a small businessman and Jacob began not as a rich man's son. As a young man, he was trained to be a qualified craftsman in the shoe-and-leather industry. He was obviously good as a cutter of leather and maker of upper parts of shoes. He purchased tanned skins which he used in his workshop. With time, he expanded the workshop and began buying and selling larger quantities of leather. His business grew, it changed from retail to a wholesale leather import-export enterprise and ended up as a factor in the Polish leather industry. I remember that as a small child I often visited the warehouse, with its large massive display tables and huge floor-to-ceiling shelves filled with folded packs of tanned leathers. The packs were folded within sheets

of brown paper with labels of assorted tanneries, Polish and foreign, among them Schmidt of Żyrardów near Warsaw and Allied Kid Company of Philadelphia. After my grandfather died in 1935, my father and two of his brothers took over the business. At one point my father decided that the business, renamed "Jacob Aleksandrowicz sons", needs to have its own proprietary brand name to place on leather purchased not from major known brand suppliers but from little known local tanneries. When my father mentioned this need at dinner one day, I suggested the use of the term "JOTAL", which I made up from the letter "J", called in Polish 'jot', and the beginning of the family surname. It tickled my fancy that my own name in Polish, "Jerzy", like that of my grandfather, Jacob, also began with a 'jot'. The brand name was adopted and the company leather was henceforth known by its logo as being from the *Jotal Kid Company*. Needless to say that, being ten years old, I was inordinately proud of having been the author of this iconic family brand. Recently, when asked to select a web address for myself, I picked 'JOTAL'. and when told is it already in use, combined it with my birth year and ended up with www.JOTAL25@yahoo.com.

At the outbreak of the First World War (1914-1918) Russia came to the aid of Serbia which was attacked by Austro-Hungary after an ultimatum dealing with the assassination of the heir to the Austrian throne by a Serbian nationalist in Sarajevo in Bosnia. Austria was joined by Germany and opposed by England and France and, eventually, by the United States. In 1914 the Tsarist armies marched into Austrian Galitzia, besieged the fortress town of Przemyśl and threatened Kraków. The Russian troops had a terrible reputation, they were said to be robbers and rapists, with only minimal military discipline and a strong anti-Semitic bend. Panic reigned among all Kraków citizens and particularly among Jews. Those who had the means escaped from the city, moving deeper into the Austro-Hungarian hinterland. The Austrian authorities encouraged this exodus. My grandfather, Jacob Aleksandrowicz, moved his entire family into Bohemia and stayed in the Czech spa of Karlsbad (now Karlovy Vary) until the threat of Russian armies abated, the Russian offensive broken and the Tsarist troops thrown back. My father, then 12 years old, fondly remembered his sojourn in the Czech resort, where he attended a German-language school. As a child he knew some rudimentary German, but was far from fluent in the language and used to recall some embarrasing misunderstandings.

In due course, all seven children of Jacob Aleksandrowicz married and all had one or two children apiece. The two older boys became lawyers, the three younger ones helped to run the family leather business. The older girl, Mania, married Isidor Wien from Stryj in Eastern Galitzia, now Western Ukraine, a co-owner of an oil-refinery in Krosno, in Southern Poland, and moved to live in Vienna. The younger girl, Lola, became an expert in pre-school education, a follower of Maria Montessori. Together with my mother, she established the first Montessori Kindergarten in Kraków in several rooms in a large apartment in the Bernardynska 11 building. Eventually, she married Professor Bruno Schall, an educator from Lwów, later director of the private Katzenelson Gimnasium in Łódź, an industrial city in Central Poland, and moved there.

For many years before he died in 1935, my grandfather instituted the custom of having his married children residing in Kraków and their families to a Sabbath eve dinner every Friday evening. We would all gather together in his great dining room, sitting at a large oval table. Grandfather was quite authoritative and attendance at dinner was akin to obligatory. Present, beside his new wife and hostess, Toni Spitzer Aleksandrowicz, were his sons Ignacy, with his wife and two daughters, Wilek with wife and son, Józek and his wife (Józek had no children then, in spite of trying), daughter Lola who was then still single, my father, mother, baby sister and I, and his youngest son Olek with his new wife. Missing was a daughter Mania, married to Isidor Wien, who lived in Vienna with her two children, Lilli born in Kraków in 1913 and Herbert born in 1915. The meal was a festive and rather formal affair, with many courses, served by a maid, on a table with lit silver candlesticks, heavy silverware, fine linen tablecloth and elegant china. Much as I remember it now with fondness, at the time for us children the long meal was a bore, and we often escaped the formality of it by climbing under the big formal table and playing there. Grandfather also held formal Seder dinners at Passover and I, as the youngest male present, used to ask the traditional "Four Questions" (*Kashes*). I also followed an old custom of hiding the traditional "*afikoymen*" (a piece of matzoh needed to complete the Passover ceremony), which grandfather then had to "redeem" from me by promising me a gift, which invariably every year turned out to be an expensive Waterman fountain pen with a gold tip.

As I stated before, my grandfather looked like a typical Austrian burger, which he was, except that he was Jewish. He had a round full face, wore thin gold-rimmed glasses and had deep penetrating black eyes. He was rotund, clean shaven and bald. He wore elegant, well-tailored suits, including a very expensive one made of natural-color silk. He was always serious: while I saw him a lot, I have never seen him laugh outright. He was reputed to be stubborn and opinionated but open to reason and able to see opposing views when these were presented to him, although that had to be done often against his wishes. He was very dedicated to his children and grandchildren, and I believe, that he was particularly fond of my father.

I know that Grandfather was not orthodox, but he was a typical modern, somewhat observant Jew. He did not normally wear a hat or a cap, not even when eating. He was cleanly shaved and did not sport a beard. He did not go to a synagogue except on special occasions and major holidays. However, he did insist on kosher meat and had his wife maintain a kosher kitchen. None of his children continued the kosher observance, except one, Józek, whose wife, Sala nee Neuman, from Radom, came from a more religious family and wanted to keep Kashruth. My father's house was completely free of religious restrictions: I ate buttered ham sandwiches or drank milk along with pork dishes without giving it any thought, just as I did not think twice before eating meat on a Friday, which was then proscribed to observant Roman Catholics. At Passover, our house constituted an oasis where my parents' friends, whose own parents were religious and who had to stick to matzohs at home, came to eat bread. I grew up with strong moral convictions, inculcated in me by both my parents, but these convictions did not arise from a traditional religious upbringing. I will have more to say about ethics and morals in my parents' home later, when discussing my childhood.

The history of Kraków during Jacob's life was intertwined with the history, first of the Habsburg Empire and then of the newly-reconstituted Polish Republic. In 1867, as a concession to the restless Hungarian patriots, the Austrian Empire was transformed into a Dual Monarchy, an Austrian Empire joined to a Hungarian Kingdom. Simultaneously, provinces of the empire were granted a great deal of autonomy. All official business in Kraków was conducted in Polish, in Budapest in Hungarian, in Zagreb (Agram) in Serbo-Croatian, in Prague in Czech. Emperor Franz-Joseph styled himself *"From God's Grace*

Hereditary Emperor of Austria, King of Hungary, Bohemia, Dalmatia, Croatia, Slovenia, Galitzia and Lodomeria, Archduke of Austria, Duke of Burgundy, Styria, Karinthia, Krajina, Grand Prince of Transylvania, Margrave of Moravia, Duke of Brabant, Limburg, Luxenburg, Geldria, Wuertenberg, Upper and Lower Silesia, Milan, Mantua, Parma, Placentia, Quastella, Auschwitz and Zator, Prince of Swabia, Hereditary Earl of Habsburg, Flanders, Tyrol, Hennegau, Kiburg, Goritzia and Gradiska, etc. etc".

After 1867, emancipated Jews were gradually allowed to live anywhere in the country. Kraków Jews elected members to the provincial parliament of Galitzia sitting in Lwów and to the national chamber in Vienna. Electoral alliances between Polish Jews and Poles were formed in the Vienna Parliament. Conflicts arose between conservatives and liberals, between religious fundamentalists and religious reformists. Often anti-Semitism reared its ugly head. For a while Austria was dominated by a strongly anti-Semitic party, allied with the Roman-Catholic episcopate and supported by the Vatican nuncio. Vienna had a mayor who owed his election to his anti-Jewish campaign. Urban Poles in Galitzia co-operated with urban emancipated Jews, while Galitzian peasants fell under the sway of a rabidly anti-Semitic priest, Stanisław Stojałowski, who was so extreme in his anti-Jewish tirades that the Vienna government was embarassed by him and is said to have asked the Vatican to help calm him down.

The power of the militaristic Prussian Junker class was rising in Berlin. In the Austro-Prussian War of 1866 the Austrian armies suffered an embarrassing defeat at Sadowa (Koenigsgraetz). The Prussian military proved the equal to any in Europe. In 1870 a Franco-Prussian War broke out and the French were beaten. The French Emperor, Napoleon III, was taken prisoner at Sedan. For a while, Paris was ruled by a Commune. It took the Prussians a year to name their ruler, Wilhelm I of the Hohenzollern dynasty as the German Emperor (Kaiser). This Wilhelm was a descendant of the prince who had received Prussia from the Polish king as a vassal and who swore eternal loyalty to the Polish Crown. When he died in 1888, his son Wilhelm II ascended the throne. In humiliated France, searching for scapegoats, anti-Semitism reigned in the trial of Captain Alfred Dreyfuss, who was convicted of treason, in spite of being innocent. Nationalist fervor was rising. Fates were not favorable to multi-national multi-ethnic and multi-lingual Austrian Empire. Before the Prussians named their king as the emperor of the German Reich (a collection of German-speaking, largely inependent kingdoms, duchies and municipalities, which included besides Prussia, Bavaria, Saxony, Wuertemberg, Hesse, Hamburg, Bremen, etc,. etc.), the Habsburg emperor Francis II abandoned his title of Emperor of the Holy Roman Empire of the German People and became an Emperor of only Austria as Francis I. In 1848 young Franz Joseph assumed that throne. In 1889 the heir to the throne, Archduke Rudolf, having been forbidden to marry his love, the Hungarian aristocrat Maria Vetsery, took her to the castle of Meyerling and there they both committed suicide. He was succeeded as heir to the throne by Archduke Francis Ferdinand who died in 1914, assassinated in Sarajevo by Gavrilo Princip, a Serbian patriot/terrorist, member of the Young Serbia Movement. The Austrian Empress, wife of Franz Josef, Elizabeth, affectionately nicknamed "Sissi", was generally well liked and admired. In 1898 on a visit to Switzerland, Sissi was murdered by an Italian anarchist.

In Russia in 1894 Nicholas II became Tsar. Three years later a Jewish Socialist Workers Party, the General Workers Bund of Poland, Lithuania and Russia was founded in Vilna. A thoroughly assimilated Jewish Viennese journalist, Theodor Herzl, wrote a

fantasy--science fiction--political tract called "*Altneuland*" (the Old-New Land), proposing a Jewish homeland in Palestine, supported economically by fees from a to-be-built canal across the Negev desert, linking the Red Sea with the Mediterranean, competing with or replacing the Suez Canal. His book exerted a powerful impact and led to the foundation of modern Zionism. The First Zionist Congress met in Basel, Switzerland in 1897. In distant South Africa British forces fought the Boers for possession of Transvaal and Oranje Free State. The Russian Social-Democratic Party split in 1903 into a Bolshevik and Menshevik factions, led by Vladimir Lenin and Sergei Plechanov, respectively. In 1904-5 the once all-powerfull Russian Empire was defeated at sea at Tsushima by a surprising resurgent Imperial Japan. In 1906 San Francisco was shaken by an earthquake which killed 700 people. In 1908 Austria annexed Bosnia and Hercegovina, antagonizing Serbs and their Pan-Slav protectors, the Russians. Tensions rose in the Balkans. There were two regional conflicts, pitting Bulgaria againt her Balkan neighbors. People read signs of impending dangers in the appearance of Halley's comet in 1910. In 1911 China underwent a revolution, with Dr Sun-Yat-Sen supplanting the Manchu Emperors and becoming President. In 1912 the unsinkable liner "Titanic" sank when it hit an iceberg. In June 28, 1914 the heir to the Austrian throne (see above) was killed in Sarajevo in Bosnia. An Austrian ultimatum to Serbia signaled the beginning of World War I. The conflict between Austria-Hungary and Serbia soon expanded. Russia, then Germany, France, Britain and Ottoman Turkey joined the ranks of the combatants. All at once, the old order in Europe ended.

The period from 1860 to 1914 saw an incredible flowering of arts, literature and science. In France Louis Pasteur proved that fermentation is caused by living organisms, Victor Hugo wrote *Les Miserables* (1862), Jules Verne published "Twenty thousand leagues under the sea" (1870), Bizet wrote "Carmen" (1876), Pierre Curie and his Polish wife, Marie Curie nee Skłodowska, isolated radium and polonium, Bleriot crossed La Manche (the English Channel) in a one-seater aeroplane (1909) and Marcel Proust wrote a monumental *A la recherche du temps perdu* starting with *Du cote de chez Swann* (1913). In Russia count Leo Tolstoy published *War and Peace* (1865-1869), an epic description of the 1812 Napoleonic campaign in Russia as seen from the Russian perspective. In England, Gilbert and Sullivan wrote "H.M.S. Pinafore" (1878), Arthur Conan-Doyle published "The Adventures of Sherlock Holmes" (1891), Herbert G. Wells wrote "War of the Worlds" (1898) and George Bernard Shaw wrote "Caesar and Cleopatra" (1898). In the United States Mark Twain published "The Adventures of Tom Sawyer" (1874). In Vienna, the daily "*Neue Freie Presse*" began appearing in 1864. My great-grandfather was an avid reader of this newspaper up to the day when Hitler entered Vienna in 1938. In 1874 Johann Strauss II entertained the Habsburg Court with his operettas; in 1875 *"The Fledermaus"* created a sensation when it was performed in Kraków. Between 1895 and 1905 Roentgen discovered X-rays, Guglielmo Marconi invented radio, Max Planck postulated the quantum theory, Albert Einstein wrote about relativity and Sigmund Freud investigated dreams and sex. In Poland and Russia a new secular Yiddish literature was being created by pioneering writers, Mendele Moykher Sforim, Yitzhok Leibish Peretz, Sholem Aleikhem and others.

The economy of the Kraków area changed after 1918. While prior to 1914 most of Kraków commerce flowed south towards Vienna and was exported through the then Austro-Hungarian port of Trieste, after 1918 most commerce moved north and east, in the direction of Warsaw, Central Poland and the port of the Free City of Gdansk (Danzig). After

1918 the Aleksandrowicz leather business imported leather from Czechoslovakia (from the *Bat'a* Company in Zlin), Germany, France, England, even the United States (from the Allied Kid Company of Philadelphia) and sold it to local middlemen and large-scale shoe factories in Warsaw and nearby Żyrardów. Customers included even the large Chech Bat'a Polish subsidiary, which found it cheaper to buy leather from the Aleksandrowicz company, thanks to the quirks of export-import laws, than from its own Czech parent company. The official Polish Business Directory of 1929 detailing Krakovian commerce, published by the Polish Government and now available on the Internet at www.Jewishgen.org/ShtetLinks/Poland/Kraków, listed the family business twice: as an importer of leather for upper parts of shoes and as a leather wholesaler.

As far as I can judge it (I was ten when my grandfather died, and fourteen when the Germans invaded Poland in 1939), Jacob Aleksandrowicz was mainly preoccupied with the family and with building up his business and did not actively participate in the lively political conflicts in Kraków. In contrast, his sons, Ignacy, Wilhelm and Maks, were very active politically, starting even before the establishment of the independent Polish State. Ignacy and his younger brothers were liberal social democrats opposed to totalitarianism and opposed the proto-communist SDKPiL (Social Democracy of the Kingdom of Poland and Lithuania), led by the Polish-Jewish radical Roza Luxemburg (1871-1919). Roza Luxemburg later moved to Germany, where she and Karol Liebknecht became important leading the Spartacus faction of the new Marxist German Communist Party. Both were killed by German militarists. There are now streets in Berlin named after both Liebknecht and Luxemburg.

In 1922 my paternal grandmother Hanna Hinda Birnbaum Aleksandrowicz, wife of Jacob, was diagnosed with diabetes. This was before insulin became available and she died on 22 October 1924 in the Austrian spa of Bad Ischl in Tirol, near the place where I was later imprisoned in a concentration camp in 1944-1945. Her husband Jacob also came down with diabetes, but by the time he was diagnosed insulin was available and he lived with it for years. Every day a nurse came and injected him with insulin. Eventually, he had an intestinal tumor and died in 1935. He was buried in the Miodowa Street cemetery and had a shiny black marble tombstone. In 1997, when I visited the cemetery, I found that the entire section where his tomb was located had been vandalized by the Nazis and there was nothing to be seen at the right spot. However, broken tomb fragments that have been found lying around have been incorporated into a "memorial wall" and I have reasons to believe that one large fragment of black marble with the letters "*...wicz / 35*" is all that is left of my grandfather's tomb (see Fig. 43 at the end of this chapter).

Other children of the second Józef Aleksandrowicz, grandson of the first Józef (Joseph), Jacob's siblings, were David, born in 1867, Hana, born 1869, Małka Reizl, born January 23, 1874, Pearl, born June 18, 1875, Shiya (later known as Jozue) born in 1877, and Ryfka born in 1879. David lived in Kraków. He became a shoemaker, married to Anna whose maiden name was Gumplowicz. I remember him from my childhood as a thin, slender man, always dressed conservatively, who came every now and then to my grandfather's store. He had a daughter named Hela. Hela Aleksandrowicz married Abraham Frisch. They had a son, Wilhelm Frisch and a daughter, Pola, who married a man named Wasserberg. Małka Reizl Aleksandrowicz, whom I knew well as great-aunt Mania or Amalia, married Isidor Kleinhandler. The Kleinhaendlers lived on Meiselsa Street in Kazimierz. When Józef became old, he lived in an apartment above this daughter. Every time we came to greatgrandfather Józef we stopped and visited the Kleinhaendlers. I never met or heard about Józef's other daughters, Pearl and Rivka. Perhaps they died young or moved away. Józef's son Shiya chose to use the more Westernized name, Jozue. He moved to Vienna, married Sophie Vortrefflich. I only met Jozue Aleksandrowicz once, when he came for a rare visit to Kraków. I remember him vaguely as a distant, formal, heavy-set, elegantly dressed man. He seemed to know hardly any Polish and spoke German with a Viennese accent. In Vienna Jozue and Sophie had four children, whom I never met: Herbert, Fritz, Franz and Lilli. Herbert Alexandrowitz (!) married his relative, Halina Weindling, a descendant of Wolf Aleksandrowicz described earlier. Herbert and Halina had a daughter, Eva Alexander. Franz died young. I understand that Fritz and Lilli survived the War but I have had no contact with them.

Jacob Aleksandrowicz and Hanna Hinda had seven children, Ignacy (recorded at birth as Izak Mendel), Mania (Amalia), Wilhelm (Wilek), Jozue (Józek), Laura (Lola), Maksymilian (my father, known in New York as Max Alexander) and Salo (Olek). My father will be described separately. For the description of his siblings, my uncles and aunts, starting with the oldest, Ignacy, see Chapter 22.

Fig. 046. Portrait of Jacob Aleksandrowicz and his wife, ca. 1900;

Fig. 047. Jacob Aleksandrowicz and his family in Kraków in 1912;

Fig. 048. Jacob and his wife in Marienbad in 1914;

Fig. 049. A fragment of memorial cemetery wall, probably from Jacob's tombstone;

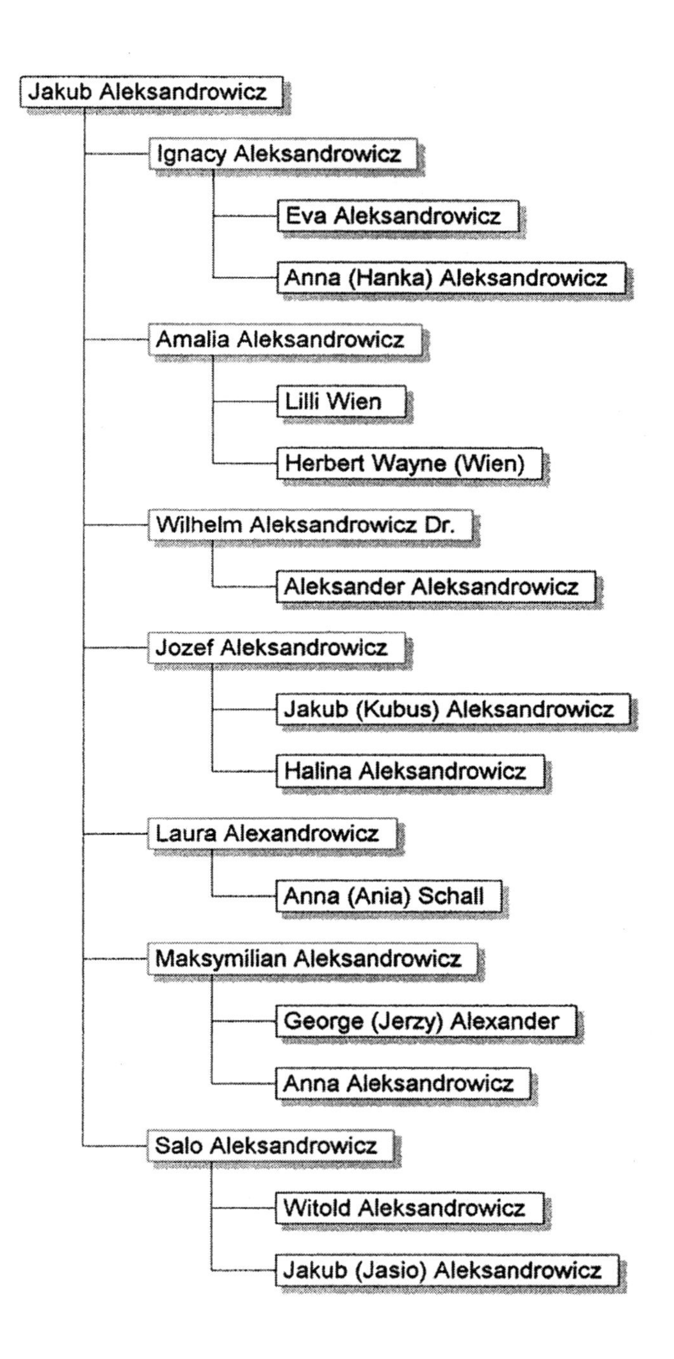

Fig. 050. Jacob Aleksandrowicz family tree

Descendants of Jakub Aleksandrowicz

Jakub Aleksandrowicz 1866 - 1935
+Hanna Hinda Birnbaum 1866 - 1923
...... Ignacy Aleksandrowicz 1891 - 1964
...... +Sala Klipper - 1942
.... Eva Aleksandrowicz 1923 - 1942
.... Anna Aleksandrowicz 1927 - 1944
...... Amalia Aleksandrowicz 1892 - 1944
...... +Isidor Wien
.... Lilli Wien 1913 -
.... +Hans Mercado
.... Silvia Mercado
.... +Maurizio Bal
.... Carina Bal
.... Alejandra Bal
.... Monica Mercado
.... +Roberto Obersky
.... Viviana Obersky
.... Enrique Obersky
.... Herbert Wien 1917 - Abt 1955
.... +Roni Golpern
.... Jeffrey Wayne
.... +Hope Queller
.... Hawkeye Wayne
.... Justin Wayne
.... Ethan Wayne
...... Wilhelm Aleksandrowicz 1894 - 1942
...... +Olga Schoenholtz - 1942
.... Aleksander Aleksandrowicz Abt 1930 - 1942
...... Jozef Aleksandrowicz 1896 - 1942
...... +Sala Neuman - 1942
.... Jakub (Kubus) Aleksandrowicz 1937 - 1942
.... Halina Aleksandrowicz 1940 - 1942
...... Laura Alexandrowicz 1900 - 1943
...... +Bruno Schall - 1943
.... Anna (Ania) Schall 1936 - 1942
...... Maksymilian Aleksandrowicz 1902 - 1968
...... +Salomea Rubin 1900 - 1942
.... George (Jerzy) Alexander(Aleksandrowicz) 1925 -
.... +Rita Birnbaum
.... Mark Alexander
.... Michele Anne Alexander 1960 - 1967
.... Anna Aleksandrowicz 1931 - 1942
...... Salo Aleksandrowicz 1908 - 1944
...... +Barbara Infeld - 1942
.... Witold Aleksandrowicz 1936 - 1942
.... Jakub (Jasio) Aleksandrowicz 1939 - 1942

Fig. 051. A listing of Jacob Aleksandrowicz descendants to the fifth generation;

Chapter 21. Lateral branch: Berek Birnbaum, his ancestors and descendants

(a) Distant ancestors: martyrs, witchhunters and storytellers

In researching the history of the Alexander/ Aleksandrowicz family I was lucky in researching a surname that is distinctive and not too common among Poles and Polish Jews. The bane of genealogical research is not a name that is rare and seldom shows up, but a name that appears so frequently that it is difficult to identify who among many individuals bearing that name is a relative and who is not, and a name that appears spontaneously in different areas. Until DNA search becomes easier and genetic data more available, disentangling the various strands sharing the same surname but little else will continue to present an almost insurmountable task. The name Birnbaum falls into the latter category. It seems to have originated independently in many places. Besides the Birnbaums in Kraków, there were Birnbaum families elsewhere in Galicia and also in Germany, Ukraine and Russia. There are many Birnbaums and descendants of Birnbaums living today in the U.S., researching the genealogy of families bearing the name. There are impressive lists of Birnbaum individuals who lived in Kraków appearing on the Internet, but also individuals who are not related to the Krakovian Birnbaums. In my personal case, my wife's maiden name was also Birnbaum. Her family came from Fuerth in Bavaria. The family has a detailed family tree, going back to 1600, but to the best of my knowledge, if the Bavarian Birnbaums were in some way related to those from Kraków, the relationship is distant and any connection occurred far back in history. To illustrate the difficulties of genealogical research when a name is very frequent, I will present below a number of Birnbaum details that we encountered in our research in Kraków, along with attempts to bring some sort of order to the available information.

Birnbaum family legends about the clan's distant history state that the family was

living in what is today borderland between Germany and France, first in Koblenz in the Rheinland and then in Alsace on the other side of the Rhine, and eventually in Frankfurt/ Main and in Bohemia. Apparently, one of our earliest legendary ancestors, a Koblenz rabbi, was murdered by participants in the Second Crusade, in the 13-th century, around 1240 A.D. Memory of his martyrdom was passed among his descendants from generation to generation. Over the years, ancestors and relatives included prominent rabbis, authors of rabbinical texts, then leaders primarily in Prague and the Bohemian countryside. It is said that the family resided in Bohemia prior to moving to Galitzia, both Habsburg territories. One prominent ancestor, the rabbi Isaiah Horowitz (Ish Horwitz), died in 1517 in Prague. His descendant, Isaiah ha-Levi Horowitz (1565-1630), was the author of the treatise *Shneh Lukot Habrit* (Two Tablets of the Covenant), and thus became known as ShLoH. Another relative of Ish Horowitz, Pincus Horowitz (died in Kraków in 1615), must have been either an important scholar or a very rich merchant, judging from his marriages and those of his children. His first wife was the granddaughter of Yehuda ben Betsalel Loew, 1512-1609, known as the MaHaRaL of Prague, famous as the reputed creator of a *Golem*, a soulless man, showing that a man, even a great, pious and learned man, might create a working human body but not its soul and spirit. After his first wife died, Pincus Horowitz married Miriam Bella, sister of Remuh, daughter of Isserl and Dina Rivka, and a niece by marriage of Alexander ha-Kohen. His daughter Hinda Horowitz married Meir Wahl son of Saul Wahl and grandson of Rabbi Samuel Juda Katzenellenbogen, MaHaRaM Padua. According to Edward Birnbaum (1855-1920), my great-uncle, who collected old musical and historic documents and who thus served as a family historian, my Horowitz/ Birnbaum ancestors, including my maternal grandmother, moved to Kraków sometimes after 1640.

In a letter written in 1948 dealing with family history Immanuel Birnbaum, Edward's son, quotes his father as stating that several siblings of his ancestors abandoned Judaism and their children became important in both Roman Catholic and Protestant theological and juridical circles. The most important of these was one Johann Pauli (1455-1530), a Rheinland monk and a preacher in Strasbourg, who became known as a collector of old German sayings and stories and a modernizer of mediaeval German language. He was essentially a contemporary of Martin Luther (1483-1546). In addition to Pauli, Edward Birnbaum mentioned another important putative Christian relative, a generation later, in Holland, an innovative protestant Dutch jurist Gerard van Geldwijk.

It took me a while to figure out why Edward Birnbaum believed that Johann Pauli, a barefoot Franciscan monk who was a scion of a Jewish Alsatian family, was important in world history and in the Birnbaum family saga. Several articles on the Internet and a published lecture delivered at a symposium at the University of Salzburg in December 2004 by Dr Irma Trattner (www.sbg.at/ger/samson/rvws2004-2005/trattner.pdf), entitled Hexenbilder (Creator of Witches) contained the answer. Fear of black magic and witchcraft was endemic in Christian Europe in the Middle Ages and earlier and it led to frequent arbitrary accusations of sorcery, mostly against old women, but it did not become formalized and institutionalized until Pope Innocent VIII issued a Papal Bull *Summis desiderantes affectibus* in 1486, named two inquisitors specifically dedicated to search for witches and mandated that church and civil authorities must give them all help necessary in their task. The two inquisitors, members of the Dominican Order, Jacobus Sprenger (Cumanus) and Henricus Institoris (Heinrich Kramer) wrote, in Latin, a compendium on witchcraft entitled

Malleus maleficarum (The Witches' Hammer). The book, with the supporting Papal Bull as introduction, was published first in Strasbourg around 1487 and republished many times subsequently. Even in Latin, it became one of the most popular books in Christian Europe, its popularity exceeded only by the Bible. This infamous manual served as a guide for inquisitors, institutionalizing torture and justifying the very existence of inquisitions. It validated the belief in witches and in satanic possessions. It led to the deaths of countless people, mainly of old women, but also of Jews, Gypsies and men accused of being warlocks. Some writers on the subjects estimate, perhaps with some exaggeration, that as many as 9,000,000 women died in the following three centuries as a result of prosecutions (www. malleusmaleficarum.org). Every prosecutor and magistrate in Christian Europe, whether theological or secular, had a copy on his desk. It described in gory details all manner of tools for detection of sorcery, signs of pacts with the devil, satanic rituals, levitation, effects of potions and philters, etc, etc. Twenty years later, in 1508, the book became the source for fire-and brimstone sermons of a popular preacher Johann Geiler von Keysersberg in Strasbourg. I do not know if this lay preacher and rabble-rouser knew how to read and write, as few people at the time could, but his sermons were written down and published in 1517, in German, by the erudite monk Johannes Pauli, our relative mentioned by Edward Birnbaum, who was in von Keysersberg's audience.

According to articles on the Internet (www.infos-aus-germanien.info, from the Wikipedia, etc), Johannes Pauli was born in Pfedersheim in Alsace around 1455 and died in Thann in Switzerland around 1530. He graduated from the University of Strasbourg and became a Franciscan monk. In 1499 he was the primary preacher in a Franciscan convent in Oppenheim, then in Bern in Switzerland and eventually in Strasbourg from 1506 to 1510. All these abbeys followed the strict bare feet and poverty vows of the order. While in Strasbourg, Pauli attended the striking, dangerously incendiary sermons delivered in the Strasburger Cathedral by Johann Geiler von Keysersberg. They warned people of pacts with the devil, of devil possessions, of hexes and evil eyes cast by old women, of man-beast conversions and werewolves, and of witchcraft in general and encouraged them to look for evidence of witchcraft among their neighbors. In 1520 Pauli published a German translation of Keysersberg sermons which thus provided them with extra wide distribution and attention. In addition, in 1522 appeared Pauli's own collectionof mixed fables, uplifting parables, but also of scary witchcraft tales, as well as of short stories, proverbs and folk sayings, comprising approximately 700 items under the title *Schimpf und Ernst heisset das Buch mit Namen, durchlauft es der Welt Handlung mit ernstlichen und kutzweiligen Exempeln, Parabeln und Historien.* This book, too, had a significant distribution. Many of its witchcraft stories, embellished in retelling, entered the European popular folklore. Several served as sources for the fairy tales of Brothers Grimm. Pauli stories and von Keysersberg sermons which Pauli published contributed significantly to the incalculable harm of inquisitorial activities and over time contributed to a number of instances of mob histeria over witchraft, possession, werewolves, etc. Burning of old women as witches became common extending, as we know, even to Massachusetts. Unfortunately, many of the superstitions popularized by Johannes Pauli persist to this day, as exemplified by the recently whipped up histeria in the United States and in France over satanic rituals and repressed memories of sexual abuse of children.

(b) Birnbaum family in Kraków (ca.1640-1939)

In November 1998 the Jewish Institute of Religion / Hebrew Union College on Wahington Square in New York City held a conference devoted to the works of the composer and collector of Jewish liturgical music Edward Birnbaum. Edward Birnbaum was my father's uncle, an older brother of my grandmother Hanna Hinda Aleksandrowicz nee Birnbaum. I was alerted to the conference by Edward's grandson and my second cousin, Henrik Birnbaum, then living in California, who asked me to go to the conference and represent the family.

The conference, which included lectures, concerts and an exhibition of rare illuminated manuscripts from the Birnbaum Collection of Jewish Music was sponsored by the School of Sacred Music of the Hebrew Union College and held at its campus near Washington Square in New York City. The Hebrew Union College located in Cincinnati, Ohio, is the main seminary training rabbis for the Reform branch of Judaism. In Cincinnati, the College maintains a collection of old Jewish music assembled in the 19-th Century by Edward Birnbaum. The conference sponsors were glad to have a representative of the Birnbaum family present. I was formally introduced as a member of the family and I welcomed the conferees in the name of the Birnbaum clan. The conference display included a selection of music manuscripts, but also of photographs and other family artifacts from the Birnbaum collection, which were specially brought from Cincinnati for the occasion. The 1998 conference was only one of my several genealogical encounters with Edward Birnbaum, the oldest brother of my grandmother. The New York display of Birnbaum medieval music manuscripts was not the first such display either. The first such display of the Birnbaum collection, according to family data, occurred in Paris as part of the *1900 Exposition Universelle Internationale* (1900 World's Fair). It was sent by Edward Birnbaum to Paris at the specific request of his friend, the contemporary foremost French literary personnage, the writer Romain Roland.

My grandfather married Hanna Hinda Birnbaum (Hancia). I never met my grandmother; she died eight months before I was born, but as a child I knew many of my Birnbaum relatives who lived in Kraków. In my genealogical research I always included the Birnbaum surname in my work. When searching the documents in the Kraków branch of the Polish National Archives with my wife's help, we encountered the surname Birnbaum for the first time in official Kraków records for the year 1806. After finding the people who then adopted this surname, we have attempted to go back in history and search for records of their ancestors. I knew that my grandmother's father was Izak Mendel Birnbaum and I knew that his father was Saul ("Reb Shioel", as my father referred to him). I found that this Saul, born around 1795, was listed in the birth record of one of his children as Saul Berkowicz Birnbaum. Since in this case the ending "*wicz*" denoted a patronymic, Saul's father must have been called Berek. Thus, my oldest assured Birnbaum ancestor, the founder of my branch of the Birnbaum family, was Beer or Berek. He must have lived around the year 1770 and earlier.

Early Krakovian members of the Birnbaum family can only be deduced, with some measure of confidence and an equal dose of uncertainty, from indications in existing Birnbaum birth and wedding certificates dated after 1806, and from the frequency of names that were given to children. The latter is based on the assumption that the children were

usually named after recently departed ancestors. Thus, Berek's wife Mirele or Mirla must have died before or in 1820, because in 1820 her son Zelig, Saul's brother, named his first girl Mirele, which he would not have done had his mother been alive. For the same reason, I believe that the original Berek must have died before 1830 when Zelig named a baby Berus. I have not been able to find out who were the parents of Berek and Mirele, Berek's wife. From the prevalence of a name that was listed as the second name of several individuals living around 1800, such as Wolf Zelig, Hirsch Zelig and Saul Zelig, often denoting the name of the father or a more distant important ancestor, I believe that the head of the family, father of Berek and Wolf, and grandfather of Hirsch and Saul Birnbaum, was named Zelig. This Zelig, the ancestor of many of the Kraków Birnbaums, must have been born around 1720 and must have died by 1787, when, his grandson, Zelig was born.

Around 1760 there were several individuals born in Kraków, whose descendants eventually assumed the Birnbaum surname when surnames became obligatory after 1806. In estimated sequence of births, starting at about 1755, these were Izak, Ensel (Anschel?), Lebel (Leib), Wolf, David and Berek. I can not be certain whether they were all children of Zelig or, even, whether they were all related, but it is likely that they were brothers or cousins and that, as a group, they decided to adopt "Birnbaum" as a surname when the Imperial Austrian authorities insisted on surnames in 1805. There was a small town named Birnbaum in Germany, located between Gorzów and Pniewy in the Poznań (Posen) district in the once Prussian part of Poland, today called Międzychód. They may have known that the family lived there at one point, but I doubt it and there is absolutely no evidence that the family even knew of the existence of this town. It is more likely that the Austrian officials assigning names picked this name, meaning "peartree", for no particular reason, except its euphonious sound. Further research may help to resolve remaining doubts. From the census listings of 1790 and 1796 and from later civil acts, I have found the names of the Birnbaum spouses. The wives' names were also of help in identifying and distinguishing these individuals and their descendants. Izak married Gitl daughter of Elias. Gitl Eliasowna Birnbaum died in 1839 (Act # 240). Ensel married Golda, daughter of Mordechai (Mordche). Lebel married Beyla. Wolf married Hanna, who died in 1834 (Act # 22) and David married Sarah daughter of Juda. Berek, as I mentioned above, married Mirele, who died in 1820. They all have had many children, some of whom died very young. Infant mortality among Kraków Jews, crowded together in the narrow confines of a Jewish ghetto, was very high. I hope that somebody will undertake a comparative study of infant mortality and sanitation and other health-related issues of Jews in Kraków, and elsewhere in Galicia in the 18-th and 19-th centuries.

It appears from extant records that Jewish families had many children, often more than a baker's dozen, many of whom died in infancy. Older surviving Polish civil records, i.e. those from before 1796, were not kept as assiduously as were those made by Austrians who occupied Kraków from 1796 to 1809 and then again from 1846 to 1918. The generation of Izak, Ensel and their brothers is represented in the civil acts by only a few entries, whereas their children's generations often shows up as having had as many as fourteen children. From the documentation we know that Izak Mendel and Gitl Eliasowna had two sons, Sandel born in 1804 and David born in 1805. Sandel married Feigl of the family of Zelig, David married Ita daughter of Mendel and Hindl. According to the act # 262, p. 88, of the year 1830, a son named Elias Józef was born on August 6 to Sandel

Birnbaum, peddler of bread, age 26, and his wife Feigl Zeliger, age 20, living in community # 6, house # 118. According to the act # 48, in the same year, David Birnbaum, 25, son of Eysik (Izak) and Gitl Elias, living in building # 118 (158?), married Yetta Lewy, also referred to as Ita Szewa (Batsheva) Peltz, age 23, daughter of Pincus and Hanna, then living in building Number 68.

Ensel's existence was confirmed by records of his daughter Golda, who was born around 1787. Thus, in 1804 Golda Enselowna, at the age of 17, married Józef, age 18, son of Salomon and Chaya, later known as Bader, living in house # 107, a member of the important Bader family, which run the Kraków Jewish ritual bath, the *mikveh,* described earlier. On February 13, 1814 Józef Bader and Golda *z Birnbaumów* (i.e. of the Birnbaums) Bader had a daughter, Henna (who in 1833 married Michael Aron Reinhold). From these records I deduced that Golda's father was Ensel, who assumed the surname Birnbaum. Józef and Golda Bader nee Birnbaum had many children, among them Juda Bader, born in 1807, who married Beyla Ringer, Ensel Bader, who married Sarah Lednitzer, Mendel Bader, who married Jachwet Birnbaum, Mordechai Bader, who married Taube Strassburger and Rubin Izrael Bader, who married Frieda Tilles, thus connecting the Birnbaum/Bader clan with many prominent Kraków families. Józef Bader had a brother, Jacob Bader, who was the official paid community *felczer*, a licensed healer. A few descendants of Jacob Bader migrated to Manchester, England, around 1850, where they changed their surname to Barder.

Lebl who married Beyla, must have been born around 1760. He must have died before 1809. He is not to be confused with his nephew Lebel, husband of Cierel (Zirl) who was born in 1782. We know of the first Lebl's existence because he was the father of Joel Birnbaum, born in 1779 or, depending on which document we accept as more accurate, in 1784. He was also probably, the father of Mordche (Marcus) born around 1792. All of them, Lebel and Beyla, as well as Joel and Mordche, lived in house # 62. In 1802, Joel Leiblowicz Birnbaum, listed as being 18, married Beila Genendel, 19, daughter of Pincus. In 1811, he was active as an employee of the Kahał, the Jewish traditional community organization. Among Joel's children was Leibl Birnbaumn, named after his grandfather, born March 4, 1809, who married Rebecca Fink in 1833. According to their descendants in the USA, this Leibl Birnbaum, later known as Leon, and Rebecca nee Fink had Joel (1841-1908), who married Hudessa (Eva) Goldberg and emigrated from Kraków to the Bronx. Mordche Marcus Birnbaum married Lieba, daughter of Lazar. He traded horses and engaged in tanning leather. Wolf Sellig, also born around 1760, lived in house # 2. He was the husband of Hanna, who died in 1834 (act # 22) at the ripe age of 75. Wolf and Hanna had a daughter, Cierl, born in 1793, and two sons, Sellig, born on March 3, 1798, and Aaron, born in 1803. Aaron Birnbaum married Friedl, daughter of Wolf and Frumetta Persigbaum, in March 1827 (Act # 220).

We know about David and his wife Sarah, daughter of Judka, from documents of his son, Hirsch (Herschel) Birnbaum, born around 1789-1794. The exact date of his birth and of his wife, is uncertain. In 1813, 23-year-old Hirsch Birnbaum made a very desirable match: he married the young, 16-year-old daughter of a famous rabbinical family, Reizl (Rela) Jonasówna Eibenschuetz, sometimes spelled Eybeschutz, even Aybuszyc. Rela, who was born in house # 70, on 4 November 1802, to Jonas Eibenschuetz, son of Jacob Eibenschuetz, and Malka Pincusówna, was a distant but direct descendant of the famous Krakovian sage and cabalist, Nathan Nate Spira, through his daughter Dobrysz (died 1642) and Dobrysz's husband, Yeshaya Ashkenazi. Dobrysz and Yeshaya's grandson or great-grandson, also

Nathan Spira (Shapiro) became rabbi of the small town of Ivancice (Ivantshitse) in Moravia, known in German (and Yiddish) as Eibenschuetz, hence the name adopted by his progeny. As described in an earlier chapter, one of the Eibenschuetz rabbi's sons, became a very learned and respected proponent of magic, cabalistic incantations and messianic fervor. Jonathan Eibenschuetz was born in Kraków in 1696, he eventually became the Chief Rabbi of Hamburg and Altoona. It was this Jonathan Eibenschuetz who conducted the dispute with opponents of the mystic strain of Judaism, led by R. Jacob Emden. At the time, as now, there was no recognized supreme Jewish religious authority that could adjudicate conflicts between the traditional orthodoxy and messianic strains within Judaism, but, at the time there was in Poland a Jewish quasi-parliament, the *Vaad Arba Aratzot*. Although it was supposed to deal mostly with taxation and maintenance of community organizations, in the absence of anything better, the Emden-Eibenschuetz argument came before this body, and supporters of Eibenschuetz carried the day. I have no independent knowledge of the respective merits of the Eybenschuetz or Emden positions, but I trust and follow the judgement of both Heinrich Graetz and Mayer Bałaban, both of whom are squarely in the Emden camp.

The age of Rela Jonasówna Birnbaum, nee Eibenschuetz, as shown in birth certificates of her children, proves the casual way in which specific age of individuals (as well as spelling!) was treated at the time. Thus, her supposed date of birth is shown in the registry of births for the 1802, under November 4. It is possible that the registration of her birth was delayed and she was actually born earlier, because in 1818 at the supposed age of 16, she is listed as "Rela z Jonasów, age 20" (Act # 154); in 1819 as Rela Jonasówna, again as 20 (Act # 428). In 1821 as Rela Eybuszówna, she is still said to be 20 (Act # 12); in 1822, as Rela Abuszytz, she is said to be 25 (Act # 288); and, finally, she is recorded in 1827 as Reyzl, age 21 (Act # 52), i.e. born in 1806 (!). Obviously, an approximate age was good enough. Rela and Hirsch had many children. One of their children, Nathan Birnbaum (1864-1937, married a relative, Friedl Eibenschuetz-Ehrenpreis, daughter of Abraham Ehrenpreis and Zisl, widow of Jacob Eibenschuetz. Nathan Birnbaum was among the earliest proponents of settling Jews in Palestine, coined the term *Zionism* for the movement advocating a return to Zion but was opposed to reviving Hebrew for everyday use and strongly felt that Yiddish is and should be the national language of the Jewish people. He helped organize the First Conference for the Yiddish Language which met in 1908 in Chernovtsy then the capital of Austrian province of Bukovina, then known in German and Yiddish as Tschernowitz, that is now a part of Ukraine.

Listed above were all the assorted Birnbaum families living in Kraków around 1800, except for the three most directly connected to my personal family tree, those descended from Lebl, Zelig and, primarily, Saul Birnbaum, all three born between 1780 and 1800. Zelig, born around 1789 and Saul, born in 1795, were the sons of Berek. I am not sure if Berek was also the father of Lebl, born in 1782, husband of Cierel (Tsirl or Zirl). Lebel and Cierel had a daughter named Hinda in 1804, another, Sarah, in 1806, a son, Moses Wulf, in 1808, and a daughter Ester in 1809. In 1817 Cierel Birnbaum, wife of Lebl, merchant, living in house # 8, died prematurely at the age of 32 (Act # 192b).

Like the other family members of his generation, Berek is known to us from the records of his children. Zelig Birnbaum, the oldest son of Berek and Mirla, married Beyla Gela Fishlowicz in 1813. She was the daughter of Izak (Icyk) Fischl and Chava. Because hand-written capital T and capital F are similar, people not familiar with the Latin alphabet easily have mistaken one for the other. The surname of Beyla Gela's parents may have been Fischlowicz or Tischlowicz and I have encountered both in some documents, along with their spelling variants, Tislovitz, even Tyslobis. A child, Berus (Little Berek) born in 1830 died in a few days; but his name indicated to me that Zelig's father Berek must have died before 1830. Some records show that Bella's (!) father was Izak (Icyk, Itzik) and Abraham Fischlowicz was her grandfather, other records call her Beyla Abrahamówna, imply that her father was Abraham. Confusingly, in August 1814 Zelig, age 24, and Beyla Gela z Fiszlowiczów, age 20, living in house # 122, had a child that they named Chaya. The registry was said to have been witnessed by the baby's grandfather, Izaak Fiszlowicz, and by Szymon Englaender. Zelig's occupation was listed as "liwerant", i.e. supplier or provider, without specifying what it was that he was delivering (in 1833 this Chaya later married Salomon Kornblum). In the same year, 1814, Beyla Gela's father, Izaak Fischlowicz, now listed as the son of Abraham and Sarah, died at the age of 54. In December 1815 and in June 1817 two boys, Mojzesz Bendet (Benedikt) and Efraim Fischl (!) were born to Zelig and Beila. In 1819 and 1820 the couple had two girls, Henna Pearl and Mirele. Zelig was then listed as a trader in grain. After 1822 he became a bar owner, but continued to deal in grain and was so listed in the "*Aufnahms-Bogen vom Jahre 1847 – Arkusz spisowy konskrypcyjny z roku 18..*". Zelig and Beyla Gela had eight more children.

My ancestor Saul Berkowicz Birnbaum, born around 1795, married Gitl Samuelowna Baum, born in 1798. Gitl was the daughter of Samuel Baum (Bałaban II, 609), who served as secretary of the *Komitet Starozakonnych* (the official replacement of the Kahał, Committee of the People of the Old Testament) from 1817 to 1822. His son Gerszon, Gitl's brother, served from 1823 as the official sworn translator of the rabbinate and it was Gerszon who translated into Polish rabbi Hirsch David ha-Levi's speeches and proclamations, including the one excommunicating followers of Hassidism. In 1820 Saul Birnbaum, whose profession was described as "spekulant", age 25, living in house # 100 and his wife Gutl daughter of Samuel, 22, had a son, named Ensel. A year later they had Abraham Szmul (Samuel) (Act # 231, p.79). Later, in 1840, Abraham Samuel Birnbaum married Rebeka Redlich. Abraham and Rebeka (Rifka) had in 1845 a daughter named Hana. In 1824 Saul, now listed as a "coral maker", 32, and his wife Gitl Baum, 30, had a son, Samuel Juda. Two years later Saul, "maker of beads", and Gitl had a daughter, Deborah (Dvoira). The next available record, in 1832 shows that a baby, named Izrael, born to Saul and Gitl *z Baumów* Birnbaum, died (Act # 301, p.101). In 1836 a boy named Wolf was born (Act # 192). Wolf Birnbaum had two children, Zdzisław and Genia. The latter married a man named Jeżower and had a daughter named Ruth. Saul and Gitl had other children, whose birth certificates I could not find. Among those listed on the Web by other Kraków researchers are Jachwet, who married Abraham Szmul Bader, Ester, who married Tobias Wechsner, and Michel Leib. These and other Birnbaum data are conveniently listed and can be accessed on the Web site <*www.isc.uci.edu/~dan/genealogy/Kraków/Families/Birnbaum.html*>). Not listed on the Web site or anywhere else, and of particular interest to me, was the birth of Izak Mendel Birnbaum, one of the apparently unrecorded children of Saul and Gitl, born around 1828, who later married twice and fathered at least eleven children, among them Edward and my paternal grandmother, Hanna Hinda Birnbaum Aleksandrowicz.

Isaac Mendel Birnbaum became a tavern keeper in Kraków. He married Małka Drezner, daughter of Shaya (Jozua) Drezner and his wife Henna nee Bader. I have dealt with

the Drezner and Bader genealogy earlier. With Małka, Isaac Mendel had seven children. When Małka died young, probably a victim of the cholera epidemic that struck Kraków in the eighteen seventies, Isaac Mendel had small children and needed help in bringing them up. He was eager to remarry. His late wife had a younger sister, Golda Feigl (Gina). A family story has it that, against her wishes, Golda Feigl was married to Isaac Mendel. Together they had four children. I have not been able to find out exactly when Isaac Mendel was born or when he died, but he must have died shortly prior to 1891, because the name was then given to one of his grandchildren, the first-born son of his daughter Hanna Hinda and her husband Jacob Aleksandrowicz. The son, Izak Mendel Aleksandrowicz, was later known as Ignacy (1891-1964) (see the next chapter).

Isaac Mendel and Małka Birnbaum's first son, Edward (Ascher/Anschel, named after Isaac Mendel's uncle Anschel) was recorded as having been born in Kraków on March 12, 1855. Before him came Hana (born in 1853), after him Golda Augusta (b. 1859), Saul (Salomon, b.1860), Gumpert (b.1864), Hancia (b.1866) and Ester Feigl (b.1868). With Gina, Isaac Mendel had Jozua (b. 1877), Abraham Joel (Adolf, b.1879), Amalia (b.1882) and Julius (b.1883). All were born in Kraków. In the Edward Birnbaum Collection of Jewish Cantorial Music preserved in the Hebrew Union College in Cincinnati there is a photograph of Edward Birnbaum and two of his brothers and four sisters: Salomon and Gumpert and Hana, Golda, Hanna Hinda and Ester. Some of the photos have come from family collection and been lent for the Birnbaum exhibition. I believe that there is some confusion about Edward's date of birth. The birth was recorded in 1855, yet his father would have been 27 then and 25 when his first sibling was born, rather old for the time. Also, in some documents Edward was said to have been born in 1848. It is possible that he was born at the earlier date but his birth was not recorded with the civil authorities until much later.

Edward Birnbaum became known as a composer, music arranger and cantor. He studied in Vienna and Breslau (now Wrocław in Poland), then served as a cantor in Magdeburg in Prussia, Beuthen in Silesia (today Polish: Bytom) and from 1879 in Koenigsberg in East Prussia (today Russian Kaliningrad). Among melodies that he has modified and arranged for modern musical instruments were such well-known traditional tunes as *Lekhu Doydi* and *El Mole Rakhmim*. His most important lasting contribution, however, was not as cantor, composer or arranger of music, but as a historian of Jewish music and a collector of old Jewish liturgical melodies. In this he was a pioneer. His collection, it is said, encompasses up to 65% of all extant historical Jewish cantorial musical documents. It is deemed of incomparable value. The collection is now preserved at the Hebrew Union College in Cincinnati and attempts are being made to obtain funds to house and display it permanently in New York, in the School of Sacred Music at the New York campus of the Reform Jewish Hebrew Union College – Jewish Institute of Religion. The Encyclopaedia Judaica (Keter Publ., Jerusalem 1972, IV, p.1039) has a biography of Edward Birnbaum, which gives his birth date as 1855. Edward died in Ostseebad Kranz near Koenigsberg in 1920. He had four children: Immanuel, Gertrud (Grete), Hans and Paul.

The oldest child of Izak Mendel Birnbaum and Małka Drezner Birnbaum, Edward's sister Hana, married Alter Weinstein. They had two sons named Ignatz and Alexander (Olek) whose children carried the Weinstein name, and three daughters who married Beck, Steinberg and Fleischer. The next child, Golda (Augusta), married Max Bader and had four children: Alexander (Alex), Rose, Sigmund (Sigi) and Charles Bader. Izak Mendel's

son, Edward's brother, Salomon (Saul), became an accountant. He never married. Their brother Gumpert was listed in the 1881 Kraków census as a brewer and distiller of alcohol. Gumpert eventually moved to Berlin. He had two sons, Max and Hans Birnbaum, both moved to New York after Hitler's rise to power an lived in Queens. Izak Mendel and Malka's daughter and Edward's sister, Hanna Hinda married Jacob Aleksandrowicz, who was her first cousin. As explained before, Jacob's mother, Rachel Drezner was a sister of Hanna Hinda's mother, Małka. Both were daughter of Shaya Drezner and Henna nee Bader, as well sisters of Isaac Mendel's second wife, Gina, also a daughter of Shaya Drezner and Henna nee Bader. Thus, the children of Hanna Hinda with Jacob Aleksandrowicz, including my father, and the children of Małka or Gina with Isaac Mendel Birnbaum were cousins, half-cousins and double cousins. It was all quite complicated. Jacob and Hanna Hinda had seven children, Ignacy (b. 1891), Amalia (b.1892), Wilhelm, b.1893), Jozue (b. 1896), Laura (b. 1900), Maksymilian (Max Alexander, b. 1902) and Salo (b. 1908). Wilhelm, Jozue, Laura and Salo died in the Holocaust. Ignacy and Maksymilian (my father) came to the US. Ignacy died in New York in 1964, Max in 1968. Amalia (Mania), emigrated from Vienna to Buenos Aires and died there in 1944. Isaac Mendel's and Małka's last daughter, Ester Feigl Birnbaum, married Henryk Mikołajewicz. They had three daughters: Mania who married Herstein, Saba who married Spatz, and Giza who married Marcel Spritzer.

Isaac Mendel and Gina Drezner Birnbaum's son Jozua became an educator and a director of a Jewish school in New York. He had two children: Ignatz and Tusia. Next son of Isaac Mendel and Gina, Adolf Birnbaum, moved from Kraków to New York in 1905 and became a designer and jeweler at Tiffany's. Their youngest son, Julius, also became a jeweler in New York. He had three children: Manuel, Joyce and Pearl. Pearl married David Horowitz, a physician. Pearl and David have four children: Alfred Horowitz in Los Angeles, Michael, Steven and Julia in Israel. Isaac Mendel and Gina's only daughter, Małka (Amalia) married Henry Kaufer. In the Edward Birnbaum Collection of Music in Cincinnati there is a postcard written by Edward around 1910 and addressed to "Fraulein Amalia Birnbaum", living with her mother, G.F. Birnbaum, in the Bauminger House in Kraków.

Amalia and Henry Kaufer settled in Vienna. They had three children: Gisela (Gisi), Helene (Heli) and Enoch (Inek), all born in Austria. The children moved to Prague where Gisi married David (Duszko) Davidson and Heli married Jirka (George) Steiner. Inek came to the United States and enlisted in the army. The Steiners had two sons, John and Charles. Just before Hitler annexed Czechoslovakia the Davidsons emigrated to America and settled in Boston, then moved to Maine. They were both physicians. Gisi became City Physician of Portland Maine. Heli and George Steiner moved from Prague to New Zealand with their two boys. Inek settled in California. Eventually, Heli and Jirka and one of their sons moved to London, the other son came to the United States.

The next generation of Birnbaums became dispersed all over the world. Edward's son, Immanuel Birnbaum married Lucia Richter. He became a journalist in Poland, Germany and Sweden. He had two sons: Karl Edouard, who lives in Stockholm and Henrik (1925-2003), who lived in California. Immanuel remarried after the war. With his wife, Alicja Orszanowska, he had Ida and Michael. Edward's daughter, Gertrud, married a man named Hilf and moved to London. Edward's son Paul died during the War in 1942. Edward's nephew, the son of his brother Gumpert, Hans Birnbaum, became a physician in Queens, New York. He had two children, Lisa and Gerry. Hans' brother Max also had two children, Gabrielle (Gaby) and Peter. Gaby married a man named Kanarek. Peter was interested in Eastern philosophies and became an expert on the old original Indian proto-EuroCaucasian language, Sanscrit.

Immanuel Birnbaum's son, Karl, who lives in Stockholm, married Britta Linder. Their children are Maria, Anja, Camilla, Daniel and Paula. Maria married Markus Keller, they have two children: Lavinia and Leon. Anja with first husband Anders Olsson has Simon and with second husband Martin Roessel has Julia. Camilla married Fredrik Pantzerhielm. They have a daughter named Laura, a son Jacob and a daughter Clara. Paula, Karl and Britta's youngest, married Pierre Guillet de Monthoux in Switzerland. She recently had twins. Immanuel's son, Henrik Birnbaum, moved to California. He died in May 2003. Henrik was an expert in early Russian and Slavic history. He published a number of historical treatises and taught at the University of California in Los Angeles. He also lectured at the Central European University (CEU) in Budapest and the Zagreb University in Croatia. Henrik and his first wife Ulla had Eva Birnbaum. Henrik and Ann Mari Nilsson had Steffan. After his death his widow, Marianna, established a foundation in his name at the CEU offering scholarship to promising students of history. Eva and Sony Goeth have Tobias and Melina. Eva and Peter Backlund have Daniella. Steffan is married to Mona and has two children, Maria and Sarah. Immanuel's youngest son Michael is married to Petra Haffa. They have Sarah, Rebecca and Layla.

Izak Birnbaum and Gina's daughter, Edward's half-sister, Amalia (Mania) and her husband Henry Kaufer, left Vienna when Hitler took over and settled in Brooklyn. Their daughter, Gisi Davidson, nee Kaufer, had two children, Minna and Carol. Minna married Lawrence Noone, she now lives near Hartford, CT. Minna has three children. Kimberly, Kristen and Karl Noone. Kimberly and husband Paul Coutinho have Nicholas and Benjamin, Karl and Susan have Tyler Burke Noone. The Kaufers' other daughter, Heli, who married Jirka Steiner, moved from Czechoslovakia to New Zealand, and eventually to London. Heli died in London in 1990, Jirka in 1992. Their son John Steiner, born in Prague, moved from New Zealand to London. He married Mary Deborah Pickering. They have three children: Michael Charles Steiner, Katherine Ann and Susan Elizabeth. Michael Charles Steiner, John's son, married Lisa Samuels. They have two small children, Dominic George and the baby, Hanna.

Jirka and Heli's other son, Charles Steiner, also born in Prague, became a physician, moved to New York and then to New Orleans. Charles Steiner married Judy Sherman, then Rosalyn Konopny. Charles and Judy have Mark Allen, Emily Susan and Rebecca Helen, all born in New York. Charles and Rosalyn have Carley Rachael and Chelsea Alexis. Charles and Judy's son, Mark Allen Steiner married Eilean (Poppy) Donan Mackenzie. Mark and Eilean have two boys, Harrison and Max. Emily Susan married David Weiner. Emily and David have two children, a boy and a baby girl. Rebecca Helen (Becky), briefly married to Dimetrius Seraphieme Koutas, has a girl, Zoe.

Amalia and Henry Kaufer's son, Enoch Kaufer married Evelyn Judis and moved to California. Enoch and Evelyn have Lanny, John, Michael and Gilda. Lanny Kaufer married Cheryl Nicoli and then Roseanne Westland and then Harmony Loup. Lanny and Cheryl have Aran, Lanny and Roseanne have Mara. Michael married Suzanne and they have a son, Jacob. Gilda has a daughter, Ara. Gilda is now married to Ben Wheeler. The Wheelers live in Seattle.

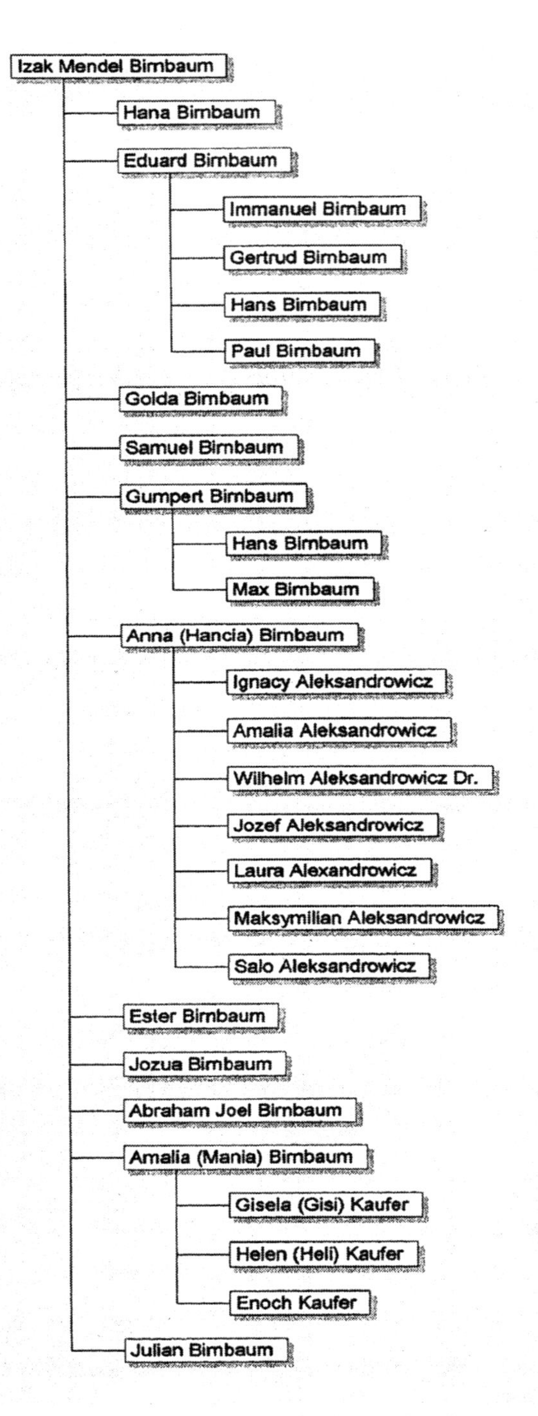

Fig. 052. Izak Mendel Birnbaum family tree

HEBREW UNION COLLEGE–
JEWISH INSTITUTE OF RELIGION

❖

Music, Spirit & Scholarship: The Legacy of Eduard Birnbaum

❖ SUNDAY, NOVEMBER 22, 1998 ❖

8:30 Registration and Breakfast

9:15 *Welcome*
Rabbi Sheldon Zimmerman, President, HUC-JIR

9:30-12:30 ***Discovering The Birnbaum Collection: Lectures with Musical Illustrations by SSM Students***
Dr. Mark Kligman, Chair

Professor John Planer, "Introduction to the Eduard Birnbaum Collection"

Professor Eliyahu Schleifer, "Dreams and Melodies: Tunes for the Priestly Benediction in the Birnbaum Collection"

Professor Edwin Seroussi, "Unexpected Contributions of The Birnbaum Collection to the Study of Sephardic Liturgical Music"

Professor Philip Bohlman, "Self-Reflecting Self: Eduard Birnbaum & The Age of Jewish Music Collection"

12:45-1:45 Lunch
Greetings
Dr. Alfred Gottschalk, Chancellor, HUC-JIR

Title page of Cantor's Manual for the complete liturgical year, handwritten and drawn by Ahron Beer (1738-1821). Writing in 1790-91, Beer compiled melodies to establish the cantor as soloist unaccompanied by the congregation.

Fig. 053. A page from the Edward Birnbaum seminar, New York 1998.

Chapter 22. Children of Jacob Aleksandrowicz and Hancia nee Birnbaum

(a) Ignacy Aleksandrowicz (Kraków-New York, 1891-1964)

The professor of economics at Hobart College in Geneva, New York in the Finger Lakes country in the years 1946-63 had a long foreign name, difficult to pronounce, impossible to spell. Students noticed, however, that the name began with an "A" and ended with a "Z". Soon, Professor Ignacy Aleksandrowicz became known as "Professor A-to-z".

My uncle Ignacy was the oldest of seven children of Jacob Aleksandrowicz and Hanna Hinda, nee Birnbaum. He was the oldest sibling of my father, Maks, eleven years older than my father, who was born in 1902. Ignacy was born in Kraków on September 16, 1891 and was given the Hebrew names of Izak Mendel, after his grandfather on his mother's side, Isaac Mendel Birnbaum. While everybody in Kraków knew him as Ignacy, he was listed on his official Polish documents which I found among his possessions after his death, as Izak Mendel. Ignacy became a prominent lawyer, a graduate of the Law Faculty of the Jagiellonian University of Kraków with the highly cherished title of *Iuris utriusque doctor*. He was interested in political science and became an expert in labor law and economic history. He was married and had two daughters. His illustrious internationally acclaimed legal career ended in 1939 with the onset of the War. While his wife and children were killed, he survived and came to the USA in 1941. As an expert not only in civil and criminal law but also in labor economics, he became a Professor and then chair of the Department of Economics at Hobart College in Geneva, in upstate New York in 1946. He retired in 1963 and died in New York City in 1964.

As a student in Jagiellonian University, Ignacy was active in the Jewish student organization *Związek* (Union) and editor of its journal. In 1911 he was among the founders of the ŻPSD (Jewish Social Democratic Party of Galitzia). In 1918 Austrian Galitzia was combined with the Russian and German parts of Poland to form the resurrected Polish Republic. The ŻPSD held a meeting in Kraków in April 1920 and decided to join forces with the Jewish Labor Bund of Poland. Ignacy Aleksandrowicz spoke in favor of forming this united Jewish social-democratic party for all of Poland, refused to become a communist and was active in the Bund. He served as a member of the regional committee of Bund in Kraków and co-editor of its monthly in Polish called *Walka* (the Fight). In 1938 he became the chairman of Kraków Bund. He ran for a seat on the City Council as a candidate of the Bund.

During the 1914-1918 war Kraków was a part of the Austro-Hungarian Empire. Ignacy was drafted into the Austrian Army and saw action on the Russian Front. As the Empire and its armies fell apart in 1918, he found himself in the Eastern Galitzian city of Lwów. Prior to 1918 the city was an important commercial hub and the capital of the constituent Habsburg Kingdom of Galitzia and Lodomeria. The town was largely inhabited by Polish Roman-Catholics and Jews, the countryside was almost totally Orthodox Ruthenian and Gutzul, now considered as subgroups of Western Ukrainians. In 1918 both the Poles and the Ukrainians hoped to establish independent countries, joining the parts that were Austrian with the parts that were ruled by the just deposed and executed Russian Tsar, Nicholas II. Ultimately, in 1918 the Poles succeeded, while the Ukrainians failed. The Poles were lucky in their leadership, and had the support of President Wilson. Poland became an independent country. Ukrainian nationalists were poorly led by the anti-Semitic *ataman* (general) Semyon Petlura, who failed to attract the critical Western support and was eventually defeated by the Red Army. As a result of Petlura's defeat, Ukraine remained in the Russian orbit for another 80 years. In 1918 the Poles and the Ukrainians were battling for possession of Lwów. Neither side trusted the Jews and both engaged in anti-Jewish excesses. Ignacy, in his soldier's uniform and with his Austrian rifle, along with other Jewish soldiers of the defunct Austrian army, organized an armed Jewish Self-Defense Force *(Żydowska Samoobrona)* and became a member of its command. The Samoobrona successfully defended the Jewish areas of the city. Its action represented a little-known instance of a vigorous and successful armed Jewish resistance to anti-Semitic attacks. To the best of my knowledge this episode has never been described in print. I would like to see a detailed study done of this proud chapter in Jewish history. After a few days the situation in Lwów stabilized. The Poles, among them teen-age children (*Orlątka Lwowskie*; Pol.: Lvovian Eaglets), were victorious, the Ukrainians withdrew and Lwów became part of Poland until 1939. As Lviv, it is now a part of Western Ukraine. The Jewish self-defence force, no longer needed, dissolved. My uncle Ignacy, demobilized, returned to Kraków.

In 1922 Ignacy married Sala Klipper, from Bielsko (Ger.: Bielitz), a mid-sized town to the southwest of Kraków. Her parents operated a hotel in Bielsko. They owned the apartment house at Wrzesińska 4 in Kraków and also Villa Jasmin in the spa of Krynica (pronounced Kree-nee'-tsah). Ignacy and Sala had two daughters, my cousins and playmates, Eva was born 14 November 1923 and Hanka was born 18 August 1927. Eva was almost two years older that I, Hanka was two years younger. All three of us were very close and played together often. In 1931, at age six, I spent an entire summer with them in their Krynica villa. I will describe the time I spent with them later, when writing about my own childhood. Ignacy's wife, Sala, was a well-known sculptress, a student of the famous artist, Xawery Dunikowski (1875-1964), who was also born in Kraków. Dunikowski, among

his other works, received the commission to sculpt the dozens of heads imbedded in the ceiling of *Sala pod Głowami* (Room under the Heads) in the Royal Palace on Wawel Hill when that palace was being renovated. Many of the heads were missing or damaged and Dunikowski and his students, my aunt Sala among them, sculpted their replacements. Next to her apartment at Wrzesińska Street Sala had a large studio, which I remember as being full of life-size statues, mostly of nudes, particularly of her own pre-pubertal girls (see sample photo below). I do not know what became of the sculptures after the War and where they ended. I assume that they were not destroyed and I would not be surprised to hear that they are on display somewhere in Poland or that they have been appropriated as war booty by the Germans and now grace some German museum. Recently, the Science and Art Publishing House PWN in Warsaw published an elaborate, pictorial art book dealing with Jewish paintings and sculpture in Poland during the last two hundred years, written by the art historian Jerzy Malinowski (2000), who collected available data about a number of Jewish artists. I was disappointed to see that none of the works of my aunt-by-marriage, Sala Aleksandrowicz, nee Klipper, appeared in this book. Malinowski mentions that the sculptor Xawery Dunikowski had seven Jewish students. In the listing of Jewish artists who displayed their works at a 1920 exhibition in Lwów, Malinowski includes a Miss Klipper (*Kliperówna).* That would have been the name under which my aunt-to-be would have displayed her works in 1920.

Ignacy opened a law office in Kraków, first on the Main Town Square and then in his family's house at 4 Wrzesinska Street. He specialized in political trials and became known as a defender of people accused of crimes against the state by the semi-fascist authoritarian Polish regime of Józef Piłsudski and his successors. He was in demand as a public speaker and he run for public office. Politically, he was strongly opposed to totalitarian communism, but he was ready to defend communists for their political views and he had many friends among famous leftists of all colors. He was among the most prominent Jewish liberal political activists, not only in Kraków, or Poland, but in all of Europe, known and respected also in the United States.

He was known as a fearless defender of civil rights. Among people he knew, who discussed politics and social theories with him and who admired him were many famous socialists and prominent former commmunist dignitaries, the latter all exiles from Russia. I remember only a few that he told me that he met and had ideological discussions with. Among them was Angelika Balabanoff (1872-1965) who had been Lenin's Soviet Commissar (Minister) of Foreign Affairs, after the overthrow of the Tsarist and Kerenski governments. In prior exile she lived in Italy, became a mentor to a young socialist named Benito Mussolini. When her new protégé later rose to power and became a fascist and a dictator, she refused to visit Italy. In new exile after disagreement with Lenin she settled in Belgium, became Secretary of the Third Socialist International. As a grand old lady, in 1940 when the Germans occupied Belgium, she ended in New York, honored by the Bundists for her past contributions to socialist thought. Ignacy, my father and my stepmother met her often and enjoyed her reminiscenses. Alexandra Kollontay (1872-1952), a more distant acquaintance of Ignacy Aleksandrowicz, was also a former Soviet Commissar (of Social Affairs) and a member of the Praesidium of the All-Russian Duma (Parliament). After Stalin took over in Moscow, she became Soviet Ambassador to Belgium and never returned to Russia. Ignacy met her in Brussels. Friedrich Adler (1879-1960), whom

Ignacy met in Vienna, was among the leading theoreticians of Austrian Social-Democratic Party and a founder of its militia, the Schutzbund. Emil VanderVelde (1866-1932), a Belgian Socialist and Secretary of the Socialist International, visited Poland and had long discussions with Bundist leaders including Ignacy Aleksandrowicz, who objected to his support of the Zionist-socialist parties for membership in the Socialist International. Leon Blum (1872-1950), a French Jewish socialist and leader of the SFIO (French Division of the Workers' International), became Prime Minister of France, leading a Popular Front government that included Communists, a move that upset Ignacy and other Polish Bund leaders who tried to dissuade him from trusting Maurice Thorez and other Communist leaders beholden to Moscow. I know that Ignacy admired Karl Kautsky (1854-1938), the Grand Old Man and theoretician of European Social Democracy, who became an exile when Nazis took over Germany and Austria. I know that he was in contact with him but I am not sure that he ever met him in person.

In Poland, Ignacy intimately knew and collaborated with many political and social activists, ranging from the Polish elder satesmen like Ignacy Daszynski and Leon Wasilewski to the young promising socialist leaders like Adam Ciołkosz and his Jewish wife Lydia, and Jewish activists, both Bundist and Zionist, like leftist lawyer Ludwik Honigwill in Warsaw and the Zionist parliamentarians Ignacy Schwarzbart and Ozjasz Thon in Kraków. Ignacy Daszynski (1866-1936) was a co-founder and pre-eminent leader of the Polish Socialist Party, early Prime Minister of newly resurrected Poland in 1919, a key architect of its liberal constitution, a member of the first Polish Sejm (parliament) and in 1929 Marshal of the Sejm, a position roughly equivalent in Poland to the Speaker of the US House of Representatives. When Daszynski's former socialist colleague and collaborator, Józef Piłsudski, led a successful putsch as an army leader, disbanded the parliament, imprisoned its leaders after the infamous *Centrolew* trial and instituted a semi-fascist government in Poland, he withdrew from politics but he was not forgotten. His funeral in Kraków in 1936 was the largest outpouring of mourning people ever seen in Poland. Like Daszynski, Leon Wasilewski (1870-1936) was also a co-founder of the Polish Socialist Party, collaborated with Piłsudski until the *putsch* and then became the leader of the opposition and editor of its official socialist organ, the newspaper *Robotnik* (the Worker). His daughter, Kraków-born Wanda Wasilewska (1905-1964), a specialist in childhood education, was more radical in her politics than her father. She was a leader of the Polish Teachers Union and editor of the official Polish weekly children journal *Płomyk* (Little Flame) which I read every week in school. She had long discussions with my mother, arguing about pre-school and early school education. During the war Wanda married a Soviet official Vasily Korneychuk, settled in Soviet-occupied western Ukraine, collaborated with the Communists and became an important member of the Soviet Duma (Parliament).

Ludwik Honigwill (1887-1950) was a prominent attorney in Warsaw. He was one of the lawyers defending opposition politicians arrested after the Piłsudski putsch in the contrived *Centrolew* trial mentioned above, along with Leon Berenson, Wacław Barcikowski and others. Among the defendants were socialists Herman Lieberman, Adam Ciołkosz, Norbert Barlicki and Adam Preger and peasant leaders Wincenty Witos, Władysław Kiernik, Józef Putek and Kazimierz Baginski. The trial ended with their convictions for anti-government activities. Only in 1939, during the War did the President of the Polish Government-in-exile offered apology and exoneration to all the defendants,

who then joined the exile coalition government, first in Tours in France and then in London. Defending in the trial meant risking arrest, but Honigwill managed to remain free and active as an attorney in political cases. He and my uncle Ignacy frequently consulted in such cases. Ludwik Honigwill escaped from Poland in 1940 or 1941 and lived in New York, where I met him. Prior to the *Centrolew* trial one of the defendants, Adam Ciołkosz (1901-1978), represented Kraków socialists in the Polish parliament and his prominence and reputation as a spell-binding speaker explained why the Piłsudski government was so eager to neutralize him. After return from jail, he continued to live in Kraków, remained active in the opposition to the regime and edited the daily opposition paper, *Naprzód.* He collaborated with Krakovian Jewish socialists, among them my uncle, my father and my mother. Ciołkosz was married to a Jewish girl, Lydia Kagan (Kraków-London, 1900-2002), a close personal friend of my mother. The two women knew each other well, visited each other often and maintained friendly relations until the War, when Lydia escaped to England, while my mother perished in the Holocaust. When I needed tutoring for an interview for admittance to the best public secondary school in town in 1937, it was Lydia Ciołkosz that taught me. During the War Adam served as a member of the cabinet in the Government-in-Exile in London and was among its primary movers. At one time he helped direct funds from London to my mother for social work in the Ghetto. After the War, Adam and Lydia Ciołkosz refused to collaborate with Soviet occupiers of Poland, refused a tempting offer to join a *Quisling* government in Warsaw and remained in London for the rest of their lives. In London they edited a scholarly monthly journal *Kultura*. By contrast to Adam and Lydia, the pre-War secretary of the Krakovian Socialist Party, Józef Cyrankiewicz, also a friend of my parents, remained in Poland during the War and led the socialist underground organization in Kraków. In this position, he insisted that the Kraków Kahał transmit some funds received from London to my mother. Cyrankiewicz was caught and imprisoned by the Germans. Liberated by the Russians, he chose to cooperate with the them, joined the Polish government and rose to become Prime Minister of pro-Communist Poland.

In the nineteen thirties in Kraków life for Ignacy, Sala and their daughters was settled into a quiet routine. Ignacy was busy with his law practice and with his political activities, Sala was busy sculpting in her studio and the girls went to school and engaged with the usual mundane after school activities except for one: they posed nude for their mother. I knew both girls intimately and played with them often. I knew that they posed for their mother but I never saw them do it. As I remember it now, neither girl was particularly pretty but they were both smart and interesting. Both were fairly athletic, adept in calisthenics, better than I in turning summersaults. The older one, Eva, was tall for her age and mature for her age, somewhat too serious for my taste. The younger one, Hanka, was my favorite. She was vivacious, cute and easy with a smile. We used to bike together in the suburbs on weekends, swim on a sandy beach in the bend of the river Vistula in the summer and ski in the nearby hills in the winter.

When the war broke out in 1939, it was assumed that the Germans would occupy Kraków. Men of military age and men politically engaged were considered at risk and advised to leave the city, but women and children were considered safe. We knew that everybody will have a hard time during the war but we trusted the Germans as a civilized nation to not unduly harm innocent people. Ignacy left Kraków and went east to Lwów, where he met all his brothers. In Soviet-occupied Lwów at the time the Soviet secret police, the NKVD, was looking for political enemies, assisted by stool-pigeons, local communists and others. Since most of the able-bodied men of military age, who have not been drafted into the Polish army, escaped from Kraków and moved eastward, many of them ended in Lwów. The Krakovian communists knew Ignacy (and my father, Maks) as staunch opponents of Stalinism. Some of them denounced the brothers Aleksandrowicz to the NKVD. Other Krakovian communists, some of whom Ignacy defended in courts at considerable personal risk, secretly passed a warning to Ignacy, that the NKVD has plans to arrest him and his brother and that both must run. In the middle of night, Ignacy and Maks quietly left Lwów, traveled north, to smuggle themselves to Vilna in the then independent Lithuania, which seemed safer. They hired a local guide to cross illegally through a heavily-guarded Russian-Lithuanian frontier in the middle of a cold winter night, wading through deep snows in dark forests. The Soviets fiercely guarded their borders and the odds were against the brothers being successful in crossing this border, but desperation made them try. In the woods they were approached by Russian frontier guards and ordered to halt and were being shot at, but luck was with them and they managed to evade the pursuing soldiers and to safely reach Lithuania.

Like Lwów, contested by Poles and Ukrainians when the Austrian Empire fell apart in 1918, Vilna was also contested by two peoples, the Poles and the Lithuanians when the Russian Empire fell apart in 1918. The town was originally founded by the Lithuanian Grand Duke, Gediminas, as a capital for his Duchy. After a dynastic union of Poland and Lithuania around 1400 A.D., Vilna continued as the capital of the Lithuanian part of the Polish-Lithuanian Commonwealth. The Lithuanian aristocracy was absorbed into and became indistinguishable from Polish aristocracy. In fact, some of the most famous Polish noble houses, the Princes Radziwiłł (one of whom married Jackie Kennedy's sister, Lee Bouvier) and the Sapiehas (one of whom preceded John Paul II as Archbishop and Cardinal of Kraków) were of Lithuanian ducal origin. In 1918 the town of Vilna (Polish: Wilno, Lith.: Vilnius) was mostly inhabited by Poles and by Yiddish-speaking Jews. The second most important Polish Catholic shrine (after Our Lady of Częstochowa), the Madonna of *Ostra Brama* (Pointed Gate) is located in Vilna. The Jews revered Vilna as a center of Jewish learning, both religious and secular, referring to it as "The Jerusalem of Lithuania". The prominent Jewish sage, known as the Gaon of Vilna, lived there in the 17-th Century. A net of secular Jewish secondary schools, the CISHO group, existed in Vilna. The Jewish Scientific Institute (*Yiddisher Vissenshaflikher Institut*, abbreviated: YIVO), now located in New York, was founded in Vilna. The Jewish Labor Bund was established in 1887 in Vilna. While the town itself was Jewish and Polish, the population in the surrounding countryside, known in the Middle Ages as Samogitia (Polish: *Żmudź*), spoke Lithuanian, an ancient Baltic Indo-European language, somewhat related to Sanskrit. After 1918 reborn independent Poland and Lithuania went their separate ways. Lithuania claimed Vilna as its ancient historic capital but resurgent Poland sent in an army under General Lucjan Żeligowski, occupied the city and created an independent enclave called Central Lithuania, which promptly opted to unite with Poland. The Lithuanians never ceased to consider Vilna as their traditional capital and when the Soviets occupied it in 1939, convinced Stalin to cede it to them. This turned out to be a Trojan Horse kind of a gift, because in 1941 the Soviets swallowed the small country and converted the independent Lithuania, along with Latvia and Estonia, into Soviet Republics. But when Ignacy and Maks arrived there,

Lithuania and its Vilna were briefly free and safe, although poor and squeezed between Hitler and Stalin. Ignacy Aleksandrowicz became the Chairman of the influential Vilna socialist Bund.

The approaching take-over of Lithuania by the Soviets meant that Ignacy and Maks would not be safe there for very long but it gave them a window of time to arrange for an escape. With Europe in flames, the easiest way to get out of Lithuania at that point was to travel by a Trans-Siberian train through the Soviet Union, but transit through Soviet lands for politically engaged individuals was risky. To get a police permit to travel through the Soviet Union it was necessary to have a valid entry visa to some foreign place and dollar funds for a ticket on the Trans-Siberian Railroad. In nearby little Kovno (Lith.: Kaunas), which served as the capital of the country while Vilna was in Polish hands, there were foreign embassies and consulates, among them consulates of the Netherlands and of Japan. The Japanese consul was a foreign ministry bureaucrat by the name of Chiune Sugihara. The Jewish Labor Bund of Poland, in which both Ignacy and Maks were active, had affiliates in New York. The American Jewish Labor Committee and a Committee to Save Endangered European Intellectuals strove mightily to provide an avenue of escape for endangered Polish Bundists. The Dutch representative in Kovno assured the Japanese consul that the Dutch colonies of Surinam and Curacao in South America require no entry visas, although they did have restrictions on entry. Sugihara was willing to issue Japanese transit visas with nebulous final destinations that might not need entry permits, such as the Dutch colonies, and he was willing to accept the Hollander's assurances. The end result was, as we now know, that at considerable risk to his career this Japanese civil servant issued many such visas, enabling thousands of stranded Jews to escape from Lithuania, just as it was about to be engulfed first by the Soviets and then by the Nazis. The Jewish Labor Committee sent to Kovno a list of about forty names of individuals whom it wanted to save and for whom it would arrange American visas. Sugihara used that list, among others, when he issued his Japanese transit visas. The names of Ignacy and Maks Aleksandrowicz were first on his alphabetized list. Armed with Japanese transit visas, the brothers received Soviet permits and traveled to Moscow, where in the American consulate they received US entry papers. In 1940 they took the Trans-Siberian Railroad to Vladivostok, a boat to Kobe in Japan and then traveled, via Honolulu and San Francisco, to New York. In New York, Ignacy became a leader of the exiled Polish Bundists and was active in the New York office of the Polish Government.

In New York in July 1943 he was named Secretary of the official *Delegatura* (Representation) of the Polish State Control Commission, the financial watchdog of the funds of the Polish Government-in-Exile. The Polish Government-in-Exile had ample funds, as the gold reserves of the Polish State Bank had been removed prior to the German onslaught and were avilable in London. Also removed from Poland and subject to the jurisdiction of the exiled government and supervision by the State Control Commission were Polish national treasures, including a royal collections of Arrases (large woven Renaissance wall hangings) from the royal Wawel Palace and the gold royal crown and royal sword, all stored for safe-keepig in Canada. Ignacy Aleksandrowicz thus had a responsible position safeguarding the integrity of the expenditures authorized by the exiled Polish leadership and of protecting Polish cultural treasures. In 1946, after the U.S. Government recognized the pro-Soviet government in Poland and withdrew its recognition of the Polish Government-in-Exile, Ignacy resigned and then joined the faculty of Hobart and William Smith Colleges, the Colleges of the Seneca in Geneva, New York.

In the meantime, Ignacy's wife, Sala, and her daughters and his sister-in-law, Sala's sister Regina Friess, and her children, Joasia and Olek, escaped from Kraków for a while to Puławy in the Lublin district in central Poland but returned to Kraków after the Polish campaign ended. The first two years of war were difficult, food was hard to get, money was tight, but they managed to pool resources and survive. In 1940 Eva Aleksandrowicz (1923-1942), then 17, volunteered to work in a public nursery for orphaned or abandoned Jewish children in Kraków run by the charitable organization called "*Centos*" on Agnieszki Street. According to a form dated December 2, 1940, a copy of which I received from the Holocaust Museum in Washington, Eva received permission to stay in Kraków. Confirmation of her work status was countersigned by a family friend, Dr. Pola Wasserberg, in her capacity as Supervisor of the "*Kinderheim*". Eva's other wartime activities, in the Underground, have been described by the Jewish secret agent, Jacob Celemenski, in his memoirs written in Yiddish and published after the War (Celemenski, 1963). In 1941, things took a decided turn for the worse. The Jews in Kraków were being herded into a Ghetto. Many of us did not trust the Germans and were afraid of being hemmed in in a ghetto. At that point, we still had options which later disappeared. Sala and her daughters, her sister and her sister's young children moved from Kraków to a nearby town of Skawina, in which they were eventually caught in the Holocaust and placed in cattle cars being sent to an extermination camp in Bełżec in Eastern Poland. The older daughter, Eva, would not leave her mother, but Sala managed to push the younger girl, Hanka, off the train. Sala and Eva were never heard from again. Hanka Aleksandrowicz (1927-1944) came to stay with us in the Kraków Ghetto for a while. Eventually, she was provided with false papers showing that she is not Jewish and sent to live as a hidden child in Warsaw, where nobody would know her. Her life in Warsaw was also described by the Underground courier Celemenski. By the time she moved to Warsaw there were officially no Jews there. The large Warsaw Ghetto and its hundreds of thousands inhabitants had been liquidated. The Ghetto Uprising had been suppressed and the Ghetto buildings razed to the ground. The only Jews there, some twenty thousand, were living in hiding or on false papers, among 600,000 Christian Poles.

Hanka, with her false baptismal papers, acted as a mother's helper with a Polish Christian family which accepted her knowing of her Jewish origin, risking their lives if detected. They treated her kindly and were very helpful. I understand that they were very protective, unfortunately, I do not know their name. We were all certain that she will survive the War there. After Poland was liberated from the German occupation by the advancing Soviet armies, Hanka's father, Ignacy, in New York received news from friends in Poland who met her in Warsaw and who assured him that she must have survived the Holocaust. However, after liberation of Warsaw and then after the surrender of Germany months and months passed with no news from the young woman. All efforts to find her, or to find out what her fate was, were unavailing. Ignacy died in 1964 without knowing what happened to his younger girl. I found out later that she died as a fighter in the 1944 Warsaw Uprising. As the Soviet armies were approaching Warsaw in 1944, the Poles wanted to liberate their capital themselves and Warsaw exploded in an insurrection by the underground Polish Home Army. The approaching Russians stopped and waited on the other side of the Vistula and did nothing to help, while the Germans methodically killed the Polish patriots and destroyed the city block by block. A lot of people were caught in this debacle, almost 200,000 people died. Years later I saw in the Bund section of the YIVO Archives, a letter sent by a combatant in the Warsaw Insurrection, Szymon Joffe, indicating that my then 17-year-old cousin participated in the 1944 battles, was wounded and taken by her comrades to a small field hospital, which was then overrun by the Germans. One such primitive field hospital, perhaps even the one in which my wounded cousin was a patient, was described by Dr. Adina Szwajger (1992), who ran one and served as a physician in it. I assume that people who died in these little hospitals were eventually given proper, probably Catholic, religious burials. At Warsaw sites at which they fought and were wounded and died there are now plaques on buildings, honoring them and listing their names. However, Hanka Aleksandrowicz was at that time living under false papers as a Catholic and her battle comrades were not told that she was Jewish or knew her real name. Since I do not know what her assumed Christian hidden child name was, I am stymied in any attempts to find out more about her fate. It is sad to contemplate that my young cousin may have been honored as a heroine of the 1944 Warsaw Polish Insurrection but as a Catholic Pole, under a name that was not really hers.

With the Holocaust and the death of his family and the take-over of Poland by the Communists, there was no way that Ignacy would want to live in Poland, but he visited the country several times. In 1947, in Kraków he tried to find the details of the fate of his family, to reclaim some of the family real estate and, incidentally, to look for his late wife's artwork. He was unsuccessful in either endeavor. He found only vague information about his family and he could not find the statues. He did find photographs of some of the statues, brought the photos to the US, and displayed them on the wall of his residence in Geneva and later in New York City. A copy of one photo is appended here. He failed to wrest any of the family houses in Kraków from the Communist administration. He accepted a position as Professor of Economics at Hobart and William Smith Colleges in Geneva, New York, where he became the Chair of the department. It was there that he was called "Dr. A-to-z". As a prominent economist and college faculty member and an expert on labor law and on socialist economic theories Ignacy was asked to comment on and review articles and books dealing with Soviet and other leftist issues. Among such articles is one, published in the Annals of American Acadmy of Political and Social Science (267, 233-234, 1950), a crotique of a book dealing with the economic theory of socialism by Oskar Lange and Fred M. Taylor. Ignacy Aleksandrowicz died in New York City in 1964.

Ignacy Aleksandrowicz is listed on page 63, Volume I, of the *Slownik Biograficzny Dzialaczy Polskiego Ruchu Robotniczego* (Biographical Dictionary of Activists of the Polish Labor Movement), published in Warsaw around 1968. He is also listed, in Yiddish, on pages 96-101 of *Doyres Bundistn* (Generations of Bundists), edited by J.S. Hertz (1968). Ignacy Aleksandrowicz and his daughters are also mentioned in several places, in Yiddish (pp.10-11, 15, 32-35, 189, 201-2, photo p. 97), in Jacob Celemenski's book (1963) and in the first volume of *Geshikhte fun Bund* (History of the Bund), by J. Sholem Hertz (1981, 32, 125).

Fig. 054. Portraits of Ignacy Aleksandrowicz and his mother;

Fig. 055. Sculpture of Ewa Aleksandrowicz at 14 by her mother, Sala nee Klipper;

Nr. 3372/37

Nazwisko Dr. Alescandrowicz

Imię Izak Mendel

Data urodzenia 17. IX. 1891.

Miejsce urodzenia Kraków

Imię ojca — matki —

Zawód adwokat

Miejsce zamieszkania —

Wzrost średni

Twarz owalna

Włosy c. blond

Oczy piwne

Znaki szczególne —

Wydany dnia 25. VI. 1937.

za Prezydenta miasta

PODWORSKI MARIAN

Kierownik Urzedu ewidencji ludnoś

ZARZĄD MIEJSKI w stoł. krol. mieście KRAKOWIE — Pieczęć gminy

(Własnoręczny podpis osoby wyszczególnionej w dowodzie)

Stosownie do art. 19 rozp. Prezydenta R.P. z dnia 16 marca 1928 r. o ewidencji i kontroli ruchu ludności (Dz. U. R. P. Nr. 32, poz. 309) zaświadcza się, że wymieniony(a) w niniejszym dowodzie p. Dr. Alexandrowicz Izak jest obywatelem(ką) polskim(ą), co zostało stwierdzone na podstawie art. 2 ustęp 1 litera b ustawy z dnia 20. I. 1920 Dz. U. R. P. Nr. 7 pkt. 44

Nr 2888/37

za Prezydenta miasta

Podpis

Dr. FRYDERYK WES

Naczelnik Wydziału

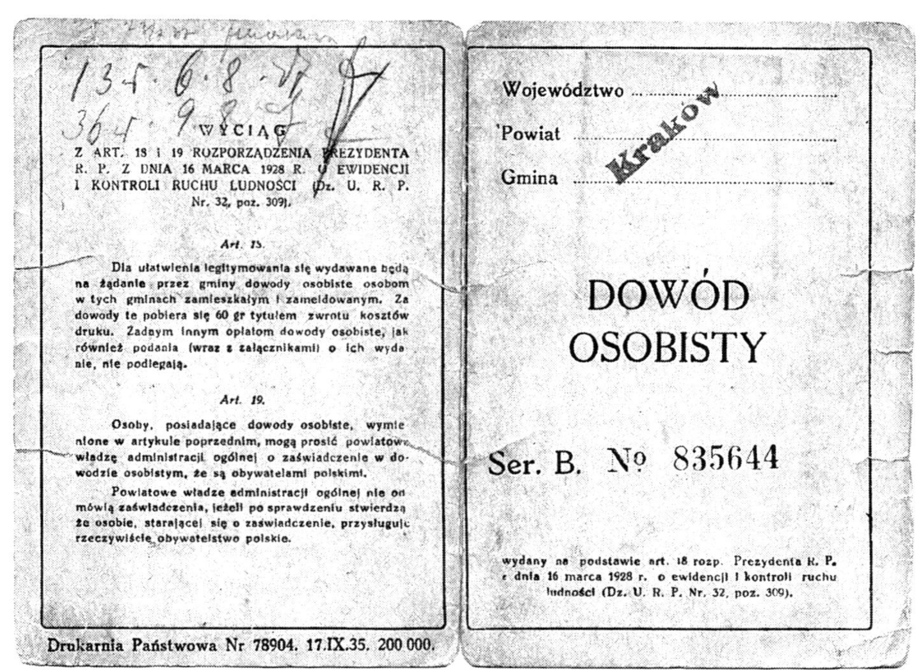

WYCIĄG

Z ART. 18 I 19 ROZPORZĄDZENIA PREZYDENTA R. P. Z DNIA 16 MARCA 1928 R. O EWIDENCJI I KONTROLI RUCHU LUDNOŚCI (Dz. U. R. P. Nr. 32, poz. 309).

Art. 18.

Dla ułatwienia legitymowania się wydawane będą na żądanie przez gminy dowody osobiste osobom w tych gminach zamieszkałym i zameldowanym. Za dowody te pobiera się 60 gr tytułem zwrotu kosztów druku. Żadnym innym opłatom dowody osobiste, jak również podania (wraz z załącznikami) o ich wydanie, nie podlegają.

Art. 19.

Osoby, posiadające dowody osobiste, wymienione w artykule poprzednim, mogą prosić powiatową władzę administracji ogólnej o zaświadczenie w dowodzie osobistym, że są obywatelami polskimi.

Powiatowe władze administracji ogólnej nie odmówią zaświadczenia, jeżeli po sprawdzeniu stwierdzą że osobie, starającej się o zaświadczenie, przysługuje rzeczywiście obywatelstwo polskie.

Drukarnia Państwowa Nr 78904. 17.IX.35. 200 000.

Województwo

Powiat

Gmina Kraków

DOWÓD OSOBISTY

Ser. B. № 835644

wydany na podstawie art. 18 rozp. Prezydenta R. P. z dnia 16 marca 1928 r. o ewidencji i kontroli ruchu ludności (Dz. U. R. P. Nr. 32, poz. 309).

Fig. 056. Polish I.D. card of Izak Mendel (Ignacy) Aleksandrowicz

(b) Amalia (Mania) Wien, nee Aleksandrowicz (1892-1944)

Amalia Wien known as Mania, daughter of Jacob and Hanna Hinda Aleksandrowicz nee Birnbaum, lived in Vienna for at least 15 years in 1938 when the weak Austrian Chancellor (Prime Minister) Kurt Schuschnigg, successor of assassinated Chancellor Dolfuss, capitulated to Hitler's demand that he resign and be replaced by an Austrian Nazi, Dr. Seyss-Inquart, as Chancellor of Austria. A reasonably honest plebiscite to decide whether Austria should join Nazi Germany was to be held, but Hitler was not going to take chances that the joining (in German: *Anschluss*) might be defeated. He ordered Seyss-Inquart to ask the German army to march into Austria and occupy its capital, Vienna. The plebiscite became a joke as, under the watchful eyes of the German Wehrmacht, 98% of the population voted for the Anschluss. When Hitler entered Vienna, he was greeted by a jubilant and histerically excited approving crowds. I believe that Schuschnigg had little choice but to comply with Hitler's resignation demand, because the Austrian state army could not have been depended upon to strongly and reliably oppose the Nazis, and the only organized political and military force in Austria that could have been depended was the Austrian workers' Social-Democratic Party. However, the party's militia, the *Schutzbund*, had been decimated earlier by Schuschnigg's predecessor, when Chancellor Engelbert Dolfuss ordered the Austrian state army to disarm the Schutzbund and use army cannons to bombard the workers' housing development, the Karl Marx Hof in Vienna, a Schutzbund stronghold.

Born in Kraków, 46-year-old, Mania Wien nee Aleksandrowicz, her husband Isidor and their two grown-up children, both born in Kraków, saw the writing on the wall and decided that there will be no future for them in Austria. Isidor, born in the southeastern Poland (now a part of Ukraine), had a Polish passport and came to Poland. He was a co-owner of an oil refinery in the central Galitzian town of Krosno. Mania and the children, however, decided not to come to Poland which was soon to become a target of Nazi Germany and wanted to go to America. The US had then a rigid quota policy, all the Wiens were born in Poland and therefore came under the Polish quota which had a long waiting list. Most of the rest of the world was also closed to them. Fortunately, a small opening appeared. It became possible for them to go to Argentina and Mania took advantage of it and she and her married daughter Lilli Wien Merkado emigrated to Buenos Aires. Her son Herbert Wien, a sportsman and an olympic swimmer with the Vienna *Hakoah* team, did manage to come to the United States and here he changed his name to Herbert Wayne,

Mania Aleksandrowicz Wien, my paternal aunt, was the granddaughter of Józef Aleksandrowicz and Rachel nee Drezner and also a granddaughter of Isaac Mendel Birnbaum and Małka nee Drezner, greatgranddaughter of Menashe Aleksandrowicz and Lea Katzner and Asher Drezner and Henna Bader and greatgranddaughter of Saul Birnbaum and Gitl Baum and, again, of Asher Drezner and Henna Bader. Mania, formally known as Amalia, was born on December 20, 1892 in Kraków. At the time the family lived on 49 Dietla Street, the wide elegant avenue with a planted garden strip in the middle, created when the Vistula River changed its flow and moved into a different channel. The old channel, which once separated

the mediaeval city of Kraków from the area of Kazimierz where the Jews lived, was filled and became a major thoroughfare. Today, in the center of the road trolleys run next to the grassy strip and, at the lower end of the street where it approaches the present flow of the river, a major bridge joins the city to the suburbs of Dębniki and Ludwinów. From across the river a great view of the City and its Castle Hill unfolds. Today, one of the luxury hotels, the Forum, is located in Ludwinów, its rooms taking advantage of the panoramic views of the city.

In Mania's birth certificate (see photostat) her father was listed as a merchant. Her mother was listed as Hanna Hinda, daughter of Izak Mendel and Malka, spouses Birnbaum, deceased. Mania was born at home, assisted by a midwife, Rachel Vogler. The witness to the birth registration was Jozua Lipsker, a cantor in Kraków. Mania was recorded as a legitimate child, an important fact attesting that Jacob and Hanna Hinda were married, in Kraków, on June 14, 1891, in a civil as well as religious ceremony.

As the older girl in a household where both the father and the mother worked in their business, Mania was expected to take care of the younger siblings. My father, Mania's young brother, Maks, who was born in 1902, remembered fondly how young Mania loved him and his sister Lola, but mostly how she cared for their much younger brother Olek, born in 1908. In March 24, 1912 Mania married Isidor Wien, son of Bluma Wien of the town of Stryj (roughly pronounced Streeh). Isidor was born on 25 April 1886. His mother was a soap maker, daughter of Rafael and Brana Wien in Stryj. Isidor and Mania moved to an apartment on Orzeszkowa Street 9, a side street off lower Dietla Street. In a little more than a year Mania and Isidor had a child, a girl whom they named Ludwika, who went through life as Lilli. Lilli was born on 28 August 1913. A son, Herbert, was born to Mania and Isidor two years later, in 1915. Soon after, Isidor and his brother Morris acquired a partial ownership of an oil refinery in the town of Krosno in central Galitzia. That refinery was producing petroleum products until the Second World War when it fell into German hands and was later destroyed in an allied bombing raid.

Isidor and Mania and the children prospered in Vienna until the arrival of Hitler in 1938, at which point Mania moved to Buenos Aires, where she died in 1944. Isidor came to Krosno and Kraków, and was trapped in Poland when the Second World War broke out in September 1939. He retreated before the Germans to Soviet-occupied Lwów, from which he was exiled by the Soviets deep into Siberia. He came back to Poland after the War but did not stay there, and moved to America. I met him in New York around 1950. Eventually he joined his family in Argentina where he died.

Mania and Isidor's daughter, my cousin Lilli Wien married Heinz Merkado in Vienna and the two of them left in 1938 for Argentina. In Buenos Aires Lilli and Heinz had two children, girls named Sylvia and Monika. With time, Sylvia married Maurizio Bal, Monika married Roberto Obersky. Sylvia has two girls, Carina and Alejandra. Monika has a girl, Viviana, and a boy, Enrique. Heinz died tragically, killed in a robbery. Lilli died in 2001. Viviana Obersky married and has a baby girl, Carolina. She moved to Israel. Carina Bal married a New Yorker, Joseph Sachs, and they now live in New York with their boy, Osher and a baby girl, Betsalel. Life in Argentina has become very difficult and of the younger generation only Enrique and Alejandra are now in Buenos Aires with their respective parents.

Lilli's brother, my cousin Herbert Wien, later Wayne, came to New York, married Renata (Ronnie) Golpern. Herbert was an athlete. In Vienna he was a member of the Hakoah olympic-class swim team. Both he and his wife were expert swimmers. In America

Ronnie became a swimming instructor. Herbert and Ronnie Wayne had one son, Jeffrey. Herbert became ill and died young. Jeffrey Wayne became a lawyer, married Hope Queller of Long Island, and moved to Hawaii. Jeffrey and Hope have three sons: Hawkeye, Justin and Ethan. The older boys continue the family tradition of being great athletes.

Isidor's brother, Morris (Moritz) Wien and his wife Rose had two daughters, Bianca and Rita. Bianca married Ludwik Gross, a physician. She and her sister Rita, married to Robert Stone, came to the U.S. They live on Staten Island. Each sister had two daughters, Bianca had Diane who married Jeffrey Marks and Marian. Rita had Debbie and Marilyn. Diane and Jeffrey have three sons, Daniel, Andrew and Joshua.

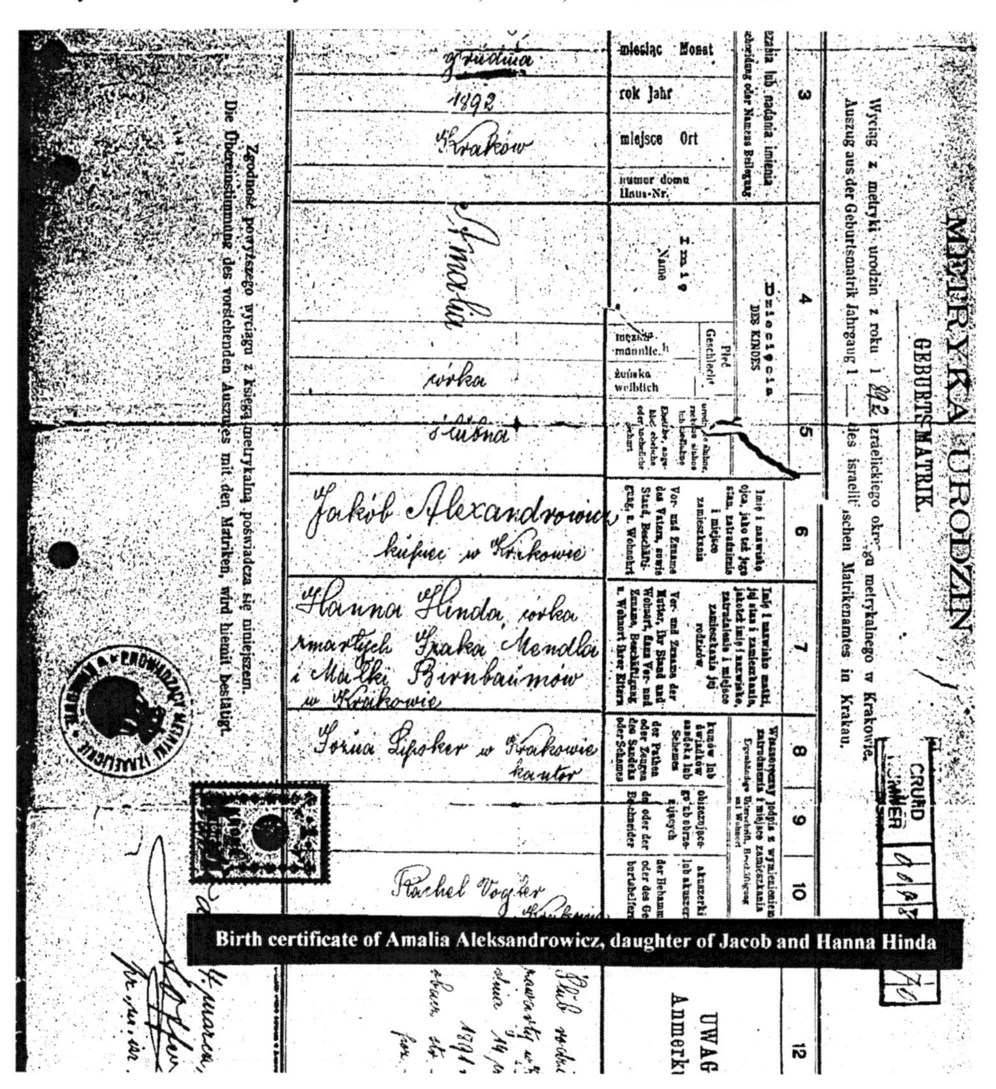
METRYKA URODZIN
GEBURTS-MATRIK.
Wyciąg z metryki urodzin z roku 1892 izraelickiego okręgu metrykalnego w Krakowie.
Auszug aus der Geburtsmatrik Jahrgang 1892 des israelitischen Matrikenamtes in Krakau.
miesiąc Monat: Grudnia
rok Jahr: 1892
miejsce Ort: Kraków
Imię Name: Amalia
Płeć Geschlecht: córka
ślubna
Jakób Alexandrowicz kupiec w Krakowie
Hanna Hinda, córka zmarłych Izaka Mendla i Małki Birnbaumów w Krakowie
Szyja Lipsker w Krakowie kantor
Rachel Vogler
Zgodność powyższego wyciągu z księgą metrykalną poświadcza się niniejszem.
Die Übereinstimmung des vorstehenden Auszuges mit den Matriken, wird hiemit bestätigt.

Birth certificate of Amalia Aleksandrowicz, daughter of Jacob and Hanna Hinda

Fig. 057. Birth certificates of Mania Aleksandrowicz

Folio 167

METRYKA URODZIN
GEBURTSMATRIK.

Wyciąg z księgi urodzin z roku 1913 izraelickiego okręgu metrykalnego w Krakowie.
Auszug aus der Geburtsmatrik Jahrgang 1913 des israelitischen Matrikenamtes in Krakau

1	2 Urodzenia / Der Geburt					3 Obrzezania lub nadania imienia / Der Beschneidung oder Namens Beilegung					4 Dziecięcia / des Kindes			5	6	7	8 Własnoręczny podpis z wymienieniem zatrudnienia i miejsca zamieszkania / Eigenhändige Unterschrift, Beschäftigung und Wohnort	9	10	11	12
Liczba porządkowa / Ord. Zahl	dzień Tag	miesiąc Monat	rok Jahr	miejsce Ort	numer domu Haus-Nr.	dzień Tag	miesiąc Monat	rok Jahr	miejsce Ort	numer domu Haus-Nr.	Imię, Name	Płeć / Geschlecht: męska männlich	żeńska weiblich	urodzenie ślubne, rzekomo ślubne lub nieślubne / Eheliche, angeblich eheliche oder uneheliche Geburt	Imię i nazwisko ojca, jakoteż jego stan, zatrudnienie i miejsce zamieszkania / Vor- und Zuname des Vaters, sowie Stand, Beschäftigung u. Wohnort	Imię i nazwisko matki, jej stan i zamieszkanie, jakoteż imię i nazwisko, zatrudnienie i miejsce zamieszkania jej rodziców / Vor- und Zuname der Mutter, ihr Stand und Wohnort, dann Vor- und Zuname, Beschäftigung und Wohnort ihrer Eltern	kumów lub świadków sandeka lub schemes / der Pathen oder Zeugen des Sandeks oder Schames	obrzezującego lub obrzezujących / des oder der Beschneider	akuszerki lub akuszera / der Hebamme oder des Geburtshelfers	dzieci martwo urodzone / Todt geborene Kinder	UWAGA / Anmerkung
500	28 dwudziestego ósmego	Lipca (Juli)	1913 dziewięćset trzynastego	Kraków	J. ul. [illegible]	drugiego	sierpnia	1913	Kraków		Ludwika		córka	ślubna	Izrael Wien, kupiec w Krakowie	Amalia, córka Jakóba Aleksandrowicza-[illegible] w Krakowie i żony jego [illegible] z Birnbaumów	Jakób Kirschbaum w Krakowie		Helena Felinger w Krakowie		Ślub [illegible] w Krakowie dnia 24 marca 1912 [illegible] 22 poz. 86

Zgodność powyższego wyciągu z księgą metrykalną poświadcza się niniejszem.
Die Übereinstimmung des vorstehenden Auszuges mit den Matriken wird hiemit bestätigt.

dnia 13 stycznia 1929

[illegible signature]

Fig. 058. Birth certificate of Ludwika Wien;

(c) My uncle Wilhelm Aleksandrowicz (1894-1942)

Wilhelm Aleksandrowicz (Wilek) became a lawyer and married Olga Schoenfeld from Tarnów. He received his law degree from the Kraków Jagiellonian University. At 18, he was drafted into the Austrian army. In the family photograph from 1912 he appears in a military uniform (see photo at the end of the chapter). As a young man he was a leader in the Kraków social-democratic student movement at the Jagiellonian University, but after his marriage, busy with a criminal and military law practice he ceased to be active. He was a defender of soldiers accused before courts-martial. In the 1930 Kraków phone directory he was listed as a lawyer with an office at 33 Rynek Główny (Main Market Square), with an apartment at 2 Jabłonowski Square, near the University. Later, prior to the Second World War he moved his office and his apartment to 15 Basztowa Street, to the so-called Phoenix Building, which housed the Kraków office of the Viennese Phoenix Insurance Company. In 1929, he and Olga had one child, a boy, Alexander Aleksandrowicz, whom we called *Aluś.* I remember Wilek as a jet black-haired man, always impeccably dressed in dark suits, wearing large dark-rimmed glasses. After his marriage to a snobbish Tarnovian, he did not have much contact with the rest of the family, As long as my grandfather lived and had the weekly Friday night dinners for all of us, Wilek, Olga and Alus came and Alus played with me. After my grandfather died in 1935, even those contacts ceased and we met only rarely. Of all my uncles I knew Wilek least.

At the outbreak of the war, in 1939 Wilek, like most Jewish men in Kraków, whether of military age or politically active, escaped from Kraków before the entrance of the German army and moved to Lwów. When Lwów became dangerous for him because he was too well-known for his background of political and legal activities, he tried to join his brothers Ignacy and Maks in Vilna in then-independent Lithuania. Ignacy and Maks were among the first Jewish activists to try to leave Lwów for Vilna, but even they found the going difficult. They escaped successfully from pursuing Soviet guards. Wilek, who tried it a little later, was caught by Soviet soldiers, imprisoned and tortured in the town of Lida. After a difficult incarceration, he managed to bribe his way out and returned to Kraków, joining his wife and son. He then took his family from Kraków, where his liberal political sympathies were known, to nearby Tarnów, his wife's town, where he thought he would have a better chance to survive the war. He did not succeed. To the best of my knowledge, in 1942 Wilek, his wife and son and his wife's family were caught in a Nazi "action" in Tarnów and died in some extermination camp. Perhaps the forthcoming opening of the Nazi files kept closed until now at Arolsen in Germany will provide us with information about Wilek and other members of our families killed in the Holocaust.

(d) My uncle Józef Aleksandrowicz (1896-1944)

Józef Aleksandrowicz (Józek), the third Józef Aleksandrowicz in the direct line of my family, was my favorite uncle. Of all my uncles he devoted the most time to me. He was married to Sala Neuman from Radom in central Poland.

For a long time he and Sala were unsuccessfully trying to have children. Not having any, they paid a great deal of attention to me. He and Sala lived next door to us on the second floor of the family residence on 11 Bernardyńska Street. Józek often took me to watch soccer (called football in Poland) games, which my father was not interested in. His favorite team was called Cracovia, which had a stadium at the entrance to the *Błonie*, the vast public meadow park west of town center. With him I rooted for the Cracovia team, and its star player named Kossock. At the beginning of the War, I was crestfallen to find out that this idol of mine, like so many sports figures, had feet of clay; he became a traitor, declaring himself an ethnic German (*Volksdeutsche*), which gave him all kinds of privileges, but made him an object of hate of fellow Krakovians. On rare occasions, Józek also took me with him to the reform synagogue of Kraków, the so-called Tempel, on Miodowa Street. Of all children of Jacob Aleksandrowicz, Józek was the most religious, partly because of his wife who came from a strongly religious orthodox family and maintained a kosher home. Even so, Józek was not particularly observant, and went to a reform synagogue and only on special occasions. My parents were atheists and never went near any synagogue or temple. The Reform Tempel, which survived the Nazi occupation intact but neglected, has been restored with funds from the Lauder Foundation. It has interesting stained glass windows. There being few Jews left in Kraków, the restored Tempel, with its great acoustics, serves as a concert hall. In fact, when we visited Kraków in October 1997, we heard a magnificent orchestra concert there.

Józek's wife, Sala Neuman Aleksandrowicz, had a brother, Shiya Neuman, who also settled in Kraków, and lived in our building on 11 Bernardyńska Street, with his wife, four daughters, Tosia, Hela, Luba, Lotka and a son Janek. Shiya Neuman had a paper goods store, a notebook factory and a bookbinding atelier. For a time during the War, I worked in his factory learning how to bind books. One of the Neuman girls, Lotka, left Kraków at the beginning of the War, moved to Lwów, was arrested by the Soviets and deported deep into Soviet Asia. She survived there, returned to Poland and now lives in England. Shiya Neuman tried to save another of his daughters, Luba, then around 25, by buying for her a foreign, Latin-American, passport, I believe Honduran. She left Kraków for an internment camp for foreign citizens. We were sure that as a foreign citizen she will survive the war, but somehow she perished. Of the rest of the family, Shiya alone survived. He died in Kraków. I found his tomb in the Kraków Miodowa Street cemetery.

To their own and everyone's surprise Józek and Sala did have a child after 14 years of marriage, a boy born in 1938, whom they named Jacob after Józek's father, my grandfather, who died in 1935. We called the child by the diminutive, Kubuś. In December 1939, after the start of the war, in difficult conditions in the Jewish Hospital on Skawinska Street in Kraków, Sala bore a girl, named Halinka. At that point mostly women and children were left in Kraków under the Germans; Józek was in Lwów. He never did get to see his little girl. From Soviet-occupied Lwów he was sent by the Russians to a *gulag* in the North, near the Russian-Finnish border, to help build a railroad towards Murmansk: the *Murmanskaya Zheleznaya Doroga*. The railhead was called Kandalaksha. He almost died there from cold and hunger. From German-occupied Kraków, in spite of all the hardships of the Nazi occupation, Sala sent some warm clothing to Józek, but I doubt if he ever received it. After Hitler attacked the USSR, Stalin released the overworked, starved and frozen Polish citizens from the gulags and Józek traveled south to Samarkand to join Polish forces being formed on the Persian border. In Samarkand he contracted typhus. In his

weakened condition, he succumbed. He is the only member of my immediate family who was not killed by the Nazis, but who died in the Soviet Union.

When Sala's brother, Shiya Neuman sent away his daughter Luba with the foreign, Central-American passport which he bought for her, she took the three-year old Kubuś with her, with papers indicating that he was her child. We were sure that as interned citizens of foreign countries, Luba Neuman and Kubuś would be treated decently and survive the War. Indeed, in my first letter to my father after the War, I so assured him and asked him to search for Kubuś, who may be going under the surname Neuman. My father, in turn, spared no effort to find Luba Neuman and Kubuś, or if Luba died, to find Kubuś who may not know his real family name, but all efforts were unsuccessful. Neither Luba, nor Kubuś, survived. Apparently, the German Gestapo did not respect the foreign passports and treated Jews with such purchased passports not differently from the rest of us. Perhaps records indicating what happened to Luba Neuman and to Kubus will be found among the papers in the Red Cross collection in Bad Arolsen, Germany, when these are released to the genealogy researchers and the public. In German-occupied Poland, in Kraków, Józek's wife Sala and her newly born daughter Halinka were sent to an extermination camp and perished.

(e) My aunt Laura Schall nee Aleksandrowicz (1900-1943)

Like my mother, my aunt Laura, whom I knew as Lola, was a fervent follower of Maria Montessori and Friedrich Froebl. With my mother, in 1929, Lola established the first Montessori kindergarten in Kraków, probably the first in all of Poland. It was located in the Bernardyńska Street family building facing the Wawel mount. There being no Montessori supplies available commercially, the two women designed their own and had them made locally. Thus, in 1929, at the age of four, I became the first child in Kraków to attend a Montessori-type kindergarten.

My aunt Lola was the closest in age to my father and was his favorite sibling. As children, they looked very much alike and they played tricks on friends by dressing in each others clothing and fooling even people who knew them well. Lola was attractive, well-proportioned but tall for a girl. She had lustrous jet-black hair and big black eyes and black eye lashes. She became a teacher, specializing in pre-school education.

In her thirties, when she must have assumed that she will never marry, Lola met and married a college professor, Bruno Schall, whose family came from Lwów. The family did not consider this marriage as very desirable, but as Lola was not young it was acceptable. The wedding took place in the palatial grand salon of my grandfather's appartment on Bernardynska 11. Bruno was offered a position as director of a private Jewish secondary school in Łódź, the Katzenelson Gymnasium, and he and Lola moved to Łódź. The marriage, I believe, was rocky and Lola's brothers were not enamored of Bruno Schall. When Lola became pregnant in 1937 she came to us in Kraków to deliver her little girl, Anna, named after Lola's mother, my grandmother, Hanna Hinda Birnbaum Aleksandrowicz. This was the

third child in my immediate family named after Hanna Hinda whom all her children adored. We called that child with the diminutive *Ania,* to distinguished her from Ignacy's daughter and my sister, both called by the diminutive Hanka. When the war broke out in 1939, Łódź, located within an easy reach of the German border, was considered at risk of being rapidly overrun by the Germans and the Schalls moved to Bruno's parents' place in Lwów, then becoming a part of the Soviet Western Ukraine. As a family of Lwów natives they avoided the Soviet-instituted deportation of Polish and Polish-Jewish refugees, like my uncles Józek Aleksandrowicz and Isidor Wien, who were taken deep into Soviet North or Soviet Central Asia prior to the German onslaught on Russia. The Schalls remained in Lwów. It turned out that the Soviets did the Schalls no favors by letting them stay in Lwów. Those Jews deported deep into the Soviet hinterland had a hard time there but most of them survived, while those who remained in Lwów came under German rule when the Germans marched in in 1943. Bruno, Lola and Ania disappeared sometimes after that, I never found out when or where.

My father, Maksymilian, was the next offspring of Jacob and Hanna Hinda; he was born in 1902. I will describe him in detail in a following chapter.

(f) My uncle Salo Aleksandrowicz (1908-1945)

In February 1939 the world ski championship of the International Ski Federation (FIS) were being held in Zakopane in the Polish Tatra Mountains. My uncle Salo Aleksandrowicz, known by his diminutuve as Olek took me with him to attend this ski meet. We spent a wonderful week in the Tatras, skiing and attending the main ski jump event, won by the then foremost Polish ski champion, Stanisław Marusarz. Polish Post Office issued an attractive colorful series of stamps and a souvenir sheet for the occasion and, as an avid stamp collector, I begged Olek to buy me the stamps. I stood in a long line at the post office to buy the stamps and get a special cancellation on them. I lost all my possessions during the War. Once in America, I tried to recreate some parts of my stamp collection, and bought from a stamp dealer a set of the FIS stamps with the commemorative cancel (see attached photostat). It serves as a reminder of the great times I had at 13 in Zakopane in the winter of 1939. One evening in Zakopane we were entertained by the most famous Polish mountaineer folklorist, story-teller and guide, Wacław Sabała Krzeptowski, grandson of the mountaineer hero, Sabała, who 100 years earlier guided the re-discoverer and popularizer of Zakopane and the Tatras, Dr. Titus Chałubiński. The Polish word for a mountain is *góra*, the mountain people are the Górals. They speak Polish in a distinct dialect, and are generally known for their fierce love of their mountains, of their freedom and their Polish patriotism. During the War, the Germans tried to "divide and conquer", by offering the Górals a favored identity as a separate ethnic group, the *Goralenvolk*. And, to my chagrin, Wacław (diminutive: *Wacuś*) Sabała Krzeptowski, betraying his Polish origin and language, became the leader of this German construct and collaborated with the occupiers. In response, in Zakopane there appeared hostile grafitti on walls, in the local dialect. The grafitti, widely repeated in Kraków, stated: "*Hey, Wacuś, Wacuś, jeszcze będziesz wisiał za cuś!* " (Hey, Vatsush, Vatsush, you will yet hang for something!).

The youngest of Jacob's children, Salo Aleksandrowicz (Olek), was born in 1908. After his father's death in 1935 Olek, along with Józek and my father, inherited the family's wholesale leather business and all three ran the store until the War. Olek was the family athlete, slim, tall, lithe and physically strong, but kind and gentle. He was a champion swimmer, a hiker and a talented skier. He married a girl with similar interests, Barbara (Baśka) Infeld, whose parents had a store of sewing supplies, wool and notions on Starowiślna Street in Kraków. The two of them took long hikes in the summer and ski trips during winter, mostly to the Polish High Tatra Mountains National Park and its resort town of Zakopane. Once, when I and my mother and 4-year-old sister went swimming in the Vistula River, my little sister got caught in a whirlpool. I was nearby and I saw her go under and, without a word because there was no time to shout a warning, I grabbed her mostly by her hair and held on to her for dear life but the whirlpool was too strong for me to get us both out and I, too, was being pulled under. It was then that Baśka on shore saw me struggle. She instantly jumped in and, strong swimmer that she was, saved both of us. As far as I can judge Olek and Baśka had a very good marriage. Eventually, they had two boys: Witold, born around 1935 and Jacob (Jasio), born around 1937.

When the war began, Olek moved to Lwów, which was occupied by Soviet troops. When the Soviets, in preparation for the coming German onslaught, began to move what they considered untrustworthy element, including refugees from Kraków, away from the borderlands and deep into Soviet hinterland and difficult existence, Olek returned to be with his wife and children and stayed in the Kraków Ghetto. In 1942, Baśka and the boys were deported to the extermination camp in Bełżec, the same camp in which my mother and sister perished. Olek and I remained in the Kraków Ghetto, then in the Kraków-Płaszów concentration camp, the one described in "Schindler's List". In 1944 we were moved to Austria, to branches of the Mauthausen Concentration Camp. At first we were in Melk, then in Ebensee. Olek, as a well-built, strong and athletic person, suffered terribly from malnutrition. The meager ration of food that kept me desperately hungry, was totally inadequate to support a strong grown-up athletic man. The hard labor and insufficient amount of food were a lethal combination. Olek died of diarrhea and starvation in my arms, in February 1945, a mere three months before the end of the war, i.e. before General Patton's Third Army marched into Ebensee. At death he weighted so little that I had no trouble carrying his emaciated body to the camp crematorium all by myself. In retrospect, I realize what a macabre picture I must have presented carrying my uncle's body to be cremated, but at the time it did not occur to me to consider it special or unusual in any way. Dozens of people died in Ebensee every day and their corpses were routinely taken to the crematorium by the prisoners detailed that day to that task. I myself, while usually otherwise assigned, did on occasion serve on this detail and thought nothing of it. The sight of the dead and dying was so ordinary that it did not create any stir.

I had previously described my recollections of Olek and his death in a short article published in "*Survivors Chronicle*", Vol. 7/2, Fall 2001, p. 9. To the best of my knowledge, my uncle Olek was the last member of my immediate family to die in the Holocaust.

Fédération Internationale de Ski

F. I. S.

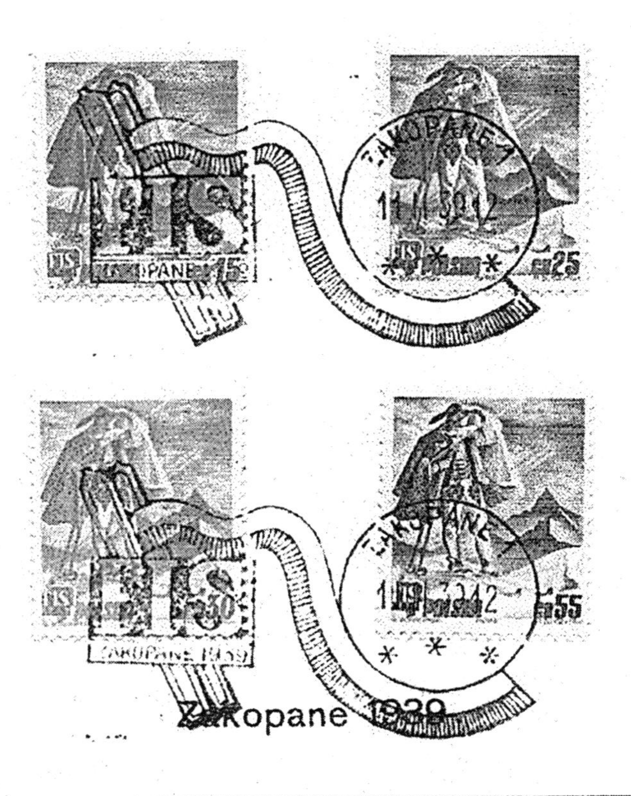

Fig. 059. Stamps issued for the FIS ski competition, Zakopane, Poland 1939;

Part VI. TWENTIETH CENTURY: RECOLLECTIONS OF MY PARENTS

Chapter 23. Maksymilian Aleksandrowicz (Max Alexander) (1902-1968)

Last time I saw my father Maksymilian Aleksandrowicz in Kraków, Poland, for a few hours was a few days before the outbreak of World War II in Europe, on 25 August 1939. He was in uniform of the Polish Army, having been mobilized, as Poland was preparing to meet the German onslaught. He was then 37 years old. I was fourteen. After this brief time together we did not meet again until after the War. The next time I saw him was seven years later, in New York City, on July 6, 1946. He was 44, I was 21. He did not see me during my adolescence, which I spent in the Kraków Ghetto and in Nazi concentration camps. During this time he was at first a soldier engaged in the desperate attempt to stop the invading German army, then a refugee in Lwów and Vilna. Eventually, he came to America, while in Europe both the Nazi Gestapo (*Geheime Staats Polizei*) and the Soviet secret police (*NKVD*) were looking to arrest him because of his prominence and leadership position in the Jewish democratic socialist movement.

My father was born in Kraków, on July 5, 1902 (although his birth was not registered until a week later, on July 12, 1902). He was the son of Jacob Aleksandrowicz, a leather merchant in Kraków, and his wife Hanna Hinda (Hancia), nee Birnbaum. Both the Aleksandrowicz and the Birnbaum families lived in Kraków for many generations. Maks, as he was known in Kraków, had six siblings, four brothers and two sisters. Maks's father and mother both came from families with many children. Jacob's parents, Józef Aleksandrowicz and Rachel, nee Drezner, had six children; Hanna Hinda's parents, Isaac Mendel Birnbaum and his two wives, Małka who died young, and her sister Dina, both nee Drezner, together had eleven children. All three Drezner women, Rachel, Małka and Dina, were sisters, so that family relationships became quite complicated but what is clear is that Maks had a whole array of cousins in Kraków. All these cousins married and all had a number of offspring. When I was little it appeared to me that all the people I met were somehow related to me, a very logical conclusion.

In the first decades of the twentieth century Poland was a poor country. Most of the population lived in the countryside and barely managed to scrape a meager living on tiny plots of land, but the country had a lot of fertile soil and availability of food was not a problem, its distribution was. There were always in rural Poland a few rich landowners and aristocrats, but besides those few, the majority of the people were peasants who owned very small plots of often intensely, though primitively, cultivated farmland. Customarily these small land holdings were routinely subdivided among the owner's children upon his passing away, ending in minuscule ownerships, often inadequate to provide a decent standard of living. An average peasant spent his life trying to somehow acquire additional land so that he could leave to his children more land that their portion of the land that he inherited. Dispersed among the peasants lived many Polish Jews, mostly located in small towns and villages, earning a living as craftsmen (cobblers, tailors, etc.), small shopkeepers, itinerant peddlers and, occasionally as inn and tavern owners and lease-holders (arrendars) of rural flour mills, lumber mills and similar enterprises owned by large aristocrats but frequently run and administered by Jews. For their livelihood the Jews depended on the peasants of the surrounding countryside, and, as that population was poor, so were the shtetl Jews. Also, because the peasants had hardly any money but had to use the services offered by the mills, enjoyed a drink of vodka in a tavern (Pol. *karczma*) and needed to buy items like shoes or fabric and notions from the Jews who controlled most of the local petty commerce, they hated the Jews and looked upon them as exploiters. Thus, it was easy for demagogues to stir up anti-Jewish sentiments, which often lead to boycotts, pogroms and other anti-Semitic outbursts.

Poland had also a few cities and a number of small towns, but these had little industry and not enough jobs. Such industry as existed, for example the textile mills in Łódź, was predominantly in German or Jewish hands, the latter compounding the innate anti-Semitism. In Kraków there was a small number of wealthy Jewish merchants and owners of buildings, but most of the Jewish population, concentrated in the area of Kazimierz, was poor. Jewish workers in the cities, being literate, became aware of the iniquity of their existence and began organizing, creating workers' parties. In the Russian zone of Poland and Lithuania, a social-democratic Jewish Labor Bund was established in 1897 in Vilna by Arkadi Kremer, Vladimir Kossowski, Vladimir Medem, John Mill and others. It was the first organization in the Tsarist borderlands of Eastern Europe to advocate the revolutionary ideas of Jewish emancipation, freedom, justice, equal rights for all citizens and brotherhood of workers of all nations. A Polish Socialist Party (PPS) also came into existence, intensely patriotic and reasonably democratic, composed of Polish workers in the cities and towns, led by Polish intellectuals with a membership which included a few Jews. In competition with the PPS and Bund, Roza Luksemburg, Karl Radek, Felix Dzierżyński and others established a more radical Social Democracy of the Kingdom of Poland and Lithuania (SDKPiL), which did not have a separate Polish and Jewish sections. In the Austrian zone of Poland, Galitzia, some Jews joined the PPS but most Jewish workers joined the Jewish Social Democratic Party (ŻPSD), co-founded by my uncles Ignacy and Wilhelm Aleksandrowicz. In addition, there existed also in Galitzia, as in Russia, several devoutly religious orthodox political parties (mostly strong in rural areas) and several popular Zionist groupings ranging from far-right Revisionists, followers of Vladimir Jabotinski, to Labor-Zionists (Poale-Zion), the latter with both left and right wings. After 1918, when Poland became independent,

joining the three previous zones, the Galitzianer Jewish Social Democracy joined forces with the Bund in one unified democratic socialist movement of Jewish workers and leftists, competing with an illegal Communist Party, successor to the SDKPiL, for allegiance of the Jewish proletariat. By 1939, the Bund, then led by Henryk Ehrlich (1882-1941) and Victor Alter (1890-1941), became the dominant Jewish political organization in Poland. I have met both Bundist leaders several times, when they visited Kraków and when my father and I traveled to Warsaw and my father took me to the office of *Naye Folkstsaitung*, the Bund daily newspaper. During the War, Erlich and Alter were arrested and killed on orders from Stalin, while most of Bund members perished in the Nazi Holocaust.

Of all the Bund founders and early leaders, my father most admired Vladimir Medem (1879-1923), an early Bund theoretician, whose family backround, education and political positions were close to those adopted by my father. Like Medem, my father as a young man was strongly opposed to joining the Communist International (the *Comintern*) which was totally dominated by Russia, and felt that the Bund must retain its freedom of action and ideology. Also like Medem, my father felt that home for Jews is where they live and that the Eastern European Jews must insist on equal rights *in situ* and that the Zionist idea that real home for Jews is in Palestine and that Eastern Europe serves only a temporary way station played into the hands of anti-Semites. Indeed, the favorite slogan of Polish anti-Semites was "*Żydy do Palestyny!*" (Kikes to Palestine!).

For obvious reasons the presence of a significant number of Jews among a deeply religious Christian population was treated by the Poles as a problem. Suggestions and attempts to solve this so-called "Jewish Question", which so interested and even pre-occupied many non-Jewish European statesmen and thinkers, including Polish ones, during the nineteenth and early twentieth century, also deeply engaged Jewish leaders, as well as some Jewish deep-pocket philanthropists. The problem was usually defined rather simplistically as being due to the skewed demographics of the Jewish population in Central and Eastern Europe. Whereas European nations consisted mostly of peasant farmers and other agricultural workers with a significant admixture of urban middle class and merchant class, a growing proletariat, a small cadre of professionals and an aristocratic elite, the Jewish society lacked the agricultural component with its fierce attachment to specific pieces of land, and was top-heavy in merchants and the so-called free professions: lawyers, physicians, etc. The predominance of Jews in the professions, way above their proportion in the general population, and the presumed Jewish rootlessness, were said to be the key causes of anti-Semitism. It seemed obvious, therefore, to many Jewish and non-Jewish thinkers that the solution must involve acquiring a piece of land for the Jews to emigrate to and settle on and encouraging them to become farmers there. Love for and attachment to their own piece of land would foster territorial feelings hitherto presumably missing among Jews and having a Jewish farmer class would make the Jews indistinguishable from other nations. Jews being like other peoples would end anti-Semitism. At the time nobody seemed to cherish Jewish cosmopolitanism, as did King Casimir the Great 400 years earlier, as a potential asset of some importance to the host countries and, in the long run, to humanity as a whole. It was this cosmopolitanism that led large numbers of Jews to become innovators in a number of fields of human endeavor ranging from religion to arts and science and to social progress in general, as exemplied more recently by the large number of Jewish recipients of Nobel Prizes in assorted fields.

The attempt to "fix" the presumed Jewish demographic deficiencies came to be referred to as Territorialism. Among the early believers in the territorial solution, who chose to act upon it, was the Jewish industrialist and philanthropist, Baron Maurice de Hirsch ((1831-1896). He immediately run into the key problem that bedeviled all future believers in territorialism, namely, trying to find an appropriately large and desirably fertile piece of land for the poor Jews to colonize. In 1891 Baron de Hirsch established a Jewish Colonialist Society, purchased land in South America, talked to the Russian government and then attempted to recruit poor shtetl Jews to become farmers in distant lands. Obviously, the historically logical place for a migration of poor Eastern European Jews was Palestine, then in Ottoman hands, because Jerusalem and the surrounding areas had sentimental value. The ancient royal city of David and Salomon, the city mentioned each year at Passover ("Next year in Jerusalem"), had an obvious appeal. However, Palestine was then essentially a small arid piece of desert land, unable to support a large population. It was sparsely inhabited by poor Arabs and nomadic Beduins, who subsisted mainly not by agriculture but by herding sheep and goats. The Turkish government, owners of Palestine, did not look favorably on a large settlement of European Jews in one of its territories. Baron de Hirsch eventually established and funded a large Jewish agricultural colony in Parana in Argentina and persuaded the Tsarist government to let some of their Jews go. He also supported a movement of Jews to Palestine, which grew to become known as *Hovevei Zion.* While the Argentine colony faltered, the movement seeking to move Jews to Palestine, which was named "Zionism" by my relative Nathan Birnbaum, was eventually successful.

Other areas, some of them quite outlandish, have been suggested for the putative Jewish territory, among them the tropical island of Madagascar located off the east coast of Africa, then about to become a French colony, now an independent Malgache Republic. Madagascar as a solution for Poland's Jewish problem was treated seriously in Poland in the nineteen twenties and thirties. I remember even a satirical novel describing a future Jewish state there inhabited by Polish Jews. In that book there was a street in Jewish Taananarivo named after a prominent Polish anti-Semite. When a surprised visitor asked why a known Jew hater was so honored, he was told that he was honored for being among those who were primarily responsible for pushing Polish Jews to settle in Madagascar. The idea of Madagascar as a heaven for Jews died a quiet death. Equally quaint, but longer lasting, was the Soviet attempt to establish a Jewish state in Central Asia. Vladimir Lenin, running the new Soviet Union as the Secretary of the Politbureau of the All-Russia Communist Party, named Joseph Stalin as Commissar of Nationalities. Stalin was not Russian but a Gruzin (Georgian). He came from Sochi in Gruzia in the Caucasus (I prefer the term *Gruzia*, which is the Russian name for this country, because the English name, Georgia, is easy to confuse with the U.S. state of the same name). Stalin proposed to solve the problem of all Jews in the Soviet sphere by creating an autonomous Jewish region (*Oblast*) in, of all places, Birobidjan, a territory located on the Trans-Siberian Railroad in distant Central-Eastern Asia. With Soviet government support and encouragement, the Birobidjan settlement was supposed to rival the Zionist settlement in Palestine. A Jewish autonomous government administered the Birobidjan Oblast. Yiddish became its official language. Yiddish newspapers appeared, a radio station broadcast in Yiddish and a sign in Yiddish graced the all-important railroad station. For all that, Birobidjan never thrived; its attraction for Jewish inhabitants of European Russia was minimal. The autonomous Oblast survives to this day, the railroad station still has a Yiddish sign and a Yiddish newspaper occasionally appears there, but few Jews live there and they form a small minority of the colony's population. Like the Parana colony of Baron Hirsch, Birobidjan failed to attract many settlers and I believe that it eventually will disappear.

Only the Zionist dream of a return to Zion managed to lead successfully to the establishment of a Jewish territorial entity. And the reputed need of the Jewish people to have a Jewish farmer class led to an idealistic movement to establish Jewish land communes in Palestine, the so-called *Kibbutzim*. Modern agricultural techniques and modern irrigation, combined with a large amount of idealism and hard work as well as considerable capital outlays by world Jewry, allowed these communes to reclaim a lot of the desert soil and plant crops. The kibbutzim served as early role models and played a key role in settling the land and defending it. Eventually, even there, the kibbutzim lost some of their luster and importance in a modern state and now constitute a small, though honored, segment of the total Israeli society. In a way, with the establishment of a sovereign Israeli state, the Territorialists have won their contest with those who, like my father, believed that Jews must fight for their rights in the countries in which they reside, be it Poland, Russia or the United States. However, while it is comforting to know that Israel exists as a Jewish territory, its existence did not solve the problem of anti-Semitism in all the various lands that Jews inhabit and even Israel's very existence depends, to a large extent, on the political and financial support of Diaspora (dispersed) Jews living as ethnic minorities all over the world, where they are a force for equality of political and economic citizenship rights. In a sense, the experience of world Jewry since the establishment of Israel proves that the mere existence of a territory that is Jewish does not eliminate ant-Semitism and does not eliminate the need for Jews to fight for equal treatment and against discrimination wherever they live, thus vindicating my father's position on the "Jewish question".

Following in the footsteps of his older brothers Ignacy and Wilek, my father, Maks, became concerned about the problems of anti-Semitism and ethnic discrimination, as well as of exploitation of Jewish (and Polish) workers by Jewish and non-Jewish employers, and became very active in the Jewish Labor Bund in Kraków. His primary language was Polish, but he learned to speak Yiddish, so that he could address Jewish workers then freshly arriving from the *shtetls*. In the process, he became a strong supporter of Jewish culture and Yiddish language and helped to set up a Yiddish secular school organization (CISHO, *Tsentrale Yiddishe Shul Organizatsye*) competing with religious yeshivas in places like Vilna and Białystok and was among the early supporters and promoters of the Yiddish Scientific Institute (YIVO) in Vilna. He was in demand as a public speaker. I remember hearing him address rallies of tens of thousands of people in the Kraków Rynek Główny (Central Market Square). He spoke in Polish or in Yiddish, on occasions such as the First-of-May Labor Day Rally or during the notorious and controversial general strike in support of the workers at the *Semperit* rubber factory in Kraków. He also traveled to and spoke on behalf of the Bund in neighboring towns, such as Tarnów, Bochnia, Wolbrom, Olkusz, Będzin and Chrzanów. He ran on the Bundist list in elections for membership in the Kraków City Council. He was particularly interested in young people and led the Krakovian Bundist youth organization, the *Tsukunft* (the Future). He and his sister, Lola, led many outings and other social activities of the Tsukunft. Even as a small child I used to join my father as he led the Tsukunftists in hikes, along the banks of the Rudawa river to

Skała Kmity (Kmita's Rock), to the Abbey at Tyniec or to the ruins of a mediaeval castle in Tenczynek. The Tsukunftists often met and played ball at the stadium of the *Jutrzenka* (the Dawn) Bundist team on the *Błonie* (the Meadows) and I became a sort of a mascot for the group. In particular, I remember one young Tzukunft girl, who must have been about 16 then, named Berta Krupnik, who used to collect wild flowers for me and play with me behind the Jutrzenka field. Berta later married Motl Księski, a master shoemaker. I worked with Motl during the War. Both Berta and Motl survived the War separately, found each other after the war and came to New York.

As a child of middle-class somewhat assimilated Jews in Austrian Galitzia Maks attended a public grammar school in Kraków, in which instruction was in Polish, with German as a second language. For a year after the outbreak of the First World War, when Kraków was threatened by the approaching Tsarist army, the Jacob Aleksandrowicz family was evacuated to the spa of Karlsbad in the then Austrian Bohemia and there the 12-year-old Maks attended a German-language school. His knowledge of German was imperfect and he had a hard time in the Karlsbad school but nevertheless he remembered his sojourn in the spa with fondness and took my mother there when she was ailing after the birth of my sister. The Aleksandrowicz family returned to Kraków when the Russian threat receded. After primary and secondary education, my father studied in the Higher Commercial Academy in Kraków. In 1924, when he was 22, his mother, my grandmother Hancia Aleksandrowicz nee Birnbaum, died as a diabetic, insulin not yet being available. When my grandfather was also diagnosed with diabetes a few years later, he had a nurse come in daily and inject him with insulin at home and he lived that way for many years, eventually dying of cancer in 1935. At 23 Maks, already an active member of the Jewish Labor Bund, had many male and female friends.

At roughly the same time, Maks met, fell in love and married a poor Jewish girl, Salomea Scheindel (Luśka) Rubin (1900-1942), daughter of Isaac Rosenberg and Keila Rubin. Luśka's father, a scion of a distinguished rabbinical family (son and grandson of the rabbis of Wieliczka/Klasno), studied the Torah all his life and died of consumption. His wife and then widow, my grandmother Keila, eked a living as a seamstress and piece-worker. She took work home. As children, my mother Luśka, and her older sister Pola helped by sewing buttons on shirts. Luśka, who grew up poor, showed political sympathies which naturally tended to the left. She flirted briefly with communism, but did not join the Communist Party because of her distaste for its subservience to Soviet totalitarianism and to the developing personality cult of Stalin. She also had no illusions that Stalin's solution to "the Jewish question", the Jewish Autonomous Region in Birobidjan, deep in Soviet Asia, would help to ease the life of Polish or Russian Jews. She became a dedicated active member of the Jewish Labor Bund, which favored fighting anti-Semitism in place, i.e. in Poland. The Bund was not only a political party but it was also active in social work and fostered Jewish culture and Yiddish as the language of the Jewish masses. In the years prior to 1939 Luska conducted free classes and she established a lending library for the Kraków chapter of the Bund in its headquarters on Dajwór Street. She kept this library open evenings two or three times a week. Like her husband, she also ran for a seat on the Kraków City Council on a Bundist electoral list. Both of my parents were convinced idealistic democratic socialists, believing in basic human goodness and advocating a reasonable equality of incomes, human dignity of labor and restraints on rapacious capital,

while supporting free press, free elections and a parliamentary system of constitutional government with guaranteed rights for minorities.

In 1924 Luśka, while still single, became pregnant and left Kraków to join her sister who moved to Paris. Maks told me that while he and my mother were a couple, as free spirits they did not believe that an official civil or religious ceremony was necessary for two people to consider themselves a marriage. However, with Luśka pregnant, he became concerned that without an official marriage registration his child would not carry his surname, so early in 1925 he came to Paris and they were joined in a civil marriage in a *mairie du Deuxieme Arrondissement* in March 1925. On June 27, 1925 I was born in Paris in a clinic at rue Santerre 15. Three months later we all returned to Kraków and moved to an apartment in Dębniki, across the Vistula from the center of the city. Obviously, Maks's father did not approved of the match or of the "premature" birth of a child, which is why the young family lived far from the family compound. However, reconciliation must have taken place, because three years later we moved to one of the family-owned houses on Bernardyńska Street, across from the Wawel Castle, the old seat of Polish Kings. Maks joined his father in his wholesale leather business located at 57 Dietla Street. In 1931 my sister Hanka was born. In 1935 Maks' father Jacob Aleksandrowicz died and Maks and his two brothers, Józek and Olek, inherited the business. All the time Maks continued to be active in the Bund, strenuously campaigning in City Council elections and in elections to the Jewish Community Council, the *Kahał.*

Our family life in Kraków was peaceful. My father was a very busy man. He took his business activities seriously, but he was even more involved in his work with the young Bundists. Everyday was somewhat similar. During the day he ran the leather business. He used to come home from the business for the mid-day meal, which was the big meal of the day, usually consisting of three courses, soup, meat with potatoes and vegetables and dessert. He used to announce his arrival by whistling a special "Aleksandrowicz" tune from a distance, so the food would be ready and on the table. After the meal he went back to the store and worked until about 7 PM. He then came home for a quick brief evening supper, always rather harried, often with his *Omega* pocket watch on the table in front of him so that he could see how much time he had before having to leave to go to the Bund. Almost every evening he went to the Bund organization where he met with his friends and proteges of the Tsukunft. My mother went with him two or three times a week to open the Bund library. We children stayed home with a live-in maid.

During the period between wars Poland was ran, rather arbitrarily, by Józef Piłsudski, the leader of the Polish legions that in 1918 helped to liberate the country first from Russian, then from German and Austrian domination. The country, at the behest of the Allied powers assembled in Versailles which officially recognized the independence of Poland, had a liberal democratic constitution, giving women the right to vote and protecting equal rights of minorities, including Jews. The first Prime Minister, was Ignacy Jan Paderewski, the pianist. The second was Ignacy Daszyński, the previously mentioned Galitzian Socialist, who used to represent Polish Galitzia in the Viennese Parliament. The first elected President of the Republic was a liberal democrat, Gabriel Narutowicz. The ideal situation did not last long. The country had four main political parties, two of them rabidly anti-Semitic: the National Democratic Party (,*Endeks*') and the Church-dominated Christian Democratic Party (,*Chadeks*'). There was also a Peasant Party, led by Wincenty Witos and

the Polish Socialist Party (PPS). Narutowicz was considered too friendly to the Jews and was assassinated by a right-wing extremist. Eventually, Piłsudski staged a *coup-d'etat* and became the sole ruler of the country. A pro-Government party, made largely of sycophants and government employees and hangers-on, was set up, called *BBWR* (Non-party Bloc for Cooperation with the Government) and from then on parliamentary elections were rigged and the liberal parties boycotted them. Piłsudski died in 1935 and lesser men took over the reins of Government. Anti-Semitism became dominant in Poland. The National Democracy, under its leader, Roman Dmowski, used the hatred of Jews as its main prop. The Church-run Catholic party was competing in this endeavor. The pro-government party, which was later called *Sanacja* and then OZON (*Obóz Zjednoczenia Narodowego*, i.e. the National Unity Camp), also began to compete in the anti-Semitic sweepstakes. Only the Polish Socialist Party tried, not very successfully, to counteract the anti-Jewish propaganda emanating from Germany after Hitler's accession to power. Anti-Jewish excesses were common. For example, I remember hearing about pogroms in a small town of Działoszyce and in Przytyk, a largely Jewish shtetl. The latter event inspired the Krakovian folksong writer, whom my parents supported, Mordche Gebirtig, to write the song "*Es brennt, mayn shtetele brennt*" (It burns, my shtetl burns). The influential Roman Catholic hierarchy in Poland was advocating a boycott of Jewish stores and Jewish craftsmen. A priest, Maksymilian Kolbe, who was killed by the Nazis and canonized by the late pope John Paul II, founded an anti-Jewish publishing enterprise and edited a journal, *Dziennik Niepokalanej* (Daily of the Immaculate), which advocated boycott of Jewish stores, hoping that boycotting the Jews will beggar them and thus induce them to voluntarily leave Poland. The Bund strenuously fought the anti-Semites and my father was prominent in that fight. The Bund responded to the pogrom in Przytyk with a general strike of Jewish workers in Poland, demanding strong government action to protect defenceless elderly Jews in the countryside. The strike was supported by both Jewish merchants and industrialists and by Polish workers organized in the socialist trade unions affiliated with the Polish Socialist Party.

The international political situation in Europe was becoming very volatile. As I mentioned earlier, in Austria the rightist fascist Dolfuss government fought an actual street battle to disarm the workers' self-defense militia, the *Schutzbund*, thus eliminating a force able to oppose Nazi street gangs, effectively disarming Austria and making it vulnerable to Nazi excesses. Dolfuss' successor, Kurt Schuschnigg, yielded to Hitler's threats and opened the way for the Austrian Nazi, Seyss-Inquart, to invite Hitler to gobble up Austria. Within months, Hitler also grabbed Czechoslovakia, with naive connivance of British Prime Minister Neville Chamberlain and French Premier Edouard Daladier in Munich. Hitler also took Kłaipeda (Memel) from the Lithuanians. Poland was next on his list. The Germans asked it to yield to them Gdańsk (Danzig), a part of Polish Silesia and a corridor through Polish Pomerania. Unlike Eduard Benes, President in Prague, the Polish President Ignacy Mościcki and the Army Chief Marshall Edward Rydz-Smigły in Warsaw, refused to yield peacefully and Poland began to mobilize. Having learned the lesson of Munich, France and Great Britain guaranteed the inviolability of Polish borders.

Emigration, whether to America or to Palestine, was not on my father's agenda. He was determined to make Poland and Russia and the rest of Eastern Europe livable for Jews as equals of Poles or Russians. He was in favor of staying in place and fighting anti-Semitism and discrimination, making sure that Jews have all the citizenship rights in their

places of residence. He was obviously an idealist, believing that when men of good will come together, hate and discrimination will disappear. Quite correctly, he was concerned that Palestine had no room for all the World's Jewry, at that time numbering between 13 and 16 million. He did not think that Zionism can represent a solution to the Jewish Question, whether in Poland, Russia or the United States. Three million Jews in Poland had to make the best of their existence in Poland, and the millions of Jews in the Soviet Union and elsewhere had to do the same. He was also aware of the fact that the Arabs of Palestine were not welcoming Jewish immigration. Indeed, in the mid-nineteen thirties, the Arabs in the British Mandate of Palestine rioted and killed a number of defenseless elderly religious Jews. The paramount leader of the Palestinians, the Grand Mufti of Jerusalem, Hadj Amin el-Husseini, visited Berlin and, inspite of being a Semite just like the Jews, was greeted with great pomp by the Nazis as an important friend and ally. Time has proven that many of my father's concerns were correct: the fact that the Promised Land had Arab inhabitants at the time is the cause of much anguish and killing to the present. The Palestinian Arab population did not decrease but increased significantly and became more nationalistic after European Jews began arriving there. My father was also correct when he said that the small land west of the Jordan River could not sustain all the Jews of the time. The numbers problem was solved, in part, by the insane though technically efficient acts of the Germans under the spell of a gifted orator and rabble-rouser, Adolf Hitler.

True to their philosophy, my parents were not only active in the Jewish Labor Bund but set out creating alliances with non-Jewish democratic forces in Poland. As long as I remember, during my childhood, my father was an active public speaker, addressing large crowds sometimes in Yiddish but mostly in Polish during general joint Polish and Jewish socialist workers' rallies. My parents had many Jewish and non-Jewish friends in the leftist intelligentsia in Kraków, among them Adam Ciołkosz and his wife Lydia and Józef Cyrankiewicz, Secretary of the Kraków branch of the social-democratic PPS, who after the War became the country's Prime Minister. Also among their friends was Prof. Stanisław Skrzeszewski, a Communist sympathizer, who after the War became Polish Ambassador to France and then Foreign Minister of Poland. Skrzeszewski's Jewish wife, Różka, nee Rosenbaum, was also a childhood friend of my mother's. Following the ascendancy of the Nazi Party in Germany, anti-Jewish propaganda increased, which led to an increase rather than a decrease, in anti-Jewish sentiments everywhere, including Western Europe and the United States (remember Henry Ford publishing the infamous forgery the *Protocols of the Elders of Zion*, Colonel Lindbergh fraternizing with Hermann Goering, , the Undersecretary of State Breckinridge Long campaigning against issuing visas to European Jews and Father Coughlin, the radio priest?), forcing my father to abandon some of his optimism about peaceful co-existence.

In Poland, the government was kow-towing to the worst right-wing elements. My father was not religious and, in fact, he opposed and fought the influence of the rabbinate and of the Jewish religious establishment, which tried to keep the Jewish masses from secular education and enlightenment. Nevertheless, he was deeply disturbed when Joanna Prystor, an anti-Semitic member of Parliament, pushed through a ban on ritual slaughter. My father saw this not as a humanitarian gesture (as it was touted), but as an expression of anti-Semitism. The Polish Government, led by Gen. Felicjan Sławoj-Składkowski and Col. Józef Beck, tried futilely to cooperate with Hitler. When Hitler's army invaded Czechoslovakia in October 1938, the Poles helped themselves to a slice of Czech territory beyond the Olza River, inhabited by ethnic Poles, the so-called *Zaolzie*. Then, the anti-Semitic Polish Government passed a law depriving Polish Jews who lived abroad, mainly in Germany, of their Polish citizenship, condemning them thereby to the status of stateless persons, who would have had to stay in Germany. Some of these people have lived in Germany for a generation or longer. Their children were born and reared in Germany and did not know any other language but German. Because of that law, they would have suddenly become an international problem. The Nazis, with their history of Nuremberg Laws and planning the soon-to-occur *Kristallnacht*, were not going to allow Germany to acquire thousands of additional Jews. On October 26, 1938, days before this Polish denaturalization law was to go into effect, they forcibly rounded up all these thousands of hapless Polish citizens resident in Germany, loaded them onto trains and shipped them, without advance notice, into the no-man‘s land at the Polish-German border town of Zbąszyn.

Thousands of desperate people, without food or shelter, stayed in the no-man's land in Zbąszyn, until international pressure forced the Poles to allow these people who were after all Polish citizens, to enter the country. The care of these unfortunates then became the responsibility of Jewish charitable and political organizations in Poland, which proceeded to assign them to Jewish households that volunteered to offer them shelter. My parents volunteered to take in one such family. A German family was brought to Kraków and assigned to live with us, probably because they had a young son, although he was older than I. The father was a Jewish tailor of Polish-Jewish origin, who forty years earlier emigrated to Germany, where he eventually married a non-Jewish German Frau. Their son, Willy, was then around 17 years old (I was thirteen at the time.). The young man spoke only German, was quite chauvinistic about German superiority over the likes of Poles and, for sure, Polish Jews. There is no question in my mind that he also considered himself superior to his hosts in Kraków and was ashamed of his Jewish father, who spoke German with a foreign accent. He hardly deigned to speak to someone so much younger and so otherwise inferior as myself.

Interestingly enough, and characteristic of the crazy times, the non-Jewish wife of our involuntary guest, smuggled herself immediately back to Germany to her old apartment. While there, she found out that by divorcing her husband, and formally claiming that the boy is not her husband's son, but the result of an extramarital affair with a pure Aryan, she can establish that her son is not even partly Jewish. Thereupon, she left her husband in Poland to an uncertain fate, and took Willy back home to Germany. We never heard from them afterwards, and I do not know what happened to them there, but later during the war some fellow Krakovians told me that they had met Willy as an SS-officer in one of the concentration camps, in the black uniform of a Nazi Storm-trooper and that he behaved abominably, being even more cruel to the camp inmates than the other Nazis.

One morning in the spring of 1939, the radio announced that Hitler's Foreign Minister, Joachim Ribbentrop, was going to Moscow to meet his Soviet counterpart, Vyacheslav Molotov, and Stalin. That morning, I remember my father saying that a Ribbentrop-Molotov pact would mean a partition of Poland and a world war. However, he also said that, if by chance, the outbreak of war is delayed, as it was a year earlier thanks to Munich, then we will not stay in Poland but leave Europe, perhaps go to America. As luck would have it, the war was not delayed, and we were all trapped in a burning Europe.

I remember my father's looks when I saw him last before the outbreak of the War. He was then well-built, neither fat nor slim, about 6 feet tall, weighing around 170 lbs. His hair was straight, jet-black, simply combed back without a part; his face was without wrinkles, and his forehead high. He was light-skinned, always clean-shaven, though his dark stubble required frequent shaving. He spoke with a clear, resonant voice, pronounced words with deliberate correctness. He spoke flawless grammatical Polish, which was his primary language. He also knew German. He knew Yiddish well enough to deliver public speeches in Yiddish and to have later a weekly political news commentary in Yiddish on WEVD radio station in New York in the nineteen fifties. Yiddish was not native to him, he learned it when, as a young man, he became interested in the Jewish socialist worker movement and it became necessary for him to be able to communicate with the Bund rank-and-file, most of whom used Yiddish in their daily lives, particularly in smaller communities and shtetls.

As a young man of draft age, my father served for a year in the Polish peacetime army and was considered a part of the reserves. In 1939, at 37, he was drafted into the Polish army as part of a general mobilization, given a uniform and an old rifle. He was stationed in the army barracks under the *Kopiec Kościuszki* (Kościuszko's Memorial Mound) outside Kraków. After the outbreak of War, his fighting unit was withdrawing eastward while trying to delay the German offensive. After the War, in New York he mentioned to me that his army unit had only one skirmish with the attacking Germans before disintegrating. Apparently, they were camping by a small country road when they were told of a German tank column approaching. They dug trenches by the roadside and waited for the enemy. Their commander, a lieutenant, was whispering orders to remain quiet until ordered to fire. Eventually, three German armored vehicles appeared, driving slowly and carefully in the potentially hostile terrain. The Polish machine gun waited until they were in front and then opened fire. The Germans were surprised and two of their vehicles were set on fire before they had time to respond. The third car did open fire but completely at random, shooting aimlessly in all directions. Dazed Germans jumped out of the burning cars and rolled on the ground trying to tamp down their burning clothing. This was my father's first and only military victory. Continuous bombing by low-flying German planes made organized concentration of forces and establishment of a front line impossible. Retreat turned into a rout. When the Soviet troops backstabbed Poland from the East and occupied the eastern part of Poland, the Polish army disintegrated. At the first opportunity, my father stopped at a Jewish household in a Jewish shtetl in Eastern Poland and got some civian clothing. He could not return to German-occupied Kraków, because he assumed (correctly) that the German Secret Police would be looking for him. In that shabby clothing he travelled to Soviet-occupied Lwów, where he met his sister Lola and her Lvovian husband and also his brothers who escaped from Kraków. His stay in Lwów was brief, because soon the Soviet Secret Police also began asking about him. He moved to Vilna, then part of independent Lithuania.

In the meantime my mother, my little sister and I left Kraków temporarily and traveled into central Poland beyond the expected frontline, to wait out the expected Polish-German war. When the Germans and Russians occupied all of Poland and there was no frontline and no safe zone, we returned to Kraków. After the Germans evicted us from our house near the Wawel Castle, we lived on Dietla Street, then briefly in a small neighboring town, Skała, and eventually in the Kraków Ghetto. In October 1942 my mother and sister

were caught in the Kraków Ghetto and shipped in cargo cars to the extermination center in Bełżec near Lublin and were never heard from again. I survived in the concentration camp in Kraków-Płaszów, then in camps in Mauthausen and its branches, Melk and Ebensee in Austria. In May 1945 I was liberated in Ebensee by the Third American Army under General Patton. Not surprisingly, I was sick, undernourished, emaciated and debilitated both physically and emotionally. All this will be described later.

When the Polish army disintegrated in September 1939, my father found himself in Eastern Poland, where most small towns were then largely inhabited by Jews. Hiding with a Jewish family, he exchanged his army uniform for civilian clothing and made his way to the city of Lwów, then occupied by the Red Army. In Lwów he found his brothers, who escaped from the Germans to the Russian part of Poland. However, many other people from Kraków also escaped to Lwów, including some Communists. Before the war my father was was strongly and publicly opposed to the Stalinist version of Communism. In Lwów, some of these Communists denounced him to the Soviet authorities, while others warned him of an impending arrest. He had to move. In this short time the entire political geography of Eastern Europe changed drastically. A new border was erected by Hitler and Stalin across what used to be Poland. Since the two dictators did not trust each other the border was continously guarded and bristled with gun emplacements, barbed wires and guard towers. Crossing it illegally was always extremely difficult and dangerous and, anyway return to Kraków was out of question for my father or uncle Ignacy because in Kraków there were sure to be arrested by the German secret police, the Gestapo, which was looking for them. Attempts to unite the family in one way or another were bound to fail. We were forced to face the future separately.

With his brother, Ignacy, who was also politically engaged, my father smuggled himself in severe winter weather, through heavy snows in the forests, to the then independent Lithuania through another new fortified border. The Lithuanians always considered Vilna, which they call Vilnius, to be their historic capital, founded by a Grand Duke of Lithuania, Mendog, and developed by a successor, Gedyminas. When Poland and Lithuania joined, around 1400 A.D. into a dynastic union, the Lithuanian Grand Dukes became Kings of Poland. Vytautas, a half-brother of Władysław Jagiełło, the first Lithuanian King of Poland and victor over the Teutonic Knights of the Cross on the plains of Grunwald and Tannenberg in 1410, tried to sunder the union. However, he suffered a devastating defeat in a battle at Worskla with invaders from the east, the Mongol Tartars and Pechenegs, and concluded that Lithuania cannot exist alone. Thus, the union with Poland remained in effect. Lithuanian nobility joined their Polish counterparts. With time, this Lithuanian nobility, along with the royal dynasty, lost its Lithuanian identity and became Polonized. Unlike the peasantry in the surrounding countryside, nobility spoke Polish, the language of the royal court. The most famous Polish poet, Adam Mickiewicz, born in a Lithuanian manor house, wrote in Polish. He began his main work called *Pan Tadeusz*, with the words, in Polish, "*Litwo, ojczyzno moja*", i.e. "O Lithuania, my fatherland". He is now honored in Lithuania, with his surname given a distinct Lithuanian ending as Mickiewiczius. The Polish (and American) national hero, Tadeusz Kościuszko (the name is distinctly Lithuanian), was born in Lithuania. The latest Polish hero, leader of the armed "legions" that succeeded in resurrecting Poland in 1918 after a hundred and twenty years of foreign occupation, Józef Piłsudski, was also born in this Lithuanian region. In addition, adding to the Lithuanian nationalist problem,

Vilna (now Vilnius) became a heavily Jewish "Jerusalem of Lithuania". It became a center of Jewish culture and of religious and secular Jewish learning and of the Yiddish language. After 1918 Vilna became a part of Poland and reverted to Lithuania only in 1939.

There would have been no safety for my father in Vilna; in a short time the Russians and then the Germans and then again the Russians occupied Lithuania. When my father came to Vilna in 1940, Lithuania was briefly independent, although the Stalin-Hitler Pact assigned it to the Soviet zone of influence and it was only a matter of time before it would be joined to the USSR. All the embassies and consulates were not in Vilna but in the small town of Kovno (Kaunas) which served as Lithuania's capital, when Vilna was not available. To get out of Lithuania while Europe was in flames one needed a foreign visa and a permit to traverse the Soviet Union. However, no country was eager at that point to issue entry visas to Polish Jews. The United States adhered to a strict quota system and the Polish quota was oversubscribed. The US State Department, under the sway of Undersecretary Breckinridge Long, was adamant in refusing admission to persecuted European Jews and Franklin D. Roosevelt was unwilling to commit his prestige to such an unpopular cause. Fortunately, there were a few places that would admit Europeans without restriction, among them, thanks to an understanding Dutch official, the Dutch colonies in South America, Surinam, Curacao and others. And, as it happened, the Japanese consul in Kovno was willing to incur the wrath of his government and issue Japanese transit visas, to people without immigration papers, but presumably going to these Dutch possessions. Among the two thousands Jews to whom Sugihara issued Japanese transit visas, on August 19, 1940, were my father, Maks Aleksandrowicz, and my uncle, Ignacy Aleksandrowicz.

Fortunately for Maks and his brother, who also came to Vilna, the Jewish Labor Committee in New York tried to save endangered Jewish activists and to find a way to provide a temporary American heaven for a list of endangered Bundist leaders. In Washington a committee was formed, under the patronage of Eleanor Roosevelt and the President of the American Federation of Labor, William Green, with the task of saving endangered European intellectuals. It was thanks to the efforts of this committee that my father and my uncle were placed on the list of endangered people to be saved. The problem of visas required for leaving Lithuania and travel through the Soviet Union was solved by Consul Sugihara. After waiting in Vilna for news from New York, the brothers Aleksandrowicz traveled to Moscow where, thanks to being on that list, both my father and uncle Ignacy received temporary American visas on January 29, 1941. They boarded then the Trans-Siberian Railroad to Vladivostok, proceeded to Japan and from Kobe in Japan they took the liner *Tatsuta Maru* on March 4, 1941 and arrived in Honolulu on March 14 and in San Francisco on March 20, 1941.

Max expected to wait out the war in the US, earning a living first by working as a tanner in Salem and Peabody in Massachusetts and then by managing a tannery in Andrews, North Carolina. As soon as he arrived in the United States he made strenuous efforts to pull his family out of Europe and bring us to America. There were no American consular offices in German-occupied Poland, the nearest U.S. office was in Berlin. I understand that some papers that would have helped us get an American visa did arrive in Berlin in November 1941, but before we could acquire the means to travel there, the Japanese bombed Pearl Harbor, Germany declared war on the U.S. and the consulate and embassy in Berlin closed. Originally, Max hoped to return to Poland after the war ended, rejoining his wife and

children there and resuming work in his business and his interest in politics. It was not to be. His wife and daughter died in the Holocaust, as did his sister, brothers, nephews, nieces and other relatives. I was the only survivor of his entire large family in Kraków and in my very first letter after the War in 1945 I told him that I will not stay among cadavers in Europe but want to come to the US. In spite of my father‘s strenuous efforts in 1945 to bring me to the US, and with the preference of being a minor child of a U.S. resident, it took me a full year to obtain a visa. I arrived in New York in July 1946. Eager to make up for my lost education I soon left to go to college in Geneva, New York. Maks was lonely in North Carolina and eager for companionship. With my encouragement, he remarried in December 1946. His second wife was an old acquaintance, Różka nee Luksemburg. In November 1950 Maksymilian Aleksandrowicz became an American citizen, abbreviating both his first name and his surname, becoming known as Max Alexander. He left North Carolina and settled in New York City. In New York he became active in the labor movement and, as mentioned above, he conducted a weekly radio program in Yiddish on the station WEVD commenting on weekly events. In a sense, he became a political commentator, a Yiddish "pundit", discussing current events from the point of view of a Jewish labor sympathizer, knowledgeable about European affairs. He served as Secretary of Local 9 of the Cloak Joint Board of the Ladies Garment Workers Union. He never returned to Poland. He died in New York City on November 10, 1968.

At the rail terminal in New York Maks and his brother were met by a relative, a cousin of their father. The relative prepared for them a list of addresses and phone numbers of relatives living in New York, who could be of help, but apparently by accident, omitted his own from the list. However, the brothers had other relatives here, including an elderly aunt, who escaped from Vienna and lived in Brooklyn who was more hospitable, and they found welcome among New York‘s labor leaders. Penniless but proud and unwilling to live off charity they immediately looked for work. As I related earlier, Ignacy remained in New York. As an important Polish political figure he became a member of the highest finance control agency of the Polish Government-in-Exile. Eventually, he was offered a position on the faculty of Hobart College in Geneva, in upstate New York, where he became a Professor of Economics. My father proceeded to New England, which was then the center of American shoe and leather industry and where he could use his knowledge of this field. As it happens, the jobs he got in Salem and Peabody, Massachusetts, were all at minimum wage, which was then 40 cents an hour, or $ 16 per week. While this was not a munificent wage, it helped him to be independent while he was learning to speak English. He also became active with Jewish groups in New York and Polish groups in New England. For example, on November 7, 1941, he delivered a lecture on the war situation in Poland to an enthusiastic Polish audience in the Casimir Pulaski Auditorium on 24 Winter Street in Peabody, MA. Eventually, my father was considered for a leadership role in the Jewish Labor Committee in New York, but instead accepted an offer to manage a tannery in a small town in eastern North Carolina, named Andrews, in Cherokee County, near the Tennessee border. He stayed in Andrews for the duration of the war. Eventually, when he found that most of his family was exterminated in Europe, he filed for US citizenship and in the process abbreviated his name to Max Alexander.

Maks Aleksandrowicz (Max Alexander) has published numerous political and historical articles in journals in Poland and in New York. He conducted a weekly news

commentary *Amol un haynt* (Once and today), on the WEVD radio station in New York. He was the subject of an article by J. Soski entitled "*Haver Max Aleksandrowicz*" in the New York Yiddish journal *Undzer Tsait (*3-4:32-35, 1999). He was also prominently mentioned in the memoir of J. Celemenski, an underground Jewish courier in German-occupied Poland (1963, 9-11, 15). His photo was featured in Volume I, p. 32 of J.S. Hertz's *"Geshikhte fun Bund*" (1981). Through the Holocaust and the Cold War, my father remained a believer in the ideals of democratic socialism and an optimist, seeing a better future for mankind and a defeat of the forces of reaction, whether black or red. He remained hopeful and continued to work for the future of Jewish culture, Yiddish language and the ideals of the Jewish Labor Bund. He continued to see the international Workers' Day of the First-of-May, widely celebrated in his youth in Europe, as an important unifying holiday of the international proletariat and liberal intelligentsia. Speaking in Yiddish on the New York radio station WEVD on the occasion of May 1, 1964, he said:

"In the seventy years since it was proclaimed as an international workers' holiday has May First strongly demonstrated its appeal. It always was, is today and will always be a symbol of the aspirations and ideals of the socialist movement striving to fully reconstruct society on the basis of freedom and justice. Hitlerists and communists have tried to take this holiday from us, but it remained the day of brotherhood and international solidarity, the fountain of our enthusiasm and our belief in a better tomorrow, a future of equality and justice for all men and all people...

...Let us extend our hand to socialists in all lands...in the spirit of international solidarity in the fight against capitalist reaction and communist dictatorships, for a world of freedom and justice. Let us express our solidarity with Jewish workers and Bundists in the whole world in their battle against anti-Semitism, nationalism and clericalism, for liberty and for continuation and development of our language and culture..."

The speech was printed, in full, in Yiddish, in the April-June 2004 issue of the New York journal Unser Tsait, Vol, 4-6, pp. 3-5 (2004), in memory of my father Maks Aleksandrowicz on the occasion of the fortieth anniversary of his delivery of this speech.

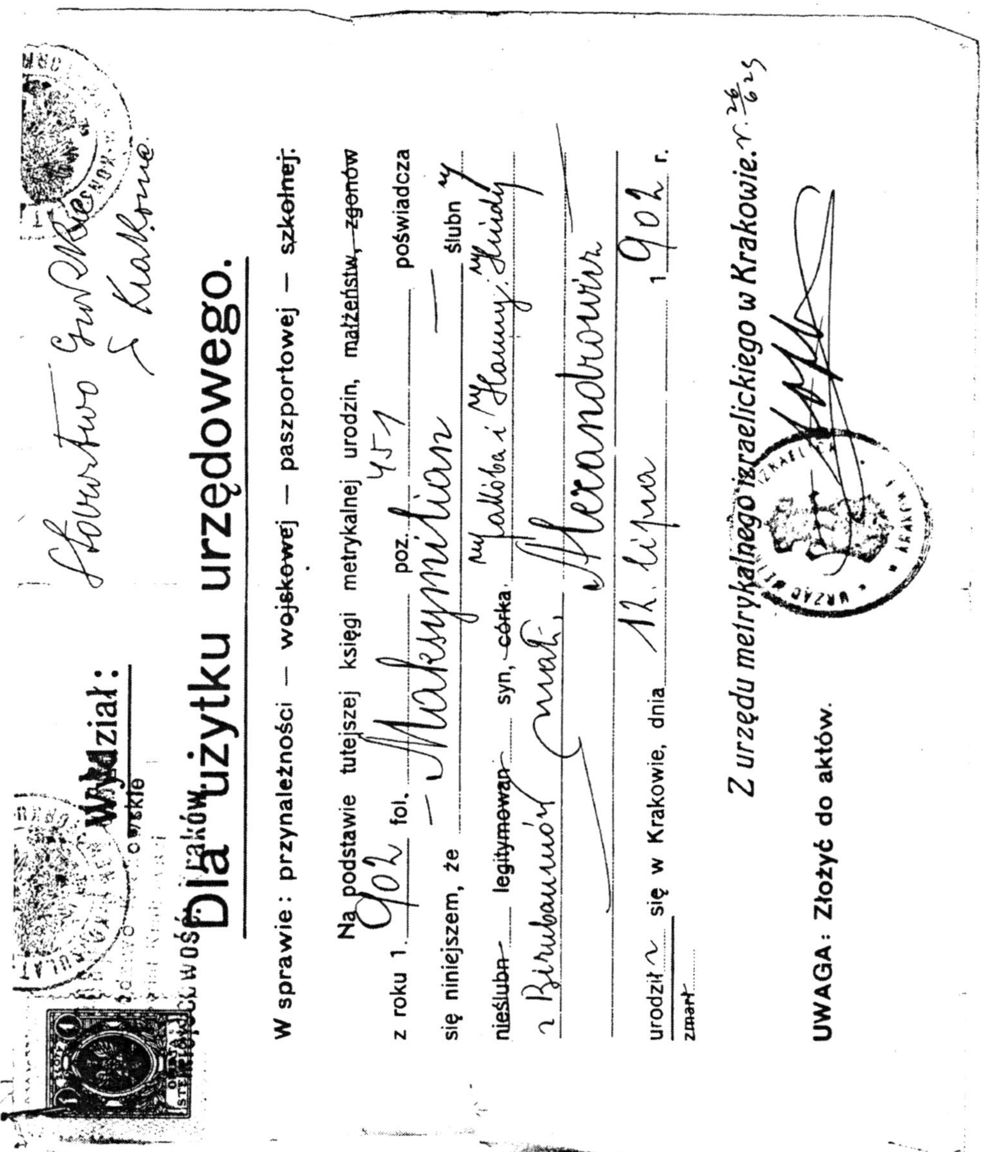

Stowarzyszenie ... w Krakowie

Wydział:

Dla użytku urzędowego.

W sprawie: przynależności — ~~wojskowej~~ — paszportowej — ~~szkolnej~~.

Na podstawie tutejszej księgi metrykalnej urodzin, ~~małżeństw, zgonów~~ z roku 1902 fol. ______ poz. 451 poświadcza się niniejszem, że — Maksymilian — ślubny ~~nieślubn~~ ~~legitymowan~~ syn, ~~córka~~ Jakóba i Hanny Hudy z Birnbaumów małż. Alexandrowicz

urodził się w Krakowie, dnia 12. lipca 1902 r.
~~zmarł~~

Z urzędu metrykalnego izraelickiego w Krakowie. r. 26/6 25

UWAGA: Złożyć do aktów.

Fig. 060. Birth certificate of Maxymilian Aleksandrowicz, Kraków, 1902

Translation of the birth certificate of Maxymilian Aleksandrowicz:

(Fiscal stamp and seals of the Kraków Administration

Office: *Municipal Administration*

<u>For official use</u>

Documenting nationality for the purpose of issuance of passport

On the basis of the local metrical record of births for the Year 1*902*, line *451* we declare herewith that

Maksymilian legitimate

son of Jacob and Hanna Hinda of the Birbnbaums, spouses

Aleksandrowicz,

was born in Kraków on the *12-th day of July, 1902.*

From the metrical izraelite office in Kraków. Y.26/629

Comment: Place in the records

Seal of the Jewish Metrical Office
Signature (illegible)

Fig. 061 Maks Aleksandrowicz with his brother Józek and brother-in-law Isidor Wien in Kraków in 1938

Paszport po wykorzystaniu należy zwrócić władzy, która go wystawiła

729E/247

SER.II. №131844

RZECZPOSPOLITA POLSKA
M. S. W.
RÉPUBLIQUE POLONAISE
M. I.

PASZPORT-PASSEPORT

Obywatel polski / Citoyen polonais } Maksymilian Aleksandrowicz

zamieszkały w / domicilié à } Krakowie / Cracovie

w towarzystwie żony / accompagné de sa femme } —

i / et de ——— *dzieci / enfants*

Paszport ten zawiera 40 stronic
Ce passeport contient 40 pages

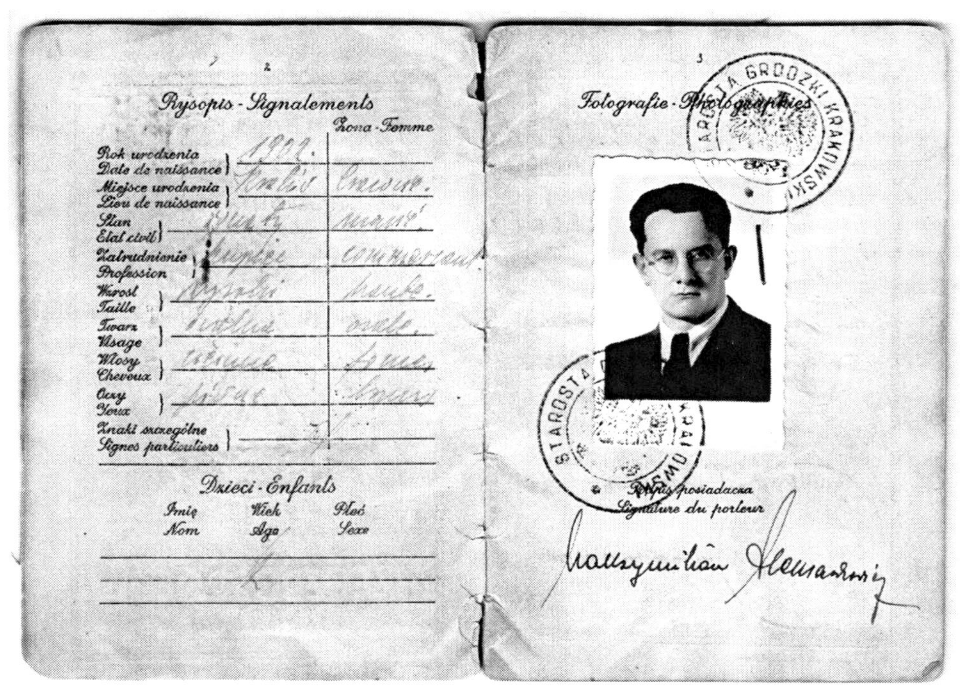

2

Rysopis - Signalements

		Żona - Femme
Rok urodzenia / Date de naissance	1902	
Miejsce urodzenia / Lieu de naissance	Kraków	Cracovie
Stan / Etat civil	żonaty	marié
Zatrudnienie / Profession	kupiec	commerçant
Wzrost / Taille	wysoki	haute
Twarz / Visage	owalna	ovale
Włosy / Cheveux		
Oczy / Yeux		
Znaki szczególne / Signes particuliers		

Dzieci - Enfants

Imię / Nom	Wiek / Age	Płeć / Sexe

3

Fotografie - Photographies

STAROSTA GRODZKI KRAKOWSKI

Podpis posiadacza / Signature du porteur

Maksymilian Aleksandrowicz

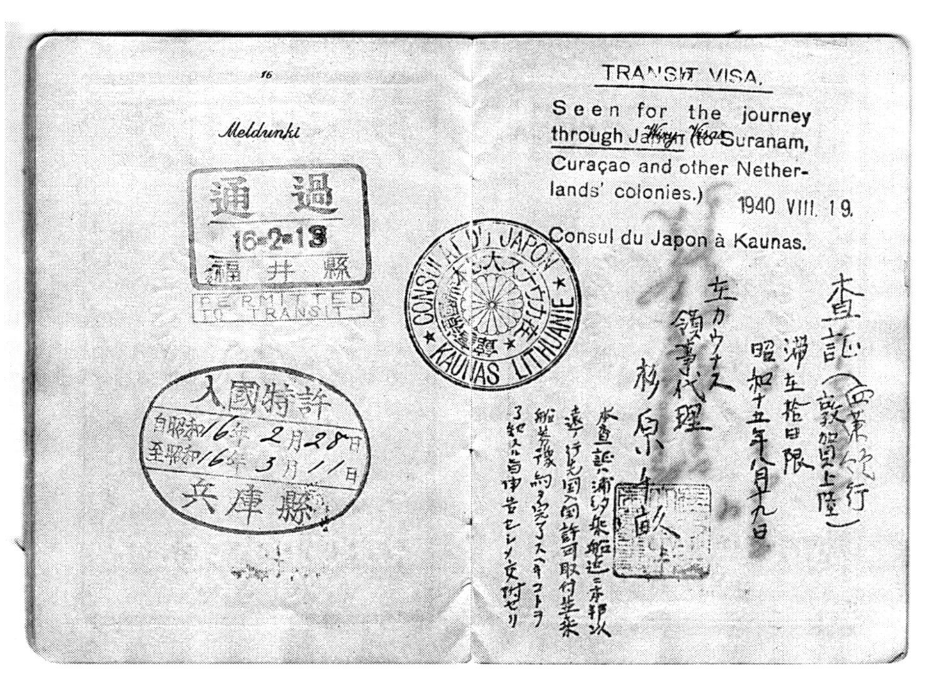

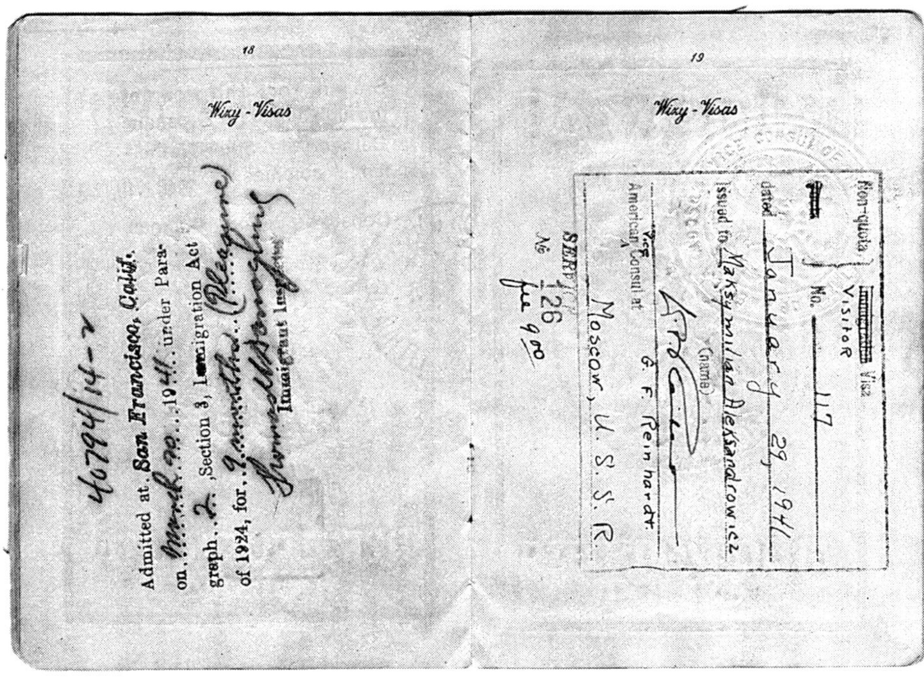

Figs. 062, 063. Pages from the Polish passport of Maksymilian Aleksandrowicz showing his Japanese and American visas

MAKSYMILIAN ALEKSANDROWICZ: PAGES FROM POLISH PASSPORT

My father had a Polish passport. In it he was described as being born in 1902 in Kraków, married, a merchant, tall, with an oval face and dark hair and green eyes. He carried this passport with him during the War and he had it with him in Vilna in 1940, when it became critical for him to get away. The only way out of Vilna was through the Soviet Union, a risky passage for somebody who was on the NKVD arrest list. Permission to cross Russia on the Trans-Siberian Railroad to Vladivostok, was given only to holders of foreign visas. The Polish immigration quota was oversubscribed and visas were routinely refused. The Jewish organizations in America were pressuring the Roosevelt Administration to issue a limited number of visitor visas to endangered European activists. My father and his brother Ignacy were on a list submitted to the Government by the Jewish Labor Committee through the Committee to Save European Intellectuals, organized under the joint patronage of Eleanor Roosevelt and Philip Green of the American Federation of Labor. The State Department, under Cordell Hull, Sumner Welles and Breckinridge Long, did not look favorably on the prospect of flooding the U.S. with Jewish refugees. Each consul had a right to interview applicants and grant or refuse a visa. The consul in Lithuania was swamped with claimants and simply was ordered to close shop. The only way to get a visa was to appear before the American consul in Moscow, clearly not an easy task, as the Soviets did not allow easy access to their capital.

Fortunately, in stepped the Japanese Consul in Lithuania, Chiune Sugihara who, out of a humanitarian impulse, defied the official policy of his government and issued Japanese transit visas, using the Dutch colonies of Surinam and Curacao as final destinations. With such a visa, it became possible to cross Russia. My father and his brother were among the first to receive a transit visa from Sugihara. They traveled to Moscow, where the US consul issued American visitor visas to them. Fortunately, the Russians were not well organized and my father traveled through Siberia and safely left the Soviet Union without NKVD interference. Both the Japanese and the US visas, stamped in my father's Polish passport, are visible in pages from that passport.

Recently, Hillel Levine published a book (see Bibliography) detailing the activities of Chiune Sugihara. In the book there is a photo of a page from Sugihara's alphabetical list of visas issued in Lithuania . The names of my father and uncle head the list.

Fig. 064. Kraków Market Square, scene of public rallies addressed by my father and his army barracks at the Kościuszko Memorial Mound

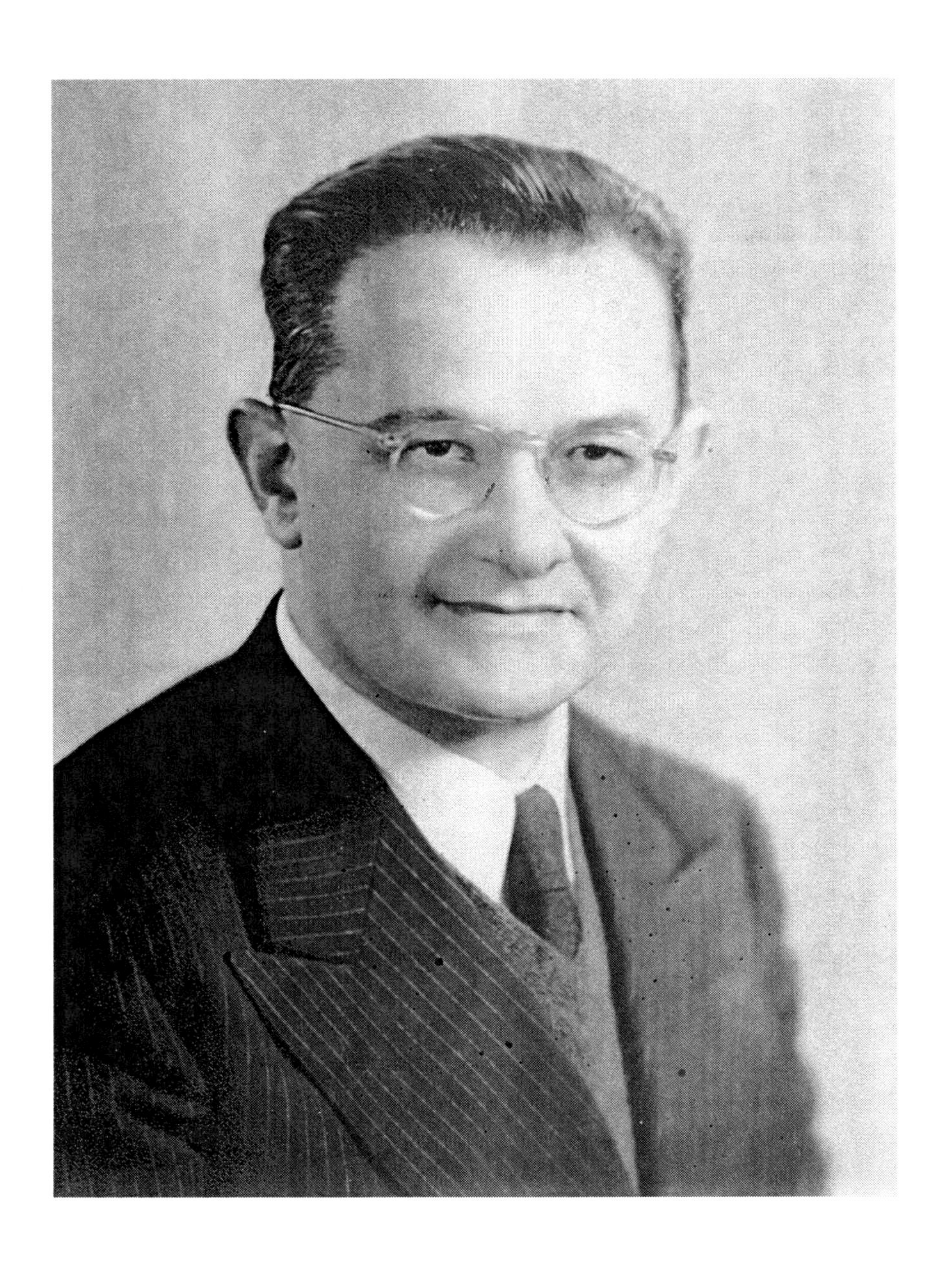

Fig. 065. Max Alexander in New York in 1945

THE UNITED STATES OF AMERICA

ORIGINAL
TO BE GIVEN TO
THE PERSON NATURALIZED

No. 6858349

CERTIFICATE OF NATURALIZATION

Petition No. 475303

Personal description of holder as of date of naturalization: Date of birth July 12, 1902 sex Male;
complexion Dark color of eyes Brown color of hair Gr-Black height 5 feet 11 inches;
weight 165 pounds; visible distinctive marks None
Marital status Married former nationality Polish
I certify that the description above given is true, and that the photograph affixed hereto is a likeness of me.

(Complete and true signature of holder)

UNITED STATES OF AMERICA
EASTERN DISTRICT OF NEW YORK } ss:

Be it known, that at a term of the District Court of The United States held pursuant to law at Brooklyn on November 14, 1950 the Court having found that MAX ALEXANDER then residing at 20-35 24th Street, Long Island City, N.Y. intends to reside permanently in the United States (when so required by the Naturalization Laws of the United States), had in all other respects complied with the applicable provisions of such naturalization laws, and was entitled to be admitted to citizenship, thereupon ordered that such person be and (s)he was admitted as a citizen of the United States of America.

In testimony whereof the seal of the court is hereunto affixed this 14th day of November in the year of our Lord nineteen hundred and fifty and of our Independence the one hundred and seventy fifth.

Clerk of the U.S. District Court.

By Deputy Clerk.

Seal

It is a violation of the U.S. Code (and punishable as such) to copy, print, photograph, or otherwise illegally use this certificate.

DEPARTMENT OF JUSTICE

Fig. 066. Max Alexander Naturalization papers

Fig. 067. Tombstones of brothers Maks and Ignacy Aleksandrowicz in New Jersey

Chapter 24. Salomea Scheindel Rubin Aleksandrowicz, (1900-1942)

My mother, Salomea Scheindel Rubin Aleksandrowicz and my sister Anna (Hanka) Aleksandrowicz, age 11, died in the Holocaust. It is hard for me even now to stop and think not about the meaning of the Holocaust as such but about the meaning of this specific event, the murder of my mother and sister. The Holocaust has simply become a part of world and my family history, something I have learned to take for granted. Yet, I find it really hard to accept that in the middle of the Twentieth Century a technologically advanced, fully developed Central European country, home of Goethe and Heine and Beethoven, driven by a set of totally irrational concepts, would have seen fit to send a highly accomplished forty two year old social activist and educator, wife and mother of two children, and her innocent cute dark-eyed sweet eleven-year old girl to their deaths, not as an individual aberrant behavior of a crazed individual criminal but as a considered legally sanctioned act of an established elected government, rapturously supported by a majority of the country's population. This is scary because it shows that a clever spell-binding demagogue can sway a majority of even the most civilized and deeply religious people to commit the most heinous of deeds simply by using patriotism and playing to an age-old widespread popular prejudice. It was the mass of ordinary Germans, not some deranged criminals, that executed (what an appropriate verb to use!) the government's orders, while the rest of the world looked on and did not even try to intervene in some way. As an addendum, let me say that I never would have believed it possible *("it can't happen here!")* that in 2006, in civilized America a legally elected government would incarcerate individuals without permission from any court and torture them in secret places with assent and even encouragement from the majority of a duly elected parliament and a sizeable proportion of the voting population.

I find it very hard to describe my mother in a few words. My mother, known to her friends as Luśka, serving as a leader of the Bundist underground organization in the Ghetto

in German-occupied Kraków, died more than sixty years ago. She was then 42 years old.

She was born on September 30, 1900 in Kraków, a Polish city, which was then in the Austrian province of Galitzia. She was the second of four children of Keila Hinda Rubin and Izak Rosenberg. Keila Rubin, sometimes officially registered as Klara Schmerler, was born in 1872 in Perehinsko, district Dolina, in Eastern Galitzia, between the towns of Stryj and Kolomea. She came to Kraków in 1897. I could find very little about her childhood or her progenitors, what I know will be discussed in the next chapter. Izak Rosenberg was born in 1866 in Klasno, a suburb of Wieliczka, a small town near Kraków, the site of an old and famous salt mine. He came to live in the Kazimierz district of Kraków in 1900. At earlier point in history, Wieliczka had a privilege of "*non tolerandis Judeis*" and all the Jews lived just outside the Wieliczka town limits, in Klasno, where the town synagogue was located. My mother told me that her father was the son and grandson of rabbis of that synagogue. It appears that his grandfather was rabbi Szymon Rosenberg (born in 1821), possibly son of rabbi Abraham Rosenberg. Izak must have been a studious but sickly young man because he died of "consumption", i.e. tuberculosis, before I was born. I was named after him. My mother's mother, whom we called "*babtsia*" (little grandma), was left with four young children. The family lived in Kazimierz, at 16 Brzozowa Street. I remember the house well, because as a child I visited my grandmother there very often. Her third floor walk-up apartment consisted of two rooms: a combination kitchen-living room and a bedroom. The entrance was from an outside walkway. Across the courtyard lived my grandmother's sister, Ester Małke, who married a man named Blonder. The Blonders had a stall selling clothing in the Sukiennice, the mediaeval Cloth Hall located in the middle of the *Rynek Główny*, the Main Market Square of Kraków. In the early nineteen thirties my grandmother still lived on Brzozowa Street, with her youngest daughter, Sonka and Sonka's husband Stephan Neuger. Sometimes in mid-thirties both Keila Hinda Rubin-Schmerler-Rosenberg and the Neugers, with their child, a boy named Ignaś, moved to the Aleksandrowicz house on Bernardynska 11, to an apartment on the ground floor, when my parents, my sister and I moved to a bigger apartment on the second floor.

A number of Aleksandrowicz family members and their relatives lived there, too. My grandfather Jacob and his second wife, Toni, lived on the second floor until his death in 1935. Afterwards my uncle Józek and his wife Sala, nee Neuman, moved into this apartment. Sala's brother, Shiya Neuman, his wife and their five children lived on the ground floor, next to my grandmother and my aunt Sonka Neuger. The six-room, fourth floor apartment was occupied by my aunt, Lola Aleksandrowicz, prior to her marriage in middle thirties. She and my mother ran a Montessori kindergarten in that space. I will describe that kindergarten elsewhere. In the next house, Bernardynska 10, also owned by my family, lived my uncle Olek with his wife, Barbara nee Infeld, and their two boys. Also, after my grandfather's death, his widow, his second wife, Toni Spitzer Aleksandrowicz, occupied an apartment on the third floor.

My mother's childhood could not have been easy. Her father, as befits a scion of a long line of rabbis, the Rosenbergs of Klasno/Wieliczka, studied the Talmud intensively but did not work for a living. His relationship with his large Klasno family was distant. He became very sick when my mother was a small child, and died of *consumption*. His widow eked out a living as a seamstress, taking piecework home. The older children, my aunt Pola, and my mother helped by sewing buttons and finishing buttonholes. While growing up poor, my mother had a thirst for knowledge, which served her well. She was thoroughly versed in Polish and Jewish history and lore. She spoke a literary Polish and Yiddish, she knew French and German and some Russian. She was familiar with Polish, French, Russian, as well as English, literature, the latter only in translation. Politically, she was close to leftist parties. At some point she drifted away from communism, because she was disappointed in its autocratic Soviet version idolizing Stalin and joined the Jewish democratic, socialist, anti-Zionist political movement, the Jewish Labor Bund. For many years she served as the librarian of the Jewish Labor Bund organization in Kraków on Dajwór Street. She remained friendly, however, with her former communist comrades and I knew many of them as a child, among them Marek Samuel and Różka Mandelbaum-Skrzeszewska. Along with my father, she became very active in the Bund and ran for city council on a Bund ticket. For both my parents, the Bund movement provided an important social activity and the intense focus of their political involvement.

I never knew how my parents met. I had assumed that it was as part of their political activities, but recently my stepmother told me a story, which has all the earmarks of being true. She said that they met in the theatre. It was customary in Kraków to get a subscription to a theatrical season and a subscription came with an assigned seat, so that at each performance the same people sat in the same spot. Young people would go to the theater with friends. My mother and her friend, Bronka Kranz, had such a subscription. In front of them sat two young men, my father, Maks Aleksandrowicz, and his friend, Emmanuel (Mundek) Scherer. The men were much taller than the young women, and obstructed their view. After much trepidation the two women gathered their courage and approached the men and asked if they could switch seats. The conversation that ensued led to dates and, eventually, the two men married the two women: Maks married my mother and Mundek married Bronka. The two couples remained friends. The Scherers moved to Warsaw and then, after the war to New York, where Mundek became General Secretary and leader of the World Coordinating Committee of the Jewish Labor Bund. He and my father remained close and continued their friendship in New York City. Both men died in New York City and both are buried near each other in a cemetery in New Jersey, as is Mundek's wife, Bronka nee Kranz.

My mother married my father in Paris shortly before my birth. I was born in June 1925. My name on my French birth certificate was Georges. This translated into Polish as Jerzy (pronounced Yeh-rzee). A diminutive of Jerzy is Jurek (pronounced Yoo-reck) and that is what I was called in Kraków. The family came back from Paris to Kraków when I was three months old. My mother had become an expert in pre-school education and was a follower of Maria Montessori. Our house was full of textbooks on pre-school education, some written by Friedrich Froebel, others by Montessori and Alfred Binet and a number of other experts. With her sister-in-law, my aunt, Lola Aleksandrowicz, my mother established in 1929 the first Montessori-style kindergarten (*Froeblówka*) in Kraków, probably in all of Poland. I was then four years old and I became their first pupil. I remember the kindergarten well. We had considerable freedom to pick any educational material from the many that were made available to us, but we also had to follow a strict routine: there was a time to play independently, a time for group activities and a time to clean up and put all the toys in their assigned places. No standard Montessori supplies or toys were commercially available, and all had to be designed by the two women and made to order for them. Among

the specially made furniture and supplies were small tables and chairs, a small set-up for washing hands and frames teaching children how to close buttons, tie bows, lace shoes, close snaps and other practical aides designed to develop daily living skills. Other toys included alphabet letters cut from heavy cardboard with color–coded front faces and sand paper backing, designed to teach the appearance and shapes of the letters through both visual and tactile exploration. Wooden building blocks and towers and a whole array of other teaching tools, all involving active voluntary participation, completed the supplies. The kindergarten routine called for the children to put everything away properly at the end, to sweep the rooms and to wash hands at a row of small washbowls. The atmosphere in the kindrgarten was warm and friendly. Other surviving pupils remember it fondly. Recently I heard from Eva Heller, now Toren, living in Israel, who has a fond recollection of her time there. In the kindergarten I met Adam Scharf, a grandson of Napoleon Telz, the owner of the foremost Krakovian printery, the *Drukarnia Narodowa*, who continued as my friend also in grammar school. I attended this kindergarten until 1931, when I became old enough to go to a public primary school. Also in 1931 my parents had a second child, my sister, Anna (diminutive: Hanka or Hanusia).

My mother was a slim attractive woman, with dark brown hair and deep dark green eyes. She was easy going and smiled and laughed frquently. She was well liked, made friends easily and had many many friends, women as well as men, many of whom I remember from my childhood. Her best friend Bronka Kranz married Mundek Scherer, a friend of my father. One of my mother's closest girl friends, Różka Mandelbaum, married Stanisław (Staszek) Skrzeszewski, a professor at Kraków's Teachers College. Staszek was not Jewish. He was what we would later call a communist "fellow-traveler". After the war, he became one of the movers and shakers in Poland's pro-Communist government. He served as Ambassador to France and then as Foreign Minister. Thus, my mother's friend, a Jewish girl from Kraków, became "*Lady Ambassador*" in Paris and "Lady Cabinet Minister, *Pani Ministrowa*" in Warsaw. I find this interesting because I remember that there was a popular novel published in Poland before the War, about a woman who suddenly found herself a *Pani Ministrowa* after a sharp change in the country's politics and formation of a very different government. In this case real events mimicked and even outshone fiction. Another of my mother's friends, Różka Goldschmidt married Leopold (Poldek) Leinkram. Her brother, Alexander (Olek) Goldschmidt was a prominent physician. Before the war he practiced medicine in the spa of Morsztyn. After the war he became an important activist, directing Polish government health policy. As I stated before, my parents were also friendly with prominent Polish Democratic Socialists in Kraków, Lydia and Adam Ciołkosz and Józef Cyrankiewicz. Cyrankiewicz was secretary of the Kraków branch of the PPS (Polish Socialist Party). Ciołkosz was a member of the democratically elected Polish Parliament in 1928. When I needed help, in 1937, to ace entry tests and interviews for the best secondary school *(gimnazium)* in Kraków, Lydia Kagan Ciołkosz acted as my tutor. During the War Adam and Lydia escaped to the West and he served as a minister in the Polish Government-in-Exile in Angers in France and then in London, and as a member of the rump Parliament-in-Exile, where he chaired the legislative budget committee. After the war, when Russia imposed a communist government on Poland, Polish (and surviving Jewish) leftists faced a choice: cooperate with the Russians or be arrested. In London Adam and Lydia Ciołkosz would not play Quisling and refused to return to Poland. They remained as exiles in London,

where they published a distinguished Polish monthly journal, *Kultura*. Cyrankiewicz, on the other hand, stayed in Poland, ran the socialist underground during the War, was caught by the Germans, sent to a concentration camp. Having been liberated by the Russians, he chose to work with them and, eventually, became Prime Minister of the pro-Communist Polish Government.

My mother had a good voice, enjoyed singing and reciting poetry. She knew an incredible array of songs in Yiddish and Polish, but also in Russian, French and German. Many of the songs were folksongs with long histories, the Yiddish ones mostly old standbys, but also folk ballads written by the contemporary Krakovian Jewish songwriter, Mordche Gebirtig, with whom my parents were very friendly. My mother admired Gebirtig and was instrumental in popularizing Gebirtig's songs, several of which she was the first to see and sing before they became widely known. I list below a few that I remember from my childhood. I have reasons to believe that my parents also helped Gebirtig financially. Among my mother's other favorites, and there were many besides the ones by Gebirtig, were two satirical poems, one of which was set to music, which I particularly liked. I well remember her helping me to recite the first one, a long Marshak poem popularized by Kadia Molodowska (1894-1975) satirizing a visit of a Mister Twister, an American millionaire, former member of the President's cabinet, to the Soviet Union (*Mister Twister, ghevezener minister, Mister Twister millionaire...gayt furn kein SSSR)*. And I remember her singing Itzik Manger's song/poem alternatively called The Golden Peacock (*Di Goldene Pave*) or *Rabeynu Tam*, about the learned Rabbi, grandson of the renown mediaeval Jewish scholar, Rashi, who presumably received a letter from the queen of Turkey, carried by a golden peacock. I still remember portions of it and can sing these excerpts today. Because the poem and the song were such favorites of ours, and I remember only small parts of them, I would like them to become generally known, I have been looking for their texts here in New York at various Jewish cultural organizations and on the Internet. Neither the poem nor the song is widely known and for several years I have not been able to find them. I have now been fortunate in having a friend in Shane Baker, Director of the World Congress of Jewish Culture in New York, and incidentally a translator of some of my articles, who found the Marshak poem through his contacts. It is too long to quote it here. And I received from my stepmother a yellowed tattered sheet containing the Yiddish text of the Manger's poem, which she found among family papers. This one I can now quote in its entirety:

Lomir zingen a sheyne lid	**Let us sing a pretty song**
Ay didl didl dam	Ay didl didl dam
Vi di goldene pave fleet	How the golden peacock flies
Ibern Shvartzn yam	Over the Black Sea
Un trogt a libes brivele	And carry a small love letter
A shayne libes brivele	A pretty little love letter
Tzum Rabeynu Tam, Oy, tzum Rabeynu Tam	To Rabbi Tam, Oy, to Rabbi Tam
Oy vay, yadiday, yadiday, oy vay, yadiday.	Oy vay, yadiday, yadiday, oy vay, yadiday.
Un ver hot dos briv geshribn	And who had written the letter
Ay didl didl day	Ay didl didl day
Dos brivele hot geshribn	The little letter was written by

Di malke fin Tierkay
Geshribn es mit roytn tint
Un farhasemt es geshvind
Mit hayse trern drei
Oy, Mit hayse trern drei
Oy vay…

Vos shteyt geshribn in brivele
Ay didle diddl day
Rabeynu Tam ikh libe dikh
Vuzheh shwaygstu nu
Ikh esse nisht, ikh trinke nisht
Ikh bin tsezetst fun benkenish

Ikh habe kayne rooh
Ikh habe kayne rooh
Oy vay…

Vuzhe zogt Rabeynu Tam
Ay didl didl day
Er glet di peyes un di bort
Un makht dray mol feh
Un dos tsighele in shtol
Un dos vaysse tsighele
Helft im mit a meh
O vay…

Vos zoogt tsi deym di rebetsn
Ay didle didle day
Zee shlugt im mit a valgherholtz
Un makht tsu im azoy
Shikses lign dir in zin
Un yakh, un yakh, un yakh wi bin
Dayn hays gelibte froy
Dayn hays gelibte froy
Oy vay…

Un ver hot dos lid gemakht
Ay didl didl day
A shnayder yoong hot es gemacht
Lekoved Rabeynu Tam
Shabes tsvishn tug un nakht
Hot a lets arayngemakht
Akurat tsum gram, oy, akurat tsum gram
Oy vay…

The queen of Turkey
She wrote it with red ink
And sealed it rapidly
With three hot tears
Oy, With three hot tears
Oy vay, etc

What is written in the little letter
Ay didle didle day
Rabbi Tam I love you
Why are you silent
I do not eat, I do not drink
I am pining with desire

I have no rest
I have no rest
Oy vay, etc.

What is Rabbi Tam saying
Ay didl didl day
He smoothes his peyes and his beard
And says three times feh
And the little sheep in a stall
And the little white sheep
Helps him with a meh
Oy vay, etc.

What says the rebbe's wife to this
Ay didle didle day
She beats him with a rolling pin
And says to him thus
Foreign women are on your mind
And where am I, am I, am I
Your dearly beloved wife
Your dearly beloved wife
Oy vay, etc.

And who has created this song
Ay didle didle day
A taylor youth created it
To honor Rabbi Tam
Saturday between day and night
He created a satire
Exactly to a tee, oy, exactly to a tee
Oy vay, etc.

Other Yiddish songs were frequently political satires with anti-tsarist, anti-Zionist and anti-fundamentalist overtones. The Polish songs were traditional folksongs and nursery songs, ballads written by the Polish bard, Adam Mickiewicz, set to music, or patriotic Polish anti-German and anti-Russian songs and hymns. She also sang simple songs written by Stefan Turski, the previously-mentioned author of Krakovian folk satirical musical plays, among them *Krowoderskie Zuchy* and *Lola from Ludwinów*, similar in a way to plays written at more or less the same time, by Gilbert and Sullivan. The German songs were all political. While the civil war raged in Spain, she also sang Spanish anti-fascist songs. She recited to us poems, among others, by Adam Mickiewicz, Juliusz Słowacki, Maria Konopnicka and Julian Tuwim, as well as by I. L. Peretz, Itzik Manger and Kadia Mołodowska and Kraków's own Mordhe Gebirtig.

Some examples from my mother's repertoir, selected at random:

Yiddish, traditional: Oyfn pripetchik s'brent a fayerl,
Yosl Behr geyt in militair,
Az der rebe Elimelekh is gevorn lustig freylekh;

Anti-tsarist: S'yogn, s'yogn shvartse volkn;
Yoshke foort avek,
Shluf Alexey yoyrish mayner;
Die Amurer batalionen gayen royt makhn di velt;

Anti-Zionist: Bin ikh mir a shloyme meene,
Zhabotinsky iz fin hayl un
Weizman fin finantsn;

Anti-Hassidic: Oyb ikh vawt geveyn da Boyre Oylom vos vawt ikh gemakht?

Mordhe Gebirtig's Kinder yorn, zeese kinder yorn;
Hey, tsiguele; Avreyml un Josele;
Shloymele liber, khvil endlokh wisn, zug mir dem emes,
vos iz mit dir...

Rayzele: Shtayt zikh dort in guesele, shtil fertrakht a hayzele,
drinen oyfn boydem-shtibl woynt mayn tayre Rayzele...
Ikh bin Avreiml, der feyigster marvikher, a groyser kinstler,
kh'arbayt laykht un zikher
S'brent, briderlekh, s'brent, inzer oorem shtetl nebokh brent...

Polish songs: Pod zielonym jaworem stoi lipa zielona; Hey tam pod lasem;
Wanda leży w Polskiej ziemi; Patrz Kościuszko na nas z nieba...;
Kto powiedział że Moskale są to bracia nas Lechitów...;
Nie będzie Niemiec pluł nam w twarz, ni dzieci nam guermanił...;

Polish childrens songs: Stary niedźwiedź mocno śpi; Nie straszny dla nas burzy czas;

Sroczka kaszkę ważyła, swoje dzieci karmiła;
Wlazł kotek na płotek i mruga, piękna to piosenka nie długa;

Polish ballad from the long poem "Konrad Wallenrod" by Adam Mickiewicz:
W gruzach już leżą Maurów posady; naród ich dźwiga żelaza;
Other ballads by Mickiewicz: Stary Budrys…;
Przysłowie niedźwiedzie;

Poems by Słowacki: Lila Weneda Ojciec zadżumionych:
Trzy razy księżyc odmienił się zloty...

French songs: Sur le pont d'Avignon;
Alouette, gentil alouette; Au clair de la lune;
Compagnons de la Marjolaine; and the anthem:
Allons enfants de la Patrie!

Russian/Ukrainian: Volga,Volga, mat' radnaya; Płacze Matka Ukraina; Słuszay;

German political song: Das Reich ist im Gefahr, das Reich ist im Gefahr;
Das Reich das niemals sich erwahr, ja, ja, sich erwahr...

Spanish anti-fascist: Ne passeron; Los Quatros generales, mamita mia;

Finally, an anti-Nazi German quattrain: Wir wollen kein Mahler aus Gotesgnaden
Wir wollen kein Fuehrer aus Berchtesgaden
Wir wollen kein Eintopfgericht mit Herring
Wir wollen so fressen wie Feldmarschall Goering.

When the war began in the fall of 1939, my father was drafted into the Polish army and my mother was left to cope alone with the cruel war conditions under the ruthless German occupation. At first we went to Central Poland, then came back to Kraków. The German occupiers were tightening the screws, food was scarce and expensive, our money supply uncertain. Life was getting dangerous. My mother tried her best to protect us, my sister who was eight in 1939 and me (I was fourteen), as well as her mother and her younger sister and child, all of whom were totally dependent on her survival skills. We were told to vacate our apartment on Bernardyńska Street, which was close to the Royal Castle Complex on the Wawel Hill that became the residence of the German governor of Poland, Hans Frank, and we moved to another Kraków apartment on Dietla Street. From October 26, 1939 all Jews, including teenagers, were ordered to engage in obligatory forced labor (*Zwangsarbeit*). From December 1, 1939 we were forced to wear armbands with the Star of David, identifying us as Jews and thus exposing us to incessant danger of beatings, arrests and random shootings. Jews were barred from many areas of the city. When it was important for us to go there to buy some necessities, the armbands had to be removed. A Jew caught without an armband was shot. We were all registered as permanent inhabitants of Kraków. In the summer of 1940 we appeared in person at the Jewish Community Center on Skawińska Street and were entered into a census. My mother registered as Scheindel Aleksandrowicz and her mother, Keila Rubin vel Rosenberg, served as a witness. One Ella Gross, whom I do not know, served as a second witness. That registration sheet with my mother's photograph and signature is preserved in the Jewish Historical Institute in Warsaw and a copy is available from the U.S. Holocaust Memorial Museum in Washington, D.C. Unfortunately, the photo is of a very poor quality and one can hardly see my mother's face.

In March 1941, when all Kraków Jews were ordered to move from Kraków proper to an enclosed ghetto in the outlying district of Podgórze, my mother decided that we should move out of the city. The entire family, including her mother, sister with son and my sister and me, moved to a nearby shtetl called Skała by Ojców, which at the time seemed safer than the very exposed ghetto inhabited only by Jews and enclosed by walls with controlled access. Skała was small enough not to warrant a German garrison, but the power of the occupier was felt there, too. As in most small rural townlets in Poland, this small town had a square in the center where a farm and notions market was held once a week. The square was paved with cobblestones and surrounded with single story wooden buildings containg stores selling food, paper goods, shoes, clothing, fabric, underwear, notions, etc. As in most small rural communities in Poland, the stores and the buildings around the square were owned and operated by Jews. At one point a group of German soldiers arrived, surprised a number of elderly religious Jews in the square and in the stores, dragged them out and proceeded to beat them, cut and tear their beards and left them all bloodied and injured, while laughing all the time as if having a time of their lives.

On German orders, Skała's mayor instituted a work obligation on local Jews and newcomers like us, including those as young as I was then. The work frequently consisted of breaking stones for road building with a hand-held heavy hammer and other work for which I had neither the strength nor the preparation. Our Skała interlude did not last long. Eventually, all Jews were forced to leave Skała, which was to become "*Judenrein*" (clear of Jews) and we had no choice but to move back to Kraków, to the Podgórze Ghetto. A brief attempt to have only me stay outside of the Ghetto and hide with a family of a municipal worker, failed when that family got frightened that somebody might denounce them for sheltering a Jew, which was punishable by death. Anyway, staying in a place illegally, not registered for a food ration, required costly food purchases on the black market which was both inordinately expensive and risky to boot, because somebody might become suspicious why the extra food was needed. While higher payments might have assuage the fears, we found the whole enterprise beyond our then limited means and the rest of the family was in the Ghetto, So, after a few weeks I joined my mother, sister, babcia and aunt Sonka and her son by smuggling myself into the Ghetto, the German-created "*Juedischer Wohnbezirk*" (Jewish Living Area), enclosed by walls with gates guarded by Jewish quislings commanded by Nazi SS-men. A small fragment of the Ghetto walls has been preserved in Kraków to this day and it displays a memorial plaque. In the Ghetto, my mother continued her underground political and social activities.

When the Germans were approaching Kraków in September 1939, all people who had been active in leftist anti-fascist politics, as well as most Jewish men of military draft age left the city and moved east, leaving behind the elderly, women and children. We all assumed, somewhat naively, that the German occupiers will make life hard for everybody,

but will not directly harm women and children. Nobody could have predicted the totally irrational demented way in which a presumably civilized Central-European nation like the Germans would engage in genocide and brazenly use poison gas to kill millions, including the very young and the very old, simply because they were born Jewish.

Even in the absence of men of military age, resistance to the occupiers began almost immediately in many ways, small and big. Passive resistance by most of the population was followed by the creation of active underground centers. With most of the male Bund activists being away, it became necessary to create a new, secret, underground organization in Kraków and my mother became one of the moving forces behind it. The illegal Bundist activities accelerated. At this time an official contact with the leaders of the Polish Socialist Party in Kraków was arranged. My mother was elected by the coordinating committee of the Jewish Socialist (Bundist) Underground to be the one to arrange and maintain contact with the Polish underground organizations connected with the Polish Government-in-Exile reconstituted in London. Pre-war Polish President Ignacy Moscicki resigned and the Poles selected the scion of a famous aristocratic family, count Edward Raczynski, as Polish President-in-Exile. All pre-War parties were represented in the Polish Government-in-Exile. However, locally only Polish Socialists were amenable to contacts with Jews. Leaders of the various Polish rightist, nationalist and religious parties were all anti-Semitic in varying degrees. Some had anti-Semitism as their exclusive political program, others had additional goals, but advocated boycott of Jewish enterprises for good measure. The rightist parties were not interested in helping Jews. The Government-in-Exile, in part for humanitarian reasons and in part because to do so was politically correct in the West, did formulate an official policy of helping Polish Jews. However, given the magnitude of the need, trying to save three million Jewish men, women and children from a cruel but efficient and determined German occupying force, that Polish Government was not in a position to do much. Saving small numbers of individuals here and there was about the limit of available help.

An official Polish underground government courier maintained formal contact between the organized military and civil resistance in occupied Poland, the so-called Polish "Secret State", and the Polish Government-in-Exile in London. His name was Jan Karski. He published recollections of his underground activities in Poland, including a transcript of a meeting with the leaders of the Jewish Resistance (Karski, 1944). He quoted my parents' friend, the chief Bundist underground leader in all of Poland, going under the alias *Berezowski*, thus: *"Our entire people will be destroyed. A few may be saved, perhaps, but three million Polish Jews are doomed. This cannot be prevented by any force in Poland, neither the Polish nor the Jewish Underground".* Before the War I knew Berezowski as Leon Feiner, a lawyer in Kraków and an elected member of the Kraków City Council from a Bund electoral list. He was a good friend of both my parents. I have reason to believe that Feiner deliberately picked the alias "Berezowski", because it highlighted the ignominious fact that the pre-War autocratic Polish government, eager to intimidate its political opponents including the democratic Jewish labor movement, arrested him and sent him to a concentration camp for political prisoners located in Bereza, which was modeled on the Nazis' notorious camp in Dachau. Feiner was the only Bundist leader sent to Bereza, so that all Bundists in Poland (and America) would immediately know who it was that was hiding under the "Berezowski" alias.

The courier, Karski, presented his information personally to both Winston Churchill and Franklin D. Roosevelt, as well as to the political and religious leaders of the Polish and Jewish communities in England and America, including Rabbi Stephen Wise. Public rallies were held in New York and London, but as we now know, nothing dramatic occurred and not much help was offered by those in positions of authority. One individual, Szmuel Zygielboym (war-time pseudonym: "Arthur"), the Bundist leader-in-exile in London, member of the Polish Parliament-in-Exile, tried to stir the world's conscience. He was continuously receiving communications from Feiner in Poland and presented this information to the Polish President-in-Exile in London, Edward Raczyński, the Prime-Minister General Władysław Sikorski, the Vice-Premier Stanisław Mikołajczyk, and the Minister of Information Stanisław Kot. He even approached the President of the Czech Government-in-Exile Eduard Benes because he thought that Benes, as a democrat, was better respected by the Allies than the somewhat autocratic Polish leaders. These officials, in turn, approached Foreign Secretary Anthony Eden and Winston Churchill. None of these efforts seemed to produce any results. In fact, the British Foreign Office issued a directive to the press asking it to downplay the horrific news dispatches arriving from Poland about Jews being killed by hudreds of thousands. Also downplayed were news from Poland in the New York Times and the rest of the American press. On August 31, 1942 Zygielboim received a coded telegram from Feiner: *"The German fury menacing the Jewish people in Poland destroys everything and increases in strength. Disaster after disaster befalls the city [Warsaw]. Now it is not thousands but hundreds of thousands of Polish Jews are dying. Almost the entire Jewish population is being exterminated, in the same manner men, women as well as children. Of the three and a half million of Polish Jews no more than one and a quarter million remain alive, and yet the massacres continue unabated*". Zygielboim went to 10 Downing Street in an unsuccessful attempt to show this dispatch to Churchill but was not allowed to see the Prime Minister. He continued to knock on doors but could not get British or American officialdom to respond to the disaster happening in Poland. In desperation, in May 1943 he took the ultimate step and publicly committed suicide hoping thus to awaken the World's conscience to the events in Poland. Sad to relate, even this desperate act failed to prod the civilized World to action.

In the meantime, my mother and Jacob Celemenski, a delegate of the central organization of the Jewish Labor Bund from Warsaw, met with Józef Cyrankiewicz, whom my mother knew from the time when he served as Secretary of the Krakovian branch of the Polish Socialist Party. During the War Cyrankiewicz became the leader of the Polish social-democratic resistance organization in Kraków. In the early stages of the War my mother frequently met with the Poles. Józef Cyrankiewicz let her know that he was aware of the existence of the Jewish Labor Underground and he was willing to make room for Jewish material in the underground newspaper, called "WRN" for *Wolność, Równość, Niepodległość* (Freedom, Equality, Independence). She frequently went to the liaison office of leftist lawyers, Emil and Aniela Steinsberg, to deal with assorted issues that pertained to Jews. At my mother's behest, Cyrankiewicz intervened with the Finance Ministry of the Polish Government-in-Exile in London. The exile government was routinely sending some financial help to the official Kraków Jewish Kahał, but that organization was dominated by its Zionist and religious members, hostile to the Bund, and refused to help Jewish socialists even while we all were the dire straits during the German occupation. Cyrankiewicz asked London to insure that my mother's Bundist organization got apporpriate monetary support for its social as well as underground activities. Cyrankiewicz's Polish socialists were ready, he said, to help with needed documents, "Aryan" identity papers, etc., even with an occasional gun for the incipient Jewish Fighting Organization. It was not easy, but a tenuous contact was maintained. Some Jewish underground activities in Kraków, among them bombing of the German officers' nightclub called Cyganeria and of the theater Bagatela on the corner of Karmelicka Street (where before the war we attended children's shows), made news, but most were kept quiet to minimize retribution.

My mother's activities in the Bundist underground resistance organization, both prior to our departure to Skała and after our return to Kraków Ghetto, were described by Jacob Celemenski, the Bundist underground courier who accompanied her on her first visit to the Polish Underground. Celemenski survived the War, came to New York and in 1963 published a book of memoirs in Yiddish, entitled "*Mit farschnittenem Folk*". Celemenski wrote (in my translation from the original Yiddish): "*... A few days later, in the apartment of Comrade M. Glazer took place the first meeting of Bundist activists. Represented were all branches of our movement. Among those present were Dr. Sziya Fensterblau, Luska Aleksandrowicz (wife of Maks Aleksandrowicz), Menashe Gumplowicz, Naftali Schisler, Motl Ksienski, Victor Wasserlauf, David Hilf, Fishel Eidelman, Max Milinski, Zygmunt Birkenfeld, Moniek (Moshe) Peltzman-Glazer, Fishek Harendorf (from the youth group), Cesia and Shlomo Yoine Blum and I. We debated two key issues: how to set up a contact with the Bundist center in Warsaw and how to arrange economic assistance for the families and the children, whose fathers were in prisoner-of-war camps or away in the Soviet zone. A special Aid Committee took on the task of finding needed medical help for women, the elderly and children. The Aid Committee was in contact with the Special Division of the Jewish Kahal. To the Aid Committee belonged Comrades Dr. Sziya Fensterblau, Naftali Schisler, Luśka Aleksandrowicz and Dr. Leon Nemer*". A small conspiratorial committee, consisting of Luśka Aleksandrowicz, Sziya Fensterblau, Moniek Peltzman-Glazer, Menashe Gumplowicz and Celemenski coordinated all underground activities.

There were many less publicized but critically needed activities of the Bundist underground in Kraków. Thanks to my mother's energy and initiative, the Jewish Labor underground organization opened a nursery for small children, whose fathers were away, unable to return. Keeping the children in a safe heaven enabled their mothers to scrounge for a living. The children, some undernourished, received a full day's food and were under proper care provided by experienced teachers. Thanks to the intervention of the Polish Socialists, the nursery received five thousand złotys from the funds provided by the Polish Government in London and that has enabled the nursery school to improve the diet, buy some toys for the children and, in a few cases, provide clothing. Celemenski described the nursery thus: "*In the darkness surrounding us, the nursery became an island of children's joy, resounding with Jewish songs – a truly warm corner where children could relax and enjoy themselves. The soul of the nursery was Luśka, by profession a pre-school educator, a young, serious woman with a tan face, deep mild eyes and a warm demeanor. She radiated energy. She showed a dedication to every single individual child. Like a devoted mother, she hugged the sad children, which did not know any closeness in their homes. When a mother wanted to scare and punish her child she would say to it: – tomorrow you will not go to the teacher Luśka*".

According to Celemenski, who visited the Ghetto in 1941 and early 1942, the Jewish community of Kraków, which prior to the War amounted to 60,000, now counted 20,000, even including those driven in from the surrounding communities. Celemenski attended meetings of the Bundist committee in the Ghetto. Present at the meetings were, besides my mother, Dr. Leon Nemer, Róźka Glazer, Israel Harendorf, David Hilf, Zygmunt Birkenfeld and Motl Księski. Celemenski stated "K*sięski reported that he is receiving underground news from the Polish Socialist Party, but that bringing these illegal documents into the Ghetto involves a great risk. The police and the Nazi-S.S. often conduct body searches at the entrance to the Ghetto. The papers are being carried by him, Comrade Księski, and by the young Yurek, the son of Maks Aleksandrowicz. They were indeed risking their lives".* ("Yurek" was how my name was pronounced in Kraków).

At the time I was a part of a small team of Jewish shoemakers who had a permit to leave the Ghetto and to ply their trade at a workshop in the center of the city. The key member of that group was Motl Księski, a master craftsman. Officially, the shop was crafting and repairing boots for the German Army, although I am not aware of any such boots having ever been handled. As a Bundist activist before the war, Księski knew and admired my father. His wife, Bertha, was the young woman, member of the Bundist youth group led by my father, who played with me when I was little. Księski suggested that I join their group as an apprentice. That is how come that I was in a position to be outside of the Ghetto and receive the underground messages and literature. All the underground newspapers were of small size, for obvious reasons. They required less paper and were easier to transport and easier to hide. The ones that I have received from a member of the Polish socialist resistance were six by eight inches in size, printed on thin shiny yellow-beige paper. The print was small, so that a lot of information was packed into a small format paper. Karski (1944), who in his book described and evaluated the underground press, gave the socialist press high marks: *"The publications of the Socialist Party contained a high level of reporting and a vigorous editorial policy. The chief organ of the party was WRN..."* The underground papers were distributed largely by volunteers, who risked their lives. I am proud to have been a small cog in the distribution chain.

To minimize risk of large disasters should a paper distributor be caught by the Gestapo, German Secret Police, individual distributor usually only knew the man who delivered to him or her and the individual to whom he /she delivered. Said Karski: *"When a paper carrier was discovered by the Gestapo, as others have been before by the Tsarist ,Okhrana', and submitted to torture...in the murder cellars by Himmler's men, he could give only these two names, no more. He did not know any more. This system worked, but only through wholesale circulation*". Indeed, I myself did not know the man who delivered the papers to me. A nameless non-descript person brought a bundle to my workplace. I do not recall anything about him. Had I been caught, I could not betray the name of my source or even provide a description. I gave my papers to an unnamed Bund activist in the Ghetto for distribution. I have no idea where the paper was printed. I could tell from its content that WRN was a national publication, but not where my copies originated. They could have been printed in one central location and then carried in bulk, at great risk, around the country, or written centrally but printed in many small local facilities. I believe the former was the procedure, and that the entire edition of the paper was printed at once. Karski (1944, 273-274) declared that *"the story of the underground press would include episodes of ingenuity and*

heroism. The boldness and enterprise that went into them was exceptional, since it functioned not merely to keep these periodicals alive but to make them in every way a provocation and threat to the Germans and a symbol of the unyielding attitude of Polish resistance. Energy was directed and dangers risked for the purpose of subjecting the Germans to contempt, and keeping up Polish morale by a defiant refusal to accept the occupation as a reality... The secret press was the means by which the underground state kept in direct contact with the large mass of population. Through it, the people were constantly kept aware of what was being done, so that their morale and hope were kept at a high pitch".

When a Jew was caught hiding on the "Aryan" side, he was immediately shot, as was the Polish family who hid him. In the Ghetto ruled the Jewish police, selected by the Nazis to help them control the populace. They acted cruelly and were thoroughly hated. Their commander in Kraków was Simkhe Spira, previously a very religious Jew, who now strutted like a peacock in a fancy yellow uniform. The members of the Jewish police, the "Ordnungsdienst", had hoped that acting for the Germans will help them survive, but the Nazis double-crossed them and killed most of them before the end of the war. These Jewish policemen, Polish policemen and German SS-men were manning the entrance to the Ghetto. Anybody arriving from the outside the Ghetto was, theoretically, subject to a body search, but such searches were conducted at random. At least one member of our small party was patted and searched each time, but youngsters were less likely to be searched than adults. Hence, as a teen-age boy of small stature, looking younger than my years, I was the one entrusted with bringing the illegal messages and literature into the Ghetto, carrying it under my clothing, on my body. The risk was obvious. Had I been caught, I would have been tortured to reveal what I might know and then killed. Many times I had stood nervously by as my companions were being searched. The illegal newspapers did not arrive daily, but at irregular intervals every few days. Fortunately, on the days that I was searched were the days that I did not have anything incriminating on me, except some food which was confiscated.

Difficult times bring the best in some people, at the same time as they bring the worst in others. Today, it is easy for us, comfortable and safe as we are, to blame people who behaved abominably in difficult times. At one point, late in 1941, we used up almost all of our resources. As befits her socialist convictions my mother did not believe in wearing jewelry, did not want any, did not buy any and often stated that her watch, an expensive *Cortebert* brand, was her only jewel. This did not matter prior to the war, but it became a drawback during the occupation when other women were converting their hoards of jewels for cash to live on and she did not have that kind of security. She was continuosly concerned with the problem of being able to pay for food and shelter but she still had one item of value, a large piece of tanned leather saved "for a rainy day" from our family's once-large leather warehouse. Leather, at that point, was very much in demand and very valuable and that one piece, which was big enough for several pairs of shoes, would provide her with money for a while. But it was dangerous for her to have it, since the warehouse was confiscated for the German Army and she was required to surrender all leather that she possessed. My mother entrusted selling that last valuable possession to a good friend of the family. He took it and she did not hear from him for a long time, after which she confronted him and he had no money for her and gave her a lame excuse about the leather having gotten stolen. My mother felt betrayed by one whom she trusted and that was the only time her children had seen her cry, losing her generally up-beat demeanor.

She could not understand how anybody could act selfishly in times in which survival depended on mutual assistance and unselfish cooperation. She herself never forgot her humanity and selflessly helped others whenever possible, even at great cost to herself. Thanks to her contacts with the Polish underground and within the Jewish secret organizations, she was in a position to save herself and her children. However, she did not abuse the trust placed in her and, at great personal sacrifice, she put others first, sent others to safety and she paid for it with her life. My mother and my little sister, along with her mother, sister and nephew were caught during one of the mass "deportations" from the Ghetto, on October 28, 1942, and sent to an unknown eastern destination, presumed to be a work and residence camp but which turned out to be an extermination center with gas chambers. The camp was located in Belżec in east-central Poland.

In Berlin in Germany there is now a large and very somber "Monument to the Six Million Murdered Jews of Europe", designed by Peter Eisenman and consisting of a very large and very somber field of cement steles, covering many blocks of desirable land near the Brandenburg Gate, which I visited recently and found very effective in evoking the horror of the Holocaust and thus very moving. Under the field of these cement monuments there is a small museum including an interactive exhibition listing, among other displays, all Nazi internment and extermination camps. In this list I found, with some effort, a general description of the Belżec camp and a slide of a color drawing of the camp. No photographs of the camp or its victims were available. Possibly there are some in the ITS collection in Bad Arolsen in Germany, but those are not yet available.

Preparing for the possibility of a deportation from Kraków to some eastern destination, perhaps a camp or a small distant village, my mother took a step to hide and take with her a small item of value that she purchased at the beginning of the war, a small gold coin, not much bigger than a dime. She got a cobbler to hide this coin by imbedding it between layers of the sole of my little sister's shoe. Clothing and shoes of those who died in extermination camps have been collected and some are now on display in museums of the Holocaust. I would not be surprised if my sister's shoe, still with its gold coin in it, graces one such exhibit, perhaps even the one in Washington, D.C.

In writing about my uncle Ignacy I stated that on the 7-th of September 1942, Eva, 19, and Hanka, 15, his daughters, along with their mother, Sala Aleksandrowicz nee Klipper, were being deported from the village of Skawina to the extermination camp in Bełżec. Riding in the train to their death, the mother managed by force to push Hanka out of the car, while the older girl, Eva, would not allow herself to be pushed out and insisted on remaining with her mother. This left Hanka alone in the Ghetto. She was a very sad and scared young woman, having lost her mother and sister, as well as her cousins, friends and relatives, except for my mother and me. She had, however, one reason to hope for a better future: she knew that her father was safe in the United States. My mother took her in and took care of her, physically and emotionally; she stayed with us in our cramped quarters. At the first opportunity that presented itself, the Bundist underground organization in Warsaw arranged for Hanka to get false papers and to be sent to Warsaw where nobody knew her and nobody could identify her as Jewish. There, they arranged for her to be a live-in maid in a friendly Polish home. Unfortunately, all that effort was in vain. In 1944 Warsaw erupted in an armed insurrection and the Germans proceeded to destroy the city, street by street, block by block. Somehow, in the upheaval, Hanka was wounded and perished.

Celemenski obviously liked and respected my mother. He was quite aware how difficult was her life: *"...Herself, Luśka had a hard life. At the start of the War, her husband, comrade Maks, was called to Polish military service, later he went from Lemberg* (Lwów) *to Vilna. Luśka was left with her two children; Yurek – 12 years, and Hanusia – 9 years old.* (actually, I was 14 and my sister was 8). *Together with them were her mother and sister, Sonia Neuger with a child of five. Luśka had to care for the entire family. At the time they lived in three rooms on Dietlowska Street. In one of the rooms Luśka ran a private kindergarten for ten children, with wealthier families paying a fee, to have the children play there for a few hours a day. This was her private enterprise. Luśka was also very active in political party work. In spite of all this hardship, she always was very optimistic. She was always very friendly with the parents of the children as well as with all her comrades and friends. She created a warm atmosphere in our difficult daily life".*

Celemenski further described my family in the Ghetto thus (p. 189): *"...I have conferred with a number of comrades, among them, Luśka, wife of M. Aleksandrowicz. She looks tired and exhausted from her heavy work. Her head is already covered with silver, but from her young face shine her mild, wise eyes. Next to her sit her children Hanusia and Yurek, and stands Hanusia – the younger daughter of Dr. Ignacy Aleksandrowicz. They all lived through difficult times. Dr. Aleksandrowicz's daughter has already lost her mother and her older sister. They were deported to the gas chambers. I can feel their pain, when Luśka asks me whether perhaps I could take Hanusia, Ignacy's daughter, with me to Warsaw. When I returned to Warsaw, indeed I have taken her with me. The comrade Luśka did not cave in, she maintained a brave front. Yurek had already been working with comrade Księski in a workshop on the "Aryan" side... Luśka and her little girl, tragically, did not avoid the bitter fate of the Jewish people... She, and her family, were deported and killed. In my memory persists the living image of that evening when we had taken leave of each other and each went our own way".*

On October 28, 1942, while I was at work outside of the Ghetto, my mother and my 11-year-old sister, Anna (Hanka), were caught by the Nazis in our appartment, assembled in a square, marched in rows of five to a railroad yard, packed in cattle cars, removed from Kraków and shipped to an unknown destination. My mother could have saved herself from the deportation, but she would not abandon her daughter, her elderly mother and her sister with the small child. We know now that they were all sent to an extermination camp in Bełżec, near Lublin in central-eastern Poland. Luśka Aleksandrowicz and her daughter Hanka, my grandmother Keila Rubin and my aunt Sonka Neuger and little cousin Ignas, were never heard from again. The extermination camp in Bełżec functioned only briefly, but that is where most of the trains carrying Kraków Jews were sent. A monument to the fallen in Bełżec was recently dedicated in the presence of relatives of the victims, the President of Poland and the American and Israeli ambassadors. My friend Guta Godstein, widow of my friend from concentration camp and post-war stay in Italy, Ludek Goldstein, has written a poem about deaths in gas chambers, which I find appropriate to quote below.

When the Kraków Ghetto was dissolved, in March 1943, I and one of my uncles, Olek Aleksandrowicz, were sent to the concentration camp built in a suburb of Kraków, called Płaszów, then to camps in Mauthausen, Melk on the Danube, and Ebensee in the Tyrolean Alps. In February 1945 my uncle Olek, died in my presence. In May 1945, thin and emaciated, barely alive, I was freed by the American Third Army. In July 1946, as the only survivor of the Holocaust in my immediate family, I came to the United States and joined my father and my uncle Ignacy. My father lost his wife and daughter, my uncle Ignacy lost his wife and both daughters. All the rest of my immediate family who resided in Kraków in 1939, my grandmothers, twelve of my uncles and aunts and all eleven of my young cousins perished in the Holocaust. Of the latter the oldest was eighteen, the youngest was not quite three.

In writing this chapter I have relied heavily, besides my own recollections, on two books, from which I have quoted liberally: the memoir of Jacob Celemenski (1963), the brave courier of the Jewish Underground during the War in Poland, written in Yiddish, excerpts of which I have translated myself, and a book by Jan Karski (1944), the messenger of the Polish National Underground State during the German occupation, who smuggled himself to the West and personally reported to Churchill and Roosevelt on the happenings in Poland, including a description of the massacre of millions of Jewish men, women and children. A brief biography of my mother Salomea (Luska) Aleksandrowicz was included in the book "*Doires Bundistn*", (Generations of Bundists) edited by J. S. Hertz (1968), including a photo with children, taken approx. in 1937. The book by J. Celemenski also includes a photo of my mother, my sister and myself.

As I stated above, I was impressed by a poem recently written in Melbourne in Australia by my friend Guta Goldstein, widow of Ludek Goldstein who was with me in the German concentation camps and later in the UNRRA camp in Italy. The poem, entitled *Genocide in Rows of Five* (Goldstein, 1999, 171) follows:

Multitudes in rows of five,
Counted like cattle
Morning and night.
In rows of five
They endured and died,
Old people and children.
In rows of five.
Young women and men
Of their freedom deprived,
Their lives as yet unlived
In rows of five.

In rows of five,
Defenceless and ill.
They were brought here
In cattle trains,
Against their will.
In rows of five.
They kept hope alive,
Their will to survive.
In rows of five.
They were led to their death
Into chambers filled with gas.

Fig. 068. Salomea Scheindel Rubin Aleksandrowicz with her newborn son, Jerzy, now George Alexander, Paris 1925;

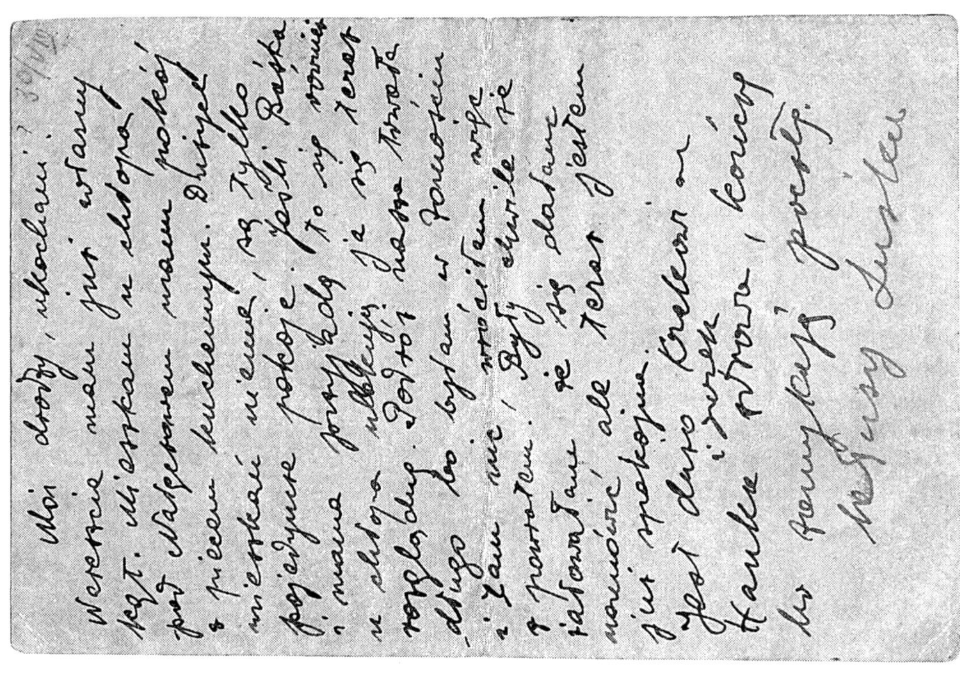

Fig. 069. A postcard dated two days before World War II began in Poland

A POSTCARD FROM MY MOTHER, DATED AUGUST 30, 1939

The Second World War broke out in Poland on September 1, 1939. At the time, my father was drafted into the Polish Army, while I, with my mother and sister, left Kraków and moved further east to avoid the incoming German Army. We rented a room from a Polish peasant, Antoni Sygnowski, in Chrószczów, near Nałęczów, in the Lublin district of East-Central Poland. The postcard is interesting because it is dated August 30, 1939, i.e. 2 days before the outbreak of the War and it carries a receipt stamp of the main Post office in Kraków (Kraków 1) from August 31, 1939, the last day before the German onslaught. I find it a tribute to the Polish mails that they functioned so efficiently even at the time of general mobilization and wide-spread panic and fear of the German bombs.

My mother wrote:

Moi drodzy, ukochani!
Nareszcie mam własny kąt. Mieszkam u chłopa pod Nałęczowem, mam własny pokój z piecem kuchennym. Dużych mieszkań nie ma, są tylko pojedyncze pokoje. Jeśli Baśka i mama przyjadą to się również u chłopa ulokują, ja się teraz rozglądnę. Podróż nasza trwała długo bo byłam w Zamościu a tam nic, wróciłam więc z powrotem! Były chwile że żałowałam że się dałam namówić, ale teraz jestem już spokojna.
Jest dużo Krakowian. Hanka i Jurek zdrowi, kończę bo zamykają pocztę.

Całusy Luśka

In English:

[My dears, loved ones!

Finally I have my own corner. I am living with a peasant near Nałęczów. I have my own room with a kitchen stove. Large apartments are not available, only single rooms. Should Baśka and mom come here they would also stay with a peasant, I will look around. Our trip was long because we went to Zamość where there was nothing so I turned back! There were moments when I regretted that I let myself be convinced, but now I am calm. There are many Krakovians. Hanka and George are fine. I am closing because they are about to close the post office

Kisses Luśka]

JÜDISCHE GEMEINDE
KRAKAU -- SKAWINERGASSE Nr. 2

PROTOKOLL

aufgenommen am 8/VIII 1940.

In der Kanzlei der jüdischen Gemeinde in Krakau erscheinen: Aleksandrowicz Scheindel aus Krakau

derzeit wohnhaft in Krakau Dietelsgasse 57 und die Zeugen:

a) Gross Ella von Beruf

wohnhaft in Krakau Dietelsgasse 9 ausgewiesen durch Ausweispass N°3629/24 ausgestellt d. die Krakauer Polizeidirektion am 1/9 1924

und

b) Rubin f. Rosenberg Keila von Beruf

wohnhaft in Krakau Dietelsgasse 57 ausgewiesen durch Ausweispass N° 4172/24 ausgestellt d. die Krakauer Polizeidirektion am 27/9 1924

Die Zeugen erklären folgendes:

Aleksandrowicz Scheindel geboren am 30/9 1900

in Krakau Stand verheiratet

Beruf aus Krakau

derzeit wohnhaft in Krakau Dietelsgasse 57

1940 registration card of mother, in the Jewish Community Council in Kraków

Obiges erklären wir, zwecks Erteilung eines Personalausweises von seiten der Jüdischen Gemeinde in Krakau in Angelegenheit der Umsiedlung des (der) Genannten von Krakau nach

Die Richtigkeit obiger Angaben bestätigen wir durch unsere eigenhändigen Unterschriften:

Ella Gross
Als Zeuge

Rosenberg
Als Zeuge

Aleksandrowicz Scheindel
Antragsteller

Fig. 070 Photostat of my mother's 1940 registration

Chapter 25. My mother's family, Rubin, Schmerler, Rosenberg

Since mediaeval times the salt-mine town of Wieliczka near Kraków boasted a privilege of *non-tolerandis Judeis*, therefore Wieliczka Jews lived just outside the township border and developed an area known as Klasno. The local Wieliczka synagogue was located on the Klasno side of the Klasno-Wieliczka border. The pattern continued into the 20-th Century. The synagogue no longer exist, having been destroyed by the Nazis during World War II. Thus it was that my grandfather Izak Rosenberg was born in 1865 or 1866 not in Wieliczka but in Klasno. Izak was the son of the Rabbi of Klasno, but apparently, his birth was not recorded with the civil authorities, because it does not appear in the civil Wieliczka/Klasno records. The state would have considered his birth illegitimate, although his parents marriage was sanctioned by a rabbi and was fully accepted in his social milieu. I found it difficult to trace his family tree, because, I assume, even had he been registered at birth he would have been entered under the surname of his mother, not his father, as did his father before him. From assorted inferences it appears likely that his grandparents were related and both may have carried the same surname. From a Jewish marriage record *(ketuba)* in possession of David M. Burns, another descendant of the Rosenbergs of Klasno, it appears that Izak's grandfather was Rabbi Abraham Rosenberg, father of Bluma, and that Izak's father, whose name may have been Juda Leib Rosenberg, was also a rabbi of Klasno. I have reason to believe that Juda Leib Rosenberg's wife, whom he married in the synagogue without registering with civil authorities, was a relative, perhaps a second cousin, and also likely to have carried the surname Rosenberg, because that was Izak's surname, and therefore it must have also been that of his mother. It seems that Juda Leib died before 1902, because then his son Izak gave that name to his son, whom I knew as my uncle Leibek, my mother's younger brother.

Izak Rosenberg became a permanent resident of Kraków in 1890. The official Kraków voter list of 1911 lists him as residing at Brzozowa 16, where his widow lived until

1935. His occupation was given as an egg dealer. The Kraków 1925 census listed him again, under item # 1658, as residing with his family at 16 Brzozowa Street in the Kazimierz area. It was noted in that listing that he was "ritually married", of mosaic persuasion, a Polish citizen of Jewish nationality, speaking in "jargon" (a somewhat disparaging term for the language we now refer to as Yiddish). I believe that he died earlier but was still carried on the books in 1925.

According to the data presented in the Polish "*Spis Mieszkańców*" (List of Inhabitants) of the City of Kraków in Poland, dated September 1925, Volume XIII, item # 1659, his wife Klara Schmerler, a seamstress, born in 1872 in Perehińsko, powiat (district) Dolina, came to Kraków in 1897, at the ripe age of 25. Perehińsko was then a small *shtetl* in the region of Northeastern Carpathia, between the towns of Stryj, Kołomyja, Drohobycz, Tarnopol and Stanisławów (today Ivanovo-Frankivsk in Western Ukraine). Once predominantly Jewish, the shtetls in the area have no Jews today. The listed towns in the area were also once predominantly Jewish.

When Klara was born in 1872 the region was a part of the Habsburg Kingdom of Galitzia and Lodomeria, with the Austrian Emperor Franz Joseph as King. Lwów (Lemberg, today Lviv) was the capital of the entire region. Kraków served as the central city of the western part of Galitzia. The area was mountainous, neglected and poor. The towns and the small townlets located north and south of the chain of Carpathian Mountains were largely Jewish; countryside was inhabited by poor, largely illiterate, peasants, Eastern-Orthodox Ruthenians, who owned very small pieces of land. They grew their own food, potatoes, rye, corn or perhaps buckwheat, had a few chicken and maybe a cow, but hardly any cash. They bartered with the shtetl Jewish shopkeepers for such few necessities as fabric for clothing and leather for a pair of shoes for Sunday and then used shtetl Jewish tailors and cobblers to convert these into a dress, a suit of clothing and a pair of shoes. There were in the area a few large estates, owned by Austrian or Hungarian aristocrats, such as the Counts Esterhazy or Zapolya. Also, there were a few large residences of Hassidic "*tzadiks*", miracle-maker rebbes, supported in style by ultra-pious Jewish followers. There was no industry except for an occasional flour or lumber mill, owned by a rich aristocrat and often leased and run by a Jewish operator. Indeed, one such mill was operated by one of my Birnbaum ancestors. Energetic young people, Jewish as well as non-Jewish, had little future in this depressed area, and migrated to larger towns, either in Galitzia, like Lwów and Kraków, to Austria proper, Vienna, or even, miracle of miracles, to America. The young Schmerler girl moved from Perehinsko to Kraków, in Western Galitzia.

After a few years in Kraków Keila Hinda Schmerler was officially recorded by Polish clerks in the 1925 register as Klara married to Izak (Yitzhak) Rosenberg in Kraków. The marriage was earlier performed by a rabbi in a synagogue and was not then officially recognized by the civil authorities. Any children of the union were then considered illegitimate by the Austrian state. In this same list of 1925, the profession of Klara Schmerler, ritually married to Izak Rosenberg, was given as "*szwaczka*" (seamstress). Also shown in the list were her children, Juda Leib Schmerler, born on August 28, 1902, whom I knew as Leibek, and Sarah, born on April 7, 1909, whom I knew as Sonka Rosenberg. Listed separately as independent individuals with a different surname under items # 1660 and 1661, were Klara's two older children, daughters, Paulina (Pola) Rubin, born on December 7, 1898 and Salomea (Luśka) Rubin, born on September 30, 1900. The latter became my mother.

I have not been able to establish where the surname "Rubin" came from, but I assume that it was among Klara's surnames. If her parents were also only "ritually married", then perhaps her father's surname was Schmerler and her mother's was Rubin, and when registering her first children they did not establish legally who the father was and, therefore, were forced to use the mother's name in registering the births. Then, either Klara's parents have established that they were married or the civil authorities began recognizing religious unions, so that the next child, a son, was registered at birth as Juda Leib Schmerler. Then Klara and Izak must have registered their own marriage with the civil authorities or these recognized the validity of their marriage so that their youngest daughter was listed as Sarah Rosenberg. I remember having seen my mother's original birth certificate as a child; it stated that she was an illegitimate child of Keila Hinda Rubin, but then the certificate added a comment that *Jako ojciec przedstawił się niejaki Izak Rosenberg* ("As father presented himself one Izak Rosenberg"). This confirms that, at the time of my mother‘s birth, my grandparents have had only a religious marriage. This was obviously quite common among strongly religious, non-assimilated Jews in Kraków. Because of that, the civil authorities considered the children illegitimate and had them registered, if at all, carrying the mother's, not the father's, surname. Confusion arose, when the family later attempted to correct that and have the children get the father's name, because, as I just stated, the parents themselves were likely to have been offspring of unregistered marriages and they, too, carried their mother's last names. In this case, Keila and Izak‘s‘ four children carried three different surnames: Rubin, Schmerler and Rosenberg.

I remember, when visiting my grandmother ("*babtcia*") on Brzozowa 16, who lived on the third floor walk-up, she used to call out to her sister who lived at the same address, but on a different staircase, across the courtyard. My grandmother was a short woman, vivacious but quiet, always cheerful and dignified. She was very religious herself, wearing a wig, praying regularly in a small local synagogue, keeping a strict kosher cuisine, insisted on fasting on fast days even when she was quite old and her children tried to convince her that she does not have to fast when it interferes with her health. My mother and I and my little sister used to worry about her on Yom Kippur and we spend a lot of time standing in front of her small prayer house on Koletek Street, ready to be there, in case of need, to help her. She would come out every now and then and reassured us that she is doing well. Her hair was shaven, which I did not know until later during the War, and I usually saw her in her plain, brown, weavy wig. As far as I can judge, her religious convictions were standard orthodox, not Hassidic. I did see, however, that for all her deep convictions, she was very understanding of people who were not religious and tolerated the fact that all her children, my mother and her siblings, abandoned all religious rituals and became essentially atheists. She loved us all fiercely and was very protective of her brood and we reciprocated and loved her in return.

In her house on Brzozowa Street there was a moving clothline strung between my grandmother‘s and her sister‘s windows, which could be pulled with the wet clothing on it. Written notes could be attached to the line and sent to the other side. It sounded to me, as a child, that "*Babtcia*" called her sister with one word, "Estomowkay", which I now translate as Ester Małke (Queen Esther). Her married name was Blonder.

When I looked up Blonder in the same 1925 listing, I found, in Volume XIII, Items # 1610-1611, Hirsch Blonder, merchant, born 1886 in Kraków, his wife Erna, born 1884 in

Perehinsko, powiat Dolina, and their Kraków-born children, Franciszka, born 2.VII.1914, Israel, born 7.VIII.1916 and Szymon, born 6.VI.1920. I know from personal knowledge that the Blonders operated a stall in the Sukiennice (Cloth Hall) in the Main Square of Kraków (Rynek Główny) – I have often stopped at their stall when walking through the Rynek, which was almost daily. The surprise of that listing was the next name, that of Cirla Schmerle (!), widow, mother-in-law of Hirsch, born 1849 in Perehinsko, resident in Kraków since 1920. I assume that the two sisters, Klara and Erna (Keila Hinda and Ester Małke), both married and with children, brought their widowed mother to Kraków, after their father died. This Cirla, then, was my great-grandmother on my mother's mother's side. I never met her, she must have died before my birth in 1925.

There are some inconsistencies in the 1925 data. I was born in June 1925. I was given my mother's father's Hebrew name, Izak or Yitzak, so her father must have died before I was born, yet he is listed in the 1925 census as residing on Brzozowa 16 (item # 1658). In 1922 my aunt Pola Rubin (item # 1660) married Maurice Falek and had moved to Paris and there had a son, my cousin Jacques, born in Paris in 1924. The census birth dates and places are correct, but the information seems to have been collected not in 1925 but earlier. I knew my mother's full maiden name was Salomea Scheindel Rubin. In May 1925 she married Maksymilian (Maks) Aleksandrowicz, son of Jacob and Hanna Hinda nee Birnbaum in Paris, France. I was born shortly thereafter. My grandmother was killed in the Holocaust, in the Bełżec extermination camp in October 1942. She was 70.

My mother's older sister, my aunt Pola Rubin married Maurice (Maniek) Falek in Kraków and the two of them then emigrated to Paris, France, where they modified the spelling of their surname to Fallick. Maniek Fallick established a furrier atelier and workshop at 271, rue St. Denis. I first met my aunt Pola, her husband and their son, Jacques, as a small child, when they visited us in Poland, in 1928 or 1929, but I have only a scant recollection of their visit because I was only three or four years old and my cousin was a year older. When the Germans occupied Paris in 1940 Pola, her husband and their teen-age son escaped from Paris and survived in a small village in Vichy France. After the war they returned to Paris. They continued to live at 271, rue St. Denis in the second arrondissement.

Eventually, my cousin Jacques married Yvonne, a multi-talented artist, born in Britany in the town of Treguier. My wife and I visited Pola and Maniek a few times in Paris and stayed with them at the rue St. Denis. Maniek died in the seventies. Since then, Jacques visited us many times in New York where he came often on business and we visited him repeatedly in Paris. My knowledge of French has decreased over the years, but both Jacques and his wife speak fluent English, so communication between us was never a problem. We enjoyed being together. Jacques acquired an old country farm 70 kilometers from Paris in a hamlet of Heurteloup, a part of the community called Longnes, not far from the small town of Anet, the site of a chateau built for the royal favorite Diane de Poitiers. Jacques is busy renovating the many buildings on the estate, while Yvonne tends to its flower and vegetable garden. They also have a pied-a-terre in Paris, fabulously located around the corner from the Champs Elysees. We visited them many times and enjoyed both places. Last time we visited my aunt Pola in Paris, in 1998, on her 100-th birthday; she was in good health. Alert, capable of walking, optimistic and cheerful, she moved from her third-floor walk-up to an old-age home, but refused to allow her son to sell her old apartment, and announced

that she will return soon to her own home and will host us there on our next visit to Paris. She died in her own room in a Rotschild Home for Seniors in Paris. Toward the end she had been very weak and she slept a lot. Pola was born on 7 December 1898. She died in mid-2005 in her 107-th year.

I have described my mother, Luśka Rubin Aleksandrowicz earlier. Her only brother, Leibek Schmerler, born in Kraków in 1902, married Rosa, whose maiden name I do not remember. Leibek and Rosa had two children, a girl, Mira (diminutive, Mirka), born in 1931 and a boy born in 1939. I remember Leibek as a pleasant, very intelligent man, deeply devoted to his children. I remember that he was of short stature, almost bald, although he was still in his mid-thirties. His wife was an attractive, dark-haired unassuming woman, usually very quiet and soft-spoken. Leibek worked as a teller in a private Krakovian financial institution, the Bank Holzera. Being a teller in a bank in Kraków in the thirties was a highly responsible occupation. Banks were not open to just anybody. They dealt mostly with wealthy businessmen issuing letters of credit, loans and exchanges and checks (*veksels*) as a form of private currency. A teller had to deal with creditworthiness and with defaults and bankruptcies, often involving very large sums of money. My uncle Leibek was also very active in Jewish politics; he was a leader of the Left wing of the Kraków Poale-Zion organization. This was the group that evolved, in Israel, into the Mapam party, strongly leftist but not communist. As a Labor Zionist, Leibek believed in workers' rights but in a Jewish state in Palestine. He often had heated discussions with my father, who thought that equal rights for Jews in Poland were of higher, more immediate, priority because Palestine does not have room for more than a fraction of the many millions of Jews from Poland, Ukraine, Russia and, for that matter, from Western Europe and the United States. Leibek escaped from the Germans in 1939 to Równe in Wolhynia, now Belarus, but the Germans caught up with him in 1941 and he did not survive. His daughter, Mirka, was the same age as my sister and the two girls were extremely close. I liked Mirka very much, she was a very pretty vivacious little girl, often mischievous and always ready with a smile. She was a frequent presence in our house and often stayed for the night in a pajama party. Mirka was 11, when she, her mother and her baby brother perished in 1942 in the Bełżec extermination camp. A photograph of Mirka, attached at the end of this chapter, taken in Kraków in 1936 or 1937 shows her at the age of approximately 5 or 6, and it proves what a pretty, delightfully pixyish child she was.

My mother's younger sister Sonka married Stefan Neuger (1906-1978). They had a son, Ignaś, born in 1934. My grandmother, Keila Rubin Schmerler Rosenberg lived with Sonka and her family, first on Brzozowa 16 and then on the ground floor of the Aleksandrowicz house on Bernardyńska 11. Sonka was a pretty blond, soft-spoken and quiet. Her husband was even quieter than she was, I hardly remember him ever speaking. After the outbreak of the war, Stefan, who was of draft age but was not drafted because time was too short, and had every reason to fear being caught under the German occupation, escaped from Kraków to the east of Poland. Eventually, he joined the leftist partisans in the eastern woods, survived the war and was decorated for bravery in battle with the Polish Knight's Cross and other medals. He was buried in an imposing tomb in the Kraków Miodowa Street Jewish cemetery. During the War his wife and child moved together with us to save money. When we had to leave Bernardyńska Street, we moved together to Dietla 57 and then for a while to a small town, Skała near Ojców. My aunt Sonka

took her husband's absence and the war conditions very hard. Without resources, she was completely dependent on my mother, and I am sure it was not easy for her. She was tense and had fits of crying. Not surprisingly, little Ignaś suffered a lot and, at 7, became very difficult to handle, particularly in our cramped war-time quarters, which did not allow for any privacy or respite from being in the continuous presence of other people. The Germans decided to concentrate all the Jews in a few large ghettos, where they would be easier to control. We now know that they wanted to facilitate assembling the Jews for transport to extermination camps. As I stated earlier, we were forced to move to the Kraków ghetto. On the 28-th of October 1942, my mother and sister, my grandmother and my aunt Sonka and Ignaś were taken to the death camp in Bełżec and I never saw any of them again.

Fig. 071. My cousin Mirka Schmerler at the age of 5;

STEFAN NEUGER
30 IX 1906 – 6 V 1978
UCZESTNIK II WOJNY ŚWIATOWEJ
WYRÓŻNIONY KRZYŻEM KAWALERSKIM O.P.
I WIELOMA ODZNACZENIAMI BOJOWYMI
DZIAŁACZ ŻYDOWSKICH ORGANIZACJI
SOCJALISTYCZNYCH I TSKŻ
DROGI MĄŻ, OJCIEC I DZIADEK

Fig. 072. Tombstone of Stefan Neuger, husband of my maternal aunt, Sonia

Part VII. JERZY ALEKSANDROWICZ (GEORGE ALEXANDER), 1925–

Chapter 26. Birth in Paris, childhood in Kraków, 1925-1939

I was between two and three years old when I received as a gift a chocolate doll in the shape of a boy, covered in silver foil. As I recall it now, the figurine was approximately 6-7 inches tall. After I stripped the foil the figure was black and I referred to it as my "*murzynek*" (little black boy). I loved the chocolate figurine, would not eat it, and for days carried it around and even took it to bed and slept with it. One evening, drowsy from sleep I must have bitten off and eaten a piece of chocolate from the figure's head. The figure was not made of solid chocolate but was empty inside and the opening in the head that I had made extended all the way to the figurine's feet. When I realized what I did I felt extremely guilty and cried that I had "killed" the little black boy. Obviously, I was very verbal at that point. Apparently, I became quite upset and could not be consoled. My mother took the figure from me and put it high up on a shelf in a china cupboard, behind glass. I remember that cupboard: it was highly varnished, veneered in walnut wood, with Art Deco inlays. It had a center mirror and its beveled glass panels were etched with a geometric design, not unlike the Frank Lloyd Wright glass patterns. Since I knew that the black boy was up there, whenever I looked up in that direction I cried and cried. Eventually, the boy disappeared from the cupboard, but I still continued to cry whenever I looked towards the shelf where it once stood. The incident must have occurred before we moved when I was close to three years old. It is my earliest recollection from my childhood.

I have now come to relate how my own experiences from birth in Paris, through childhood in Kraków and wartime struggles during the Holocaust illuminate the over-all history of Krakovian Jewry during the mid-twentieth century. Of course, large portions of my story have already been told as parts of my desciptions of the lives of my parents and cousins. To protect myself and to keep my emotions in check, I have tried to present my own life in a reasonably detached manner, in keeping with the style of the rest of

this history of my city's and my family. My recollections, as I suppose is only natural, tend to concentrate on pleasant memories and give rather short shrift to the difficult times. Unlike the accounts of many Holocaust survivors, most of them very emotional, providing a plethora of horror stories, mine will not dwell on the horrors of the time, which were real enough. I aim to present remembered events as dispassionately as is possible for me, today, after more than sixty years had elapsed.

In 1924 my parents were in love but did not get married in Kraków, because of strenuous objections of my father's father. My grandfather, Jacob Aleksandrowicz, was well off at the time. He had seven children and expected all of them to marry well, i.e. to offspring of rich important families. All did, except my father, who wanted to marry a poor girl whose father, while of important parentage (son and grandson of Rabbis Rosenberg of Wieliczka/Klasno, a town near Kraków), was sickly and had died, leaving a widow with four children who eked a living by doing piece-work as a seamstress. She earned a meager amount by working at home so that she could stay with her young children. Her two older girls, Pola, born in 1898, and my mother, Luśka, born in 1900, as they were growing up, helped with the work by sewing buttons and eventually by sewing shirts on an old foot-pedaled Singer sewing machine.

This proposed marriage was especially galling to my grandfather, because my father was, as I could tell even as a child, his favorite. It is my definite impression that Jacob Aleksandrowicz considered two of his sons, Ignacy, and my father, Maks, as smarter than his other children. He trusted my father's intellect. Years later when in his will he left his leather business to his three younger sons, it is to my father that he entrusted the direction of the business. He relied on my father's business acumen throughout.

He was, therefore, upset that my father wanted to marry a poor young woman. But, to no one's surprise, my father was stubborn and eventually he did marry my mother, if not in Kraków, then in Paris. In particular, after I was conceived in 1924, as my father told me, he was eager for me to carry his surname and, his father's opposition or not, he was determined to marry. My mother, because she was pregnant and not married, left Kraków and went to stay with her older married sister. By 1925, my mother's married sister, Pola Fallick (Falek) nee Rubin, lived in Paris. The ostensible reason for my mother's trip to Paris was to study at the Sorbonne, the famous Parisian university. Whether she actually took many courses there, in view of her pregnant state, I cannot tell for sure. However, it is likely that she did, because my mother was strong, stubborn and determined, and would not allow such a minor inconvenience as pregnancy to keep her from pursuing things that interested her, including an opportunity to take courses at the Sorbonne. She was forever taking courses and studying as long as I remember. She was remarkably well read and informed. She was an expert on pre-school education, a follower of Friedrich Froebel and Maria Montessori. Among subjects that she knew was library science and, I am aware of, her fluency in French, German, Yiddish and Russian. Sometimes in the spring of 1925 my father came to Paris and in May a civil marriage ceremony was performed in Paris. I was born on 27 June 1925. As a child, I saw a copy of my original birth certificate issued in 1925 (not the one shown below, a copy issued in Paris in 1946), which stated that on June 27, 1925 was born in Paris, at rue Santerre 15, Georges, "*du sexe masculin*", son of "*Salomea nee Rubin et Maximilian Alexandrowicz, maries*". My father did not tarry in Paris but returned to Kraków and my mother and I followed when I was three months old.

Because my grandfather and my father were angry at each other, my parents did not move to an apartment in grandfather's house, but rented a small place in an outlying district of Dębniki, located far from center of town. We stayed there for three years, during which time a reconciliation of sorts must have occurred because we then moved to one of the family houses, at 11 Bernardynska Street, across from the Royal Castle. I have only a vague recollection of the Dębniki apartment. Most of my recollection is based on one incident, which trivial though it was, must have been traumatic for me at the age of two and a half or so. The incident with the black chocolate doll was described above.

When I was almost four years old, my mother and my aunt Lola set up a kindergarten, following the then innovative Montessori design. I became their first pupil and thus the first Montessori pre-school "*bambino*" in town. Kindergarten supplies were made following my mother's design. I recall blocks and frames with shoelaces, with snaps, with buttonholes, with hooks and other training aids, as well as letters and boards lined with sandpaper, etc. The kindergarten had a row of small sinks for washing hands and small child-size tables and chairs. Among the pupils, I remember Ewusia Heller, Lilka Anisfeld, Adaś Scharf and my cousin Eva Aleksandrowicz, daughter of my uncle Ignacy. In the kindergarten I learned the alphabet and began to read childrens books. Among my favorites was *O krasnoludkach i sierotce Marysi* by Maria Konopnicka (Of elves and orphan Marysia) and a novel for children by the famous educator Janusz Korczak entitled *Król Macius Pierwszy* (King Matty the First). During the War Korczak ran a orphanage for Jewish children in the Warsaw Ghetto. When the Nazis ordered the children deported to an extermination camp, probably Treblinka, they offered to allow Korczak to stay behind but he refused to abandon his charges and went to his death hugging and comforting the children. I also read avidly the entire series of Jules Verne's science fiction novels in Polish translation and also bowdlerized versions of *Robinson Crusoe* by Daniel Defoe and of *Gullivers Travels* by Oliver Swift.

It was our family custom to spend the summers away from Kraków on a farm or in a resort area. Usually, we rented a house for the summer, with my mother and me staying in that rented house, while my father, like other husbands, would come on weekends, a custom not very different from the one in the Catskills during the same period. When I was four years old in 1929, we stayed is a resort village of Sucha, in the foothills of the Carpathian Mountains. Sucha was a railway hub south of Kraków and was easy to reach by a trainride of around one hour. I do not remember much of Sucha, except that my aunt Pola and my cousin Jacques came from Paris and stayed with us for a month. Jacques was one year older than I. He spoke only French and I spoke only Polish, but we apparently had no difficulty in communicating. By the end of the month Jacques could speak a fractured ungrammatical but understandable Polish. We stayed in Sucha for almost three months.

Next year we spent our summer in a village appropriately called Kalwaria Zebrzydowska, a place famous for pilgrimages, dotted with 42 small local shrines, built as a form of penance by the Polish aristocratic owner of the area, named Zebrzydowski, who rebelled against the King Jan Kazimierz in XVII-th century and came to rue it. Kalwaria was not only a summer vacation retreat for Kraków families, it was also a religious center where Roman Catholic families routinely came with their children to pray and walk from one shrine to another to do so. Apparently, that summer, among the families that came to Kalwaria was one named Wojtyła from Wadowice near Kraków, with a boy named Karol, a little older than I. For all I know, our paths may have crossed while we were there. Obviously, young Karol Wojtyła remembered fondly his visit to Kalwaria. Recently, in the summer of 2002, during his final visit to Poland and Kraków, my "landsman" Karol Wojtyła, the late Pope John Paul II, made a pilgrimage to this Kalwaria, which he knew from his own childhood.

In 1931 our family did not go away on vacation because of the aftermath of my mother's pregnancy and for a while I was sent by myself to stay with my cousins, daughters of my uncle Ignacy and for a while with my grandmother Schmerler in Czerna near Ojców. From that time forward, we changed our custom and took shorter summer vacations, but all together, including my father. In 1932 we went, all four of us, for two or three weeks to the spa of Krynica, referred to as the Polish Karlsbad, an elegant resort with mineral springs. Krynica landscape was very green, mountainous, woodsy and very beautiful. While we were there, the heiress to the Dutch throne, Princess Juliana and her new husband, Prince Bernhard, spent their honeymoon in Krynica. Other famous guests included the then famous singer Jan Kiepura and the actress Martha Eggerth. Our other vacations were spent in small mountain resorts. Hiking and climbing the mountain peaks was our main occupation there. I was very proud of my tenacity, endurance and climbing ability. A big incentive to the climbing was my wooden walking stick shaped like a mountaineer axe (*ciupaga*). As was the custom all over Europe, Polish mountain refuges sold little round embossed metal souvenir shields, approximately one-to-two inches across, which were nailed to the cane. I remember that my cane was full of such shields and I was working on a second one. Among the mountains south of Kraków of which I had shields on my canes were Pilsko, climbed from Jeleśna (elev. 4,800 feet) and the Babia Góra, climbed from Zawoja (5,250 feet). We also spent some time at the source of the river Vistula at the foot of Barania Góra.

After 1932, we settled on vacationing in the mountain resort of Zakopane, high in the craggy Tatra Mountains. Zakopane was, and still is special, both in summer and in winter. It was in Zakopane that I attended the International Ski Federation competition with my uncle Olek, described earlier. The Tatra Mountains above Zakopane are high rocky crags, composed of granite, sculpted by wind and water, covered with snow most of the year, rising way above the tree line. At lower elevations Zakopane has many woodsy and rocky trails which follow fast flowing mountain streams, among them the Trail of the White Stream, the Valley of the Strążyski Stream and others. Hiking in the woods to waterfalls was delightful, hiking in the high mountains challenging, with stony trails above the tree line, which reward hikers and climbers with spectacular views of permanent snows and glaciers. In openings surrounded by high peaks are many deep and dark ice-cold or frozen mountain lakes. On the way to the Zawrat Pass, I remember climbing past the Gąsienice Meadow Mountain Refuge (*Schronisko na Hali Gąsienicowej*), the Valley of the Five Gąsienice Ponds, the Black Pond and the frozen small *Zmarzły Staw*. Another hike that I remember fondly was hiking the trail to the *Szpiglasowa Przełęcz* (Szpiglas Pass) from Hala Gąsienicowa to *Dolina Pięciu Stawów Polskich* (Valley of Five Polish Ponds). The most spectacular and most scenic of the mountain ponds that we visited was (and is) the *Morskie Oko* (Eye of the Sea), arguably the most beautiful mountain sight that I have ever seen. We went to Zakopane both in summer to hike and in winter to ski. Zakopane became for me and for my family a memorable beloved place, second only to Kraków itself.

My pre-school career ended when I became six and eligible for the public grammar

school. A month before my sixth birthday I received a special present, a baby sister.

On April 8, 1931 my sister, Anna Aleksandrowicz, called Hanka (diminutive *Hanusia* or *Haneczka*), was born. She was named after my father's mother, Hanna Hinda, called Hancia, whom my father adored. I was almost six years old then. I looked forward to my sister's birth and I was not disappointed. I guess at that point I was old enough and secure enough, having been the only child for so long, that I never looked at her as a rival for my parents' attention. To the contrary, I loved her fiercely, and was devoted to her and she was so much mine that my parents had to restrain my interest in her and protect her from too much of my constant protection and attention. She was a beautiful baby and grew up to be a beautiful little girl, kind and sweet. She had big black eyes, very straight dark brown hair, and a cute round face. She certainly reciprocated my attention to her: I was her idol and she duly adored her big brother. We were extremely close.

My mother's pregnancy was difficult, as I mentioned before, she needed rest and recuperation. For one month, as I judge now, it was probably July 1931, I was sent to stay with my cousins, daughters of my uncle Ignacy, in their summer home in Krynica. I was then exactly six years old. My cousin Ewa was almost eight, my cousin Hanka (also named after the same Hanna Hinda, who was also Ignacy's mother) was four. We were, of course, very familiar with each other, because we often played together. They lived in Kraków within an easy walking distance from us, on Wrzesińska 4, in a house owned by the in-laws of my uncle Ignacy, the Klippers. In Krynica, their villa was called "*Jaśmin*". As was then the custom also in New York, only the women and children stayed in Krynica, the men worked and only came for brief visits on week-ends. In addition to Ewa and Hanka and their mother Sala (nee Klipper), in the "*Jaśmin*" also was Sala's sister Regina, wife of Mundek Friess, a physician, with her two children, Joasia, age three and Olek, a year-old baby, who crawled around on all four.

This was my first experience of being away from my mother and it was not easy. I objected to a lot of rules that governed the household. I still remember my protests at having to go to bed for a nap in the afternoon. I did not take naps. Being six years old, I considered myself too old for that. However, my cousins did take naps, even the eight-year-old, and I was told that a rule is a rule, and I was sent to bed. I retaliated by refusing to fall asleep and merely waited in bed until the required hour or two were over. Other problems involved food. I was always (and still am) a picky eater and the food that I got in Krynica was not to my liking. Somehow, however, I survived the month there and returned to my parents undamaged.

Because my mother was still not feeling well, she could not breast-feed my baby sister who was, therefore, fed from a bottle. In August, my father took my mother to recuperate away from both of us. He took her to Karlovy Vary, the spa in Czechoslovakia which we still knew as Karlsbad, while I and my 5-month-old baby sister were left with mother's mother, "*babcia*". A cabin was rented for us from a farmer in Czerna near Ojców, a pretty village in a wooded valley, which was the site of a famous Carmelite monastery. The monastery was open to visitors only one day a year, during its annual Public Fair. We were lucky to be there during this event and I remember the rather modest whitewashed buildings housing the monks and a number of tables set up in the courtyard with merchandise, mostly related to the church, i.e. candles, little statuettes of the Madonna, etc. I do not remember seeing any chapel or church on the grounds. I am sure there was one, but my grandmother,

as a religious Jewish woman, would not have taken us there. We spent a month in Czerna. The cabin had a kitchen and my grandmother cooked for us – she was quite religious and the meals were strictly kosher. While at home, we paid no attention to Kashrut and enjoyed ham and cheese or pork loin sandwiches and ate meat and drank milk in any meal. However, when we visited my maternal grandmother or my grandfather Aleksandrowicz and his second wife, "aunt" Toni, we got kosher meals so that I was quite used to them and I enjoyed my grandmother's cooking. Eventually, my mother came back from Karlsbad and joined us in Czerna for a while.

A year later during the summer we again rented a house in Kalwaria, the place of pigrimages. By this time I was seven and my little sister was 16 month old and I took care of her all the time, keeping her entertained. Among the activities, I used to line the farmer's wheelbarrow with pillows and blankets, then I put my sister in it and pushed the wheelbarrow around. She was getting prettier all the time, with big shiny eyes and long straight hair, a smooth complexion and a sunny disposition. She laughed a lot and served as a wonderful living toy for me. I loved her and protected her from everybody, even from any potential scolding by our parents. Unfortunately, I have lost all my possessions during the War, including family photographs, so I am unable to show how pretty was my little sister. After the War my father got copies of a few family pictures from his aunt, Amalia Kaufer, the one who came to New York from Vienna in 1938. She brought with her all her belongings, including such pictures as we sent her to Vienna from Kraków. I enclosed those of my early childhood and those that show my sister at the end of this chapter. I only wish I had more pictures of my mother and of my sister. Those that I have do not do them justice.

In September of 1931 I went to a public primary school. The school was rather far away from my house but it was special; it took me almost three-quarters of an hour to walk to school, rain or shine. If it really poured I could take a trolley, but that did not help much. I had to walk ten minutes to the end of our street to the trolley stop, then change to a different line in the Main Market Square and then walk another few minutes to school. It usually did not pay me to use the trolleys. There was a reason why I went to a school located so far (there were several schools nearer): it was an experimental school and was considered by far the best in town. The school was called *Swiętego Wojciecha* (i.e. St. Adalbert's), and was located in an old wooden building, one story high. The Director was a kind but stern educator, a lame man named Harassin. My primary teacher was Mrs. Maria Malinowska-Rewera, a remarkable educator, a very kind person and an innovative teacher, a co-author of a book on modern teaching methods. She was like a second mother to us, deeply caring and warm. She worked together with Prof. Franciszek Głębowicz. I enjoyed the school and went there happily, for six years, from 1931 to 1937. It was strictly a boys' school. Public schools in Poland were not co-educational.

The school was demanding. We received an excellent education, in spite of the fact that our class had 64 students. It is of interest, and, in retrospect, probably not a coincidence, but the number of Jewish children in the class, 14, seems to mirror the percentage of Jews in the over-all Kraków population at the time. I remember the names of only a few of my 64 colleagues, mostly those, children of middle class, with whom I identified. Among my classmates in the grammar school was my relative Richard Aleksandrowicz, son of David and grandson of Wolf. Other Jewish student was Adam Scharf, grandson of Napoleon Telz, owner of the largest and best Kraków printery, whom I knew from kindergarten.

I also remember Józek Rakower, whose relatives owned a delicatessen on the Square of All Saints, where we used to go for free samples of sausages, and Marek Lichtig, Ben Teufel, and Richard Weinsberg, whose family owned a brick factory "*Bonarka*". The latter lives now in New York. Among the non-Jewish students was Kazimierz "Kazik" Kowalski, son of a Professor at the Jagiellonian University. Kazik became a professor at the Mining Academy (*Akademia Górnicza*) and president of the prestigious *Polska Akademia Umiejętości* (Polish Academy of Arts and Sciences) in Kraków. One classmate who always drew pictures and became a talented graphic artist, was Jerzy Skarżynski, son of Professor Bolesław Skarżynski, a prominent biochemist at the Jagiellon University whom I met after the War in Vienna at an International Biochemical Congress. Jurek Rewera, son of the teacher Mrs. Malinowska-Rewera and Stanisław Kaifasz, my rival for the title of top student in class, complete the roster of the few whose names I remember.

In school, we were offered all kinds of tasks, which today would be called enrichments for "gifted" students. I remember one in particular, which must have occurred when I was entering the fifth grade, i.e. two years before graduation. This particular project dealt with a globe for the geography class. The school had a huge blank floor-standing globe, approximately six feet in diameter, which towered over our heads, appropriately tilted on its axis, which could be rotated so that different parts of it were facing the front. The globe was covered all over in dull pale blue paint. Then it became a task for a few students who were good at and interested in geography to paint on it the outlines of the continents, then major physical features: mountains, plains, rivers, in color, and, eventually, mark political country boundaries and the more important cities. It took us the entire school year to complete the task. I remember painting the Himalayas in strong red and brown as opposed to Mid America which was deep green. We worked very hard and for long hours after classes, but we were told that our effort was important and that we are making a valuable contribution to the school, which will benefit countless generations of students in the future. With deep pride we finished the globe just as the school year ended. I still remember vividly my upset and dismay, when I came back to school next fall to see that our work was erased, the globe had been again covered with pale blue paint all over and the next class of students was put to work outlining its geographical features. Obviously, this was one of ongoing enrichment projects, available each year to the fifth grade geography class. A class monthly newspaper was another. I do not recall any other specific enrichment projects, but there were many.

As a class we also took many day trips to places within the city and beyond. Among those that I remember were several to the Słowacki Municipal Theatre to see famous actors in stage shows of Polish and foreign classics, some by Alexander Fredro (A Man for All Seasons), by Stanisław Wyspianski (The Wedding) and other Poles, as well as plays by Shakespeare, Rostand, Moliere, etc. As a class we also visited the Zieleniewski Ironworks in the Dąbie area (now expanded and developed as Nowa Huta) and we hiked in the Wola Forest (*Las Wolski*) west of Kraków.

While hiking in this lovely forest I tripped, fell and broke my left wrist. It immediately swelled and hurt considerably but, at 10, I was not about to complain or notify the teacher who acted as chaperone on this excursion, instead I quietly whimpered because it hurt. Eventually one of the other children did tell the teacher, Professor Głębowicz. He was upset and angry and scolded me for keeping it secret. He could not leave the

class in the woods but arranged immediately for me to be accompanied by two of my classmates and go to town to the municipal first aid station (*Pogotowie Ratunkowe*) located in the Fire Department building (*Straż Pożarna*) on Andrzej Potocki Street, now renamed Westerplatte Street. There they immobilized my wrist with a splint in a protective bandage and told me that they are only a first aid station and I need a surgeon to reset my fractured bone. I went home and to bed with my arm on a pillow and that is how my mother found me when she came home. Next day a surgeon with a nurse came to our house (in those days physicians did come to peoples' homes) and pulled my hand and rotated it until the wrist bone snapped into its proper position, wrapped the area in a gypsum cast which I wore for three weeks. This was followed by a long period of exercises, massages and heat treatments, all at home. My wrist fully recovered and I never had any problems with it after the convalescence period.

In addition to this ill-fated hiking trip, with my classmates I enjoyed other hikes and, as a class, exploration of the salt mines in nearby Wieliczka by Kraków. The salt mines had a distinguished history and were important to Polish economy for long centuries – at one point income from this enterprise sustained more than 40% of the royal budget and it paid for building the Kraków University and the royal palace. The mines were large and most impressive, on several levels, with many deep shafts, long corridors and enormous caverns, halls and chapels dug out over the centuries from rocksalt-bearing layers of soil and rock. Legends had it that the mines were discovered when Blessed Kinga, wife of the Duke Bolesław Wstydliwy (Boleslaus the Bashful, ruled 1243-1279) threw a gold ring in Kraków and it rolled and rolled and was discovered when it fell into a cavern opening. The cavern walls were made of rocksalt. I remember that as children we used to joke that Duchess Kinga was blessed because she died a virgin and she died a virgin because Bolesław was "bashful". The truth about the mine discovery is more prosaic. Salt was being dug at that location from pre-historic times. The mines were listed in records of the Krakovian Duke Kazimierz I Odnowiciel (Casimir I the Restorer, 1038-1058), two hundred years before the rule of Bolesław and Kinga. The salt mines became a royal monopoly, leased for exorbitant fees to be run by private enterprise, often leased to rich Jews, among them my distant relative, Saul Wahl, a descendant of Meir Katzenellenbogen of Padua. Saul Wahl is said to have served one night as a royal substitute during the interregnum caused by departure of King Henryk Walezy prior to the election of Stephan Bathory in 1575. It may even be that he acqired his nickname *Wahl*, meaning "election" in Yiddish and German, because of his importance during this election, when the entire nobility of the Polish-Lithuanian Commonwealth gathered to pick a new king.

I found school challenging but enjoyable. I liked discovering new things. I was lucky because my parents provided me with a warm and supporting home environment but allowed me the freedom to grow and develop confidence in my abilities and in my judgement. I walked to school alone and even in this I learned early to depend on myself. This early development served me well during the turbulent time of the German occupation and subsequently. As I said, school was fun, although not always. Once I had a big fight with my relative Richard Aleksandrowicz. And once I was embarassed before the whole class by mispronouncing a French word. I was reading aloud from a Polish text in class and came upon a word spelled in italics. The word was "*mademoiselle*" and I read it phonetically the Polish way, *mah-deh-moy-sehl-leh.* The teacher said that this is not how it is pronounced

and asked Stan Kaifasz, whose family was wealthy and who had a French governess, to read it the right way as *mat-moo-ah-zel* and pronounced it colloquially as *mamzel.* Kaifasz was my main competitor in class and I was crushed, in particular because this was a French word and I was very proud of having been born in Paris. I determined right then and there to learn and become profficient in French, a dream that I realized a few years later in secondary school. All told, considering the class size and the poverty and backwardness of the country at the time, we received an outstanding education. I graduated from the primary school after having completed six years in 1937.

Life at home followed a quiet simple routine. My mother was not interested in household chores such as cleaning or cooking or even planning meals and shopping for food. We had a maid, as did most families of my friends. Young peasant girls from surrounding villages were eager to get away from their depressed communities and considered entering service in the city a step forward and an opportunity to learn, to advance their social status and to find desirable marriage partners. The girls were not expected to help sustain their farm families and did not send any money home. Hence, the wages they earned in the city did not have to be particularly high, but consisted of room and board and a small amount of monthly cash, which the young women saved to form a type of dowry. Hence, hiring a maid was generally affordable for families such as mine. Because my mother wanted our young woman to do more than was usually expected from a simple peasant girl, the person that I remember we hired was attractive, very bright, experienced, trustworthy and with a pleasing personality. Her name was Tosia, a diminutive of Antonia. Tosia had considerable autonomy, was given money to do shopping for food and was trusted to arrange for proper meals all by herself.

Our appartment consisted of a living room-dining room combination, with two large windows and a balcony facing the castle, two bedrooms both with windows on the castle, one for my parents and one for the children, a long hallway, a kitchen with a balcony facing the courtyard and a small cubicle for the maid, a bathroom with a sink and bathtub and a separate cubicle with a toilet. The living-dining room room furniture consisted of a large, heavy wooden rectangular extension dinner table with six chairs and two dark mahogany credenzas, one horizontal and the other one upright. The upright one had a top section with a mirror flanked by cabinets with glass fronts etched in a pattern somewhat reminiscent of Frank Lloyd Wright glass designs. My parents bedroom had a large *tapczan*, a bed with what we would have called today a kingsize mattress and the children room had a small bed for my sister and a daybed for me, a desk and a free standing armoire with drawers for underwear and clothing and shelves for books. Coats hung in a closet in the foyer. The bathroom had a gas-fired water heater, which had to be lit to provide hot water.

The kitchen had a coal-fired stove with an oven, and an ice-box, not a refrigerator. A bloc of ice was brought daily by the ice-man. Coal, delivered by a horse-drawn cart, was stored in the basement and Tosia brought each day an amount needed for that day. The house was heated with hard coal. In the corner of each room stood a tall upright stove, covered with attractive decorative tiles and lined inside with fireproof bricks. In winter, first thing in the morning Tosia would fill the lower part of these stoves with some wood and coal and light a fire. The coal would glow for several hours and heat would rise within the elaborate inner chimney within the tall tile stove heating the inner bricks. The stove would radiate heat for most of the day. The house was well insulated, all windows were double.

Bed linen was hung in open windows every morning, even in winter. Carpets were taken to the courtyard frequently, placed over a bar and shaken with a carpet-beater. Winters were severe, cold but dry. It snowed frequently, but the winter sun shone often. If dressed warmly, playing outdoors was no problem and winter sports were as popular and pleasant as summer sports. Long walks were as easy in winter as in summer. Streets were covered with snow most of the winter and many of the horse carriages (*droshkes*) for hire changed from wheeled vehicles to sleds. Snow banks lined the sidewalks and it was possible for me to put on my skis in front of the house and ski all the way out of town to the nearest slope, or put on my skates and walk in deep snow to the skating rink. On particularly cold windy winter days my mother would cream my face with vaseline for protection.

To go to school in winter I was wormly dressed, in woolen long pants and a woolen sweater under a warm havily-lined navy blue overcoat. The overcoat imitated real Navy outfit, it had epaulets and golden buttons with an anchor design. The rest of the year I wore a white shirt and dark short pants. My underwear consisted of a cotton tee shirt and cotton underpants. When I was small my mother, as an experienced seamstress from her childhood days, sewed my clothing, even the heavy navy-like overcoat which we called *montyniak*. When I went to secondary school (gimnazjum) at 12, I wore an obligatory uniform, a navy jacket with the school shield and number on the upper part of the sleeve and so-called *pumpy*, long pants with elastic at bottom, worn with that bottom hiked to just below the knee. The uniform was completed by regulation dark socks and laced ankle-high shoes. My little sister wore very short colorful dresses, also mostly sewn by our mother. In winter she wore warm woolen pantyhose-like gaiters, mostly dark beige. For underwear she wore a contraption consisting of a sleeveless white cotton bolero-shaped top with a button on each side near the waist. Her cotton underpants had two flaps, front and back, each with buttonholes on the sides, which buttoned to the top.

Every day we received freshly-baked small breakfast rolls delivered to our door, pleated poppyseed rolls, crisp rounds and square rolls, crescents, caraway rolls, saltsticks, whole wheat Graham rolls, and a number of other creations. I miss these breakfast rolls to this day. With fresh butter, sold to us by peasant women who brought it from the Krakovian countryside wrapped in cabbage leaves, and salt, they provided a treat that is hard to match. Breakfast invariably consisted of these rolls and eggs, fried in individual-size small frying pans. When I was small I could only have one egg, when I ate two I broke out in a rash. I outgrew that allergy as I got bigger. My parents drank coffee brewed with chicory with hot milk for their breakfast, I got a cup of ersatz coffee, made from roasted grains by a company called Kneipp, of course with plenty of hot milk and sugar. I took with me to school a sandwich and a fruit to eat during a break between classes, referred to as a second breakfast. The sandwich was either a roll or two slices of buttered rye bread or black peasant bread, with ham or cheese. There were many cheeses available, ranging from pressed country cottage cheese to imported Emmenthaler. The fruit was mostly an apple, occasionally a pear or a few cherrries.

We ate the big meal of the day at midday, between one and two in the afternoon. It consisted of a soup, a main course, cooked fruit desert and hot tea. The meal began with potato soup, pea soup, sourgrass soup (*shchav*), which I hated, vegetable-rice soup, chicken noodle soup with unborn chicken eggs, mushroom soup with barley, etc. The meat course (ground beef with spices formed into a patty, meatloaf with a hard-boiled egg in the middle, veal chops, roast porkloin known as *polędwica wieprzowa*, chicken, goose, beefsteak, pot roast, goulash, pork sausage or frankfurters called *parówki* in Kraków) was mostly accompanied by potatoes, boiled or mashed, occasionally with chicken fat and fried chicken skin pieces, called *grieven* in Yiddish. Sometimes potatoes were replaced by rice, home-made egg noodles or macaroni or any number of varieties of kasha, from coarse groats to yellow finely cut grain, similar to Moroccan couscous. We had no lamb dishes because my father would not eat it. Also fish were seldom eaten for the same reason. Exception was made for canned sardines packed in their own oil which were served on bread as they came from the can or mixed with cottage cheese and spices. Meat was not cheap by local standards and poor Jews often had to make do with salt herring which came stacked in flat wooden boxes and was considered a poor men's substitute for meat. With the meat also came cooked vegetables, such as a variety of stringbeans, brussels sprouts, cauliflower, lima beans, fava beans, peas, carrots, beets, mushrooms and a salad either of lettuce or of cucumbers soaked in vinegar called *mizeria*. The first three were served Polonaise style, i.e. with bread crumbs sauteed in butter. Carrots also came raw, grated, with raisins, sugar and lemon juice. My mother and sisters also ate raw tomatoes, which my father disliked and I, therefore, refused to eat. Condiments included horse radish, mustard and pickles, caraway and assorted other seeds and spices. A special meal was called *bigos*. It was akin to French *choucroute garni*, and consisted of pork sausage, other meats, sourkraut and potatoes, with caraway seeds and apple pieces, cooked together for hours. We also had vegetarian meals, in which the main course was replaced by a dish of pasta or potato-and-flour fingerlings served with browned bread crumbs and crumbled country cheese, buttered kasha and with a sunnyside fried egg on top or a rice-and-apples casserole with eggs, raisins, sugar, milk and cinnamon, shaped in a circle, baked crisp on the outside and cut into pie shaped wedges. For desert we had home-made apple sauce, compotes of cooked cherries, rhubarb with gooseberries, fresh apples, pears, raspberries, blueberries, blackberries, boysenberries, strawberries, wild strawberries (*poziomki*) with sour cream, apricots, plums, or tangerines, bananas, oranges, etc. In the summer, I particularly enjoyed a drink made with tap water and a large dollop of raspberry syrup or sour milk akin to buttermilk, and yogurt or kefir. Evening meal, a supper, was usually modest, either a sandwich or some of the left-overs from the midday dinner and tea. As is obvious from the above, we were not short of food until the Germans marched in. Poland was an agricultural country and, unlike some imported manufactured goods, food was plentiful and generally not beyond reach of even modestly well-off families.

Sunday being the maid's day off, we routinely ate the Sunday dinner in the evening in a restaurant. We invariably had it in the same establishment, a place called Weissbrot's on the northeast corner of Starowislna and Dietla streets. We always sat at the same table and were served by the same elderly waiter, who knew, without being told, what we wanted. My father got *flaczki z kiszką w sosie gulażowym* (tripe with stuffed derma in brown goulash gravy), I got a children's portion of the same tripe dish and my mother shared her half chicken with my little sister.

My sister, Hanka, was growing up, she was 8 years old when the War broke out and she finished third grade in primary school. We continued to be very close. She was very beautiful, with a round face, straight hair, big eyes, clear skin. She was usually cheerful and friendly, but quiet, surrounded by girl fiends from school or from the neighborhood, all of them either her exact age or a little older. Her closest friend and companion was her cousin Mirka, daughter of my uncle Leibek Schmerler. Mirka was the same age as my sister, the two girls having been born within a few weeks of each other, The Schmerler family lived on Starowislna Street, a 20 minute walk from our house. Mirka spent many a night in our house, with both girls running around evenings either in warm pyjamas in winter or in short nightshirts in the summer, with their cute behinds flashing as they run and played games. While my sister was usually a calm and serious child, Mirka, in contrast, was a vivacious, pert and sassy child. I often entertained both of them, primarily by creating cardboard doll houses and helping them with cutouts of shapes and figures from colored papers, which were glued to cardboards to form artwork that was then proudly displayed in both our and Mirka's households. Both my sister and I attended gym classes in the afternoon, I went to a Swedish calisthenic class in the *Sokoł* (Polish branch of the Scouting movement, the word itself means falcon)) building on Wolska Street, my sister was enrolled in rhythm and dance class run by a known dancer and artist, Maria Bilig (*Bilizanka*) in the Bagatela Theatre building on the corner of Karmelicka Street. In keeping with the purpose of the Sokoł organization, a Latin motto *In corpore sano, mens sana* (In healthy body, healthy mind) was inscribed on the Wolska Street building. My parents acquired a grand piano, which occupied a corner of our living room and Hanka had a piano teacher come to our house to give her lessons. As far as I can judge, she was not very good at it, but being able to play the piano was considered a part of education of a young woman, just as the rhythm class was supposed to help a girl's posture and ability to move gracefully.

I had a bicycle and on spring and fall weekends I took long rides into the surrounding countryside. Obviously, the country-side was considered completely safe. There was never any question about my biking out of the city alone or in company of my young cousin. Often, my cousin, also named Hanka after my paternal grandmother, came with me. She was the daughter of my uncle Ignacy. Hanka was two years younger than I, but she was a good biker and had no trouble keeping up with me. I enjoyed her company. I was fourteen in 1939, my cousin Hanka was twelve. Near the end of World War II Hanka, then 17, lived as a hidden child on false non-Jewish papers in Warsaw. She died as a fighter in the Polish Warsaw Uprising in 1944. In summers, in addition to biking I also enjoyed swimming. Kraków had a large public swimming pool in the Jordan Park on the Błonie and a sandy river beach on the Vistula. In the park I was taught how to swim at around five or six and I became a good swimmer. I was never very good as a ball-player and I generally avoided competitive sports. In winter, I was also a good skater and a moderately expert skier. We lived a block away from the Kraków Maccabi soccer field on Koletek Street that was hosed down and flooded in winter and allowed to freeze, becoming a public skating rink. Given the pretty and hilly Kraków surroundings, cross-country skiing was easy on the dry, crisp sunny days of Polish winters. Each winter we spent some time in the ski resort of Zakopane in the Tatra Mountains, a trainride from Kraków. Zakopane had easy as well as expert ski trails, rope tows, an inclined railway to the Gubałówka Hill and a cable car to Kasprowy Wierch. Easy skiing was near our hotel on a small hill called Wilcznik, more expert skiing called for a trip to Gubałówka a tow rope or following a horse-drawn sled. The run from the Kasprowy Wierch cable-car station called for real expertise. All that made downhill skiing exciting and cross-country skiing enjoyable. Also, Zakopane had horse-drawn sleds in winter for countryside rides and for *ski-ring*, i.e. pulling a number of skiers in tow.

As I stated before, my father was a prominent activist in the Jewish Workers Bund. While the Bund was primarily a democratic socialist political party, it also was a large social and educational organization, sponsoring various cultural activities for working adults, sport organizations and classes for youth and courses and summer camps for workers' children. It set up a convalescent resort for recovering tubercular youngsters in the pine woods of Miedzeszyn near Warsaw. This Medem Sanatorium eventually evolved into a general summer resort for Jewish workers' children, with varied recreational and sport activities combined with clean air and ample, healthy food. It used Yiddish as the primary language of communication. The Sanatorium became an exemplary gem of a place, well organized and aware of the latest educational ideas. For example it had a children-run self-government that consulted with the faculty and staff. Twice I spent a month at this place, at the age of 10 and 11. My father hoped that in the Medem Sanatorium I would be exposed to a Yiddish-speaking milieu and become more familiar with the language. In furtherance of the educational and recreational ancillary aims of the Bund, my father conducted seminars for members of the Young Bund "*Tsukunft*" (the Future) and led weekend excursions into the countryside. As I mentioned earlier, I went along with the teen-age and young adult groups into the countryside, among them day-long hikes along the shores of the little Rudawa River to Kmita's Rock, to the Tyniec Cloister and to the ruins of Tenczynek Castle. My mother established and ran a lending library for the Kraków Bund. My uncle Ignacy conducted a course for older secondary school and university students in political economic theories, including capitalism, fascism, socialism and communism, which I was allowed to attend, although I was considered young for it. In this course I read excerpts from Adam Smith, Max Weber, the *Communist Manifesto* and *Das Kapital.*

At home we subscribed to three daily newspapers and a number of periodicals. In Polish we received the Nowy Dziennik, ostensibly apolitical but with an obvious Zionist slant. It had the advantage of being published right near us in Kraków. It was a quality paper and, allowing for its slant, a reliable daily source of news. Our other Polish paper had a definite political outlook. It was the official daily organ of the Polish Socialist Party. In Warsaw it was called *Robotnik* (The Worker). We received its Kraków edition which was called *Naprzód* (Forward). I remember many of its political polemics but also many of its informative educational articles on assorted subjects from history and travel to economics and science. In addition, my parents read the Bundist daily *Naye Folkstsaitung* (New People's Gazette), published in Yiddish in Warsaw, which arrived a day late by mail. In school I received a weekly children magazine called *Płomyk* (small flame).

As ardent supporters of Jewish culture, my parents were eager for me to become fluent in Yiddish, "the language of the Jewish working masses in Poland". In addition to my two stints at the Medem Sanatorium, they also hired a tutor to teach me Yiddish at home. The tutor, a Vilner "Lutvack", named Bursztyn, introduced me to classic Yiddish literature, including works of Mendele Moykher Sforim, Yitzhak Leibish Peretz ("*Monish*"), and Sholem Aleykhem ("*Tevye der Milkhiker*", Tevye the milkman), as well as to Sholem Ash and Yitzhak Bashevis Singer and David Opatoshu. With my mother, I also read poems by Itzik Manger ("*Goldene Pahveh*"), memorized one popularized by Kadia Molodowska ("*Mister Tvister*") and others. During the summer of 1939, the last summer before the War, I also attended a one-week camp of Bundist scouts, members of the Bund child group (*Skiff),* in the woods in the hills of Sub-Carpathia. In camp, we slept in a converted barn, prepared our own meals and sang songs around a campfire in the evening. I remember the camp fondly and I remember how cold I was during my shift of guarding the camp at night. As a child I was always aware that Yiddish as a folk language is full of particularly pungent sayings and proverbs which loose a lot of their flavor in translation. I will quote only a few. On the use of best ingredients in cooking: *Az me laygt arayn, nemt men aroys* (If one puts it in, one takes it out); on bringing up children: *Kleine kinder kleine tsures, groysse kinder groysse tsures* (Small children small problems, big children big problems); on the surprising altruism of some rich Jews: *A yiddishe kishke kem'en nisht shetsn* (A Jewish "gut" cannot be predicted); on Jewish existence: *S'iz shver to zayn a Yi*d (It's hard to be a Jew).

On my own, throughout my childhood I read voraciously, including Polish classics, like Mickiewicz's *Pan Tadeusz*, Sienkiewicz's *Trilogy, Quo Vadis*, and *W Pustyni i Puszczy* (In Desert and Jungle), Prus's *Pharaoh,* Raymont's *Chłopi* (The Peasants), Żeromski's *Wierna Rzeka* (Faithful River), Wittlin's *Sól Ziemi* (Salt of the Earth), the poem *Lokomotywa* by Julian Tuwim and a number of others. I also enjoyed foreign novels and plays in Polish translation, among them classical Greek works by Homer, Aeschylus, Sophocles and others, plays by Shakespeare, Moliere and George Bernard Shaw, and novels by Defoe, Swift, Dickens, Galsworthy, Heinrich Mann, Edmund Rostand, Marcel Proust, Lew Tolstoy, Fyodor Dostoyevski, Herman Hesse, Karl May, Jack London, James Fenimore Cooper, Mark Twain, Upton Sinclair. I read the almost complete set of science-fiction novels of Jules Verne, Edgar Rice Borroughs and H.G. Wells. As I mentioned earlier in connection with my visit to the ski championship in Zakopane, I was an avid philatelist, collecting stamps of the entire world and learning geography in the process. I lost my stamp collection during the War and tried to recreate it after my arrival in the United States, where I joined the American Philatelic Society.

The Bund chose to boycott the rigged national parliamentary elections, but it ran candidates for local City Council elections, which were fair and open, and for elections to the Jewish Community Councils, the Kahałs. Both my parents ran in those, as did three of my uncles. In the 1938 elections to the Kahał, the Bund was the overwhelming choice of Jews in Warsaw (16 of 20 seats went to Bundists), Wilno, Białystok and elsewhere, but not in conservative Kraków where most of the seats went to the so-called "General Zionists" and to religious parties.

Clouds of War were assembling over Europe. My father was getting more and more concerned. The prognosis was grim for all of Europe and for Polish Jews in particular. Anti-Semitic propaganda was coming from Germany in waves. In Berlin a charismatic demagogue and a rousing orator named Adolf Hitler rose to power. Hitler became the "Fuhrer" of a party, which he called National-Socialist German Workers Party or NSDAP and the Germans began routinely to greet each other with a "*Heil Hitler*" salutation. Hitler became Chancellor (a post similar to Prime Minister) of Germany. Upon the death of President Hindenburg in 1933, he assumed dictatorial powers. Hitler and his party used the arson of the Parliament Building in Berlin (the "Reichstag Fire") by a feeble-minded man as an excuse to arrest political opponents and establish a totalitarian state. The assassination of a German consular official in Paris by a young Jew in 1938 served as pretext to burn synagogues, rob Jewish stores and break windows all over Germany in a *Kristallnacht* of pillage and destruction of November 9. 1938. France and Britain were gripped by indecision and domestic left/right conflicts. America was desperately eager

to remain uninvolved, although the President, Franklin Delano Roosevelt, was aware of the coming conflict and tried to prepare the country for it. Isolationist politicians were campaigning against any involvement of the United States in European conflicts. There was in the United States a sizeable public sympathy for the Nazis. Colonel Lindberg, a national hero after his solo crossing of the Atlantic, was friendly with Hermann Goering, also a flier, who was the Number Two Nazi after Hitler. Lindbergh and Goering used to hunt together. Among prominent anti-Semitic public figures was Father Coughlin, the "radio priest" and Henry Ford. The latter did not hide his overt hostility to Jews. His newspaper, the *Dearborn Independent*, published a stream of anti-Semitic invective, including that notorious forgery, the *Protocols of the Elders of Zion,* originally popularized by the Tsarist secret political police, the *Okhrana.*

In 1935, Italians led by a Fascist dictator, Benito Mussolini, who styled hiself *Il Duce* (the Duke), invaded Ethiopia (Abissynia). Its ruler, the Negus Haile Selassie, vainly appealed to the League of Nations in Geneva, asking for sanctions that would prevent Italy from getting petroleum products, which it desperately needed for its tanks and trucks. The League proved ineffectual in this endeavor, thus earning public contempt, a fact that led to its eventual unlamented demise. After some initial successes, the Ethiopians were overcome by the superior armament of the Fascist army led first by Marshal de Bono and then by General Badoglio, the same general, who later succeeded deposed Mussolini and surrendered Italy to the Allies in World War II. Ethiopia became an Italian colony until liberated by the British during the 1939-1945 War. In 1936, a Civil War broke out in Spain, with fascist generals vowing to overthrow Spain's legitimately elected republican government. The Generals, Queippo de Llano, Mola and Francisco Franco, followers of the extreme rightist political movement founded by Jose Antonio Primo de Rivera, the *Falange*, managed to occupy half the country but not the capital city, Madrid, or the Catalan areas centered around Barcelona. The Government, President Asana and Prime Ministers Largo Caballero, then Juan Negrin, moved from endangered Madrid to Valencia. The treasonous generals set their headquarters in Burgos, named Franco *El Caudillo* and requested and received help from Hitler and Mussolini, while the European democracies, riven by internal conflicts, declared their "neutrality". Volunteers from Europe and America came to help. The Soviet Union did send aid to the Spanish Republic, not so much to defend Spanish democracy as to advance the interests of Spanish communists, among them the famous Dolores Ibarruri, known as *La Passionaria.* The Spanish Civil War received an appropriate literary elaboration in Ernest Hemingway's "*For whom the bell tolls*". In one of the most poignant events in this war, the town of Guernica was destroyed by German airplanes in April 1937. It's fate has been depicted in a large canvass by Pablo Picasso. For a long time Picasso's *Guernica* was on proud display loaned to the Museum of Modern Art in New York. It now has the pride of place in the Museo Reina Sophia in Madrid. It is sad that the Spanish republic was unable to overcome the combined forces of Spanish Falange militarists, Italian Fascist arms and German Nazi warplanes, and, after a valiant defense, succumbed. Barcelona and Valencia, then Madrid fell and Franco remained as *el Jefe* of Spain until his death in nineteen-seventies. Picasso's *Guernica* remained in New York until Spain was rid of Generalissimo Franco, the Falange and its fascist supporters.

In Eastern Europe the Soviet Union was riven with internecine struggles, with Stalin getting rid of his rivals by conducting show trials in which the prosecutor Andrey

Vyshinski accused old heroes of the Communist Party of treason and of supporting fascism and Nazism. Assassins were sent to kill exiled Leon Trotsky. Executed in Moscow were fabled Soviet revolutionary leaders, Bukharin, Zinoviev, Kamenev, Radek and Rykov as well as the leader of the Red Army, Marshall Tukhachevsky. Chiefs of Soviet Secret Police, variously known as Cheka, then as NKVD, Yagoda and Yezhov, were executed in turn. The whole country was in turmoil, its prisons and labor camps (*gulags)* overflowing. On the other side of the world, the Imperial Japanese army invaded China and occupied all the coastal areas, including Peking, Shanghai and Nanking. Generalissimo Chiang-Kai-Shek moved the Kuo-Min-Tang Government of China inland to Chungking. The Japanese sank an American U-boat, the *Panay*, in the Yang-Tse River and killed many civilians during the infamous "Rape of Nanking". In the United States, mired in a continuing economic depression, isolationism reigned supreme, even while Franklin D. Roosevelt was being re-elected over and over again.

In Poland, we have tried desperately to make light of the situation, pretending that everything was going to be all right and that the winds of conflicts will blow away. We even made feeble attempts at jokes about Hitler at that time, pretending that, as a dictator, he was hated by most Germans and that he was quite stupid. I remember the joke that went this way: Hitler and Hermann Goering (his associate, a pilot, Prime Minister of the key German constituent state, Prussia, and chief of the Luftwaffe, i.e. German Air Force) were travelling past a farmhouse, when a dog run out and was killed by their car. Hitler sent Goering to the house to apologize and pay for the dog. Goering did not come back for a long time and then arrived with his hands full of gifts: sausages, a wheel of cheese, basket of fruit and flowers. Hitler asked what happened and Goering answered: "I do not understand it. I entered and said ‚Heil Hitler. The dog died‘ and they all jumped and hugged me and kissed me and showered me with gifts". Another joke: Hitler asked Goebbels, his propaganda chief, how come that the Jews are so much better at commerce than the Germans. Goebbels replied that it is hard to explain but offered to take Hitler shopping and demonstrate it. They came to a German china shop and asked to see a porcelain tea set. Then Goebbels told the shopkeeper that his friend is left-handed and he needs a set for lefties with all cup handles directed to the left. The shopkeeper replied that he did not know that such sets existed and regretfully he does not have one in stock. Then they came to a store owned by a Jew. When Goebbels repeated the request, the Jew excused himself for a moment, took the set to the back of the store, turned all the cups so that all handles faced left and brought it out. After they paid and were outside Goebbels turned to Hitler and said "Now you see why the Jews are more successful?". And Hitler replied: "I do not see that this proves that the Jew was smarter. He just happened to have had such a set in stock, while the German didn‘t! ". How sad and pathetic these attempts at humor sound to us now but I remember that at the time, I and my friends considered them hilarious. Of course, we were then 12 years old. The Jewish refugees from Germany who came to Kraków also brought with them the quattrain that my mother picked up: "*Wir wollen kein Mahler aus Gottes Gnaden*".

Having finished the primary school, I enrolled in a public secondary school also located far from my home, but which enjoyed an excellent reputation, the Third Public Liceum and Gimnazjum named after King John III Sobieski, who ruled Poland in the Seventeenth Century. I attended this Gimnazjum for two years, at which point the Second World War broke out and all my formal education stopped. The school was indeed very good, quite demanding and there I have learned a lot. Among the subjects covered, were Polish language, grammar and literature, mathematics, physics, chemistry, biology, ancient history, religion, French language and Latin, as well as calisthenics and vocational training (carpentry and associated skills). Also, as every school in Poland was obliged to do, the gimnazjum taught the tenets and history of the Roman-Catholic Church. For Jewish students the Chief Rabbi (in Polish *Nadrabin*, in Yiddish *Oberrabbiner*) Schmelkes came once a week and gave us lessons not in religion but in Jewish history, using Prof. Mayer Bałaban's *Historia i Literatura Żydowska* as a textbook The gimnazjum professors were good and the schooling that I acquired, before the outbreak of War interrupted my education, served me well in my later life. A well-known poet, Tadeusz Szantroch, conducted the course in Polish Literature while the premier expert on Polish grammar, Professor Zenon Klemensiewicz, used his own text in class. Biology was taught by Stanisław Mikstein. Professor Mickstein was admired by students, not so much for his educational abilities, which were not special, but for his knowledge of postage stamps. Mickstein was a prominent philatelist, an expert on recognizing fakes of the so-called "Kraków overprints", a series of stamps of Austria overprinted in 1918 with the words "*Poczta Polska*", which became rare, very desirable and subject to many forgeries. French was taught by a talented mimic, Professor Marian Deszcz, who never spoke Polish to us but only French, yet somehow managed to convey meaning and in the process taught us a great deal of conversational French. Professor Deszcz helped me to realize my long-held desire to learn French, though not without amusing incidents. Since he never spoke Polish and never translated what he said, at times we faced frustration. In the very first lesson he used a term which I understood as "*zhumele'ff*" and I could not figure out what he meant. I came home to my mother, who was fluent in the language, but she did not know such a word. Finally, she asked me for the context in which Prof. Deszcz used the term. I explained that he asked the whole class to stand up and say it in unison. It was only then, that my mother said: Aha, you were saying "*Je me le've*", translated as "I am getting up". Because it was apparent to my parents that I was eager to really know French, they hired a private tutor for me, an elderly Frenchwoman, who married a Pole and lived in Kraków. For the next two years until the outbreak of the War, I studied French intensively, with lessons both in school and at home and what I learned stayed with me for the rest of my life. I do not remember the name of the old gimnazjum professor who taught Latin but I remember his opening statement on the first day of classes that we should not expect good grades from him, because "at best students can get to know Latin for a C or a D, he himself knows it for a B and only God Almighty knows it for an A". In the religion class Dr. Schmelkes wore heavy glasses and we believed that he cannot see much. One of my classmated never studied for the course but kept an open copy of the textbook in front of him and, when asked a question, always knew all the right answers because he read from the book. He was surprised when he got a D grade. When asked, Dr. Schmelkes explained that in this case, the author of the text, Mayer Bałaban got an A but the student deserved no more than a D.

As I was getting older I was given a weekly allowance of 25 *groszy* so that I could buy myself a soda or a piece of candy. Most candies cost 5 groszy and I could treat myself to one every school day, except that the candy that I really liked and wanted was a *Danusia*, a bitter chocolate confection filled with soft sweet chocolate cream, but Danusia was very expensive and cost 25 groszy so I could afford it only seldom, after having no treats for a week. On occasion I bought an ice cream cone for 5 groszy and, instead of sweets I often stopped on my way to school at the *Ziarno* cooperative grocery store on lower Grodzka Street and bought myself a sour pickle straight from a barrel and ate it right there in the street. The pickle also cost 5 groszy. As a special treat, I would stop at a bar on Starowislna Street and buy a snack which sat in a tray on the counter, obviously meant to accompany a shot of vodka. The snack consisted of a chunk of Polish sausage pickled in vinegar with a slice of sharp pickle on top held by a toothpick and a dollop of mustard. At times, my father would take me with him when he enjoyed a *widelec* (Polish word for a fork), a snack in a bar on Sienna Street, a steamed frankfurter on a crisp roll with sourkraut and mustard.

I have encountered a general impression among Americans, including Jewish-Americans, that a majority of Polish Jews in the years 1918-1939 were very religious and observant, strictly keeping religious commandments, including eating only kosher food. Polish Jews were said to be oddly dressed, wearing black old-fashioned caftans and *yarmoulkes* (caps), sporting long beards and side-curls (*peyes*). Indeed, Jews all over Poland were like that several generations earlier. While many remained like that in small backward *shtetls* and in religious hasidic *yeshivas* and some rural newcomers in towns may have also been so attired, most of the Jewish population in a city like Kraków was indistinguishable from the rest of the general European population, just as were Jews of Germany, France or England. My family was fully "European" in dress, behavior and interests. My mother, whom I described in detail above, was fluent in French and German, besides flawless Polish and Yiddish. She was fully conversant with both classical European litterature, and the latest prize-winning French novels. My father was a thoroughly modern businessman and political leader, following European and American politics with keen interest. I spoke, and still do, flawless grammatical and accentless Polish. I expanded my reading to include Herman Hesse (*Siddharta*), Leon Feuchtwanger (*Jud Suess, Geschwister Opperman*), Heinrich Mann (*Young Henry of Navarrre*) and Arnold Zweig, Jean Paul Sartre (*Huis Clos*), Mihail Sholokhov (*Quiet flows the Don*) and Maxim Gorky, the Indonesian patriot Multatuli, *Kristin Lavransdatter* by Sigrida Unset and short stories by Selma Lagerlof, Jack London (*Martin Eden, Call of the Wild*) and Ernest Hemingway, as well as the trilogy by Shalom Asch (*Moscow, St, Petersburg, Warsaw*), all in Polish translation. In my newly acquired French I read the *Lettres de mon moulin* of Alphonse Daudet, and his Tartarin de Tarascon stories. As part of a group taught political and economic history by my uncle Ignacy I also read the *Communist Manifesto* of Karl Marx and Fredric Engels, long excerpts from *Das Kapital* and Max Weber's writings on what was published in an English translation as *The Protestant Ethic and the Spirit of Capitalism*, which greatly influenced my subsequent political and economic convictions. I also read and recited new Polish and Yiddish poetry. What is germane here is that my family was far from unique. All my childhood friends, whether Jewish or not, came from similar backgrounds; middle class or upper middle class, with not much attention to religion, but with knowledge and awareness of latest developments in Western civilization. All of my classmates in public school, Jewish and Roman- Catholic, were keenly aware of and following local and world events, including, for example, the Italian invasion of Ethiopia, the Spanish Civil War or the Japanese occupation of coastal China. In this we were rather typical of a large part of the population of Kraków, Jewish or otherwise. In secondary school I had 14 Jewish classmates (out of a class of 64), not one of them was wearing a yarmoulke or followed

orthodox religious dietary rules. As a group, in dress, diet, interests and behavior, we were totally indistinguishable from our Christian classmates although we were all very aware of our Jewish origins.

It must by now be obvious to my readers that formalized religion did not play an important role in my life, not before the Holocaust and not since. I was asked if my Holocaust experience brought me "closer to God", or conversely, made me "angry with God and loose any faith in Him". The answer is: neither. While conversant with Jewish history and ethics, I did not have any religious upbringing prior to the Holocaust, so I did not have faith to loose and I did not have religion to turn to for comfort. Therefore, I did not become religious as a result of my wartime experiences either. I grew up in a home with no religious observances, but a home in which ethical and moral considerations were always very strong. It was obviously possible for my parents to have a definite set of ethical rules without following a specific faith and to bequeath to their children an all human, all encompassing, humanistic morality without basing it on any specific religious considerations. In fact, I came to the conclusion as a youngster, and I still believe, that being moral without the expectation of reward or fear of punishment by a deity, represents a higher level of morality and asks for a greater exercise of free will and personal responsibility. It does not matter whether the faithful believe that such reward or punishment will be administered immediately or in afterlife. I feel that non-believers are more ethical than the most religious – they behave properly because it is the moral thing for a human being to do and not because their deity requires it and a priest, rabbi, guru or mullah preaches it, promising salvation or invoking fire and brimstone.

Of course, as a broadly educated person, a scientist and an amateur historian, I am fully aware of and interested in the exceedingly important role that religion has played in the history of civilizations. Obviously, there must exist some deep primal instinctive need in most people both to explain and defang the threatening natural phenomena that are not understood and to provide some meaning to prosaic human existence that is larger than oneself. People find it satifyingly comforting to believe that some beneficent intelligence is watching over them and will protect them from malevolent influences. The need must be felt very strongly and is instinctive and atavistic, and only tangentially cultural, inasmuch as most cultures seem to have independently invented supreme beings for themselves. Of course, the fact that religious beliefs were among the most important expressions of developing civilizations and that they arose in so many cultures, does not make them true. It only speaks to the desperate need for reassurance that is characteristic of our species. In fact, I believe that as a corollary to this need for assurance and security, it appears that it was not God, who created man, but that it was man who invented god(s) to satisfy his deeply felt needs.

Men created the concept of god, because of feelings of insecurity and need for protection and because of a need for a reason for being, a need for a cause transcending selfish temporary daily concerns. Every human group, every isolated tribe, seems to have devised its own protective deity or deities, which would help it to overcome its enemies. Usually, even in societies which worshipped many gods, one of them became dominant, serving as the chief protector or protectress. The presence of such a protector must have been very welcome, putting to rest profound anxieties and satisfying a need for reassurance. The monotheistic concept of one God, omnipresent and omnipotent, without a physical

localized presence, was slow to develop. One small and weak tribe, in an inhospitable near-desert land, surrounded by powerful enemies, imagined for itself just such a comforting tribal deity. At first this god was very personal, vengeful and dangerous, residing in one holly place, requiring temple sacrifices and blind obedience and ritual obeisance. However, over the years, this god, while a protector of his chosen people, became more and more concerned with ethics and morality, was less attached to a specific location and became definitely more universal, omnipresent and omnipotent. It is interesting that this concept of deity, developed by an insignificant desert tribe, became the dominant concept of the three so-called Abrahamitic religions. The Jewish God, with minor modifications, became the God of Christians and Moslems. For Christians, the Jew Saul of Tarsus, later known as St. Paul the Apostle, made the Jewish God acceptable when he modified the Jewish idea of a Messiah by adding to it the concept of a Redeemer. For Moslems, the Arab warrior Mohammed of Mecca became the last and thus, the most important in the long line of biblical prophets.

I find it fascinating that of all the possible permutations of the concept of deity, it is the Jewish concept that won such a wide acceptance. I believe that it was Ogden Nash, who phrased it succinctly, when he wrote the quatrain:

How odd
of God
to choose
the Jews.

While a non-believer myself, nevertheless I have always been fascinated by the variety of religious expressions and impressed with the power, for good and evil, exercised in the name of religion. Philosophy, ethics and morality owe a great deal to religion. Even those of us who do not believe, have been, consciously or unconsciously, affected by the milieu in which we grew up. There is no question in my mind, that the Judeo-Christian thought has influenced my ideas of good and evil and had, to a large extent, guided my own personal behavior from early childhood. The inner strength of my moral upbringing guided my behavior during the difficult days of the Holocaust, when I never acted with total disregard for others. I have watched so many previously religious men callously betray their brethren to gain even a most minor advantage. As I saw it, a religious background seldom prevented people from behaving abominably, while the opposite was also true: many non-believers acted nobly and sacrificed themselves for the common good. I can state proudly that my moral and ethical upbringing served me well during the War. Even in the most trying circumstances in concentration camps I have never done anything to be ashamed of or anything that I would come to regret in retrospect. I have never taken unfair advantage of anybody and I was always as helpful and considerate of others as I possibly could have been in those horrible days.

While my ethical behavior was not due to my belief in, or fear of God, I was always painfully aware that religion could be a force for good as well as evil. I am aware that we, as a civilization, have good reason to be grateful to religious fervor of the past, as well as be afraid of it. Religious beliefs led to the creation of some of the greatest human achievements, which would not have been created otherwise, among them some of the great works of art,

music, literature and architecture. In art, my personal idiosyncratic selection includes the stained glass windows of Sainte Chapelle on the Ile de la Cite in Paris, the Last Supper of Leonardo da Vinci in Milan, Michelangelo's Pieta and the ceiling of the Sistine Chapel in the Vatican, the Byzantine mosaics in the Church of San Appolinare Nuovo in Ravenna, the Sarajevo Haggada, the modern Haggadah of Arthur Szyk, and the Wit Stwosz wooden altar in the Church of Our Lady in Kraków. The religious music masterpieces that I love include Bach's St. Matthew's Passion, the Ave Maria of Schubert and the traditional Jewish devotional tune, Lekhu Doydi, which was transcribed for modern instruments by my great-uncle Edward Birnbaum. World literature owes its inspiration to that great tribal chronicle of my people, the Bible, which is particularly poetic in English in its St. James version. In my opinion, the religious fervor expressed itself best in grand architectural monuments, meant to evoke awe and admiration for a specific deity. A list of great religious edifices that I have visited and admired is large. It includes, in no particular order, the Parthenon in Athens, Angkor Temples in Cambodia, Menakshi Temple in Madurai in South India, Shwa de'Gon Temple in Rangoon in Burma, Mosque of Omar in Jerusalem, Suleymaniye Mosque in Istanbul, Bibi Khanum Mosque in Samarkand, Tanah Lot seaside temple in Bali, Borobodur on Java, Yo-mei-Mon Gate in Nikko, Japan, Dohanyi Street Synagogue in Budapest, the recently-attacked Ghriba Synagogue on Jerba Island in Tunisia, Pecherskaya Lavra Monastery in Kiev, Saint Basil's in Moscow, Gaudi's Sagrada Familia Church in Barcelona and the Duomo in Milan. The list is endless and I have been hard put to limit my selection only to those, which I consider as the most spectacular. All these architectural monuments were created thanks to organized religion.

On the other hand I am also aware of the terrible damage that religious fervor has caused and is still causing in the world today. The absolute belief in one definitive truth confers on believers not only the right but the obligation to force that truth down the infidels' throats, by persuasion if feasible, by force if necessary and by murder if required to save "immortal souls". New ideas were considered dangerous to status quo organized religion more often than not. Heretics were burned at the stake; books, like the Talmud, were burned in *auto-da-fe's*. Religious wars like the Crusades led to massacres and created lasting animosity that hurts us even today. More people have been tortured and killed in the name of religion than for any other cause. Burning of Joan of Arc was not unique. The Spanish Inquisition was not unique. The Taliban and Al-Qaida are not unique. Religion served as a cover for sadists and torturers and bigots in many lands and in many periods. The Jews, having lived for two millennia as a minority among Christians and Moslems, had particular reasons to experience and fear religious fanaticism. In fact, the entire Jewish history, from the time of the destruction of Herod's Temple to the Holocaust, consists of one long series of religiously inspired persecutions. The Holocaust, while the largest and most ominous, is not even the last in the series. One can look at the anti-Jewish excesses that took place since, in Argentina, in Stalin's Russia and in the Moslem Middle East, as a continuation of religious attacks. The 1941 pogrom in Jedwabne that I mentioned before, while horrible in its own way, represented only a minor episode in the long history of my people. The Church-inspired antagonistic behavior of Polish anti-Semites towards Polish Jews before the War, fit perfectly with the position of the Roman Catholic Church for most of the last two thousand years of Jewish history. It is of interest that anti-Semites, while complaining of the Jews' "alien" appearance and sacrilegious beliefs, never made any

meaningful distinction between those Jews who adhered to their traditional black clothing and ancient religious customs and those who abandoned both and blended into the general population. Certainly, the Nazis made no such distinction. I appreciate the recent attempts being made in Poland to modify the latent anti-Jewish feelings, which I experienced as a child in Kraków. In particular, I appreciate the efforts of the late Pope John Paul II and of the Polish Episcopate to moderate the long-standing anti-Semitic feelings of a large proportion of the Polish nation.

This brings me to the fact that I am a Jew, even though I am not a Jew by religion. I have always been aware of my Jewish origin, even as illustrated by the anecdote about the priest who asked me if I am a *Starozakonny*. I did not as a child and I do not now follow any of the external requirements of Mosaic faith, as they are generally understood. I do not cover my head, do not attend any formal house of prayer, do not eat exclusively kosher food, do not keep meat and milk separate, do not fast on religiously designated days, do not put philacteries on my forehead and arm for prayer, etc., etc. I am not a Jew because of religion, I am a Jew because I was born to Jewish parents and am a descendants of a long and proud line of Jews. I am a part of the Jewish people. I consider my being a Jew an outcome of my belonging to a national or ethnic group, not a religious one. Much as I do not observe this or any other particular religious faith, I have no doubt that we, the Jews, survived as a separate entity over two millennia (a *relic,* as the historian Arnold Toynbee once wrote!), largely thanks to the tenacious adherence to the ancient religion. We did not get submerged in the sea of surrounding nations mainly because of persecutions that we encountered. I believe that, even though a non-believer, I am a Jew. I was a Polish Jew and am now an American Jew, because my parents were Jews. Religious beliefs can be changed or abandoned, but the fact of national origin is rooted in the past and as such can be ignored but can not be changed. In the same vein, an Italian-American or an Irish-American, who was born a Catholic, can convert, say, to Buddhism, and thus cease to be a Catholic, yet he remains an Italian-American or Irish-American, because the latter is based on the fact that his ancestors were Italians or Irish. To many Jews being Jewish means both belonging to the Jewish ethnic group and following the Mosaic faith. To me and many like me, only the former is relevant.

It is of interest that to anti-Semites in Poland and elsewhere Jews were an enemy as an abstract concept. Having Jewish friends and knowing Jews as they really were did not change the concept and seldom altered anti-Semitic beliefs. Indeed, many anti-Semites who had Jewish friends made an exception for *them*, but still were against the Jews as an impersonal construct. The previously mentioned Polish novelist, Zofia Kossak-Szczucka, was a case in point. She was highly educated, of upper crust family, a gentlewoman in origin and behavior. Before the War she was convinced that "Jews" were harmful to Poland and that Poland would be better off without them and joined the main anti-Jewish political party. During the War, appalled by the murderous German treatment of Jews, she risked her life to lead an underground Committee to Help Jews, yet did not change her political inclinations and remained convinced that Poland as a country would be better off without Jews. Prejudice is a very strong emotion, often impervious to logic, especially an ingrained one, carried from one generation to the next. Unfortunately, it is easy for demagogues to stir up ancient hatreds and exploit them for personal gain. In Poland some of the politicians may have honestly believed in the poison that they spread, among them the above-mentioned

Kossak-Szczucka and perhaps Roman Dmowski, but many others did not and simply used it as a tool. We know that the Tsarist government consciously used anti-Semitism as a tool to divert attention of poor peasants and workers from its own incompetence, absolutism, corruption and mismanagement and stirred the masses and encouraged pogroms. Jews were always a convenient scapegoat. Even now, the Middle Eastern governments find it convenient to inflate the importance of the small Jewish state in their midst and use it as an excuse for their own ineptness and corruption and an excuse for doing nothing to modernize their economies and allow their people more political freedom.

In 1939, Poland, unlike the United States, could not afford the luxury of isolationism. On its eastern border the Soviet Union was self-destructing with the so-called Moscow trials of old Bolsheviks and military leaders, yet remained poised to swallow little Poland. On the other border, Hitler's Germany was evidencing a bigger and bigger appetite. It swallowed the Saar and militarized the Rheinland. In 1938 it grabbed Austria. It took the harbor city of Klaipeda (Memel) from Lithuania. The British under Prime Minister Neville Chamberlain and the French under Premier Edouard Daladier were not prepared militarily or psychologicaly for war. Fearing what Hitler might do if opposed, they forced independent Czechoslovakia at a meting in Munich to yield large areas to Germany. The Czech fortified border in the Sudeten mountain range was surrendered to the Germans, leaving the Czechs defenseless. Unable to oppose, not only Hitler and Mussolini, but also Chamberlain and Daladier, the Czech President Edouard Benes, Masaryk's successor, resigned allowing Hitler to set up a puppet government in Prague under Emil Hacha. Within months, the independent Czech Republic became a German Protectorate of Bohemia and Moravia. A puppet government under Father Tiso was set up in a satelite state of Slovakia, thus surrounding Poland with German troops from the North, West and South, with Soviet troops in the East. Nazi propaganda in Poland was spread by the Polish fascists and by the small German minority in the Polish-German borderlands. In the resort spa of Szczyrk south-west of Kraków, where we were vacationing in the summer of 1939, Nazi posters in Polish and German festooned local walls and roadside telegraph poles. I recall how they angered my father who was pulling them down.

Unlike Austria and Czechoslovakia, Poland did not cave in, but it stood quixotically ready to resist the German onslaught and refused to give up its access to the Baltic Sea, Danzig and Pomerania or to allow Soviet troops to march through its territory to confront the Germans. The British Government, finally waking up to the fact of Nazi duplicity and unlimited appetite, in 1938, rather late, guaranteed the inviolability of Polish borders. Within months, in a stunning and totally unexpected reversal of policy for both dictators, Germany concluded a pact with Russia. Stalin shed his long-time Foreign Minister, an old Jewish communist, Maxim Litvinov, and named as Foreign Minister his loyal subject and comrade, the stolid Vyacheslav Molotov, who was blindly obedient and whom the Russians knew as a mental lightweight and called "Molotov *durak*". The German Foreign Minister, Joachim von Ribbentrop traveled to Moscow to confer with Stalin, and concluded a pact, not-so-secretly dividing the area between Russia and Germany into "spheres of influence", within which each would have a free hand. Poland was to be partitioned, with Russia getting the eastern half. Russia was also given a free hand in the Baltic States, Lithuania, Latvia and Estonia. Assured of Russia's benevolent neutrality, and knowing that the French and the British were not militarily ready and therefore not prepared to start a Western front,

Hitler wanted to finish Poland off in a hurry and then turn to face the Allies in the West. Poland was invaded on September 1, 1939, without a declaration of war. The German propaganda claimed that the Poles were abusing the German minority in Poland which was minute and used this as the pretext for attacking. The British and the French were indeed not prepared but bound to honor their recent guarantees to Poland, on September 3, 1939 declared war on Germany. Thus began the Second World War in a generation.

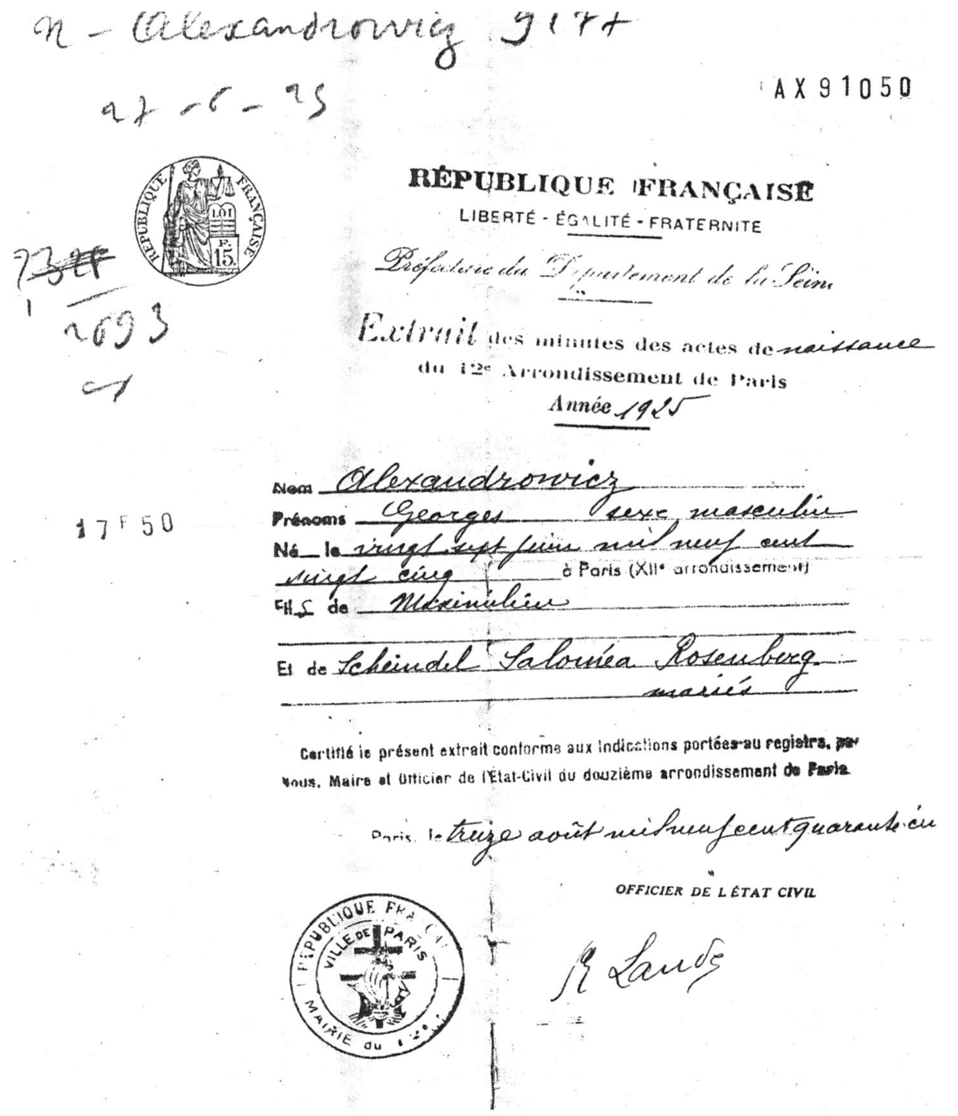

N - Alexandrowicz 9177
27-6-25

AX 91050

RÉPUBLIQUE FRANÇAISE
LIBERTÉ - ÉGALITÉ - FRATERNITE

Préfecture du Département de la Seine

Extrait des minutes des actes de naissance
du 12e Arrondissement de Paris
Année 1925

Nom Alexandrowicz
Prénoms Georges sexe masculin
Né le vingt sept juin mil neuf cent vingt cinq à Paris (XIIe arrondissement)
Fils de Maximilien
Et de Scheindel Salomea Rosenberg
mariés

17F50

Certifié le présent extrait conforme aux indications portées au registre, par Nous, Maire et Officier de l'État-Civil du douzième arrondissement de Paris.

Paris, le treize août mil neuf cent quarante cinq

OFFICIER DE L'ÉTAT CIVIL

R Lands

Fig. 073. Birth certificate of Georges (Jerzy) Alexandrowicz, Paris 1925;

Fig. 074. Jerzy Aleksandrowicz at 3 witn a teddy bear

Fig. 075. Jerzy at 5 with cousins, Eva, 7, and Hanka, 3, and a maid;

Above: from the left, Adam Scharf, the author (age 4) and my cousin, Ewa Aleksandrowicz;
Below: Foreground, the author and Adam Scharf;
Background, my mother and aunt Lola Aleksandrowicz

Fig. 076. In my mother's kindergarten in Kraków, 1929;

Fig. 077. My sister Anna at 5, with uncle Józek Aleksandrowicz and great-aunt Amalia Kleinhaendler;

Fig. 078. Kraków 1938, a professional portrait with my sister

Chapter 27. Kraków, a Central European City, steeped in history

While I was born in France, I grew up in Poland. My parents were from Kraków, the family sojourn in France was brief and we all returned to Kraków when I was three months old. Hence, as a child I only knew Kraków as the city of my childhood. The ramparts of Krakóws castle towered over the windows of my room from early childhood until the outbreak of the Second World War.

The earliest Krakovian castle located on a hill called Wawel was likely to have been made of wood and defended by a palisade. The site itself, a chalky Karst hill at the bend of the river, was easily defended. It had, however, according to legends one major drawback: a fire-breathing dragon that lived in a cave under the hill. The dragon, of course, required that young boys or, more likely, girls be provided to him. It took a brave and wise prince, conveniently named Krak or Krakus in the legend, to slay the dragon by a ruse, offering him a sheepskin filled with sulfur, swallowing which caused the beast such thirst that it died of too much of the river's water. The cave under the castle hill is today among Kraków's tourist attractions: in the cave large bones of prehistoric beasts have been found, probably giving rise to the dragon legend. On the shore of the Vistula, below the castle, today a black metal statue of a skinny dragon spouts fire from its mouth every few minutes. It is likely that a tribe and a ruler named Krak really existed, inasmuch as there is an ancient memorial mound dedicated to Prince Krakus, located in the southern part of the city. Large memorial mounds were an old pagan Slav tradition, which has survived to the present day. Kraków and its vicinity have three additional memorial mounds, including one for a prehistoric pagan princess, Wanda, one for the national hero, Tadeusz Kościuszko, and one, created in the late 1930's, for the Polish liberator and strong-man, Józef Piłsudski. A mound seems to serve purely as a monument or a lookout point, even the old ones were not used as graves. The Krakus Mound had been dug up and searched, but no tombs, no burial goods and no items of archeological interest have been found, only soil.

Kraków, (in Polish, pronounced Krah'-koof), the centuries-old hometown of my family, the Aleksandrowicz family, and home of one of the largest, culturally important, Jewish populations, is a city in the southern part of Poland known as Lesser Poland and called Galitzia by the Austrians prior to 1918. Formerly a royal capital and currently the site of the second oldest university in Central Europe (after Charles University in Prague), it is to this day *the* center of Polish culture. It was throughout most of its history Poland's most important city, referred to in Latin as *urbs totius Poloniae celeberrima* (the most famous city of all Poland). Called in Latin Cracovia, in English Cracow, in German Krakau, in French Cracovie, it is called in Yiddish Krooh-keh. I chose to use the Polish name throughout, rather than the English Cracow, because I found that with today's easy travel, the Polish name somehow fits better. References to the city on the Internet, such as those in the <Jewishgen.org> site use the Polish form, although without the accent over the "o". Kraków's international airport has the call letters, KRK, reflecting its Polish name.

Obviously, I have warm feelings for the city: my childhood there, before the onset of World War II, was happy and protected. I remember my days in Kraków with fondness, as do many former Jewish Krakovians. Recently, I found that we are not the only ones to have sentimental feelings for that city. A recently deceased prominent former citizen of Kraków who moved to Rome, also seemed to have harbored similar feelings for the city – in the summer of 2002, the late Pope John Paul II, a former Krakovian Archbishop and Cardinal, had completed a very emotional pilgrimage to Kraków, his last, indicative of how strong is the emotional impact of this attractive city on its former residents. It is said that the Pope wanted to be interred in Kraków, presumably in the crypt under the Wawel cathedral, but the Vatican objected and he was buried in Rome.

The origin of the city's name is lost in antiquity, as is the origin of the name of its river and of Wawel (pronounced Vah'-vel), the hill dominating the city, which was from the earliest times the site of the ruler's castle. No definite historical records exist, but legends abound. I have always been interested in the derivation of words and names. I have expended considerable effort, even as a child, researching various secondary sources to discover the origin of the name of the city and of its castle hill. I have been unsuccessful. I know of no common Polish or Slavic root words, which might resemble the word *Kraków*, with the possible exception of the cry of the ravens, said in Polish to sound like *kraah, kraah.* The name of the city is said to be derived from the name of its legendary founder, Prince Krakus or Krak. The Polish ending "*ów*" denotes a second case plural, i.e. genitive plural, a possessive responding to the query "*whose?*". Thus, the name Kraków may imply "a city of the ravens or of Krak people or the Krak dynasty", Possibly, there once existed an ethnic group or old Slav tribe of Kraks, but I am not aware of any. There are many Polish place names ending in *ów*, for example Piotrków (city of the Peters), Opatów (city of the Abbots), Lwów (Latin *Leopolis*, i.e. city of lions).

There seem to be a number of parallel Slav terms in Poland and in the upper Balkans. Thus, I was struck by the close relationship between the languages of South Slavs (Serbs and Croats) and of Poles, separated as these people are by German speaking Austrians and by Hungarians. To me the vocabulary of the distant Serbo-Croatian spoken on the coast of the Adriatic seems closer to Polish than the vocabulary of the neighboring language of Russia. I found it interesting that the latest thinking about population migrations in Europe beween 500 and 700 A.D. postulates that the South Slavs came to the Balkans from the shores of the Baltic, the land between the rivers Elbe and Vistula, some of them perhaps specifically from the area around Kraków, where they lived for centuries. This would explain the persistence of similar names on the shores of the Baltic and the Adriatic. Thus, we know that some old pre-historic Slav tribes along the Baltic called themselves Sorbs and Veneds, strikingly similar to names now found on or near the Adriatic. We know that a number of important population centers arose between 500 and 700 A.D., probably including Kraków as well as Dubrovnik in Dalmatia, named after the Slav word for oak tree (*dąb* in Polish, important in the Slav pagan religion) and the lagoon community of Venice, possibly given its name by arriving Slav tribe of Wendts or Weneds (for example, the name of Venice in German is Wenedig). I find it interesting that the main street in Kraków leading from the Royal Way and the royal enclave to the Jewish area in Kazimierz is called Stradom, so reminiscent of the main street of Dubrovnik called the Stradun. In paralleel with the name Kraków (and KRK, Kraków airport call letters), the name of the largest Adriatic island off the coast of Dalmatia is Krk. The Krk island was a historically important center of Croation culture and language, source of the early documents in old-Slav Glagolithic alphabet and site of the oldest preserved text in Croatian, the *Bashka Tablet* dating to the 11-th century. The early importance of the island of Krk can be gaged by the fact that it became a seat of a mediaeval bishopric as early as 900 A.D., before either Gniezno or Kraków in Poland warranted such a church honor. There is also in Croatia a river called Krka flowing to the Adriatic at Sibenik. Similar place names occur also in Bulgaria. Similarity of these names is likely to be more than a co-incidence. I believe that a relationship between early Slav Polanians and early Southern Slavs, in particular between Krakovians and Dalmatians, deserves to be investigated, perhaps with the aid of DNA studies of both populations. To the best of my knowledge, no prehistoric tribe of Kraks has been mentioned in early Slav records, not in Poland and not in Croatia, but perhaps one could be postulated. Besides the name of the city, I have looked for the origin of the names of its river or its castle hill, but found no information, not even any suppositions for the words *Wisła* and *Wawel*.

Kraks‘ town must have become important and wealthy enough to merit not just wooden but stone buildings, a rarity in those days. The oldest surviving stone structure, discovered in digging under the Wawel Hill, is the small round Romanesque chapel dedicated to Sts. Felix and Adauct, dating to the 9-th or 10-th century, built of flat, worked stone. As a child I visited the ruins of that little chapel, which were uncovered buried in the ground underneath the existing castle. Old legends also tell of conflicts between inhabitants of Kraków and German-speaking invaders, even in pre-historic times. The princess honored by a mound, Wanda, was said to have died rather than marry a German robber baron. To save her country from the German margrave, who pursued her and insisted on marriage, she jumped from the Hill to the river below. This patriotic self-sacrifice by a beautiful Slav girl is celebrated in songs ("*Wanda leży w Polskiej ziemi, bo nie chciała Niemca...*" , i.e. Wanda is buried in Polish soil, because she did not want a German), and commemorated every June in Kraków in an evening ceremony and fair called "*Wianki*" (wreaths), with fireworks, with elaborately decorated lighted boats on the river and with a large number of wreaths with lit candles floated down the river. As a child I enjoyed observing the fireworks and the floats from the balcony of our house which was located above the river bend.

Kraków, an important town at least since the VIII-th century, royal capital of Poland from 1040 A.D. to 1595 A.D., royal coronation and burial site thereafter, has retained its romantic medieval character to the present day. It is the seat of one of Europe's oldest centers of scholarship and higher education. It showed a significant Jewish presence from the earliest times. As I reported earlier, the first recorded appearance of the city of Kraków on the world scene occurred in the 10-th Century in the account of a Jewish merchant explorer, representative of the Arab Caliph of Córdoba in moorish Spain. Almost immediately, Poland appeared as a recognized power on the European scene, when in 966 A.D. the Duke Mieszko I converted to Roman Catholicism and married a Czech princess, Dąbrówka. The route from Prague to Mieszko's realm led through Polish (or Great Moravian?) Kraków.

Within a generation, in 1025, Mieszko's son, Bolesław Chrobry, was crowned as King of all Poland, with the blessing of the Pope and a grudging approval of Otto III, the ruler of the Holy Roman Empire. Besides the Polish lands, Wielkopolska (Greater Poland) with Poznań and Gniezno and Małopolska (Lesser Poland) with Kraków, Bolesław also ruled over the so-called Red Rus which included the "Chervenian" (Ruthenian) Castellanies of Halich and Vladimir. We know that at one point he conquered Kiev, today the capital of Ukraine, where he damaged his sword by striking it against the fabled Golden Gate of that city. He also conquered and for a while occupied lands belonging to the Great Moravian Kingdom, a major power at the time. In his time, Kraków became an important center of wealth and political activity and from his time on for several centuries most of the Polish historical events took place in Kraków. In time Kraków also became the site of a large and influential Jewish community, which, eventually included my ancestors.

Bolesław's descendant, another Bolesław, known as *Smialy*, i.e. "the Bold", formally moved the country's capital to Kraków. It was in Kraków that the next drama of Polish history took place. Partly according to later recorded oral history and partly according to legend, King Bolesław the Bold, facing a rebellion of powerful warlords and churchmen, killed or ordered the killing of the haughty aristocratic bishop of Kraków, Stanisław, head of the important Kostka family. The Church responded with excommunication, freeing the king's vassals from obedience and forcing Bolesław to abdicate and escape to a monastery. The Church not only had the martyred bishop canonized, but made him the patron saint of Poland. The murder is said to have occurred in a church on a small rock (in Polish: *Skałka*) on the banks of the Vistula in Kraków. Now the church of St. Stanisław "*na Skałce*" (on the Little Rock) serves as a place of pilgrimage and the burial place of Poland's famous artists and national heroes. Recently, historians began a re-evaluation of the entire event. Bolesław the Bold is now said to have been a very capable monarch, enlightened for his time, trying to impose royal hegemony over local warlords and church leaders. Bishop Kostka was both a churchman and a powerful magnate. His opposition to the king was political, not religious, and his execution may have been warranted for reasons of state.

Bolesław's nephew, Duke Bolesław Krzywousty (the Hare-Lipped), divided the country among his sons, but decreed that Kraków be considered as the official central capital of all Polish principalities. His sons ruled in Kraków in succession. It was during the time of the last of his sons, Mieszko III the Old that the first known Polish coins were issued, presumably in Kraków. They were apparently prepared by Mieszko's Jewish mintners and they had Hebrew inscriptions. This was the time of the Crusades and of the concomitant pogroms and great persecution of Jews in Western Europe. A great many Jews migrated east, looking for security and economic opportunities. As traders and craftsmen, generally able to read and write and keep records and having international connections, they were welcomed by the Polish princes and nobility, including the rulers of Kraków. Obviously, Jewish population became substantial and important, because in 1264 the Duke of the small principality of Kalisz felt the need to issued a decree, the so-called "*Statut Kaliski*", regulating Jewish commercial rights and offering Jews the sovereign's protection of life and possessions. Similar decrees were issued by several other Polish princelings. King of all Poland, Kazimierz Wielki (Casimir the Great), ruling from Kraków, extended the validity of the Kalisz Statute to the entire country. Eager for commerce and trade, Kazimierz encouraged persecuted West European Jews to settle in his kingdom, thus fostering commerce in Poland's cities and creating a class of merchants who were totally dependent on the good will and protection of the ruler and who helped to enrich the royal treasury. Like Alexander the Great much earlier, he established several new towns, naming them after himself "*Kazimierz*", all brick-walled, with many defensible brick buildings, mostly royal granaries, but also with churches and synagogues. One of these cities, Kazimierz Dolny on the Vistula, located approximately 100 miles northeast, downriver from Kraków, has a defensive brick synagogue dating to the time of its founding. The other, better-known Kazimierz, located just across the Vistula from Kraków proper, was incorporated into the Kraków municipality in 1791, when Kraków expanded, the river changed its course and the old river bed was filled in. The latter town of Kazimierz, which also has an old defensive brick synagogue (*Stara Bóżnica*), eventually held the largest concentration of Jews in Poland, if not in all of Europe. The policies of King Casimir the Great, including his encouragement and patronage of Jewish traders, resulted in a general increase in the country's wealth and power. He is remembered as one, who "found the country made of wood and left it made of brick".

Jews in Kraków settled in the area bounded today by St. Anne (then called *Yiddishe gas or Judengasse*), Jagiellońska and Gołębia Streets. At a time of great persecution of Jews in Western Europe, Casimir's Poland offered them a welcome refuge and the Jewish population grew rapidly. As in Worms in Germany, manning one defensive tower and gate in the wall surrounding mediaeval Kraków, the one nearest to their living area, was the responsibility of the Jews. The Jewish area, near the city center, was in demand. Jealous non-Jewish burgers wanted to have their Jewish competitors expelled. The Kraków Jagiellonian University wanted to take over the area. Eventually, in 1495, three years after the expulsion of Jews from Spain, the Polish King Jan Olbracht expelled the Jews from Kraków proper, moved them to the nearby Kazimierz, and gave their land to the University. The old university buildings are still located there.

The Jewish and the non-Jewish merchants feuded continuously. Accusations of poisoning wells, of using blood of children in matzos, of desecration of religious wafers and of sacrilege were often hurled at the Jews. Individual Jews suffered terribly, many were jailed and tortured, many were martyred, but somehow, others managed to surmount all the obstacles and enmity of the Church and of the competing merchants, and continued to conduct business, commerce and crafts in Kraków. Among them were my ancestors. I believe that my putative ancestors were active in Kraków prior to the fifteenth century, probably much earlier. As described above, a prominent Jewish merchant named Alexander was active in Kraków in the 16-th Century. His sons, including the great merchants Baruch and Marek ben Alexander ha-Kohen and the famous scholar Jozue Falk ben Alexander ha-Kohen,

must have been referred to by their patronymic as the *ben Alexander* or *Aleksandrowicz* brothers. The first properly recorded appearance of the family name Aleksandrowicz, *as a surname* in Kraków dates to the year 1807, when Joseph Aleksandrowicz, born around 1783, registered a daughter, Temerle. There are many earlier indications of the presence of family's ancestors in the city, but in the early times surnames were not routinely used and future family surname can only be inferred. It is obvious, however, that my family and the city were bound in multiple ways. Generations of family members interacted with the city, influenced it and were, in turn, influenced by it. My own childhood was spent there and every corner of the inner city still evokes fond memories, as reported below.

To the best of my recollection, when I lived in Kraków, 1925-1940, the city was administered by a City Council and a President (Mayor). The Mayor's name was Mieczysław Kaplicki, said to have been a Jew, Kapellner by name, who converted to Catholicism and modified his name. Another converted Jew, General Mond, was the chief of the Kraków military district. As a measure of the interaction between the city and my family, in the last election to the City Council prior to the Holocaust, in 1938, six of my relatives run for seats on the council: my father Maksymilian Aleksandrowicz, my mother Luśka Aleksandrowicz, my uncles Ignacy Aleksandrowicz, Wilhelm Aleksandrowicz and Leib Schmerler and my cousin twice-removed Zygmunt Aleksandrowicz.

(a) Rynek Główny (Main Market Square)

As can be seen in a photograph of the city from the air, the center of town is pear-shaped and surrounded by a belt of greenery called "*Planty*", located over what used to be the fosse and the defensive walls of the mediaeval inner city. When I was a child there, strolling in the Planty was a standard relaxation and social occupation for Krakovians. As a child, I used to walk under the large horse chestnut trees in the Planty and collected their fruit, the shiny brown horse chestnuts, for use in making necklaces and as raw material for a glue which I used to make cardboard castles, cut-outs and other assorted toys. In the middle of the city is a large open Main Market Square, one of the largest in Europe, called "*Rynek Główny*". This Rynek is approximately 600 feet wide on each side. Near the bottom of the photo is the river, Wisła, pronounced Vee'-swah (Vistula). Above the river rises the Wawel Hill crowned with the Royal Castle complex. Facing the Castle from the south, opposite the round crenellated keep, are two cream-colored apartment houses that belonged to the family Aleksandrowicz prior to the outbreak of World War II in 1939. The name of the street separating the residence of the Aleksandrowicz family from the Royal Compound is Bernardyńska Street, named after the Bernardine cloister and church located at the other end of the street. The address of the house I lived in is Bernardyńska 11. Other Aleksandrowicz residences were scattered around the city.

Today, as in the past, Kraków is a quiet and dignified city, very "Central-European" in flavor. The Main Market Square, is indeed square-shaped, and surrounded by old burger houses dating back many centuries, as well as palatial town residences of Polish nobility. The sidewalks around the square are lined with outdoor cafes in the summer. A lively

Fig. 079. Kraków, view of the city center from above.

flower market is on one side. Ubiquitous crowds of pigeons hover over the square. In the center of the square is a 300 feet long, cream-colored, mediaeval, XIV-th Century, arcaded building called *Sukiennice* (Cloth Halls). The very name is indicative of Kraków's role as a center of the European cloth trade in the Middle Ages. Today the Sukiennice building houses an elegant café and souvenir stores under the arcades. Small stalls with assorted souvenir merchandise occupy the inside of the Cloth Halls and a branch of the National Museum is located on the second floor. On the outside, Gothic Sukiennice, rebuilt in the XVI-th century by Giovanni Maria Padovano in a Renaissance style, are decorated with coats of arms of the royal city of Kraków and with a number of carvings and gargoyles. The pillars between the arcades are garlanded with floral designs, except for the two central ones, which are topped with carvings of heads of Poland's kings and queens.

The patisserie known as Kawiarnia Noworolskiego is located at one end of the Cloth Halls. It is another of Kraków historical places. Its interior is old-fashioned, comfortable and dignified, its ceiling carved and covered with colorful murals. Noworolski Cafe prides itself on its coffee, fresh *"pączki"* (a type of jelly donuts) and tasty, extremely sweet pastry tarts and cakes. The small stalls inside the Sukiennice, built into the sides of the structure, perhaps as many as sixty, specialize in amber jewelry, arts and crafts, leather clothing and woodcarvings. In 1939, most of these stalls were operated by poor Jewish stall-keepers. Today there are no Jews there. Prior to 1939, one of these stalls, selling fabric and simple ready-made clothing, was run by Hirsch and Erna (Ester Małke) Blonder. As I stated before, Erna was my mother's aunt, a younger sister of my mother's mother, Keila Rubin. As a child, when walking in the Main Market Square, we often stopped to say hallo to the Blonders. When I was small, two of my father's brothers, both graduates of the Jagiellon University Law School, Ignacy Aleksandrowicz and Wilhelm Aleksandrowicz, had their law offices in buildings lining the Rynek and I remember visiting them there from time to time. I remember that the law offices had walls covered floor-to-ceiling with book shelves full of heavy tomes of law books.

A small but important branch of the *Muzeum Narodowe,* is located on the second floor of the Sukiennice. I visited it before the War and made a point to see it recently on my trips to Kraków and to make sure that I take there friends who accompany me on tours of the city. It contains several important patriotic Polish paintings, including two large canvases by the foremost Krakovian painter, Jan Matejko (1838-1893), "Hołd Pruski" and "Kościuszko at the Battle of Racławice", both depicting great moments in Polish history. The first painting depicts the formal public homage paid in 1525 on the Kraków Square to the Polish King Sigismund the Elder by his nephew and vassal Albert von Brandenburg-Hohenzollern, the Duke of Pomerania-Magdeburg, a duke whose descendants rose to become Kings of Prussia and eventually German Kaisers. The painting is quite detailed, showing all the foreign and domestic dignitaries invited to witness the occasion. Prominent among these degnitaries was the papal legate, Cardinal Possevini. The second painting shows Tadeusz Kościuszko, a hero of the American Revolution and a leader of Polish armies in 1794, during a victorious battle of Polish Army with the Russian Tsarist forces at Racławice near Kraków. Prominently displayed in this painting are peasants in Kosciuszko's army, armed with scythes set *na sztorc*, thus being used as bayonets. Both canvasses are enormous, each one occupies a large wall. The painter, Jan Matejko, was trying to awaken pride in Polish past and patriotic fervor in the present. Another large painting by Matejko, depicting past triumphs of Polish arms, shows King John III Sobieski saving besieged Vienna from the Turks under Kara Mustapha in 1684. That painting is now in Warsaw. As a proper Polish patriot of his time, Matejko was not favorably inclined towards Polish Jews. Unlike his contemporary artist, the sculptor Xavery Dunikowski, who had several Jewish students including my aunt by marriage Sala Klipper Aleksandrowicz, I could find no record of there being any Jews among Matejko's large number of acolytes.

In front of Sukiennice is a monument to the greatest Polish poet and patriot, Adam Mickiewicz (1798-1855). Mickiewicz was born in the Lithuanian area, near Wilno (now Vilnius), in the manor of Zaosie. He always considered himself a Lithuanian, yet his langage was Polish and all his poems were in Polish. At the time, the Lithuanian aristocracy spoke Polish and only peasants spoke Lithuanian. Indeed, as I mentioned earlier, the main work of Mickiewicz, the long epic poem called *Pan Tadeusz* begins with the phrase *Litwo, Ojczyzno moja* (O Lithuania, my fatherland), ironically written not in Lithuanian but in Polish. To this day, Lithuanians have mixed feelings about Mickiewicz, although Vilnius has retained a street named after him, the Mickievicius Gatve and preserved his Vilnius home and a pre-War statue. The Poles never had any doubt about Mickiewicz Polish patriotism and honor him as the national bard. I understand that during the War ocupying Germans destroyed the statue in front of the Sukiennice in the Main Market Square of Kraków but it has been fully restored. That Mickiewicz statue stands high on a pedestal made of a series of marble steps. Prior to 1939, huge political rallies were held in the Market Square and the speakers availed themselves of the pedestal as a rostrum and stood on it while addressing the crowds. I remember standing in the square and hearing both my politically active father and my equally involved uncle Ignacy, delivering speeches to 40,000 or more people from the steps of the Mickiewicz monument, denouncing home-grown fascists and German Nazis as menaces to civilization. Forty thousand was an enormous audience, given the fact that the entire population of Kraków at the time, men, women and children, was about 260,000. The rallys were called by leftist democratic political parties, including the PPS (Polish Socialist Party) and the Jewish Labor Bund. Both my father and my uncle spoke Polish, although, on occasion, my father also addressed the Jewish workers in literary Yiddish. My uncle Ignacy did not feel comfortable speaking Yiddish and often admixed Germanic phrases in his speeches. I specifically remember him, when speaking in Yiddish, referring to the continent of Europe, not as *Oyropeh* in Yiddish but as *Europah* in Germanic usage.

In addition to the Cloth Halls, Kraków's Rynek Główny boasts two other structures, a solitary clock tower, the sole remnant of its mediaeval, 13-th century Town Hall and a small Romanesque church dedicated to St. Adalbert, Poland's first saint. The Town Hall Tower used to serve, in Austrian times until 1918, as the "*Odwach*" (a guard post), a symbol of Imperial Austrian presence, with an armed soldier always standing stiffly at attention on guard there. I believe that during the First World War, my uncle Wilek Aleksandrowicz, drafted to serve in the Austrian Imperial Army, stood guard at the Town Hall. I wish I had a photo of him standing at the Odwach. Today the tower houses a small museum and, in the basement, a nightclub and a restaurant. To the side of the Town Hall Tower, a memorial plaque imbedded into the ground identifies the spot on which, in 1794, Tadeusz Kościuszko, newly returned from America, swore to take up his sword and lead an army, including peasants and Jews, in a fight against invading armies of Tsarist Russia. The fight, initially successful against overwhelming odds (see mention of the painting

"*Kościuszko at the Battle of Racławice*" above), eventually ended in defeat and the second partition of Poland.

In a corner of the Square stands the little church of St. Adalbert, the oldest in the city, dating to the 12-th century. The church now lies way below the street level showing how much accretion of land occurred over the ages. St. Adalbert (*Swięty Wojciech*) gave up his position as Bishop of Prague and retreated to the quiet of the Monastery of Monte Cassino in Italy. Afterwards, he became a missionary. In 997 A.D. he went to baptize the pagan Slavic Prusan people on the shores of the Baltic Sea and was killed for his efforts. King Bolesław Chrobry rescued his remains and had them interred in a golden tomb in the specially built cathedral in Gniezno, Poland's early religious capital erected at the site of a previous pagan center. Many miracles were associated with the missionary's tomb. This was at the very beginnings of the existence of the Polish State. Bolesław invited the German Emperor Otto to make a pilgrimage to the Saint's tomb in Gniezno, impressed the Emperor with his wealth and power and received from him an acquiescence to a royal crown for Poland, denoting independence and sovereignty, and indicative of the wealth, power and importance of this early Polish mediaeval ruler.

In a corner of the Krakovian Square stands the Basilica of the Ascension of Notre-Dame (*Kosciół Mariacki*, i.e. the Marian Church) dating to the 13-th century. The church building is surmounted by two towers, one much wider than the other but shorter, ending abruptly. One of the many legends that I remember from my childhood in Kraków had it that two brothers were competing which one can build a higher tower. The brother who had been losing became jealous and killed his more successful sibling, with the outcome that the larger tower ends abruptly, while the narrower one continues harmoniously and proportionately to its spire and golden crown (see photo at the end of chapter). As part of an old tradition, scrupulously maintained over the centuries, every hour on the hour a trumpeter climbs the taller tower and plays an ancient melody four times to the four directions of the world and each time the melody breaks abruptly. According to legend, in 1241 the Mongol Tatars under the over-all command of Batu Khan, a grandson of Djingis Khan, were approaching Kraków and would have conquered the sleeping city, had not an alert trumpeter seen them and warned the defenders from the tower with his "*Heynał*". A Tatar arrow hit his throat and abruptly ended the signal. Presumably, since then, every hour, twenty four hours a day, seven days a week, the *heynał* is being played over the Market Square sky and it is now broadcast nationally by the Polish state radio every day at noon. This sounds very romantic and the story may have some truth to it. Kraków boasts many other legends and festivals and ceremonies and several of them relate to what must have been a very traumatic Mongol invasion of 1241. Among the commemorative events is the annual "Lajkonik" festival, where a man dressed as a Mongol rides a festively caparisoned wooden horse. A widely told story, commemorated in the name of a white rocky Karst formation near Kraków, has it that the Tatars were chasing a group of nuns who were miraculously saved by the "Maidenly Rocks" *(Skały Panienskie)* which enclosed them and protected them from their pursuers.

Inside, the Marian Church is dark and moody, but it contains a stunning medieval masterpiece, a large polychromic wooden altar carved in Kraków over a dozen years by the Nurnberg and Kraków master carver Wit Stwosz (Veit Stoss) and his aides, between 1477-1489 (see photo below). This altar, which I remember from 1938 as being made of impressively aged and largely colorless wormy wood, has in the 1950's been restored to its gaudy shiny multi-colored state, which it presumably originally had. While the excessive brightness of the restoration has dulled somewhat by now, I nevertheless much preferred its old unpainted and ungilded look. We have seen a similarly restored much smaller wooden altar in a church in Levoca in Spisz (Speiss) area of Slovakia, south of the Carpathian Mountains.

The north side of the square is lined with cafes. We used to call it Linia A-B. Young people used to promenade along the Linia A-B, displaying their finery, somewhat like they do in provincial towns in Mexico along the sides of the Zocalo. I am not sure whether the custom survived to this day, because today Linia A-B is crowded with tourists, both Polish and foreign. On the west side of the Square is the well-known restaurant, Hawełka, continuing in the same location for several generations. This restaurant was a favorite haunt of the city elite, serving such rare delicacies as lobster. It still is expensive. The ground floor dining room is presided over by two large painted portraits, one of the last Polish King, Stanisław August Poniatowski, and the other of the Austrian Emperor Franz Joseph, who reigned over Kraków from 1848 to 1916. This sets the tone for the place and tells you immediately what to expect. An elegant, very wide carpeted staircase leads to the large formal dining room on the second floor, where we enjoyed a fine meal during our visit to Kraków in 1997. At the large landing on top of the stairs prior to the entry to the main dining room hangs an upright copy of a larger-than-life-size oil painting of my cousin twice-removed, Róża Aleksandrowicz, daughter of Wolf Aleksandrowicz, by a well-known Polish artist, Jacek Malczewski (1854-1929) (see photos). This painting of a specifically named young member of the Aleksandrowicz family in such a central location, serves as one good indication of the intimate connection between my family and the city. Further along the west side of the Square is the historic aristocratic palace *Pod Baranami,* including today a basement night club and cabaret, a site of concerts and shows.

On the south side of the square, among the many old buildings I remember one known as *Kamiennica Hetmanska* (Hetman building), having once been owned by the *Wielki Hetman Koronny* (Grand Crown Marshal) Jan Klemens Branicki. In the XVI-XVII-th centuries the powerful armies of the Polish-Lithuanian Commonwealth were commanded by four men, known as *hetmans*, two for Lithuania and two for the Polish crown lands. Branicki was the Grand Marshal of the crown armies. On the ground floor of the building is a large bookstore, once known as Friedlein, then as Gebethner and Wolff, where I used to buy books as a child. To the right is a telephone office from which you can conveniently call abroad and, in the Wierzynek building, another Kraków landmark, the restaurant Wierzynek, where we had an epicurean meal in 1997. Nicholas Wierzynek was a rarity, a Polish (not German or Jewish) burger in Kraków around 1365 A.D. He was not a nobleman, but he was rich. When King Kazimierz the Great had a number of crowned heads of Europe visiting Kraków, Wierzynek invited the King and his guests to a feast at his house on the Rynek and impressed all of them with his wealth and savoir-faire as well as with his menu. Among the invited royals were Emperor Charles IV of Habsburg, King of Bohemia John of Luxemburg, King of Hungary Louis of Anjou, King of Denmark Waldemar, King of Cyprus Peter de Lusignan, Duke of Austria Rudolf IV, Margrave of Brandenburg Albert, Duke Otto V Wittelsbach of Bavaria, Duke Ziemovit III of Mazovia, Duke Bolko II of Swidnica, Duke Władysław of Opole, Duke Kaźko of Stettin and others.

There are records indicating that Wierzynek borrowed money from Levko son of Jordan, the King's Jewish financier and thus it is likely that Jewish money helped fund the feast. Obviously, this *Uczta u Wierzynka* (Feast at Wierzynek's) was quite an event and the memory of it is still being cherished in Kraków. The restaurant bearing Wierzynek's name, located in the original restored Wierzynek building, still serves fine food.

As I stated before, King Kazimierz was a wise ruler and during his reign the country prospered. He had a Jewish financier. Lewko Jordanis. Even ordinary town people did well. This, after all, was the wise king who, at a time of persecution and expulsion of Jews in Western Europe, invited the hounded Jews to settle in his realm and establish commerce. As we can personally attest, the tradition of fine feasts continues to this day at Wierzynek's. The Wierzynek restaurant is the most elegant, with crystal chandeliers and fine décor and is the most expensive in town.

Finally, the south side of the square boasts many historical buildings showing their age by having been built with supporting heavy butresses. Among the buildings two, in particular, demand attention. One is the *Szara Kamienica.* the Grey Building, owned by the previously mentioned Jewish Feintuch family which converted to Catholicism. Stanisław Feintuch adopted the surname Szarski from the name of the family building and location of its colonial merchandise store. Nearby is the Montelupi building, owned by the Italian Montelupi family, which once ran the royal Polish postal system. When queen-mother Bona Sforza died, her son King Zygmunt August inherited some of her possessions in Italy and needed a system of rapid communication with Italy. In 1558 he asked one of his courtiers, the *nobly-born* Prosper Provana, an Italian resident of Kraków, to establish a regular weekly communication service from Kraków to the nearest Italian commercial center which happened to be Venice. To have the royal service pay for itself the King allowed it to accept letters and parcels for private citizens and businesses for a fee. Provana arranged to have fresh horses available at regular intervals and the mail moved from Poland to Italy through Vienna in five days, a record speed for the period, compared with the nine days it took the imperial Turn-und-Taxis post to deliver imperial mail from Vienna to Venice. After Provana, the Polish post was ran by the Montelupi family and from 1569 the Kraków terminal for the post was at the Montelupi house on the Rynek Główny. The Polish Post celebrated its 400 years in 1958.

The atmosphere of the Rynek Główny (Main Market Square) of Kraków, with its old burger buildings, its outdoor cafes, the *heynal* from above, the flower stands, even the pigeons, adds up to a very pleasing harmonious whole. I remembered the Square with pleasure and my impressions were confirmed when I visited Kraków in 1997. The Main Market Square is a rare gem, grand, yet built to human scale and meant to be enjoyed and cherished.

Fig. 080. Kraków Main Market Square (Rynek Główny);

Fig. 081. Rynek: Cloth Hall (Sukiennice) and Marian Church with its altar;

Portrait of the Austrian Emperor Franz Joseph

Hawełka

31-010 KRAKÓW
Rynek Główny 34
Telefon:
(012) 22-06-31, 22-47-53
Fax (012) 22-58-64

Rachunek nr 021624

NIP = 676-007-86-14
RACH.NR 11 STRONA - 1
02.11.97 K-202 RACH NR 24

1 GOL.Z GRZYB. 8,00B
1 PAPRYKARZ 8,00B
1 ZIEMNIAKI 3,00B
1 HAWBSVAAWELK 5,00B
RAZEMHERBATA 35,80A
1 MLEKO 0,50A
PODSUM.-ROON 6,97 1,53 28,50
PTU B 7% 25,23 1,77 27,00
PTU 3,30
ZŁ
OGÓŁEM GOTÓWKA 35,50

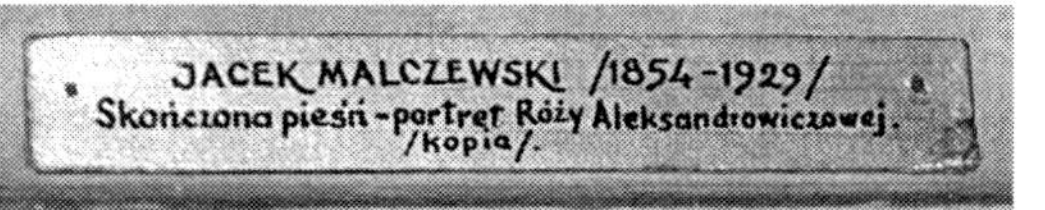

JACEK MALCZEWSKI /1854-1929/
Skończona pieśń - portret Róży Aleksandrowiczowej.
/kopia/.

Fig. 082. Hawełka Restaurant and its painting of Róża Aleksandrowicz.

(b) Old Kraków-Sródmieście (Central City)

In New York City, in Central Park on a rise over the lake, near the Meteorological StationI there is an equestrian statue of a crowned knight in armor with two crossed swords. The statue was funded by the Polish community in New York to commemorate one of the most important events in Polish history, the victory almost six hundred years ago by combined Polish-Lithuanian forces of Władysław Jagiełło, King of Poland and Grand Duke of Lithuania, over the German army of the Teutonic Order of the Knights of the Cross (known in German as Kreuzritter) at Grunwald in East Prussia. The memory of this great victory is kept alive in Poland to this day. At the time the Germanic order of armed knights grew so powerful that it threatened to integrity and territories of both Poland and Lithuania. It took the combined armies of both countries to oppose the Knights. The two swords in the King's hands relate to a snide remark made by the Grand Master of the Order, Ulrich von Jungingen, before the battle. He was so sure of victory and so contemptuous of the inferior armament of the Polish forces that he offered the Poles two swords prior to the battle. The Poles won, the Order was decimated and the Grand Master himself was slain during the fight. To this day, in New York, King Jagiełło holds the two Teutonic swords in his raised arms. A similar monument commemorating the victory at Grunwald was set up in Kraków, north of the old city walls and a Barbican, on the 500-th anniversary of the battle, in 1910, when Poland did not even exist as an independent country and the event led then to a great outpouring of Polish patriotism in Galitzian Kraków. Among participants was the then famous Polish-American pianist, Ignacy Jan Paderewski, who helped to fund the monument. The Grunwald Monument in Kraków was destroyed by the Nazis and restored after their defeat.

The old part of Kraków has many similar reminders of the past located beyond the Main Market Square in the eleven streets fan out from it. All these streets are lined with old buildings, as are cross-streets and neighboring plazas. Because the administrative capital of the country was moved to Warsaw in the 17-th Century, a lot of Kraków remained unchanged. Large portions of the old town of Kraków have been preserved. Even the German occupiers during the Second World War did not harm it much. Not only the Main Market Square but also the streets fanning out from it are of tourist interest. They all contain old structures of historic value, churches, palaces, burger homes, even fancy boutiques and restaurants that add to the charm of Kraków. All of them are steeped in history and tradition. I remember them all fondly as they all carry important connotations for me.

Three streets lead north from the Main Rynek: Floriańska Street, Swiętego Jana Street and Sławkowska Street. Floriańska Street leads from the Rynek to the Florian Gate, the one surviving gate of the mediaeval defensive walls that surrounded old center of Kraków (see photo). Beyond the Gate is a round defensive structure, the Barbican. The street is now a pedestrian promenade, among the main shopping and restaurant streets of the city. It is lined with many elegant stores, including Kraków branches of Paris fashion boutiques, several expensive restaurants, two hotels and a historic Kraków institution, the *Jama Michalikowa (*Michalik's Cave). The latter is a bohemian nightclub that once served as a hangout for a whole generation of Polish poets and painters and is today a tourist attraction. In October 1997, my one Aleksandrowicz relative still living in Kraków invited me, my wife and a visiting Israeli couple, Joseph Aleksandrowicz and his wife Tithy, to meet in the Michalik's Cave. It was a memorable evening: there weren't that many people named Aleksandrowicz in Kraków since 1939. The place has dark wood walls. Elaborate ceilings and rather modern stain glass windows. Located outside the mediaeval walls, beyond the Florian Gate, the round fortress, the Barbican, built in the 13-th century, has a special meaning for me. I remember that in the late 1930's it was the site of a mediaeval pageant, a part of the *Dni Krakowa* (Days of Kraków) Festival, with costumed actors recreating events from the Middle Ages and participating in pageants and other festivities. As a 12-year-old I have attended an open-air presentation of the *Till Eulenspiegel* story in the Barbican, in which the actor playing the mediaeval town mayor was so corpulent that he had to carry his belly in front of him in a wheelbarrow.

The next street, Swiętego Jana (St. John's) Street, leads from the Rynek to the Czartoryski Museum, a public museum that contains the art collection of the old Polish aristocratic house, the Czartoryski family. The caliber of the collection is a testimony to the Czartoryski taste as well as wealth. Among the museum's gems is a "Landscape with a Good Samaritan" by Rembrandt and a Leonardo da Vinci portrait of Cecilia Gallerani, seated, holding an ermine and appropriately called the "Lady with Ermine" (*Dama z łąsiczką)* (see photo below). I always deemed the Kraków Leonardo to be equal in quality to the Mona Lisa in the Louvre and the Ginevra dei Benci in the Metropolitan Museum in New York. The Krakovian "Lady with Ermine" has recently (2003) visited the United States. It toured three museums (Milwaukee, Houston and San Francisco) in an exhibition called "Splendors of Poland". The New York Times (Travel section, September 8, 2002, p. 3) referred to this Leonardo portrait as a "Mona Lisa rival" and confirmed my opinion of its quality by stating: "Many people, including experts, consider ‚Lady with an Ermine' Leonardo's most beautiful". The Czartoryski Museum also contains a collection of old armor, including a full hussar armor with its famous heavy wings that lent the hussar troops their weight and power, as well as historical military flags and costumes. It is located in a grand old building with an arched passage above the cross-street, Pijarska Street, which runs along the few remaining sections of the city's mediaeval defensive walls. Under the walls is a display of street art for sale, a veritable riot of color (see photo). Most of the paintings are only good as souvenirs, but it is possible to find some pleasing works of art among them.

On Sławkowska Street is the palace that houses the Polish Academy of Arts and Sciences. As a school child I visited the Academy with my classmates. It houses a Museum of Natural History, including a complete body of a Siberian mammoth on display, which was originally preserved frozen with flesh and skin intact. When I visited Kraków in 1997, a former classmate of mine from grammar school and gymnasium, now Prof. Kazimierz Kowalski (*Kazik*), rose to serve as President of the Academy. Sławkowska Street crosses the *Planty* garden and its extension north is called Długa Street. On the corner stands the building of the Chamber of Commerce and Industry. The entire street level floor of this building was occupied by the wholesale-and-retail stationery store of Róża (Regina) Aleksandrowicz, widow of Wolf, and her sons, which I described when talking about Wolf, son of Menashe, the youngest brother of my great-grandfather Józef. Nearby is the Kleparz Square, a daily farmer's market, where we bought fruits and vegetables and flowers during our stay in Kraków in 1997.

The three streets that issue from the Rynek to the West, are Szczepańska Street, Szewska Street and St. Anne (*Swiętej Anny*) Street. Szczepańska Street widens, past the old Poller's Hotel into Szczepański Square, on which is located the Municipal Theater, named after Poland's great poet, Juliusz Słowacki. The theater building is modeled after the old Paris Opera. Its interior is very elaborate, even gaudy, with gilded statuary, painted ceilings, dark upholstered seats, opera-like loges, etc. The solid fire-proof curtain separating the stage from the audience was painted by Henryk Siemiradzki, a painter I mentioned earlier. As a child I attended many performances in this theater, some with all my classmates as a school activity, among them "A Man for All Purposes" by Alexander Fredro. In 1997 we saw there a folk-art performance of a staged mountaineer wedding, complete with food, singing and dancing, in which we, the viewers, were treated to food and beer, like guests at an actual wedding.

The next street, *Szewska* (Shoemakers' Street) is also lined with shops, including several bookstores, where in 1997 I bought books by the Nobel Prize winning Polish writer, Henryk Sienkiewicz, author of the book "*Quo Vadis*". On an earlier visit to Kraków, in 1958, we bought a Polish woolen kilim rug at a *Cepelia* store on Szewska Street. The kilim was hand-made by mountaineers in Zakopane at the foothills of the Tatra Mountains. Szewska Street crosses the *Planty* promenade. In the Planty at this point there was an outdoor cafe before the War, Drobner's Pavillion, where my father took me on Sunday mornings. He enjoyed coffee and read foreign newspapers, I had ice cream in the form of frozen layered coffee with milk and whipped cream on top, served in a tall glass. In the Planty, in a spot near the restaurant, there is now a plaque indicating that on this site once stood the city's defensive walls. As I mentioned before, the defense of the tower at this specific location was the responsibility of the Jews, whose original area was nearby. The tower was called, appropriately enough, "*Żydowska Baszta*" (Jewish Tower). We saw a "Jewish Tower", presumably similar to the one that existed in Kraków, in the German city of Worms. In 1997, at the entry to the Planty sat an old peasant woman with a basket, selling a mountaineer specialty, a goat cheese called *Oszczypek*. That cheese is hard, pungent and strongly smoked, a delicacy that I remember from my childhood, like no other. It is produced individually in small quantity and hence, except for this old woman coming from the mountains, it is not available anywhere, except in the Polish Tatra mountain resort of Zakopane. Beyond the Planty stands a small theater called "*Bagatella*", which used to have children plays and which during the War served as a German recreation center that was bombed by fighters of the Kraków Jewish Underground. Further on, on the corner of Karmelicka Street and Podwale was a studio of the dancer Maria Billig (Billiżanka), who was my little sister's dance teacher. On Podwale was a teachers' college, in which my parents' friend Staszek Skrzeszewski was a professor. As I related before, after the war, Skrzeszewski joined the Polish pro-Communist government and served as Ambassador in Paris and as Foreign Minister. Not a Jew, he was married to a Jewish girl, Bronka Mandelbaum, a close childhood friend of my mother's. Further on, Karmelicka Street is crossed by Rajska Street. During our stay in Kraków in 1997, we lived in a rented apartment on Rajska 10. Every day we walked from our apartment, turned onto Karmelicka, crossed the Planty, past the woman selling "*oszczypki*", continued on Szewska and crossed the Rynek Główny on our way to the National Archives palace on Sienna Street to research old documents dealing with my family history.

Further along the side of the Rynek, past the *Palac pod Baranami* (Rams' Heads Palace) is the street of St Anne. It leads to the present-day campus of the Kraków Jagiellonian University. The oldest university buildings date to the 16-th century. The area was originally, prior to 1495, inhabited by Kraków Jews, with synagogues, ritual baths and a cemetery. The street now known as St Anne's was called *Judengasse.* The university always wanted the place, because of its central location and, eventually, arranged to have the Jews expelled from Kraków to the neighboring Jewish community in the town of Kazimierz, across the Vistula River. Later, after the Vistula changed its course, in 1791 Kazimierz was incorporated into the City of Kraków. The area at St. Anne Street remains in University's hands to the present. For years after 1495 Jews were not allowed to live in Kraków proper but stayed in the nearby Kazimierz, although they continued to conduct their commercial activities in the city center, a 15-20 min walk from their new homes.

Kitty-corner with St. Anne's is Wiślna Street. As the name implies, it leads to the river. Its natural extension is Zwierzyniecka Street, which, in turn, leads past the Abbey of the Norbertan Sisters, via the George Washington Boulevard, towards a Memorial Mound dedicated to Tadeusz Kościuszko, a hero of both the American Revolution and the Polish National Insurrection against the Tsar in 1794. The Kosciuszko Mound is surrounded by military fortifications. At the beginning of the War in 1939, when my father was drafted into the Polish Army, he was stationed in the Army Headquarters at the Kościuszko Mound. Not far from the end of Wiślna Street began a street of many names. I remember it as Wolska. My friend and classmate Adam Scharf lived there. His grandfather, Napoleon Telz, owned Kraków's most elaborate printing establishment on Wolska Street, the *Drukarnia Narodowa.* Napoleon Telz, a Jew, was a strong Polish patriot and many Polish patriotic pamphlets were printed in his shop, which occupied a large building. The company was equipped to print elaborate pictorial books and most of the elegant Polish illustrated tomes were produced here. Professor Mayer Bałaban's classic two-volume history of the Jews of Kraków was printed there, and, incidentally, financed, in part, by the R. Aleksandrowicz wholesale stationery store, which donated the paper. Just before the war in 1939, Wolska Street was renamed Józef Piłsudski Street after the late patriot, military hero, liberator and then strongman of Poland. The Communists called it the Street of the July Manifest. It reverted to its last pre-war name and it is again called the Józef Piłsudski Street. Further on this street is a building of the Polish Falcons. As a child, I used to go there for calisthenics. The street opens up into a wide meadow, called *Blonie.* The late Karol Wojtyła, Pope John Paul II, served as Archbishop and Cardinal of Kraków before becoming Pope. When he visited Kraków for the first time as Pope, he celebrated a Mass on the Błonie, and the entire huge area was full of admiring celebrants. There is now on the Błonie a monument commemorating this event, a huge inscribed boulder. The Pope also held a Mass here during his 2002 visit to Kraków. The Latin motto on the Sokoł buildings reminded me that many buildings in Kraków had Latin proverbs on them and as a child I used to collect and cherish these sayings and I still remember some of them. A few examples: on the Lutheran Church of St. Martin it said: "*Frustra vivit, qui nemini prodest*" (He lived in vain, who was of no use to anybody), on the headquarters of the V-th Army on Stradom Street it said: "*Si vis pacem, para bellum*" (If you want peace, prepare for war).

The street next to Wiślna, fanning out from the Rynek is Bracka Street. On Bracka Street there used to be a small private lending library, owned by the Gumplowicz family,

where as a child I used to borrow books, both fiction and non-fiction. I know now that this library was established three generations earlier by Ignacy Gumplowicz, brother of Ludwik Gumplowicz, the founder of modern science of sociology, described in an earlier chapter. The library played a large role in acquainting Kraków Jews and non-Jews with the world literature and political thought and it facilitated communication between Kraków Jews and Poles and introduced Jews to modern Polish and Western European writings. The grandfather of the Gumplowicz brothers, Jacob Gumple, was a rich Kraków merchant, born in the city prior to the Partitions of Poland. Jacob's daughter, Dobrysz Gumplowicz, married my great-great-great-grandfather Joseph Aleksandrowicz. Thus, Jacob Gumple is my ancestor and the Aleksandrowicz and Gumplowicz families are distantly related. I met a direct descendant of Jacob Gumple, Jan Imich, who now lives in England. Another descendant, that recently wrote to me, lives in Washington, D.C.,

Back in the Rynek, to the left of the Marian Church, stands a smaller church, dedicated to Saint Barbara, patroness of miners, including those of the famous large ancient salt mine in Wieliczka near Kraków. The street next to St. Barbara's church leads to a smaller square, appropriately known as Mały Rynek, i.e. Small Market Square. It is not really small, except in comparison to the Main Square. This smaller square is used for special events, fairs and exhibitions. The street north of Mały Rynek, Szpitalna (Hospital) Street used to be lined with "*antykwariats*", antique stores and old bookstores. The other street fanning out from Mały Rynek, Sienna Street leads to the Main Post Office, the Old Vistula Street and, in the distance, to one of the bridges over the river. At 16 Sienna Street, in a small palace, is the Kraków branch of the Polish National Archives, where my wife and I spent many hours, having the thrill of handling delicate old original documents describing my family's past and the past of Kraków's Jewry.

The main street from the center square going south, the only street that is not geometrically at right angles to the square, Grodzka Street (*Gród* means castle or fortress), leads directly to the entrance to mount Wawel, which is surmounted by the royal castle complex of Kraków. Many old buildings, several churches and palaces are located on the Royal Way which is the Grodzka Street. Where Grodzka Street crosses a wide opening, there are two squares flanking it and on them two old churches. To the right is the All Saints Square, with a 13-th century Franciscan Church, the 17-th century Wielopolski Palace housing the Kraków City Hall and the palace of the Roman Catholic Archbishop of Kraków. Karol Cardinal Wojtyła, Pope John Paul II, lived in the latter as the Archbishop of Kraków and he stayed there when visiting Kraków as pope. To the west of Grodzka Street is the Dominican Square with the Dominican Church. In the Franciscan Church are the Art Nouveaux stained glass windows designed by Stanisław Wyspiański (1869-1907), a multi-talented painter, designer, poet and writer. In the Dominican Church there is a stone tomb of the Kraków Duke, Leszkek Czarny (Leszek the Black), from 13-th century. The US consulate in Kraków is located in a side street near the Dominican Church, on Stolarska Street. Grodzka Street continues after crossing Poselska and Senacka Streets (named for the members of Lower and Upper Houses of Parliament). It passes the baroque church of Sts. Peter and Paul, the gothic church of St. Andrew, the Lutheran church of St. Martin and the small medieval church of St. Jude. Beyond it is a monument to the victims of the Katyń Massacre, where the Russians executed thousands of Polish army officers in 1940. The street widens to a magnificent plaza with a view of the Royal Palace on a hill. Beyond

the Royal palace, the street changes its name to Stradom and then to Krakowska Street, the main border street at Kazimierz, in what used to be a Jewish area of the City. The Jewish Community Center is located on Krakowska Street.

Fig. 083. Medieval Florian Gate and art display under the old walls.

Fig. 084. The Czartoryski Museum with Leonardo's Lady with Ermine

(c) The Royal Complex on Wawel Hill

I grew up in the shadow of Wawel Hill. It shaped my entire childhood and was inordinately important to me and to my family. It is, in a way, the epitome of my connection to the city of Kraków and to Poland. As it happens, the Wawel Hill also represents the core of Polish history and culture. The complex of structures on Wawel Hill, incorporating the early medieval, gothic and then Renaissance Palace of Polish Kings and their coronation cathedral, both established prior to the tenth Century and enlarged and decorated in the XVI-th century, at the time of Poland's greatest glory, is deeply imbedded in the Polish psyche. It is, by far, the most important expression of Polish nationhood, representing the quintessence of everything that is important to being Polish. And it is that complex that has also so much meaning for me. During all my happy years before the War, I played on Wawel's ramparts and fantasized in its shadow. My home stood facing the castle. From my bedroom, every morning, upon awakening, I gazed at the crenellated castle walls and the round mediaeval tower standing guard over my window.

The Wawel Hill, surrounded by crenellated ramparts, contains within its old medieval fortress walls crowned by defensive towers, a largely Renaissance Royal Palace and Baroque Cathedral, the residence, coronation and burial places of Kings. Both edifices were old when converted to their present Renaissance style. As a child, I and all the local children, considered the whole Wawel complex as our own grand medieval playground. We played under the walls and climbed over them. As I stated before, my family owned two large houses directly facing the castle. From the top of the castle walls one can look into the windows of the third floor apartments in the family buildings and conversely, from the third floor balcony of my aunt Lola Aleksandrowicz, I looked over the top of the castle ramparts under the round keep of the tower. A more romantic surroundings for one's childhood would be hard to imagine. I still have a warm feelings for the family homes, I consider that I have a valid claim to them in spite of their having been taken over, during Communist rule, by the Polish National Treasury as "abandoned property". The claim of "abandonment" rings hollow, given the fact that my family members and I myself have tried to recover them and futilely traveled to Kraków many times to reclaim them. The photos at the end of this chapter show the location of the castle hill above the river and some of the fortifications that I used as my playground. They also show the Aleksandrowicz houses on Bernardyńska Street, located directly opposite and below the round tower of the castle.

Directly opposite the Aleksandrowicz house at 11 Bernardyńska Street starts a steep and narrow but attractive path leading up to the summit of the Wawel Hill, past the crenellated walls to a heavily overgrown, ivy-covered entry gate to the palace grounds. From the spot beyond the gate it is possible to see the roofs of the Aleksandrowicz houses, and peek into the apartments there. To the right, under the Hill, flows the Vistula River. Beyond the river is the area of Dębniki, where my family lived in 1925-8. Today, on the other side of the river stands the Forum Hotel, distant from the center of the City, but with a great panoramic view extending to the castle hill. Proceeding on the hill, past the Sandomierska and, then, the Złodziejska Towers, near the entrance to the Dragon's Cave, one enters a broad area, with an exterior view of the Renaissance Palace and the cathedral with its side chapels crowned by roofs covered with gold. There is a small cafe in the opening and a number of huge canons from various military engagements over the centuries.

The Royal Palace in its present form dates to the XVI-th Century rule of King Sigismond the Old and his wife, Bona Sforza, daughter of the Duke of Milan. Bona Sforza brought Italian architects, Francesco di Firenze and Bartolomeo Berecci, to Kraków. They converted the existing gothic structure into an expansive Renaissance complex, with an arcaded courtyard, one of the largest and best preserved in Europe. In the courtyard the City of Kraków used to, and still does, present outdoor costumed mediaeval spectacles. I remember attending, as a child in 1938, a chess game with living actors in elaborate costumes as chessmen, as part of the festival of "Kraków Days" celebrated every June. In 1997 we saw, in this courtyard, the re-enactment of a mediaeval wedding of a Bavarian prince and the daughter of a Polish King, performed by a visiting cast of hundreds, all dressed in elaborate period costumes, who came from the Bavarian town of Landshut. The walls of palace rooms are decorated with Belgian Arras tapestries from the XVI-th Century. They contain collections of historical objects, ranging from the sword of King Bolesław the Bold, warped when he hit the Golden Gate of Kiev with it in the 12-th Century, to the huge blue silk tent of the Turkish Vizier Kara Mustafa that King John III won at the battle of Vienna in 1684. The chambers have been abused over the centuries of Austrian occupation and only recently restored to some of their old splendor, indicating how rich the country must have been at the time of the glory days of the Polish-Lithuanian Kingdom around 1525, when its lands extended from Courland (today's Estonia) on the Baltic to Valachia on the Black Sea and from Silesia on the west to the Dnieper River on the east. The tapestries are spectacular and rival the famous "Red Unicorn" series in the Louvre.

One of the royal chambers, the Poselska Room, which was apparently used as a royal courtroom, had a ceiling decorated with 194 carved heads, presumably of royal courtiers and the queen's ladies-in-waiting, set in wooden squares. Over the years many of the heads disappeared and many of those remaining were damaged. In 1925, during a restoration of the palace, the chief architect in charge of the project, Prof. Szyszko-Bohusz, wanted to have the missing heads replaced. He asked the foremost Polish sculptor of the day, Xawery Dunikowski, to undertake this task. Dunikowski and Szyszko-Bohusz decided that the replacement heads should not be exact copies of the surviving heads but should be in the same style. Dunikowski, who had many students and acolytes, used his students and his friends and acquaintances as models. Since he surrounded himself mostly with other artists and young women students, the heads that he carved, 60 of them, are likenesses of some of his contemporary artists and of many of his girl students. His students and assistants are known to have participated in the work. My aunt, Sala, wife of my uncle Ignacy Aleksandrowicz and an accomplished sculptress in her own right (see more about her in an earlier chapter), was then, at twenty, a student of Dunikowski. I have a book of the Dunikowski heads (see Bibliography, under Walicki) and I have carefully looked at them to see if, by chance, my aunt served as a model for one of them, but I did not see any ressemblance. It is, however, likely that she helped to sculpt some of them.

The religious edifices on the Wawel Hill began in the seventh-to-tenth centuries with a pagan temples, then a wooden church, replaced in the XI-th century with the previously-mentioned round Romanesque chapel of roughly-hewn stones, the Chapel of Sts. Felix and Adauct. The present Cathedral of Wawel, the see of the Archbishop

Cardinal of Kraków, was built in gothic style, supplemented with Renaissance and Baroque additions. It served as a coronation and burial place of Polish Kings for six centuries. The cathedral contains many elaborately carved silver and marble burial monuments of royal personnages, starting with King Casimir the Great. The last two kings of the Jagiellonian dynasty, Zygmunt the Old and Zygmunt August, who ruled when Poland‘s power was at its zenith, are buried in separate Renaissance chapels adjacent to the main body of the cathedral, each richly decorated and with roof domes covered with gold. The maze of cathedral crypts, located deep beneath the floor, contains the tombs of kings, among them Casimir the Great and Sigismund the Old. Other crypts contain tombs of famous Poles, including Tadeusz Kościuszko, Józef Poniatowski (leader of Polish army and Marshal of France under Napoleon), Józef Piłsudski (liberator of Poland and military strongman, 1918-1935) and poets Adam Mickiewicz (the one honored by a monument in the Main Market Square) and Juliusz Słowacki for whom the City Theatre is named.

Beneath the hill is a large cave, called *Smocza Jama* (the Dragon‘s Cave), which can be visited and explored. Large bones of pre-historic mammoths have been found in the cave. The entrance is through a narrow winding staricase from the top of the hill, the exit is down below the hill towards the banks of the Vistula. Below the exit stands now a metal statue of a skinny dragon, which spouts a flame every few minutes. The banks of the river are now a promenade, the river bed is below. As a child I used to swim on a beach, on the banks opposite the castle hill, at a bend in the river. The beach was sandy, but not very safe, because the river created eddies and sudden deep spots and whirlpools. It is at one of such whirlpools that my sister almost drowned and I tried to save her but could not pull us out of the water and had to be rescued by my aunt Baśka, who was a very strong swimmer. I mentioned the incident, when writing about my uncle Olek, Baśka‘s husband. As I stated above, I share with most Polish patriots the warm feeling for the Wawel Hill. I remembered the warm feeling when I found a fragment from the Wawel among embedded fragments of palaces and monuments from all over the world n the Chicago Tribune Building on Michigan Avenue in Chicago.

Fig. 085. Photos of the Wawel Hill, with the Royal Castle, Palace and Cathedral;

Fig. 086. The ceiling of the Room under the Heads in the Royal Palace

Fig. 087. The Aleksandrowicz house facing the round tower of the Castle

Fig. 088. The Round Tower of the Castle above the Aleksandrowicz building;
Rita Alexander in Kraków in 1997;
Views of the Aleksandrowicz House in Kraków, 11 Bernardyńska Street

(d) The Jewish areas of Kraków

After their forced resettlement in 1495 from the area now occupied by the Jagiellonian University, Kraków Jews lived in a Jewish enclave in the township of Kazimierz by Kraków. The move to Kazimierz, which had a large Jewish community already, was certainly not welcome and caused obvious hardships including overcrowding, but it did not prevent the Jews from continuing to trade within the city. The Jewish area of Kazimierz was at first separated from the center of Kraków by a narrow river bed spanned by wooden bridges. That bed was eventually filled up to become a broad avenue, the Dietla Street. The entire area was not far from the Royal Wawel Hill and within a walking distance of the center of the city. In 1791, after the river changed its course and moved beyond Kazimierz, it no longer separated the two and Kazimierz was formally incorporated into the City. The main Jewish settlement started around the wide longitudinal area known today as *Szeroka* (Wide) Street. The oldest extant solid brick synagogue was built at the south end of Szeroka Street during the reign of Casimir the Great and renovated around the end of the XVI-th century. It is known as *Stara Bóżnica* (the Old Synagogue) (see photos at the end of chapter). The sturdy seven-centuries-old building has been restored and serves now as the Jewish branch of the Polish National Museum in Kraków. Around the Szeroka Street are two more synagogues: the 500-year-old Remuh Temple, still occasionally active, and the newer Popper Synagogue, now hidden behind a pseudo-kosher restaurant. Behind the Remuh synagogue is an old cemetery, vandalized by the Nazis, now partially restored. In this cemetery are the tombs of the Kraków sage, Reb Moses Isserles (Remuh), and his father, Israel nicknamed Isserl (photo). Also, there are tombs of a woman named Dobrysz, daughter of the cabalist Nathan Spira, who claimed to be a descendant of the mediaeveal Jewish scholar and rabbi, Rashi. As described elsewhere, a family legend says that we are related to Remuh. Also, my first ancestress to carry the surname Aleksandrowicz had "Dobrysz" as her first name. Inasmuch as Kraków Jews routinely named their children after deceased relatives, it is easy to surmise that Dobrysz Aleksandrowicz, nee Gumplowicz, could have been a descendant of Dobrysz, daughter of Natan Spira.

When the Jewish community outgrew the old Remuh cemetery around 1800, a new cemetery was created at the north end of Miodowa Street. The German occupiers during the Second World War destroyed most of the tombstones, including that of my grandfather, Jacob Aleksandrowicz, who died in 1935. After the war an attempt was made to restore this cemetery and today it is a properly quiet, green, treed, dignified and restful place. Tombstones that the Nazis broke have been incorporated into a "memorial wall". I believe that some of the black marble fragments of this wall have come from my grandfather's grave.

The Jewish area expanded as the population grew. According to a list of inhabitants quoted in the third volume of the work "*Dzieje Krakowa*")(Bieniarzówna and Małecki, 1979), in 1810 Kraków had a population of 23,612, of which 5,014 or 21.2% were Jewish. By 1847 the Jews constituted 32% of the population. In 1939, Kraków had approx. 260,000 people, including 65,000 Jews or 25%. In 1939 the bulk of the Jewish people still lived in Kazimierz, which was, however, considered the location for poor Jews. Well-off Jews lived all over town, although mostly in the area called Stradom, located between Kazimierz and the Royal Hill. Stradom extended from the corner of Dietla Street, the alley with narrow grassy strip in the middle, the street that was created when the river changed its course, to the corner of Gertrudy and Bernardynska Streets at the foot of the *Kurza Stopka* part of the royal palace on Wawel Hill. My family's leather business was located on Dietla Street. On the corner of the Stradom and Dietla streets stood an old church in a large yard. When the area became largely Jewish, the church lost its parishioners. Ecclesiastic authorities declared the building not needed and it was eventually sold to be used as a warehouse and craftshop. Apartment buildings were built on land in front of it, obscuring the old structure. Among owners and users of the land and the church structure was the well-known Krakovian Jewish family, the Schamroths. A drive to renovate that old church is now in progress.

In 1939 the main Jewish area extended from Starowiślna Street to the north to Krakowska Street in the south, from the present river bed of the Vistula separating Kraków itself from the area called *Podgórz*e (in Pol. mountain foothills) to the site of the old defensive walls, now marked by the Planty longitudinal garden along St. Gertrud and Bernardynska streets. The area was busy and vibrant – economically, politically, socially and culturally active – a living organism, where life was getting better and more interesting every day. One of Poland's best daily newspapers, a Jewish newspaper in Polish, *Nowy Dziennik* (the New Daily), was published here. There was an important privately funded Hebrew Gymnasium (secondary school), several theatres and movie houses, a number of synagogues, a large reform temple, many Hassidic religious prayer houses (*shtibls*), dozens of kosher and kosher-style restaurants and hundreds and hundreds of stores. Jewish political parties thrived and competed fiercely. Political rallys and demonstrations occurred often. It is hard to imagine today how vibrant this large Jewish community was and how much was lost because of the Holocaust.

The streets in the Jewish area were full of food stalls and hawkers. I fondly remember the sounds and smells of the street life. I used to buy hard yellow salted peas and warm Fava beans ("*bobes*") from street vendors, which they served in a sheet of newspaper rolled into a cone. Other vendors sold bagels and pretzels. What we called bagels in Kraków was very different from the New York variety which, I believe, came from Czerniowce (Tschernowitz) in the Bukovina, now in Ukraine. The Kraków bagels were baked, shaped in a circle, pleated from two or more strands of dough, crisp on the outside but soft inside, and heavily salted like pretzels. On rare occasions, when I got a five groszy coin and told to buy myself a candy, I bought instead a sour pickle from a barrel and ate it in the street. As I mentioned earlier, the candy I liked best, but bought seldom because it was expensive, was called "*Danusia*", coated in bitter dark chocolate with chocolate cream filling. In a bar on Starowiślna Street I used to buy a savory snack, a piece of sausage with a pickle. This item was obviously there to accompany a vodka, but as a youngster I had to be satisfied with only the sausage. On Sundays, the maid's day off, my entire family went to the Weissbrot Restaurant on the corner of Starowiślna and Dietla streets. Food in the Weissbrot Restaurant was not kosher but the place tried to stick to traditional Jewish style of cooking, thus being somewhat "kosher-style". I got a smaller portion of the same dish that my father got, the stuffed *derma*, and I always remonstrated with the waiter that I do not want a child's portion but an adult one, he always agreed with me and he winked at my parents and they all knew what he would do.

On the Stradom, within easy walking distance form my house, there was a movie house, which often was used for live performances, and I remember seeing there two famous Jewish commedians from Warsaw, Djigan and Schumacher. I also attended other Jewish theater performances, including a recitation by Rachel Holzer, An'ski's *Dybbuk* and American Jewish films, among them "*Yidl mitn Fidl*" with Molly Picon. In the Wanda cinema house on Gertrudy Street I saw many movies with Charlie Chaplin (Modern Times), Paul Muni (Pasteur), Errol Flynn (Captain Blood), Clark Gable (Gone with the Wind) and Greta Garbo (Ninotchka). The last one I saw there was an American anti-Nazi film, whose title I do not remember, about the Nazi spy activities in America and the help they got from the German-American Bund. That movie was still playing in the *Uciecha* Theatre on Starowislna Street when the War began and was immediately confiscated by the incoming Germans.

Of course, the Nazis put an end to Jewish Kraków. During the war most of the Kraków Jews were expelled, some forcibly moved to Podgórze, the area beyond the Vistula, where a Ghetto was being created, and most were eventually killed. A fragment of the Ghetto wall has been preserved to this day and a commemorative plaque erected on it (see photos). Also in Podgórze, on the *Plac Bohaterów Ghetta* (Heroes-of-the-Ghetto Square), there is now a small museum on the site of a pharmacy, which once stood at the border of the Ghetto. Further, south of the city, in the suburban area of Płaszów, the German occupiers created a concentration camp, known as Kraków-Płaszów. A replica of this camp was featured in the movie "Schindler's List". Today, there are no original camp buildings left. The area's rolling hills and meadows are grassed in. Two monuments stand there: a large one erected by the Polish authorities in memory of all the victims in the Płaszów camp and a small, modest one, erected by the Jewish community to honor the Jews, like me, who suffered there (photo) and those who died there. I spent a part of my war years in this camp. My visit to the camp area was emotionally draining and difficult for me, perhaps the most difficult moment during my recent visit to Kraków. In the camp, the Germans and their Latvian and Ukrainian guards were cruel, beatings were frequent, killing and dying was a part of daily existence. Re-living all this, even 55 years later, was not easy.

Fig. 089. Photos of the Old Synagogue of Kraków;

דא געלעבט,
געליטן און אומגעקומען
דורך די הענט פון די
היטלעריסטישע מערדער
פון דאנען האט זיי געפירט
דער לעצטער וועג צו די
לאגערן פון אומקום
דער פראגמענט פון די יידיש
געטא-מויערן
TU ŻYLI, CIERPIELI
I GINĘLI Z RĄK
HITLEROWSKICH OPRAWCÓW.
STĄD WIODŁA ICH
OSTATNIA DROGA
DO OBOZÓW ZAGŁADY
FRAGMENT MURÓW
GETTA ŻYDOWSKIEGO
1941-1943

Fig. 090. Photos of preserved small fragment of the 1943-4 Ghetto wall;

Fig. 091. Photos of Isserl family tombstones in Remuh Cemetery and of monuments at the site of the Kraków-Plaszów concentration camp

Chapter 28. World War II (Kraków Ghetto, Holocaust, Concentration camps)

After the Molotov-Ribbentrop pact was signed in 1939, the Germans issued an ultimatum to Poland to yield the so-called "Polish Corridor", the Pomeranian area of North Poland, separating the main area of Germany from the German East Prussia, as well as the Polish rights in the Free City of Danzig (Gdańsk). These rights were given to Poland at the Treaty of Versailles in 1918 to provide Poland with an outlet to the Baltic Sea. Unlike Czechoslovakia, Poland was not going to surrender to Hitler's demands and was preparing to fight. It received offers of support from Great Britain and France. It became clear that a German invasion of Poland was imminent. Kraków, located close to the German border and the border of German-occupied Czech "Protectorate of Bohemia and Moravia" and the German-controlled Slovak Republic, was at risk of being captured by the invading armies within a very few days after the onset of war. Poland mobilized. My father, then 37 years old, was drafted into the Polish army, given an ill-fitting uniform and an obsolete gun and stationed in barracks on the outskirts of the city. Somewhat naively, we all believed that the Germans will slice rapidly into Poland, go probably as far as the middle of the country, then stop for winter, while the Polish Army will regroup on the Vistula line. In the meantime, the Western Allies will open a second front in France and the war will drag on for a while. Thus, my father believed that the safest course for his wife and children would be to go to the central-eastern part of Poland, beyond the Vistula line, and to wait out the war there, while his brothers would temporarily relocate to eastern Poland, to the old Galitzian city of Lwów where they would join their sister and her Lvovian husband.

Thus, late in August of 1939, my mother, my sister and I boarded a train going east. It turned out to be a nightmare journey because the trains were overloaded, since we were not the only people who tried to escape east. The first town that we looked at for shelter, Zamość, was overrun by refugees, and we could not remain there. Eventually, we stopped in a pretty spa and resort community called Nałęczów, not too far from Lublin and about one hundred miles south-east of Warsaw, well east of the Vistula River. The spa had a number of hotels, which, however, were all requisitioned by the Polish Government, because Nałęczów was designated to be the place to which the Government and all the foreign embassies would evacuate from Warsaw to avoid the expected bombing raids. Since we could not stay in a hotel, we found cheaper accommodations: we rented a room in a peasant home of one Antoni Sygnowski in Chruszczów on the outskirts of Nałęczów. We have never before been to Nałęczów, but the spa was known to us from a Polish classic novel written by Stefan Żeromski, about an idealistic physician, Dr Judym, fighting the effects of greed and pollution, in which Nałęczów was very obviously featured under a fictitious name.

In the morning of September 1, 1939, in Nałęczów, we heard over the radio a solemn announcement by the President of the Polish Republic, Ignacy Mościcki, that Poland's eternal enemy ("*wróg nasz odwieczny*") indiscriminately attacked and bombed defenseless open cities, destroyed airplanes on the ground, killed numberless civilians, and invaded western reaches of Poland, all without a declaration of war. Skeptic that I am, and must have been even then, I was not at all sure that Britain and France will honor their commitments to Poland and declare war on Germany, but they did it after three days. The Second World War had began.

As we feared, Kraków fell to the Germans in 5 days. The Polish army, outgunned and outnumbered, retreated eastward. My father's unit did likewise. In Nałęczów everything was quiet for several days, then a number of limousines came, some with foreign flags mounted on their roofs. Almost immediately German warplanes appeared in the sky. The limousines stayed for only one day and then left toward the Rumanian border, the only neutral border crossing open to Polish officials and foreign diplomats. At one point I saw a dogfight in the air above Nałęczów, between a modern fast German Stuka plane and an old-fashioned slow Polish biplane. It was not a fair fight. When the Polish plane swooped down low I could see the fear and the desperation in the face of the Polish pilot. I doubt that he survived the encounter. Anyway, the Germans destroyed most Polish airplanes on the ground on the first unannounced day of attack. Poles prided themselves on the skill and training of their fliers, a point that they proved later when Polish pilots were using British planes to fight in the Battle of Britain. Unfortunately, the caliber of the obsolete Polish planes did not match the skill of the pilots. Poland tried to build up a more modern air force, even asking its citizens for public donations to a special fund, *Liga Obrony Powietrznej i Przeciwgazowej (LOPP)* (League of Air and Poison Gas Defense) to which we all contributed, but the effort came too late and Poland's industry was no match for the German industrial war machine.

The German-Polish campaign did not last for weeks or months as we expected, because the Polish army was stabbed in the back by Soviet troops, which marched into Poland from the East and began disarming and interning Polish soldiers. Except for isolated islands of resistance, Polish army ceased to exist. The city of Warsaw, the fortress of Modlin on the Vistula and the small garrison on Westerplatte on the Baltic held out for a while, but eventually, all formal armed resistance in Poland ceased. The French hunkered down behind their Maginot Line and had no intention of attacking Germany. The Germans and the Russians were cooperating, with the Russians providing the Germans with grain and oil. For a while we were not even sure whether the area that we were in, the Lublin

district, was going to be occupied by the Russians or the Germans. As it turned out, it was the Germans who marched in. Since we were therefore no better off in Nałęczów than we would have been at home in Kraków, we had no longer any reason to stay there, and we started to look for transportation to return home to Kraków. At first there were no moving trains, and those that eventually began moving, were mobbed. After several weeks of waiting, we did manage to come back to Kraków and to our home on Bernardyńska Street, opposite the Wawel Castle.

The Palace on the Wawel became the official seat of the German government for the occupied Polish territories, the so-called General-Gouvernment. In the city, the Germans requisitioned whole apartments, as well as individual rooms in apartments, to quarter occupation officials and German secret police and high army officers. We lived near the German government bureaus, hence our place was very desirable. One room in our apartment was requisitioned immediately and in it lived a very high German army officer, I believe, a general. He was unfailingly polite, but demanding. He expected to be served. Our peasant maid Tosia (we had one for years, and she was still with us) cleaned the German's room, polished his boots and ironed his clothing. At fourteen, I was naive about such things, but I now believe that the pretty, healthy Polish farmer's daughter eventually also came to share his bed.

In November 1939 the occupying Germans ordered all Jews to wear an identifying mark to make it easier to harass them in the streets. The mark was a white band with a blue Star of David. Wearing of the band created many problems. Wearers of the band were forbidden to enter the Main Market Square, were forbidden to use the Main Post Office. Small annoyances included a ban on sitting on park benches, riding the trolleys or wearing fur. From the very beginning of the occupation, Jews were required to step off a sidewalk for a German soldier and subjected to a dozen other small and petty humiliations. More seriously, wearers of the band were often badly beaten in the streets not only by Germans but also by Polish hooligans, usually without any reason except for their Jewishness. Wearers could be beaten and robbed with impunity. They had no civil rights of any kind whatsoever. Refusal to wear the band was risky. Being identified as a Jew without one often meant being shot on the spot. While Germans did not know how to recognize a non-observant Polish Jew when the Jew was dressed like everybody else on the street, Polish hooligans often could tell. Without compunction, they proceeded to extort money for their silence, and if refused, denounced the hapless Jews to the nearest German Nazi officer.

The location of our apartment was very conveniently close to the Castle Hill and, in February 1940, we were ordered to vacate all of it within 24 hours. We were forbidden to take more than one suitcase with personal clothing and had to leave behind all our furniture and belongings, and, interestingly, the above-mentioned maid, who decided to stay with her German. Dispossessed from our own apartment in our own apartment building, without any compensation or rights to complain, we found a small place on the second floor of the house on Dietla Street 57, a house that was familiar to us, because it was the location of my father's business. The business, which dealt with wholesale leather import and export, was already closed. The vast merchandise storehouse was confiscated for boots for the German army and removed. Obviously, leather was important for the German war effort and it was scarce and valuable. I do not know which German office was responsible for the removal of all the leather stored in our warehouse, worth hundreds of thousands of 1939 dollars.

While I believe that the Germans were quite meticulous about such things and therefore proper records of the confiscation probably exist, I have not been able to find out where such records are likely to be preserved today, whether in Berlin, Warsaw, Moscow, maybe even Washington. Of course, we were never compensated for the confiscated goods.

Money was becoming a problem. Prices of food were rising. Savings could only go so far, given the inflation. It was then that my mother, who was a trained kindergarten teacher, decided to open a small, unregistered private nursery in our apartment on Dietla Street. Since everybody needed to hustle for a living, having a place to deposit small children was important and worth the required small payment. Thus, my mother's kindergarten had no problem getting enough kids and provided us with a modest income. Since there was no school, I studied a little on my own, but I was available to go to work to earn some money and I became a paid apprentice in a bookbinding and notebook factory, owned by our former neighbor from Bernardyńska Street, Szyja Neuman. Neuman was distantly related to us, his sister having married my uncle Józek. In this workshop, I learned how to operate a machine that automatically put staples into school bluebooks and how to fan stacks of sheets of paper to better count them. Most importantly, I learned how to sew pages of printed books, prepare hard book covers and then bind the sewn pages into the covers. This binding of books the old-fashioned way turned out to be a skill that has come handy since as a hobby. To save money, my grandmother (my mother's mother) and my aunt Sonka and her little son, moved in with us. In this small apartment, shared by the enlarged family and the kindergarten, we stayed for several months.

In August 1940, the Germans ordered all Jews living in Kraków to register with the Jewish Community Council, then still located in its pre-War (and current) quarters on the corner of Krakowska and Skawińska Streets and to carry proof of the registration. Of course, nobody trusted the German intentions and we were all sure that nothing good could be in store for the people who register, but staying in Kraków without being registered seemed even more dangerous. The question was intensely debated as to which is safer: to register or to ignore the request and stay in Kraków illegally. Many of our friends refused to appear at the Registry Office. Apparently my mother decided that registering was the safer course to follow, because on August 8, 1940, my mother and I, my grandmother and aunt marched to the Council office and filled the required forms. In them, we provided the occupying Germans with our addresses, dates of birth, places of birth, marital status and occupations, all in the presence of two witnesses. We provided small passport-size photos, which were glued on the form. After the War some of these forms found their way to the Jewish Historical Institute in Warsaw and their microfilmed version has been deposited with the US Holocaust Memorial Museum in Washington. Among the forms in the Museum there is one of my mother's (see photostat in the chapter about my mother) and one that is mine (see below), copies of which I have received from Washington. In those copies the photo of my mother is very dark and unrecognizable, while my photo is a little clearer. No registry forms of my grandmother and aunt have surfaced, although I am positive that they also registered. In fact, my form has been witnessed and signed by my grandmother, who was obviously present in the Registry Office with me, yet her own form is missing. Researchers should be aware that absence of a form does not mean that the individual did not live in Kraków in 1940. The Washington Holocaust Museum has microfilm copies of some additional German documents from 1940, specifying occupations of registered Jews,

their employers, their earnings, veteran status and health. The copy, which I filed then, specifies that I was an apprentice in fabrication of school notebooks and other paper goods. I was then fifteen.

Life for Jews under the Nazis was difficult from the very beginning of the occupation and it became progressively worse. There were all kinds of chicanery, searches, confiscations, restrictions, humiliations and physical attacks. At times, the streets where most Jews lived were closed off and German soldiers ransacked them. Apartments were searched, property confiscated, inhabitants humiliated by having to undergo strip searches, while the soldiers were presumably looking for hidden guns and for jewelry hidden in body orifices. White armbands with a blue Star of David became a part of existence. The Central Square being off limit to Jews, including those who had stores there as my mother‘s maternal aunt, Ester Małke Blonder did, lost all means of earning a livelihood. Stores everywhere were being expropriated. Streets have become dangerous. Cruel beatings were becoming more frequent and more brutal. Occasionally, people were shot without reason, as part of a policy to terrorize the Jewish population. And it was announced that all Kraków Jews will be forced to live in a walled, enclosed, isolated area, like a mediaeval Ghetto, in an outlying district of Kraków, in Podgórze. Without waiting to be immured in such a Ghetto, we decided in 1941 that we might be better off not in Kraków but in some smaller nondescript community that would be of little interest to the occupiers. My mother explored several places nearby and settled on one approximately 20 miles from Kraków. Thus, my entire extended family moved from Kraków to the small town called *Skała koło Ojcowa*, i.e. Skała near Ojców. Ojców was before the War and is now a well-known tourist destination with a Renaissance castle called Pieskowa Skała and many Karst caves, one of which had a historic significance as the hiding place of the Polish King Władysław Łokietek (Ladislas the Short) in the 1300‘s. The townlet of Skała to which we moved, was a typical *shtetl* with central square stores mostly owned by Jews and a surrounding area inhabited by Polish peasants who came to Skała on market days to sell farm produce and buy shoes and clothing (and vodka) from the Jews.

In Skała we found accommodations not in center of town but in a safer and quieter area on the outskirts. We rented an apartment with a kitchen from a peasant, Szymon Trzcionka, at 7 Mydlarska Street. We stayed in Skała for approximately a year. Even in Skała, the German-instituted restrictions on Jewish existence were being felt. Skała did not merit a permanent German occupation force, but from time to time a detachment of young Teutonic storm troopers, in their all-black uniforms and their skull-and-bones insignia, would suddenly appear in the town center square, grab a few elderly religious bearded Jews from the streets or from their stores and proceed to have “fun”. This cruel fun accompanied by much laughter consisted on beating them with clubs and forcibly tearing out their beards, leaving them bleeding and dazed. It is hard for me now to appreciate how anybody could have considered this activity amusing and leading to loud laughter, but it did. Most of the Polish population of Skała did not watch this sport but chose to hide and stay indoors as soon as the Germans appeared. The German occupation authorities promulgated all kind of general restrictions on the Jews, including a labor obligation imposed not on individuals but on the entire Jewish community, and these restrictions and obligations pertained to Skała as well. I often had to join a road gang, breaking stones and doing other heavy manual labor for which I was totally unprepared. Special rules humiliated Jews by considering

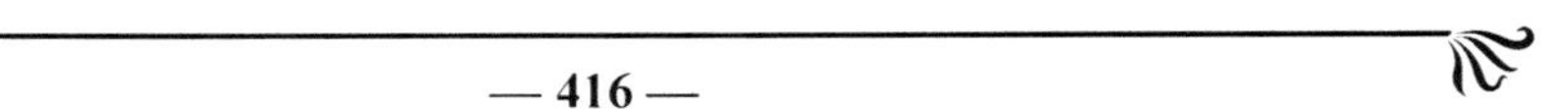

all of them as dirty and as carriers of disease and requiring them to go to public delousing stations, whether they needed it or not. I remember that the town Mayor tried to mitigate some of the anti-Jewish excesses. He was a physician, and his name was, interestingly, Dr. Kościuszko, although he was not related to the famous Polish (and American) hero, Tadeusz Kościuszko. Overall, however, by having moved to Skała we had bought some time and saved some money, for Skała was much cheaper than the Kraków Ghetto. But the relatively quiet time in Skała did not last.

At the beginning of 1942 the Germans decided to collect scattered Jewish communities into a few larger, easier to control, concentrations. Skała, as well as most small towns and villages, were to become "*Judenrein*" i. e. "clean of Jews". Being discovered in one of those places that were declared free of Jews was punishable by execution on the spot. And it was a given that some local anti-Semite would denounce your presence to the German authorities or some greedy ruffian will try to extort money from you by threatening to expose you and after getting all your money, denounce you anyway. In Skała, Jews were ordered to assemble for transport to the central ghettos. Again, the choices we faced were grim. Staying and hiding in Skała after all the Jews have left was more than risky. There was almost no doubt that eventually, even with all the good will on the part of the population, some of our Polish compatriots would denounce us to the Germans, who would, without any compunction, shoot us. Going to the place of assembly was equally risky. We did not trust the Germans, because we knew that in some places the assembled Jews were simply massacred or shipped to parts unknown and not heard from again. At best we would have been deported to some undesirable distant location in the forbidding East.

My mother decided on a third choice: we would all try to get to Kraków on our own and penetrate into the Ghetto. There, at least we would be with a large number of compatriots and friends. Obviously, we assumed at the time that while the Geremans had shot individuals and even massacred groups of individuals, they would not kill thousands upon thousands of people. Thus, we were then naive to believe that there was safety in numbers. The travel on our own from Skała to Kraków itself, however, was dangerous. According to German orders we were not supposed to travel on our own, but were ordered to appear for a group transport. We knew that if caught en route, we would be shot. It is hard to describe the difficulties involved in arranging the transport for our entire family. For example, my old grandmother or my little cousin could not walk all the way. My mother hired a horse-drawn cart to take us to Kraków. It was exceedingly risky for Jews to be seen on the road, but it was also very risky for the peasant whose horse and cart it was. If caught, he, too, could have been shot for helping Jews. For a large fee, one peasant agreed to take the risk and the trip was arranged. The cart was one of those ladder carts, then typical of the Polish countryside, with wooden ladders forming both sides, a wooden plank placed on the bottom mounted on an undercarriage of wooden wheels with metal rims (shades of the founder of the first Polish royal house, Kołodziej Piast!). I felt that it was extremely dangerous for all of us to go together, because my we were so obviously a fleeing Jewish family, even from a distance. What I argued for, is for me and my little sister to strike out on our own, separately from the rest of the family, dressed somewhat like peasant children. We would try to reach Kraków slowly walking through the fields, avoiding roads and avoiding people, sleeping in the fields if necessary. I felt that we would have a better chance that way than being all together on the overloaded one-horse driven cart. With a very heavy heart, my mother, seeing the logic of my arguments, agreed, although it could not have been an easy decision for her. My sister trusted me and was willing to go with me. I was then 16, my sister was ten.

My mother and grandmother, aunt Sonka and her Ignas on their cart got to Kraków within hours and managed to enter the Ghetto without too much effort. It took me and my sister several days walking through and sleeping in the fields. We were not used to walking barefoot, but we took off our shoes to look like peasants, carrying the shoes tied by their laces and slung over our shoulders. I do not think we could have fooled anybody. It was obvious from our skin, not exposed to much country air, and from our soft hands, obviously not used to field work, that we are city children. We succeeded only by avoiding people and sleeping in the open. At one point a group peasant kids, perhaps 10-12 years old, saw us in the distance, started shouting: "Jews! Jews!", and chased us. There was no way that we could have outrun them. We were sure that this will be the end, but we ran for our lives, and then hid in a groove between some tall densely growing tomato plants. We fell flat to the ground, breathing as quietly as we could. Time passed. We could hear them encouraging each other to persevere in the hunt. They searched for us and searched for us. At one point they passed very close but did not see us. They passed and continued the search further and further away from our hiding place. They must have misjudged the distance at which they spotted us. Eventually, after a long time they tired of the game and left. We waited forever in the tomato field and then resumed our trek. At the time, the peasant kids treated this as a game but for us it was a matter of life and death Betrayed to the Germans we would have been shot on the spot for trying to avoid the deportation orders. During these few days my mother could not have been sure whether she will ever see us again but luck was with us at this time and we were reunited in the Kraków Ghetto, although not without problems. Happily, entering the Ghetto was easier than leaving it. Guards stopped you before leaving, you had to have all kinds of permits and documents, but they largely ignored you if you joined an entering work group and sneaked in.

The Kraków Ghetto, where we had many friends and former neighbors, was very crowded, but welcoming. Food was scarce and expensive. Housing was not available and we had to double up with friends, not being able to have a place of our own. With help from friends, we managed to receive official permits to live in the Ghetto. The Ghetto was enclosed within strong brick walls. The gate to the Ghetto was guarded by Nazi-SS stormtroopers. The SS-men wore all-black uniforms decorated with the infamous skull-and-bones death insignia. They were assisted by unarmed Polish police wearing their pre-War navy-blue uniforms (hence referred to as the Blue Police), and by a newly-created uniformed Jewish auxilliaries, the so-called *Ordungsdienst,* dressed in bright yellow-orange, rather ridiculous and pompous, costumes.

An attempt was made to have me hide outside the Ghetto, on the so-called "Aryan side", and for several weeks I stayed hidden with a Polish family of a worker of the Kraków Municipal Gas Works, who sheltered me in spite of the risk of his entire family being shot if I were found out. He did it partly from conviction, but more for the money that he was paid. I did not have any papers showing that I am not a Jew. Often, when somebody rang a bell, I had to hide in a closet. This attempt to have me stay outside the Ghetto did not work out too well. We did not then have enough money to keep it up for any length of time and hiding meant just that, hiding. There was to be no such thing as going out or being seen by neighbors. And the risk was considerable and avoidance of detection difficult, if for no other reason, then because a hidden person had to be fed, yet food was being rationed, bread, flour, meat, sugar, fat. Food had to be provided for the unregistered guest, but buying a lot of it on the black market risked revealing the presence of a fugitive, besides being inordinately expensive. So, after a few weeks of being a hidden child, we gave up and I returned to the Ghetto.

In the Ghetto, my mother served as one of the leaders of the Jewish Underground and I served as a courier for the Underground. That sounds heroic and dramatic but in reality the details show it as fairly prosaic. Being the son of a leather merchant who was also a leader of the Jewish Labor Bund, I was well known among the merchants, master craftsmen and unionized cobblers in the Kraków shoe and leather industry. One of my father's friends, a Jewish master shoemaker, Motl Księski, always had a workshop in the center of the City, on Szewska Street, near the Rynek, way outside the Ghetto. When the Nazis came, he arranged to have one of his non-Jewish journeymen listed as the official owner and operator of the workshop, with himself and his Jewish employees to continue to ply their trade as before. He then proceeded to arrange for a contract with the Germans to make and repair German army officers' boots. This gave the shop a privileged status and secured its Jewish workers a permit to get out of the Ghetto every day and march through the City to the workplace. Thanks to my absent father's reputation, I was invited to join the group as an apprentice shoemaker. My only qualification was that I was my father's son and my family was a prominent member of the shoe and leather industry in Kraków.

Every morning, our small group of five or six, left the Ghetto and every evening we walked back, sometimes bringing food. We were often, but not always, searched on arrival at the Ghetto gate and the food would be confiscated. Still, it was worth the risk. On days that we were not searched, we managed to bring it in, and food was much cheaper outside the ghetto. There was another risk that I took, one to which I have alluded earlier. A courier from the Polish Socialist Party (PPS) underground, then known by its conspiratorial initials WRN (for *Wolność, Równość, Niepodległość*, i.e. Freedom, Equality, Independence) visited us at the workshop and delivered underground communications, including messages, instructions, pamphlets and newsletters, which I then carried to the Ghetto. I was chosen to carry them as the youngest member of the group, on the assumption that the Nazi SS guards would not frisk me as often as they would the adults. Being found out would have meant torture and a certain execution, but I was glad to do it and never considered refusing. We lived on the edge of a volcano anyway, and people were often shot for no reason except their Jewishness, so I felt that the extra risk was not worth worrying about. And being a courier of the underground and serving as a link between the Polish and Jewish Undergrounds was reward enough. My small service with the Underground was mentioned, as I said earlier, in the memoirs of the heroic secret underground Jewish social-democratic agent, a war-time friend of my mother, Jacob Celemenski, published in Yiddish after the War in New York by the Ferlag Unser Tsait (1963). I have translated the parts of Celemenski's book that deal with my family and me. Some of these excerpts were included in the chapter dealing with my uncle Ignacy and his daughter and more in the chapter about my mother, Salomea Scheindel Rubin Aleksandrowicz. I consider it one of the most historically important books written about the Holocaust. Recently, most but not all, of the Celemenski book has been translated into English and published in Melbourne, Australia.

From Celemenski's book I found out that my mother, who was always politically active, continued her activities during the war, both before we left Kraków for Skała and after our entry into the Kraków Ghetto. In fact, she was the key member of the Jewish Socialist (Bundist) Underground, maintaining contacts with the Polish Underground in Kraków. Her Polish contact, who provided the Jews with some false non-Jewish documents, with propaganda material and financial aid, was the pre-War Secretary of the Polish Socialist Party in Kraków, my parents' acquaintance from before the War, Józef Cyrankiewicz. After the War, Cyrankiewicz became Prime Minister of Poland. For obvious reason, my mother's underground activities were kept somewhat secret from me, although now, in retrospect, I can see when and where she did what she did. Somehow, we have been aware of underground activities before they became public knowledge. For example I knew about disruptions of rail communications in the Płaszów-Bonarka rail hub which led to a derailment of an ammunition train. I found out more about my mother's secret work from Celemenski's book.

When the Polish army disintegrated in 1939, my father found himself in Eastern Poland, part of the old Pale of Settlement, where most small *shtetls* were inhabited by Jews. Hiding in a Jewish house, he took off his army uniform and donned civilian clothing and made his way to the city of Lwów, then occupied by the Red Army. Returning to Kraków was out of the question. The German secret police, the Gestapo, was looking for him. Because of his pre-war political involvement, we had in the hallway closet of our house on Bernardynska Street some political duplicating equipment, consisting of a ribbonless typewriter, wax sheets for cutting stencils, a mimeographing machine with inking rolls, a small printing press and ink and paper supplies. When the Germans came we were concerned that should they find it, we would be accused of underground activities, questioned, tortured and killed, To the best of my knowledge the equipment was not in use, although it might have been without my knowing it, after all I was only fourteen then and while I considered myself reliable and worthy of full confidence, there might have been others who preferred that I be kept out of the loop. Anyway, the Germans did not discovered the equipment while we lived there and, since it was bulky and heavy and we lived so closed to the German headquarters, we had no means of taking it with us when we were expelled from the apartment, so we left it there in our hallway closet. It is tempting to think that the Nazi secret police, the Gestapo, found all this material after we left and shot the German army officers then living in our apartment. As related earlier, my father was opposed to both fascist and communist totalitarianisms, therefore not only the German but also the Soviet secret police was looking for him. In Russian-occupied Lwów he was warned of an impending arrest, smuggled himself to Lithuania, and from there he moved, via Moscow and Kobe, Japan, to the USA. In this trip, he was aided by the Japanese Consul in Lithuania, Chiune Sugihara, and by the Jewish Labor Committee in New York. He arrived in America in March of 1941. We knew all this. Until Pearl Harbor, we were able to correspond with him. From Skała, we sent him regular reports and received his letters. Things became more complicated after Pearl Harbor when the US declared war on Germany and after we moved to the Ghetto.

After the Japanese attack on Pearl Harbor, on December 1941, the US and Germany were at war. All postal communication between the US and Germany and the German-occupied European territories ceased. At the time, my mother, my 10-year-old

sister and I were in occupied Poland, while my father was a refugee in the United States.

Originally, we had no problem corresponding with my father in America. The mail was censored, but it moved until the declaration of German-USA war in December 1941. All exchange of mail ceased. It was then that my father remembered that he had a business associate, Gustav Fehrlin, in the Swiss city of St. Gallen. He wrote to Mr. Fehrlin, and asked him to serve as an intermediary. For many months, Mr Fehrlin accepted our letters from the German-occupied Polish territory, transferred them to Swiss envelopes, franked them with Swiss stamps and forwarded them to New York. Conversely, he took my father‘s letters from the US and forwarded them to us in Swiss envelopes. Seeing those envelopes with Swiss franking on them was for us a great morale-builder. We were duly grateful to Gustav Fehrlin. This arrangement continued until my mother‘s deportation to an extermination camp in October 1942 and my confinement in the Kraków-Płaszów concentration camp. Further correspondence became impossible after my mother‘s death in October 1942 and my transfer to the concentration camp. The fact that I knew that my father was safe in America, however, helped to sustain my morale in the dark days ahead.

I never managed to thank Herr Fehrlin for his kindness and consideration. His help during the war was of tremendous psychological value. Seeing those Swiss stamps on the envelopes containing my father‘s letters from America, was an incomparable morale sustainer. Now, as some of the Swiss war-time behavior and business activities have been questioned, I believe it is only fair that I mention this one small way in which the Swiss neutrality was of benefit to one beleaguered European Jewish family and the way that at least one Swiss citizen did what he could to be of help. I assume that Gustav Fehrlin is no longer with us, but perhaps his children live in St. Gallen and they should know that their father helped one family of Polish Jews during World War II, and that this help was appreciated.

In March of 1942 all residents of the Ghetto were required to receive new extra special permits to stay in Kraków, others were deported to parts unknown. In June 1942 the Germans ran one of their many terrorizing actions, meant to scare and dehumanize the ghetto population. The entire area was surrounded by troops and nobody was allowed to leave. Soldiers roamed the Ghetto, shooting people at random, and beating those caught in the streets. They marched into the office of the Ghetto administrative center, the *Judenrat*, and shot its chairman, Dr. Arthur Rosenzweig, a man whom they themselves appointed a short time earlier. Apparently, Dr Rosenzweig was not subservient enough and has retained a measure of decency and civilized behavior. In the street they caught and killed my parents‘ friend, the famous Krakovian Yiddish poet and writer of folksongs, Mordkhe Gebirtig. Gebirtig was unschooled, did not know musical notation, but he had an enormous talent that conquered all obstacles and he became famous and his songs were very popular. My mother supported Gebirtig, recommended him to all her friends and used to sing many of his works. Many of Gebirtig‘s songs were published in New York after the War. The most famous of them, written after a 1937 or 1938 pogrom in a small town in Poland called Przytyk, was entitled “*Es brennt, mine shtetele brennt*” (It‘s burning, my little shtetl is burning).

With the expulsion of 6,000 people, who were sent to the Bełżec extermination camp, the Ghetto population decreased and the Germans cut the size of the Ghetto, thus continuing the overcrowding, the lack of hygiene, as well as the starvation and despair and disease. At some point the younger Ghetto inhabitants concluded that quiet passive

opposition is pointless and set upon more active, desperate acts against the German occupiers A Jewish Fighting Organization (*Żydowska Organizacja Bojowa or ŻOB*) was formed, manned mostly by members of young Poale-Zionist groups along with a somewhat separate Bundist outfit. The two groups coordinated their activity and for a short time used my mother's connection to communicate with the Polish Underground. The cramped size of the Ghetto and the known German practice of responding with draconian punishment completely out of proportion to the offense, intended to terrorize the population into submission, made it impractical to conduct an uprising in the Ghetto, as was, for example, done in the much-larger Warsaw Ghetto. Instead, the Kraków Ghetto Jewish Fighting Organization settled on a different tactic and decided to conduct acts of sabotage outside the ghetto. I have mentioned some of the acts of the ŻOB above when talking about my mother's participation in the Underground. When the train at the Kraków-Bonarka railroad station was derailed, the Germans responded by arresting 150 Jewish men at random and tortured them to reveal the names of the culprits, which the hostages did not know. The Germans also advertised to have the guilty ones surrender, but the fighters knew from previous experience that, should they reveal themselves, the Germans cannot be trusted to release the hostages, and indeed, they shot all 150 innocent people. Other acts of sabotage followed, including a bombing of city restaurants, movie houses and clubs frequented by German officers. In one of the successful attacks, on the nightclub called "*Cyganeria*" (Gypsydom), eleven German officers were killed and many more wounded. At one point, one of the young leaders of the Krakovian ŻOB, Lolek Liebeskind, engaged in a street shoot-out with the Germans trying to arrest him, killed a number of them and died in the resulting fusillade. For safety reasons my mother notified the Polish Socialist underground press about a successful exploit but requested that it not be separately credited to Jews to avoid German reprisals. The Germans, apparently, were not fooled.

On October 28, 1942, a day I am not likely to forget, I left for work as usual. When I came back, I found that my mother, my little sister, my grandmother and other relatives, along with a number of other Ghetto inhabitants, have been removed from the Ghetto during the day and taken to a train to be transported "east". I never saw any of them again. Eventually, I found out that they were sent to the extermination camp in Bełżec in the woods of central-eastern Poland and perished there. My mother was among the heroines of the Kraków Jewry: a prominent political activist, a cultural icon, an innovative educator and a selfless leader of the War-time underground resistance. She was also a warm likeable person and a wonderful wife and mother. I missed her terribly.

I was then seventeen. I stayed in the Ghetto by myself, helped along by a few friends and one close relative, my father's youngest brother, my uncle Olek (Salo Aleksandrowicz 1908-1945). In March 1943, the Ghetto was liquidated and its inhabitants forcibly transferred to a newly created concentration camp at Płaszów, a southern suburb of Kraków. The camp was most depressing, the primitive barracks cramped and inhospitable, the atmosphere grim. There was no more any possibility of working outside the camp. Even the favored few, for example, workers in the Schindler Emalia Factory or the Madritsch Factory, were confined to the camp. A few people were left in the Ghetto, given the task of collecting the remaining belongings, finding any valuables and, in general, cleaning up. A few people escaped from the Ghetto through the sewers. These people were then faced with the daunting problem of finding shelter, possibly with the few courageous non-Jewish

friends who were willing to risk their life in that endeavor, and continuously avoiding betrayal by local anti-Semites and low-life extortionists and blackmailers. Among those who managed to escape that day and managed to survive, was my second cousin once removed, Dr. Julian Aleksandrowicz, and his family. Julian was a physician in Podgórze, the outlying district of Kraków on the other side of the Vistula, the district in which the Germans constructed the Ghetto and to which they moved all the Krakovian Jews. Julian was running a hospital in the Ghetto. Before the war he had mostly non-Jewish patients and found some of them willing to be of help by hiding his wife and son. Julian himself joined the partisans in the forests, and served as a physician in the underground army. After the War he received Poland's highest military medal, the order of *Virtuti Militari*. There is now in Kraków a street named for him, using his war-time alias, called Dr. Twardy Street. As a physician, he was among the few Jews who safely joined a partisan unit. I understand that many others were killed by the very partisans whom they tried to join to fight a common enemy. Not being sure of any outside Polish friends who would be courageous enough to hide us, and not willing to risk exposing any to the test, my uncle Olek and I did not attempt to escape, we marched out of the Ghetto, under armed escort, to Płaszów.

I have been asked why we did not fight or why we did not escape from the Ghetto and the camp. Only people who were not there and have no way of knowing the conditions in which we existed then, could ask such questions. Many wrong, even ridiculous, explanations have been given by psychologists and other self-appointed experts. Many analyses have been made. Long-term conditioning, passivity, depression, have been mentioned as having played a role. One key reason for me, though, was my awareness of the efficiency, might and unbounded cruelty of the occupiers who did not hesitate to kill hundreds of hostages when a single Jew managed to escape. Without any compunction, shame or fear of reprisals from the civilized world, the Germans announced in advance that they would execute hundreds of innocent hostages should a prisoner escape from camp, and indeed did routinely execute hostages in cases of escapes. This alone, I understand, kept some highly ethical people from escaping or taking up arms. In addition, as I mentioned before, the Germans announced with great fanfare that they would execute entire families of those Poles who dared to help Jews and indeed did carry out many such executions of Polish men, women and children and published the details in the daily press. Such executions and their public knowledge served as a strong deterrent preventing decent but fearful people from taking an active role in moderating the Holocaust and kept some Jews, like myself, from exposing our potential friends to the risk. Without assurance of shelter, few escapes from camp were successful, most escapees were caught with the help of denunciations by Polish criminals and extortionists and, when brought back, were hanged with great ceremony in front of the entire assembled camp population. This highlights some of the reasons which kept me from escaping or from taking up arms. As we now know, a few Jews, with hardly any weapons, in utter desperation and without any hope, did confront what was then, without any doubt, one of the best equipped, best trained and disciplined and most indoctrinated armies in the world. A small armed group in Kraków and larger ones in Warsaw and Vilna and some detachments in the forests fought the German enemy and thus provided us with examples of courage and heroism against all odds. These instances of resistance now are duly celebrated, but the effort did not then change our situation in any way and, besides saving honor for posterity, did not produce any obvious benefits at the time.

The act of escaping *per se* was not difficult, particularly in the early days in the Ghetto, and I was confident that, should I decide on it, I could manage it successfully. But I was very aware that escape would only be my first and easiest task. The main reason why escape was not a solution for me, was the fact that I had no place to go after the escape. I was overwhelmingly aware that after escaping I would have been surrounded not by comforting Polish compatriots and friends, but more likely by apologetic embarrassment, hesitation, fear and indifference. I was absolutely certain that I would be exposed to hostility, blackmail, extortion and denounciation. As I stated before, the Germans made it crystal clear that entire Polish families found protecting Jews will be killed and proudly advertised such killings. I could not have been sure whether our Polish friends and acquaintances have been ready to take such risks, and I did not have the confidence that, should I ask them for help, they would pass the test. I also felt that I do not have the right to present them with such a test and demand such sacrifice from them. Only much later in the War, did some organized help appear in the form of an official underground Council to Help Jews organized by the Polish Government-in-Exile in London. By the time awareness of such help became known, however, I was no longer in Poland, but in the tightly controlled camps, deeply in Hitler‘s Alpine redoubt, surrounded by hostile Germans and even more hostile (and anti-Semitic) Austrians, where escape was not an option.

In Płaszów, my uncle and I were assigned to work in a shoe-and-leather barrack, referred to in German as *Schuh-und-Leder Gemeinschaft*. The atmosphere in the factory was grim, but the work itself, while unpleasant, was not physically taxing, because we did not exert ourselves to produce anything for the Nazis. The camp, anyway, was designed more to humiliate, whip, torture, intimidate and shoot people a random, than to produce anything worthwhile. The camp, described in the book and movie called "Schindler‘s List", was a nightmare of tortures, beatings, shootings, insufficient food and inadequate clothing. The camp commander, Amon Goeth, and his German, Ukrainian and Latvian guards behaved in a calculated sadistic manner, designed to cow and dehumanize the prisoners. The living conditions were horrible and random torture and shootings were common and scary because of their unpredictability. Walkways in the camp were paved with tombstones from a Jewish cemetery. The camp commander accompanied by his two vicious dogs marched through the camp and picked people at random to be beaten with horse whips, humiliated and, as often as not, shot. Inmates who tried to escape and were caught were publicly stripped and whipped and then hanged in the presence of all assembled prisoners. For all this, the Płaszów camp was reasonably benign, as we discovered when we were moved to camps in Germany and Austria. The death rate in Płaszów was not overwhelming. For all the cruelty, deliberate extermination of prisoners was not among the camp‘s objectives, the camp had no gas chambers and most inmates survived for periods of time.

When the Russian armies were coming near, the Płaszów camp was liquidated, the sick and disabled were shot and able-bodied prisoners moved to camps in Hitler‘s "Alpine Redoubt". Instead of shifting badly needed troops from the Eastern to Western fronts, where the Allied forces landing in Normandy were vulnerable, the German dictator chose to use his scarce remaining railroad resources which survived Allied bombings to move Jews from camps in the Polish territories deeper into Germany, just so that they would not be saved by the approaching Soviet troops. This indicates that the Nazis had a most perverted set of priorities. One could postulate that Hitler‘s obsession with Jews was partly responsible for the speed of Germany's collapse, once the Allied landings took place and broke out of the hedgerow-covered site of landings in Brittany,

The voyage from Płaszów was memorable for its horror. I wish I had the skill to report it as it deserves to be reported. Red rail boxcars meant to carry goods but also labeled as being meant to carry "forty men or eight horses" were used for prisoner transport. They were packed with more than one hundred and twenty people, providing standing room only. Doors were sealed shut. Only tiny openings allowed some air, but food and water were not provided. Travel took days. People were dying like flies and even then remained standing, for there was no room for them to fall to the floor. Our train from Płaszów was first sent to Auschwitz (Polish name for Auschwitz is Oświęcim; there were two camps there: Auschwitz and Birkenau, Oświęcim and Brzezinki). These Auschwitz camps being overcrowded, their administration refused to accept us. Our train stood at a siding in Auschwitz for two or three days, sealed, while people were dying of thirst. Because the cars were not opened and we were not registered at Auschwitz, we did not receive the tattooed numbers on our left arm which was the hallmark of the Auschwitz camps. Eventually the train rolled on and we ended the journey, more dead than alive, in Mauthausen on the Danube, near Vienna. That cruel trainride remains as one of my most vivid and haunting memories of the Holocaust. A car, very much like the one in which I rode, is on display in the U.S. Holocaust Memorial Museum in Washington, D.C. On my visit to that museum, entering that car and re-living its horror was my most difficult and emotional experience during my visit to that Museum. I would not have visited the Museum, except that I was asked to do so at the behest of the Service Employees International Union (SEIU) and of my union, the Public Employees Federation, which wanted to have me, as a member and a Holocaust survivor, observed during the visit and arranged to have me accompanied by a writer and a photographer and I felt that it is my obligation to the victims of the Holocaust to comply. A description of that visit written by Peter Pieragostini was published in the SEIU journal *Union* (1993).

Like Dachau, Mauthausen was a major Nazi concentration camp, a permanent installation, towering over a small pretty Austrian town. The camp was enclosed by high stone walls. In one place, the wall overlooked a rocky ravine, with a deep drop of a hundred feet. Apparently, prisoners have been thrown from that wall, because when Mauthausen was finally overran by American soldiers the ravine was covered with bones and body parts. In Mauthausen, on August 11. 1944, a transport of 4,590 Polish Jews, mostly from Kraków and its surroundings, was met with typical German method and efficiency. We were registered, showered, deloused, shorn, dressed in fresh prisoner garb, carefully questioned and assigned prisoner numbers. I became prisoner No. 84,314. We were not kept in Mauthausen, but sent to a branch camp in Melk, a tourist mecca on the Danube, the site of the summer palace of Archbishops / Cardinals of Vienna. The palace, a stop on every present tourist cruise on the Danube, is said to boast 365 windows, so that the Archbishop can look from a differnt window each day of the year. One can assume that His Eminence had the daily privilege of looking from windows of his palace at a line of bedraggled, starving prisoners, dressed in striped clothing, being cruelly beaten by their surrounding guards, barely dragging themselves from camp to work site in the morning and back to camp in the evening. I remember vividly marching through the pretty town, under the unblinking stares of its stolid citizens. In Melk I have witnessed and participated in a phenomenon that

I have not heard of before and would not have believed in, had I not been a part of it. I have heard of people falling asleep while they remain standing, but in Melk I experienced the phenomenon of being one of a whole column of men, marching in lockstep, while asleep. It is hard to believe that it is possible, but I was a part of that column. We were so food- and sleep-deprived and so exhausted and so weak, that we slept while marching and never missed a step. I estimate the surviving number of prisoners in Melk at less than 10,000. The unstoppable march of the Soviet armies towards the heart of Germany and Austria finally brought them towards Melk and, true to their crazy credo, the Germans moved us from Melk deeper into the Austrian Alps, to another branch camp of Mauthausen, located in the Tyrolean resort town of Ebensee on the Traunsee, near Gmunden and Bad Ischl. That trip, too, was memorable for the deplorable conditions of the journey. At first we traveled to Linz on one of the Danube pleasure boats, packed unbelievably tight with prisoners. From Linz we simply marched, all of 80 kilometers, forced to move by guards, who shot anyone unable to continue the walk. The description of my experiences in Ebensee follows in the next chapter. In May 2005, in Mauthausen, a ceremony was held to mark the 60-th anniversary of the liberation of the notorious camp. Former prisoners mingled with soldiers of the U.S. Third Army, 11-th Armored Division, who entered the camp 60 years earlier and who recounted the horrific sight which greeted them. The President of Austria, Heinz Fischer, spoke, as did the Cardinal of Vienna Christoph Schoenborn, alluding to the responsibility of many Austrians for the horrors. Incidentally, this is the same cardinal who recently, after the death of John Paul II and ascension of Benedict XVII, questioned acceptance of the theory of evolution, indicating that the Church may yet ally itself with fundamentalists who reject Darwinism and support belief in divine creation of Adam and Eve and their descendants.

After the War, the son of Julian Aleksandrowicz, then ten years old, testified to the horrors of being hidden as a non-Jew during the War and Julian himself published a book, entitled "The memoirs of Dr. Hardy" (1967). In 1997 my New-York-born wife and I stayed in Kraków while researching the history of my family. While there, we visited the Bernardyńska and Dietla streets where I lived, as well as the area of the former Ghetto in Podgórze. A part of the wall that surrounded the Ghetto has been preserved and now contains a memorial tablet. Also preserved as a small museum is the pharmacy that served the Ghetto on what is now called the Heroes of the Ghetto Square. We also visited the area of Płaszów near Kraków where the concentration camp was located; it is now an area of rolling hills, covered in grass. There are no camp buildings left, but two monuments stands at the site, a large official monument honoring all the victims of the camp and a small stone erected by the Jewish Community of Kraków devoted to the memory of those Jews who suffered there. That latter visit was not easy for me but it took the form of a pilgrimage to a site of martyrdom. I never returned to Mauthausen, Melk or Ebensee and I have refused to visit Bełzec, the site where my mother and sister died.

I have written about my own and my family's experiences under the German occupation but did not mention the fate of those of my relatives and friends who found themselves under the Soviet rule. I did not meet the Soviet soldiers and thus have no personal stories to tell. I do know, however, from tales of others who did experience Soviet rule, that it was no picnic. While, other than the murder of Polish army officers at Katyn, there were no outright mass killings on a scale of those in the German zone, there were

mass arrests, investigations and tortures by the secret police, the *Narodny Commissariat Vnutriennykh Dyehl* (NKVD). Polish officers were interned and executed. Most civilian Polish-Jewish refugees from German zone of Poland were deported deep into Soviet interior, to Siberia and elesewhere. Stalin ruthlessly pursued Polish patriots, including army officers who were murdered by the Russians in the Katyn forest in Byelarus. He also held a grudge toward Jewish democratic socialists who refused to collaborate with the Communists. He ordered the arrest and execution of the two most prominent leaders of the Jewish Labor Bund in Poland, Henryk Ehrich and Victor Alter. My uncle Józek Aleksandrowicz was sent, without proper clothing or equipment, to build a camp and a railhead in the frozen area near Murmansk near the White Sea, facing the North Pole. Eventually, released but exhausted by the ordeal, he fell victim to a typhus epidemic and died in Samarkand. Two of my other uncles by marriage, Isidor Wien and Stefan Neuger, were sent to Siberia. They suffered a great deal but survived and returned to Poland. Isidor left Poland after the War and came to New York and then went to Buenos Aires. Stefan joined the Partisans in the forests, distinguished himself and won a medal for bravery. After the War, he lived in Kraków until his death.

JÜDISCHE GEMEINDE
KRAKAU -- SKAWINERGASSE Nr. 2

PROTOKOLL

aufgenommen am 8/VIII 1940.

In der Kanzlei der jüdischen Gemeinde in Krakau erscheinen: Aleksandrowicz Jerzy

aus Krakau

derzeit wohnhaft in Krakau Dietelgasse 57 und die Zeugen:

a) Gross Ella von Beruf

wohnhaft in Krakau Dietelgasse 9 ausgewiesen durch Ausweispass Nr. 628/24 ausgestellt d. die Krakauer Polizeidirektion am 1/9 1924

und

b) Rubin f. Rosenberg Keila von Beruf

wohnhaft in Krakau Dietelgasse 57 ausgewiesen durch Ausweispass Nr. 4187/24 ausgestellt d. die Krakauer Polizeidirektion am 23/9 1924

Die Zeugen erklären folgendes:

Aleksandrowicz Jerzy geboren am 27/6 1925

in Paris Stand ledig

Beruf aus Krakau

derzeit wohnhaft in Krakau Dietelgasse 57

zuständig nach ist uns persönlich bekannt.

Wir Bestätigen die Personengleichheit obiger Person mit untenstehendem Lichtbilde.

Obiges erklären wir, zwecks Erteilung eines Personalausweises von seiten der Jüdischen Gemeinde in Krakau in Angelegenheit der Umsiedlung des (der) Genannten von Krakau nach

Die Richtigkeit obiger Angaben bestätigen wir durch unsere eigenhändigen Unterschriften:

Ella Gross
Als Zeuge

Rosenberg
Als Zeuge

Aleksandrowicz Jerzy
Antragsteller

Fig. 092. Jerzy Aleksandrowicz, 1940, Ghetto Registration in Kraków

Translation of the 1940 Record from Kraków, obtained from the Museum in Washington.

The original is kept in the archives of the Jewish Historical Institute in Warsaw.

Jewish Community Council
Kraków – Skawina Street 2

Record of Inquiry (Protokoll)
Taken on 8 August 1940

In the Chancellery of the Jewish Community Council in Kraków appeared

Aleksandrowicz Jerzy

of Kraków, currently living at *Dietl Street 57*

and witnesses : (a) *Gross Ella,* living in Kraków *Dietl Street 9,* established with an *I.D. Nr. 629/24 issued by the Kraków Police Administration on September 1, 1924*

and (b) *Rubin f. Rosenberg Keila,* living in Kraków *Dietl Street 57 established with an I.D. Nr. 4197/24 Issued by the Kraków Police Administration on September 23, 1924*

The witnesses declared the following: ***Aleksandrowicz Jerzy*** born on *June 27, 1925* In *Paris,* status *single, c*urrently living at *Dietl Street 57* is known to us personally.

We confirm the likeness of the person with the picture below. We declare the above facts for the purpose of issuance of an I.D. on the part of the Jewish Community Council in connection with expulsion of the above-named person from Kraków to ------ (blank).

We confirm the accuracy of the above information with our signatures:

Ella Gross, as witness

Rosenberg, as witness

Aleksandrowicz Jerzy, Subject of the Inquiry

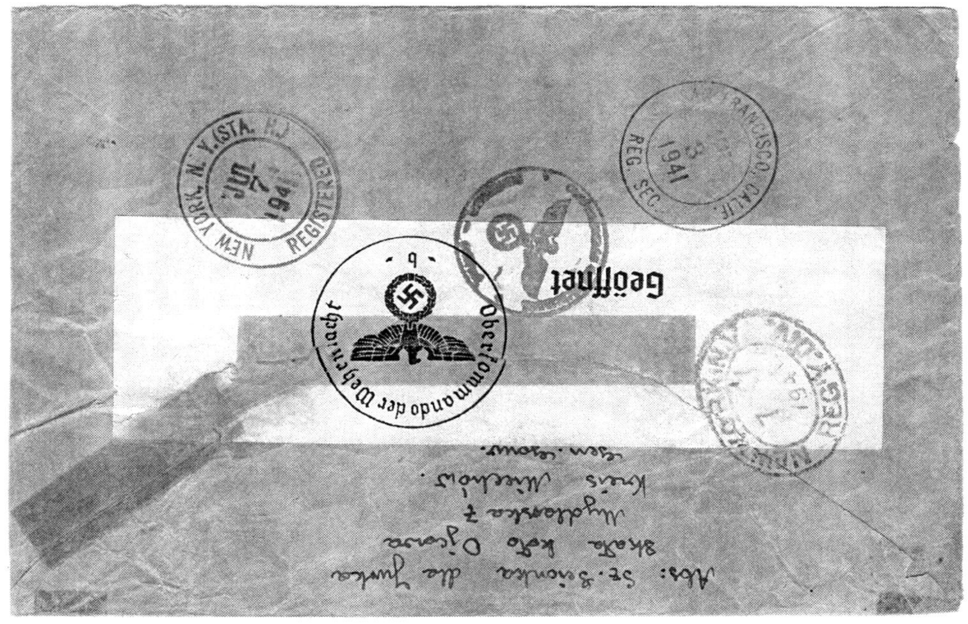

Fig. 093. Envelope of my letter from Nazi-occupied Poland to my father in the U.S.

Part VIII. VIGNETTES FROM CONCENTRATION CAMPS, 1942-1945

Chapter 29. Burning Europe; Horrors of German Concentration Camps

The prisoners were dying from starvation and overwork, from depression, exhaustion, insufficient food, beatings and torture. Innocent people, men, women and children, were killed by the millions, with gas, in the service of an insane ideology. A technologically adept nation placed its scientific and organizational ability in the service of that insane ideology. It was a time when a gifted but crazy orator swayed large number of otherwise ordinary people to run amok. I was caught in the middle of all this insanity, as a young Jew in German-occupied Poland from September 1939 until liberation from a concentration camp in Austria by the American Army in May 1945. My mother and my 11-year-old sister, my grandmothers and many of my uncles, aunts and cousins were killed in the extermination camp in Bełżec, Poland. I was interned in one concentration camp after another. At first, I was in the Kraków-Plaszów camp, described in the book and film "Schindler's List", then in branch camps of Mauthausen in Austria.

I was born in 1925, which means that when the World War II began in Europe in 1939 I was 14. For the next six years I was undernourished and remained short and thin. When sent to the camp I looked younger than my years. I survived because I was small and the amount of food that was disastrously inadequate for grown men, was merely insufficient for me. I was starving but I managed to survive. In addition, I used to exchange a ration of cigarettes to supplement my daily ration of food. Also, I was of an age where I was strong enough to survive the hardships, yet young enough to not fully appreciate the dimension of the disaster that befell my family, my people and humanity as a whole.

In the camps, each morning we received a small slice of bread baked with an admixture of sawdust as an extender and a hot cup of thin grain coffee, black and unsweetened. In the evening we got a bowl of watery soup made from potato peels. The camp guards got the potatoes, the prisoners got a soup made from the peels boiled in salt water. Inasmuch as there were ten times as many prisoners as guards, there were not too many peels in that soup, it was mostly dirty salty hot water. However, in addition, in their wisdom, in some camps the Germans issued each male prisoner a daily ration of two low quality cigarettes. I understand that not all of the German prisoners everywhere received cigarettes, but I certainly did in one of my camps. It is a sad commentary on the addictive properties of nicotine and the desperation with which some prisoners needed those cigarettes that many were willing to barter their meager one daily slice of bread for the cigarettes. The exchange rate was one slice of bread for the two cigarettes. Since I was young and I have never smoked, I had no need for the cigarettes and I exchanged my cigarettes for bread every day. I never had any trouble finding takers. In this manner, I could eat my own bread in the morning and keep the second slice for evening to have with my soup. More often than not I did not have the will power to keep the second slice until evening and gobbled both slices in the morning. In the camps I was sick, undernourished, overworked and underdeveloped. Without that second slice of bread a day, my chances of survival would have been slim. I believe that I owe my surviving the Holocaust to my being able to barter cigarettes for food. Ever since then I have looked at cigarettes with disdain and I never could start smoking.

In the winter of 1944-1945 I was a prisoner in the Ebensee camp, a branch of the Mauthausen concentration camp. Today Ebensee is a resort located in the Tirolean Alps. While the village itself is very attractive with its timbered Alpine houses and picturesque inns, the approximately thirty thousand prisoners did not have time to admire the beauty of their surroundings. The camp was located in a particularly unhealthy wet forest, leaning against a tall mountain, which stopped all the prevailing winds. All the rain clouds discharged over the area. Thus, from the camp we could see that the village and the lake had decent, mainly sunny weather, in the camp it was often raining. The jerry-built barracks were always wet, cold and gloomy.

The prisoners' moods matched the weather. Work was hard and food woefully inadequate. Starvation, beatings and exhaustion took their daily toll. Thousands of prisoners, among them my uncle, my last surviving relative caught by war in Poland, died of starvation in Ebensee only a few weeks before the end of the war. The work in the camp consisted of digging deep tunnels into the mountain. Presumably, the tunnels were going to be used for an underground airplane factory, but the work by the emaciated prisoners was slow and the tunnels were far from finished when the war ended. Some of the tunnels were dry and some encountered underground streams and their ground was covered with icy, muddy, slowly running water.

Every morning the prisoners lined up to march to work. Some lines were going to the dry tunnels, some to the wet ones. The guards did not care in which line any given prisoner stood. Thus, every morning at dawn I had a choice between comfortably warm and dry tunnels and cold, damp watery tunnels where one stood ankle deep in icy water. But each type of tunnel had its advantages. In the dry tunnels it was easy to see how much soil was moved. Thus, the prisoners had to work hard or suffer severe beatings. The prisoner *capo* (foreman) of my group favored a rubber truncheon, which he used to hit people over the head. In the wet tunnels the water covered everything and it carried away most of the dug up soil. When the guards or the prisoner's foreman turned his attention elsewhere, nobody could tell if the prisoners dug anything or just whiled away time, standing ankle-deep and freezing in the icy stream. When I felt strong, which was not often, I obviously

preferred to go to the dry tunnels, but mostly I chose the wet ones to conserve my waning strength. In the dry tunnels I had another choice to make. I could pick up a pneumatic hammer and stand in place and drill into the hard compacted clay, or I could pick a shovel and load soil dug up by others onto wagons for removal. Handling a hammer may seem to be the easier of these tasks, but I was small for my age and thin from undernourishment and underweight and the heavy vibrating hammer shook my whole being to such an extent, that I more often chose to shovel than to drill.

Lack of food was a constant nagging companion. Food was constantly on our minds, we dreamed about and talked about it endlessly. Although smaller and needing less nourishment than mature men like my uncle who died, I always went hungry and I believe that I would not have survived except for another lucky break, the Allied bombing of the Attnang-Puchheim railroad station and the rice that I managed to get there. The Allied bombing of the German war machine was increasing in frequency and ferocity. Every night American airplanes hit another strategic target. Eventually it was the turn of the important railroad junction of Attnang-Puchheim in Austria, a pivotal point on the Linz-Salzburg rail line. The Allies hit Attnang-Puchheim at a particularly effective time: the bombing caught a fully-loaded freight train at the station. The cargo was particularly important, because it consisted of increasingly scarce foodstuffs, mainly sacks of rice.

As daylight dawned, the local authorities were very eager to save the shipment of rice, but the rail cars were smashed by the bombs, the sacks of rice were lying in the open and some were torn and their contents were spilling on the ground. Because of the war, manpower was not easily available. All the able-bodied men from the countryside had been drafted and were serving in the Wehrmacht. Somebody suggested bringing in the prisoners from the nearby concentration camp at Ebensee, a mere few miles away. I was included in the prisoner detail sent to clear up the bombing mess. Lifting the heavy sacks of rice was backbreaking but the opportunity to go outside the camp was welcome, and seeing the damage done to the German rails by the Allies was good for our morale and heartening. At one point I encountered one of the torn sacks from which rice was spilling. Alas, the rice was pearly, almost tranparent, dry and hard and when I tried a mouthful I found that I cannot chew it and digest it. The prisoners had absolutely no way to take it somewhere and boil it. In fact, being caught with some of it would have meant a certain beating if not execution on the spot.

And then, to my joy, I discovered that when I took a mouthful of this dry rice and held it in my mouth for several minutes, my saliva would soften it sufficiently, so that with effort I could then chew and swallow it. All day, while carrying sacks of rice and other bags, my mouth was full of rice that was being digested by my saliva and in this manner I ate my fill. I honestly believe that this rice meal was among the most significant factors that allowed me to survive. It quenched my hunger and restored some of my strength for a few days and, in this manner, from one day to the next, prolonged my ability to function for a little while longer. I published a brief description of my experience at Attnang-Puchheim in the *Survivors Chronicle* (see Bibliography). The American army liberated the Ebensee camp on May 5, 1945, and I was among the survivors..

Suicide was never far from my mind. The technical aspect of committing one was never a problem. It would have been easy to do; all that it called for was a walk towards the barbed wire surrounding the camp pretending an attempt at escape and one of the guards stationed with machine guns in the turretted towers would have been sure to shoot one to death. However, I was very aware of the final nature of death, never believing in life in the thereafter. Life was very difficult, escape by dying had its appeal, but the finality of it made me postpone it from day to day. Every day I considered the suicide option and every day I decided to wait one more day. When my life really and truly reached the stage when continuing the struggle had become impossible and further existence was too difficult, with my health totally deteriorated, my strength gone and a deep depression set in, thus, when, as I now see it, a suicide was morally and realistically justified, I found that I could not do it. What I did not realize then, is that a suicide is an act of will. In reality, it turned out that it is not an easy, almost passive act, but to the contrary, an act requiring a strong affirmative action, a positive commitment to the deed. What I discovered, is that when a total physical debilitation is accompanied by a total depression and life seems not worth living, then the strength of will to actively end it just is not there. At that point I simply did not care whether I live or die, whether I eat or not, whether I continue to suffer or not. I just became completely passive and let events wash over me without any active participation of my real inner self. Fortunately for me, this stage, which was a definite indication of approaching death, set in at the very end of the War, just prior to the entry of American troops. The sight of Americans entering the camp instantaneously erased any and all feelings of depression, replacing them with a desperate will to survive, to recuperate and to resume life as a human being. It took the Germans five-and-a-half long years of battering my feeling of self-worth and my will to survive, during which I fought for every bit of advantage in a desperate fight against overwhelming odds, to bring me to this state. It took only a momentary glimpse through the trees of a tank with the American flag to instantly banish depression and to revive my ability to take up the struggle to get well physically and psychologically and to return to normal civilized existence.

At the beginning of 1945 I was getting weaker and weaker with each day. At first, we had reserves, we were physically and psychologically strong. We were healthy, well nourished. We had a good life, strong family ties, reliable support groups. Then, once the Germans began their campaign of degradation, humiliation and brutality, which included beatings and arrests with tortures, we kept our spirits and waited for the War to end, confident that Germany will eventually loose. The deprivation of food and physical resources was harder to endure. Our resolve to survive was not sufficient to overcome the physical obstacles to survival. Our strength ebbed and the likelihood of survival began to be measured against the duration of the War. Will the War end before all our strength is gone? Which will come first, the end of the War or our demise? My uncle Olek, who was with me in Ebensee Concentration Camp, suffered terribly, much more than I. A tall, once lithe and muscular man in his prime, 34-years-old, he found the physical deprivation regimen deadly. The same food ration which was woefully inadequate for me, a thin small underdeveloped teenager, was a daily torture for him. In addition, because he was tall and appeared strong, much more was expected from him than from me. For example, at one point we had a young Polish *Capo,* a prisoner who was appointed as group leader. He was arrested in Poland as a common criminal and sent to the camp, as what the Germans called a *Berufsverbrecher*, a professional criminal, perhaps a murderer. This illustrates the system that the Germans instituted, using criminals to intimidate and brutalize camp inmates. The young *capo* was certainly brutal. He picked on my uncle as his particular victim, and beat him all the time with a wooden or rubber truncheon. My uncle's strength was no match for the beatings and the starvation. He became weaker, his metabolism ceased to function and he died in my arms in February 1945, barely three months before the end of the six-year War. I held him in my arms as he stopped breathing. We were so used to people dying in the camp that his death was not particularly noticeable, except for me, for he was the last member of my family that I then had. I well remember how thin and light he was. When I carried his emaciated body to the camp crematorium to have it incinerated, it weighted so little that I did not need help to carry it. I was left all alone.

On May 5, 1945 I was lying in my bunk in the barracks of the concentration camp in Ebensee in the Austrian Tyrol, too weak to get up. I was in the bunk, sick, hungry, emaciated, depressed, when suddenly, through a crack in the wall, among the trees, I saw a big gray-green moving tank and then I saw that it was waving a big American flag. I realized that the American Third Army has just liberated Ebensee and that I have survived the War. After the War my friend Sam Goetz tried for years to find any of the American soldiers who liberated the camp and thus saved our lives. Recently, he heard from Bob Persinger, who was the young U.S. seargeant leading the tank troop that entered the Ebensee camp on that fateful day. The story appeared in the Los Angeles Times of November 4, 2005.

I was in bed, because I was totally exhausted and dying and could remain prone because all the work in the camp has stopped. The Nazi SS commander of the Ebensee camp and the German guards had run away before the arrival of the Americans. A few days earlier, the commander gathered all prisoners, about thirty thousand of us, and ordered us to go into an unfinished tunnel we dug out into a mountain. He claimed that the approaching Americans carpet-bomb the ground before conquering it and that he is sending us into the tunnels for our own protection. We suspected, however, that he intended to kill us in the tunnel, that he wanted to gas us all there, and we refused to follow his command. We much preferred to take our chances with the American bombs. Incensed, he ordered his soldiers to shoot, but the guards refused to obey his orders and he could not force us. Previous guards, disciplined Nazi Storm-troopers, have been sent to the frontlines, the guards at this point were mostly elderly civilians drafted with little training to serve on the home front. The camp commander gave up, got into his car and drove off. I understand that he was caught a few days later by the American army and went to trial for the war-time criminal excesses.

Ebensee was not unique. It was one of several sub-camps, divisions of the main concentration camp at Mauthausen on the Danube. Mauthausen had high solid stone walls and permanent structures and was meant to be a permanent Nazi camp for political opponents and social and religious outcasts, which by some fluke, included some surviving Jews. By contrast, Ebensee was a temporary entity, created to house able-bodied inmates who were to build an airplane factory underground. As such, Ebensee did not have torture devices, interrogation chambers, gas chambers or gallows. However, it did have a crematorium, which it needed because the death rate among inmates was so high. We were forced to work extremely hard, without proper equipment, without adequate housing or clothing, in the cold, with little sleep, and almost without food. The rate of death from starvation was staggering. At liberation, the weight of the walking skeletons of prisoners, once-healthy grown up men, hovered around eighty pounds. The average survival rate among the prisoners was a few weeks. I survived because I was small, underdeveloped and did not need as much food as fully-grown men. Like my uncle Olek, prisoners developed diarrhea, the bane of undernourished starving inmates, and died. I was not doing too well myself but I did manage to survive.

The American soldiers were horrified, seeing all these walking skeletons, hardly alive from starvation. They did what comes naturally. They cooked up a rich soup, full of meat and fat and all kinds of good food and offered it to the liberated prisoners, who formed a long line at the field kitchen. I was, however, too sick and too weak to get to the line in time. By the time I dragged myself from my bunk, I was among the last few to stand in line. To my horror, they run out of soup before my turn came. This was for me an unbelievable reverse, and I cried. Eventually, the kitchen scrounged up some leftovers and prepared a thin watery soup and I got a bowl of that. What I did not know, and what the helpful American liberators obviously did not realize, is that the exhausted and starving individuals were in no position to digest a rich soup and most got diarrhea and some died. The thin warm broth that I got, was what the doctor would have ordered for empty stomachs and was much better for me. It may even be that, given my emaciated condition then, the fact that I did not get the rich soup may also have been among the factors that saved my life.

In general, the decompression after liberation led many people to get seriously ill. Almost to the end, I was somehow able to work when I had to in order to stay alive, I survived on nerves, guts and a daily outpouring of adrenaline. Soon after liberation, however, I found how weak and how sick I really was. I was subject to continuous fainting spells, headaches, migraines, exhausing cough attacks, circulatory problems, occasional convulsive seizures, as well as a general malaise and weakness in the joints. I had a number of incompletely healed scars on my head and neck, and an open sore on my shin from beating and accidents. I had trouble walking and trouble breathing. In a word, I had a long way to go to full health. In a small field clinic set up in Ebensee by the American Army I was X-rayed and diagnosed as having tuberculosis, in addition to all the more obvious problems. I still remember what the army physician wrote in Latin on a piece of paper that he handed me: "*tb pulmonis dextra, verisimiliter activa*". The doctor advised me to enter a hospital immediately, which, of course, I did not do. There was too much for me to do, too many urgent matters to take care of. I had no time to be sick.

My first order of business was to get somehow in touch with my father who, I knew, was in America. I had memorized the address of a distant cousin, who was a professor at the City College of New York. Getting a letter to New York, was, however, next to impossible. There was no regular mail in newly conquered Austria and the available Red Cross mail took weeks, if not months. Eventually, I found an American soldier of Polish-Jewish extraction, who took one of my letters and send it through army mail to New York. In that very first letter I informed my father that I am the sole survivor of the whole extended family and that I have no intention of returning to Poland, but would like to join him and create a new existence for myself in the United States.

Nobody from my immediate family survived in Poland. My mother, my grandmother and my little sister perished in the extermination camp in Bełżec in Poland in October 1942. All other relatives died, probably also in Bełżec. As described above, my last relative to die, my uncle Olek, died a few weeks before liberation, cradled in my arms in Ebensee. The prisoners in Ebensee came from all over the occupied territories. Besides Polish Jews, there were Poles, Frenchmen, Greeks, Russians and a sprinkling of other nationalities. The Poles set up a refugee camp nearby, the rest of the liberated prisoners, including Polish Jews, formed a second camp. As a Polish citizen and as a Jew, I qualified for residence in both camps, registered in both and, thus, managed to receive a double ration of food. I found a few kindred souls, young Polish Jews like myself, orphaned and alone. We formed a support group for ourselves.

Eventually, the camps maintained by the army and then by UNRRA, the United Nations organization in charge of refugees, began emptying out. As communications were opening up, trains were beginning to run, however irregularly. Prisoners of all nationalities were returning home. With time, the Frenchmen were returning to France, and, with more difficulty, the Eastern Europeans to Poland, Ukraine and Russia. Only the Jews had no place to return to. They would not return to places where their entire families were exterminated. Gradually, however, even they were being shifted by the United Nations Refugee Administration to different, less makeshift, facilities.

I found out that my aunt in France has survived, with her husband and son, and I was ready to go to France, but always with the idea of eventually joining my father in the United States. Then I found out that, being French-born and of draft age, I may have trouble leaving France while the war with Japan was still going on. Also, it was easier for me to get an American visa if I remained a homeless refugee. At the time, in 1945, there were no American consular offices in Austria yet, but there were in Italy, occupied earlier. I understood that it might be easier for me to get a US immigrant visa if I went to Italy. The Jewish soldiers from Palestine, who served in the British armed forces, were very active in trying to get Jewish refugees to go to Palestine. This was a clandestine effort, against the wishes of the British and in spite of British active opposition and blockade. In Ebensee, the effort took the form of sending trains of Jews to Southern Italy, as a trans-shipment point for Palestine. With several of my new friends from Ebensee, I boarded one of these trains and traveled via the Brenner Pass and the length of Italy to the heel of the Italian boot, to the resort of Santa Maria al Bagno, near Nardó in the province of Apulia, where a semi-permanent UNRRA camp was being set up. I remained in Santa Maria for several months, some of my friends stayed there for several years.

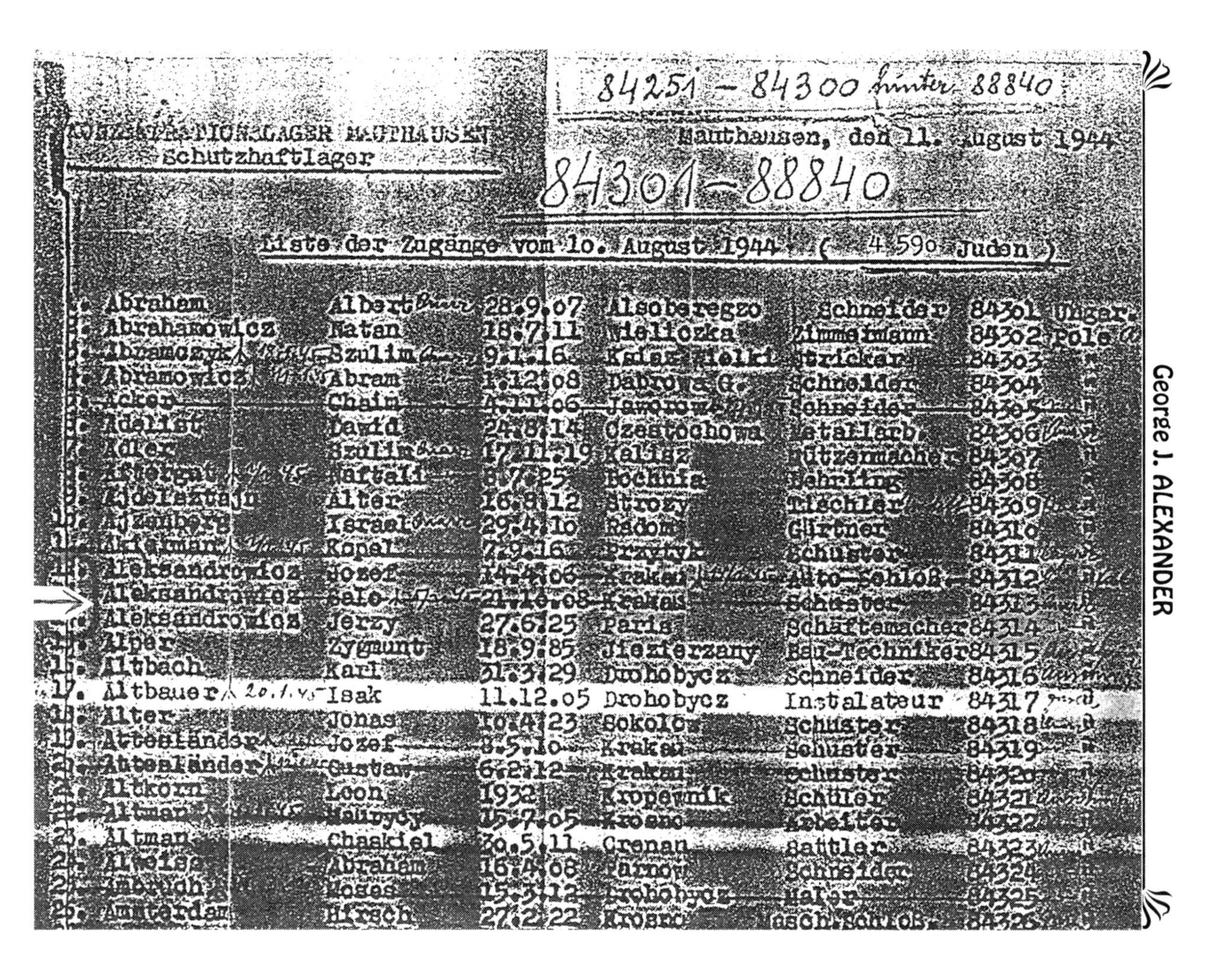

84251 – 84300 hinter 88840

KONZENTRATIONSLAGER MAUTHAUSEN
Schutzhaftlager

Mauthausen, den 11. August 1944

84301 – 88840

Liste der Zugänge vom 10. August 1944. (4 590 Juden)

No.	Name	Vorname	Geb.	Ort	Beruf	Nr.	
1.	Abraham	Albert	28.9.07	Alsoberegzo	Schneider	84301	Ungar
2.	Abrahamowicz	Natan	18.7.11	Wieliczka	Zimmermann	84302	Pole
3.	Abramczyk	Szulim	9.1.16	[illegible]	Stricker	84303	
4.	Abramowicz	Abram	1.12.08	Dabrowa G.	Schneider	84304	
5.	Acker	Chaim	4.11.06	Jaworow	Schneider	84305	
6.	Adelist	Dawid	24.8.14	Czestochowa	Metallarb.	84306	
7.	Adler	Szulim	17.11.19	Kalisz	Mützenmacher	84307	
8.	[illegible]	Naftali	8.7.25	Bochnia	Lehrling	84308	
9.	Ajdelsztajn	Alter	16.8.12	Strzyz[illegible]	Tischler	84309	
10.	Ajzenberg	Israel	29.4.10	Radom	Gärtner	84310	
11.	[illegible]	Kopel	7.9.16	Przytyk	Schuster	84311	
12.	Aleksandrowicz	Jozef	14.4.06	Krakau	Auto-Schloß.	84312	
13.	Aleksandrowicz	Salo	21.10.08	Krakau	Schuster	84313	
14.	Aleksandrowicz	Jerzy	27.6.25	Paris	Schäftemacher	84314	
15.	Alper	Zygmunt	18.9.85	Jezierzany	Bau-Techniker	84315	
16.	Altbach	Karl	31.3.29	Drohobycz	Schneider	84316	
17.	Altbauer	Isak	11.12.05	Drohobycz	Instalateur	84317	
18.	Alter	Jonas	10.4.23	Sokolow	Schuster	84318	
19.	Attesländer	Jozef	8.5.10	Krakau	Schuster	84319	
20.	Attesländer	Gustaw	6.2.12	Krakau	Schuster	84320	
21.	Altkorn	Leon	1932	Kropewnik	Schüler	84321	
22.	Altman	Maurycy	15.7.05	Krosno	Arbeiter	84322	
23.	Altman	Chaskiel	30.5.11	[illegible]	Sattler	84323	
24.	Alweiss	Abraham	16.4.08	Tarnow	Schneider	84324	
25.	[illegible]	Moses	15.3.12	Drohobycz	Maler	84325	
26.	Amsterdam	Hirsch	27.2.22	Krosno	[illegible]	84326	

Fig. 094. Page from German record of the Mauthausen concentration camp, arrow to Aleksandrowicz entries, and a hand-written note of death of my uncle Olek

Ausweis — Certification.

Herr / *Mister* Aleksandrowicz Jerzy

geb. am / *born* 27.6.1925 in / *at* Paryż (Francja)

zuletzt wohnhaft / *last domicile* Kraków, Bernardyńska

wurde vom 13.4.1943 bis 6 Mai 1945

in nationalsozialistischen Konzentrationslagern gefangen gehalten und vom **Konzentrationslager Mauthausen** in Freiheit gesetzt.

was kept in captivity from 13.4.1943 *to* 6 May 1945 *in Nazi-German concentration camps and was liberated from the concentration camp of Mauthausen.*

Untersdiriften und Stempel: / *signatures and stamps:*

Lagerkomitee / *Camp Commite*

Lagerkommandant / *Camp commandant*

Mauthausen, am — 6. VI. 1945

1786 45

Provisional identification card for civilian internee of Mauthausen.

Vorläufige Identitätskarte für Mauthausen, Gruppe Zivilinternierte.

Current number / *Laufende Nr.* 3312 Internee number / *Häftlings-Nr.* 84374

Family name / *Familienname* Aleksandrowicz

Christian name / *Vorname* Jerzy

Born / *geboren* 27 June 1925 at / *in* Paryż (Francja)

Nationality / *Nationalität* Polish

Adress / *Adresse* Polish Camp of polit. exprisoners in Ebensee

Fingerprint: / *Fingerabdruck*

Signature: / *Unterschrift* Aleksandrowicz Jerzy

Mauthausen, am — 6. VI. 1945

Fig. 095. Mauthausen/Ebensee identification certificate – 1945

Part IX. FROM CONCENTRATION CAMPS TO AMERICA

Chapter 30. From camps in Austria to Italy, then to New York

The World War began for me on September 1, 1939, when German troops invaded Poland, and it ended almost six years later, on May 6, 1945, when the troops of the American Third Army liberated the concentration camp in Ebensee in Austria, where I had been imprisoned. The War in Europe came to an end, but my problems continued, although they were of a significantly different nature.

No longer did I need to fear being shot because I was a Jew. No longer was my life in any direct danger. Each minute did not bring fresh menace and fresh panic. Desperate hunger ceased to be a problem. I did not have to scrounge for food scraps as I had to before. I was not subject to beating and malnutrition and overwork. But, the relaxation following liberation brought its own dangers. One famous one, that I and others have described before, concerned the immediate danger of very rich nutritious food that our poor emaciated bodies were not equipped to digest.

For the last few days prior to liberation, I have been sick and depressed, pretty close to death, but I managed to walk and work through sheer flow of adrenaline stimulated equally by a balance of fear of beating and torture, the pain of dying a slow and painful death and the residue of a desperate innate will to survive at any cost. Only a few weeks earlier, my last surviving relative, uncle Olek, died after a slow inevitable progression of malnurition, exhaustion, beating, and, eventually, diarrhea. I knew that I can not and will not live much longer, but the liberation came just at the last minute, as the Germans fled and the Americans took over. The sudden decompression, the removal of unbearable tension, was too much. I became extremely weak and stayed in my bunk in the barracks. I was too tired, too sick, too exhausted to drag myself out of the bunk, too weak even to stand in line for the life-giving American soup. A lot of people died that day, not necessarily just from diarrhea and stomach upset caused by the unaccustomed food, but, in general, from decompression, from accumulated effects of malnutrition, exhaustion and maltreatment. I survived. Not in the greatest of shapes, but alive. I was subject to fainting spells, convulsive seizures, migraines and exhausting tubercular cough attacks. My body needed time and rest to recuperate.

I was eager to go to the United States, but I was aware that American visas were difficult to get. The Polish quota was over-subscribed for years, but I was born in France, and in the American system I came under the French quota and I was a minor with a father residing in the States. Still, the wait for a visa promised to be long and I contemplated going to France and stay with my aunt, uncle and cousin until it came time to join my father. These plans did not work out. France was still at war, I was of military age (I was 20 at the time). Although as a former concentration camp inmate I would not have been drafted into the French military, as a young man of draft age and as one born in France and subject to French laws, I would have been prevented from leaving France for America as long as the war lasted or until the defeat of Japan. So, instead of going to France, I left Austria for Italy, which by this time converted itself from a defeated enemy into a recovering country which has managed to find an accommodation with the U.S.A., exchanging diplomatic relations. In Italy I could find an American embassy and a consul who would get me a visa for U.S.A.. From a prisoner/refugee transfer center in Austria, with a few hundred liberated Polish Jews but mostly in company of four or five young men of my own age and similar background, I boarded a train to Italy. We were, of course, refugees, with uncertain future, but we were young and resilient. Our train was not a regular scheduled train, it often stood at sidings and in cities en route and we were quartered in local schools or barracks until the train could move again. Thus, in Milan we were quatered in the Scuola Cadorna. We took advantage of the stopovers and the delays and managed to do some sightseeing. In this way I saw war-damaged Milan, including the Duomo, the Galleria, the railroad station where Benito Mussolini and his mistress Claretta Petacci were hanged and daVinci's *Last Supper*, pale and damaged in the refectory of a bombed church. I also saw Bologna, Florence and Rome, where we stayed in Cinecitta, a movie-making campus, used then to house refugees. The journey ended at a United Nations refugee camp in Santa Maria al Bagno, near Lecce, at the very south of the heel of the Italian boot, in the province of Apulia. The sandy, dry and warm Mediterranean climate served as a balm for my tortured lungs. It was a good warm, dry, sunny location, perfect for a person with tuberculosis. In a few months in this beach paradise, I took deeper and deeper breaths, began to take long swims in the warm Mediterranean waters and I largely recovered my strength. As I got more confident of my health, I began to consider my future, which presented obvious challenges. I was contemplating going to the US without knowing the language, the customs or the expectations of the country. I lost six years of my life, including six years of schooling, six years of growing up, maturing as an adolescent. To compensate for that I had obvious strengths: the war made me very resourceful, independent, more mature and more serious than I would otherwise have been. I would not have been the first immigrant to America, all of whom managed well there, and, of course, my father had been there for several years, and I had hoped that he might be able to help me orient myself in the strange new land.

Santa Maria al Bagno, part of the community of Nardó in the Apulian heel of the Italian Peninsula, was a pre-war beach resort favored by Italy's fascist elite, which was taken over by UNRRA, the United Nations agency charged with taking care of war victims, and converted into a refugee center, mostly for Jews. It received, housed and fed the Holocaust survivors who arrived on the train from Ebensee. And it tried to mend their broken lives. While used by UNRRA as a camp for refugees, it did not look like one. It was originally a small attractive Italian village, a resort on the Ionian Sea. I assume that its normal population was small, though it swelled significantly during the summer season. Most of the houses were empty because their rich Fascist owners were either in jail or in hiding, although a few locals who took care of the houses must have been around. The sea front was mostly rocky, with the waves breaking against the rocks. The main area of the resort fronted on a pretty little sandy beach. The Allies largely emptied Santa Maria of its few inhabitants, confiscated all the empty summer homes and assigned these houses to refugee families or groups. The house assigned to me, in which I lived for several months, was a villa located one block away from the beach. It housed five young men. While the dispossessed locals were surely unhappy about the camp, there was no overt hostility shown to us. To the contrary, everybody was polite, even friendly. Post-war Italy was impoverished and in need, even food was scarce, but the camp was provided with supplies and the Allies, mostly British, saw to it that the formerly starving liberated Jews had plenty of basic foodstuffs. In 2005 the President of the Italian Republic Carlo Azeglio Ciampi recognized the basic decency of the people of Nardó toward the Jewish refugees who found themselves in their midst and awarded them a Gold Medal of Civic Merit for their demonstration of "human solidarity and civic virtue" toward the Jews.

The Santa Maria seashore location turned out to be ideal for people whose lives have been as severely disrupted as ours were. The five men sharing the house lost their families in the Nazi Holocaust. All of us were liberated in the Ebensee Concentration Camp in Austria. We all came from similar backgrounds and got along very well together. As I stated elsewhere, the five of us formed a mutual support group and formed particularly profound friendships that would last a lifetime. Three of us, Yurek Wahrhaftig (1924-1972?), Ludek Goldstein (1926-2003) and I came from Kraków, Oscar came from nearby town of Przemyśl and Samek came from Tarnów. Ludek had an interesting experience toward the end of the war. In Kraków, he was employed in Oskar Schindler's Enamel factory, but when it came time to be saved and evacuated to a safe heaven in Bohemia with other Schindler employees, he did not have the wherewithal to bribe Schindler's Jewish bookkeeper who assembled the list and he was bumped from it. These corrupt machinations by Schindler's trusted assistant were understandly omitted from the glorified and simplified version of history in the film *Schindler's List*. Like me, Ludek ended in the Mauthausen concentration camp and was sent from Mauthausen to its satellite camps in Melk and Ebensee and, like me, he barely survived the war in the latter. The pre-war backgrounds of all five of us were similar, we all came from not religious middle-class Jewish families, reasonably well-off until the Nazi invasion. While we all had a rather similar view of our Jewishness, we widely diverged in our political attitudes and in our expectations for the future. Yurek Wahrhaftig was an ardent Zionist eager to go to Palestine to volunteer for a Jewish army and eager to help establish an independent Jewish state. I, on the other hand, had valid expectations of being able to emigrate to the United States. My father was in America and I hoped to join him there. Samek knew that he had an uncle in New York, the only surviving member of his immediate family, and he also wanted to go to America. The other two men also preferred to go to the United States, if at all possible. A brief story that I wrote about the five young men of the Santa Maria camp appeared in *Survivors Chronicle* in the Fall of 1998.

Gradually, as I became stronger physically and psychologically, I began to swim every day. I was a good swimmer before the War, enjoying long leisurely swims. Obviously, although six years have elapsed since the last time I enjoyed a swim, I have not lost the ability. With time, I took longer and longer swims. At a high point I undertook a long trip from Santa Maria by sea to the neighboring resort of Santa Croce, a distance of several miles. While I swam along the shore, my friends walked on the shore keeping me within sight at all times. It took me several hours to complete the trip. I encountered a school of jelly fish (medusas) and had to swim right through it, which felt like swimming in a sea of jelly. I did not know then that these creatures can be dangerous and that the sting of their tentacles can hurt, even kill. Fortunately, I did not suffer any ill effects from this particular experience, I assume that these jelly fish were young and not very poisonous. I am still proud of this long-distance swim in Santa Maria, among the longest I ever did.

The five of us took trips from the camp, to Nardó, Gallipoli, Brindisi and Bari. Once we went together to Naples. Since this was soon after the battles between the Germans and the Allies up the Italian Peninsula, train transportation was disrupted and recovering gradually. The trains did not follow any dependable schedule. Trains, often consisting of only cargo cars, came and went at odd intervals. Sometimes, only an engine traveled on the tracks, without any cars. This did not stop us – we did not follow any specific schedule, either. Once, we traveled from Brindisi northwest to Naples in the cabin of a coal-fired locomotive, watching coal being shoveled into the maw of the engine and we ended up covered with soot. In Naples I visited the National Museum, the castle of Maschio Angioino, the Vomero residential area and the Posilippo peninsula. On my own, I climbed to the crater of Vesuvius, visited the volcanic area of Solfatara in Pozzuoli, and with some effort, found a boat to take me to the Isle of Capri. There were no regular tourist excursions to Capri at the time, but I was very eager to see it and I managed to find a small local student group, boys and girls, getting into a private boat leaving from the Mollo Beverello for Capri and I asked to join them. They were very gracious and invited me to come along. Once there, we hired a fishing boat to take us into the Blue Grotto. In the grotto the color of anything immersed in the water was incredibly blue, reflecting the sunlight dispersed in the water. The oars, the lower part of the boat itself, our hands in the water were vivid blue. The boatman suggested that we jump in for a swim. We were dressed in our street clothing, so he took us into a dark corner of the Grotto to change into bathing suits, and then we went for a swim, a luxury that today‘s masses of tourists are not permitted to enjoy. Then, we were the only people present. The experience was incredible. I still remember the color of my arms and the rest of my body in the Grotto water. Obviously, in spite of everything that I have lived through during the War and Nazi occupation, my capacity to enjoy beauty or my thirst for knowledge and interest in sightseeing had not dimmed.

One day in Naples the five of us went together to the famous used merchandise market. We were forewarned about the omnipresent thieves in the market. As I was considered the most reliable of the bunch, I was entrusted with all the money we had. My pants were tight and the side pocket had a very narrow opening so that I could barely squeeze my hand into it. When my hand was in the pocket it was impossible for anybody to reach inside. I took the wad of lira notes that we had and held it between my thumb and my fingers squeezing it tightly inside the pocket. I kept my hand in the pocket all the time we were there. After a while I became aware of a space between my thumb and fingers, a feeling of emptiness. I

took my hand out, unbelieving that it could have happened, and looked at my hand to see that, sure enough, there was no money in it. I have no idea how it could have happened. My pants were intact with no rent in the fabric. The talent of the Neapolitan pickpockets was truly amazing. I immediately stated that I would happily pay a sum equal to the one I lost, just to be shown how it was accomplished. These people were true artists, not like some thieves today who use brute force and intimidation to rob tourists.

Life in Santa Maria was peaceful, food was provided by UNRRA, and swimming in the warm waters of the Ionian Sea, was restorative. The warm and dry sandy climate of Santa Maria was good for my condition and it did arrest my tuberculosis, causing calcifications in my lungs which, many years later, gradually dissolved. Social life in the camp was lively. In the camp, my friend Samek met the young woman who later became his wife. While young children (there were a few) went to local school in Nardó, there was no opportunity for me to go to school. I stayed in this UNRRA camp for a while, but as I gained strength I became concerned that the camp offered me no education of any kind. Anxious to resume my formal studies I left the camp and moved to Rome where there was a Polish school (see below). As a minor child of a U.S. resident I received a visa after one year of waiting and came to New York in July 1946. Samek came to America a year later. Yurek, who wanted to go to Palestine, got his wish: he was spirited by the Zionist underground, past the British blockade, and joined the Jewish secret army, the Hagana. He eventually became a pilot. The others languished in camp. In spite of U.S. affidavits that my father had sent them, they could not get to the U.S., because immigration was controlled by national quotas, and the Polish quota was hugely over-subscribed. Tired of waiting, they eventually took advantage of an opportunity to go to Australia and ended in Melbourne.

When my wife and I visited Israel in 1971 I wanted to find Yurek, whom I have not seen since 1946. I knew that he hebraicized his name. An Israeli friend suggested that he may have simply translated the name to its Hebrew equivalent. "Wahrhaftig" in German or Yiddish means "truthful". Sure enough, I was told that there is an Air Force officer called Yerucham Amitai, and, when I telephoned him, he turned out to be my friend Yurek. He met us and told us about his air force service, leading a squadron of fighter planes and about his work as a paratrooper trainer. Among his students, he recalled, was a young Ugandan, named Idi Amin. He also told us that he helped to build the airport in Entebbe in Uganda. However, he was very reticent and rather vague about his then current service. This latter became clear to me, when I saw the book "90 Minutes at Entebbe" by William Stevenson (1976) which was dedicated to the memory of Yerucham Amitai, late Deputy Chief of the Israeli Air Force. It appears that, when we were in Israel, Yerucham was directing Israeli Air Force Intelligence. No wonder that he was vague about his activities. After the highjacking of an airplane to Entebbe, Yerucham was among those who contacted Idi Amin, then President of Uganda, unsuccessfully trying to convince him to help free the passengers. Yerucham was also helpful by drawing a plan of the Entebbe airport, which was used by the Israeli paratroopers in their rescue mission. My friend Yerucham Amitai was killed in 1972 in a car crash that, I suspect, may not have been entirely accidental.

I have kept in touch with Samek who lives in California. While I dealt with my memories of the Holocaust by burying them in my subconscious and refusing to join any organization of Holocaust survivors, Sam did just the opposite. He has taken time out from his distinguished professional career as an eye specialist and became very active in making sure that the memory of the Holocaust survives. He was active in establishing a Chair of Holocaust Studies at the UCLA and was a member of the Presidential Commission, which set up the exhibits in the National Holocaust Memorial Museum in Washington.

Oscar and Ludek emigrated to Melbourne. With them went our friend, Natek. Natek believed that he was the sole survivor of his family. Efforts to unite survivors were, as we know, reasonably thorough, but nevertheless incomplete. I can imagine Natek's surprise and pleasure when accidentally, on a street in Melbourne two or three years after the war, he met his brother, who also believed that he is the only one to survive. Somehow, by coincidence, each independently ended emigrating to Melbourne. Oscar died in Australia and I never had a chance to see him again. I met Ludek, a Melbourne resident, after forty years, in 1985, during his visit to New York. The forty years seemed to have melted immediately. We revived our friendship with the greatest of ease. We hit it off and enjoyed each other instantly. In addition, our wives, whom we had married years later, also found that they liked each other. The four of us became close friends. Our friendship was reinforced when we vacationed together. We met Ludek and his wife, Guta, in Melbourne, in 1986 and again spent a month with them sharing a beach bungalow and exploring the Great Barrier Reef, north of Cairns in Queensland, Australia, in 1989. We vacationed together in 1993 in Czechoslovakia, visiting Prague, Karlsbad, Marienbad and climbing the Tatra Mountains in 1994. We arranged to meet again in Sri Lanka, in 1996, then in Montreal, Quebec and Tadoussac in Canada in 1998 and met again in 2000 in Australia. We did not let the distance between New York and Melbourne to keep us apart. My friend Ludek died in 2003 at the age of 77. His wife, Guta, lives in Melbourne. I have quoted a poem that she had written in the chapter describing my mother. We travelled to Australia in 2004, met Guta in Cairns and spent some time together in a resort on Dunk Island.

Five young men, five Holocaust survivors, five friends. Different personalities, different career choices. What we had in common was an inner strength, a determination not to give in, a determination to succeed, a determination to make our lives worthwhile. In this, I have reason to believe, we were typical of so many of Holocaust survivors.

After a few months stay in Santa Maria, as my health improved, I felt stronger and more adventurous. I began to be very concerned about my interrupted education and very eager to catch up. I left my new friends in Santa Maria and moved from the isolated camp to Rome. In Rome there was a Polish secondary school maintained by the Polish Army in Italy. That army, commanded by General Władysław Anders, was recruited earlier by the British from former Polish prisoners-of-war in Soviet lands. At one point after Hitler attacked the Soviet Union, the Prime Minister of the Polish Government-in-Exile in London, General Sikorski, met with Stalin, and arranged for the Soviets to release interned Polish citizens from the Gulags and allow them to assemble near Samarkand in Soviet Central Asia. Among those released and travelling to Samarkand was my uncle Józek Aleksandrowicz (see above chapter about my grandfather and his children). However, he was emaciated and exhausted from the ordeal in camp, contracted typhus and, in his weakened condition, succumbed in Samarkand. At the time, the Soviets were desperately fighting the Nazi onslaught and did not have resources to spare, such as uniforms, guns, canons, tanks or transportation for a Polish contingent, and this incipient army languished in Samarkand for a while. Eventually, Stalin agreed to let it move to the British zone in Iran, which was then jointly occupied by the British and the Russians to prevent it from falling into German hands, the way Iraq did in a pro-German coup by an Arab soldier-of-fortune named Kawutli. This Polish army numbered several tens of thousands of soldiers and included a large number of Polish Jews, all eager to see action against the hated Germans. Equipped by the British, this army moved from Iran, through Palestine to join the British in fighting in the African campaign against the Germans commanded by General Edwin Rommel in Tobruk, El Alamein and in Tripoli in Libia. After Rommel's defeat, this army fought its way up the Italian Peninsula. Its most important battle occurred at the mountain pass at the Monastery of Monte Cassino, from which one thousand years earlier a monk named Adalbert traveled to the shores of the Baltic Sea where he was martyred and became Poland's first Roman-Catholic saint. At Monte Cassino many Poles and Polish Jews perished. An elaborate cemetery at Monte Cassino is a testimony to the bravery of these expatriate warriors fallen in a common Allied cause.

After World War II ended the Anders Army stayed in Italy in camps near the southern end of the peninsula, in Barletta and Trani near Bari, where some schooling was being offered to the soldiers, mostly young men without any special skills other than soldiering. These soldiers were caught in a terrible fix. They were justifiably afraid to return to Poland, which by then had become a Soviet satellite. They saw that leaders of the Polish Underground Home Army were arrested and tried as enemies of the State and shot. Some soldiers of the Anders Army who dared to return to Poland were greeted with suspicion and arrested. Britain felt responsible for these troops which fought bravely for Britain and eventually moved them all to Scotland. I understand that these young men had little education and no easy way to earn a living, and in Scotland they fell on hard times. For a while I was getting letters from some of my friends among them describing their depression and their difficulties.

The Polish Secondary School in Rome, supported by the Anders Army, was meant primarily for children of high army officers and was run by Polish Jesuits and nuns from the contingent serving at the Vatican. The students, without exception, were children of generals and colonels, mostly of aristocratic origin, such as one girl whose father was a general before the War in charge of the Vilna military district. I was the only exception, the only Jewish student in the school, a survivor of the Holocaust, who appeared at the school office one day and asked, as a right for a young Polish citizen, to be enrolled in its classes. It never ocurred to me that somebody has to pay for this schooling. The school administration was very gracious about it and I was welcomed and treated with every courtesy. I find it hard to believe that of the many young Polish Jews, Holocaust survivors, living then in camps in Italy, I was the only one to think of enrolling in this school, although its existence became well known. The school offered not the usual curriculum but a strongly condensed, accelerated program. Having completed two years of secondary education prior to the War, I was enrolled in a combined third and fourth year class. I studied in this school for several months, graduated with good grades, and received a certificate of having finished four years of secondary school comparable to the program designed to follow both the pre-War Polish and then current Italian curriculum. My education was somewhat comparable to the American High School, although cosiderably foreshortened.

As the only non-Catholic student in school, I presented a certain problem for the administration. Classes of religious education were mandatory, according to both pre-war Polish and then current Italian curricula. A grade indicating completion of religious studies was required for graduation. Everybody tried to be helpful and it was suggested that I procure a letter from a rabbi, certifying that I am conversant with the tenets of Mosaic religion. That would have been acceptable to excuse me from classes in religion and I would be given a passing grade at the end of the term. I went to the main Roman Synagogue, located on the banks of the Tiber, and I met a distinguished elderly Rabbi, the Chief Rabbi of Rome, whose name I do not know, and explained to him, in my broken Italian what it was that I needed from him. I told him that I am a Polish Jew, a refugee, a Holocaust survivor, and that I need a certificate from him for my school. I treated this request for a certificate purely as a formality. He did not take it as such. With all the earnestness of a man used to communicating with God, he took out a *Siddur*, a prayer book printed in Hebrew, opened it at random at a page of prayers and asked me to read it and to recite the prayer.

As it happened, the type of Jew that I am, not having ever been a believer, I never attended a synagogue and I never prayed. I did not then and do not now know any Hebrew. I know how to read Yiddish, which is written in Hebrew alphabet, so I know the letters, but that does not mean that I can read or understand Hebrew. To describe it simply, Hebrew is usually written with only consonants. There exist diacritical marks, which might represent vowels, but these are hardly ever used in prayer books, because it is assumed that believers know most prayers by heart. As I have mentioned before, this absence of vowels allows readers to pronounce words differently and leads to the creation of dialects, most significantly, the Ashkenazic and the Sephardic. Kraków Jews pronounced their prayers in the Ashkenazic way. The revived Hebrew used in Israel today is pronounced more like the Sephardic dialect, perhaps because scholars decided that it is closer to the ancient Biblical way. Yiddish, in contrast to Hebrew, uses vowels as well as consonants, so it is easier to read and leaves fewer options in reading. For example the Hebrew/Yiddish word for Saturday was pronounced *"Shabes"* in Kraków and is now pronounced *"Shabat",* the word for "generations" was pronounced in Kraków as "*doyres*" and is now pronounced in modern Hebrew as "*dorot"*.

To go back to my encounter with the Chief Rabbi of Rome, I. told him regretfully that I cannot read his text but that I still would like him to certify that I am Jewish and familiar with my people's history and culture. To make a long story short, he considered my request impertinent, refused to write anything and, not so politely, threw me out. I went back to the Polish school, told the administration that the rabbi refused to provide me with the needed letter and offered instead to take the course in Catholic religion that the school offered, which at that level dealt with the history of the Church of Rome. I actually enjoyed the course, because I liked history and I did very well in it. I had pleasant discussions with the Jesuit priest who taught it, except for one discussion on the need for and the actions of the Spanish Inquisition, in which we agreed to disagree.

For a few intense months I took an accelerated course of general humanist education, including not only math and science and religion but also European history, Latin and even Classical Greek, trying to compensate for my lost years. Thanks to my strong motivation and eagerness I managed to cover most of regular secondary school program. With the solid background of my pre-War education of six years of exemplary primary school and two years of high-standard Gimnasium (secondary school), with all the reading that I did on my own during the early years of the War and with the addition of the few months of this very intense attempt at catching up in Rome, I had no trouble in keeping

up with my fellow freshmen in college in the United States. In the few months in Rome I managed to cover a lot of what I missed in formal schooling. In addition, I was very busy socializing, acting out as a late-blooming teen-ager surrounded by cute high-school girls. But that is a story for another book.

My first letter from Europe did not reach my father in America until weeks after my liberation which occurred on May 5, 1945 in Ebensee in Austria. In that letter, I told my father that I am the only survivor of the entire large family in Poland. My mother, my little sister, my grandmother, all my aunts and uncles and cousins who were caught by the war in Poland, perished in the Holocaust. I also told my father, who during the war expected to return to his family and his business and his political activities after the war ended, that there is no family, no business and no political future in Poland. I stated that I will not go back to live in Poland, not even temporarily. I wanted to start a new life in the United States. Also, I told him that several of my friends in Santa Maria want to go to the US and need affidavits of support.

My letter was not the first notice that my father had that I had survived. The first notice consisted of a list, one of many printed in the New York Jewish Daily Forward in 1945, enumerating survivors in the various camps, as they were being liberated. The lists were usually provided by Jewish soldiers in the American army. The list from Ebensee was printed incorrectly. I was listed as being 25 years old. At the time I was twenty, but I was born in 1925. A check of the original hand-written notes from the soldier showed the correct data and proved that the mistake occurred in transcribing and that I was indeed the person listed.

My father immediately began an effort to contact me. His friends in the military traveled specially to Ebensee to see me, but in the meantime I had left Austria and moved to Southern Italy, to the UNRRA camp in Santa Maria at the heel of the Italian peninsula. Eventually, we did get in touch and began a correspondence marred by difficult and unreliable mails.

As soon as my father found out that I was in the south of Italy and that the nearest American Consulate was in Naples, he began bombarding the Consul, Harold M. Granata, with letters importuning him to facilitate my coming to the United States. I have a copy of one personal letter that he enclosed with an affidavit sent September 20, 1945 (see enclosed photostat). Having been born in France and thus subject to a French quota and a minor and son of a US resident I was entitled to a preference, non-quota, visa. The problem was, however, that there was no transportation for civilians, all ships being used to return G.I.s home and the State Department was not eager to allow a flood of refugees, most of them Jews, to enter the US. The consul, whom I met many times, kept saying that he can not issue a visa without authorization from Washington, which was not forthcoming and without access to civilian transportation which was not available.

My father was then living in a small town of Andrews in Cherokee County of North Carolina, near the Tennessee border where he managed a tannery that was the main employer in the place. As such, he was an important man in town, even if not yet a citizen. He was in a position to get the US Senator from North Carolina by the name of Mead to write a letter to the Consul in Naples requesting that he help me get to the US. Had my father lived in New York where so many people had relatives in Europe whom they wanted to bring over, I doubt if he could have gotten a New York Senator to write such a personal

note, but in North Carolina my situation was unique. Between my father‘s letters and Senator Mead‘s letter, the consul, Mr. Granata, got to know me and was eager to help. He promised me that he will issue a visa as soon as possible and he kept his promise, although it took a year. I was among the first to get a visa after the State Department authorized their issuance. My visa was the second American immigration visa issued in Italy after the war.

In the meantime, both my father in the US and I in Italy, were getting impatient and frustrated with the delays. My father could not understand what is holding up the works. On October 16, 1945 I received a telegram in Santa Maria, stating "Have sent you by air mail affidavit. Apply immediately for visa at American Consul in Naples to whom copy of affidavit has been sent. Do not go to France if you have prospect to get American visa in Naples. Affidavits for your friends follow shortly. Love – Max Aleksandrowicz". On February 10, 1946 I got one that said "Advise whether consul cabled or wrote to Washington for quota number. Advise if possible for you to get airplane reservation.... Inform Jacob Lasker in Santa Maria that Mister Kilker Frash in Murphy North Carolina is looking for him. Love Max" and on May 11, 1946 I got one with "Cable whether visa received and what are your transportation prospects. Reply nightletter = Aleksandrowicz 536 West 112 Street NewYorkCity". Once I received a letter from the Italian branch of the International Rescue Committee (IRC) in Rome, offering help and asking me to visit their office to receive a letter from America. The IRC was established in the United States around 1936 to help refugees and fugitives from Nazi Germany. It boasted a distinguished patronage of Albert Einstein, Reinhold Niebuhr Upton Sinclair, Jack London and many many others. It did then an invaluable role in sheltering, aiding and protecting asylum seekers and other political or ethnic refugees. I am aware that it continues this work to this day.

On May 16 1946 I received a letter from the Consul that he received a quota number for me (see photostat) and I went to Naples to get my visa. On 27 June 1946 I received a "war ship ticket" for travel from Leghorn, Italy to "the first US port" (as it happened, it was to be New York City) on a ship called ‚Hobart Victory‘. The ticket was issued by the American Export Lines, as agent for the War Shipping Administration. The price of the ticket was $200 plus $8 in taxes. I left from the port of Livorno (Leghorn) on Hobart Victory, in company of seven young Italian war brides of American G.I.'s and myself as the only passengers, along with war materiel being returned to the States. We arrived in New York late in the afternoon on July 8, 1946. It was too late in the day for the ship to enter the harbor and it remained outside at St. Ambrose light for the night, but the eight passengers were brought in a small boat to the Battery, the pier from which tourist boats now leave for the Statue of Liberty. My father waited for me at the pier.

While I stayed in the UNRRA camp in Santa Maria in Southern Italy described earlier, I traveled to Naples a few times. In Naples I visited the American Consulate and took advantage of the stay in this beautiful city to do some sightseeing. Eventually I moved to Rome to attend the Polish school. In accelerated study I acquired enough formal knowledge, so that when I came to the United States I was able to become a freshman in college and to keep up with the studies there. As an inmate in concentration camps I have lost all my personal possessions, including any identification documents. After liberation, I received two different Refugee Identification numbers from the UNRRA and also a statement from the American occupation authorities confirming that I have been a camp inmate. While in Rome I registered with the Polish Interest section of the British Embassy and then took advantage of the opening of a Polish Embassy and applied for and received a temporary Polish passport proving my Polish citizenship. I felt that I need such a passport to receive an American immigration visa, which was usually applied to a valid citizenship document. It was with this passport that I applied in the US Consulate in Naples for the American visa.

In UNRRA camp food and lodging were provided. When I left the camp I depended on my father to send me from America a few dollars and packages which I could exchange for things that I needed which were very modest. Still, I felt that I should try to earn my keep and I decided to look for a job, while being very aware of the fact that I have no special qualifications and have no way to fully maintain myself or earn a living. I took inventory of my strengths and weaknesses and hoped that I could use my knowledge of Polish, French and a smattering of English, self-taught during the early days of the War, and of German which I acquired by having been forced to deal with German oppressors during the War. I offered to serve as an interpreter for the Allies in Naples and was directed to a British unit quarding German prisoners-of-war. My knowledge of both English and German turned out to be very limited, but fortunately one of the German prsoners had lived in America and was fluent in both German and English. As a prisoner he was not trusted, however, and it became my task to check his translations to make sure that he is not cheating. The British commander, knowing that I just came out of a concentration camp, was very sympathetic and understanding, but eventually, after a few weeks in the job, we both decided that I am not up to it and we parted company. From Naples I moved to Rome and the school described earlier.

My birthday is on the 27-th day of June. On June 27, 1946 I was going to be 21 years old. That would have made me legally an adult and not entitled to the extra special treatment reserved for minor children of citizens or permanent residents of the USA. It took the American Consul in Naples a year to get a visa number for me. Time was getting short. As it happened, I left Italy for the US on June 26, 1946. On leaving, I was still under 21 years old, and thereby a minor going to join a father, entitled to special consideration and a non-quota immigration visa. One day later I would have become of age and lost that preference, at least in theory. In practice, once I had a visa, nothing much mattered. The trip lasted ten days. The sea was rough. The ship, a Victory class cargo boat, carried mostly army equipment being returned home and 8 civilian passengers, the seven Italian war brides and me.

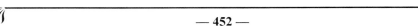

When I came to New York in 1946, I was very eager to continue my schooling. I enrolled in Hobart College in Geneva, New York and graduated *cum laude* in three years. I did my graduate work at Rutgers University in New Brunswick, N.J. My thesis professor was the Nobel Prize winner Selman Waksman, the discoverer of streptomycin. My thesis dealt with the fate of animal cholesterol once it finds its way into the soil. The thesis was accepted and I received a doctorate in Microbiology and Organic Chemistry in 1953. I spent four years at the Worcester Foundation of Experimental Biology in Massachussets at a very exciting time – the Foundation worked on the development of *The Pill*, the contraceptive pill which was to free women and revolutionize sex mores in the United States and the world. In 1958 I joined the faculty of the College of Physicians and Surgeons of Columbia University and the staff of the New York State Psychiatric Institute. I taught medical students and spent most of my time performing biomedical research. The results of my research into brain metabolism, biosynthesis of cholesterol, chemistry of learning and memory, action of hallucinogens and related subjects have been published in over 150 professional papers. I retired in 1994 as Associate Clinical Professor of Biochemical Psychiatry at Columbia. I continue my research as a volunteer at the Institute of Basic Research of the New York State Office of Mental Retardation and Developmental Disabilities located on Staten Island, New York.

I arrived in New York late in the afternoon on July 7, 1946. The ship remained at Ambrose Light and we, the passengers, were brought by a small passenger boat to Pier 1 at the battery. My father, who was waiting for me at the pier looked older than when I last saw him seven years earlier; he had some gray hair and to me he looked distinguished in his American suit and tie, but I had no trouble recognizing him; he really did not change that much. I assume that I must have looked very different to him: he last saw me at fourteen and here I was arriving a 21-year old. We hugged and had tears in our eyes; it was quite a reunion. My father lived then in Andrews, North Carolina where he was managing a tannery, but he flew in to New York City to meet me.

My father arranged a room for us at the old Biltmore Hotel near the Grand Central Terminal. We took an elevator, which stopped once or twice and then we were in our room. I rushed to the window to look at the street, assuming that we are on the second or third floor. I craned my neck and craned and craned and saw that the street was far below. It turned out that our room was on the 14-th floor. The hotel must have had separate express elevators that did not begin to stop until a high floor. Way down below tiny people were crossing the street, avoiding tiny little toy cars. This was my first impression of New York and my introduction to American skyscrapers. We stayed a few days in the city. I met my father‘s friend, Roza Luxemburg, who later became his second wife. I met my great-aunt Amalia Kaufer, whom I never met before. Although she was born in Kraków, she lived in Vienna. I mentioned her before when writing about my greatgrandfather Birnbaum and his children. When the Nazis came to Vienna in 1938, aunt Amalia emigrated to America. I also met my cousin, Herbert, the son of my father‘s sister Mania Wien. The Wiens also lived in Vienna and in 1938 Mania and her daughter Lilli moved to Argentina, her son Herbert came to New York.

My father‘s oldest brother, my uncle Ignacy, left New York a few weeks earlier, having accepted a faculty position at Hobart College upstate, in Geneva, NY, in Finger Lakes Country. I wrote about Ignacy before. He was very close to my father, they always had a lot in common. In Kraków, they followed the same political paths. My father admired his older brother. As a child in Kraków I knew Ignacy well and played often with Ignacy‘s two daughters, both of whom were killed in the War. Ignacy alone survived, along with my father. I have become the only member of the next generation who has survived the War. Now that I came to America it became natural that I have to see uncle Ignacy. Therefore, after a few days in New York City my father and I proceeded to Geneva, in North-Central New York State, and spent a few days with Ignacy. One day the three of us traveled to Niagara Falls. Thus, during the first few days in America, I saw the two arguably most renowned sites in the country: the largest city and the greatest natural wonder.

My father had to go back to work, so we left Ignacy and traveled to Andrews, North Carolina and the tannery. Andrews, then a town of approximately 1,500 inhabitants, is located in Cherokee County, near the Tennessee border, in the beautiful Smoky

Mountains. The tannery was the biggest employer in town. As I am now aware, Andrews was a very traditional place, conservative and Republican even then, being in that part of the mountainous South that remained loyal to the Union and did not join the Confederacy during the Civil War (pardon me! the War Between the States). This part of the country did not grow cotton, did not have slaves. There were hardly any blacks in Andrews. The population was thoroughly homogeneous, of English and, perhaps, Scottish stock. My father was well liked and everybody was very friendly, displaying southern hospitality at its best. The town was a part of the Southern Bible belt. There were roadside signs imploring us to believe in Jesus and to prepare to meet our maker. This is the area which made news recently when the right-wing terrorist who bombed abortion clinics and set off a bomb at the Atlanta Olympics hid in the Smoky Mountains near Andrews and obviously had a lot of local support.

As I stated, we were treated with Southern hospitality and encountered no problems. To the contrary, everybody was helpful. The town was run, like a fiefdom, by one wealthy family who owned everything worth owning, a lot of real estate and many houses, as well as the local bank and the local independent telephone company. The tannery that my father ran was previously owned by this family, which had sold it to some New York interests. The family matriarch represented Andrews in the State Legislature, almost as a right. Her family always sent a member to the State Senate. My father became very friendly with the powers that be, which had the additional advantage that their younger generation was well educated and a pleasure to talk to. They were sympathetic to his concerns about the family left in Poland, and were aware of the progress of war, they knew of the Holocaust and were abreast of local politics. They were the ones who got North Carolina‘s Senator Mead to write to the consul in Naples about me, which must have been helpful.

The other people in town that my father became friendly with were the principal and teachers in the local High School, primarily the Social Science teacher. I came to Andrews in the middle of July 1946. I was going to attend college in the fall, but the local High School classes began in August and I was invited to audit some classes, to become familiar with the sound of spoken American English, which I had trouble understanding, especially in its Southern version. I remember being in one social science class where the teacher was talking about the inequalities of treatments of different races. As an example, she mentioned that Andrews has a High School for its hundred or so white students but that the five black Andrews students have to be bussed to a black school in Robbinsville, more than an hour away, which took a lot of their time. All the students in class agreed that this was unfair and that Andrews should build a school for them. The teacher commented on the expense this would entail but the students felt that fairness demanded that it be done. Then, out piped up George Aleksandrowicz and said that, since there was plenty of room in our classroom, why not invite the blacks to join us. As soon as I said it I noticed the consternation and the total silence in class. Obviously, in 1946 this idea was unthinkable, inconceivably strange to the students. After a long silence, the teacher quietly said “George doesn‘t know our customs here” and that was that. The discussion continued and my contribution to it was ignored. This was my introduction to Jim Crow.

Fig. 096. Five young men in Santa Maria.
From left: Sam Goetz, Jurek Aleksandrowicz, Oskar Hanner (standing), Ludek Goldstein (seated) and Nathan Kohn.

Fig. 097. George Alexander in an overcoat in Rome

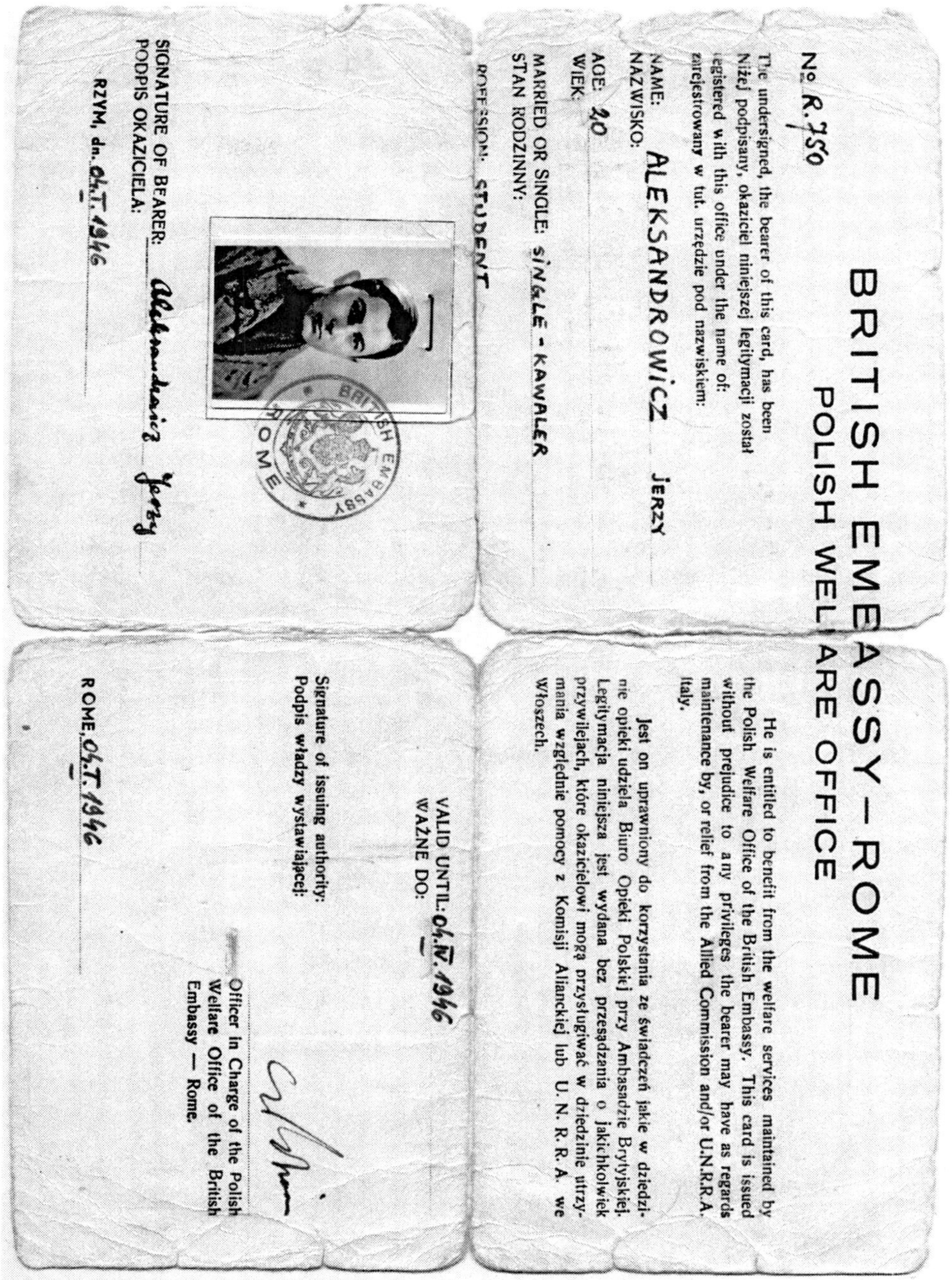

BRITISH EMBASSY – ROME
POLISH WELFARE OFFICE

№ R.750

The undersigned, the bearer of this card, has been
Niżej podpisany, okaziciel niniejszej legitymacji został
registered with this office under the name of:
zarejestrowany w tut. urzędzie pod nazwiskiem:

NAME: ALEKSANDROWICZ JERZY
NAZWISKO:

AGE: 20
WIEK:

MARRIED OR SINGLE: SINGLE - KAWALER
STAN RODZINNY:

PROFESSION: STUDENT

SIGNATURE OF BEARER: Aleksandrowicz Jerzy
PODPIS OKAZICIELA:

RZYM, dn. 04.I.1946

He is entitled to benefit from the welfare services maintained by the Polish Welfare Office of the British Embassy. This card is issued without prejudice to any privileges the bearer may have as regards maintenance by, or relief from the Allied Commission and/or U.N.R.R.A. Italy.

Jest on uprawniony do korzystania ze świadczeń jakie w dziedzinie opieki udziela Biuro Opieki Polskiej przy Ambasadzie Brytyjskiej. Legitymacja niniejsza jest wydana bez przesądzania o jakichkolwiek przywilejach, które okazicielowi mogą przysługiwać w dziedzinie utrzymania względnie pomocy z Komisji Alianckiej lub U. N. R. R. A. we Włoszech.

VALID UNTIL: 04.IV.1946
WAŻNE DO:

Signature of issuing authority:
Podpis władzy wystawiającej:

Officer in Charge of the Polish Welfare Office of the British Embassy — Rome.

ROME, 04.I.1946

BRITISH EMBASSY ROME

Fig. 098. ID issued by Polish Welfare Office of British Consulate

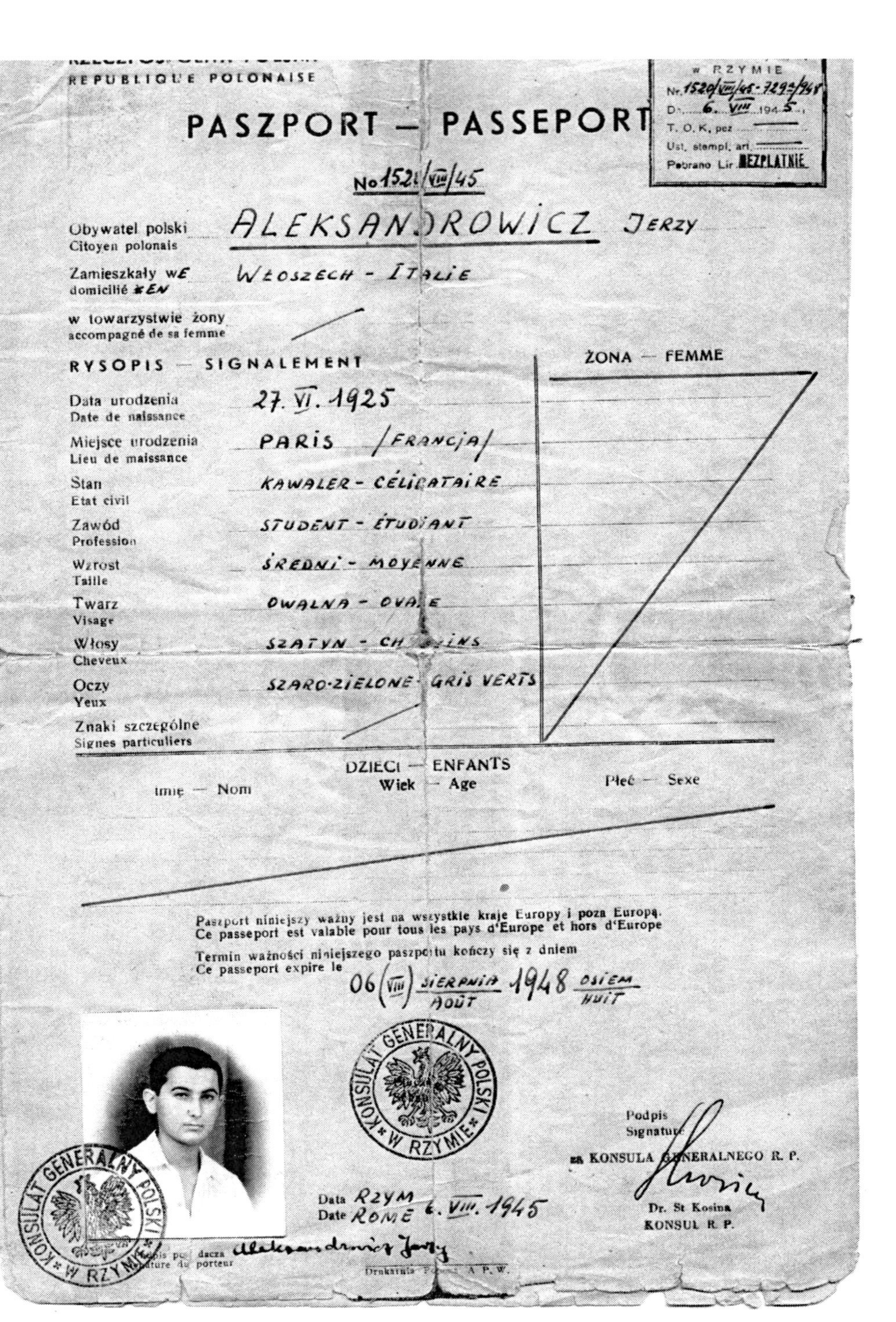
REPUBLIQUE POLONAISE

W RZYMIE
Nr. 1520/VIII/45-7292/945
Dn. 6. VIII 1945
T. O. K. poz
Ust. stempl. art.
Pobrano Lir. BEZPŁATNIE

PASZPORT — PASSEPORT

No 1521/VIII/45

Obywatel polski / Citoyen polonais: ALEKSANDROWICZ JERZY

Zamieszkały we / domicilié en: WŁOSZECH - ITALIE

w towarzystwie żony / accompagné de sa femme: —

RYSOPIS — SIGNALEMENT

ŻONA — FEMME

Data urodzenia / Date de naissance	27. VI. 1925	
Miejsce urodzenia / Lieu de naissance	PARIS /FRANCJA/	
Stan / Etat civil	KAWALER - CÉLIBATAIRE	
Zawód / Profession	STUDENT - ÉTUDIANT	
Wzrost / Taille	ŚREDNI - MOYENNE	
Twarz / Visage	OWALNA - OVALE	
Włosy / Cheveux	SZATYN - CHÂTAINS	
Oczy / Yeux	SZARO-ZIELONE - GRIS VERTS	
Znaki szczególne / Signes particuliers	—	

DZIECI — ENFANTS

imię — Nom | Wiek — Age | Płeć — Sexe

Paszport niniejszy ważny jest na wszystkie kraje Europy i poza Europą.
Ce passeport est valable pour tous les pays d'Europe et hors d'Europe

Termin ważności niniejszego paszportu kończy się z dniem
Ce passeport expire le 06 (VIII) SIERPNIA / AOÛT 1948 OSIEM / HUIT

KONSULAT GENERALNY POLSKI * W RZYMIE *

Podpis / Signature za KONSULA GENERALNEGO R. P.

Dr. St Kosina
KONSUL R. P.

Data / Date RZYM / ROME 6. VIII. 1945

Podpis posiadacza / Signature du porteur: Aleksandrowicz Jerzy

Drukarnia ... A. P. W.

Fig. 099. Temporary Polish Passport of Jerzy Aleksandrowicz

Maksymilian Aleksandrowicz 308
Andrews, North Carolina
U. S. A.

September 25, 1945

American Consulate
Naples, Italy

Dear Sir:

My son, George Jerzy Aleksandrowicz, born on June 27, 1925, in Paris, France, has been liberated by the American Army from the Nazi concentration camp in Ebensee, Austria, and he is now in an UNRRA Camp and his address is: UNRRA IT. 34. HQ. AC. CMF. He would like to come to me and to live in the United States.

Six years ago in August 1939 I parted from my wife, daughter and the above mentioned son, who was at that time fourteen years old, and joined the Polish Army. This was the last time I have seen my family. While they found themselves soon under German occupation, I retreated with the Polish Army to the Eastern part of Poland. After my unit exhausted its ammunition and has been dissolved, I found myself under Soviet occupation cut off from my people by the new frontier line. In 1941 I succeeded to come to the United States on a visitor visa which has been changed in 1945 to an immigration visa. I received already my first papers and am holding a managerial position with the Andrews Tanning Company, Inc. in Andrews, North Carolina.

According to information received from Poland, no one of my family is there and my son is the only survivor of the whole family. I am anxious to bring him over to have him with me, to give him the best care a father can give his only son and to heal the wounds of the inhuman sufferings in the Nazi Concentration Camp. I would like to give him back the faith that he has the right to live as a free man.

I am enclosing herewith my affidavit, the certificate of my employer, a statement from my bank, copy of my income tax return for 1944, a list of war bonds I own and I ask you to give my son the immigration visa so he can join me and live with me. I am the only person he has in the whole world and he is also my only hope. I trust that you will have the most understanding for my request and you will grant my son the right to be with me.

Thanking you wholeheartedly, I remain

Very sincerely yours,

Maksymilian Aleksandrowicz

Maksymilian Aleksandrowicz

Fig. 100. Letter to American Consul in Naples

IN REPLY REFER TO

FILE No. 811.11 - ALEXANDROWICH, George Jerzy.
HMG:cs.

THE FOREIGN SERVICE
OF THE
UNITED STATES OF AMERICA

DEPARTMENT OF STATE

AMERICAN CONSULATE GENERAL

Naples, Italy, May 16, 1946.

Mr. George Jerzy Alexandrowich,
42 Via Simon de San Bon,
Rome, Italy.

You are informed that this office is on receipt of your quota number.

In order to obtain an immigration visa it is necessary for you to forward to this Consulate General the sum of $9 (2025 Lire). On receipt of such a sum said visa will be mailed to your address.

Very truly yours,

for the Consult

Harold M. Granata,
Vice Console Americano.

Fig. 101. Consul's letter announcing issuance of visa

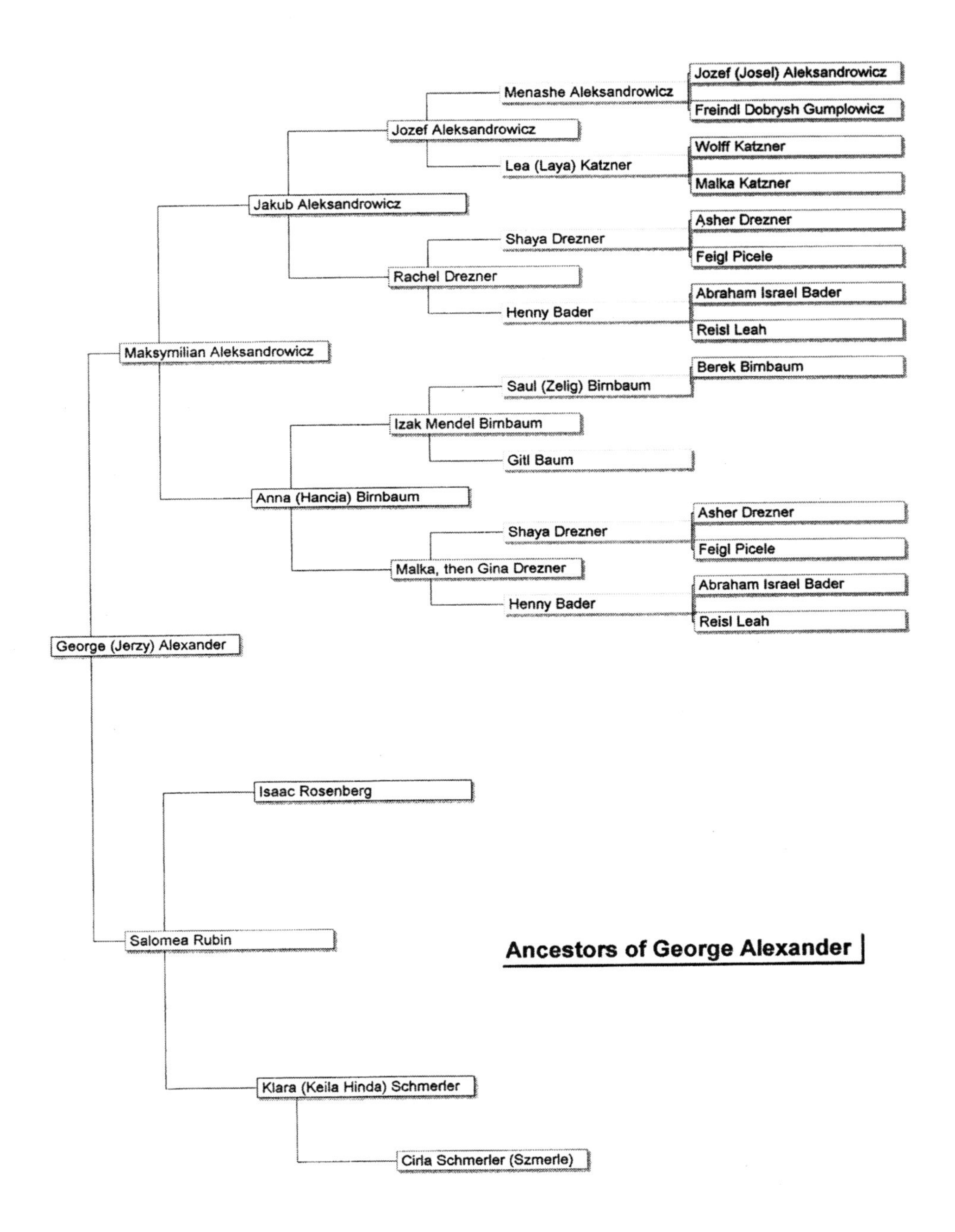

Fig. 102. Ancestor tree of George Alexander

EPILOGUE

Small and large ethnic and religious conflicts are tearing humanity apart and have to be better understood so that they can be better dealt with. Otherwise, it is hard to be overly optimistic about the future of humanity. On the wall of the U.S. Holocaust Memorial Museum in Washington, there is a quote from General Eisenhower who said "Never again!", after his personal experience with the Holocaust. He expressed a noble sentiment. I wish that he were right, but he was not. Smaller, but cruel massacres are occurring today with frightening frequency. Jews have been killed because they were Jews, in the Middle East, in Argentina, in France and elsewhere. But not only Jews. Shiites and Sunnis, Ulster Catholics and Protestants, Turks and Kurds, Serbs and Kossovars, Russians and Chechens, Tamils and Sinhalese, Hindus and Moslems,, Hutus and Tutsis, Sudan Arabs and Darfur Blacks and many others are engaged in mutual slaughter. Larger conflicts pitting fundamentalist Moslems against Christians and Jews loom over the horizon. Attempts at resolving these ancient conflicts have not been conspicuously successful.

My interest in history led me to write about both the one thousand years of Jewish existence in Kraków and about the tragic end of this millennial history, which I witnessed. I put down my thoughts as a Polish Jew about Polish-Jewish coexistence prior to and during the Holocaust, which is often misunderstood. I wrote in the hope that my work will prove of interest to all those interested in hostile interaction and conflict as well as cooperation and tolerance between ethnic groups. Jews have lived in Kraków, Poland's royal capital, for a thousand years and constituted up to 30% of its population. The Polish-Jewish coexistence was never easy and commercial competition was fierce but a certain amount of mutual understanding and tolerance developed over the years. The Nazi pogrom ended all of it. There are now hardly any Jews in Kraków, but there is a revival of interest in things Jewish among educated young Poles.

The Holocaust was made possible by a terrible concatenation of events: at base, the existence of a centuries-old ingrained Church-fostered anti-Semitism in Europe, the deep resentments by Germans after their defeat in World War I, the rise there of a dangerously spell-binding anti-Semitic demagogue, and, finally, the absence of restraints normally imposed by aroused world opinion in a world distracted by a desperate world-wide conflict. One might hope that no such concatenation is likely to ever occur again in the "developed" countries, but similar events are occurring elsewhere, albeit on a significantly smaller scale. I have no confidence whatsoever in the ability of the locals or of the current US government to properly respond to any of these conflicts and only scant confidence in any succeeding US administrations. I do believe that studies of these conflicts might, just possibly might, help us understand how different peoples learn to coexist and how, every now and then, forces arise that drive humans to these vortices of destruction. I have tried to demonstrate how two inimical ethnic groups, in this case, Poles and Jews, have learned, over long years, to coexist and establish a form of modus vivendi, as each group got used to the presence of the other and how and why this mutual understanding often broke down, quite apart from the orgy of terror and slaughter brought about by an invading enemy. I hope that works such as mine, delineating the development of such coexistence and its shattering at times, will eventually help us learn how to bring hostile ethnic populations to better control their murderous impulses and lead to the development of tolerance and thus lead humanity to a better future.

Scarsdale, New York, 2008

BIBLIOGRAPHY

In preparing this book I relied mainly on the following original documents:

1790-1792 "Spis Ludności w Mieście Żydowskim Kazimierzu, przy Krakowie, w Województwie i Powiecie Krakowskim leżącym przez Rabina Synagogi i Duchownych czyniony" (in Polish) (Census of population of the Jewish Town Kazimierz by Kraków, in the Province and District of Kraków, prepared by the Rabbi and Clergy of the Synagogue). Preserved in the local branch of the Polish National Archives in Kraków, Poland (PNA/K), very difficult to decipher and interpret. Some transcribed data from this census are available on the Web at <www.Jewishgen.org/ShtetLinks/Poland/Kraków>.

1796 "Verzeichnis der saemtlich in der Judenstadt Kasimir, der Vorstaedten und nahen Dorfen befindlichen Juden" (in German)(List of Jews found in the Jewish Town Kazimierz, suburbs and near villages) [selected pages]. Only half of this census survived. Written in Old German. Some transcribed data from this census, are available on the Web at <www.Jewishgen.org/ShtetLinks/Poland/Kraków>.

1788-1808 "Akta Urodzin/Gmina Starozakonnych w Krakowie (Geburtsbuch fuer der Kasimirer Juedengemeinde 1788-1899" (Polish/German) (Birth records / Old Covenant Community in Kraków (Book of Births for the Kazimierz Jewish Community). Includes some records of marriages and deaths. Available at the PNA/K. Many of these records, as well as wedding and death records are also available on the Web.

1812-1831 "Akta urodzin stanu cywilnego" (Civil birth records). These are individual yearly bound volumes, one for each year. Births are recorded in detail, in elegant calligraphy, in time sequence. Some volumes have an alphabetical index by first letter, which is, however, random within each letter. (in Polish, at the PNA/K).

1845 "Akta urodzin stanu cywilnego" (Civil birth records). (in Polish, at the PNA/K).

1847	"Arkusze spisowe konskrypcyjne z roku 18..; AufnahmsBogen vom Jahre 1847/ Land Galizien, Kreis Krakau, Ort Judenstadt, Herrschaft Krakau" (Military induction record sheets, Year 1847 / Country Galitzia, District Kraków, Location Jewish Town, Sovereignty Kraków). (Polish/German, at the PNA/K).
1847	"Wykaz alfabetyczny Nazwisk i Imion Osób Wyznania Mojżeszowego, których Akty Urodzenia w tej Księdze wedle Przepisów Prawa w Ciągu Roku 1847 zapisane znajdują się" (Alphabetical Index of Family Names and First Names of Persons of Mosaic Faith, whose Birth Records for year 1847 are in this book, according to law, inscribed). (In Polish, at the PNA/K).
1850	"Index spisu mieszkańców Kazimierza przy Krakowie, A do L" (List of inhabitants, Kazimierz by Kraków, A to L). (in Polish, at the PNA/K).
1870	Addressbuch fuer Oesterreich-Ungarn (in German, book of addresses for Austro-Hungary). Available at the New York Public Library.
1880	"Indeks spisu mieszkańców miasta Krakowa, tom I" (List of inhabitants of the city of Kraków, volume I). (in Polish, at the PNA/K).
1881	"Lista mieszkańców dzielnicy VIII w Krakowie" (List of inhabitants of area VIII in Kraków). (in Polish, at the PNA/K).
1900	"Spis mieszkańców, tom XV, dzielnicy VIII/"Kazimierz" (List of inhabitants, vol. XV, area VIII / Kazimierz), (in Polish, at the PNA/K). 1905, 1909, 1910 "Księgi adresowe, Kraków i Podgórze" (Books of addresses, Kraków and Podgórze) (Podgórze is a suburb, which was incorporated into the city in 1891). In Polish, available at the New York City Public Library).
1913	Skorowidz Galicyi, pp. 572-4 "Skóry" (Leather). (in Polish, at the NYC Public Library).
1921, 1932	"Księgi adresowe mieszkańców Krakowa" [Books of addresses of inhabitants of Kraków). (in Polish, at the NYC Public Library).
1926/1927	"Księga adresowa Polski" (Book of addresses of Poland). This is available on a microfiche at the New York City Public Library Slavic Division.
1930	"Urzędowy Spis Abonentów Sieci Telefonicznej Okręgu Kraków/Katowice" (Official list of subscribers to the net of telephones in the Kraków/Katowice region). This, too, is available at the New York City Public Library.
1938	Spis mieszkańców, Kraków Dzielnica II Wawel, Ulica Bernardyńska. Kept at the Kraków Municipal Records Office, Lubicz Street, inspected at the Municipal Records Office, in the Kraków Magistrat on the Plac Wszystkich Swiętych.

1939 Nowy Cmentarz Żydowski, Spis Nagrobków. (New Jewish Cemetery, List of tombs). In Polish. The only book saved from the Nazis, kept in a chimney, partly singed. Preserved at the Jewish Community Center, Kraków, Krakowska Street.

[The Family History Center of the (Mormon) Church of Jesus Christ of the Latter Day Saints (LDS) has many birth records from Kraków and Western Galitzia on microfilm (1798-1878), and some marriage and death records are also available there, but no census, conscription, tax, business, cemetery or telephone lists. All the Mormon records can be requested from the Family History Center in Salt Lake City, but many are available at the New York City LDS Center in Manhattan, opposite Lincoln Center. The personnel at that center is always very helpful and I would like to take this opportunity to thank them for their kind assistance to non-Mormon genealogists.]

Secondary sources for this work, including general background data:

Abramski, C., Jachymczyk, M. and Polonsky, A., Eds. The Jews in Poland. Publ. Basil Blackwood Ltd., Oxford 1986 (includes an article by Ciechanowiecki about ennobling of converted Jews);

Aleksandrowicz, Julian. Kartki z Dziennika Doktora Twardego. (Pages from the dairy of Dr. Hard). Wydawnictwo Literackie. Kraków 1967. (A war-time memoir of my father's second cousin, a war-time physician with the Partisans in Polish forests).

Bałaban, Majer: Historia Żydów w Krakowie i na Kazimierzu, 1304-1868. Vol I. Wydawnictwo "Nadzieja" Kraków 1936. (History of Jews in Kraków and Kazimierz, 1304-1868. Vol.II. Publishing House "Nadzieja"). Available in the New York Public Library, in Polish. This is the basic, classical history and primary source for Kraków Jewry.

Barnavi, Eli, Historical Atlas of the Jewish People. Schocken Books, New York 1992;

Beider, Alexander. Jewish Migrations to Eastern Europe. Avotaynu 13(3):12-18 (1997);

Biderman, Israel, M. Mayer Bałaban, Historian of Polish Jewry. Wydawnictwo DiG, Warsaw 1994.

Bieniarzówna, Janina and Małecki, Jan M. Dzieje Krakowa. Tom III. Wydawnictwo Literackie, Kraków 1979. (Kraków History, Vol. III.).

Bogdanowicz, Halina. Wawel. 2-nd ed., Wyd. Sport i Turystyka, Warsaw 1965.

Brook, Kevin Alan. The Jews of Khazaria. Jason Aronson Publ., Northvale, N.J. 1999.

Celemeński, Jacob. Mitn Farshnitenem Folk (In Yiddish)(With a decimated people). Farlag Unser Tsait, New York 1963; an incomplete version was recently published in English in Melbourne, Australia by the Jacob Celemenski Memorial Trust under the title: Elegy For My People, Caulfield, Vic., Australia; 2000.

Cymbler, Jeffrey, K. Nineteenth and Twentieth Century Polish Directories as Resources for Genealogical Information. Avotaynu 13(1):25-33 (1997);

Dawidowicz, Lucy. From that Time and Place. Bantam Books, New York 1989. (A memoir of a mission to Poland at the start of World War II by my father's friend and historian of the Holocaust).

Dimont, Max. Jews, God and History. Simon and Schuster, New York 1962;

Dobrowolski, Tadeusz. Sztuka Krakowa. (Art of Kraków). 2-nd edition. Wydawnictwo Literackie. Kraków 1957.

Donat, Alexander. The Holocaust Kingdom. Holt, Rinehart & Winston, New York 1963.

Dubnow, Simon M. History of the Jews in Poland and Russia. The Jewish Publication Society of America, Philadelphia 1918 (6 vols.); republished in one volume by Avotaynu, Inc., Bergenfield, NJ 2000. (A modern history of Eastern European Jewry).

Ehrlich, Mark. Honoring the Past to Change the Future: Solidarity and the Warsaw Ghetto. Tikkun, 3 (5):23-27 (199?)

Encyclopedia Judaica. Vols. I-XIX. 4-th Printing. Keter Publishers, Jerusalem 1978.

Epstein, Helen. Where She Came From. Penguin Putnam /Plume Book, New York 1998. A daughter's search for her mother's story.

Fischler-Marinho, Janina. Have You Seen my Little Sister? Vallentine Mitchell, London 1998. (A memoir of a Kraków girl child who survived the Holocaust).

Fuks, Marian, Hoffman, Zygmunt, Horn Maurycy and Tomaszewski, Jerzy. The Polish Jewry/History and Culture. Interpress Publ., Warsaw 1982.

Glueckel of Hameln. Memoirs (Zichroines), transl. M. Lowenthal, Schocken, New York 1977; (Dairies of a remarkable Jewish woman, written 1690-1719).

Goetz, Samuel. I Never Saw My Face. Rutledge Books, Danbury, CT 2001. Autobiography of my friend, a Holocaust survivor.

Goldberger, Janka. Surviving With Uncle. Janus Pub., London 1995. A semi-fictional account of a victim of the Holocaust, written by his wife.

Goldstein, Guta. There Will Be Tomorrow. Makor Jewish Community Library Publ., Melbourne, Australia 1999. (A lyrical book by a Holcaust survivor).

Goodman, Paul. History of the Jews. E.P.Dutton, 8-th Ed., New York 1953.

Graetz, Heinrich. History of the Jews. Six vols. Breslau 1891. The Jewish Publication Society of America, Philadelphia 1956. (First modern re-telling of the entire Jewish history).

Greenfeld, Howard. The Hidden Children. Houghton Mifflin, Boston 1993;

Gross, Jan T. Neighbors/The Destruction of the Jewish Community in Jedwabne, Poland. Princeton University Press, Princeton & Oxford, 2001. A study of a major pogrom in war-time Poland.

Grun, Bernard. The Timetables of History. Simon and Schuster / First Touchstone Edition (based on Werner Stein's Kulturfahrplan), New York 1982;

Hertz, J.S., Ed. Doires Bundistn (in Yiddish)(Generations of Bundists). Publ. Farlag Unser Tsait. New York 1968, pp. 96-101; 261-2.

Hertz, J.S. Di Geshikhte fun Bund (in Yiddish) (History of the Bund), Vol. I, p.32, photo p.125. Publ. Undzer Tsait, New York 1981.

Historical Atlas of the Holocaust. US Holocaust Museum, Publ., MacMillan, NY 1966;

Jasienica, Paweł. Polska Piastów. (Poland of the Piasts) [Piasts were the first Polish royal dynasty]. Publ. Zakład Narodowy im. Ossolińskich, Wrocław, Poland 1961;

Katz, Dovid. Words on Fire/The Unfinished Story of Yiddish. Basic Books, New York 2004

Kantor, Mattis. The Jewish Time Line Encyclopaedia. Jason Aronson, Northvale N.J. 1992; (This book deals mostly with religious events and rabbinical data).

Karski, Jan. Story of the Secret State. Riverside Press, Cambridge, MA 1944. (Story of a Polish underground courier who entered a Nazi extermination camp and came West to tell about it; he personally notified both Roosevelt and Churchill).

Kertzer, David I. The Popes against the Jews. Alfred A Knopf. New York 2001.

Koestler, Arthur. The Thirteenth Tribe. Random House, New York 1976.

Levine, Hillel. In Search of Sugihara. [Chiune Sugihara was the Japanese Consul in Lithuania, who issued visas to Jews in 1940-1]. Publ. The Free Press, New York 1996.

Małecki, Jan and Szlufik, Elżbieta. Handel Żydowski w Krakowie w końcu XVI i w XVII wieku. (Jewish commerce in Kraków at the end of 16-th and during the 17-th century). Publ. Polska Akademia Umiejętności, Kraków 1995. (in Polish and English).

Malinowski, Jerzy. Malarstwo i Rzeźba Żydow Polskich w XIX i XX Wieku. (Painting and sculpture of Polish Jews in XIX and XX centuries). PWN, Warsaw 2000.

Morris, Jan. The Venetian Empire/ A Sea Voyage. Harcourt Brace Yovanovich, New York 1980.

Olson, Steve. Mapping human history / Genes, race and our common origin. A Mariner Book. Houghton, Mifflin Co., Boston, NewYork 2002.

Panchyk, Richard. Hello, Cousin: the Mathematics of Ancestry. Avotaynu 13(1): 34-35;

Passlecq, Georges and Suchecki, Bernard, Die unterschlagene Enzyklika der Watikan und die Verfolgung der Juden. (in German), Publ. Carl Hauser, Munich 1997.

Pieragostini, Peter. Memoirs of the Holocaust. SEIU Service Employees Union, 1313 L St., Washington, D.C. Summer 1993. 7 (3): 20-24.

Polish-English Dictionary. Wiedza Powszechna, NTC Publ., Lincolnwood, IL. 1993.

Polski Słownik Biograficzny. Vol. I, p.70. Polska Akad. Umiejętności, Kraków 1935.

Preker, Teresa. Konspiracyjna Rada Pomocy Żydom w Warszawie 1942-1945. (Secret Council to help Jews in Warsaw 1942-1945). History of Żegota, an official organization to save Jews set up and financed by the Polish Government-in-Exile.

Rajduch-Samek, Izabella and Samek, Jan: Katalog Zabytków Sztuki w Polsce. Tom IV. Miasto Kraków. Część VI. Kazimierz i Stradom. Judaika – Bóżnice, Budowle Publiczne i Cmentarze. Instytut Sztuki Polskiej Akademii Nauk. Warszawa 1995. (Catalogue of art monuments in Poland. Vol. IV. City of Kraków. Part VI. Kazimierz and Stradom, Judaica - Synagogues, Public Buildings, Cemeteries. Art Institute of the Polish Academy of Sciences. Warsaw 1995).

Rosenstein, Neil. The Lurie Legacy. Avotaynu Publ., Bergenfield, N.J. 2004. A detailed story of the Luria family from King David to the present.

Rottenberg, Dan. Finding Our Fathers. Random House, New York 1977. (An early bible of Jewish genealogy; the book that started it all).

Rowinski, Aleksander. Życie i śmierć Zygielbojma (Life and Death of Zygielboim). Oficyna Literatów "Rój", Warsaw 2000. (The story of a heroic Polish-Jewish leader who gave his life to alert the West to the Holocaust).

Rubin, A.P. Scattered among Nations/Documents affecting Jewish History 49 to 1975, Jason Aronson, Publ., Northvale, N.J. 1995. (Includes excerpts from the Statut Kaliski issued in 1264 by Duke Bolesław Pobożny of Kalisz);
Shereshevsky, Esra. Rashi / the Man and his World. Jason Aronson, Northvale, N.J. 1996.

Shmeruk, Chone. The Esterke Story in Yiddish and Polish Literature. Zalman Shazar Center, Jerusalem 1988. (The legend of the Polish King Casimir the Great and his Jewish mistress).

Sliwowska, Wiktoria, ed. Dzieci Holocaustu mówią (Children of the Holocaust speak). Publ. Stow. Dzieci Holocaustu w Polsce, Warsaw 1993. (Text of testimonies presented in 1946 to the official Polish Regional Historic Commission in Kraków)

Słownik Biograficzny Działaczy Polskiego Ruchu Robotniczego, I : 63. (Biographical Dictionary of Activists of the Polish Labor Movement). Publ.: Książka i Wiedza, Warsaw 1968?

Soski, Joseph. Haver Maks Aleksandrowicz. (in Yidish). Journal Undzer Tsait, New York 1999. Vol. 3-4:32-35.

Stevenson, William. 90 Minutes at Entebbe. Bantam Books, New York 1976.

Szwajger, Adina Blady. I Remember Nothing More. Touchstone Book/Simon and Schuster, New York 1992

Walicki, Michał and Wojciechowski, Aleksander. Xawerego Dunikowskiego Głowy Wawelskie (Wawel Heads of Xavery Dunikowski). Wyd. Sztuka, Warsaw 1956.

Wolak, Arthur J. Forced Out: The Fate of Polish Jewry in Communist Poland. Fenestra Books, New York 2004.

Zeiden, Herbert Guy. Khazar/Kipchak Turkisms in Yiddish. The Journal Yiddish, publ. by Queens College, New York, 1998, Vol. II 1-II 2 , pp. 81-92.

Zoellner, Frank. Leonardo da Vinci, 1452-1519. Barnes and Noble Books. New York 2004.

Żbikowski, Andrzej. Żydzi Krakowscy i ich gmina 1869-1919. (Kraków Jews and their commune). Wydawnictwo DiG, Warsaw 1994.

[In addition, a great deal of information has recently become available on the Internet scattered at assorted Web sites, some of them very useful and some less reliable. I can recommend the Web site of the Jewish Genealogical Society, <www.Jewishgen.org>, and in particular its "Shtetlinks/Poland/Kraków" section. There is a group of Kraków genealogical researchers, who have amassed a large amount of data on the origin of many Kraków families. <Jewishgen.org> also has some useful links to other sites.

Previously published historical articles by George J. ALEXANDER:

1. How I found a new ancestor in Kraków, Poland. Avotaynu (International Review of Jewish Genealogy). 155 N.Washington Ave., North Bergenfield, NJ 07621. Vol. XIV/4: 65-66, 1998;

2. Five young men: From an UNRRA camp in 1945 to the present. Survivors Chronicle (Published by the Queens (NY) Chapter of Holocaust Survivors, Hanka Hirshaut, Ed.,) P.O.Box 800-157, Elmhurst, NY 11380. 4/2 : 6-7, 1998.

3. Attnang-Puchheim or how to use uncooked rice. Survivors Chronicle 5/2 : 12, 1999.

4. Mishpokhe vormlen fin der Aleksandrowicz familie. (in Yiddish). (Roots of the family Aleksandrowicz). Undzer Tsait. 25 E. 21- St., New York. 9-10 : 17-19, 1999.

5. Yidn in Kroke (a historish un persenlekh kvershnit). (in Yiddish). Jews in Kraków (a historical and personal review). Undzer Tsait 1-2 : 25-29, 2000.

6. Geshikhte fin a yidisher familie in Poiln. (in Yiddish).(History of a Jewish family in Poland). Undzer Tsait 1-2 : 26-30, 2001.

7. My uncle Olek. Survivors Chronicle 7/2 : 9, 2001.

8, Searching for Roots in Kraków, Poland, an essay.
www, Jewishgen.org/ShtetlLinks/Poland/Krakow/Images/Essays>

9. Kraków Buildings. Aleksandrowicz Residences 1802 – 1939
www, Jewishgen.org/ShtetlLinks/Poland/Krakow/Images/Essays>

10. Kraków Jews Around 1800 – A Web of Relationships.
www, Jewishgen.org/ShtetlLinks/Poland/Krakow/Images/Essays>

Index

C

D

H

I

J

K

L

M

Q

R

S

T

U

V

W

Y

Z

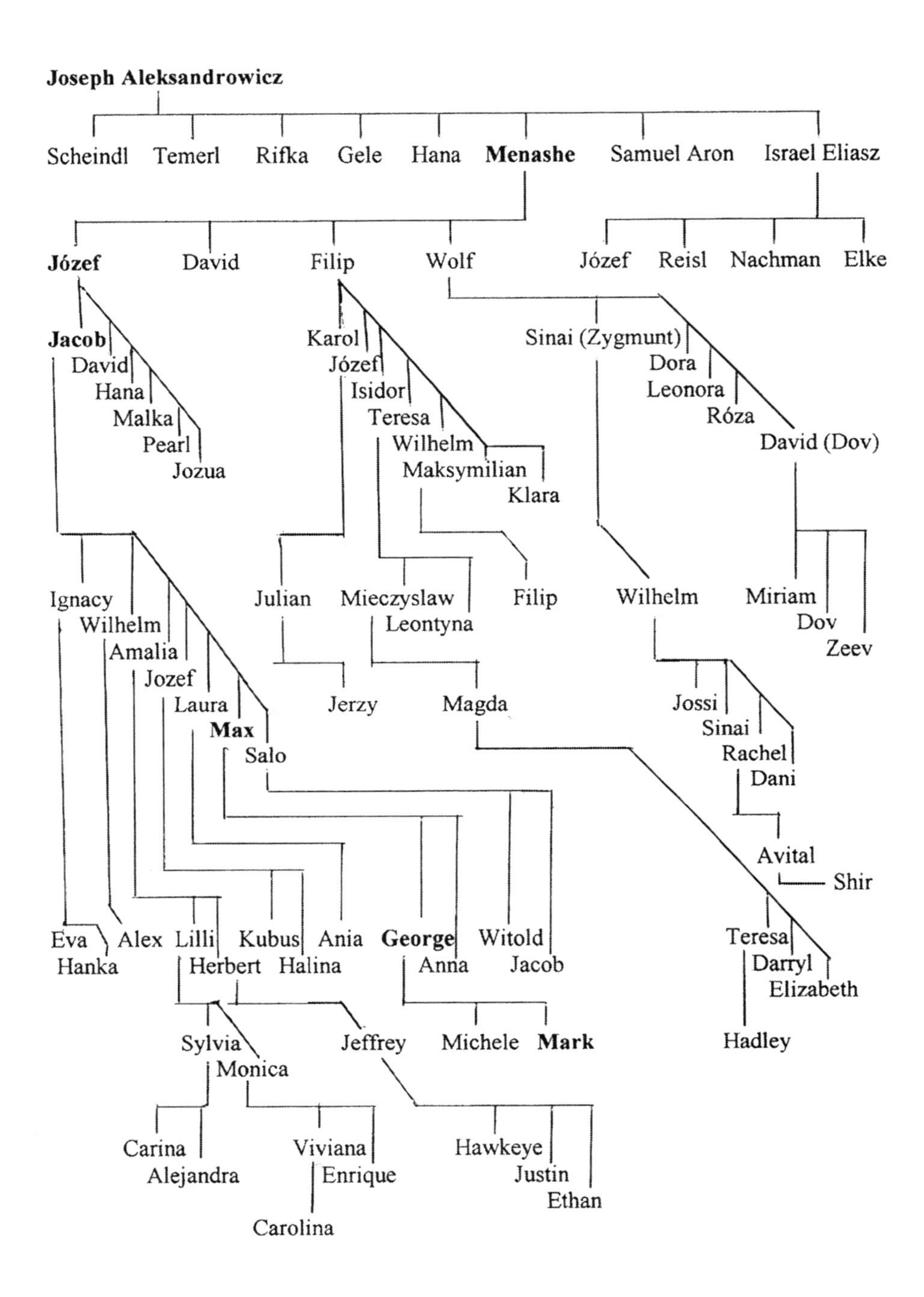

Joseph Aleksandrowicz
Scheindl
Temerl
Rifka
Gele
Hana
Menashe
Samuel Aron
Israel Eliasz
Józef
David
Filip
Wolf
Józef
Reisl
Nachman
Elke
Jacob
David
Hana
Malka
Pearl
Jozua
Karol
Józef
Isidor
Teresa
Wilhelm
Maksymilian
Klara
Sinai (Zygmunt)
Dora
Leonora
Róza
David (Dov)
Ignacy
Wilhelm
Amalia
Jozef
Laura
Max
Salo
Julian
Mieczyslaw
Leontyna
Filip
Wilhelm
Miriam
Dov
Zeev
Jerzy
Magda
Jossi
Sinai
Rachel
Dani
Avital
Shir
Eva
Hanka
Alex
Lilli
Herbert
Kubus
Halina
Ania
George
Anna
Witold
Jacob
Teresa
Darryl
Elizabeth
Hadley
Sylvia
Monica
Jeffrey
Michele
Mark
Carina
Alejandra
Viviana
Enrique
Carolina
Hawkeye
Justin
Ethan

Time line for the Aleksandrowicz family of Kraków, Poland

	900	
966 Polish Duke Mieszko baptized		955 Ibrahim ibn Yakub, Jewish traveler - first mention of Kraków and Poland
	1000	1016 End of the Khazar Empire (began 700 A.D.
		1040 Rashi, sage of Worms, born in Troyes
	1100	
1096 First Crusade		1170 Coins with Hebrew letters in Poland
	1200	
		1264 Charter issued to Jews of Kalisz by Duke Boleslaw the Pious
1295 *Zohar* written by Moses de Leon Start of the Kaballah	1300	
1306 Wilhelm Tell - birth of Switzerland		1335 King Casimir the Great found Jewish Town in Kazimierz near Kraków
1364 Founding of Kraków University	1400	1453 Antisemitic rabble-rouser John of Capistrano (Saint John of Capistrano) in Kraków
1431 Joan of Arc burned at the stake		
1492 Jews expelled from Spain		1495 Jews expelled from Kraków to Kazimierz
	1500	
1521 Martin Luther at the Worms Synod		1525 Remuh (Reb Moses Isserless), born in Kraków
1530 Copernican theory postulated		1549 Jewish Parliament in Poland (Vaad Arba Aratzot) meets until 1764
1554 Joseph Caro writes *Shulkhan Arukh*		1574 Alexander ben Jozue ha-Kohen died
	1600	1626 False Messiah Sabbatai Tzvi
1627 Taj Mahal built in Agra, India		1636 Alexander Jozefowicz, merchant in Kraków
		1648 Chmielnicki's Cossacks massacre Ukraine Jews
		1648 Dr. Samuel ben Baruch ha-Kohen died
	1700	1750 Baal Shem Tov, founder of Hassidism
1776 Birth of the United States		1772 First Partition of Poland
1787 Austrian Emperor requires surnames		1783 Joseph Aleksandrowicz born in /Kazimierz
1794 Kosciuszko Uprising		1784 Dobrysh born to Jacob Gumple and Sara Abele
1796 Austrian army occupies Kraków	1800	
		1802 Joseph marries Dobrysh (later Gumplowicz)
1809 Kraków joins Varsovian Duchy		1805-1813 Births of Joseph and Dobrysh's daughters
1812 Napoleon retreats from Moscow		
1815 Congress of Vienna, creation of an independent Kraków city-state		1817 Menashe born to Joseph and Dobrysh
1818 Karl Marx born in Trier		1845 Józef born to Menashe and Lea nee Katzner
1846 Kraków annexed to Austria		1847 Rachel born to Jozua Drezner & Henna Bader
1848 Franz Joseph becomes Austrian Emperor at 18		1849 Filip born to Menashe and Lea
	1850	1852 Wolf born to Menashe and Lea
1867 Emancipation in Galitzia		1866 Jacob born to Józef and Rachel nee Drezner Hanna Hinda born to Izak Mendel Birnbaum and Malka nee Drezner
		1877 Synai (Zygmunt) born to Wolf and Regina
		1878 Józef born to Filip and Dorothea nee Frankel
		1888 David (Dov) born to Wolf and Regina
		1891 Ignacy b. to Jacob and Hanna Hinda Birnbaum
1897 Zionism born at Basel Congress Labor Bund born in Vilna	1900	1902 Max born to Jacob and Hanna Hinda
		1925 George born to Max and Salomea nee Rubin

The Congress for Jewish Culture was founded in 1948 to promote Yiddish language and culture in the United States and throughout the world. Today the Congress conducts a full year of programming in Yiddish and on Yiddish themes, publishes the journal Di Tsukunft (The Future) as well as monographs, and administers the CYCO (Central Yiddish Culture Organization), Manhattan's only bookstore devoted exclusively to the Yiddish word.

For more information, please visit
www.congressforjewishculture.org

Printed in the United States
216941BV00002B/12/P

9 780972 456562